MICROCOUNSELING

Foreword by

Bernard G. Guerney, Jr., Ph.D.

Professor, Human Development
Head, Individual and Family Consultation Center
College of Human Development
The Pennsylvania State University
University Park, Pennsylvania

Introduction by

Dwight W. Allen, Ed.D.

Professor, Education
University of Massachusetts
Amherst, Massachusetts

With Contributions by

Norma B. Gluckstern, Ed.D.

University Research Corporation
Chevy Chase, Maryland
Adjunct Assistant Professor
Institute of Criminal Justice
University of Maryland
College Park, Maryland

Kay Gustafson, Ph.D.

Staff Psychologist
Veterans Administration Hospital
Omaha, Nebraska

Jerry A. Kasdorf, Ph.D.

Program Manager
Drug Abuse Services
Department of Mental Health
San Bernadino County
San Bernadino, California

Second Edition

MICROCOUNSELING

Innovations in Interviewing, Counseling, Psychotherapy, and Psychoeducation

By

ALLEN E. IVEY, Ed.D.

Professor, Counseling and Mental Health Administration
Human Services and Applied Behavioral Science
University of Massachusetts
Amherst, Massachusetts

and

JERRY AUTHIER, Ph.D.

Departments of Family Practice and Psychiatry
University of Nebraska Medical Center
Omaha, Nebraska

CHARLES C THOMAS • PUBLISHER
Springfield • Illinois • U.S.A.

Published and Distributed Throughout the World by
CHARLES C THOMAS • PUBLISHER
BANNERSTONE HOUSE
301-327 East Lawrence Avenue, Springfield, Illinois, U.S.A.

© *1971, 1978, by* CHARLES C THOMAS • PUBLISHER
ISBN 0-398-03712-4
Library of Congress Catalog Card Number: 77-21556

With **THOMAS BOOKS** *careful attention is given to all details of
manufacturing and design. It is the Publisher's desire to present
books that are satisfactory as to their physical qualities and artistic
possibilities and appropriate for their particular use.* THOMAS
BOOKS *will be true to those laws of quality that assure a good
name and good will.*

Printed in the United States of America
N-1

Library of Congress Cataloging in Publication Data

Ivey, Allen E
  Microcounseling

  Bibliography: p.
  Includes indexes.
    1. Interviewing—Study and teaching. 2. Counseling—Study and teach-
ing. I. Authier, Jerry, joint author. II. Title.
H62.I85 1978   658.31'12   77-21556
ISBN 0-398-03712-4

To Our Great Teachers

those with whom we have worked personally . . .

Edith Dowley	Phillip Anast
Francis Keppel	William Banaka
Eugene Oetting	Bob Innes
David Tiedeman	Lew Yager

and those with whom we have worked
through literature and films . . .

Fritz Perls
Carl Rogers
B. F. Skinner

FOREWORD

As a guide to conceptualizing the etiology of emotional and interpersonal problems, the disease model is dead. Like the mummified remains of some saint it is paraded about whenever it can work to separate third parties from their money. But as a model to inspire robust concepts, hypotheses, and paradigms for psychosocial services, it can work no more. The learning model has replaced it, permanently.

The end of the competition between the disease model and the learning model has had, however, surprisingly little effect on the struggle between the larger, parent models — the medical versus the educational models. Whether it be due to cultural lag or some other reason, the fact is that the great majority of practitioners who reject the disease model and accept the learning model conceptually nevertheless use the medical model exclusively in the way that they organize and implement their practice. The competition between the medical and educational models as *systems of service-delivery* has only just begun in earnest.

The question at the heart of the struggle is this: Will the practitioner tend to look upon potential clientele as an unfortunate minority who have fallen accidental victims to psychic injury, or will he or she regard clientele as those who seek more understanding and skill in order to lead more satisfying lives, emotionally and socially? The former perspective will, as it has done in the past, dictate a model of delivering service in which clients will be treated as physicians treat patients. The latter perspective will dictate a model of delivering service in which clients will be educated as educators teach students.

The medical model of service, regardless of whether it is applied to small groups or to individuals, calls for diagnostic-prescriptive services specifically tailored to the individual: the cause of the specific trauma or malfunction must be determined and a specific remedy administered accordingly. Conceptually and in practice, this model is very appropriate and highly effective for curing physical illness (and, incidentally, I believe there are psychotic and affective disorders which have biochemical causes and remedies that have not yet been discovered). The model is, however, totally unsuited for dealing with the *psychosocial* problems of individuals, and it is the psychosocial problems which consume the major portion of the time of counselors, psychologists, and even psychiatrists.

We will never succeed in helping the general public solve their nonorganic emotional problems through a system of delivering service based on an assumption that individual diagnostic-prescriptive procedures are required to overcome some sort of psychological abnormality or malfunctioning. It is like battling a continental-sized Hydra. As one works to slowly help an individual or small group of individuals as if each person had unique problems or deficits, many of these people within their families are inadvertently growing unhappy souls to take their place should they ever in fact be "cured."

The educational model, in contrast, shows us that it is natural for all people to have problems and frustrations while (a) the social systems in which they function are being redesigned to meet their emotional needs for self-determination and self-esteem and (b) they are learning to control themselves and their interpersonal environment to optimize the satisfaction of such needs. We must think not in terms of two static *states,* the abnormal and the normal, but of a continual *process* of self-improvement. An unchanging personal agenda or a fixed institutional curriculum is the equivalent of death. Politicians and revolutionaries have as their primary business helping people accomplish changes in the social structure, and psychosocial service providers have primary responsibility for helping them accomplish control of self and their immediate interpersonal environment.

Thus, the educational model calls for teaching basic psychosocial skills to every adult (and child) who wants to learn them as soon as possible, dropping stigmatizing labels such as "neurotic" or "maladjusted" and making no greater distinction among clients than would be made between those in a class for the mathematically inclined versus those who don't like math. In place of a one-by-one system of treatment, curricula with appropriate texts, films, behavioral homework, etc., would be designed to be used on a massive scale. Each program would be so designed as to encompass a broad range of individual differences in capacity for learning those particular behaviors. Eventually, individual tutoring would be reserved for those who already had failed to benefit from the programmatic group instruction (or for those who desire and could afford the luxury of private tutoring). When basic psychosocial skill programs — for example, communication skills, such as are taught in microcounseling, and interpersonal problem solving skills, such as are taught in Relationship Enhancement programs, and habit-control skills, such as are taught in certain behavior modification programs — are in wide use, the professional could afford to spend more and more time developing effective mass programs for skills in less wide demand. Eventually, one can hope that all of the problems currently dealt with by psychotherapists in untried and unsystematic ways can be overcome through systematic programs of instruction.

We never could have taught the general public to read, write, and do arithmetic (and then, later, chemistry and physics) if we had been misled into thinking that each individual had to demonstrate a deficit before being educated and so had to be individually studied, and prescribed for, before any teaching could take place. Yet we have been similarly misled by the medical model when it comes to teaching people psychosocial skills.

The more sophisticated programmatic instruction becomes, the more each program can encompass a wide range of individual variations within it (as witness the recent development of what is unfortunately termed "prescriptive" education). The more sophisticated the program, the less the need to consider a special program for each individual, because there is enough structured flexibility built into the system to accommodate almost anyone. Programmatic efforts can provide a very fine individual fit. The key difference between programmatic efforts and the case-by-case approach is whether one has to improvise to get a fit or whether there is a wide array of already prepared effective components from which to choose, so that one can nicely fit almost anyone efficiently without having to improvise. The improvisational approach is expensive. It can help the rich, but only a programmatic thrust can slay the Hydra.

What can we expect when the educational model does replace the medical model? When treatment is replaced by skill training, fear of stigmatization will be replaced by ambition and the desire to get ahead emotionally. The demand for psychosocial services will be expanded enormously, and the efficiency of the educational model of service delivery will permit that demand to be met. As the general public flocks to the psychosocial educator, the ken of personality theorists no longer will be limited to the college sophomore and the white rat. Designers of personality tests will begin to have more viable criteria — specific attitudes and skills with behavioral referents — around which to construct and validate their measures. Perhaps most pertinent of all, the development of clearly defined and systematic programs to help people develop their emotional and interpersonal potential will vastly expand the opportunities for controlled, replicable scientific research into methods of helping people to develop constructive personal attitudes and behaviors. This should significantly increase the pace of the development of vital, highly efficient programs for helping people.

And where does this auspicious chain of events begin? Before anything else can happen, the psychosocial educators must themselves receive training consonant with an educational model. It is their training that will give shape in turn to the type of training received by their professional trainees and clients.

Hence, the significance of this volume extends far beyond the realm of professional training as such. The authors have developed training methods which can be used by people from all walks of life. We can be especially grateful that Ivey and his colleagues have been so thoughtful, careful, thorough, and effective in developing microcounseling techniques. In this volume, it is easy to see the high productivity, the quality, and the heuristic nature of the research generated by microcounseling in recent years. Microcounseling itself, and the research to which it has given rise, are a *reflection* of the power of the educational model, and at the same time, they will serve as significant *stimuli* for further growth and development of the educational model.

No practicing professional and no student of counseling or allied professions could be considered knowledgeable in the most sophisticated and advanced methods of training in counseling-related communication skills without a thorough knowledge of microcounseling methods, the range of application of these methods, and the research supporting microcounseling as these are described in this book. Fortunately, the acquisition of this knowledge is made easy and most interesting by the directness, clarity of writing, and aptness of example the authors provide. The impact of microcounseling already has been profound, and this book doubtless will further broaden its highly beneficial influence.

BERNARD G. GUERNEY, JR.

PREFACE

THIS BOOK deals with interviewing, counseling, and therapy skills. Microcounseling is centrally concerned with identifying the components of the effective helping session. Research studies and countless clinical training workshops have led us to realize that the systematic approach of microcounseling "works" with populations as varying as medical students and nurses, clinical psychologists and school guidance workers, peer drug counselors and parent volunteers, and social workers and teachers.

Out of ten years of study of the interview has come an increasing realization that the components which make for effective helping also work toward effective interpersonal communication. In effect, the skills of helping as manifested in the interview have rather direct implications for everyday personal interaction. People who have worked with microtraining have found themselves conducting training sessions with highly skilled clinicians one day and then using the same or analogous concepts to teach communication skills to lay people the next.

The psychoeducational or "training as treatment" model has arrived. Work started by Bernard Guerney is coming to fruition. More and more professional helpers find themselves not only working in one-to-one and group counseling and therapy sessions, but also training fellow professionals, paraprofessionals, and lay groups in helping skills. James Hurst (1976) has gone so far as to suggest that terms such as "counseling" and "therapy" are limiting and indicates strongly that other intervention strategies for helping people may be as effective or more effective than traditional routes to personal change.

I do not believe that there is a conflict between training as treatment and one-to-one helping, nor do I believe that systematic workshops in skill training will ever replace the need for effective counseling and psychotherapy. In fact, early data suggest that effective psychoeducational programs often expand the use of traditional helping services. It is my contention that one-to-one and small group counseling and therapy will remain central aspects of the professional helper's role. However, professionals are increasingly finding themselves sharing their important expertise with others. As they do so, they find the joy of teaching and "making a difference" in the lives of people *before* serious problems erupt. Further, as the helping process becomes more defined as effective communication, more and more professionals will be anxious to share what they know with ever-enlarging groups of individuals.

Thus, training as treatment is not a challenge to the sacred role of the professional. Rather, it is a new opportunity for service, consultation, and scholarship. It may be anticipated that the helper of the future will spend increasing amounts of time training and teaching others the skills of living and working as a consultant to less skilled helpers. The scholarly opportunities lie in defining even more precisely what it is that makes for effective and satisfactory interpersonal communication. What skills, what qualititative conditions, what theories are most applicable to which groups of people under what conditions? The precision of microtraining and the potential of the training as treatment movement combine to suggest many new directions for the professional helper, whether researcher or practitioner.

However, before we become too enamored with newness and innovation, it seems wise to recall that one of the facts of any professional's life is reinventing the wheel. In some ways, there is really nothing in this book that hasn't been said before. I am especially appreciative to John Darley, former Executive Officer of the American Psychological Association and Professor at the University of Minnesota, who shared with me his twenty-five-page pamphlet, "The Interview in Counseling," published by the U.S. Department of Labor in 1946. In this early and excellent statement, one finds clear descriptions of helping skills such as questions, reflecting feelings, and the use of silence. There is also discussion about distribution of talk-time, the significance of the personal pronoun in the interview, and highly specific suggestions for practice role-plays. Darley suggests use of a stopwatch to note the talk-time of the interviewer, an observer who counts personal pronouns in the helping session, an observer who counts the number of topics discussed in the interview, and an observer who "counts the number of times the 'interviewer' uses questions that can be answered by 'yes' or 'no' . . ." The parallels between these recommendations and the detailed micro-counseling workshops presented in this text are immediately apparent. Darley's early efforts should have been followed up more carefully. Unfortunately, however, professional helping moved primarily toward theoretical explanations of the helping process in the following years and away from skills. While this exploration has been helpful, of course, it seems time to join theory and practice more closely.

Thus, the Second Edition of *Microcounseling* takes theory more into account, whereas the prior edition was centrally concerned with technique. Several alternative approaches to helping are presented with an analysis of interviewing behavior from a microcounseling point of view. In truth, microcounseling is a structural framework upon which many different and even antagonistic theories may be examined. As microcounseling has now ventured into the area of theorizing about helping processes, this text is on less stable ground than was the First Edition. However, we have tried to present microtraining as an evolving meta-theory about the helping process, and with this statement we invite others to join us in the search for a unified theory of helping.

A unified theory of helping must take cultural factors into account. The word *culture* barely appeared in the first edition of this book but has become central in this venture. As we search the literature, we find extensive comments about the importance of considering cultural differences in helping, but we find very little to help us think through *how* we may take such differences into account in the helping interview. Microtraining research on this topic is limited but nonetheless sufficient for a chapter in this text. I am personally convinced that different helpees need different theoretical orientations and different patterns of skills usage in the interview. However, our research on this topic is now only in the primitive stages. I anticipate major developments in this area to be forthcoming.

Thus, psychoeducation, a new emphasis on theory and meta-theory, and cultural factors represent the primary added dimensions of the new edition of this text. Other changes center on the provision of a demonstration interview so that specific examples of skills in operation may be seen, addition of new materials on other systematic training programs in helping skills, and a vastly enlarged section on research in microtraining thanks to many colleagues who have examined the framework in detail. The Appendix adds a complete workshop for those who wish to teach others helping skills and contains several instruments useful for analyzing both the helping interview and, I believe, two-person and small group communications as well.

Teaching of microtraining in interviewing skills courses, psychotherapy seminars, and paraprofessional workshops is increasing. This book has been designed for classroom as well as general reference use. Particularly important for professors using this text may be Appendix VII where specific behavioral competencies expected from trainees using these materials are defined. The essence of the defined competencies is that the effective student will be able to: (1) define his or her *own* unique interview behavior; (2) identify its effect on the client; and (3) demonstrate other interviewing and therapeutic styles and identify their content and effectiveness. In my courses in counseling and therapy, I now have all students provide typescripts and scoring of their behavior throughout the course. This material proves invaluable for student learning and for research purposes enabling further improvement in instructional programs and changes in the microtraining course.

This book would not have been possible without the energetic and scholarly involvement of Jerry Authier. Jerry first came to my attention by way of his stimulating thesis on microcounseling, completed at the University of Portland. Since that time, I have followed his career with interest. He has constantly helped me to enlarge my view of the helping profession, he has challenged my ideas (and my writing style!), and he has developed several new strands of thinking which enable me to make more sense of the helping process in general. His review of the psychoeducation process (Authier et al., 1975) will become a classic of the profession. I feel very lucky and humble that he was able to share this exploration with me.

Norma Gluckstern, Kay Gustafson, and Jerry Kasdorf have been central to the development of the ideas in this book. Norma helped make microcounseling more precise through our joint work as we delineated via video modeling tapes the concepts which are discussed in this book. Kay has completed valuable research in microcounseling and, in addition to writing some excellent chapters, she also assisted greatly through comments on the manuscript. Jerry, along with Kay, has completed an excellent and challenging review of the now extensive literature on microcounseling and microcounseling-related research. It is tempting to find only those facts which support one's case. They have found a good balance between supportive and critical research which should be valuable in delineating the microtraining models of the future.

I feel lucky and rich in the professional companionship that these colleagues have provided in the development of this work and delighted that they were willing to share their expertise. Microcounseling and microtraining have now taken much more of my life and time that I ever anticipated. This work has put me in touch with dedicated and aware professionals and lay people throughout the country. The growth and change in this volume comes from relationships with people and their ideas. Microtraining is not fixed and final; it is a fluid program which will be constantly shaped and adapted by those who work with it. I am willing and anxious to work with students and professionals who examine this book and wish to conduct workshops or research. Share your ideas with Jerry Authier and me; we are anxious to work with you and to learn with you.

ALLEN E. IVEY
Amherst, Massachusetts

INTRODUCTION

MICROCOUNSELING AND ITS EDUCATIONAL
IMPLICATIONS

M ICROTEACHING was designed as a new approach to teaching
facilitative classroom instructional skills. In the early phases of
our experimentation and research, we deliberately eliminated
conceptual frameworks and theoretical constructs as we searched
for a method which consistently showed results — a system that
"worked" was needed rather than one which was theoretically
sophisticated. Our belief was that a theoretical structure for
microteaching would evolve out of application and practice.

The publication of the second edition of this work brings the
microtraining paradigm to a new level which illustrates even
more clearly its adaptability to an almost infinite number of
training situations. Further, we are beginning to see the development of a systematic rationale and theory underlying the teaching
of single skill units. While the technology and training units presented by Allen Ivey and his colleague Jerry Authier are powerful, the evolving metatheory which describes commonalities and
differences among many approaches to helping may ultimately be
the major contribution. Technology without a direction and goal
is a potentially dangerous tool; the goal concepts of *cultural
expertise* and freeing the individual to create new and unique
responses represent general themes which permit the comparison
of alternative forms of treatment and teaching. Thus, we who
have been committed to microtraining approaches find ourselves
at a new and important beginning.

Cultural constraints are a constant in any helping or teaching
situation; we have long talked about culture as having vital implications for our work, but very few of us have been able to synthesize and demonstrate *how* cultural factors can be systematically

included in our training programs. While microtraining is still at an early level in working with cultural issues, the system's very precision and clarity will continue to force increased awareness of cultural, sexual, socioeconomic, and other contextual constraints. Some have said that the precision of microtraining results in missing many important dimensions. While this statement has a grain of truth, we have found that precision results in increased awareness of what *must* be included in training. And, it seems, for every answer that microtraining provides, a whole new set of questions arises. It was out of the precision of attending behavior that a formal way to include cultural differences in helper training was developed. Simply put, attending behavior as described in the first edition of this book does not adequately describe the wide individual and cultural variations in eye contact, body language, and patterns of appropriate verbalization. Testing of these constructs with many populations has helped broaden the concept; attending behavior has not been discarded and in fact may be a cultural universal which plays itself out in an infinite array of manners among individuals and peoples. One of the major strengths of this new volume is an effort to attack vital cultural issues; a good beginning has been made, but much more work lies ahead for both microcounseling and microteaching.

Another important implication of this book is the emphasis on using microtraining to teach individuals the "developmental skills of being people." This book has extensive clinical and research data to validate this approach as a viable alternative and/or supplement to psychotherapy and counseling. In fact, the psychoeducational model must now be regarded by all professional helpers as an alternative treatment method in much the same way as all psychotherapists need to understand behavioral, analytic, humanistic, and transpersonal approaches to helping. If anything, Ivey and Authier do not give enough emphasis to "media therapy" and "step group therapy" in this work. These modes of therapy, plus training workshops in communication skills, are the real wave of the future for the helping professions.

My own work has more recently focused on the "teaching

clinic." Here we take teachers, videorecord them in action, use systematic feedback techniques, and then develop individually prescribed routes toward teaching effectiveness. I contend that microcounseling needs to become more involved in such procedures; specifically, I am impressed by the development of "human relations learning units," where communication skills are taught not only to clients but also to those in schools and government and to individuals in business and personal services. The teaching clinic concept, along with media therapy and step group therapy, offers an important vehicle to impart skills to the general public. As one example of this, special note should be taken of the discussion of teaching sales techniques via microtraining in Chapter 13. There is no reason that systematic training of all members in a school or community could not be undertaken. Psychoeducation models need not be individual training and treatment events; they can be shared openly and widely with the lay public.

Microteaching and microcounseling may now best be conceptualized within the larger paradigm of microtraining — a systematic method of skills acquisition designed to equip the individual not only with tools but also with the freedom of choice required to be fully human. Microtraining has demonstrated its utility far beyond our original work with teachers at Stanford University. In the Introduction to the First Edition, I stated, "I anticipate a time when the microtraining paradigm helps us see more clearly the relationships between the teaching and counseling processes, sales training and interviewing, and training couples in effective marital communication and psychotherapy." The publication of this volume brings that prediction to fruition, for Ivey and Authier have indeed clarified the underlying connections between these diverse areas. One of the great strengths of this book and the microtraining paradigm is the amount of information that can be accounted for and the number of new hypotheses developed.

In a sense, work on microtraining is still at the beginning stages. While we have answered many questions in the past ten years, many more issues need further exploration. Particularly, we need more data on the effect of skilled counselors on client verbal and nonverbal behavior, on the pattern and effectiveness of alternative skill use as manifested in differing theoretical orientations to helping, and on the generalization and maintenance of learned behavior. It can be seen that microtraining is not a closed framework but rather an opening to new ideas in an apparently ever-expanding system which can account for more and more data.

From the above, with Allen Ivey and Jerry Authier, I would like to commend a view toward microtraining which asks the reader *not* to use these procedures in a set, prescribed manner. Rather, use the framework and basic ideas to expand and develop microtraining in your own unique fashion. This means developing new skills to be used in differing settings, writing new manuals or adapting existing materials, and challenging the practical and theoretical ideas expressed here. Microtraining is at its most effective when each individual uses it in his or her own style and simultaneously encourages that same freedom of expression in others.

The First Edition of *Microcounseling* was an important contribution. It brought together considerable research and clinical ideas and set the stage for the future. However, this volume represents a major scholarly and practical contribution to the literature of helping. The breadth of ideas presented by Ivey and Authier can only lead to further discoveries and clarification of the helping process. This work belongs in the library of every practicing counselor, therapist, and researcher in applied helping processes.

I hope you find a way to use microcounseling techniques to develop new approaches, as a stimulus to new mechanisms of microtraining and not simply as a recipe for a narrow range of counseling and interviewing skills. To go beyond these ideas — to make them obsolete as Ivey, Authier, and many others have as they have amplified early work in microcounseling and microteaching — is the one ultimate compliment you can give this work.

DWIGHT W. ALLEN

ACKNOWLEDGMENTS

Microtraining rests heavily on the ideas, research, and clinical efforts of many individuals — so many, in fact, that the first draft of this section once reached nine pages and was still growing. Clearly, it is no longer feasible to mention all of those who have helped to clarify and extend the concepts of microcounseling and microtraining. Only a few central individuals can be mentioned, and we also thank the many others who have contributed to this work. Microtraining has become an interdependent enterprise, too large a movement for any individual or group to be full "owner." We invite the reader to join us in the search for further expansions and clarification of the ideas in this book.

Dwight Allen and Edward Brainard were the ones who worked first to see that microcounseling was developed as a concept. Dwight Allen had done basic work in microteaching at Stanford University and must be credited with the technology underlying this system of training. Edward Brainard brought funding from the Charles F. Kettering Foundation and personal support in the early phases of the investigation.

The Colorado State University Counseling Center was the location of the original microcounseling studies. Dean Miller, Weston Morrill, and Cheryl Normington were coinvestigators on the original microcounseling grant, while Eugene Oetting, Charles Cole, James Hurst, and Richard Weigel helped clarify our work with constant admonitions and advice. The University of Massachusetts brought Allen Ivey together with Jeanne Phillips, Jeff Lockhart, and John Moreland, and out of this contact came the conceptual framework for the attending skills so important in microcounseling training and research. Richard Haase and Max Uhlemann were graduate students on the original project and since that time have made several important independent contributions to the framework.

Dean Norma Jean Anderson, Judy Katz, Joan Chadbourne, Billy Roberts, Bailey Jackson, and Jude Berman of the University of Massachusetts did not all work specifically on microcounseling as such but are directly responsible in their own unique ways for bringing an awareness of cultural and racial issues to the helping process. Paul Pedersen of the University of Minnesota, Dermod McDermott of Full Circle Associates (411 East 10th Street, New York, 10009), Derald Sue of California State University, Hayward and Alice Snyder of the University of Hawaii have provided clear and explicit ideas for making ideas of cultural awareness mesh with microtraining.

The personal support and challenge of many professional colleagues has been important. Leo Goldman of the City University of New York, Steve Weinrach of Villanova University, Tom Magoon of the University of Maryland, David Danskin of Kansas State University, and Larry Brammer of the University of Washington have been especially helpful. Al Alschuler, Sid Simon, and Gerald Weinstein, faculty in psychological education at the University of Massachusetts, provided a frame which has helped move microtraining more to an educational/developmental model. We especially recognize three colleagues in systematic training of helpers: Robert Carkhuff, Steve Danish, and Norman Kagan. Their model of excellence and innovation is inspiring.

This book presents several instrumentation thrusts useful in microtraining research. Richard Haase, Cheryl Normington, Stephen Rollin, and D.Y. Lee have contributed their efforts. Ruth G. Matarazzo of the University of Oregon Medical School shared her "Therapist Error Checklist." Robert R. Carkhuff allowed "The Scale for Empathic Understanding" to be reprinted here. Norman Kagan of Michigan State University wrote a section for us on the "Affectivity Sensitivity Scale" and the "Counselor Verbal Response Scale." We are pleased to summarize the interesting instrumentation thrusts of the able innovator in family training and psychoeducation, Bernard Guerney and his associates.

Audrey Konicek of Amherst is the photographer. Bruce Oldershaw of Springfield College provided technical assistance and advice in the development of videotapes discussed in this book.

In their own unique ways, Elizabeth, Bill, and John Ivey have contributed to this book . . . Betty through patience, several substantive contributions, and her model of excellence, Bill through sensitivity and perspective, John through enthusiasm and achievement-motivation. Their influence is ever-present throughout.

Karen Jane, Gabriel Joseph and Sarah Ann have also participated. Gabriel Joseph arrived January 6, 1977, in the middle of manuscript exchanges, wild searches for lost references, and last-minute insights. His birth and Karen's understanding provide a new beginning as we end what has been a most smooth and enjoyable venture in coauthorship.

ALLEN E. IVEY
Amherst, Massachusetts

JERRY AUTHIER
Omaha, Nebraska

CONTENTS

SECTION II.
THE CONCEPTUAL FRAMEWORK AND SKILLS
OF MICROCOUNSELING

SECTION IV.
ALTERNATIVE APPLICATIONS OF MICROTRAINING IN TEACHING AND RESEARCH

MICROCOUNSELING

SECTION I

INTRODUCTION

The purpose of the first section of this book is to set the stage for in-depth examination of microcounseling and microtraining in ensuing sections and chapters.

Chapter 1 introduces and defines microcounseling as a technology for helper training and as a beginning metatheory of the interviewing process. This is followed by delineation of specific aspects of the microcounseling model and examination of alternative uses for the framework. The chapter concludes with a brief summary of the research potential of microcounseling.

Chapter 2 explores microtraining in a historical context. Traditional training programs in psychotherapeutic skills are first explored, followed by a discussion of the major innovations of the Rogerian client-centered school. Experiential-didactic training and modern innovations are presented as important background methods for the recent innovation of microcounseling. The psychoeducation model of helping — teaching as a preferred mode of helping — is explored in preliminary form.

Microcounseling is an open system. Techniques, skills, and conceptual frames have always been open to change and modification. Shape the ideas and concepts of this book in your own style. Microtraining used mechanically and "by the book" will be less effective than if artistically shaped by the individual helper or helper trainer.

Chapter 1

MICROTRAINING AND MICROCOUNSELING: DEFINITION AND PROMISE

How does one become a helper? Is helping a natural way of being or can it be learned? If helping can be learned, what is the most appropriate educational route? Should helping be taught from a commitment to a single theoretical orientation, or should we identify specific skills common to many theories? Finally, if helping skills can be identified and taught, with whom should these skills be shared?

Microcounseling is one route which seeks to explore the answers to the above questions. Microcounseling is a systematic approach to training which appears to facilitate natural helpers in becoming more effective and assist less skilled would-be helpers to become effective. The central purpose of this book is to present microcounseling and its many applications for the training and education of interviewers, counselors, and psychotherapists.

Undergirding microtraining and microcounseling is a constant emphasis on teaching helping dimensions to others. If the skills of effective helping can be clearly delineated, it is only logical that they be shared with as many people who can benefit from these skills as possible. Microtraining gives considerable credence to the psychoeducator model of helping. The psychoeducator model is concerned with teaching individuals how to be more competent in their own lives and moves from a medical model of illness→diagnosis→prescription→therapy→cure to an educational model of client dissatisfaction (or ambition)→goal setting→skill teaching→satisfaction or goal achievement (Authier, Gustafson,

Guerney, and Kasdorf, 1975). This teaching model of helping does not preclude or oppose counseling and psychotherapy. Rather, the psychoeducational model demands the same exacting skills from the professional helper and can be used to complement and supplement the interviewing process.

Microtraining is evolving toward a metatheory of helping — a theory about helping theories. Evidence is beginning to accumulate that microtraining concepts and skills underlie many differing approaches to helping. Early data seem to suggest that very different methods of counseling and therapy can be examined in the light of basic microcounseling skills. Further, cultural, sexual, and racial communication patterns appear to be clarified through the lens of microtraining's conceptual framework. A secondary thrust of this book is to explore microtraining's relationship to many other processes of helping and training.

At the outset we should state that microcounseling as presented here is not in its "final state." A system which is closed to change and development is dying or dead. We urge constant examination and challenge to the ideas presented here. Through research and comments from colleagues and microtraining students, the present framework has developed. It will continue to develop *if* people modify and change the concepts and use them in their own unique manner.

We have set the stage for a metatheory of helping and a broader role for the professional helper of the future. It now seems appropriate to turn to microtraining and develop through step-by-step procedures the framework which makes the essence of helping as explicitly teachable as possible.

MICROCOUNSELING IN PRACTICE

A young man is talking intently about his attitudes toward a recent job; a novice interviewer appears to be listening closely. With some heat and emotion, the young man tells about a conflict with his supervisor. The interviewer does not respond, and an awkward pause occurs. The interviewer breaks eye contact, shifts uncomfortably, then asks the client what some of his objectives in his next position might be. A supervisor is recording the session with a portable videotape recorder and takes notes on the novice's and the client's behavior.

Shortly after, the session is terminated. The young man completes an evaluation form and leaves the room. The supervisor and the interviewing trainee discuss the session, examine the client evaluation form, and view parts of the videotaped session. The client is then interviewed again, and the process of recording and feedback is repeated. In the second session, the novice interviewer appears more relaxed and able to listen. When the conflict with the superior again appears, the trainee listens more fully to the client and does not shift topics when emotions appear. The client is able to express attitudes and hopes more fully.

This process, a scaled-down interviewing session, is microcounseling. In such microtraining techniques, a beginning counselor talks with a volunteer client about real problems. The interview occurs in a setting which provides interviewing practice with maximum opportunity for immediate feedback and trainee growth. The compressed nature of the situation allows a focus on specific dimensions of interviewing skills and does not demand that the trainee respond immediately as a fully professional counselor.

Microtraining may be compared to the traditional approach to interviewing training in which the beginning interviewer, counselor, or therapist is quite literally "thrown in" to the first session with a long list of caveats, concepts, and suggested methods. The beginning interviewer is expected to sort all this information and act effectively. Teaching beginning counselors and therapists how to interview is one of the more complex and challenging issues facing the helping profession (Krumboltz, 1967; Matarazzo, 1971; Matarazzo, Wiens, and Saslow, 1966; Wrenn, 1962). Most would agree that counselor and interviewer training have not generally been efficient or economical of human resources. Beginning interviewers often find their first sessions confusing. They frequently have trouble in defining their own role in the interview and in getting the client to talk.

In effect, microcounseling provides an opportunity for those who are preparing to counsel to obtain a liberal amount of prac-

tice without endangering or offending clients. While microtraining has other possible purposes and uses, its principal aim is
to provide experiences which serve as a bridge between classroom
or textbook theory and actual practice in interviewing and counseling. Too many enter the helping fields without supervised
practice in interviewing skills.

MICROTRAINING: A TECHNOLOGY AND A METATHEORY

Cartwright (1968), in a review of psychotherapy research,
singled out the educational process for training novice clinicians
as being in particular need of systematic study. Instruction in
basic clinical and interviewing skills is carried out in educational
institutions with students preparing for many professions, including psychological and educational counseling, medicine, nursing,
psychiatry, clinical psychology, the ministry, and subprofessional
helping roles. Industry and the United States Employment
Service are greatly concerned with interviewing and have given
considerable thought to methods of improving training in this
field.

Microtraining and microcounseling techniques are direct attempts to develop a systematic approach to interviewer *and* interviewee training. Microtraining has evolved from a list of skills
of helping accompanied by a powerful technology of training
(Ivey, 1971) to its present state of a metatheory of helping — a
theory about helping theories. This book will present both the
technology of microtraining and an evolving theory which, we
believe, will explain several commonalities and differences of
alternative therapeutic approaches. Further, this theory will
present a conceptual format for consideration of outcome of
helping — the culturally effective individual. Effective helpers
produce competent people; a major thrust of this book is to explore desired outcomes of helping processes.

Microtraining (or microcounseling — the two words will be
used interchangeably) is two things:

First, microtraining is a *technology*, a systematic format for
teaching single helping skills. It uses videotape, step-by-step
training manuals, and self-observation. It is a *structure* for teach-

ing an infinite variety of skills.

Second, microtraining is a *conceptual framework and theory* concerning the basic skills of the helping process. Specific skills of helping, e.g. questions, reflection of feeling, directions, and interpretation, which are and can be used by helpers of widely differing orientations, are outlined in this text. These skills serve as the basis for effective helping. Moreover, if these skills are taught in the psychoeducator model to helpees, they will result in effective individuals. The effective helper and effective helpee demonstrate analogous communication skills and competencies.

Within both definitions, microtraining techniques should be considered structural or methodological approaches to interviewing skills training. The technological structure provides a framework for teaching an increasingly wide array of skills and techniques to many populations. The conceptual framework and theory underlying the specific skills in this text provide an overview for a more detailed examination of what transpires between a counselor and a client.

The technology of microtraining is relatively simple and can be applied to virtually every area of human endeavor. Microtraining techniques have been used to teach firefighting skills, sales techniques, dental teaching skills, parent communication skills, and the most complex interviewing techniques. Regardless of the level or complexity of the skill being taught, the microtraining framework of interview-training-reinterview remains constant.

The conceptual framework of microcounseling provides a structure wherein the helping process is broken down into specific components which can be taught as single units and later integrated into meaningful gestalts. The specific skills of microcounseling as defined in this book form an intrastucture underlying the total helping process. Chapter 7 demonstrates how the specific skills of microcounseling are used in different helping theories. Thus, the conceptual framework of microcounseling provides a systematic format for examining the commonalities and differences of alternative theories of counseling and psychotherapy.

Microtraining offers an important new role for the future of the helping professions — that of teaching communication skills to helpees. The counselor or therapist is becoming increasingly a teacher of skills. Patterson (1969) was among the first to suggest such an emphasis: "Perhaps therapy is not necessary! What we may need is direct training or education of everyone in the conditions of good human relations — not only normal people and children but the emotionally disturbed as well" (1969, p. ix). Authier, Gustafson, Guerney, and Kasdorf (1975) have reviewed over 100 articles discussing this issue and conclude that teaching of skills for effective living — the psychoeducator model — is a major direction for future helping. A major thrust in this Second Edition of *Microcounseling* is exploration into the uses of microcounseling's technology and conceptual framework for the direct teaching of skills to client populations. Microcounseling skills have been taught to children, teenagers, parents, psychiatric patients, older workers, and many other people. The real future of microcounseling is undoubtedly in the direct teaching of skills as a new model of helper functioning evolves.

In this book, the words "interviewing," "counseling," and "therapy" will be used interchangeably. We define *interviewing* as a process of information seeking (most typically in a personnel or placement situation), *counseling* as seeking to understand another person more fully (school guidance, college counseling), and *therapy* as helping another person change pathological behavior (analysis, long-term treatment, behavior modification). "Helping" is a broader concept, including these terms, and may even be extended to any relationship wherein one individual assists another (medicine, welfare work, law, family relationships, etc.). Despite these differences, all interviewers, counselors, and therapists must learn to listen, to ask questions, to attend to feelings, and to interpret their clients' statements. Therefore, the skills outlined in this book should be useful to those who work with people in many settings.

THE BASIC MICROCOUNSELING MODEL

While many variations are possible, most research and methodology in microcounseling has been conducted in a situation in which the trainee goes through the following progressive steps:

1. Baseline interview of five minutes on videotape
   The trainee interviews a volunteer client about a real or role-played concern. Depending on the situation, a specific issue may be agreed to by both participants before the session begins, or a simple, unstructured/unplanned interview may be held.

2. Training
   A. A written manual describing the *single skill* to be learned is read by the trainee.
   B. Video models illustrating the specific skill are shown to the trainee and discussed with reference to the single skill being taught.
   C. The trainee views the original baseline interview and compares his or her performance with the modeling tape.
   D. The supervisor/trainer maintains a warm, supportive relationship with the trainee, stressing positive aspects of the performance while constantly focusing on the single skill being taught.

3. Reinterview
   The trainee videotapes another session and gives special emphasis to the single skill being learned. This tape is reviewed with the supervisor/trainer.

The systematic technology of microtraining has a special benefit in that the beginning helper is not overwhelmed with the necessity of doing everything "right" in the first interview. *The task is simple and direct — learn one skill at a time and gradually develop a repertoire of competencies in helping.* The time required for this process is approximately one hour. If the trainee does not demonstrate competence in the skill at the end of the first trial, the process may be recycled with more training and re-interviews.

It may be observed that the training procedures involve cue discrimination and specific suggestions for improvement, video models (Bandura and Walters, 1963), written materials, and supervisor's comments. Operant techniques (Skinner, 1953) are stressed, in that appropriate interviewer behavior is rewarded; the emphasis is on positive growth, and relatively little attention is paid to interviewer errors. The positive approach of operant psychology coupled with specific suggestions is important in rapid trainee growth.

However, microcounseling training also involves important *relationship skills* on the part of the supervisor. It is possible for a routine to develop in which the teacher of skills loses personal involvement with the trainee. When this happens, the trainee may still learn the skills but appears to have trouble generalizing them to actual interviewing settings. Therefore, a friendly, warm, and genuine attitude on the part of the individual supervising a microtraining session is essential. *Most important, the supervisor in a microcounseling training session must model the skills he or she is teaching.* If the supervisor does not attend to the trainee when teaching attending behavior or note appropriate emotions and feelings when teaching reflection of feeling, little learning in the situation will occur. Rogers (1957a) might term this supervisory behavior as genuineness or congruence. Regardless of whether one favors the precision of learning theory or the warmth of phenomenology, it seems essential for successful microcounseling training that the supervisor be congruent with his trainee and model what is taught.

Even though the above comments are important, it is possible to vary styles of supervision, to use multiple supervisors, or even to eliminate the supervisor. A programmed text has been successfully used in place of the written manual in some studies (cf Goldberg, 1970; Frankel, 1970; Authier and Gustafson, 1976b). The extent of video feedback and the number of models shown to the trainee can be varied. In some cases, role playing and rehearsal of the specific skill to be demonstrated have been utilized as an additional step before the trainee returns for another counseling session.

With some trainees, it is possible to teach more than one skill at a time. With others, it is desirable to break a skill into even smaller component parts before the central skill is practiced. For example, some interviewers may need to learn how to maintain eye contact before they can attempt general listening skills. Considerable variation has been observed in the skills individuals bring to microtraining sessions. However, with apt supervision, careful selection of skills leading to more complex behaviors, and ample practice, we believe that virtually every person can significantly improve his or her interviewing skills.

Microcounseling is based on several essential propositions. First, it is possible to lessen the complexity of the counseling or interviewing process through *focusing on single skills.* The goal of the trainee is to master one skill at a time rather than to demonstrate competence in all areas simultaneously. This provides the student with an opportunity to see immediate improvement in one area, which helps in developing more difficult skills at later training stages.

Second, microtraining techniques provide important opportunities for *self-observation and confrontation.* Immediately after engaging in a counseling session, the trainee and the supervisor have the opportunity to view the trainee's behavior and the client's reactions. Provision of instantaneous feedback serves as a guideline to future interview performance.

Third, interviewers can learn from *observing video models* demonstrating the skills they are seeking to learn. Each specific skill is demonstrated on videotape by a skilled counselor. Not only does the trainee hear what good techniques in counseling are but also sees them in action.

Fourth, microcounseling is a method which can be *used to teach interviewing skills in a wide area of diverse theoretical and practical frameworks.* Indeed, not only can psychoanalytic interpretation skills, Rogerian reflection of feeling, interpretation of vocational tests, and asking questions in an employment interview all be taught to trainees within a microtraining framework, but these skills can also be taught to patients, clients, or anyone who could profit from training through the psychoeducator model.

Fifth, microtraining sessions are *real interviewing.* While role-played or simulated counseling sessions are sometimes used in this method, the trainees soon assume a real counseling role. Frequently, volunteer clients find themselves discussing actual problems. A common finding is that clients appear to appreciate the opportunity to have someone listen to them and volunteer to return for more sessions of this type.

GROUP INSTRUCTION IN MICROCOUNSELING SKILLS

Microcounseling, as apparent from the previous outline, was originally conceived as a means for individual counselor or therapist training. The detailed supervision and demand for specific competencies may be cost-effective in terms of client benefit, but not all settings have sufficient staff and videotaping stations for the full implementation of an individualized micro-counseling training program. Thus, Ivey and Gluckstern (1974a, b; 1976a,b) have developed a systematic program of group instruction in microtraining skills. The program has proven effective in classroom and workshop settings (cf Gluckstern, 1973; Hearn, 1976; Scroggins and Ivey, 1976). It is sufficiently flexible that extensive videotape equipment may be used but organized so that a single closed-circuit unit may be sufficient to promote group and individual learning.

Group instruction in microcounseling skills involves the same dimensions as the one-to-one approach but supplements the basic framework with elements of group process. The specific methods of group process in teaching microtraining are outlined in detail in Chapter 12. Trainee groups as small as three or four or as large as one hundred or more have participated successfully in microtraining using group methods. Client populations for group training have included professional groups as varying as medical students and secondary school counselors, nurses and resident dormitory assistants, and paraprofessionals and directors of clinical training programs in professional settings.

Within the psychoeducator model, microtraining skills have been taught to hospitalized psychiatric populations (Ivey, 1973b), parent effectiveness groups (Bizer, 1972), elementary school children (Goshko, 1973), couples groups (Andes, 1974), and many other lay populations. With careful use of small group interaction and follow-up on levels of competency, trainees can achieve communication skills equal to those of persons trained via one-to-one microtraining.

VALUES AND USES OF MICROTRAINING

Microcounseling is designed to bridge the gap between theory and practice, between classroom and interview session, between what is said and what is done. Following are some settings in which microcounseling has demonstrated its usefulness.

Safe Practice in Counseling and Interviewing Skills

Many are concerned about "unleashing" the beginning therapist on the first client. The casual observer of a novice clinician often wonders if the wrong person is doing the interviewing. Full of anxieties, trying to remember a list of do's and don'ts, the beginning interviewer is often most ineffective. While not all interviewers or therapists go through this experience, most would admit that awkward early sessions happen all too often.

As a result of this confusion, clients are lost and sometimes never return to another therapist. Good candidates for a job are missed; a student may end up in the wrong college. If the counseling profession is capable of helping clients, it is also capable of damaging them.

Similarly, interviewers may be injured by their first session or sessions. A cycle of self-doubt and self-blame may be generated such that they may leave the field. Perhaps even more serious, they may stay but never learn the meaning of counseling or interviewing. Who has not contacted an employment or guidance counselor who knows very little about counseling? School guidance counselors often retreat into administrative-aide work and schedule students from class to class because they do not know how to listen or talk with students in a counseling relationship. The personnel director may retreat to objective testing and interview job candidates only perfunctorily.

Much of this loss of client and counselor functioning can be alleviated by more effective training programs. Microtraining provides a setting in which individuals may practice skills and see themselves improve. Counselors build self-confidence as they see self-growth and become more effective in each interview. They learn they are not expected to be perfect and may begin a pattern in which they realize that counseling is a lifelong endeavor of growth rather than a short-term situation with definite answers.

Perhaps even more important is the responsibility of the counseling profession to its clients. The short sessions, while usually covering meaningful material, do not expose a client in depth to the beginning counselor. The client has the opportunity to give feedback to the counselor, and a more mutual relationship between counselor and client can be established. Further, a supervisor is close at hand to assist the trainee in handling difficult problems that may arise.

In-service training within the microcounseling framework is also helpful. While interviewers may learn a new method or idea in a classroom or book, they are sometimes hesitant to try it on their regular clientele. Further, in the regular session, the opportunity for feedback and consultation is not present. An analogy might be drawn to the quarterback thrust into a football game without practicing a new play. It is hard to implement a new idea unless you have had the opportunity to learn the basic skills and practice them. Hearing or reading about an idea is not enough.

Allen and Ryan (1969) point out that other professions have built opportunities for safe practice into their training programs. One can think of Link trainers for aircraft pilots, rehearsals for actors, cadavers for medical students, and the moot court for lawyers. The airline stewardess serves real meals in a mock cabin to real people. However, teachers, counselors, and interviewers usually learn their skills on the firing line of the classroom, therapy session, or job interview. Microtraining is a way of bridging the gap between classroom and practice. Further, it is a system which is real and provides opportunity for experiential learning for professional and personal growth.

Focusing Experientially on Specific Skills

Polanyi (1966) believes we have made a false assumption in thinking that we acquire knowledge best by studying it. He points out that chess players can best understand the expertise of the chess masters by entering into a "master's spirit by rehearsing the games he played, to discover what he had in mind." In essence, Polanyi is stating that we can best understand knowledge by experiencing it.

Microtraining is experiential in nature. While cognitive written materials are available for each skill of interviewing, the major emphasis is on participation and action by the trainee. He or she conducts an interview, reads a short written manual, talks with a supervisor, views an example of the skill to be learned, compares him or herself as an interviewer with the expert, plans new approaches, rehearses the next session, and practices until the skill in question is learned.

Microcounseling demands active involvement. Within the demand for involvement, the situation is made simple and clear so that the person is not confused and overwhelmed by data. Counselor trainers have demanded involvement, but they describe and present the interview in an almost mystical fashion. What actually happens in an interview or the behaviors a counselor engages in are not stressed. There exist relatively few counselors or interviewers who can define what they have done to make an interview successful.

Defining skills of interviewing demands a more precise vocabulary. An important aspect of training in microtechniques is knowing what you are about and being able to define it in operational terms. "If you can't teach someone else what you are doing, you don't understand it yourself" is a motto of those committed to this type of approach. Microcounseling forces one to identify what one is doing.

Thus, microcounseling skills in this book are presented in terms which are definable and replicable in many situations. The application of any one skill is not counseling or interviewing; it is practice in a specific skill. Counseling and interviewing exist at a higher level, one in which the individual has many skills and uses them appropriately in response to the unique interviewing situation. The skilled counselor or interviewer does not necessarily think of the skills used.

The concept of tacit knowing as used by Polanyi may help show the relationship between the specific experiential skills of microcounseling and the skilled counselor who has many skills available. When one swings a golf club well, sings a song beautifully, or responds appropriately to a client, there is tacit knowledge of what one has done. Moreover, if the golfer, singer, or interviewer thought in detail of all the actions or specific behaviors engaged in, achieving the same high quality of the action would not be possible. Many specific behaviors have been integrated into one large natural action.

It must be recognized that there is more than one alternative route to excellence in golf, singing, or interviewing. Some come by these skills naturally; their life experience seems to be such that they need not think about what they are doing. Even they, however, often have to go back and practice details before they can integrate difficult concepts or problems into their behavior, e.g. the golfer practicing putting if he or she feels "off," the singer rehearsing a difficult passage, the therapist reflecting on what went wrong in the last session. Moreover, many people do not come by complex skills of living naturally and easily. Direct training in skills is viewed as the most efficacious method of improving interpersonal functioning. Microtraining is proposed as one method through which people can develop new skills which otherwise might not be possible and as a means for experts to improve on already existing skills.

Tacit knowing and smooth integration of learned skills does not always happen immediately with every individual. For example, consider the "millipede effect" in microtraining:

> An old fable talks about the fly and the millipede. It seems the millipede was walking along the road when a fly came buzzing by and landed. The fly looked the millipede over and marveled at the way the millipede could coordinate a thousand (or so it seemed) legs.
>
> "Pray, millipede," said the fly, "how dost thou work all those many legs together so smoothly?"

"No sweat," said the millipede, "I just do it."

The fly flew away marveling at the coordination of the many-legged creature.

After the fly left, the millipede began to ponder the conversation. "Now just how do I move all those legs so marvelously? Do I do three left and three right and then alternate down the line . . . or perhaps it is one at a time?"

And as the millipede examined how he did it, he fell in the ditch (Ivey and Gluckstern, 1974b, p. 12).

The moral, then, is that as one consciously examines how one does something, performance may become slowed or awkward. The microtraining emphasis on single skills sometimes makes interviewing awkward and uncomfortable for the trainee; we have found that high functioning people have actually had temporary performance decrements during microtraining workshops. Yet, with further practice (just as in golf or singing), these behaviors eventually become integrated into a larger and even more effective whole and no longer need to be stressed, as they have become part of the now more effective person. Low functioning people, on the other hand, show immediate, rapid, and lasting increments in their performance after training in these skills.

In essence, then, it is the experiential nature of microtraining which makes possible the integration of learned skills with other natural behaviors. Toward this end, doing rather than talking is stressed within microcounseling. As such, the breaking down of complex verbal and nonverbal behavior into concrete dimensions with immediate and in-depth experience can result in growth for both naive beginners and the most advanced professional.

A Research Tool

The microtraining framework provides a useful laboratory for interviewing research. A major problem in counseling research is the isolation of the many variables involved in the counselor-client interaction. When viewed over a fifty-minute session, the complexity of the interview becomes almost overwhelming. Variables in the interviewing process can be sorted out more easily in the microtraining framework, thus allowing the researcher to investigate the specific area of interest more closely. Control of

verbal comments or nonverbal communication by the counselor
is more easily obtained. Variables such as length of session,
varieties of training techniques, client problems, and a host of
other variables can be more easily manipulated.

Microtraining offers a framework for a host of controlled
studies in counselor training and counseling itself. What are the
important dimensions of learning in microcounseling? Is it supervision? Is it feedback? Is it viewing the models? Or is it perhaps
the interaction of these factors with a particular trainee? What
interviewing skills seem to help which client at what time? The
short-term sessions provide an excellent laboratory for the study
of mutual reinforcement patterns of counselor and client. These
and other research possibilities will be considered in more detail
at a later point.

The microcounseling framework provides an opportunity to
test laboratory research in a more applied setting before direct
translation to operational practice is made. Various problems of
applying research to practice can be studied and resolved in the
more controlled and standard situation provided by microcounseling.

SUMMARY

This chapter has identified microcounseling as a systematic
technology useful in many skill training situations with a multitude of content dimensions. Microtraining has also been discussed as metatheory of helping which can be used to explain and
compare alternative approaches to helping. Through careful
identification of underlying structures and qualities of helping
relationships, microtraining makes concepts previously only
implicitly understood explicit and measurable.

The focus on specific skills as opposed to the totality of the
interview allows one to approach the interview more analytically
and to develop a more sophisticated understanding of one's own
skills and limitations. Microtraining is useful for research and as
a framework for in service or preservice counselor training.

The multidimensional training approach of microcounseling
utilizes several aspects of learning theory, the most important of
which is experiential. The trainees have the opportunity to

practice and demonstrate that they have learned the skill in question. In addition, they have the opportunity to look at themselves in comparison to expert counselors. While the basic microcounseling model as outlined has many alternatives, evidence suggests that the multimedia, multifaceted approach of the basic model is most effective.

It is important to note that structural innovations are highly subject to value decisions made by the individual using the approach. It is conceivable that one could use a microcounseling framework to teach counselors skills which are irrelevant or even damaging to the client. While this may be unlikely, the possibility of using this method in unwise ways must be considered. Further, it is not a panacea which will make everyone a skilled interviewer. It should, however, be a useful tool to help interviewers become more effective.

Chapter 2

MICROCOUNSELING IN PERSPECTIVE

To GAIN A grasp of the development and impact of microcounseling, one needs to focus on both the academic and therapeutic arenas. Regarding the former, counseling and interviewing skill training is carried out in educational institutions, with students preparing for widely varying professions. The personnel executive, the psychotherapist, the school counselor, the nurse, the social worker, the physician, and the vocational counselor, just to name a few, all require interviewing training. Moreover, the increased complexity of technology in the world and the difficulties with the interface of the human being with such a complicated environment has led to the demand for "lay therapists," "indigenous helpers," and other paraprofessionals who also require interviewing training. In conjunction with this growing demand has been the recognition that a more efficient and effective means of training professionals and paraprofessionals is needed to meet the many requests of people seeking to comprehend their world.

A simultaneous outgrowth of the need for a more efficient and effective means for training in basic helping skills was the determination that likewise a more direct, efficient, and effective means of helping people to cope with their environments was also needed. The *psychoeducator model* has developed as one approach to meeting this need (cf. Ivey and Alschuler, 1973; Carkhuff, 1971c; Guerney, 1969; Guerney, Guerney, and Stollak, 1971; and Mosher and Sprinthall, 1971). Most of the advocates of this model agree that instead of viewing their function in terms of abnormality (or illness), diagnosis, prescriptions, therapy, and cure, they view it in terms of client dissatisfaction or ambition, goal setting, skill teaching, and satisfaction or goal achievement. The skill teaching portion of the psychoeducator model is that in which we are most interested here. The development of the skills taught as well as the structure utilized to teach the skills closely parallels the development of the increasingly more effective skill training programs in educational settings. Indeed, many of the changes in formal interviewing training programs paved the way for the psychoeducator model. Some of the historical and theoretical dimensions of the development of approaches to both the educational and psychoeducational arenas will be discussed in more detail in this chapter, with the overall goal of placing microcounseling as both a training and a therapeutic process in proper perspective.

UNDERLYING ISSUES IN HELPER TRAINING

With regard to interviewing training, it was less than two decades ago that most instruction in basic interviewing or psychotherapeutic skills was of a hit-or-miss apprentice type, with intuition or clinical arts stressed over precise and defined behaviors and trial-and-error learning over systematic teaching. Rogers (1957b, p. 76) lamented the state of training procedures in psychotherapy:

> Considering the fact that one-third of present-day psychologists have a special interest in the field of psychotherapy we would expect a great deal of attention might be given to the problem of training individuals to engage in the therapeutic process. . . .For the most part this field is characterized by a rarity of research and a plentitude of platitudes.

The situation a decade later had not improved much, as indictated by Matarazzo, Wiens, and Saslow (1966, p. 608) in their conclusion following an extensive review of literature:

> From the studies cited and from our review of the literature we have concluded that there is essentially no published research regarding the teaching of psychotherapy, the supervisory process, how learning effective psychotherapy takes place and how to teach psychotherapy efficiently. Many reports of training programs are available and it is evident that many psychotherapists talk about teaching, but few report systematic innovations, comparison of method, and/or student skill before and after a course of instruction.

Whitely (1969) reached much the same conclusion after reviewing the counselor education literature.   Even as late as 1971,
Matarazzo, although being heartened by recent changes in psychotherapeutic skill training, concluded that teaching of such skills
was still in its early stages.   This was demonstrated by her review
indicating that there were few systematic programs with measurement of training effects.   Fortunately, there have been great
changes made with regard to the training and research of various
counseling and interviewing skills since that time, but that is the
subject matter of another chapter.   Let us turn then to some of the
factors which appear responsible for the lack of systematic training and research in psychotherapy prior to the 1970s.

Perhaps the first deterrent was the notion held by many that
psychotherapy was a private interaction between therapist and
patient and therefore should be removed from any form of public
scrutiny.   The supervisory process, with regard to training such
skills, was therefore seen in the same light.   Of course, such pervasive attitudes were responsible for excluding researchers and
other observers from the therapist's inner office, thus restricting
any consensus being developed with regard to what actually
occurs in the therapeutic process.   Indeed, it is our contention
that lack of knowledge regarding the explicit nature of the interviewing process resulted in the traditional therapeutic training
approach viewing the acquisition of conceptual strategical skills
and the resolution of the trainees' countertransference feelings as
the proper content of the supervisory process.   That is, since the
specific behaviors involved in the therapeutic process were un-
known, traditional therapeutic training had to rely on its theoretical bases as the content of its training format.

Recent studies in microcounseling have demonstrated, however, that there are specific behavioral skills which an interviewer
can utilize to facilitate a client's self-exploration.   Logically, then,
these identifiable skills ought to be the content of the supervisory
process.   Furthermore, when this is the case, it would seem that
these skills would serve as a bridge between the trainees' classroom training and applied training experiences, thereby making
the transition from the classroom to the therapy session much

smoother than the more traditional approach of supervision of psychotherapeutic skills has allowed in the past. Based on recent data that a patient's reaction to the initial stages of therapy is crucial in determining its outcome (Strupp, 1970) and indeed that even experienced counselors or therapists sometimes have a detrimental effect on clients, it would seem that a smooth transition from the classroom to the clinical experience is paramount. Before beginning a discussion of microcounseling, which we contend helps bridge the gap from the classroom to the clinic more smoothly due to the instructional technique and the content emphasized, a review of various existing models of therapeutic training may prove beneficial in placing this approach to interviewing and clinical skill training in a broader perspective.

TRADITIONAL TRAINING PROGRAMS IN PSYCHOTHERAPEUTIC SKILLS

The format of traditional therapist education is essentially the grandparent of counselor and interviewing skill training, and it is fitting to turn to it first. A prerequisite for students trained under the traditional system is the possession of a highly developed, refined, conceptual grasp of psychotherapeutic theory. A model of supervision outlined by Ekstein and Wallerstein (1958) exemplifies the traditional training format. Although based on psychoanalytic psychotherapy, the format of Ekstein and Wallerstein is very similar to those used by others, regardless of theoretical orientation or discipline. Under this model, the student attends innumerable lectures and seminars on psychoanalysis and psychoanalytic psychotherapy prior to being assigned the first control patient. Once a trainee begins seeing patients, the student recounts from memory what transpired in the therapy session to the supervisor. Thus, the student's self-report serves as the sole data upon which learning within the supervisory process is based. Of course, the shortcoming of such a case presentation approach is that students consciously or unconsciously tend to distort what actually occurred in therapy. This notion is supported by the now classic study of Blocksma and Porter (1947) which demonstrated that there was little relationship between what the students reported they would do and what they actually did do in an interview.

The traditional training format also often had an experiential component. Under this model, the supervisory process itself is seen as a means of helping the student recognize and refine conceptual-strategical skills to deal effectively with the phenomena of transference and countertransference. As such, a large portion of the supervisory process involves the trainer helping the trainee first to work through transference feelings toward the supervisor. Thus, in essence, the trainee-supervisor relationship is of a therapeutic nature, aiming to help the student work through transference and countertransference phenomena, thereby allowing the student to describe patient sessions to the supervisor spontaneously, clearly, and cogently. Once this goal is accomplished, it is expected that a generalization of this experience to the student's own interviews will occur and somehow be reflected in the trainee's actual therapy behavior. However, since during this process there is no attempt to observe or modify the student therapist's behavior with the patient, nor have any behavioral end products been stated explicitly, one can only conclude that any changes in therapeutic behavior on the part of the student are largely due to internal conceptual changes which have been made. Finally, since the student therapist is not allowed to practice those things stressed during supervision prior to meeting with patients, it is questionable whether the transition from training to the interview can truly be smooth.

Mueller and Kell (1972) represent an updating of this format. They provide in-depth discussion of such issues as differentiation between supervisor and student, countertransference and transference between the student and the supervisor, and even include a lengthy discussion of terminating the supervisory relationship. The supervisor-student relationship in this model, then, is considered roughly analogous to the issues which occur between patient and therapist. While traditional, it must be stressed that this approach to training is still very much in evidence.

ROGERIAN CLIENT-CENTERED TRAINING

Perhaps the first major deviation from the traditional interviewing training format was that offered by Rogers (1957b). The strength of Rogers' client-centered approach was his willingness to open to public scrutiny what occurs in psychotherapy, thus allowing for the compilation of objective data about the therapeutic process and thereby paving the way for more systematic training procedures. This training model allows students to learn to discriminate between facilitative and nonfacilitative sessions by having them listen to recordings of experienced and inexperienced therapists conducting therapy. Additionally, the students observe a series of interviews conducted by experienced therapists, participate in group therapy, and/or undergo individual therapy as a means of obtaining an experiential understanding of what therapy is about. The final stage of his training model involves the trainee being allowed to carry on psychotherapy under the direct supervision of an experienced therapist. Teaching devices such as tape recorded interviews and multiple therapists' cases are utilized as beneficial learning vehicles during this phase of training.

It is readily apparent that Rogers' training program was a marked departure from the traditional interview training model. Perhaps more important than the changes which allowed the supervisory process to be more systematic is the change in the content. That is, the content of Rogers' training program is geared to helping the novice acquire the skills of a good therapist. It is unfortunate, however, that the discrimination training aspect of the program is not as systematic as it might have been, thereby leaving open to question how well the student therapists learned facilitative interviewer behavior. In this model, the specific skills differentiating the skilled from the unskilled helper are not as well defined for the student as they can be. A student may be able to discriminate between the effectiveness and ineffectiveness of a session but may not be able to identify what he or she did during the session to result in positive or negative evaluation. Moreover, the student is not given explicit instructions and/or practice in how to manifest these behaviors. This seems some-

what surprising in that several investigators (Snyder, 1945; Seeman, 1948; Fiedler, 1950a,b; and Strupp, 1955a,b,c) had identified specific behaviors used by therapists as well as the factors
which were aspects of a good therapeutic relationship regardless
of theoretical orientation. Nevertheless, even though Rogers' approach to training future therapists did not teach discrimination
as systematically as it might have, it was revolutionary in that it
was one of the first attempts to establish a formal training bridge
between the classroom and the actual therapeutic interview situation.

EXPERIENTIAL-DIDACTIC TRAINING

Another marked departure from the traditional training approach which did attempt to teach discrimination of facilitative
behavior conditions was that of Truax and Carkhuff (1967).
Their experiential-didactic training program is the best-known
early attempt to identify and train therapist qualities which differentiate successful from unsuccessful therapists, thus to some extent filling the void left by Rogers' training program. The
therapeutic qualities which they attempted to train were warmth,
empathy, and genuineness, since a number of studies demonstrated that therapists who were rated high on these qualities had
positive therapeutic outcomes while therapists who were rated
low on these dimensions were not effective or, worse, had a detrimental effect on their patients (Truax, 1961; Truax and Carkhuff, 1967; Truax, Carkhuff, and Kodman, 1965). Initially, they
suggest that new students listen to selected audiotaped therapy
sessions, thereby learning what constitutes high and low levels of
warmth, empathy, and genuineness. The student therapists are
then taught to discriminate these qualities by learning to rate
audio tapes on a seven or nine-point scale designed to measure
these three central therapeutic ingredients. A third phase of
training entails having the student therapist undergo a group
therapy experience. Finally, once the trainee has actually begun
doing therapy, the supervisor relates to the student in a highly
warm, empathic, and genuine manner, forming another aspect of
the experiential portion of training. In essence, then, the Truax

and Carkhuff training program, although somewhat similar to the psychoanalytic and Rogerian training program in that it helps trainees learn to deal with feelings and conflicts elicited by the training experiences, has emphasized more than Rogers the acquisition of specifiable, facilitative interviewer skills. Moreover, the supervisor not only provides the trainee with an appropriate role model but also establishes the conditions under which the novice can most easily engage in self-exploration. As such, their approach is one step closer to bridging the gap between the classroom and the actual therapeutic interview session.

In spite of the primary advantage of specifying facilitative therapeutic conditions in their training format, Truax and Carkhuff fail to explicitly define the behaviors constituting the global characteristics of empathy, warmth, and genuineness. That is, they assume that if students can learn to recognize the presence or absence of these qualities in other therapists, they will automatically incorporate these qualities into their own interview behavior. Yet, as with most assumptions, unless this is proven, the validity is questionable. For this reason, it seems that a more appropriate approach would be the direct training of the behavioral components of these more global interpersonal skills. Fortunately, Carkhuff (1969a,b) has taken a step toward this end by refining his operational definitions of empathy, respect, and genuineness, plus he has extended the therapeutic equation to include counselor initiative dimensions of confrontation and immediacy. Further, in their recent work, Carkhuff and Berenson (1976) present an elaborate conceptual scheme for counselor training based upon many studies related to these methods. In this vein, perhaps Carkhuff's most significant contribution to the training of future therapists may be his emphasis on evaluating the results of counselor training programs and then modifying or changing these programs in order to produce more effective counselors. His recent statements emphasize even more strongly the role of the helper as a teacher of skills. Even with these recent advances, it seems there is room for further innovations which would either supplement the existing programs or be effective in themselves, and it is to these that we now turn.

INNOVATIONS IN INTERVIEWING TRAINING

Innovations in psychotherapeutic and/or interviewing skill training can be discussed considering two dimensions: (1) the increasingly specific behavioral nature of training and (2) the use of observational media to enrich training programs. The behavioral program stressed in studies by Phillips and Matarazzo (1962) and later by Matarazzo, Phillips, Wiens, and Saslow (1965) can be construed as the first program measuring actual student therapists' behaviors and relating change in these behavior patterns to the students' training. The training program consisted of obtaining pre- and posttraining measurements under two supervisory conditions. One program consisted of four students who reported their interviews to their supervisors and, on the basis of their reports, received conceptual and technical suggestions. The other program consisted of four students who were observed by the supervisor as they performed an interview once a week, with each observation followed by a discussion between the supervisor and the student regarding the student's actual interview behavior in which the supervisor made recommendations for specific behavioral change. Results indicated the students undergoing the latter approach increased their use of nondirective communication facilitating techniques and were more active and influence-oriented during their interviews than the students receiving the former supervision. Furthermore, students in the latter condition whose training was primarily behavioral in substance developed interview behaviors which more closely resembled behaviors of Strupp's (1970) experienced therapists.

These studies were useful in terms of identifying the specific behaviors of novice interviewers. More importantly, they demonstrated that if a specific behavior change is desired, then specific behaviors should be taught. Additionally, the studies illustrated the possibility of isolating, defining, and teaching concrete behaviors which are basic to any novice interested in acquiring clinical interviewing skills. The training, however, was not as behaviorally specific as is now possible, and the instructional approach relied on delayed rather than immediate feedback.

Recent innovations in the use of observational media in psychotherapeutic and/or interviewing skill training programs has helped to overcome these two primary criticisms. Prior to this, even though specific behaviors could be identified and defined, their complex nature often made them difficult to impart to trainees. Immediate, point-by-point supervision was also next to impossible. Reivich and Geertsma (1969) describe a training model based on the use of videotape which incorporates such features as videotaped demonstrations of the desired behaviors and self-observation by videotaped feedback, thus compensating for the shortcomings of the previously discussed behavioral model of training. The Reivich and Geertsma model does not replace the traditional emphasis on assisting students to acquire conceptual, strategical skills, but it facilitates and elaborates on this important area. They feel utilization of observational media enhances the trainee's ability to translate behavioral events into theoretical concepts as well as conceptions of therapists' activities into behavioral events. Kagan and Krathwohl (1967) also discuss the use of videotape to help novice interviewers learn to counsel by observing their own sessions. More recently, Kagan (1972; 1973; 1975a) has developed a training manual entitled "Interpersonal Process Recall," which systematically teaches trainees by having them observe themselves in a counseling session and receive point-by-point feedback from a supervisor and the client. Kagan also uses stimulus affect films as a means of helping the trainee become more aware of personal feelings in the helping interview. Specific details of his program and other "packaged" programs used as adjuncts to counseling training will be discussed in a subsequent chapter.

A shortcoming of some of the work using observational media stems from the lack of "model tapes" which clearly identify those specific behaviors which can effect constructive patient change. Since microcounseling is an interviewing training paradigm which has as one of its components stressing specific behaviors using video examples, it seems appropriate to place microcounseling in perspective prior to moving on to the discussion of the teaching of specific behaviors to client populations.

MICROCOUNSELING

Microcounseling is an innovative approach to instruction in basic clinical skills which is based on the assumption that interviewer behavior is extremely complex and therefore can best be taught by breaking the interview down into discrete behavioral units. It should be stated explicitly at this point, however, that interviewing is more complex than merely emitting "canned" or mechanical behaviors at the appropriate moment. Therefore, we see the instructional approach as simply providing the vehicle for students to gain necessary skills which, once delineated and mastered, can be incorporated into a style which allows a person to be maximally facilitative as a professional or a paraprofessional helper. The approach accomplishes the delineation necessary by incorporating as part of the training format the use of observational media and behavioral content in such a way that many of the problems mentioned above are overcome. That is, feedback on specific behaviors is immediate, since observational media are used both to model specific interviewer behavior and during the supervisory process when videotaped practice sessions are reviewed. Additionally, the use of observational media allows for an effective division of interviewer behavior into small units so that skills can be focused on directly. The trainee is encouraged to internalize individual skills so they can be emitted appropriately and spontaneously as new natural skills of the helper. Indeed, it is the shaping process by which such integration occurs which makes the microcounseling paradigm such an effective means of training interviewers, thereby making the transition from the classroom to the clinical setting smooth, natural, and powerful. By practicing these skills in a systematic way, microtraining provides trainees with the opportunity to master the skill prior to going into the clinical setting, thus helping to build response repertoires, without which the trainee could not be spontaneous in the clinical setting.

Microtraining in its most recent version (Ivey and Gluckstern, 1974a,b; 1976a,b) adds to the breadth of the system; that is, not only does it include focus on specific behaviors and the use of observational media as a way of "shaping" the trainee's counseling skills, it also involves the best of the traditional system in terms of enhancing supervisor-student relationships. Moreover, a new emphasis on peer supervision of counseling practice sessions provides an opportunity for the group process experiential dimension stressed by Kagan and by Truax and Carkhuff, thereby enhancing student-student relationships. Finally, many of the new skills taught under the current microcounseling paradigm represent the behavioral components of the central therapeutic ingredients mentioned by Rogers, i.e. nonpossessive warmth, empathy, and genuineness. As such, microcounseling now more than ever represents a blend of traditional and innovative procedures which perhaps more effectively and efficiently serve to help the trainee become a spontaneous helper in his/her respective clinical setting.

Evidence has amassed demonstrating that microcounseling is both an effective and efficient modality for teaching various kinds of clinical skills. However, since both the various skills taught by this paradigm as well as the research comparing microcounseling to other training formats will be presented in separate chapters, only a few of the original studies demonstrating the effectiveness of microcounseling will be cited here.

Ivey, Normington, Miller, Morrill, and Haase (1968) were the first to demonstrate the efficacy of microcounseling training both as an instructional medium for the acquisition of basic psychotherapeutic skills and as a research paradigm. They utilized the microcounseling technique to teach three different groups of beginning counselors one of the following three interviewing skills: attending behavior, reflection of feeling, or summarization of feeling. The results indicated microcounseling to be effective in three veins: (1) beginning prepracticum counseling students showed significant changes in all three skills in just five hours total training time; (2) every pre- and posttraining comparison of clients' reactions to the interviewers was positive and significant; and (3) microcounseling with its emphasis on specific behaviors was a viable research paradigm. Thus, not only were Ivey et al. able to define in concrete terms the interview skills of attending behavior, reflection of feeling, and summarization of feeling, they also demonstrated that these skills could be taught effectively and efficiently to student interviewers within the micro-counseling paradigm. Demonstrating that the clients' reactions to the student interviewers were significantly more positive once students acquired the specified skills attested to the validity of the program and met Cartwright's (1968) reminder that the goal of training and research must be to connect studies of effective instruction to specified client behavioral changes.

Another study which has contributed to the validity of the instructional method of microcounseling is the study by More-land, Phillips, Ivey, and Lockhart (1970). Their training in-volved teaching a minimal activity skill, an open-ended question skill, and a paraphrase skill in addition to the three skills taught by the Ivey et al. study to first-year clinical psychology graduate students. This study was the first to demonstrate that the effects of microcounseling training generalized from the instructional lab to actual interview situations with patients. This finding adds support to the notion that the microcounseling approach serves as a bridge between the classroom and the clinical situation.

A study by Haase and DiMattia (1970) is another of the original studies which demonstrates that microcounseling training is effective in imparting skills of attending behavior, reflection of feeling, and expression of feeling. Their study is important in that it demonstrates that paraprofessionals can learn basic clinical skills via the microcounseling paradigm. Further, a more recent study by Gluckstern (1973) demonstrates that, given adequate opportunity to counsel on the job, paraprofessionals maintain their skills over time. A number of "packaged" programs useful in the training of paraprofessionals have been developed since these original studies, and they will be discussed in detail in Chapter 11. Moreover, several studies have been conducted evaluating the microcounseling training paradigm and comparing it to these other therapeutic and/or interviewing skill training approaches; this material is presented in Chapter 13. Therefore, at this point, we will move to a second major thrust of this chap-ter—the training of interviewing and/or counseling skills directly to clients.

TRAINING IN "COUNSELING SKILLS"
AS A THERAPEUTIC MODALITY

The psychoeducator movement has as its basis giving training of "counseling-related skills" to clients or patient populations. Psychoeducation draws from the tenet, if therapists, counselors, interviewers, etc., can be trained to be more facilitative interpersonally, perhaps it is also possible to directly teach the same skills to patients, clients, and the general lay population. This notion has logical appeal in that most authorities view the manifestation of certain interpersonal skills as a necessary component of good mental health. Sullivan (1953), Coleman (1965), and Foote and Cottrell (1955) all define lack of mental health as "faulty interpersonal relations," "social ineffectiveness," and "interpersonal incompetence" respectively. On the more positive side, Maslow (1955) describes a self-actualized person, one who epitomizes good mental health, as being capable of "deeper and more profound interpersonal relations than any other adult." Further, Jahoda (1958), in her comprehensive review of the positive mental health literature, discusses the theorists who advocate adequacy in interpersonal relations and empathy or social sensitivity as criteria of mental health. Finally, Rogers (1959) and colleagues Truax and Mitchell (1971), as well as Carkhuff (1971b), talk about the global interpersonal skills of empathy, respect/warmth, and genuineness as components of good mental health. If then, as these authorities propose, interpersonal skills are important aspects of good mental health, and if one assumes that facilitative behavior in a counseling or therapeutic situation is a way of enhancing interpersonal competence, then it would seem that direct training in many of the interpersonal skills taught helping professionals would be a logical goal of a psychotherapeutic approach. However, several factors mitigate against this natural sequitur.

Training in interpersonal skills of helpers has only recently been refined to the degree that it is possible to consider similar training for clients; the newness of the concept is a major impediment to the psychoeducator movement. In addition, though, there were several historical and theoretical antecedents which inhibited psychological practitioners and health professionals from using direct training as a therapeutic approach to help people deal with their complex world. Certainly, many of the attitudes of the professional therapy movement work against psychoeducation. Important among these are viewing the psychotherapeutic process as a private interaction, the attitude that change has to be internal rather than interpersonal, and the resistance to defining interpersonal skills in terms of concrete behaviors. More specific to the use of direct training in counseling skills as a preferred mode of treatment with psychiatric patients, though, is the belief or attitude that psychiatric patients are incapable of learning in a direct, systematic training program. Moreover, specific to the learning role in general, there is a strong cultural norm that learning, i.e. going to classes, is mostly a childhood activity, and therefore, to employ a direct training approach to an adult population is to violate this cultural norm. Additionally, there is an attitude that we "naturally" learn social and emotional coping skills without explicit instruction; providing explicit instruction in such skills is thus in opposition to this cultural norm.

Finally, and perhaps most important in delaying the psychoeducator model, is the role of the therapist as a teacher, which requires therapists to challenge many basic norms in their own thinking and world views. Such a role change demands a giving up of the medical model and the status which accompanies this, i.e. "being a doctor." Likewise, it requires therapists to view the "patient" not as someone who is "sick" but rather as someone who is "lacking in interpersonal skills." With this acknowledgment, the emphasis of interpersonal skill training as opposed to "insight" is required and violates the theoretical and value structure of many professional helpers.

Just as Rogers (1951) was largely responsible for opening therapeutic interaction to public scrutiny, so was he instrumental in changing an attitude regarding the patient, namely that given the "proper interpersonal climate," it was the client who had both the right and the best aptitude for solving his or her own problems. The willingness to encourage clients to choose their own goals knowledgeably and a high degree of respect for the client's own ability to reach them is thus the attitude which Rogers and his followers (Rogers and Dymond, 1954; Truax, 1961; Betz, 1963; Truax, Carkhuff, and Kodman, 1965; Truax and Carkhuff, 1967; Carkhuff, 1971b) have not only advocated but also have provided empirical evidence to support.

While the nondirective school provided the impetus for this change, the operant school led by Skinner, which eventually became known as "behavior modification," took a more direct approach to see that the client actually worked on the behavior which needed to be changed. Further, this school underscored the notion that it was the client who had the best potential to change behavior. The behavior modifiers were eager to suggest that if things weren't working out right, it was the helper who must be first to change his or her ways. Moreover, followers of this school of thought were even less inclined than other "therapeutic schools" to act as high priests or keepers of the secret flame. Indeed, they have been among the first and foremost (e.g. Lindsley, 1966; Zimmerman and Zimmerman, 1962; Patterson and Brodsky, 1966; Ayllon and Azrin, 1968; Phillips, 1968) in wanting to give their skills away to whomever might wish to use them. Finally, just as the nondirective therapists deliberately rejected the term "patient," behavior modifiers have deliberately rejected many medical analogies and terms such as "symptom," "cases," "therapy," etc., as a way of demonstrating that an educational model may perhaps be the more effective approach to the delivery of mental health care.

In spite of the nondirective and behavior modifier schools of thought helping them to view the person with whom they worked as more of a learner than a patient, few therapists have reconceptualized their role as that of a teacher. Perhaps the difficulty with such a reconceptualization is that although most people in a helping role use elements known as components of an educational model such as guidance, modeling and feedback, or evaluation of the helpee's actions or statement, viewing the therapist's role as that of a teacher in many therapy systems has a forced, imposed quality rather than flowing easily from descriptions of their own work. Thus, although many people have been discussing training as a viable therapeutic modality, few if any of the advocates of the psychoeducator movement have made clear how the adoption of such a model would change the role of the psychological practitioner. Instead, most of the proponents have been content merely to list some of the programs using such a model without delineating the specific teacherlike tasks which were involved in the procedure, e.g. Carkhuff, 1971c. Others, e.g. Ivey, 1974b, have been quite specific in terms of delineating the specific therapist's tasks within that particular education model approach but have failed to make the conceptual shift from therapist to teacher on a more general level, especially in terms of how the therapist-trainer's tasks are really teaching tasks, calling for the use of teaching modalities. Carkhuff and Berenson's (1976) and Ivey's (1976) most recent statements seem to be important steps in more clearly delineating the helper as a teacher.

Fortunately, a systematic reconceptualization of the therapist's role to that of a teacher's role has recently been made (Authier, Gustafson, Guerney, and Kasdorf, 1975), and with this clarification in the recent literature perhaps more practitioners will be inclined to utilize the direct training approach as a therapeutic modality. If so, they will of necessity need to incorporate some of the components of the previously described training programs to implement effective interpersonal skill training to a client population. Indeed, many of them have already been modified for this purpose, but since a future chapter will discuss microtraining in alternative settings, the purpose of this section will mainly be to outline some of the original approaches which can be conceptually viewed as offshoots of these counseling and/or interpersonal skill training paradigms.

Donk (1969; 1972) was the first to use a modified microcounseling format to teach hospitalized mental patients the skill of attending behavior. His results indicate that not only was this new interpersonal skill acquired but that it generalized to the patients' ward behaviors. In a related study, Haase, Forsyth, Julius, and Lee (1971) showed that clients at a university counseling center trained in the skill of expression of feeling prior to being seen by a counselor expressed more feeling in their initial counseling session than did clients who did not receive such training. A study by Higgins, Ivey, and Uhlemann (1970) was another important variation of the use of the microcounseling paradigm with other than a counseling trainee population. They instructed students in the interpersonal skills of "direct-mutual communication," which are closely related to dimensions emphasized in encounter groups. This study was especially important in that it demonstrated that microcounseling could be used to train clients in quite complex interpersonal skills. In addition, Higgins et al. raised the possibility that microcounseling could be used to train clients in therapy to use more effective interpersonal skills in their everyday extratherapeutic interpersonal relationships. Confirmation of this notion has been demonstrated in a study by Ivey (1973b), in which "media therapy (discussed in greater detail in Chapter 10) has been an effective means of helping psychiatric patients with their "back-home" environments.

Carkhuff and his followers also applied a "counseling skill training program," or at least modifications thereof, as part of training clients in interpersonal skills. Carkhuff and Bierman (1970) offered systematic training in interpersonal skills to ten parents of emotionally disturbed children. The results indicated that there was significant improvement in the level of communication and discrimination between parents but that changes in the level of communication between parents and their children, although in the predicted direction, were not nearly equal to that of the change between parents. Additionally, changes in the child's behavior on more traditional indexes indicated general improvement, but the changes were not significant. Pierce and Drasgow (1969) studied the effects of the experiential-didactic training program on the level of facilitative interpersonal functioning of psychiatric inpatients. Their results indicated that the training group demonstrated significant improvement, as demonstrated by pre- and postobjective and subjective interviewee measures of interpersonal functioning. Moreover, these patients improved significantly more than any of the four control groups, which were receiving more traditional forms of treatment including drug administration and individual and group therapy.

It becomes readily apparent that direct training formats as preferred modes of treatment are limited only by the "teachers' " abilities to isolate and operationally define specific behavioral units of interpersonal skills and to use teaching modalities (especially audio and video feedback mechanisms) as a means of helping people live in a complex and complicated world. Although but a few studies in direct training have been discussed here, Authier et al. cite over 100 references on this issue in their comprehensive review of the historical background of the psychoeducator model. Programs described in this chapter are not the only programs of value but rather are forerunners of many formats which are in operation today and which will be presented in a future chapter. We want to make clear, if it is not already apparent, that we are not arguing which training or direct treatment method is best or right. We recognize that different treatment modalities are frequently appropriate for different problems. Moreover, more often than not, a combination of training or treatment methods is most appropriate, and this is often the case when the more traditional models are used along with the direct training models. It is our hope, therefore, that our readers will utilize those aspects of each program which will help them be the most effective helpers and reach a maximum number of helpees, clients, or patients.

SUMMARY

Initially, this chapter discussed various psychotherapeutic training programs which were designed to help train many types of professionals or paraprofessionals in the art of interviewing or in basic clinical skills. It was emphasized that the more traditional approach was helpful in focusing on the conceptual strategical skill areas and to some degree the experiential area of interviewing but lacked specification of facilitative and interpersonal behavior. Further, this more traditional approach seemed to lack a reasonable transition from the classroom to practice. Finally, traditional training in psychotherapeutic skills seemed to be less systematic than might be possible. It was noted that Rogers opened the door for scrutiny of the therapeutic interaction and that later his followers, especially Truax and Carkhuff, began to fill these voids by focusing on the facilitative conditions of empathy, respect/warmth, and genuineness in a systematic way. In spite of these advances, however, even the experiential-didactic approach to training appears to suffer from the inability to isolate and specify discrete objective interviewer behaviors which the novice can be taught, the acquisition of which lead to predictable changes in client behavior, either outside the counseling situation or within a counseling session.

Recent innovations in interview training, especially the use of observational media as a modality and specification of behavioral content during training, have paved the way for microcounseling. Studies of specific interviewer behaviors were instrumental in suggesting that novice interviewer behavior was identifiable in rather concrete terms and therefore could serve as the content of interview training. Further, the simultaneous application of audio and video media was of benefit in helping to define more clearly the specific behavior on which the novice was to focus. Microcounseling's unique contributions lie in the fact that it combines these two innovative training techniques in a systematic way, which allows the teaching of positive facilitative interviewer behaviors rather than relying on the students acquiring the skills in a trial-and-error fashion. Further, the microcounseling paradigm uses the observational media during a micro-practice session, thus giving the student a chance to practice what the program is trying to effect. Microcounseling is seen as an important training technique which can help beginning counselors, regardless of theoretical orientation, bridge the gap between classroom learning and initial clinical experiences. Even though several of the original studies demonstrating the efficacy of this approach were cited, the thrust is not to present microcounseling as a training alternative but rather as a supplement to existing programs.

A simultaneous and logical extension of the evolution to more effective interviewing training programs is the growth of the training of clients and patients in interpersonal and/or counseling related skills. A reconceptualization of the role of the psychological practitioner is called for which emphasizes the "therapist" as a "teacher." In conjunction with this change, cultural attitudes that learning, especially of interpersonal skills, is not an adult task must be challenged. With the gradual erosion of many entrenched attitudes, the direct training of interpersonal skills to all people experiencing difficulty in living in this complex world is beginning to take shape. Doubtless, as the movement takes more definite form, other and more complete historical perspectives than this will be delineated. Still, the movement is on, and alternative uses of microcounseling and interviewing training are cited as some of the forerunners of the psychoeducator model.

SECTION II

THE CONCEPTUAL FRAMEWORK AND SKILLS OF MICROCOUNSELING

The first section, with its definition of the structural and conceptual components of microcounseling as well as its discussion of the historical-theoretical base of the paradigm as both an educational and therapeutic modality, has set the stage. Microcounseling is a conceptual framework representing an array of skills and qualitative conditions associated with effective helping. This section presents the many skills of the microtraining framework with specific illustrations of the skills within an actual interview. Data presented here are primarily in a white middle-class framework, and cultural considerations will be examined in Chapters 8 and 9.

Basic to all microcounseling skills are the concepts of attending behavior and attention which are explored in detail in Chapter 3. Simply put, *clients in the helping process talk about what helpers listen to.* This chapter explores the process of listening or attending and points out how nonverbal and verbal attention patterns influence the behavior of the helpee.

Chapters 4 and 5 present the microtraining skills of attending and influencing. An overview of these skills may be found in Figure 1 (Chapter 4). Skills such as open and closed questions, paraphrasing, and reflection of feeling are explored in the chapter on attending skills. The chapter on skills of interpersonal influence stresses such concepts as effective self-expression, directions, self-disclosure, and interpretation. Within both chapters, the interview is presented as a process of interpersonal influence, and emphasis is placed on locating and recognizing what a helper does consciously and unconsciously to determine what happens in a helping session.

Empathy is an important but all-too-vague construct of the helping professions. Chapter 6 examines empathy and presents new conceptual frames from microtraining to operationalize empathy, respect, immediacy, and other "core facilitative conditions" of the helping process. Also, Chapter 6 starts to give attention to the issues of alternative theoretical orientations to counseling and psychotherapy and provides a beginning discussion of some of the dimensions of helping which appear to transcend differences in theoretical orientations. This point will be elaborated upon in Chapter 7, where the microtraining skills used by different helpers will be considered. At this point, it appears that helpers of different schools use vastly different microtraining skills but often (but not always) come together when qualitative dimensions of helping are considered.

Some readers will find it helpful to read Appendix III concurrently with Chapters 4, 5, and 6 of this section. A typescript of a demonstration interview is presented which provides specific illustrations of most of the concepts discussed.

Finally, it is important to state that the skills listed here represent only one presentation or categorization of verbal and nonverbal dimensions of helping. While we have found this particular conceptualization of skills useful and fruitful for training and research, we are also aware that other frames for conceptualizing helping exist. We have found that each person who uses the *technology* of microtraining operates best when he or she adapts existing skills or revises *conceptual frame or theory* to fit special needs and interests. Do not let the discussion in the following chapters limit the potential of the technology for identifying new dimensions for analyzing and teaching the helping process.

Chapter 3

ATTENDING BEHAVIOR: AN UNDERLYING
CONSTRUCT OF MICROTRAINING

MICROTRAINING PROCEDURES focus on specific skills and behaviors which can be defined, seen in operation, practiced, and evaluated. Rather than confuse the interviewing trainee with an overwhelming amount of data, the component-skills approach breaks interviewing into workable and observable dimensions.

The basic question asked by the research team (Ivey, Normington, Miller, Morrill, Haase, 1968) who first explored this area was What *are* the specific component skills of counseling? The search for skills to teach within the microcounseling framework began in traditional interviewing, counseling, and therapeutic texts. Many descriptions and theories were examined, but none was sufficiently specific or behavioral to be taught as a microtraining skill. The search next centered on direct observation of interviews, but these original efforts in observation proved fruitless. It was easy to rate an interviewer as "good" or "bad" but almost impossible to decide on what behaviors were indicative of effective counselors.

The breakthrough which resulted in the concept of attending behavior occurred with one of our secretaries, whom we shall call Mary. Frustrated with our lack of success in identifying skills of counseling, we decided to teach some interviewing skills to our secretary, who was unfamiliar with counseling procedures. Mary was asked to talk with a volunteer client and attempt to interview him; the session was to be videotaped. Mary began with "What's your name? Where are you from? What year in school are you?" The client responded pleasantly and positively, but after he answered the third question, an awkward pause occurred. Mary appeared tense and uncomfortable; her eyes wandered about the room as she searched for something new to say. Shortly, she dredged up a new question, and the interview proceeded for a short time until another awkward break occurred. The interview continued in this stilted fashion for the remainder of the five-minute session. On only one occasion did Mary seem at ease; the client asked her a question and Mary momentarily forgot herself, relaxed, and talked about herself. While this may be appropriate social behavior, it is generally not considered interviewing.*

Mary illustrated many of the behaviors of the beginning counselor. She focused on herself and her responsibility for conducting the interview to the extent that it was almost impossible for her to listen to the client. Awkward pauses, loss of eye contact, physical tension, and talking about oneself rather than listening have been noted as common characteristics of the beginning interviewer.

After the first five-minute session, Mary received impromptu microcounseling training. While no written manual describing what was to be called attending behavior was available, we talked with her about finding a more comfortable, relaxed position and maintaining eye contact with the client so that she could communicate attentiveness and interest. Mary was instructed not to add new topics but simply to ask questions or make comments concerning something the client had already said. A videotape of experienced counselors was shown to Mary stressing these three concepts: (a) a relaxed, attentive posture, (b) eye contact, and (c) verbal following. Mary then viewed a videotape of the first session and analyzed her performance with the help of the supervisors. It might be observed that when we saw Mary failing to exhibit specific interviewing behaviors, it became possible to identify and teach them to her.

Following the training session, Mary returned to reinterview the same client. After a brief moment of artificiality, Mary began

---

*However, later research and evaluation suggest that talking about oneself at appropriate times may be a most useful interviewing skill (Higgins, Ivey, and Uhlemann, 1970; Ivey and Gluckstern, 1976a,b) .

to respond in highly impactful ways. In fact, she looked like a highly skilled, experienced counselor. The change was not only dramatic, but when we began to consider the twenty minutes of training it was almost shocking! We have had less change of behavior in some practicum students in an entire year. A pause occurred when the student had exhausted the last question, and Mary's lack of training in counseling skills again became apparent; however, after a short struggle, she asked a question regarding something that had been said earlier in the session, then relaxed, and the interview continued smoothly.

Interestingly, the behaviors learned in the interview generalized to other situations. The following Monday, Mary could not wait to tell us about attending to people over the weekend. She had developed a new behavioral repertoire which was reinforced by a new kind of excitement and involvement with other people. Generalization to some degree is expected, since Mary is of the white middle-class culture and microcounseling concepts of attending behavior were generated from class-related helping theories of the meaning of verbal and nonverbal communication. However, it is important to note that attending behaviors vary cross-culturally. Discussion of the need to adapt the training to specific cultural demands is not warranted here since it is presented in a subsequent chapter. Suffice to say that patterns of verbal following, eye contact, and nonverbal communication are culturally related. Hall's primer of cross-cultural communication, *The Silent Language* (1959), is basic reading for any professional helper who would teach communication skills to other groups or truly understand the nature of communication in any helping interview. The fact is that patterns of attending and communication differ widely from culture to culture and from individual to individual. Thus, for the most part, the remaining section of this chapter will present attention as studied within a white middle-class culture.

Further, the stress in this chapter is on three channels of communication: eye contact, nonverbal communication, and lexical usage. Other channels of communication such as vocal intonation, speech rate, use of different languages, proxemic and space variables, and time sequence are not discussed. These variables are culturally important and may even take precedence at times over the three central dimensions of attending behavior stressed in this section, particularly in cross-cultural situations. For practical purposes in training both helpers and individuals in communication skills, we have found that stress on the three components of attending behavior is sufficient. As workshops and training progress, trainees begin to develop intuitive and practical knowledge in other channels of verbal and nonverbal communication. For further examination of these issues, Hall (1959; 1976), Mehrabian (1972), Wiener and Mehrabian (1968), Birdwhistell (1967), and Ekman, Friesen, and Ellsworth (1972) provide helpful data. Scheflen's (1973) in-depth analysis of psychotherapy transactions is perhaps the most relevant.

ATTENTION AS A POTENT REINFORCER

Rogers (1951, p. 349) has made the following statement:

> In work with various groups it has been sobering to observe how little the members attend to what others say. Without attention there can be no understanding and hence no communication. Apparently the act of attending carefully to another person is a difficult task for most people. They are usually thinking what they will say when the speaker stops.

Rogers goes on to point out that attending to a person is not enough; one must demonstrate to the other that one *has* listened. He suggests looking at the speaker and nodding one's head as giving some proof that one has listened. "If, however, the leader paraphrases the speaker's comment, he thereby furnishes conclusive proof that he has attended" (p. 349-350).

An important aspect of establishing a relationship with the client is being aware of, and responsive to, the communications of that individual and communicating this attentiveness. The communication of attentiveness is a potent reinforcer in counselor-client interaction and plays an important role in the establishment of a relationship. Skinner, in *Science and Human Behavior* (1953, p. 78), has discussed the concepts of attention as follows:

The attention of people is reinforcing because it is a necessary condition for other reinforcements for them. In general, only people who are attending to us reinforce our behavior. The attention of someone who is particularly likely to supply reinforcement—a parent, a teacher, or a loved one—is an especially good generalized reinforcer and sets up especially strong attention-getting behavior.

The research literature strongly supports the value of attention in promoting human behavior change. For example, Allen, Hart, Buell, Harris, and Wolf (1964) demonstrated that teacher attention was maintaining the peer isolation of a nursery school pupil. When the teachers switched their approach to giving the child attention when she was interacting with other children but not when she approached the teachers, her isolation behavior disappeared. Kennedy and Thompson (1967) used attention to modify the behavior of a hyperactive first-grade child. Whitley and Sulzer (1970) used attention to help teachers reduce disruptive classroom behavior. Wahler (1969) has trained parents in the use of differential attention to shape the behavior of "oppositional children." Similar approaches in the use of attention with children have proven equally effective (Quay, Werry, McQueen, and Sprague, 1966; Zimmerman and Zimmerman, 1962).

Evidence for the use of attention as a reinforcer of *verbal behavior* was first provided by Greenspoon (1955) when he successfully demonstrated that a subject's speech may be modified by minimal nonverbal and verbal cues. Extensive research since that time has demonstrated a wide variety of methods through which human behavior may be modified by verbal and nonverbal attention patterns. Excellent reviews of the literature in this field are provided by Bandura (1969), Phillips and Kanfer (1969), Ullmann and Krasner (1965), and Bergin and Suinn (1975).

Content analysis of interview typescripts reveals that counselors either directly or unconsciously selectively condition client responses to suit the counselor's theoretical orientation (Bandura, Lipher, and Miller, 1960; Murray, 1956; Rogers, 1960). Bandura (1961, p. 154) has noted the following:

> . . . the results of these studies show that the therapist not only controls the patient by rewarding him with interest and approval when the patient behaves in a fashion the therapist desires but that

he also controls through punishment in the form of mild disapproval
and withdrawal of interest when the patient behaves in ways that
are threatening to the therapist or run counter to his goals.

A BEHAVIORAL EXAMINATION OF ATTENTION

Despite the emphasis on attention as a generalized reinforcer,
relatively little thought has been given to the definition of the
behavioral components of attending. The three behaviors identified with Mary and subsequently studied by Ivey, Normington,
Miller, Morrill, and Haase (1968) are considered important by
others as well. The following discussion provides a framework
wherein the behavioral aspects of attention may be systematically
considered.

Pepyne and Zimmer (1969) have given special attention to
integrating *verbal conditioning and the counseling interview*. In
their review, they conclude that counseling appears to be emerg-
ing as a process in which specific changes in a client's verbal
behavior can be predicted as well as explained. Kennedy and
Zimmer (1968) found that a paraphrase and a neutrally toned
"mm-hmm" utterance were effective reinforcers with respect to
self-reference statements; however, "mm-hmm" with an affirming
head nod and "I see" were not. They also found that different
counselors obtained significantly different results from comparable subjects. This work has been extended by Crowley (1970),
Hackney (1969), and Pepyne (1968), who have further demonstrated specific aspects of the conditionability of response classes
(topics) in the interview and emotionally laden and nonfeeling-
tone statements.

Exline has given detailed study to *eye contact* and visual interaction patterns (Exline, Gray, and Schuette, 1965; Exline and
Winters, 1965) and finds that eye contact between people represents generally more positive attitudes. Out of this general finding, a variety of other studies detailing the complexity of eye contact patterns are continually arising. Exline and his coworkers,
for example, found that competitive and "Machiavellian" subjects
tend to maintain eye contact longer under stressful conditions.
If an interviewer comments about an interviewee unfavorably,
the interviewee will decrease his or her amount of eye contact.

Ivey and Gluckstern (1974b) point out that the timing of eye contact breaks often illustrates to the careful observer topics which are uncomfortable to the speaker *or* listener.

Physical components of attending behavior also have a research background which justifies their importance. Nonverbal communication patterns have shown themselves to be amenable to direct study (Duncan, 1969). Condon and Ogston (1966) have demonstrated that the physical movements of one member of a group or dyad affect others. Birdwhistell (1967) and Scheflen (1969) as well as Ekman and Freisen (1974, 1975) have demonstrated how to systematize body postures and have shown the importance of nonverbal communication in interpersonal relationships.

The literature on nonverbal communication is ably summarized by Mehrabian (1972). He notes that forward trunk lean and a relaxed body posture are received favorably by the observer and are considered indications of interest. Additionally, a frequently quoted study by Haase and Tepper (1972) found the combination of eye contact, forward trunk lean, closer distance, and positive verbal message was rated as demonstrating the highest degree of empathic understanding. Indeed, they found a positive verbal message was vitiated when not accompanied by nonverbal behavior reflecting good attending skills. A similar study by Bayes (1972) found body, head, and hand movements and smiling to be indicators of high "warmth" ratings. The evidence presented by these studies aptly demonstrates the importance of a formalized interviewing training program including a focus on the nonverbal aspects of an interviewer's behavior.

Individuals give attention to one another by many different means. While these can be divided into a variety of conceptual frameworks, the concepts of attending behavior (eye contact, physical attention, and verbal following behavior) appear to be central aspects by which people relate to, reinforce, and interact with one another. This brief summary of the research literature suggests the power of this means of interpersonal influence. Effectively combining the three dimensions into one larger construct would seem to provide an important vehicle for describing much of what happens between individuals in the interview, as well as in many of life's other interactions.

Attention is central to the interaction between interviewer and client. Unless the interviewer listens or attends to the client, little in the way of understanding will occur. Too many beginning counselors and interviewers fail to listen to their clients.

Attending behavior coupled with microtraining techniques offers a new approach to many problems. Attending can be taught as technique, but unlike pure technique ("say the client's name at least three times"), attending implies real interaction. In order to engage in the skill of attending to client comments, the person must listen to content. To follow communication of feeling by appropriate changes in voice timbre and quality and by appropriate statements, one must attend to the feeling that is being communicated. The person who is incongruent or attending inwardly rather than to the client will be unable to listen. Once it is initiated, attending seems self-reinforcing and may even provide an approach that can be used regardless of the theoretical framework or applied work situation of the trainee.

Some may question the possible artificiality of attending behavior or other skills suggested in this book. They validly object to seeing life as a series of exercises in which the individual constantly dredges into a "handbag of skills" to adapt to each life situation. Our experience has been that individuals may sometimes begin attending in an artificial, deliberate manner. However, once attending has been initiated, the person to whom one is listening tends to become more animated, and this in turn reinforces the attender, who very quickly forgets about attending deliberately and soon attends naturally. A variety of our clients and trainees have engaged in conscious attending behavior only to find themselves so interested in the person with whom they are talking that they lose themselves in the other.

Polanyi's (1966) concept of tacit knowing discussed in Chapter 1 provides a useful explanation of this phenomenon. As in the golf swing of the talented professional, the specific behaviors of attention have been integrated (unconsciously if you will) into a larger, perhaps more meaningful gestalt. Sparking deliberate and distinct behavioral acts into a new whole is the relationship (or mutual reinforcement pattern) between the individual who first started attending and the person to whom that individual attends. Koestler (1964) describes similar phenomena under the concept of the habit hierarchy and points out that the bringing together of formerly distinct behaviors into a new whole frees the individual for creative exploration of larger and more complex issues.

In summary, attending behavior could be defined as simple listening. However, the three central aspects of attending behavior provide a specific set of behaviors through which listening may be taught. Too often interviewer trainers have said "listen," without defining what the act of listening is. The counselor should look at the client to note postural movements, gestures, and facial expressions which give important indications concerning the client. Eye contact need not be constant, nor should it be fixed staring; it should be a natural looking at the client. Secondly, postural position and relaxation are important. Unless the interviewer is relaxed, it will be difficult to focus on the client. When a helper is tense in an interviewing session, attention is often focused on personal concerns rather than on the client.

Finally, verbal following behavior demands that the counselor respond to the last comment or some preceding comment of the client without introducing new data. Topic jumping or asking questions in a random pattern is a common occurrence among beginning interviewers. If the interviewer attends to the client's comments and does not add new information, it is surprising how well he or she gets to know the client. In our society, few people really listen to one another; when someone attends to us, it is a powerful reinforcer to keep talking.

ATTENDING, ISLAND, AND HIATUS BEHAVIOR*

Audiotapes of counseling sessions have tended to give the impression that the counseling interview is a continuous process.

*Portions of the following section are included with permission of the *Journal of Counseling Psychology* American Psychological Association. This section is rewritten from a paper, "Attending, Island, and Hiatus Behavior" (Hackney, Ivey, and Oetting, 1970). Th basic concepts of this paper were developed by E.R. Oetting and originally presented to the American Personnel and Guidance Association (Ivey and Oetting, 1966).

With videorecording, the counseling session is not seen as a continuous unit but as a series of islands and hiatuses.

The island consists of a topic (response class) or a series of very closely related topics, sometimes small, sometimes broad in nature. The island is clearly a unit, and there is almost complete agreement among observers of a tape of the point where the counselor and client reach the end of an island. At this point, a hiatus occurs, a pause or respite. The hiatus may be very short, or it may be extended; it may be represented by the uncomfortable period where the novice therapist desperately searches for something to say while the client anxiously awaits another go-ahead signal, or it may be a comfortable period of reflection between an experienced therapist and the patient in the midst of profitable long-term therapy.

The hiatus appears to be a period of negotiation between the counselor and client, a negotiation in which new response classes or topics are sought. Both counselor and client become acutely aware of both verbal and nonverbal cues during this negotiation. The client in search of a new topic may present possible alternatives to which the therapist has the choice of attending or ignoring (reinforcing or extinguishing). A typescript of this type of interaction might read as follows:

> *Client:* Well, I can't think of anything else to say.
> *Interviewer:* (Silence.)
> *Client:* I think I'll go shopping this afternoon.
> *Interviewer:* (Silence.)
> *Client:* Except I don't like to go shopping alone and all my friends have classes this afternoon.
> *Interviewer:* It's not fun to do things alone.

In this example, possible topics (shopping, class schedule, friends, and being alone) are treated differently by the counselor. By silence, the interviewer extinguishes certain topics. When the interviewer does reinforce the client's last comment by attending, the potentially emotionally loaded topic of lack of companionship is selected. If the client responds to the counselor's statement, the negotiation, and thus the hiatus, is concluded, and a new island emerges.

The island, of course, represents a series of interviewer-client utterances on a similar topic. It appears to flow smoothly until that topic is exhausted and a new hiatus or negotiation takes place.

It is now possible to return to Mary, our secretarial interviewer-in-training. When a topic was launched and Mary was attending, she appeared almost as a professional counselor. However, when a hiatus was reached, her lack of training in counseling skills became apparent. The hiatus called for initiation of new areas, and Mary did not follow one of the counseling or interviewing traditions. If she had, she would have waited for the client to respond (nondirective), initiated an expression of her own feeling state (recent client-centered), directed attention to an early experience (analytic), presented a discriminative stimulus to elicit verbal responses which could be reinforced (learning theory), brought out a Strong Vocational Interest Blank (vocational counseling), or asked a question about previous job history (employment interviewing for job placement).

Mary actually began to talk about an interesting experience in her own immediate past (standard social behavior). However, since she was still attempting to engage in attending behavior, when the interviewee responded to her, she listened to him, reinforced his comment, and once again *looked like* the highly skilled interviewer.

The concepts of island and hiatus in interviewing provide useful speculations for research in counseling and therapy. Some of the contradictory research findings in content analysis of counseling may be explained with these terms. It is possible that those studies showing highly consistent counselor behaviors between theoretical disciplines have focused on behaviors characteristic of islands, and those studies showing differential behavior for counselors of differing persuasions have focused upon behaviors characteristic of the hiatus.

All successful interviewers, counselors, and therapists have basic attending skills. They are good listeners, are relaxed and natural in the interviewing session, maintain some type of consistent eye contact (in some cases, it is recognized that therapists avoid eye contact but still maintain attention), and verbally attend or follow through with clients.

However, it is equally clear that interviewers, counselors, and therapists of differing persuasions and differing skills do indeed differ. It is likely that they differ in what they attend to or reinforce in the client's behavior. An employment interviewer may notice the nonverbal cues of the interviewee but ignore them if they are not job-relevant, whereas an existential therapist may pay considerable attention to these same cues. An analyst may attend to statements about a person's work primarily in terms of analytic significance. The hiatus or negotiation period provides the clearest opportunity for observation and study of differential reinforcing or attending patterns of interviewers.

The concept of attention provides an explanation for the success of the many varieties of counseling and interviewing approaches. For example, it has been pointed out that an analytic client dreams in Freudian symbols, a Jungian client in mythological symbolism, and a Gestalt client in parts and wholes. The therapist at key hiatus points has simply selectively attended or reinforced the client's verbalizations which support his or her theoretical framework. A Freudian client may have a mythological symbol in a dream, but if mention of the symbol is met by silence on the part of the therapist, it is not likely to figure prominently in the session.

Similarly, vocational counselors demonstrate differential attending or reinforcement patterns. One counselor may attend primarily to past work history and factual information about job progression, noting and reinforcing client comments about skills and competencies developed. Another counselor may attend to client comments related to attitudes and emotions toward the supervisor. Thus, typescripts of vocational interviews conducted from different attentional frames reveal marked differences in content, although both counselors might be very effective in attending behavior.

ATTENDING BEHAVIOR AND INTENTIONALITY

Ivey (1970) and Ivey and Rollin (1974) have discussed the *intentional individual,* the fully functioning person, in the following way:

> The person who acts with intentionality has a sense of capability. He is one who can generate alternative behaviors in a given situation and "come at" a problem from different vantage points. The intentional individual is not bound to one course of action but can respond in the moment to changing life situations as he looks forward to longer-term goals.

Microteaching in interviewing techniques draws on a similar concept. Counselors often cannot act with intentionality; they do not have a sufficiently varied behavioral repertoire and so tend to act in a stereotyped fashion, using one or two types of interview leads. Training in the specific skills of microcounseling gives the beginning counselor a series of behaviors which can be drawn on to facilitate interviewer-client interaction.

The model of the intentional interviewer supplies a general frame of reference for the objectives of an interviewing or counseling training program. Most interviewer trainers wish to help their trainees develop a unique approach to interviewing. While the supervisor may occasionally serve as a beginning model for the novice therapist, the supervisor is most effective when trainees develop their own behavioral repertoire or interviewing style. Fully professional counselors are their own persons. While they understand and appreciate the skills of others, they are capable of making their own unique synthesis in the actual interview.

The specific objective of microtraining is to supply beginning counselors or interviewing trainees with an acquaintance of and experience in a variety of interviewing skills. It is anticipated that no one student needs, nor will be interested in, all the skills which could be taught. Microcounseling, then, is concerned with introducing trainees to a variety of skills in the expectation that each individual will eventually develop a unique and personal behavioral repertoire.*

---

*Intentionality forms a part of the concept of communication competence and the "culturally effective individual" explored in Chapter 9.

Mary's behavior could also be viewed from the framework of intentionality. When the hiatus was reached during the first session, her behavioral repertoire as an interviewer was limited, perhaps nonexistent, and she had no readily available response. Hence the awkward pauses, talking about herself, and topic jumping. When Mary was given the one additional skill of attending behavior, response possibilities were greatly increased, the conversational islands lengthened, she talked less, and the individual with whom she was talking enjoyed the session more.

As one swallow does not make a summer, neither does attending behavior make an interviewer. Additional skills, practice, and experience would be necessary before Mary could demonstrate fully effective interviewing techniques. Mary's intentionality as an interviewer was increased by adding attending behavior to her repertoire, but it would require more skills to give her more choices if she were to become fully intentional. One cannot be free or make choices unless one has alternatives available.

Then what is the relationship between attending behavior and intentionality? The interviewer's use of attending behavior in the interview determines the direction and content of the session. Zimmer and his students (Crowley, 1970; Hackney, 1969; Pepyne, 1968) and Miller et al. (1973) demonstrated that selective attention or reinforcement profoundly influence what happens in the interview. Through use of attention and the constructs of attending behavior, the intentional counselor can lead the interview in many directions. Through use of selective attention and a variety of behavioral skills, the counselor may be of maximal benefit to a maximum number and type of clients. The one-tool counselor who may lack intentionality, the ability to focus attention, and accompanying behavioral skills is less flexible and less able to deal with new and unusual occurrences during interviews. Further, the range of clients who may be helped is reduced. Unable to attend to the variety of responses and behaviors the client emits, the individual who lacks intentionality is unable to respond to all dimensions of the individual's experience.

ATTENDING BEHAVIOR, ATTENTION, AND OTHER FRAMES OF REFERENCE

Attending behavior is considered here primarily from a behavioral frame of reference. The related construct of attention has been an issue in psychology for a considerable period of time. There are important distinctions between attending behavior and attention as the following definition by William James (1890, pp. 403-404) illustrates:

> Everyone knows what attention is. It is the taking possession by the mind, in clear and vivid form, of one out of what seems several possible objects or trains of thought. Focalization, concentration, of consciousness are of its essence. It implies withdrawal from some things in order to deal effectively with others, and it is a condition which has a real opposite in the confused, dazed, scatterbrained state which in French is called *distraction* . . .

Attention appears to describe the functional significance of attending behavior in that it is a way in which the conscious organization of experience may be described. Much of Luria's (1969) work describing the development of cerebral organization in children could be viewed from a similar frame of reference, although he does not emphasize the term "attention."

Attending behavior is directly observable and measurable, while attention remains a more subtle area of study. It is possible, for example, for an interviewer to be engaging in attending behavior in terms of all physical and verbal manifestations while primary attention is directed elsewhere. The Skinnerian view of attention is one which is best observed in the behavioral relationship of one individual to another. The focus of attention as described by William James, however, remains a more intuitive, inner-directed matter, less subject to direct observation.

The literature on attention has been diverse and has demonstrated a lack of synthesis over the years. Woodworth and Schlosberg (1954, pp. 72-73) made the following comment:

> In spite of the practical reality of attending, the status of attention in systematic psychology has been uncertain and dubious for a long time. Early psychologists thought of it as a faculty or power, akin to the Will. . . . Any such view was strongly opposed by the association-

ists who wished to recognize as forces only sensory stimulations and association. The Gestalt psychologists have regarded any force of attention as extraneous to the field forces which in their view are the dynamic factors in human activity. The behaviorists have rejected attention as a mere traditional mentalistic concept.

Recently, however, attention has been examined in more depth. Norman (1969) has developed a comprehensive model for attentional processes and presents valuable data on selective attention, the acquisition and processing of information, and memory. Trabasso and Bower (1968) have studied the relationship of attention to learning. Both works summarize much of the literature on attention. A major symposium on attention was held at the 1969 International Congress of Psychology in London. The review by Swets and Kristofferson (1970) should also be cited. It appears that attention as a construct is gaining increasing popularity.

Attention is also an important construct in more esoteric areas of psychology. Maupin (1965), for example, examined the concept of attention in relationship to Zen meditation exercise. Kasamatsu and Hirai (1966) found that the focused attention of Zen exercises resulted in predictable patterns of brain-wave alpha rhythm. Shor (1962) relates hypnosis to concepts of attention. Deikman (1963) discusses mystical phenomena as being founded initially on focused attention and cites hypnotic concepts of automatization similar to the integrative constructs of Polanyi (1966) and Koestler (1964) mentioned earlier. Discussing autogenic training, Luthe (1969) describes many studies in which passive concentration, special types of attention, and related methods have resulted in drops in blood sugar, decreases in muscle potential, changes in peripheral circulation, rise in skin temperature, respiratory changes, and other physical phenomena. Instruction in such inner attentional processes may someday become part of every person's experience.

Biofeedback is still another esoteric area of psychology in which attention plays an important role. The process, for the most part, entails providing the patient with relatively immediate information or feedback of some bioelectric response. Biofeedback training itself has three main goals: (1) the development of increased awareness of some internal physiological function, (2) the establishment of control over this function, and (3) the transfer or generalization of this control from the training site to other areas of one's life. It is obvious that although a conglomeration of variables is operating during biofeedback training, attention is *sine qua non*. As such, attention is becoming important in the treatment of various psychosomatic disorders. Indeed, a review of the clinical applications of biofeedback training (Blanchard and Young, 1974) cites evidence demonstrating biofeedback training to be an effective treatment procedure for such diverse diseases as hypertension, migraine headaches, cardiac arrhythmias, and epilepsy. They conclude that although it would be premature to hail biofeedback as a panacea for psychosomatic and other disorders, the evidence is often interesting and provocative. Since the role of attention is so important in this procedure, perhaps now more than ever instruction in attentional processes needs to become a part of every person's experience.

Attention and existentialism also deserve consideration. The French *distraction* described by William James as a confused, disordered state is closely akin to Roquentin's experience of decomposition in the following passage from Sartre's *Nausea* (1964, p. 128):

> Existence is a deflection. Trees, night-blue pillars, the happy bubbling of a fountain, vital smells, little heat mists floating in the cold air, a red-haired man digesting on a bench . . . In vain I tried to *count* the chestnut trees, to *locate* them by their relationship to the Velleda, to compare their height with the height of the plane trees: each of them escaped the relationship in which I tried to enclose it, isolated itself, and overflowed.

It may be observed that the inability of Roquentin to focus on or attend to his surroundings has been important in his inability to organize his world. Similarly, the inability of the three principals to commit themselves to action in *No Exit* (Sartre, 1946) is another powerful description of the inability of man to maintain attention or commitment to the environment in a focal manner. It is interesting to observe that participants in sensory-restriction experiments tend to experience problems of attention not unlike those described above (Zubec, 1964a,b,c). Understimulation appears to produce a similar problem in developing consistent attentional processes.

The French existentialists suggest that the way out of man's dilemma is action in an absurd world despite possible awareness that the action itself may be absurd. The route to action is existential commitment or, alternatively defined, the focalization of one's attentional processes to one dimension of the multitude of possibilities which exist in one's environment. The analogy between the existential paradox "to live is to die" and the need for withdrawal from other stimuli if one is to concentrate on one stimulus in James' definition should be apparent.

Intentionality is, of course, a concept prominent in the writing of some existentialists (May, 1969). The more behavioral definition of intentionality presented here may not be much different from that of the self-actualized individual. The truly effective or actualized interviewer will have many alternative behaviors and the capability to engage in these behaviors with satisfaction to self and others. The concepts of intentionality, attending behavior, and attention suggest some areas of agreement, or at least discussion, among differing views of humankind.

Conscious, deliberate attending behavior may be viewed as one route out of the existential dilemma. Consider the beginning interviewer beleaguered by a multitude of stimuli from a talkative client. The interviewer may be unable to organize or synthesize any meaning from the client's comments. Clearly, the client is in control of such a session (even though seeking help from the counselor). The counselor who supplies a variety of leads and responses to the client without any effort at organization may confuse both him or herself and the client. By deliberate focusing on one dimension of the client's experience, the counselor can help bring the interview under control; once the interview has been focused, it is possible to build gradually to the most important and relevant dimensions and to help the client grow.

SUMMARY

Attention and the accompanying constructs of attending behavior provide a comprehensive framework for the intentional interviewer. Counselors of varying orientations and areas of expertise may be distinguished by the issues of content and feeling to which they attend and thus reinforce. As such, attending behavior does not explain varying counseling theories nor does it suggest that one type of interviewing is more effective than another. Attending behavior simply illustrates an important common denominator in a variety of counseling and interviewing approaches. It also provides a systematic way to test the validity of alternative approaches.

More than one approach to human behavior change is effective. At a minimum, there is clinical evidence indicating that approaches as varying as psychoanalysis, trait-factor vocational counseling, and behavior therapy do assist individuals. The important question may be which therapist, with what treatment, is most appropriate, at what time, with what important situational variables, and with what client? If this highly individualistic approach to interviewing and behavior change is accepted, the intentional counselor, who is able to direct responses in a variety of directions, may well be the most successful and facilitative helper.

Chapter 4

ATTENDING SKILLS IN THE
HELPING PROCESS

MICROTRAINING TECHNIQUES are based on a component-skills approach in that the broad complex of helper interview behavior is divided into single units. The most basic unit of microcounseling is attending behavior, the careful listening to the client. The beginning counselor who is able to attend to and hear the client is equipped to start counseling sessions. Without the ability to attend, the helping interview—regardless of theoretical orientation —becomes an empty sham.

This chapter presents the several attending skills with accompanying illustrations of the skills in an actual interview. The following chapter presents the skills of interpersonal influence, e.g. self-disclosure, interpretation. The complete picture of attending and influencing skills may be viewed in the Ivey Taxonomy (Fig. 1). The format of attending and influencing skills presented in these pages should be seen as only one view of the organization and the nature of skills involved in the processes of counseling, interviewing, and therapy. Those with a behavioral orientation may find attending behavior and its many possible variations most valid; reflection of feeling and paraphrasing are most related to the nondirective and client-centered orientation; adaptations of interpretation skills will be most relevant to dynamically oriented individuals. Further, the skills suggested here may be reconceptualized or rejected by some readers, especially those who disagree with the emphasis throughout on attending behavior and attentional processes.

Attending skills are closely related to the construct of basic empathy, the accurate sensing of the world of the client "as if" the counselor were in the client's world (Rogers, 1961). To hear the client with full empathic understanding, one must attend to the client. The importance and effect of empathic understanding is reviewed in Rogers (1975), and it has been demonstrated that empathy facilitates self-exploration and later interview success. Rogers states clearly that empathy is related to positive outcome.

Empathy, however, is an ambiguous construct, hard to define and describe to beginning helpers. The oft-described "put yourself in the client's shoes" simply is not sufficiently descriptive for many people learning the helping process. It is crucial in empathy to hear the world as the client sees it. The skills of paraphrasing, reflection of feeling, and summarization described in this chapter are foundation stones of empathy. Further, to be empathic, the counselor or therapist must *focus* on the client and the client's personal experience. The attending skills presented in this chapter are not empathy but are basic to the development of this central core condition of helping, therapy, and interviewing. In Chapter 6, the construct of empathy and its relationship to qualitative dimensions of microtraining skills are explored further.

This chapter describes six attending skills which are basic to empathy and have been identified as central to the microcounseling paradigm. The skills are organized into the beginning skills of interviewing and skills of selective attention. A section on *focus,* the subject of the interviewer statement, concludes the chapter.

BEGINNING SKILLS OF INTERVIEWING

Studies of novice interviewer behavior by Matarazzo, Phillips, Wiens, and Saslow (1965); Matarazzo, Wiens, and Saslow (1966); and Phillips and Matarazzo (1962) have revealed that novice interviewers tend to make many communication errors. Most notably, beginners frequently cut off interaction with their clients by asking closed-ended questions or by making long, awkward speeches. When one speaks with novices after these sessions, they often report that they were most uncomfortable and could not get the client to talk. Stories of errors made by beginning interviewers

THE TAXONOMY OF MICROTRAINING
QUANTITATIVE AND QUALITATIVE SKILLS[1]

A. *Basic attending and self-expression skills.* Underlying all attending and influencing skills are culturally appropriate patterns of eye contact, body language, and verbal following behavior. Vocal tone, speech loudness and rate, and proxemic variables are also important but are not stressed in beginning phases of helper training.

B. *The microtraining skills.* Different helpers use different helping leads. The single skills of microcounseling categorize helper behaviors into teachable units divided into attending and influencing skills.

Attending skills:

CLOSED QUESTIONS. Most often begin with "do," "is," "are" and can be answered by the helpee with only a few words.

OPEN QUESTIONS. Typically begin with "what," "how," "why," or "could" and allow the helpee more room for self-exploration.

MINIMAL ENCOURAGE. Selective attention to and repetition back to the helpee of exact words or phrases. May also be represented by "Tell me more . . ." or "Uh-huh."

PARAPHRASE. Gives back to the helpee the essence of past verbal statements. Selective attention to key *content* of helpee verbalizations.

REFLECTION OF FEELING. Selective attention to key affective or emotional aspects of helpee behavior.

SUMMARIZATION. Similar to paraphrase and reflection of feeling but represents a longer time period and gives back to client several strands of thinking.

Influencing skills:[2]

DIRECTIONS. Telling the helpee or helpees what to do.

EXPRESSION OF CONTENT. Giving advice, sharing information, making suggestions, giving opinions.

EXPRESSION OF FEELING. Sharing personal or other people's affective state in the interview.

---

[1]Examples of scoring of these skills may be found in Appendix III.

[2]Self-disclosure and direct-mutual communication are not listed as they are combination skills consisting of clusters of quantitative skills and qualitative dimensions.

Figure 1.

INFLUENCING SUMMARY. Stating the main themes of the helper's statements over a period of time.

INTERPRETATION. Renaming or relabeling the helpee's behaviors or verbalizations with new words from a new frame of reference.

C. *Focus dimensions.* The main theme or subject of the helpee or helper's sentence often determines what either individual will speak on next.

HELPEE. The helper's statement focuses on the client. May be demonstrated by the helper using the client's name or the personal pronoun "you". In the case of the helpee, this focus is generally manifested by an "I" statement.

HELPER. The helper makes an "I" statement, or the helpee may focus on the helper through "you" or the helper's name.

DYAD (GROUP). The predominant theme is an "I-you" focus with both helper and helpee ideas or their own relationship being examined. In group counseling, the words "group" or "we" will appear.

OTHERS. The subject of the sentence is some other individual not present.

TOPIC. The subject of the sentence is a special topic or problem such as job search, tests, an abortion.

CULTURAL-ENVIRONMENTAL-CONTEXT. The subject or main theme of statements focus on the surrounding culture or environment. "This is a *situational* problem" or "*Women* often have this concern."

D. *Qualitative dimensions.* It is also possible to rate helper (and helpee) state ments for the quality of response. Microtraining has attempted to provide single skill units for several underlying facilitative dimensions of helping.

CONCRETENESS. The statement may be vague and inconclusive or concrete and specific.

IMMEDIACY. Statements may be rated for tense—past, present, or future.

RESPECT. Enhancing statements about the self or others are considered to repre- sent respect, while negative statements or "put-downs" indicate an absence of this dimension.

CONFRONTATION. Discrepancies in the self or between self and others are noted.

GENUINENESS. There is an absence of mixed verbal and nonverbal messages. In particularly effective communication, verbal and nonverbal movement syn- chrony between helper and helpee may be noted.

POSITIVE REGARD. Selective attention to positive aspects of self or others and/or demonstrated belief that people can change and manage their own lives.

Figure 1 (continued).

and novice therapists are legion. Most of these problems can be
traced to the fact that the beginner simply did not know what to
do and did not have a beginning behavioral repertoire to rely on
when awkward moments or hiatuses appeared.

It seems necessary and helpful to equip the neophyte counselor or interviewer with some survival skills so that the first
sessions are not disastrous to the trainee or the client. Patterson
(1968) explores this isssue in detail. He cites evidence indicating
that counseling or psychotherapy can lead to client damage even
when practiced by experienced counselors or therapists. Thus,
the importance of providing new interviewers with interviewing
skills cannot be denied. Three beginning skills are suggested
here. These are attending behavior, open invitation to talk, and
minimal encourages.

Attending Behavior

Attending behavior is a basic skill underlying many dimensions of counseling. It has been taught to a wide variety of individuals, including advanced clinical psychology graduate students, paraprofessionals, and fourth graders, with success. It is an
especially clear skill, can be taught to individuals or small groups,
and is easily learned in a one-hour period.

Attending behavior serves many functions for the beginning
interviewer. The experience of success and seeing oneself improve rapidly is highly reinforcing. For more sophisticated
trainees, attending behavior can be presented as an introductory
skill, one which will enable them to become acquainted with the
microtraining format and see themselves on television for the
first time.

Most important, attending behavior gives trainees something
to do when they simply do not know what to do in the session.
In such awkward moments, the interviewer can simply maintain
eye contact, retain a relaxed, easy body posture, think back to
something that interested her/him in the client's earlier discussion,
make a comment about it, and the interview then can proceed.
One of the most important skills that advanced therapists or
personnel interviewers have when pressed in the interview is the

ability to relax, reflect on the session, and then respond to the client in some appropriate fashion. One cannot help but think of the many interviewers who have used their pipes as a method to put themselves together before responding to the client.

For those who are oriented to behavioral approaches in the interview, a wide variety of adaptations and extensions of the use of attending behavior as a reinforcer are feasible. Following a model suggested by the studies of Crowley (1970), Hackney (1969), and Pepyne (1968), it would be possible to develop microcounseling skills in which trainees would demonstrate their ability to alternately reinforce various types of affective and cognitive content. For example, trainees could demonstrate their ability to reinforce emotional comments about parents. This then could be extinguished through lack of attention, and then again reinforced. Beginning or experienced counselors who demonstrate this type of control in the session can be expected to gain considerable confidence in their ability to handle difficult situations. A variety of skills using attention as a reinforcer can be developed to allow trainees to sharpen their ability to shape client behavior in a multitude of directions.

At another level, attending behavior can be viewed more simply as listening thoughtfully to another person. An emphasis on being with the client, hearing thoroughly, and noting experience, when coupled with attending behavior training in microcounseling, can lead to a phenomenological or existential orientation. In dynamic orientations, attending behavior could best be considered a general listening skill, primarily used by the therapist to gain information.

Attending behavior's main components of eye contact, physical posture, and verbal following behavior can be taught separately if a trainee is functioning at a low level. In teaching some psychiatric patients the concepts of attending behavior, we have found that teaching three concepts simultaneously may be too demanding. Similarly, some interviewing trainees may need special advice and assistance in developing appropriate eye contact patterns or physical attending behaviors, especially if they demonstrate unusual patterns in their interviews.

Appendix III presents a typescript of a helping interview scored for the several dimensions of attending behavior and the attending and influencing skills. Here it may be observed that the helper is engaging primarily in attending behavior but at three points clearly changes topic. These changes of topic represent hiatus points where one can obtain a particularly clear view of the nature of the helper's orientation or an indication of problem areas which the supervisor can use to help the trainee improve interview flow.

The first topic change (Al 18) occurred just after the following exchange:

Al 17: You said you'd like to deal with it. Ah, am I hearing you accurately? That you'd like to deal with him more effectively, or be with him more? (Open question, attends to helpee's previous statement)

Joan 17: Yeah. Or must tell him to get out of my life. I don't know which I want to do.

Al 18: Okay. Let's not try to resolve that right now. Let's do an exercise that we've done in the past. Stop for a moment. And would you just sort of close your eyes and just sort of imagine what you might like your relationship to be like. Regardless of how it is now— what would you like it to be? How would you like to respond to him? Just think for a moment. (Direction)

The clear topic change indicates that the helper does not hesitate to be direct and tell the helpee what to do. A nondirective or client-centered helper might have reflected the ambivalent feelings (e.g. "Joan, right now you're undecided and confused. One side of you says that you want a relationship with a man, the other that this man may not be for you."). An interpretive helper might have attended to the immediate situation and might have provided an interpretation (e.g. "You're showing your unwillingness to be close to a man.").

The preceding topic jump provides an idea about the theoretical orientation or world view of the helper. The following topic jump provides an indication of a problem area for the counselor and is important data for the counselor or therapist trainer:

(Joan has just viewed a videotape in which she saw her tight posture and tenseness associated with the man discussed in the previous paragraph.)

Joan 25: I'm feeling very strongly right now that what I need to do is say good-bye to him. But it really—that this isn't a situation that I can continue to work on or that's profitable to continue to work on. And that it's not time for me to be that involved anyway. (Expression of feeling, some reinterpretation)

Al 26: How would you like to respond to him? I mean first I've got to say that I've heard you say that you really want to be done with it. How would you——(Open question, pharaphrase).

Joan 26: Hmm.

Al 27: How would you like to respond to him? What might he say to make you come across like this? (Open question) .

Joan 27: Would you repeat the question?

Here the helper has made an attempt to hear the helpee and attend at Al 26, but he completely fails to attend to the helpee at Al 27, resulting in a sidetrack and a disruption to the session. At points such as this, one can learn much about the helper and his reasons for failing to attend. Supervision with this helper would focus on basic attending skills and the need to hear the client's central topic.

The topic jump is an excellent place to study the helper in training and note patterns which may need further development or changing. Similarly, breaks in eye contact or sudden changes in body language represent the nonverbal equivalents of failure to attend. The study of these nonverbal components will provide vital data about helpers and their basic interviewing styles. Some helpers have trouble maintaining eye contact when discussing subjects which are difficult for them personally. They then wonder why their helpees seem to avoid certain areas when they themselves have constantly extinguished helpee exploration in difficult areas. Similarly, some people are so attuned to certain issues that they will provide supportive eye contact and body language only on certain topics. These more aggressive helpers are essentially determining what their helpees will talk about. Some helpers may never have clients who talk about sex, others may have clients who talk about nothing else. The pattern of attending behaviors is key to explaining the difference between the two.

Vocal tone is not ordinarily stressed as one of the main components of attending behavior, but it must be observed that sharp changes in pitch, resonance, or volume are indicators of attentional patterns much as are topic jumps, eye contact breaks, and shifts in body position.

The simple construct of attending behavior, then, may not necessarily be all that simple. At the early levels of training, stress on the importance of eye contact, body language, and staying on a single verbal topic produces improvement in beginning helpers. At a more sophisticated level, attending behavior constructs provide useful ways to analyze the pattern of helping of even the most skilled professional.

The Issue of Silence in the Interview

Many people have raised the question of the place of silence in the microtraining framework. Is silence a skill? We believe that silence is best considered a part of attending behavior (and at a later point, self-expression behavior). Silence, the absence of verbalization, obviously does occur in the interview. Any time the helpee is talking, the helper is usually silent. When the helper talks, the helpee usually listens. When one observes silent periods between helper and helpee, counselor and client, therapist and patient, it becomes apparent that silent times in the interview are not truly silent in that nonverbal communication is still taking place. *Thus, silence in the microtraining framework is considered another part of nonverbal communication and is a dimension of attending behavior.*

The meaning and power of silence in the interview have been best described by Matarazzo, Wiens, Matarazzo, and Saslow (1968) and Matarazzo, Wiens, and Saslow (1966) in their pioneering work on the laboratory correlates of speech and silence behavior. It is this group which has conducted some of the most significant studies of the impact of nonverbal behavioral messages in the interview. Among their important findings was that therapist percent of talk-time was a useful variable for study. They documented the important, but often forgotten fact, that therapist talk-time and talk patterns determine heavily what helpees will do.

They also discussed the importance of "reaction time latency," the time between when one speaker stops talking and the other begins. Observation reveals that naive beginning counselors often have quick reaction time and speak before their client is truly finished. The extreme of rapid reaction time, of course, is the interruption before the client has even finished speaking. They stress that reaction time is a more important variable than mutual silence and indicate that few experienced interviewers wait so long as ten or fifteen seconds before responding. Rather, the response times in their studies ranged from a low of one second to a high of slightly over four seconds for a patient-therapist pair.

They also studied length of utterance and found that such simple interviewer behaviors as head nodding, "Mm-hmm," or longer speech durations on the part of interviewer led to longer verbalizations on the part of the interviewee. Finally, study of reaction time patterns also revealed that if an interviewer reduced reaction time to less than one second, reaction time patterns were changed on the part of the interviewee in the same direction. Moreover, if an interviewer increased reaction time to a full five seconds, the helpee in 25 percent of the instances would initiate a new utterance.

These and other data from the Matarazzo group lead to the clear conclusion that silence is not the absence of behavior but rather the presence of some extremely complex human interaction patterns. When these data are combined with the important nonverbal dimensions of the helping interview, it is clear that we have no periods where there is an absence of behavior. An excellent current review of this work may be found in Matarazzo and Wiens (1977).

If a microtraining skill of silence were developed, some important dimensions of instruction for beginning helpers would include the array of nonverbal dimensions mentioned in this and the preceding chapter. The reaction time between the point at which a client stops and the interviewer makes a comment would also be important. The desirability of interviewers lengthening their reaction time, thereby keeping their talk time at a minimum in the early stages of helping, may also be stressed.

Open Invitation to Talk

This skill, which was developed by Phillips, Lockhart, and Moreland (1969b), is specifically concerned with teaching the beginning interviewer to ask open-ended questions and encourage clients to talk and explore their thoughts and feelings. An open invitation is best understood when compared with a closed approach to interviewing:

> *Open:* Could you tell me a litle bit about your last job?
>   How did you feel about your wife's ignoring you?
> *Closed:* Did you like your last job?
>   Do you get angry with your wife's ignoring you?

Phillips, Lockhart, and Moreland observe that open comments provide *room* for client exploration without categories being imposed by the interviewer. An open invitation to talk allows the client many alternatives for self-expression. The closed question, on the other hand, tends to be factual and can often be answered with a yes or no. Interviews focusing on closed questions often give the client a feeling of interrogation. Employment interviews which stress past job history, educational background, and related factual information represent a prime example of closed communication. In such sessions, the interviewer fails to obtain a real understanding of important attitudes, feelings, and experiences of the applicant or employee which might be vital to eventual placement.

In summarizing open invitation to talk, Phillips, Lockhart, and Moreland (1969b, p. 1) conclude the following:

> Crucial to the giving of open-ended questions is the concept of who is to lead the interview. While the interviewer does ask questions while using this skill, his questions are centered around concerns of the client rather than around concerns of the interviewer for the client. Questions should be designed to help the client clarify his own problems, rather than provide information for the interviewer. . . . If the interviewer relies on closed questions to structure his interview, he usually is forced to concentrate so hard on thinking up the next question that he fails to listen to and attend to the client.

Open invitation to talk may be viewed as an extension of attending behavior in that it directs attention to the client's needs and wishes rather than to those of the interviewer. By focusing attention on the client's communication, it becomes possible to understand more fully the ideas presented.

Phillips, Lockhart, and Moreland point out additional values of open invitation to be considered. They assist the beginning counselor start an interview ("How have things been on the job these past few days?" as opposed to, "Is your job going well?"). They may be used to help the client give specific examples of behavior so that the interviewer is better able to understand what is being described ("Could you give me an example of what you mean when you say you don't get along with your roommate?"). Finally, open invitations can be especially useful in helping the client focus attention on emotions ("What are you feeling as we talk about this?" as compared to, "Do you feel anxious now?").

However, closed questions are also appropriate at times. Closed questions used appropriately, following an extended rambling discourse, can help the client focus attention on central issues. Then, when the client has a "fix" or focus around which he or she can think, open invitation to talk may again be utilized. Skilled interviewers use a balance between open and closed questions to facilitate the growth of their clients; varying types of interviews will obviously require differing proportions of open versus closed interview leads.

Closed questions most typically begin with "is," "are," "do," or "did." Examples might include the following:

"Do you mind if I turn the television unit on and record this interview?"
"Are you angry now?"
"Is your sister the cause of your difficulties?"
"Did you follow my suggestion?"

All these questions can be answered with a brief "yes" or "no." Closed questions are typical of beginning helpers. They may ask a barrage of closed questions on perfectly good topics and then wonder why the clients do not express themselves more fully.

Open questions most typically begin with "what," "how,"

"why," or "could." Observation of numerous interviews on questions has revealed that *what* questions are often associated with facts and the gathering of information, *how* questions with process and feelings, *why* questions with reasons, and *could* (or *would*) questions with a maximum amount of "room" for client self-exploration. In addition, "could" questions provide the client with an implied right not to answer the question, thus providing even more freedom. For example, compare the possible effects of open questions in response to Joan 14:

> *Joan 14:* (I'm) frightened that he could ooze into my life and take over. And also disgusted that why should I have to deal with that in order to have a warm relationship with a man.
> *Helper:* What does he do to give you that feeling? (Brings out facts)
> How can you deal with that? (Leads to process and often emotions as well)
> Why do you feel that way? (Looks for reasons and may put client on the "spot." Some helpers prefer to avoid why questions.)
> Could you explore that issue further? (Maximum room for exploration)

Each of the open questions leads the helpee in very different directions, all of them potentially useful depending on one's own theoretical orientation. Closed questions in response to the helpee might be useful, but could possibly put the client in a "box." For example. "Do you bring out that behavior in him?" "Are you frustrated with him?" and similar questions all rely heavily on the helper's view of the world and lead the client in very specific directions.

However, closed questions are not necessarily unwise in the helping interview. As stated previously, they provide focus and clarity and help narrow the area of conversation, particularly with a client who is talkative and confusing. Closed questions which attend to the client's past comment may be used to "cool the temperature" of an overheated interview in which the beginning counselor feels threatened by client verbalizations. For example, the client may be talking in heavily emotional terms about fears of homosexuality and the beginning helper may be incompetent to work in that area. Instead of continuing with open questions or other helping skills, the beginner may use closed questions to re-orient the interview to ground where the helper is safer and later refer the client elsewhere. For example:

Helpee: "Am I a homosexual? I'm scared to death. . ." (breaks into tears)

Helper: (After waiting for an appropriate moment) What are you scared of? (Open question oriented to facts)

Helpee: My family will reject me.

Helper: Does your family live near here?

The above example does *not* represent good counseling but does illustrate how factually oriented questions and closed questions can very quickly take the emotion out of an interview. In addition, the above excerpt does not deal with homosexuality as an alternative lifestyle meaningful to many individuals. However, when beginning helpers find themselves overwhelmed by situations or find themselves faced with situations or data that they do not understand or with which they feel incompetent, the skillful use of closed questions can move the session to safer ground.

Experienced helpers may use open and closed questions in a similar fashion. A client may move too rapidly in early portions of a helping interview, and a closed question can slow down client talk. Later, an open question will provide an opportunity to return to the same issue. Dudley (in press) examined beginning and advanced psychiatric residents at the University of Mississippi Medical School and found that beginning residents tended to ask many closed questions. However, advanced residents began their interview with open questions and later used closed questions to confirm or reject aspects of their preliminary diagnosis.

Finally, it must be mentioned that not all helpers believe in the use of questions. Nondirective, client-centered, and existentially oriented individuals tend to avoid questions for the reason that questions alomst invariably come from the counselor's view of the world rather than from that of the client. As such, questions, no matter how open, may place the client in the counselor's control.

Yet, it must be recognized that trait and factor, behavioral, many analytic, and other helpers and therapists use questions as an important interviewing skill.

Minimal Encourages to Talk

This skill is concerned with helping the client to keep talking once he or she has started to talk. Some beginning counselors are effective at using attending behavior and open invitations to get clients talking but then lapse into nonparticipation, failing to encourage the client to keep going. Minimal encourages to talk, also developed by Phillips, Lockhart, and Moreland (1969a), focus on helping the trainee become more active and involved in the session while remaining centered on the client's needs and wishes.

Examples of minimal encourages include simply an "umhmm," repetitions of one or two words from what the client has just said, one word questions, head nods, and a variety of body postures and gestures. By using such minimal encourages, the interviewer is showing interest and involvement but is allowing the client to determine the primary direction of the interview. More advanced trainees may wish to study the use of minimal encourages in detail.

Minimal encourages also serve as important reinforcers for client behavior. The integration of minimal encourages with reinforcement concepts helps the behavioral counselor direct the interview more effectively. Those of a phenomenological bent often use minimal encourages as a manifestation of their involvement, interest, and caring for the client.

Phillips, Lockhart, and Moreland stress that "the successful usage of this technique presupposes that the interviewer has tuned in to what the client is discussing." Randomly encouraging the client to talk will not facilitate either the growth of the client or the direction of the interview. Minimal encourages should follow directly from what the client has said. In this way, they can help the clients express themselves more clearly and provide an avenue whereby the counselor or interviewer can express an interest in clients and assist in continued self-exploration.

LISTENING SKILLS: SELECTIVE ATTENTION

Once the beginning counselor can attend, can open the client to talk, and can encourage talk to continue, the question of direction or focus for the interview then becomes paramount. To what should the interviewer attend? What should the client be encouraged to talk about? How can the client be helped to explore the personal self in more depth?

Skinner (1953) suggests that attention in itself is not a sufficient reinforcer for human beings. He indicates that approval is another generalized reinforcer which may be used to shape the behavior of others. "Another person is likely to reinforce only that part of one's behavior of which he approves, and any sign of his approval becomes reinforcing in its own right" (p. 78). The literature on verbal conditioning suggests that individuals in interviewing sessions will respond and talk about areas which the counselor responds to and reinforces.

The preceding discussion of minimal encouragement stressed this skill as merely a means of keeping the client talking. At a more advanced level, minimal encourages also serve as selective reinforcers of what clients actually discuss. The selection of a key word may be crucial in determining the flow of the interview for the next hour. Detailed examination of numerous typescripts reveals that helpers tend to select certain types of words consistently for their minimal encourages. Thus, once again, an elementary skill has sophisticated and important implications beyond the introductory level.

Consider the following exchange in the typescript from the Appendix.

Al 2: Could you tell me how things have been going? (Open question)

Joan 2: Well, things have been going generally pretty well. I'm clerking now. The children are all in school. Seem to be okay. And my life generally seems pretty good, except now that I'm in a man's world, uhm, my life is really different. I—before I was doing paraprofessional work with women and was in women's groups, and really my whole life evolved around women. And now I'm working with men, and I've started seeing men, ah . . .

and I'm not quite sure how to handle some of these men-women relationships.

Al 3: You're not quite sure how to handle some of these new relationships?   (Minimal encourage)

On the face of it, it would appear that the helper simply used a minimal encourage to keep the helpee talking.   However, many minimal encourages could have been brought out from that statement which would have led the interview in vastly differing directions.   For example, some possibilities include "You're clerking now," "The children . . .," "Life is pretty good," "Your whole life evolved around women," and "You're working with men now." All of these are minimal encourages, but each could take the client for the remainder of the hour in vastly differing directions. A particularly useful task for any helper, interviewer, counselor, or therapist is the careful analysis of the selective attention shown by minimal encourages.   Their use by the helper says more about the helper than it does about the client.

This section discusses three other skills that are central aspects of focused listening, all of which were part of the initial series of microcounseling studies conducted by Normington and Miller (Ivey et al., 1968).   Two of these central aspects of focused listening are reflections or responding to feeling and the paraphrase, which focuses on cognitive content of the session.   These concepts are discussed as microtraining skills, followed by a presentation of the broader focusing interviewing skill—summarization.

Reflection of Feeling

Attending behavior could be described as being with the client physically and verbally.   The construct of reflection of feeling (Rogers, 1961) is often viewed as related to empathy or being with the client emotionally.   It could be also described as *selective attention to the feeling* or emotional aspects of the client's expressions.   By selectively attending and reflecting observed feeling states to the client, the interviewer is consciously reinforcing emotional states while simultaneously extinguishing more cognitive aspects by ignoring them.

Accurate reflection of feeling was the second skill focused on

by microcounseling research. Originally developed by Normington (Ivey et al., 1968), this skill was chosen because of the important part it can play, in Rogerian terminology, in communicating to the client that "I am with you . . . I can accurately sense the
world as you are feeling and perceiving it." Such communication
is considered important in the development of empathic understanding, a key aspect of an effective interpersonal relationship.

The following client statement and examples of possible interviewer responses illustrates how selective attention may explain
and help make operational the sometimes mystical concept of reflection of feelings.

> *Client:* So I'm wondering if you can help me find a new major.
> *Counselor:* (Silence.)
> *Client:* I suppose if I did find one, I'd just bungle things again.
> *Counselor:* You feel discouraged;
> > *or*
> You feel that it's pretty futile to try again.

Both of the suggested alternatives focus on feeling and emotional
states and tend to ignore cognitive aspects of the client's communication. If followed by further emotional reflection, the client may
move to depth exploration of feelings of inadequacy. The statements above may vary in quality, but both selectively attend to
emotional aspects of the client's comment.

Alternatively, selective attention to cognitive content (paraphrasing) could help change the direction of the same session.
Counselor comments selectively attending to other aspects of client
communication would lead in other directions. Examples of this
might include "You'd like me to help you" (leading to discussions
of possible dependency and the counselor-client relationship).
The open invitation to talk, "What majors have you considered?,"
is another alternative which opens the individual to a different
type of exploration (redirects attention to the issue of future
directions and may lead to discussion of future alternatives).

In this comparison, reflection of feeling becomes clearer. The
task of the interviewer is to note emotional aspects of the client's
comments and present them in clear form so that the client may
better understand them. In this view, the value of the Rogerian

mirror becomes more clear. The most skillful reflection of feeling is the one which is attuned to the client's present emotions. This is easily distinguished from cognitive content or substantive questions raised in other portions of the same interview.

The following example from the Appendix typescript provides an opportunity to examine the structure of a reflection of feeling in more detail. The exchange below follows a self-disclosure on the part of the helper.

> *Joan 14:* It's funny. I can really believe that about you, but somehow for him—I'm just so frightened of him—that that may be it, but I don't want to deal with his insecurity. I guess——
> *Al 15:* Right now you're saying that you really feel frightened of him. (Reflection of feeling)
> *Joan 15:* Frightened that he could ooze into my life and take over. And also disgusted that why should I have to deal with that in order to have a warm relationship with a man.

Al 15 offers some interesting dimensions of reflection of feeling. He selectively attends to the word "frightened" and adds the words "right now" which emphasize present tense "here and now" experiencing. The word "really" adds to the intensity of the reflection. Important also is the use of two personal pronouns "you're" and "you." Informal observation on the Microcounseling Skill Discrimination Index (see Appendix IV) reveals that more effective reflections and paraphrases tend to have more frequent use of personal pronouns and the person's name. It should be noted at Joan 15 that the reflection of feeling leads the helpee to a more in-depth and clarifying exploration of her relationship with the man.

The essential dimensions of a reflection of feeling include (1) the direct labeling of the emotional state of the client and (2) some reference to the client via a name or personal pronoun; these may be supplemented by (3) present tense reflection of here and now states for more powerful experiencing (of course, past or future tense may also be used) and (4) the addition of certain paraphrased elements of the client's past statement(s).

Virtually all interviewers, counselors, and therapists reflect or summarize their client's feelings from time to time. The personnel interviewer, perhaps interested in a job applicant's attitudes toward a stressful executive post, finds it helpful to reflect feeling states for better understanding of the applicant. In turn, one may use this same information to help the applicant understand the self more fully. Most counselors and therapists use reflection of feeling statements from time to time, although the emphasis and number of statements of this type vary with theoretical persuasion.

Much of interviewing is centered on feelings and emotions. Selective attention to emotions as taught through the micro-counseling framework provides a useful conceptual tool to help the beginning interviewer develop the skills of reflection and summarization of feelings.

Occasionally, reflection of feeling proves too complex a skill for a beginning trainee to learn readily. Haase, Forsyth, Julius, and Lee (1971) have developed and tested the microtraining skill of "expression of feeling." In their model, beginning counselors first learn how to recognize and express their own emotions before they practice reflection of feeling. Working with subprofessional counselors, Haase and DiMattia (1970) found that training in expression of feeling facilitated later growth in reflection of feeling skills. Ivey and Gluckstern (1974a,b; 1976a,b) also provide systematic training in personal exploration of emotions as a way of aiding helpers to feel more comfortable using the reflection of feeling skill. A sample exercise of this procedure may be found late in Appendix V.

Paraphrasing

Paraphrasing, a technique used by almost all interviewers, could be considered an attempt to feed back to the client the content of what he has just said, but in a restated form. Used in this manner, this skill, developed by Ivey, Moreland, Phillips, and Lockhart (1969), is functional in clarifying confusing verbal content, tying a number of recent comments together, and highlighting issues by stating them more concisely.

Paraphrasing is also a variation of selective attention. Paraphrasing is a skill designed to help the counselor and client clarify what is said through selective attention to objective verbal content.

Paraphrasing centers more on cognitive than affective components. Just as reflection of feeling entails some reiteration of content, so paraphrasing entails some recognition of the client's feeling. The primary distinction is emphasis.

Paraphrasing could also be termed "restatement of content" and is the interviewer lead most often associated with the jokes sometimes made about nondirective counselors. Typescripts containing many paraphrases have sometimes been criticized as simple repetition of what the client has just said. Paraphrases at their worst do indeed represent mere repetition.

Good paraphrases, however, require the interviewer to reflect to the client the essence of the last comment or last few comments. If the paraphrase helps the client move further and talk more deeply about the subject at hand, it may be considered a successful lead. Whereas reflection and summarization of feeling can serve as a sufficient method for some counselors and therapists, skillful paraphrasing may serve as an adequate interview method for the job counselor, personnel director, or guidance counselor seeking a more complete understanding of a situation.

The distinction between paraphrasing and reflection of feeling is illustrated in the following examples:

Client: I don't know about him. One moment, he's nice as can be, and the next he treats me terrible.
Interviewer: He's pretty inconsistent, you don't know what to do. (Paraphrase) You feel confused. (Reflection of feeling)
Client: I'm afraid I will flunk my geometry course.
Interviewer: The geometry course is pretty rough. (Paraphrase) You're worried. (Reflection of feeling)

Both examples above provide the individuals with opportunities to keep exploring their problems. Reflection of feeling stresses emotional aspects of the client's communication, whereas paraphrasing stresses more objective content and the immediate problem to be faced, although allowing the individual to replace them with emotion if he or she wishes.

In the earlier example of reflection of feeling at Joan 14, it would have been possible to paraphrase instead of reflect. Some possibilities for paraphrases would include "His insecurity is an issue for you," "Joan, as I hear you, it sounds as if coping with his insecurity is a major issue with you right now," or "You can believe that I (the helper) may feel that way, but you don't want to deal with him from that perspective (of insecurity)." All three paraphrases most likely would have led the helpee to discuss material on a more objective, decision-oriented level.

As with the reflection of feeling, the use of the name or personal pronoun helps personalize the relationship. In addition, instead of labeling feelings, the paraphrase seeks to identify the problem, issue, or concern. Crucial to paraphrasing is finding the *essence* of what has been said. The first paraphrase above tends to focus more on the man rather than Joan. The second paraphrase has three references to the helpee and returns the issue squarely to Joan. The third paraphrase represents a dual focus on Joan, the helpee, and other people, i.e. the helper and the man. Any one of these paraphrases might be useful in clarifying the situation, but each paraphrase leads in varying directions. As with reflections of feeling, paraphrases which clarify issues in the here and now tend to be more powerful.

The Issue of Distortion in the Helping Process

Both paraphrasing and reflection of feeling depend on the helper to provide clear and accurate summaries of what the helpee has said. However, many helpers—particularly beginners—have real problems in hearing the client accurately. The distortion of the helpee's experience or statement can result in very real dangers and can hinder personal growth.

Distortion may be defined as the inaccurate hearing of what the client has said coupled with the conscious or unconscious feeding back of the client's statement as if that were what the client had really said. Out of this distortion, many clients come to believe that the counselor or therapist distortion is their own real experience. Following is an example of how distortion could be used with the helpee at Joan 14:

> *Helper:* Joan, you really sound afraid of men. I sense your fear. Sounds like you are saying you don't want to be touched by anyone.

Joan: Is that how I come across? Wow . . . I had never thought of it that way.
Helper: I'm just feeding back to you what you are saying.
Joan: Oh. . .

Out of distorted interactions such as this, helpees learn misshaped self-perceptions which may remain with them for years. In the example above, a supposedly warm, empathic helper has distorted the helpee's statements and unsettled her to the extent that she may be soon believing the distortion is true of her.

Beyond this, it seems important to state that distortions are similar to interpretations in that both provide a new frame of reference for the helpee to view life. However, an interpretation is deliberate and often is identified as an interpretation or alternative view, whereas the distortion is presented as reality and all too easily becomes the client's new reality.

To sense the power and danger of distortion, Ivey and Gluckstern (1974b) suggest the following exercise:

Step 1. Listen carefully to the person with whom you are talking. Hear the message as accurately as possible. Use attending, questions, paraphrases, or other microcounseling skills to make sure you have heard the other person accurately.

Step 2. After listening further, *deliberately distort* the message you have heard, adding some value or meaning which is different from what the helpee expressed.

Step 3. The helpee will often be caught off-balance and be confused. You follow up this confusion with other listening skills and some of your own ability to influence another. In many cases, the individual comes to believe your distorted perception of reality. *Immediately debrief your practice helpee.*

This exercise will help clarify the distinction among paraphrasing, reflection of feeling, and distortion. It is possible to use microtraining skills to make people less than they are, and an exercise such as this points out clearly the dangers of ineffective helping.

Summarization

The third microcounseling study designed by Normington and Miller (Ivey et al., 1968) focused on summarization of feeling. Summarization was once separated into summarization of feeling and summarization of content (Ivey, 1971), but examination of summarizations reveals that most involve both affective and cognitive dimensions and that the distinction between summarization of feeling and summarization of content was inappropriate.

Summarization involves attending to the client, accurately sensing the feelings and content being expressed, and meaningfully integrating the various responses of the client. In summarization, the counselor is attending to a broader range of events and information than in a paraphrase or reflection of feeling. Basic to summarization is the skill of bringing together seemingly diverse elements into a meaningful gestalt.

Summarization can be exemplified by possible counselor responses in an interview in which a client expresses many feelings and attitudes toward an employer and provides extensive information about the job situation. Both reflection of feeling and paraphrasing (plus the use of questions and minimal encourages) will help the client express many concepts. In addition, the interviewer may have observed nonverbal communications of the client which strengthen understanding of the total situation. A summarization statement takes these many points and illustrates the diverse and complex issues and feelings of the client in such a way that the client may say, "That's *right*, I never looked at it that way before," and continue on with discussion of the issue.

As indicated above, by using a summarization skill, the interviewer seeks to attend and selectively reinforce client comments and behavior in such a fashion that an overall picture of the client's feelings and experience is obtained. The counselor then integrates these specific behavioral observations into a total picture, which is then summarized for the client. The summary reviews the essential content of the session and may be particularly helpful to the client about to make a decision or in need of clarifying confusing content, tying a number of comments together, or seeing the total situation more clearly. Equally important, summarization provides an opportunity for the interviewer to determine how accurately he or she has heard the helpee.

The Appendix III typescript provides illustrations of how a summary can be used in an ongoing counseling session. Periodically, through the interview, the helper summarizes the essential dimensions of what has happened so far. It would be helpful to examine the summarizations at Al 6, 12, 31, 32, and 41. It may be observed that these summarizations are designed to focus the interview more clearly (Al 6, 12, and 41) and to check on the clarity of perceptions of the helper (Al 31 and 32).

The Concept of Focus

Although not technically a microtraining skill, the concept of focus—the selective attention to verbal topics—has claimed increasing importance in microtraining workshops. In the new series *Basic Influencing Skills* (Ivey and Gluckstern, 1976 a,b) it moves to an equal place with other microcounseling skills. Focus first appeared in microcounseling literature as a result of studying the way in which counseling clients talked about their concerns. It was found that some helpees tended to avoid self-exploration while others discussed personal issues in considerable depth. Factor analytic study of effective and ineffective communication patterns (Crowley and Ivey, 1976) were crucial in delineating the concept. This study found the simple and seemingly obvious point (at least obvious now) that effective interpersonal communication involves frequent use of personal pronouns—"I" and "you" statements.

The most simple definition of focus is that for a helpee to talk about him or herself, the sentence must contain frequent self-reference pronouns. Similarly, for a client to talk about self, it is necessary that a counselor focus on the client and use the client's name and/or the pronoun "you." Examination of video and audiotapes of beginning and advanced helpers revealed all too frequently an emphasis on the content of the helping interview—the "war stories" of the patient—rather than emphasis on the client as an individual. A simple example should illustrate the point clearly.

Helpee: My wife just left me. I'm lost.
Helper: Where did she go? *or* When did that happen? *or* Did she take the children with her?
Helper: You say your wife is gone . . . you feel confused, lost.

The first set of examples all lead to discussion about the wife and will bring out information about reasons, present status, etc. While such may be valuable, the focus is on the wife, not on the client. The latter statement (note the use of three personal pronouns) focuses on the helpee and his immediate experience.

Selective attention is critical to determining the focus of a client's conversation. If the helper consistently reinforces (i.e. selectively attends) client talk about problems, other people, or distant situations, the client will talk very little about self, make few "I" statements, and in general avoid self-exploration. The simple addition of the word "you" to the helper's vocabulary provides the cue to the client that he or she is to talk about personal views rather than external issues.

Another example illustrates what happens all too often in personal counseling:

Helpee: I just had an abortion. It was a terrible experience.
Helper: Where did you get it? Tell me more about it.

Once again, we see the helper focusing on "war stories," the facts of the problem rather than the person experiencing the concern. Some examples which focus on the helpee could include "What did getting an abortion mean to *you*?," "It was terrible for *you*," "Sounds like right now *you're* feeling a lot of things."

In vocational counseling, the same problem appears so regularly that attention to the individual may be considered a rare event.

Helpee: I haven't had a job in years. It's not my fault.
Helper: What kind of job was the last one?

Once again, the emphasis is on objective content, issues external to the individual. Attitudes toward jobs may be more important than factual information, and a simple "*You* say *you* feel it's not *your* fault?" may be effective in making the session more personal.

Several studies have demonstrated the importance of focus in distinguishing effective from less effective helpers. Gluckstern (1972; 1973) with paraprofessionals, Hearn (1976) with nurses, Chadbourne (1975) with teachers, and Sherrard (1973) with professionals have shown that focus analysis is a viable method of analyzing the microtraining process.

Ivey and Gluckstern (1976a,b) propose six classes of focus analysis which are in essence verbal response classes. The six categories are helpee focus, helper focus, other individuals focus, mutual or group focus, topic focus, and cultural-environmental-contextual focus. Through focus analysis, it is possible to determine the areas the helper (or helpee) is most interested in and willing to explore. Through selective attention to these verbal response classes, the helper determines what the helpee will talk about.

Focus analysis of the Appendix typescript provides a useful summary to this section and illustrates the importance of this dimension. The client's first comment follows:

Joan 2: Well, things have been going generally pretty well. I'm clerking now. The children are all in school. Seem to be okay. And my life generally seems pretty good, except now that I'm in a man's world, uhm, my life is really different. I— before I was doing paraprofessional work with women and was in women's groups, and really my whole life evolved around women. And now I'm working with men, and I've started seeing men, ah . . . and I'm not quite sure how to handle some of these men-women relationships.

Helpee focus: Joan, *you're* not sure how to handle *your* relationships with men.

Helper focus: *I've* had similar experiences to yours. *My* wife is working too. *I'm* not quite sure how to handle this situation either.

Other individuals focus: Your *children* are in school. Tell me more about *them* and how *they* react in this situation.

Mutual or group focus: The *two of us* are now in relationship. *My* experience of *your* experience is that *we* play out some of these same male-female relationships in *our* counseling hour.

Topic focus: How are things going in *law school?* What are some of the *problems* you have?

Cultural-environmental-contextual focus: This sounds like a *woman's* issue. A lot of *women* have gone through similar experience. Is it really a male-female issue or is it an issue of a *woman* asserting herself in a male world?

Obviously, each focus or verbal response class leads the helpee in very differing areas of conversation. As counseling is most often thought of as a one-to-one situation, individual focus may be most appropriate to teach beginning helpers. This is particularly so as many beginning helpers focus on the topic (standard social conversation) or on other people almost exclusively in early helping sessions. The task of the helper is first to get the helpee to explore him or herself as an individual before attacking the problems and issues.

Mutual focus represents the "I-Thou" communication of Martin Buber and may present itself extensively in existential helping sessions. The mutual focus is also important in encounter group work. In fact, the focus on the *group* is perhaps the major verbal difference between individual and group counseling. Sherrard (1973), for example, noted that a Tavistock group leader used the group as the focus of his sentences for almost every helping lead (which were mostly interpretations). The group leader who ends up doing individual therapy in a group would do well to examine his or her verbal utterances and will almost invariably find that the word group or subgroup is absent.

The most difficult focus concept to present to beginning or professional helpers is the cultural-environmental-contextual. This aspect of focus emphasizes that the individual operates not only as an individual but also within a socio-cultural-economic context. Feminist counseling—the emphasis on women's issues—is perhaps the clearest example of cultural-environmental-contextual focus. Radical therapists, e.g. Steiner (1975), give special attention to these issues. Trait and factor helpers and employment counselors give lip service to the cultural-environmental context but often fail to act in this area. Existential helpers may talk about the *eigenwelt* (individual), *mitwelt* (relationship), and *umwelt* (world) aspects of helping, but examination of typescripts and texts will result in finding mainly an emphasis on individual and relationship issues with "being in the world" given scant attention.

Truly effective helping must ultimately consider all six aspects of focus analysis. Helpees, clients, patients are people with problems who exist in relationship in a cultural-environmental-context. (The latter will be discussed in more detail in a subsequent chapter.) Failure to cope with the totality of human existence in a series of helping sessions may be to deny full humanness. Focus analysis provides a rather simple, yet powerful, method to check on the balance of emphasis in helping sessions.

SUMMARY

This chapter has presented the several attending skills. All are based on the assumption that attending and listening are *active* empathic stances for the beginning and the professional helper. The nature of attending behavior on the part of the helper determines very much what the helpee will talk about and do next. While hearing the helpee thoroughly is basic to any helping process, attending is not a passive act; it serves as the medium through which the important construct of empathy may be fully communicated.

The verbal and nonverbal behaviors of attending were presented as examples of areas where both beginning and advanced interviewers may learn more about themselves and their influence on helpees. Eye contact, body language, and verbal following were stressed as basic to attending behavior.

Open and closed questions and minimal encourages were discussed as important skills to open an interview. The paraphrase, reflection of feeling, and summarization were presented as more advanced skills of attending and stressed as useful tools for enriching the interview. Nondirective and client-centered helpers may use these three skills almost exclusively.

The concept of distortion is important, as it helps distinguish facilitative and effective listening from destructive intrusion into another person's experience. A basic exercise for separating distortion from interpretation and paraphrasing was presented.

The final part of this chapter discussed the concept of focus analysis as a means whereby one can understand the topics which appear in both helper and helpee utterances. Through selective attention to helpees' statements, helpers heavily determine the emphasis of subsequent interview behavior.

Chapter 5

BEYOND ATTENDING:
SKILLS OF INTERPERSONAL INFLUENCE

ATTENDING SKILLS — the accurate hearing of the client — are basic to any helping system. Unless one first hears the client and communicates that the client is heard, very little progress will occur in interviewing, counseling, or therapy. Quality use of attending skills will result in empathic understanding and may be sufficient in itself to produce positive helpee growth.

However, growth and change solely via attending skills and empathic understanding can be slow and tedious. Rogers himself has recognized this, and his more recent writings on encounter group process (e.g. Rogers, 1970) reveal more stress on self-disclosure and active feedback. When the counselor or therapist moves to more active involvement in the session, he or she becomes directly engaged in *influencing* the process of change.

The skillful use of the therapist as a person and/or as a skilled professional with important insights into the human condition *adds* to basic attending skills and primary empathy as described in the preceding chapter. Through experience and training, the advanced helper can bring in new experience, new perceptions, new theories of humanness which enrich the client and promote more rapid and solid growth. Carkhuff (1969a,b) speaks of "additive dimensions of helping," and Egan (1975) talks of "advanced accurate empathy." A still broader view of the helper as a person of influence is provided by Brammer (1973) who speaks directly about such helper dimensions as "leading," "confronting," using "feedback and opinion," "mediating," "interpreting," and "problem solving." Brammer suggests that if the helper is to be truly

93

empathic, he or she will move beyond passive attending and listening to advocacy for the client in any reasonable way possible.

The fact that many helpers *do* influence their helpees consciously and directly cannot be denied. The clearest example of influence, of course, is that of Perls' Gestalt therapy (Perls, Hefferline, and Goodman, 1951), where helpees receive minimal attending skills but extensive directions and interpretations from the experience of the helper. Review of typescripts and theoretical comments indicates that analytic therapists, behavior modifiers, trait and factor counselors, rational-emotive counselors, and existential helpers all share themselves and their knowledge in the interview. In fact, it may be suggested that only true passive nondirectivists do not share themselves in some fashion in the interview. Further, careful analysis of Rogers' classic text (1961) on nondirective helping reveals relatively frequent interpretations on his part.

The interview, then, can be considered a process of interpersonal influence. Through selective attention and the attending skills, even the most nondirective helper determines what the client talks about. However, most counselors and therapists involve themselves in the interview actively. They give directions, they interpret, they share their personal experience and views of the world. This addition of self and self-knowledge to the interview can produce important and lasting change for the client or patient. As has been observed by many in the helping professions, these changes can be "for better or worse." For if a helper can influence a person to change, the direction of that change can be negative as well as positive. (The following chapter on the "quality of helping" examines the issue of producing positive change in helping.)

This chapter presents the skills of interpersonal influence as defined in the microtraining paradigm. The concept of self-expression — parallel to attending behavior — is presented first, followed by specific discussion of the skills of directions, expression of feeling, expression of content, self-disclosure, interpretation, and direct-mutual communication.

SELF-EXPRESSION

Basic to client change in any helping session is a helper who is believable, communicates assurance, and "comes across" as a person who can make a difference in the client's life. The constant emphasis in professional helping training programs on theory, saying the "right" thing and being "correct," and being rigidly "professional" has resulted in the castration of the natural effectiveness of many beginning helpers. People who start out with a natural interest in others and a solid desire to help all too often learn fear and hesitation as a result of training.

The helper who appears uncertain, weak of voice, and lacks assurance cannot and will not effect positive change in the helpee. Missing from most helper training programs is the importance of clearly projecting to the helpee that the helper knows what he or she is doing. Physicians know the importance of the professional "white coat" effect. When a prescription is given, the physician must communicate to the patient that the prescription will be effective. This is done through clear communication and positive body language and eye contact. If the physician were to wring his or her hands, look at the floor, and state "perhaps this might be helpful" in a tentative vocal tone, the prescription (if taken at all) is less likely to be effective than if it had been presented with assurance.

Similarly, the therapist must communicate confidence. This does not mean that one must fake what does not exist. If one does not know what to do next or is lost in the interview, a frank, strong, and honest admission of that fact can be used to advantage. No one has to be perfect. What is crucial is *how* the therapist communicates what is known and not known.

Specifying what is necessary to communicate confidence and ability to helper, Ivey (1971) cites the following personal experience:

> . . . I was about to make a presentation to an important audience and felt myself awkward, tense, and stumbling over my words. I thought to myself of the concepts of (self-expression). I realized I was paying so much attention to the audience that I was forgetting myself as a

person. I believed in what I had to say. How could I put it across?
I deliberately relaxed to put myself together (It could be observed
easily by anyone in the audience) and took a deep breath. I deliberately put my thoughts in myself and started talking about what I
cared about. For a short time it was awkward, but soon I forgot that
I had engaged in deliberate behaviors and was "turned on" and
"turning on" the audience (pp. 166-167).

The specific concepts referred to in the above excerpt are eye contact, body language, verbal following behavior, and vocal tone.
The same dimensions as attending behavior are stressed, but in
this case the focus changes to the speaker.

The most dynamic and charismatic therapist (at least to many
observers) was Fritz Perls. His assurance, his constant flow of
knowledge, his wise insights constantly led to "magical" changes
in his patients. Much of the appeal of Gestalt therapy is in the
action dimensions and the power this approach gives to the
helper. But what was Fritz Perls doing? He had powerful searching eyes — when he looked at you, you felt looked at. His body
posture was assured, with a frequent forward trunk lean. He used
his gestures and facial expressions as symbols of confidence. His
vocal tone was strong, yet it changed appropriately in each situation. Taking verbal and nonverbal cues from the patient, i.e.
careful attending behaviors, Perls was able to add insights from
his experience. He was able to follow his own topic and bring
patients into his newer and more rewarding frame of reference.
However, if patients were not willing to "work," i.e. attend to
Perls' verbalizations and follow his directions, they were summarily dismissed from the therapeutic encounter.

We would not suggest that helpers become miniature Fritz
Perls. The aping of another person's lifestyle is one of the banes
of the helping professions. Rather, we ask that each would-be
helper going through microtraining sessions examine patterns of
eye contact, body language, vocal tone, and verbal following behavior. Specifically, if one is to give a suggestion or direction to
a helpee, is eye contact maintained appropriately and confidently?
Is the body language facilitative; does it communicate confidence?
With influencing skills, a trunk lean more forward than the

attending posture appears appropriate. Further, are the gestures congruent and confident? Is the vocal tone positive and assured? The voice's tone is an instrument and perhaps communicates warmth and understanding as much or more than anything else the helper does. We have observed at a clinical level that symmetry and harmony with the client can be communicated through vocal tone alone. This dimension requires further in-depth research. Finally, the words of the effective helper must not be projected in a halting fashion but must be projected confidently and follow appropriately those of the helpee. For example, if engaging in a self-disclosure, the helper's comment on his or her own personal experience should be related to the level of self-disclosure of the helpee. If too distant, the comment will be of little use to the client. In the same fashion, the directions of the behavior modifier must relate to the client's present experience.

The concepts of self-expression discussed here are based heavily on clinical work with psychiatric patients (Ivey, 1973b). Routinely, with depressed, schizophrenic, or manic patients, some disorder of self-expression skills was immediately observed in videotaped sessions. Rather than immediately focusing on the "why" of the disorder, microtraining programs were instituted in the behavioral skills of self-expression. Systematic plans were developed to produce generalization of the learned behavior to the ward and to life outside the hospital.

During these training sessions observations were made indicating that therapists also break eye contact frequently when they are not sure of themselves. Patients perceive this insecurity. In the same fashion, weak vocal tone, incongruent gestures, and inappropriate communications to the patient are perceived as indicators that the professional helper does not know what is happening. As soon as the patient senses this lack of confidence, the patient can take charge of the session, play games with the therapist, or simply leave the helping interview. Conversations with patients on any psychiatric ward will reveal that they have considerable insight into their therapist's "condition."

As such, microtraining sessions need to explore in detail the personal communication style of each trainee, be it patient or counselor-in-training. While it is essential that the potential helper determine how he or she wishes to express self in the interview, videotape analysis and training in the skills of self-expression can be invaluable in giving helpers a view of themselves as others see them. Out of training in self-expression skills, coupled with observations from the trainer, the helper-in-training can decide how best the skills of self-expression can be used.

Grinder and Bandler (1976) provide invaluable insights into the verbal and nonverbal communication channels of the individual. They speak about identifying "paramessages" which can be *seen* (hands, breathing, legs and feet, eye fixation patterns, head/neck/shoulder relationships, and the facial expression) and *heard* (vocal tone, speech tempo, and specific words and sentences used). A special interest of Grinder and Bandler is incongruities among the several channels of communication. We have found in microtraining sessions that work in self-expression provides many helpers-in-training with an awareness of their verbal and nonverbal incongruities. A variety of methods ranging from direct practice in resolving these incongruities via conscious behavior change to Gestalt techniques may be employed in connection with microtraining procedures.

DIRECTIONS

The clearest example of influence in the interview occurs when the helper tells the helpee what to do. The giving of directions to the helpee is not often mentioned as an interviewing skill, yet the examination of numerous typescripts, videotapes, and films clearly reveals that helpers are constantly telling their helpees what to do. As such, directions has been introduced in the Second Edition of *Microcounseling* as an important helping skill.

Sherrard (1973) provided the impetus for the inclusion of this skill within the microtraining paradigm. He was examining the verbal behavior of four group leaders (Carkhuff-type, Tavistock, client-centered, and vocational). Up to this point, directions had been included as a subcategory of expression of content. However, 40 percent of the helper leads of the Carkhuff group, 4 percent of the Tavistock, and 12 percent of the client-centered group clearly represented giving of directions to the group. These data clearly indicated that giving of directions was an important enough skill to stand in its own right as a basic microtraining skill.

Once again, we find that Fritz Perls is the master direction-giver. His interviews are full of directions which specifically tell the helpee what to do, how to move, words to say. Moreover, it must be recognized that behavior therapists frequently give directions, trait and factor helpers may occasionally give directions, and the growing group of family therapists and individual therapists within the double-bind school (e.g. Haley, 1963, 1973; Grinder and Bandler, 1976; Satir, 1964, 1972) use directions in unique and impressive fashions.

Ivey and Gluckstern (1976b) define the skill of directions as consisting of four key dimensions. The first of these is effective self-expression skills. If one is to give directions, one must be believable and must present the directions with appropriate eye contact, body language, and verbalizations. Second, the structure of a direction must be considered. Basically, the counselor giving a direction says *"You do this"* in a variety of forms. Some examples of directions would include the following:

"Repeat what you just said three times."

"Move over to that chair and become your father."

"A major problem you have been having with your parents is fighting and arguing. Next week, I want you to deliberately start three fights with them. Make them as rough as you can."

"Relax your forearm. Continue deep breathing."

Thirdly, Ivey and Gluckstern stress the importance of concrete as opposed to vague directions. If a direction is to be effective, it must be specific and clear to the helpee. The above directions are all concrete. They could be made vague as follows, by making the specific semantic referents less clear:

"Repeat something you've said in the past."

"Try becoming someone else. Let's see what happens."

"Next week, try to figure out your parents."
"Relax."

A fourth dimension to effective direction giving is the "check-out." If a direction is to be effective, the helpee must be asked explicitly or implicitly if the direction was heard. "Could you repeat what I just said?" or "How does that come across to you?" are ways to check out the clarity of the direction. If the helpee follows the direction immediately, of course, the check-out is not necessary.

The Appendix typescript presents two examples of directions. The first suggests a fantasy exercise to provide a picture of helpee goals.

> *Al 19:* Okay. Let's not try to resolve that right now. Let's do an exercise that we've done in the past. Stop for a moment. And would you just sort of close your eyes and just sort of imagine what you might like your relationship to be like. Regardless of how it is now — what would you like to be? How would you like to respond to him?* Just think for a moment.

This exercise includes the four dimensions of effective direction giving presented. The helper presents himself as sure and confident. The sentence structure "you do this" is present. The direction is clear. There is opportunity immediately to check out to determine if the direction was heard.

The second direction occurs at Al 23 and represents a clear topic jump, i.e. lack of attending, from what the helpee was just saying. The helpee views on videotape her tight and troubled physical reactions to the man who has been dating her. The helper through his use of directions has drawn an implicit parallel between the positive relaxed fantasy above and the current actual tense situation between the helpee and her manfriend. When she

---

*A special comment on unconscious sexism in the interview should be made here. The words "How would you like to respond to him" (which the helper unfortunately restates several times in the next few leads) place the woman in a passive rather than active role. With a woman less strong, such behavior on the part of the helper might reduce her capacity for growth. Interestingly, this same type of sentence structure has been observed in several feminist helpers. This would seem to illustrate how pervasive sexism is in our culture.

becomes aware of these discrepancies, the helpee is able to make a new and independent decision to move out of the relationship. Crucial to identifying the discrepancy in the case were the two directions by the helper.

Directions, then, can be considered an important and powerful part of the helper's skill repertoire. At the same time, the charismatic unethical helper who uses this skill successfully is in a strong position to manipulate and take clients to places which meet the helper's needs rather than those of the helpee. Directions are used in many helping schools and should be used carefully and wisely. Many humanistically oriented helpers, particularly nondirectivists, encounter group members, and existentially oriented helpers, of course, believe strongly that directions on the part of the helper are inappropriate and unwise.

EXPRESSION OF FEELING

First used successfully by Haase, Forsyth, Julius, and Lee (1971) to teach clients how to express their own feelings in a counseling interview more easily and directly, this skill has increasingly shown promise and importance as part of counselor training. In client-centered and existential-phenomenological psychology, the expression of counselor emotions is sometimes used as a facilitating dimension of the interview. For beginning counselors who have difficulty reflecting a client's feeling, direct training in expression of feeling may serve as valuable pretraining.

This skill is an analogue of reflection of feeling with the exception that the trainee places emphasis on personal feeling states and attitudes. Training in expression of feeling encourages the expression of emotions as opposed to cognitive content. A topic is selected, and stress is placed on distinguishing feeling from emotion. The following is a typical example in which the trainee is attempting to discuss feelings toward high school teachers.

Expression of feeling: I really liked Mr. Brown and Mr. Smith. They understood me. It made me feel good to walk into their classes. I really wanted to try hard for them.
Expression of content: I had two good teachers in high school,

> Mr. Brown and Mr. Smith. I took physics and chemistry from
> them.

Many individuals when attempting to discuss their emotions will almost immediately revert to a discussion of objective content. Training in expression of feeling appears to facilitate self-expression.

Haase and DiMattia (1970) trained paraprofessionals in expression of feeling and found that it facilitated their learning reflection of feeling. They noted this skill helped trainees to "discriminate between content and affect, and to be able to accurately sense, identify and verbalize the affective component of a verbal message." Ivey and Gluckstern (1974a,b; 1976a,b) have developed systematic formats for training beginning helpers in identifying and labeling emotions. A video vignette ranging in length from thirty seconds to two minutes is presented. Trainees then go through the following steps: (1) labeling the emotion of the individual on the television screen, (2) developing a reflection of feeling to indicate their ability to facilitate client exploration of emotion, (3) labeling their *own* emotions and reactions to the individual, and (4) expressing their own affective state in an appropriate fashion to the vignette. At beginning phases of this training program, some helper trainees literally recognize only two emotions — "good" and "bad" feelings. With training and experience, marked increases in sensitivity to interpersonal affect can be developed. One example of this training program is included in Appendix V (see p. 536).

At more sophisticated levels, adaptions of the expression of feeling conceptions may prove useful in aiding client-centered or existential-phenomenological therapists to express their own feeling states more relevantly in the interview. Not too long ago, expression of counselor attitudes was prohibited by much of counseling theory. With the change in emphasis, methods and training materials are needed which stress counselor reactions in interviewing leads.

The typescript in the Appendix reveals a clear example of an expression of feeling by the helper. Joan, the helpee, has just observed herself on videotape. She has been talking about her relationship with the man discussed previously, and in the video excerpt she sees herself sitting rigidly and tightly. The helper responds as follows:

Al 24: I know I'd *feel awfully uptight* if I looked like that. Sometimes I do look like that.

Joan 24: Yeah. My whole back is straight and tight.

Joan uses these data to go on and make a decision about her relationship with this man. The helper's expression of feeling was closely parallel to her immediate feelings in the interview.

From a nondirective point of view, such an expression of feeling would be considered totally inappropriate. A behavioral therapist would be more interested in the observable elements of the experience and again would not be expected to share immediate or past reactions to the helpee. The Gestalt therapist would most likely be assembling data for the "hot seat" and thinking how to get the helpee into even more powerful and immediate experiencing of the relationship. The analytically oriented therapist might consider the above lead naive and damaging. However, the more existentially oriented helper or encounter group participant might very well respond in a manner similar to this example. Implicit in Al 24 is the "My experience of your experience . . ." constructs of Laing (1967). It may be easily seen that many different evaluations of the helper's comment can be made and that these depend heavily on the theoretical orientation and value structure of the observer.

Expression of therapist's feelings in the interview offers a powerful tool for modeling interpersonal openness. At the same time, the same skill may be used to express feelings about the client's family members or friends. In the example above, the helper might have said, "I think the man you are dating is uptight and defensive." This too may be scored as an expression of feeling, as affective words are included in the helper statement. Yet, it must be recognized that this expression is far more distant from the helpee's experiencing. In the early interviews, a cautious helper may prefer this type of lead which can result in client's verbalization of emotion rather than sharing his or her own experience. Further, when helpers are themselves not comfortable with issues, the more indirect expression of feeling may be wise.

EXPRESSION OF CONTENT

When one expresses an opinion, gives a suggestion, explains some information, gives reassurance, gives advice, or perhaps even threatens the client, an expression of content has occurred. Most approaches to helper training separate these dimensions into different skills, but our experience in microtraining is that they are all closely related and difficult to separate in practice. Further, if one gives full attention to each of these skills, it is possible that interviewing training will become heavily overbalanced toward the influencing dimension of helping. Despite our belief in the interview as a process vehicle for interpersonal influence and change, we still emphasize the importance of careful attending *before* one seeks to influence another.

In its most simple definition, expression of content is simply a verbalization from the helper which brings in data from the helper's experience or knowledge which does *not* contain affective words. A teacher's classroom lecture would represent the most classic form of expression of content. A behavior modifier laying out a treatment plan for the client is engaging in expression of content. A vocational counselor providing occupational information is expressing content, as is a sex counselor providing data on impotence for a client.

The clear expression of findings and results is important in vocational-educational counseling, personnel interviews, and presentations of diagnostic reports so that others can understand them. Miller, Morrill, and Uhlemann (1970), for example, have developed a general training program in test interpretation in which beginning counselors are taught several skills of communicating test results to clients. In their program, they used half-hour microtraining sessions in the belief that more complex skills require longer periods of time. In a refinement of the above study, Miller et al. (1973) taught beginning counselors the relatively specific skill of reinforcing clients' emotional attitudes toward psychological tests. One of the important skills of test interpretation is recognizing client attitudes toward tests; if the client can honestly express how he or she feels toward tests, there is greater likelihood of the client listening more carefully to the test interpretation given later. Similarly, it is suggested that first hearing the client's needs and ideas carefully before expressing content is vital to that same client eventually hearing and acting on what the helper suggests.

Unfortunately the typescript in Appendix III presents no clear expressions of content. In each case, the expressions of content were mixed with expression of feeling. Joan 12, however, offers an opportunity for a variety of expressions of content. She talks about her relationship with a man:

> *Joan 12:* Yeah. It's like parading me down the street. You know — there's my property. That's part of it. Now, you know, now, "Joan I want you to do this." But, you know, even when he gives me something, it's like "Come over right now. I have something for you." And I might be in the middle of doing something.

Alternative expressions of content:

Advice: Joan, I think you'd be well to get rid of him. Here's how . . .

Opinion: He doesn't sound good for you. I wouldn't like the way he treats you. An absolute male chauvinist.

Reassurance: It will work out somehow. Have faith.

Suggestion: Next time he does that, why not tell him how you feel?

Threat: If you go out with him again, you're heading for trouble.

Expression of feeling: I'd be *furious* if he treated me that way. I'd be so *angry.*

While the several possibilities for expression of content above seem clear, we have found that in practice such sharp distinctions for rating purposes are almost impossible. Thus, the more general category of expression of content is suggested as more appropriate for microtraining sessions. However, a rewarding part of this training may be discussion of the array of possibilities for reaching a client via this skill area.

THE INFLUENCING SUMMARIZATION

A summarization within the attending skills framework is the bringing together of relevant client data in a brief statement. The data could cover a total interview, or they could cover several sentences. The influencing summarization is parallel to the attending summarization with the exception that the focus of the summarization is on what the helper has said.

Just as the attending summarization can include both affect and content, the influencing summarization can also include both dimensions. However, the influencing summarization is a skill which appears relatively infrequently in most helping theories and methods. It is most likely to appear at the close of an interview with a directive helper. A college counselor planning a series of tests as part of a vocational guidance program may end the interview by stating, "We have discussed several issues in this interview, and I have suggested that you do the following before you return: (1) take four interest and aptitude tests with our psychometrist, (2) discuss your possible change of major with your old and new department head, and (3) examine our vocational information file." This summary ties the interview together and provides a structure for the student to follow before the next meeting. Needless to say, such a summary could well be enhanced by also summarizing what the student had to say. If this were done, the helper would be engaging in both attending summarization and influencing summarization.

In a similar fashion, behavior therapists may summarize their treatment plans and programs for their helpees, a rational-emotive therapist may summarize "homework assignments," or a reality therapist may summarize a behavior change plan and the agreed-upon evaluation schema. This summary statement of the therapist's actions helps place the interview in perspective and reinforces client learning.

Similarly, summarizations during the interview may prove useful as perception checks for the counselor. If the counselor has been giving any separate bits of advice or information, a summarization can help bring the ideas together for the client. Careful observation of the nonverbal behavior of the client will help determine how well the summarization was received. The same effect of summarization could be obtained by asking the client to summarize her or his perceptions of what the counselor has been saying. This latter approach may be a more effective perception check than the clearest of summaries by the counselor.

The Appendix typescript does not have summaries of this type by the helper. However, the helpee at Joan 30, 31, and 32 provides some excellent examples of client summaries. As such, it is important to note that the microtraining framework can also be used to score the behavior of the client.

> *Joan 30:* And it seems like maybe, maybe it isn't just something wrong with me. That this is a special kind of interaction between him and me that really isn't very good.

In this statement, the helpee sums up the essence of how she views her decision in relationship to the man and begins to clear up the confusion that he has been causing her. She expands her summarization in the following comment after the helper's attending summary.

> *Al 31:* So what I hear you saying is that you basically are putting your own new views on this situation. Before I heard you struggling this way and that way. Now I hear you saying I'm going to look at this a little differently. You will reinterpret the situation. Ah, is this the way I want to be? Ah, you know, you could perhaps be with him, you know, more strongly, relaxed, but you're telling me, I hear you pretty clearly that that isn't something that you want to do.
>
> *Joan 31:* I'm not ready to do that now. The relationship isn't important enough. My career is more important, and my children are more important. And that's where my energy should be going rather than my energy to hold myself — defend myself — from some person.

Thus, it may be seen that microtraining skills are also skills which effective helpees, clients, and patients can demonstrate. In the early phases of this session, the helpee would have been unable to bring together the several elements of the interview in such a fashion. The attending skills of the helper plus the two specific directions facilitated her self-discovery. The ineffective helpee — the person less able to "work" and conceptualize personal experience — would not have been able to demonstrate this type of summary until many interviews had passed.

Similarly, effective helpers who use the skill of summarization will be able to distill succinctly their work and the client's progress in relatively brief statements which help the client map the world. Out of this map, the client may be able to discover new insights, try new behaviors, or recapture the essence of the session or sessions.

SELF-DISCLOSURE

Self-disclosure is based on the constructs of expression of content, expression of feeling, and summarization. It is considered a broadly based skill which is appropriate for advanced helpers, primarily in the existential-humanistic schools. Jourard (1971a; 1971b) has been the primary exponent of self-disclosure in the helping interview. His theoretical discussion of the need and importance for interpersonal openness between helper and helpee is basic to the developing of extensive literature in professional journals. Laing (1967), recent statements by Rogers (1970), and the clearly stated work on self-disclosure of Carkhuff (1969a,b) are some other important theoretical statements on the value of self-disclosure in the helping session. The sharing of personal experience in the encounter group is in the tradition of self-disclosure, but group leaders within the encounter group movement vary in their opinions as to the wisdom of leader self-disclosure. The radical psychiatry movement (e.g. Steiner, 1975) does not give the term self-disclosure important play but does lay stress on the helper and the helpee moving toward a more mutual relationship.

The ultimate use of self-disclosure may be found in reevaluation co-counseling (RC) (Jackins, 1965). Although the RC movement contains a leadership hierarchy, the actual counseling enacted within its framework is done by two clients, each helping the other. The partners face each other, hold hands, and one serves as the helper for one-half hour. A systematic, eclectic set of helping leads are prescribed by RC which lead to extensive catharsis and reenactment of past personal traumas. At the end of the thirty-minute period, the partners switch roles, and the former helper becomes the new helpee. The mutual self-disclosure of RC, coupled with very specific techniques of questioning, directions, and interpretation, can result in powerful and meaningful changes for both participants. Unfortunately, we know of no research data available on the effectiveness of this increasingly popular method of helping.

Microtraining defines self-disclosure in terms of four key dimensions. The first of these is the personal pronoun "I." If a helper is to make a self-disclosure, it must be from an "I" reference. Personal self-reference pronouns such as "my," "mine," and "I'm" are necessary for self-disclosure statements. These words, of course, may be implied from the context of the helper's speech.

The second dimension of self-disclosure is the inclusion of an expression of content or expression of feeling statement. The helper may state information or opinions from an "I" reference or express feelings and emotions through affective words. Both expression of content and expression of feeling may be considered self-disclosures. However, the direct expression of personal feelings is the more impactful and true self-disclosure as it exposes the helper to a more vulnerable and open position.

A third dimension of self-disclosure is the object of the sentence. A self-disclosure may be about one's own experience ("I have had a similar problem in my life.") or one's personal experience of the helpee's experience ["My reaction to you (the helpee) is . . ." or "My experience of your experience is . . ." (Laing, 1967)]. Both are self-disclosures; the second type involves the helper or therapist at a deeper level with the helpee and can produce immediate transference-countertransference experiencing. From another and more humanistic-existential point of view, the second type of self-disclosure brings two human beings into close communication with one another, perhaps even at an "I-Thou" level (Buber, 1970). The first type of self-disclosure permits the helper to disclose self in a safer fashion and to model interpersonal openness. This modeling of interpersonal openness on the part of the helper often facilitates helpee self-disclosure and self-exploration (Yalom et al., 1967; Authier and Gustafson, 1973).

The final dimension of self-disclosure stressed in microcounseling training is the tense of the statement. Self-disclosures may be in the past tense, present tense, or future tense. Self-disclosures in the past tense tend to be safer for the helper (and sometimes for the helpee). An example of a past tense self-disclosure would be "I have had that problem with my wife too. She . . ." or "When I was your age. . . ." The potential problem with past tense disclosures is, of course, exemplified by the latter statement. Nonetheless, such self-disclosures can be helpful in modeling openness and aiding helpees in looking at themselves more fully. Present tense disclosures are more powerful and impactful. Further, they are much more difficult for the helper to fake in an unreal fashion. "Right now, I'm feeling very deeply the hurt you experienced with your parents" or "As you say that, I feel tears coming to my eyes."

The latter two comments combine the four dimensions of self-disclosure. The second, of course, is more direct and potentially impactful and implies the "my experience of your experience" concept mentioned previously. These leads also demonstrate that not all professional helpers would use this skill. Psychoanalytic helpers, behavior therapists, trait and factor helpers, Gestalt therapists, nondirectivists, and others might consider such helping leads as inappropriate and unprofessional.

Finally, self-disclosure is the basic skill of the effective helpee. Extremely troubled patients or clients begin therapy frequently with difficulties in making "I" statements, expressing emotion, and speaking in the present tense. Haase, Forsyth, Julius, and Lee (1971) used microtraining as a format to pre-train counselees *before* they initiated counseling sessions in a university counseling service. They found client expression of feeling facilitated by such training.

It is now appropriate to turn to self-disclosures by the helper and the helpee in the Appendix typescript. The helper's first real self-disclosure occurs at Al 14, just following the helpee's statement of how the man she has been dating has been interfering in her life. Joan 14 reveals her self-disclosure in relationship to him.

Al 13: I see. Okay. Could I share one of my own experiences like this? This is from the past. I know that I had a need, and maybe I still do, to control, to own, my wife. And I can remember in the past where I've set up conditions and so forth where she was to do things. And . . . looking back on it I know that for me this was coming from my own point at that point from the feeling of not being sure of myself in my relationship with women. Ah, how does that come across to you?

Joan 14: It's funny. I can really believe that about you, but somehow for him — I'm just so frightened of him — that that may be it, but I don't want to deal with his insecurity. I guess — —

The helper's self-disclosure in this session was designed to illustrate (1) an "I" statement, (2) a mixed expression of feeling and content, (3) a self-disclosure about a roughly parallel experience, and (4) a past tense self-disclosure. As noted earlier, this type of self-disclosure tends to be less powerful than the more immediate type of expression. The helpee, on the other hand, illustrates (1) an "I" statement, (2) primarily an expression of feeling, (3) both the helper and the helpee's manfriend are objects of her feelings and attitudes, and (4) she is speaking in the present tense. Despite the relatively weak helper self-disclosure, the helpee is able to take the helper's statement and go farther with self-exploration. This is the sign of the effective and forward-moving client.

Al 33 and 34 illustrate a useful form of self-disclosure. In the preceding several client-counselor interchanges, the helper had difficulty in hearing the client and made what many would call a "therapeutic error." After some inappropriate questions and a topic jump, he returned to attending skills (Al 29, 30, 31, 32) to recover an understanding of the helpee. Microtraining stresses the importance of this tack when the interviewer does not feel fully in tune with the helpee. "When in doubt, or if a helping lead fails, return to attending skills." Having finally heard the helpee, the helper at Al 33 openly expresses his feelings of confusion in the here and now, relates this confusion to the helpee, and provides the helpee an opportunity for immediate here and now reaction to his experience. The open admission of helper error is often helpful to helpee growth and is one useful approach when the helper is out of touch with the helpee.

Al 33: Okay. Ah, let me just check out a little bit more, and then I think you better respond to me honestly. You perhaps sense a little puzzlement in my face right now? I hear you really loud and strong saying — —

Joan 33: You've said that three times!

Al 34: I've said that three times. I'm not used to people, and you've done it in the past sometimes, becoming quite that definitive that quickly. And my experience is, is that where you're really at? How do you react to my doubting you a little bit and so forth?

Important in Al 34 is the "check-out" which encourages the client to react directly to him.

In summary, it must again be stressed that self-disclosure in the interview—particularly here and now immediate self-disclosure of the helper's personal experience of the helpee—remains a controversial issue in the professional helping field. Clearly, further research on the impact and value of such helping leads is needed. One advantage of the microtraining paradigm is that the relatively vague construct of self-disclosure is made more precise, thus enabling research on alternative types of self-disclosure. For example, Authier and Gustafson (1976b) in a recent study included self-disclosure as one of the skills they researched. They defined self-disclosure as containing the above components and trained raters to code trainee utterances as self-disclosures if they contained these criteria. Unfortunately, a problem in researching the influencing skills is that criterion segments are often relatively brief. Skills such as self-disclosure should not be expected to appear frequently in microsessions evaluating real interviews. This is generally true of all the influencing skills. For example, it seems inappropriate for the helper to offer five or six interpretations, directions, or self-disclosures in a brief ten-minute segment of the interview. This is especially so as one effective influencing skill lead can sometimes take a helpee through an entire interview.

Nevertheless, the study did demonstrate the viability of researching self-disclosure training and its use with clients via a microcounseling paradigm. Perhaps this is possible since although self-disclosure contains many dimensions and types, microtraining allows breaking down self-disclosure so that it can be defined more precisely and the effectiveness of different types of self-disclosure can be studied. Unfortunately, however, most research in self-disclosure simply uses the term "self-disclosure" without adequate definition. An examination of these pages suggests that practically any helper statement beginning with an "I" statement could be rated as a self-disclosure. As alluded to, the nature of the self-disclosure can be delineated far more precisely using the several dimensions suggested here, thus making for more meaningful research.

INTERPRETATION

Interpretation involves both attending and self-expression and is a broader skill than any discussed thus far. Successful interviewers must be able both to listen to clients and to express new ideas so that the client understands them. The skill of interpretation was developed by Moreland and Ivey (1969) and has proven to be the most challenging and complex skill within the microcounseling paradigm. Conceptually, interpretation is based on an adaption of Levy's stimulating work, *Psychological Interpretation* (1963). Levy has said, "To sum up, psychological interpretation, viewed as a behavior . . . consists of bringing an alternate frame of reference, or language system, to bear upon a set of observations or behaviors, with the end in view of making them more amenable to manipulation" (p. 7).

While interpretations may vary in content, depending upon the theoretical orientation from which they are drawn, they all have a common element. When interviewers make interpretations, they are presenting clients with a new frame of reference through which clients can view their problems and, hopefully, better understand and deal with them. Seen in this light, an interpretation is not unlike either a paraphrase or a reflection of feeling. However, the new frame of reference is also tied to the interviewer's perception of the situation. As such, self-expression skills become especially important.

One function of both the paraphrase and the reflection of feeling is to crystallize for the client either the objective content or the feeling components of what has just been said. In paraphrasing and reflection of feeling, the interviewer remains, for the most part, within the client's *own* frame of reference. However, in interpretation, the interviewer provides the client with a *new,* potentially more functional frame of reference.

At this point, it appears useful to discuss some characteristics which distinguish interpretation from paraphrasing and reflection of feeling.

> *Client* (who has had a record of absenteeism) : I really feel badly about missing so much work.
> *Interviewer:* You're really troubled and worried.   (Reflection of feeling)
> You've been missing a lot of work. (Paraphrase)
> You've missed a lot of work and you are aware of how the company views absenteeism. This gives you concern as to where you stand. (Interpretation)

Reflection of feeling takes data from the client and focuses on emotional aspects. The paraphrase focuses on the content of the problem. Interpretation attends to both emotional and objective components; in addition, the interviewer's observations and frame of reference are added.

Another example from psychotherapy is as follows:

> *Client* (with agitation) :   My wife and I had a fight last night after watching a sexy movie. I tried to make love, and she rejected me again.
> *Counselor:* You're upset about and troubled about what happened. (Reflection of feeling)
> Your fight followed a sexually exciting movie. (Paraphrase)
> The movie stimulated you sexually and you sought to make love, expecting your wife to reject you once again.   (Interpretation)
> You've mentioned several times that you are interested in making love with your wife after some external sexual stimulation.   You've never mentioned your wife as being sexually exciting. (Interpretation)
> The feelings of rejection trouble you. Are these feelings similar to some feelings you mentioned in the dream last week?   (Interpretation)
> As I see you here and now, you seem very upset. Your hand is clenched. You'd like to do something right now but you don't know what. (Interpretation)

In each example of interpretation, the interviewer takes a part of the essence of what the client has said (both emotionally and intellectually) and summarizes it, adding other data which are considered relevant. A multitude of interpretations are possible with any client utterance and will vary with the theoretical orientation of the interviewer.

In microtraining, interpretation is taught as a general skill rather than one associated with a particular discipline. Thus, trainees are encouraged to free themselves and give a variety of alternative interpretations to the same behavior in a practice situation. In microtraining sessions, a role-playing client gives a standard stimulus to which the trainee can respond with a variey of interpretations. At the beginning levels, the more interpretations that a trainee can present, the better. When a large group of interpretations have been generated, the supervisor and the trainee can review the interpretations. Out of this review, the trainee will begin to get a picture of how he or she views the world and the theoretical orientation which is being applied to most clients. Too many helpers involve themselves in interpretation without having fully considered the theoretical/world view from which these interpretations come.

An interpretation is, by definition, a semantic integration of cognitive and affective states. Interpretations do not emphasize feelings as distinct from interview verbal content; interpretations attempt to present the essence of helpee experience as seen from another vantage point. The beginning helper needs to have an array of interpretations available; the skilled therapist needs to know what he or she is doing and why.

Interpretation can be taught from specific theoretical disciplines. The same data events from the helpee will result in widely different interpretations on the part of helpers with differing world views. Let us once again consider the helpee with the difficulty with his wife, but this time, specific interpretations from alternative theoretical orientations will be considered.

Client (with agitation): My wife and I had a fight last night after watching a sexy movie. I tried to make love, and she rejected me again.

Analytic therapist: This would seem to tie in with your dreams of flying and crashing you have been having all week. It also relates to your conflict with your father and his desires of achievement for you. As you know, you deliberately failed in school to avoid meeting his expectations. Are you again deliberately avoiding becoming what you want to become?

Transactional analysis counselor: I hear your parent judging you
again. You're talking about sex with your wife, but you seem
to be blaming yourself more for not achieving your goals.

Existentially oriented helper: You use the word "tried." I hear
you "doing to" the world and your wife rather than "being in"
the world and with your wife. You're still avoiding here and
now experience. Even at this moment, I see you physically
moving away from me.

Behavioral therapist: You don't yet have the skills you need to
accomplish your goals. You probably were tense and tight.
You'll need more training in relaxation and referral for sex
therapy. A systematic program for resolving this problem can
be developed.

Feminist helper: Once again, we see you as the male who thinks
he must dominate and "take" the woman. Always "trying,"
you seem sensitive neither to yourself nor others. Men are condi-
tioned to think of sex in these terms. This makes it difficult for
women to respond.

Obviously, in this brief space, it is not possible to do full
justice to the several theoretical orientations presented. However,
it may be clearly seen that each interpretation could be made
based on the theoretical orientation of the different helpers.
Different theories see the same situation differently. Which is
"right" will depend on the value structure and world view of the
observer. Microtraining programs can be developed to teach a
specific theoretical orientation or may be used to teach a more
general orientation to the skill.

The value of a reflection of feeling or paraphrase is gauged by
the client's reaction to it — be it verbal or nonverbal. The same
basic criterion can be used to gauge the value of an interpretation.
Does the client use it to cope more effectively with the problem,
discuss issues in more depth, or develop new and unique personal
insights and behaviors? Some people will respond best to an
analytic interpretation, others to a behavioral or existential frame
of reference. The actual determination of which is the "best"
interpretation will depend on future research and the examination of which interpretation is appropriate for which individual
at what time under what conditions.

Another issue in interpretation is the depth of an interpretation. Moreland and Ivey (1969, p. 1) have made the following comments:

> Interpretation has traditionally been viewed as mystical activity in which the interviewer reaches into the depths of the client's personality and provides him with new insight. However, when one conceives of an interpretation as merely a new frame of reference, the concept of depth takes on a much less formidable aura. Viewed in this light, the depth of a given interpretation refers to the magnitude of the discrepancy between the frame of reference from which the client is operating and the frame of reference supplied by the interviewer. For example, a client may report a dream in which a seedling he had planted grew into a tree and was mysteriously cut down. The interviewer could make a number of interpretations which vary in terms of their depth.
>
> 1. You lost something you really cared about.
> 2. Your life has had a number of disappointments.
> 3. You're very unsure of your successes.
> 4. You're afraid of losing your penis.

In the early stages of therapy, the first interpretation is most likely the most appropriate, whereas in later stages, the more in-depth interpretation may be suitable. The timing of interpretation is crucial. Another criterion for the validity of an interpretation is the interviewer's personal comfort with her or his view of the client's world. If the interviewer is not comfortable and congruent with both self and the client, the interpretation is less likely to be accepted and to be useful.

Interpretation also has validity in interviewing situations which are not necessarily therapeutic. The employment interviewer may believe he or she is talking with a malingerer. The interviewer may note several comments, threaded throughout the session, suggestive of a person who is not telling the truth. When the interviewer sums up these separate but related comments, adds a personal evaluation of them, and allows the individual to rethink these ideas, he or she is engaging in an interpretation. The interpretation is most effective when the helper is comfortable with the perception and feels the client can use the interpretation to explore the issue in more depth. It may be seen that the interviewer has taken an *ad hoc* theoretical framework developed from personal experience, integrated it with data from the interviewee's conversation and behavior, and provided the interviewee with an interpretation of the situation in the hope that further discussion of the issue will occur.

The most effective use of interpretation is often in those unique insights provided by the helpee rather than those provided by the helper. The helpee who is able to find a new frame of reference to interpret old experience is well on the route toward effectiveness. Through the skillful use of attending skills, directions, self-disclosure, or interpretation itself, the helper can aid helpees in making their own interpretations and insights. Particularly useful in facilitating helpees' developing their own unique approaches to their world is the microtraining attending skill of summarization. Here the helper takes main trends, feelings, and facts from the helpee's verbalizations and summarizes them for the helpee. The helpee then may spontaneously put these facts together in a new and meaningful gestalt which leads to action and personal changes in life style. It may be observed that Gestalt therapy provides directions and role enactment experiences which lead the helpee to generate spontaneously new and important insights and relationships among old facts and feelings. There is obviously more than one route toward helpees generating new interpretations.

Unfortunately, the Appendix typescript provides no clear interpretations on the part of the helper. The demonstration interview, despite its professed purpose to exemplify each of the microtraining skills clearly did not produce an interpretation which stands solely by itself. An example of a helper lead which is scored as both an attending summary and an interpretation occurs at Al 12. The preceding comments are provided so as to give a context for the summary and interpretation.

Al 10: I can't help but wonder — would you share a little bit about how that makes you feel inside? Even right now as you talk, I see something.

Joan 10: There's tension right here, and I feel like going . . . Leave me alone. Get away from me. You're intruding into my life. And, it's, it's, I feel tight and defensive. It's like I don't want anybody to get in if that's the way. I'm going to be taken advantage of that way. Nobody's going to get in. But ——

Al 11: I get the feeling right now that you feel you just want to close him off. Yet at the same time, I hear something else. . . . But, it's almost an unheard thing.

Joan 11: Unheard thing is, ah, . . . but I don't want to spend the rest of my life alone. Ah, I do want a relationship with a man. Ah, is it just this man, or is it, is it that I need to be so separate.

Al 12: Hmm (pause) Let's stop for just a moment and let me just feed back to you what I've been hearing so far. You've been saying that you're in your new law apprenticeship? Okay. And yet the real issue is this man. And how can you be yourself and be a professional. And how can you put yourself in a warm, human way with him as well. And, undergirding it is that feeling that he really wants to control you rather than allow you to be. Am I hearing you accurately?

Joan 12: I guess I don't feel that it's so much control as really own.

Al 13: Own, even more than control, then?

Joan 13: Yeah. It's like parading me down the street. You know — here, here's, here's my property. That's part of it. Now, you know, now, Joan I want you to do this. But, you know, even when he gives me something it's like come over right now. I have something for you. And I might be in the middle of doing something.

At Al 11, we see what is scored as a paraphrase and reflection of feeling. However, the words "unseen thing" could be described as the beginning of an interpretation. The unseen dimension becomes important and is clarified through ensuing discussion and the fantasy exercise at Al 18 along with videotape feedback at Al 22. The helper defines this unseen dimension as "control" (note that this is a word which comes primarily from the helper's frame of reference and not the helpee's). The helper has taken the helpee's verbal descriptions of the manfriend and interpreted his behavior as controlling. While the interpretation was not "on target," the word that the helpee substitutes for "control" is "own," which is her perception of the relationship. In this case the formerly "unseen thing" is interpreted by the helper first as control and then by the helpee as own, a much stronger interpersonal issue than control.

The helper's interpretation can be viewed as successful, as the helpee has clarified her feelings and been able to supply a more succinct "name" which defines the relationship.   The helper would have been guilty of psychological imperialism and forcing his ideas on the helpee if he had insisted on control as the issue for discussion.   Instead, at Al 13, we see him acknowledge the helpee's view through a minimal encourage reinforcing her statement of meaning.   The helpee at Joan 2 used the word "own," as did the helper at Al 4 and 5.   Nonetheless, this interchange clarifies the importance of that definition of the relationship.

Through the use of directions and attending skills on the part of the helper, the helpee at Joan 25 redefines, i.e. reinterprets, her relationship with the man in a totally new fashion.   At this point, she makes a decision to terminate the relationship.   This is a clear example of a helpee taking all available data and redefining the situation from her own perspective.   Effective, forward-moving helpees are able to take data from their life experience and redefine their life in their own terms.   At several points in this session we see the helpee take old data and apply a new frame of reference which is more useful as a way to interpret the world.

In summary, interpretation can be said to involve several distinct attentional frameworks.   First, the interviewer attends to and reinforces a variety of client comments through paraphrasing and reflection.   Simultaneously, the interviewer is relating data provided by the client to past information and his or her own theoretical framework.   When the interviewer makes an interpretation, observations are summarized in a frame of reference which gives the client a new way of viewing self and situation.   Finally, once having made an interpretation, the counselor should be able to attend to the client's verbal and nonverbal reactions and revise interpretations as appropriate.

Psychological interpretations demand important skills on the part of the interviewer.   Microtraining techniques will not develop fully skilled interpreters, but defining more precisely the nature of the interpretative process should help the beginning counselor and interviewer.

DIRECT-MUTUAL COMMUNICATION*

While not originally developed as a microcounseling skill, training in direct-mutual communication may now be considered a relevant skill for counselor and interviewer training, particularly for those interviewers interested in interpersonal openness and directness of expression. Modeled on behaviors taught in sensitivity, encounter, and T-groups, direct-mutual communication is concerned with the interviewer and the interviewee *both* receiving microtraining. If communication is to be mutual, both parties should have the benefit of training. As such, work with interviewers has centered on giving two individuals the opportunity to learn the skill together.

The skill focused on in direct-mutual communication was described by Higgins, Ivey, and Uhlemann (1970, p. 21) as follows:

> The skill(s) focused on in this study is one in which two individuals attempt to focus on their interaction as they perceive and feel it, and attempt to share with each other their experience of the other. Rather than talk about politics, their liking of certain movies, books, classes, etc. (the content of most typical conversations), they are to react to the experiences they have (or have had) with each other. They are to share personal feelings with each other and to respond to these shared feelings with new and past reactions to these feelings.

From a psychoanalytic point of view, direct-mutual communication is a frank analysis of the transference relationship occurring between two human beings. Viewed from learning theory, direct-mutual communication is teaching people another way of developing mutual reinforcement modalities with an emphasis on affective comments. Existentially, direct-mutual communication with its emphasis on here and now feelings and experiences may provide interviewers with insight into themselves and the nature of their own existence.

A programmed text integrated with videotape models was developed for direct-mutual communication. A research study by Higgins, Ivey, and Uhlemann (1970) examined the effectiveness

*Portions of this section are taken from Higgins, Ivey, and Uhlemann (1970) and used by permission of *The Journal of Counseling Psychology* and the American Psychological Association.

of the method and compared the following three approaches to teaching this skill: (A) full treatment in the traditional micro-training paradigm, (B) programmed text and video models only with no supervision or video feedback, and (C) reading material only. It was found that the full-treatment group doubled the amount of direct-mutual communication (100% increase); group B increased 50 percent; and group C did not change. While validating the general premise of the study, it seems possible that a completely programmed approach to direct-mutual communication may be feasible and that eventually only a technician or paraprofessional may be required to teach this skill, if under the supervision of a skilled clinician.

An illustration from a typescript of one of the sessions from the full-treatment group may serve to clarify what happens in training in direct-mutual communication. One of the experimental couples was from the Far East and chose to discuss the issue as to whether or not they should return to their homeland.

SESSION 1

Husband: Don't you think that the individual makes a good contribution to his old country when he goes back? Rather than staying here?

Wife: Yes, he would. But then he would not get material gain, he would not get so much money.

Husband: But money is not everything.

Wife: It isn't everything, but it is . . . you want to give the family good educations, good living and everything else, and you can't do this back there.

Husband: But it depends on what we mean by good education, and good living.

(The couple continued this discussion for five minutes with a consistent pattern of "yes, but" with one individual trying to put his point over on the other. Some heat was generated between them. This discussion was basically a confrontation of two opposing points of view.)

SESSION 2

Husband: How do you feel about people staying here in this country and not returning to their native land?

Wife: I personally feel that I would like to stay here, but at the same time I want to return to ———. Of course, I miss my family, but I would like to stay here for some time and make a good living and then take what we need for a good living at home back with us.

Husband: But what about the idea of the "brain drain"? Shouldn't people return to their own country?

Wife: I don't care. Let them stay. If they stay, it is their personal opinion.

Husband: You feel indifferent about it.

Wife: Yes. I don't think we can make others go back to ——, but if they don't, I can't help it. They can stay here.

Husband: I agree with you that this feeling of indifference is quite true. But shouldn't we try to get them to go back?

(It may be observed in this session that the couple for the first time made an effort to look at *feelings*. There is the beginning of some listening to one another. However, there is also a tendency to generalize their particular feelings to others rather than looking at their own interaction.)

SESSION 3

Husband: We both seem to have this fear of going back home. I don't think it's really the fear of going back, but a fear of the . . .

Wife: Instability?

Husband: Yes, the fear of instability there, and then the feeling of not having really accomplished to a certain extent what other people have done. And at the same time, this nagging thought comes to my mind always, you have to go back. You have to go back. What do you feel about this fear?

Wife: I feel insecure too. I don't know what will happen if we go back. I really want to go back today to —— if we have things, but I am very scared. What will we do? We don't have anything back home.

Husband: Yes, what is your feeling now at this moment? You can think about what we would have and what we would not have. What do you feel about not having it?

Wife: There is just a blank. I see nothing. The future makes me afraid. We have no definite opportunities even in —— or here.

Husband: It makes me feel right now that I'm not capable of doing it. How does my inability make you feel?

Wife: I feel sorry. And I want you to do something about it. Keep trying and somehow we will manage it. If you can't, we both can do something.

(The couple went on to constructive discussion of the problem at hand, more fully aware of the issues underlying this complex decision. It may be observed in this third session that the couple was able to share feelings and attitudes of fear and, at the same time, to listen constructively to one another. An increased emphasis on feelings may be observed. Feelings, however, are viewed in a context of life and are used positively to establish a closer relationship and make a more sound decision.) (Higgins, Ivey, and Uhlemann, 1970, p. 24)

Direct-mutual communication has been used in counselor and therapist training with some dramatic results. Therapists who have a special interest in encounter groups or existential psychology may find that the often highly charged, dramatic methods of this microtraining skill may prove helpful in making their concepts more explicit. The methods of direct-mutual communication also provide a laboratory in which the behavioral aspects of interpersonal openness may be systematically explored.

Direct-mutual communication is a synthesis of many microtraining skills plus several of the qualitative dimensions of helping stressed in the following chapter. The programmed text as currently revised may be viewed in Ivey and Gluckstern, 1976b. Two examples of direct-mutual communication were scored on the typescript. However, Chadbourne (1976) reports that Al 11 was experienced by her as mutual communication despite the fact that the content was not the relationship between helper and helpee. Al 46 is the clearest example of direct-mutual communication in the interview. It should also be observed that the helpee rejected the invitation to this type of relationship at Joan 46. This is appropriate, for early in helping sessions, direct-mutual communication should not be expected between helper and helpee. It is to be reserved for those who have gradually developed a trusting relationship over time and are willing to expose themselves completely to one another in the here and now or to those who volunteer directly for training in the general skill.

Al 46: You mentioned that I am a man. I guess that's obvious. You're a woman. Ah, I like it. I like you the way you're responding now. You're coming across soft and easy to hear. At the same time, I like you when you come across strong and sure of yourself. I find myself being a little wary of you becoming superstrong. And I also find myself a little puzzled when you come across superunsure. You haven't been much of that today. Ah, so you come across to me in many, very different ways. And I guess, underlying that, my reaction to you is a very positive feeling. And yet, as a man, I kind of, as a person, I sometimes wonder just where you're going to jump next. Where you're going to jump next. And this puzzles me. In a sense this makes me close up. How do you respond to that?

Joan 46: I think that's one of the reasons why I say that I'm going to sit here and wait. Because somebody has to, uhm, . . . it's hard to follow me. I never know what to expect next. So how could you know what to expect next? And you have to be very facile and easy on your feet, or, or else not attend to me a lot. And that's okay not to attend to me a whole lot.

The specific dimensions of Al 46 which represent direct-mutual communication include (1) the frequent use of the pronouns "I" and "you" which are basic to this type of communication and form the foundation for an "I-Thou" relationship, (2) feedback of personal content and affect to the helpee in terms of a reflection of feeling, (3) self-disclosure of content and affect from the helper's experience of the helpee, (4) a here and now, immediate, present tense statement coupled with some reflection of past experience as it relates to the present, and (5) provision of a specific opportunity and invitation for the helpee to participate in the same set of verbal interactions: "How do you respond to that?" Joan 46, primarily using the pronoun "I," describes herself more in terms of content than affective-emotional process and primarily talks in the past tense.

This example of direct-mutual communication in the interview may be especially helpful, as it provides a clear model of both how the skill can be integrated into the interview and how many helpees will find this open presentation of self and free feedback of data threatening. Used effectively, direct-mutual communication can be one of the most powerful types of helping relationships that any helper can develop. It is most appropriate for those interested in personal, mutual encounters and in the humanistic-existential orientations to helping. Behavioral, analytic, nondirective, and other approaches to helping would perhaps consider such interview behavior inappropriate and unprofessional. Yet it is these very issues which are ultimately dealt with in transference/counter-transference dimensions of in-depth psychotherapy.

However, direct-mutual communication is most properly conceived as a systematic training program for teaching two or more people how to communicate more fully and effectively. For the interviewer in training, experience in direct-mutual communication may aid in confronting a passive, hostile client with honest perceptions. The video models and accompanying materials (Ivey and Gluckstern, 1976a,b) serve as models of interpersonal openness and directness; after viewing them, the novice may begin to realize that one of the most important dimensions in the counseling and interviewing process is the immediate interaction between helper and helpee. Further, the specificity of behavior provided by training in direct-mutual communication facilitates the generalization of the learned behavior to daily life, whereas the more mystical approach of encounter groups often leaves people with a troubling feeling of "crashing down to earth" without knowing what happened.

Finally, direct-mutual communication when used effectively resembles very closely the "level 5" communication described by Carkhuff (1969a,b). Careful examination of the facilitative conditions scales will reveal that level 5 communication in all the separate facilitative conditions is closely related to the more behavioral direct-mutual communication presented here. High level communication demands, from Carkhuff's point of view, a helper and a helpee involved in mutual exploration.

Kagan (1975a) describes his systematic method of Interpersonal Process Recall and emphasizes the importance of mutual recall. Again, careful examination of the mutual recall sessions between counselor and client will reveal levels and types of communication closely akin to direct-mutual communication or Carkhuff level 5 communication. It seems clear that three distinct systematic routes now exist toward the same goal of close and honest communication between helper and helpee.

SUMMARY

The microtraining skills of attending and influencing provide a system whereby the interview may be viewed systematically and precisely. The skills presented illustrate the possibilities for introducing novice interviewers to the complex processes of human interaction. Microcounseling has deliberately kept itself non-aligned with a specific theory; it is a general training model adaptable to a variety of theoretical orientations.

The influencing skills presented in this chapter — self-expression, directions, expression of content, expression of feeling, self-disclosure, the influencing summarization, interpretation, and direct-mutual communication — are focused on demonstrating that the professional (and nonprofessional) helper can be a person of influence. The helping process exists to influence others in positive directions. An effort in this chapter has been to show that different theoretical orientations to helping favor different skills. The analytic helper will give special attention to interpretation, the behaviorist and Gestaltist to directions, the vocational counselor to expression of content, the existentially oriented therapist to expression of feeling, self-disclosure, and possibly direct-mutual communication. This pattern of different helpers using differing skills will be detailed in Chapter 7. For the moment, it is suggested that it is important for the beginning helper, counselor, or therapist to identify clearly what he or she is doing and what effect this has on the helpee, client, or patient.

It is possible to develop advanced versions of these skills for the technically proficient expert helper who may be interested in developing new ideas and methods. At another level, it is equally feasible to develop simplified versions of skills which can be taught to individuals who serve as counselor aides or paraprofessionals. Finally, clients and patients may be taught microtraining skills if suitable adaptations are made within the psychoeducator model. Microtraining is most effective when adapted to meet the needs of individuals concerned and is only meaningful when it meets both trainer and trainee needs.

Chapter 6

THE QUALITY OF HELPING:
MICROTRAINING AND
THE CONSTRUCT OF EMPATHY

MICROTRAINING FOCUSES on quantifiable measurable skills. Implicit in this training is the belief that people trained in the use of skills will use them to benefit clients. This has been borne out in research. People trained via this route prove more empathic and facilitative to others, often more so than those trained via other routes (Dunn, 1975; Hearn, 1976; Moreland, Ivey, and Phillips, 1973; Toukmanian and Rennie, 1975).

However, the fact remains that microtraining is centrally a quantitative factual approach to counselor training. Clearly, some attention should be paid to the more subjective qualitative dimensions of helping. The purpose of this chapter is to consider dimensions for improving the *quality* of helping relationships. Central attention will be given to the concept of empathy. This discussion will be followed by examination of other aspects required to produce a quality approach to the helping professions. It must be kept in mind, however, that the qualitative dimensions of helping are also heavily laden with cultural values. Quality relationships among one cultural group do not necessarily mean quality relationships in other cultures or groups.

EMPATHY

Probably the major contribution of Carl Rogers to the helping profession is the concept of empathy. In 1961, he wrote, "To sense the client's private world as if it were your own, but without losing the 'as if' quality—this is empathy" (Rogers, 1961, p. 284).

Rogers expands in depth on this basic defintion, pointing out that the therapist is able to "understand the patient's feelings," closely follows the meanings of each client statement, and through tone of voice communicates this understanding at an emotional level.

More recently, Rogers quoted a training manual on "Absolute Listening" as a good contemporary definition of empathy:

> This is not laying trips on people . . . You only listen and say back the other person's thing, step by step, just as that person seems to have it at that moment. You never mix into it any of your own things or ideas, never lay on the other person anything that person didn't express . . . To show that you understand exactly, make a sentence or two which gets exactly at the personal meaning this person wanted to put across. This might be in your own words, usually, but use that person's own words for the touchy main things (Gendlin and Hendricks, *Rap Manual,* undated, cited in Rogers, 1975, p. 5).

These definitions relate closely to the concepts of attending behavior and the attending skills. If one is to be empathic, it seems essential that one be able to hear the other person accurately. Attending behavior and the attending skills represent effective listening, the foundation of accurate empathy. Zimmer and his colleagues (Zimmer and Park, 1967; Zimmer and Anderson, 1968) factor analyzed counselor communication in an attempt to isolate dimensions of empathy and found that verbal skills such as minimal activity (the minimal encourage), unstructured invitation and interrogation (the open question), clarification (paraphrase), and reflection of feeling appeared prominently in the factor structure. Moreover, the previously discussed study by Haase and Tepper (1972) found nonverbal components such as eye contact, trunk lean, and distance, elements of microcounseling attending behavior, important in displaying high levels of empathy. These data, from different methodological and/or theoretical structures, clearly support the constructs of attending and attending behavior presented throughout this text.

Carkhuff (1969a,b) and Egan (1975) discuss and label the attending type of responses as "interchangeable," "level 3," and as "primary empathy." They state that the helper who serves solely as mirror and does not share the self is not being fully effective in the helping interview. While accurate listening may indeed be helpful to the client, it may also be slow and tedious if used as the sole medium for helping.

Effective, dynamic helping demands more than listening. Carkhuff talks about "additive dimensions" of helping and Egan about "advanced accurate empathy." Both authors clearly state the importance of the helper involving him or herself actively in the interview sharing experience and giving of self directly to the helpee. The sharing of self as a part of empathic understanding may be through self-disclosure, interpretation, and/or directions. The sharing of self may be through the giving of appropriate advice, information, or suggestions at an appropriate time.

> Detailed examination of the Carkhuff levels 4 and 5 and Egan's advanced accurate empathy reveals that the helper is expected to be able to assist the helpee in exploring areas of human existence which have not yet been considered. *As part of this experience, focus must be also on the helper's own world view and perceptions.* The helper must share him or herself to assist the helpee grow. This sharing may take a wide variety of forms ranging from the direct intervention of the behaviorist, to the personal sharing of the existential helper, to the interpretive style of the psychoanalytically oriented (Ivey and Gluckstern, 1976b, p. 16).

The skills of interpersonal influence, then, may be considered additive dimensions of helping where the interviewer, counselor, or therapist adds personal knowledge or experience to that of the helpee. Attending skills by themselves can result in personal growth, but the additive dimensions of interpersonal influence can move an interviewer faster and to more depth. At the same time, it must be stressed that the ineffective use of interpersonal influence skills can be damaging to client growth and to the helper-helpee relationships. Ineffective and inappropriate influencing skills can destroy the results of effective attending skills.

The "1-2-3 pattern" has been proposed as a systematic format for providing an interactive relationship between counselor and client to prevent the potentially disruptive use of influencing skills:

1. The helper must attend accurately and empathically to the helpee and communicate this attention via the attending skills. Success-

ful attending can result in Carkhuff's level 3 helping, Egan's primary empathy, or the basic empathy described by Rogers. Occasionally, effective attending can lead to even higher levels of communication.

2. The helper then may, as appropriate, share him or herself via the influencing skills of directions, self-disclosure or interpretation. This additional dimension permits a higher level of empathy to develop involving not only the client's world, but also the helper's world.

3. The helper then "checks-out" the accuracy or reasonableness of attending or influencing skills (e.g., "How does that sound to you?") thus allowing a mutual "I-you" or "I-Thou" exploration. Further, the tentativeness in the check-out allows room for mutual growth (Ivey and Gluckstern, 1976b, p. 32).

A similar three-step structure for the interviewing lead is suggested by Bandler and Grinder (1975) and Grinder and Bandler (1976). Step 1 is defined as listening to the client, step 2 as the therapist processing the data and adding new data where appropriate, and step 3 as testing to see how the lead fits into the ongoing world of the client. Brammer (1973) stresses the same point in the perception check, "Solicit the *helpee's reactions* to your interpretations" (p. 106).

In summary, empathic understanding or empathy is considered to be an extremely broad qualitative dimension of the helping process which involves the interviewer and the interviewee in a mutual process of discovery of understandings, meanings, and directions. Elementary empathy may be demonstrated through attending skills, but advanced empathy requires dimensions of interpersonal influence.

However, the definition of empathy presented here is still elementary, and it should prove helpful to examine other related constructs of helping such as positive regard, respect and warmth, concreteness, immediacy, confrontation, and genuineness for more complete understanding of the helping process.

POSITIVE REGARD

The concepts and labels of Carl Rogers are central to the qualitative examination of the helping process. At the same time, his terms are often "warm fuzzies" which leave the beginning helper confused yet full of admiration and hope. Positive regard is a construct which is central to a Rogerian view of helping yet which remains all too mystical and elusive. As such, it is easy for the "hard-core," scientific helper to disregard such subjective dimensions and stress more observable dimensions.

However, rather than listen to what Rogers *says*, we have examined what he *does*. The careful examination of Carl Rogers in a helping interview almost immediately reveals that he maintains a constant emphasis on the positive assets of the helpee.

> From a first glance, one would think that the helpee has no assets, no hope. But, out of a dark morass of discouragement, Carl Rogers seems always to find something positive in an individual and highlights that positive dimension via a reflection of feeling and (more recently) direct personal feedback. We believe that the selection of the positive dimensions from a client statement can be described as an operational definition of positive regard (Ivey and Gluckstern, 1976b, p. i).

Selective attention to positive client statements is crucial in nondirective or client-centered helping. When one applies the precision of behavioral approaches to a Rogerian interview, the somewhat mystical concept of positive regard begins to take focus. An example can be taken from the Appendix III typescript:

> *Joan 34:* Lots of people seem to doubt, but when I make a decision that comes from my gut, it's made. And I don't make it from my head. It's a whole decision, and most people don't understand how I do that, but that's a process that works for me, and I really need somebody to help me start feeling, and experiencing, and seeing myself. Sometimes it happens, and sometimes it doesn't. But, yeah, you really helped me make a decision then.
>
> *Al 35:* So another way to look at it: as we began by saying you were afraid of this guy owning you. And we end by saying you want to own yourself.

In the above example, the helper selectively attends to the positive, forward-moving aspects of the helpee. If the helper had selectively reinforced via a minimal encourage, "Lots of people seem to doubt," and continued to emphasize how people doubted the helpee, it may be anticipated that the helpee would eventually begin to doubt herself. *The selective attention to positive aspects*

*of helpee verbalizations can be considered an operational defini-
tion of positive regard.*

The concept of positive regard, of course, is derived directly
from Carl Rogers' clearly stated world view and philosophy.
People are seen as positive, growth-centered individuals aiming
to be helpful to themselves and others. By focusing on the positive dimensions of personal experience, Rogers is merely directing
attention to what the people already know and are.

Behaviorists, of course, would define Rogers' behavior as
simply reinforcing positive verbal statements from the helpee.
At the same time, it must be recognized that behaviorally oriented
helpers do much the same thing that Rogers does. They focus on
positive things which the client can do to improve his or her
personal condition.

*Both the Rogerian and behavioral counselor operate on the
assumption that people can be helped, that helping can make a
difference in a person's life. This faith and trust in people's
ability to change may be as important or more so than the technology one uses to produce change. If one is to be a helper, one
must believe that people can be helped.*

Other approaches to helping share the same emphasis on
positive aspects of the individual and the person's ability to
change. Transactional analysts (e.g. Berne, 1964; James and
Jongeward, 1971) stress the importance of "strokes" and the
"stroke economy." A vocational counselor in an employment
service must believe in positive change to be of value in a complex
employment situation. Laing (1967) sees madness and insanity
as sane responses to an insane world and uses these responses to
bring people to fuller awareness and control of their own lives.
The family therapists (e.g. Satir, 1964; Haley, 1973) assume that
families can grow and change. Even the more pessimistic psychoanalytic philosophy makes the assumption that people can change
and adapt to a somewhat gloomy world.

One of the more useful summaries of positive regard and the
counselor's place in facilitating client growth may be found in
Tyler's (1953) classic introductory counseling text. Talking
about "minimum change therapy," Tyler emphasizes the impor-

tance of finding positive assets in the client and communicating these positive assets so they are realized. Then, equipped with this knowledge and increased belief in self, the client can move on to solve ever larger and more complex problems of living. The minimum change becomes a maximum change over time.

Positive regard is a basic ingredient of all helping theories, although it may not be stated as such. A microtraining skill such as interpretation, minimal encourage, or question could be used to enhance or to detract from another person. In the most recent microtraining materials (Ivey and Gluckstern, 1976a,b), qualitative dimensions of helping are stressed as integral to the microtraining process. A qualitative dimension such as positive regard may be operationalized and then practiced in much the same way as the attending and influencing skills. For example,

1. A video model of lack of positive regard and a video model demonstrating positive regard as defined here may be easily developed.
2. A written manual based on the constructs of this (or other) section may be developed.
3. Microtraining workshops or individual training may proceed as usual.

Indeed, the Authier and Gustafson (1973) program has demonstrated the viability of such an approach.

Thus, formerly subjective qualitative conditions may also be taught using the microtraining format of systematically delineating the skill, modeling it on videotape (or audiotape), and providing sufficient opportunity for mastery. It is also possible to teach these formerly subjective conditions using a variety of theoretical perspectives.

RESPECT AND WARMTH

Closely related to positive regard are the constructs of respect and warmth. Rogers talks about respect in terms of the therapist holding "attitudes of deep respect and full acceptance for the client as he is" (Rogers, 1961, p. 74) and a similar range of attitudes toward the client's ability to manage his or her own life.

Warmth is commented on as related to these attitudes of acceptance sufficient so that they may be transformed "into the most profound type of liking or affection for the core of the person" (Rogers, 1961, p. 75).

Needless to say, these terms could benefit by further operational definition. The Carkhuff (1969b) scale on respect is useful and provides five check points on a subjective scale, but at the highest level Carkhuff again talks about "caring deeply" for the client. "Caring deeply," "full acceptance," and related concepts are certainly desirable qualities of the effective helper but are rather hard to define and measure precisely.*

Respect may be defined in a more simple and direct fashion: "Our definition of respect is that different perceptions of the same event must be listened to, honored and appreciated" (Ivey and Gluckstern, 1976b, p. 137). This general statement is in turn further operationalized when respect is compared to lack of respect. The clearest examples of lack of respect show in "put-downs" (negative statements about the self or others) predominant in United States society.

---

*The following exercise has proven most helpful in aiding beginning (or advanced) helpers to define vague constructs such as respect or warmth in more precise terms:

1. Start with the statement, "Have you ever seen a warmth? We all know the construct exists, but what do you *see* or *hear* that specifically tells you that this individual is demonstrating warmth?" (or positive regard, or lack of motivation, or incongruence, etc.).

2. The individual or group will usually begin to identify specific observable verbal and nonverbal behaviors which gave them the clue that the concept, in this case warmth, was present or absent. List these specific behaviors on the blackboard or on newsprint.

3. A model tape then can be produced in which the role-played helper first presents what warmth is not in terms of observable behavior and then presents what it is in terms of concrete actions.

4. Trainees may then practice the presentation of the construct in their helping sessions or note their own behaviors in a helping session.

This simple exercise has consistently proven useful to people working at an abstract level in aiding them to define the helping process more precisely. In virtually every case, it is possible to take subjective constructs and find specific elements which lead to more concrete specifications. This process of clarifying helping dimensions is very close to what Grinder and Bandler (1976) term denominalization, the active clarification of sentence meaning on the part of the helper.

Lack of respect shows in statements such as "You're not able to do that," "Stupid," or "Asians are all mysterious people, I don't trust them." These comments may be turned into statements of respect through the following changes: "Right now, you are having a hard time doing that. But with practice you can do it," "You got that answer wrong technically, but you did have an interesting point. Let's talk some more about it," and "I've not known many Asians, but I know that stereotypes are dangerous. Perhaps I ought to learn more."

Two basic types of comments communicating respect are *enhancing* and *appreciation of differences* statements. Enhancing statements include "You express your opinion well" and "Good insight." Appreciation of difference statements include "I don't see it that way, but I can imagine how you could arrive at that opinion" and "I may disagree with what you say, but I will support your right to say it." It may be seen that respect and positive regard are closely related.

Respect involves the helper attending to the world of the helpee and communicating that attention through paraphrases, reflections of feeling, or summarizations. Then, the helper *adds* dimensions of respect through a positive valuing of the helpee's experience or, if differences of opinion are present, appreciates the helpee's right to be different and supports differences actively. It may be seen that respect is a further refinement of the concepts of positive regard discussed in the previous section.

Warmth, in Roger's definition, is a subjective inner condition completely unobservable to the external observer. However, examination of videotapes suggests that warmth is *communicated* primarily through nonverbal means. The vocal tone, the degree of trunk lean, the gestures used, the facial expression, the act—in some cases—of physically touching the helpee are all means whereby the interviewer can communicate the "core condition" discussed by Rogers. Warmth, then, is viewed as being communicated primarily through nonverbal channels. This notion receives empirical support from Bayes (1972), who found frequency of smiling and body and head movements and hand motion were among those cues most related to warmth ratings. She concluded,

The finding that smiling is the best single predictor of warmth supports the repeated suggestion in the literature (Birdwhistell, 1963; Davitz, 1964; Ekman and Friesen, 1968; Mahl, 1968; Watzlawick et al., 1967) that nonverbal behavior has a central role in the communication of emotion and interpersonal relationships (p. 335).

Respect and warmth, of course, are closely related. One can respect differences but still maintain a "cold," distant exterior. If the respect for differences is coupled with a smile or a touch, the "warmth" of the communication makes for a higher level of respect and communication.

Lack of respect and warmth is shown in the exchange following the viewing of the videotape in Appendix III presented below, where the helpee notes her reactions to the manfriend and decides to terminate the relationship. The helper topic jumps, his vocal tone is out of synchrony with the helpee, he seems to try to impose his views. Al 26 and 27 represent clear examples of lack of warmth and respect.

Al 23: Let's stop and take a look at the videotape and let's take a look at yourself in that "what's-coming-next?" posture, and so forth. (The videotape is rewound briefly.)
You might want to move out front so you can see a little bit, Joan. I'd just like you to tell me if this is the way you come across to him quite often.
(The videotape is viewed briefly.)
That's back a little farther. We'll come up to it in a minute. (pause) Let's move ahead just a little bit.
(The videotape is viewed and then "stop-framed" on Joan who is holding her shoulders tightly.)
Is that the type of experience that you have in relationship to him . . . quite often?
Joan 23: Um-hm.
Al 24: I know I'd feel awfully uptight if I looked like that. Sometimes I do look like that.
Joan 24: Yeah. My whole back is straight and tight. (pause)
Al 25: Okay? . . . Let's turn the videotape on again. Ah . . . you say that you find yourself responding to him a lot like that? Is that right?
Joan 25: I'm feeling very strongly right now that what I need to do is say good-bye to him. But it really—that this isn't a situation that I can continue to work on. And that it's not time for me to be that involved anyway.

Al 26: How would you like to respond to him? I mean first I've got to say that I've heard you say that you really want to be done with it.

Joan 26: Hmm.

Al 27: How would you like to respond to him? What might he say to you to make you come across like this?

Joan 27: Would you repeat the question?

Fortunately, through a self-disclosure at a later point, the helper recoups and uses his failure to attend and maintain respect and warmth as here and now data, which helps the client see how people may respond to her quick decisions. Warmth and respect are manifest in the following exchange in which helper and helpee finish one another's thoughts.

Al 35: So another way to look at it is we began by saying you were afraid of this guy owning you. And we end by saying you want to own yourself.

Joan 35: I do own myself.

Al 36: . . . That you own yourself, and you know where you want to go.

Joan 36: Yeah. That was really good.

Al 37: You sound very sure.

Joan 37: I feel very, very sure.

Regardless of theoretical orientation, for effective communication, some degree of warmth and respect must be communicated. The synchrony of verbal and nonverbal patterns shown in this exchange is also common in the concept of genuineness to be discussed later.

CONCRETENESS

Many helpees come into the interview with vague complaints; they are unable to articulate clearly and concisely what troubles and concerns them. If the helper also operates at a vague level, the session will maintain itself at a most superficial level and be highly abstract. Generally speaking, then, specificity of expression is important in effective helping sessions. From an attentional point of view, it is vital that the helper and helpee give concrete and detailed attention to the specifics of client comments in the interview.

Concreteness or specificity of response is a fairly easy construct to teach. As in most other microcounseling skill areas, concreteness is most easily taught in contrast to its polar opposite, vagueness. The helpee may state, "I'm scared." At a surface level, the statement appears clear and direct. Yet, on closer examination, the statement is vague and inconclusive. We do not know how scared the helpee is, what specifically is frightening, whether the immediate situation is scary or whether the fright is in the recent or distant past.

The helper who reflects feeling with a minimal encourage, "You're scared," is reinforcing vagueness and unclear exploration. The helper who asks, "What specifically are you frightened of?" or "What scares you?" is moving toward concreteness of expression. Ivey and Gluckstern (1976b) delineate a variety of exercises for the exploration of the concept of concreteness. Egan (1975) presents a valuable array of exercises, and Carkhuff (1969b) presents a five-point scale for the evaluation of degree of concreteness.

Bandler and Grinder (1975) offer a useful conceptual frame for concreteness, although they do not use the term itself. They speak from a framework of transformational grammar (Chomsky, 1965, 1968) and discuss the example above ("I'm scared") as a sentence which presents only the *surface* as opposed to *deep structure*. A sentence which contains only a surface structure is incomplete, as the sentence deletes from, distorts, or overgeneralizes the client's experiential world. Thus, they suggest that the task of the therapist is to assist the client to realize the full deep structure of key verbalizations. In the example above, "I'm scared of spiders" would be a fuller, more concrete sentence for describing the world of the helpee. Further interviewing can make the sentence even more complete by finding out the deeper meaning within the statement. For example, under what specific conditions does the fear arise, what are the antecedents in the past history of the client, etc.? Grinder and Bandler provide a detailed series of methods for examining helpee sentences and a set of exercises designed to teach therapists how to identify when they have complete (or concrete) sentences. Bandler and Grinder's work is important as it moves the concepts of concreteness beyond general impressions and suggests specific means for evaluating the degree to which a sentence is complete (or concrete).

For the beginning helper, however, the relatively simple concepts of concreteness and vagueness are sufficient. They may be taught quickly and efficiently in the microtraining paradigm or in other systematic approaches. A specific example of concreteness appears in the Appendix III typescript at the following point early in the interview. The helpee has just introduced several potential areas for discussion and is talking in a relatively vague fashion about relationships in marriage. The helper at Al 6 summarizes what she is saying and then at Al 7 asks for a more specific, i.e. concrete, example. Following this question, the helpee moves to considerably more concreteness. Her sentence structure is no longer vague but becomes elaborated and more complete.

Joan 5: Yeah, and it's tight, and it's a question and I guess because you're a man, and I know that you have a good marriage. It's—I'm sort of wondering—that's not the way it's supposed to be, is it? I mean, good marriages don't mean that you own each other? Do they?

Al 6: So, if I can put it together, what you've been saying is that this business of ownership has really got you going emotionally. And at the same time, you're not really quite convinced that that's the way it has to be.

Joan 6: I hope not.

Al 7: Maybe it would help if you could give me a more specific example of what's been going on?

Joan 7: Well, a clear example. Ah . . . this man whose name is George was very, very busy for awhile and I didn't see him. And that was fine. I had briefs to prepare, and I just, I was very, very busy with the girls and my work. That was fine with me not to see him. And, all of a sudden he's not so busy, and he called me up and said, "You know, I'm coming right over" after three weeks of not seeing him. "I, you know, I want to be with you. And I have three weeks free, and I want to be with you as much of the time as possible." And I said Heyyyyy. Now I have a case to prepare. Now I'm busy. He said, "Oh, I won't interfere, but, you know, I'd like to be here all the time." That doesn't seem fair.

Generally speaking, concrete expressions are desired in the helping interview. However, should the interview become overly emotionally charged—especially in the early phases of helping—vague, more abstract expressions may occasionally be more appropriate.

A central purpose of helping is to facilitate more complete and concrete sentence structure and action, regardless of theoretical orientation. The routes toward concreteness and complete sentence structure vary greatly. The behaviorist most certainly is aimed toward concrete behavioral action which can be seen. The analytic therapist, on the other hand, also aims for concreteness, but it is a concreteness rooted in the past, and the search for the underlying structure of the vague sentence will be in the roots of childhood experience. The existentialist focusing on here and now experience will be interested in knowing the underlying structure in concrete terms of how that sentence "I'm scared" is played out in the present. The Gestalt therapist is most interested in bringing that term to life in role enactment, perhaps through the exciting exercise of the "hot seat."

It may be clearly seen that the additive theories of helping all amplify the sentence structure of the helpee in vastly differing ways. Those from a more nondirective or client-centered point of view are interested in having the clients describe their experiences in their own unique fashion. Concreteness of expression, while vastly different in differing theories, is basic—the underlying meanings of the client's behavior and verbalizations must be known.

IMMEDIACY

Just as various therapeutic approaches facilitate concreteness differently, so do they operate with differing time emphasis. Psychoanalytic theory (at least in the early years of a long-term analysis) operates primarily in the *past* tense and focuses on past experience. Gestalt therapy and existential helping focus on the *now* and give special attention to what is happening to the client in the immediate "here and now" world. Behavioral helpers and vocational counselors may delve into the past but are often primarily interested in facilitating client self-expression in the *future*.

The tense of discussion in the helping interview determines

heavily the nature of the client-counselor interaction. Consider the following:

> *Client:* I'm scared.
> *Analytic helper:* Free Associate to your earliest childhood experience which relates to that feeling.
> *Existential helper:* You're scared. What does that mean to you right now?
> *Behavioral helper:* What do you want to do about it?

Each helping lead might be facilitative. For example, each helping lead is concrete and tends to be positive in that a respect for the client's ability to act and do something about the fear is shown. However, each lead goes in very different directions. *The focus of attending behavior, of attention, is given to differing time dimensions.* Once again, we see that concepts of attention are closely related to qualitative dimensions of helping.

Immediacy relates to self-disclosure, and the more immediate, i.e. present tense, the helper statement, the more potential impact it has. Those oriented to a Gestalt approach stress the importance of *integrating* past and present experience. Thus, in Gestalt therapy, the goal is to bring both past and present experience to the fore so that future experiences can be coped with at that time in the present tense without the encumbrances of the past . . . "here and now, I and Thou." Observation of particularly effective helper and helpee statements reveals that the most insightful comments often integrate several tenses into one statement.

Wiener and Mehrabian's (1968) *Language Within Language: Immediacy, a Channel in Verbal Communication* provides more in-depth understanding of immediacy than provided by most approaches to the issue in the helper training field. While present tense expression is the most direct means of bringing immediacy to the helping interview, other verbal dimensions of immediacy are also important. Wiener and Mehrabian stress an active sentence structure as important in more immediate and powerful types of statements. For example, "My father made me do it" places the client as object of the sentence. The more active "I did what my father told me even though I didn't want to do it" places the client in control of his or her own behavior.

Wiener and Mehrabian also talk about directness of expression. The classic example of indirect expression is "Do you like him (or her)?" followed by the indirect answer, "She's (he's) a nice person." The question has not been answered, and the issue has been avoided. The client who says, "Someone should tell my boss what she is really like" could become more immediate in expression if the statement were "I would like to tell my boss what she is really like, but I am afraid to because I would be fired for sure."

Another important point of Wiener and Mehrabian is the use of vague modifiers. "Probably," "perhaps," "kinda," "rarely," "occasionally" are all examples of vague modifiers. Consider the following:

Vague: I'm kinda mad about you.
Specific: I'm really angry at you right now.
Vague: I seldom masturbate.
Specific: I masturbate twice a week.

Although the helper will want to assist the helpee "pin down" those areas he or she may be vague about, it is important for the helper to do so tentatively. This enables the helper to avoid "prescribing" how the person feels as well as facilitating the helpee's determining the nature of the concern and real feelings and thoughts about that concern. It may be seen that the broad linguistic definition of immediacy proposed by Wiener and Mehrabian is closely related to many of the concepts of concreteness.

The Appendix III typescript provides an example of the helper talking in the present tense while simultaneously searching for a more complete and concrete sentence or statement from the helpee. Note that the helpee becomes more concrete and speaks of herself in the present tense. Note especially Al 10 and 11.

Al 8: So what you're saying is that it was okay for him not to see you when he was busy, but now when you're busy he doesn't come across that it's okay with him.

Joan 8: It's like my work isn't important but his is.

Al 9: Your work isn't as important, but his is.

Joan 9: Yeah.

Al 10: I can't help but wonder—would you share a little bit about how it makes you feel inside? Even right now as you talk, I see something.

Joan 10: There's tension right here, and I feel like going. . . . Leave me alone. Get away from me. You're intruding into my life. And, it's, it's, I feel tight and defensive. It's like I don't want anybody to get in if that's the way. I'm going to be taken advantage of that way. Nobody's going to get in. But——

Al 11: I get the feeling right now that you feel you just want to close him off. Yet at the same time, I hear something else . . . But it's almost an unheard thing.

Joan 11: Unheard thing is, ah, . . . but I don't want to spend the rest of my life alone. Ah, I do want a relationship with a man. Ah, is it just this man, or is it, is it that I need to be so separate?

Immediacy obviously offers many complex areas for the professional helper to study his or her language patterns and to observe the manner of expression of helpees. Experience in microtraining sessions reveals that present tense emphasis is the quickest and most efficient way to teach beginning helpers the power and meaning of the concepts of immediacy. Differing theories will use immediacy constructs very differently. Each theory has its own set of metaphors to describe the world, and in turn, this metaphorical use of language provides a unique richness appropriate for certain clients. As a general rule of thumb, the more immediate one's conversation, the more potential it has for impact. At the same time, immediacy can be overdone. For a helpee about to start talking on very difficult areas of exploration, a nonimmediate helper response may be useful. As trust develops, a return to more immediate, present tense discussion may ensue. However, if one were treating a client in the Gestalt mode, the preceding statement would be seen as invalid or inappropriate. Once again, different theories have very different views of the world and what constitutes effective action in that world.

CONFRONTATION

Some would argue that the most important and basic purpose of a helping interview is to assist the helpee to resolve incongruities within the self and in relationship to others. Authier and Gustafson (1973) hold to this tenet as they stress their "confrontation skill" as the most viable means of breaking through a person's defenses, thereby facilitating honest, open communication. This view is also expressed strongly by Grinder and Bandler (1976) in the second volume of *The Structure of Magic,* where a full half of the text is devoted to issues of incongruity and the resolution of such issues as being grist for the therapeutic mill.

Before defining confrontation, it is appropriate that we examine the concept of incongruity or discrepancy. An incongruity or discrepancy can be defined as follows: An individual may present discrepant or ambivalent verbal messages. The patient may say, "I really love my wife, but . . . " or "My thoughts about my son are all positive, but he gets to me sometimes." These mixed feelings or thoughts are clear discrepancies; it is not often in therapy that such clear incongruities appear. More likely, the individual will have incongruent nonverbal and verbal behavior. The statement may be "I love my wife" with a simultaneous crossing of the arms over the chest or a harsh vocal tone. Finally, there may be mixed or incongruent nonverbal messages. The right hand may be open and relaxed, but the left is closed and rigid. In each of the preceding, verbal or nonverbal communications are incongruent with one another. The individual is expressing two messages, most often without direct awareness that the two messages are in conflict.

A confrontation at its most effective level occurs when the helper *confronts* the helpee with direct, behavioral observation of the discrepancy *or* facilitates a situation so that the helpee makes his or her own independent discovery of the lack of congruency. Confrontation is usually defined as a challenge or as an opposition. The therapist who says "You're full of shit" thinks that he or she is confronting the patient when in actuality all that is being done is the microtraining skill of expression of feeling. A professional confrontation which *helps* is far more complex than simple expression of emotions or saying where one "is at."

"A confrontation is defined for purposes of microtraining as *the pointing out of discrepancies between or among attitudes, thoughts, or behaviors.* In a confrontation individuals are faced directly with the fact that they may be saying other than that which they mean, or doing other than that which they say" (Ivey and Gluckstern, 1976b, p. 46). Confrontation involves careful attending to the helpee. The helper must selectively attend to discrepancies and point them out clearly. The beginning helper, with a more narrow view of the world, may selectively attend only to one dimension of helpee experience, failing to see the totality and the discrepancies demonstrated by the helpee.

Most effective approaches to personal change through counseling or therapy utilize the confrontation in some form to make clients more aware of their behavioral and verbal incongruities. The client-centered or nondirective helper is interested in reflecting back incongruent verbalizations so that the client will spontaneously see the discrepancy and take steps to resolve the differences. Special attention is given to incongruencies between self-concept and ideal self-concept (Rogers, 1957a). The behavioral helper is interested in identifying specific behaviors which are incongruent with client goals. The Gestalt counselor gives major attention to the resolution of incongruity through various exercises such as the "hot seat," group dreamwork, role playing, etc. Underlying these and other theoretical approaches to helping is a common desire to help the client or patient resolve incongruities into a new and more powerful synthesis for action.

The full video typescript presentation, Appendix III, provides a broad example of a helpee resolving discrepancies in the self. At the beginning of the session (Joan 5 and 7), we see verbalized discrepancies. The helpee states a desire for a relationship with a man, some positive things about this man, and several negative things. The directed fantasy at Al 18 provides a picture of a desired state on the helpee's part (Joan 18) of comfort and satisfying human relationships. The viewing of the videotape at Al 23 provides a contrast between what she wants and what she sees she has. In sum, the fantasy and the video viewing demonstrate in more complete and concrete terms the incongruity discussed at Joan 5 and 7. Out of this incongruity, the helpee is able to resolve the issue and make her own choice for a new direction in her life. The confrontations provided by the helper in this case were not typically in response to a single helpee statement but in terms of an overall helpee issue. Helpers of other theoretical orientations would likely work on different issues and with varying techniques. The issues considered important for confrontation vary with the theoretical orientation of the helper.

Thus far, we have explored the concept of incongruity within the helpee. A person (helper or helpee) may also be incongruent in a relationship. In the Appendix III typescript, the helper becomes incongruent with the helpee at Al 26 when he is surprised at her quick resolution of her personal incongruity. Over the next several leads, it is the *helper* who is incongruent and must take steps to regain congruency with the helpee. After considerable effort at Al 33 we see the helper confront himself in a here and now relationship with the helpee.

> *Al 33:* Okay. Ah, let me just check out a little bit more, and then I think you better respond to me honestly. You perhaps sense a little puzzlement in my face right now? I hear you loud and strong saying——
>
> *Joan 33:* You've said that three times!
>
> *Al 34:* I've said that three times. I'm not used to people . . . and you've done it in the past sometimes, becoming quite that definitive that quickly. And my experience is, "is that where you're really at?" How do you react to me doubting you a little bit and so forth?

This self-confrontation opens the interview for a new and more mutual exploration. Specific analysis of the components of the self-confrontation may be useful in terms of placing the qualitative dimensions of the intervention into proper perspective. First, the microtraining skills used are expression of feeling and expression of content—the focus of the sentence is primarily on "I" (the helper)—but there is also a secondary focus on "you" (the helpee). The tense of the statement is present, with a secondary emphasis on past. The "1-2-3 pattern" of empathy cited earlier is present (1. listen; 2. self-disclose; 3. check out). The statement is relatively concrete. Most importantly, the statement confronts the discrepancies in the helper in that he first comments on the puzzled look on his face and then explains the puzzlement and how it was different from the experience of the helpee. The check-out provides an opening for a mutual exploration of differences.

In a similar fashion, confrontation can be used by a helpee to explore contradictions in self and in a relationship. People with differences of opinion can openly and frankly confront discrepancies and discuss the differences between them. The pattern of the broad skill of direct-mutual communication provides a format wherein confrontation of incongruities between individuals or among groups may be explored.

The techniques to achieve integration of incongruities will vary with the theoretical orientation of the therapist or helper. Grinder and Bandler (1976) believe that the major goal of examination of incongruities is establishing a "solid contact" between the polarities or incongruities and that out of this contact will result a new synthesis of self which integrates the discrepancies in a unique and more satisfying manner than previously known. This synthesis, of course, is closely related to the discussion of interpretation and creativity in earlier chapters. A new meaning is created by the helpee through the creative resolution of a discrepancy. Bandler and Grinder suggest a variety of tactics for the therapist to help the patient establish contact among or between incongruities. These include comparing "paramessages" (in essence, reflecting back to the helpee via paraphrase and reflection of feeling the ambivalent messages put forth), questioning techniques ("How do you feel about . . . ?"), and a variety of fantasy, psychodramatic, or role enactment techniques similar to those of Gestalt therapy.

The integration of polarities, the resolution of incongruities, the examination of discrepancies, the detailed study of varied nonverbal and verbal behavioral patterns all fall into the province of confrontation. The effective helper of any of a wide variety of theoretical orientations (perhaps even all) will confront the helpee with observed discrepancies and take action to assist in the resolution of those discrepancies. The example cited here where the helper examines a discrepancy with the helpee would appear most frequently in existentially or encounter-oriented therapeutic relationships but may be present at times in any of a variety of helping situations. We have viewed psychoanalytic therapists make serious errors in the practice of analysis and then salvage the interview and series of sessions by using their error as a basis for exploration with the analysand. Common to all therapeutic orientations seems to be an open, relatively unemotional labeling of the incongruities on the part of the helper. The helpee, on the other hand, may and often does react strongly and emotionally to the direct and factual confrontations of the helper. It is at this time especially that the helper needs to respond spontaneously, thereby manifesting genuineness. But there is more to being genuine, so let us now turn to that qualitative dimension.

GENUINENESS

Flowing directly from the concept of confrontation is genuineness, which Rogers once listed as the "third condition" of the "Necessary and Sufficient Conditions of Therapeutic Personality Change" (Rogers, 1957a). In this piece, Rogers states that the therapist in the helping relationship should be "a congruent, integrated person. It means that within the relationship he is freely and deeply himself, with his actual experience accurately represented by his awareness of himself. It is the opposite of presenting a facade either knowingly or unknowingly" (p. 97).

This definition of genuineness is something less than behavioral, but fortunately Rogers suggests specific measurements of genuineness which provide useful hints for establishing the construct on a firmer basis. He indicates that a measure of genuineness is using the Q-sort techniques of Fiedler (1950b, 1953) and having the interviewer rate him or herself with the instrument. Several observers can then rate the interview on the same dimensions, and if observers and the interviewer are congruent in their ratings, this may be considered a "crude" definition of genuineness. Thus, despite the fact that he speaks about genuineness as an internal state, Rogers' operational definition is partially external.

Searching for a more precise definition of genuineness, Ivey once again suggests that one look at the opposite of genuineness. One immediately notes that the opposite of genuine is falseness, "phoniness," or fakery.

Genuineness is *not:* being defensive and evasive, being "professional" and planned, keeping one's own opinion to oneself, talking only in the past, expressing mixed verbal and nonverbal messages without awareness. Lack of genuineness is failing to be real, sincere, and authentic.

Genuineness and congruence, then, could be described as being open, spontaneous, sharing one's thoughts and opinions, being in the here and now, expressing congruent verbal and nonverbal messages (or if incongruent, verbalizing awareness of one's own mixed feelings and thoughts), being real, sincere, and authentic (Ivey and Gluckstern, 1976b, p. 156).

Two types of genuineness are explored. The first is genuineness in relationship to self. This is most clearly represented as the polar opposite of incongruity discussed in the preceding section. The person presents integrated verbal and nonverbal behavior. Genuineness in relationship to self requires an absence of mixed messages and a lack of discrepancies.

The second type of genuineness exists in relationship to another person. The helper who is genuine in relationship is similar to the typescript example discussed in the previous section where the helper noted his failure to be congruent and openly discussed this issue with the helpee. However, whenever the helper is in synchrony with the helpee both verbally and nonverbally, this represents the clearest example of genuineness. In such cases, the helper and helpee may mirror one another's posture and may even complete sentences for each other; they seem to have an understanding which transcends the immediately observable situation. Yet, at the same time, many direct behavioral measures may be used to determine the degree of synchrony. The most precise method for determining nonverbal synchrony of movement is that of Condon (1970; 1975) and Condon and Sander (1974), who have clearly demonstrated that vocal patterns and movement patterns of one person affect the other. Scheflen (1973) is another useful source of data. Careful observation of videotapes in microtraining will reveal that a helper and helpee who are moving smoothly through the interview will have a pattern of positive movement synchrony, and as difficulties appear in the interview, helper and helpee movement patterns become less synchronous (see the illustrations on pages 273-275 for examples of movement synchrony). Examination of the videotape cited in the Appendix III typescript reveals this type of interaction clearly. Such examples are shown most clearly at Al 11, where the helper describes the interaction in the immediate here and now. The helpee describes experiencing this moment as particularly close and helpful (Chadbourne, 1976). Other moments demonstrating genuineness are the back-and-forth interaction of Al 21 to Joan 22 and Joan 38 to Al 40.

Each qualitative condition relates to attending behavior and attention. Elizabeth Ivey of Smith College has pointed out that the person who is synchronous or genuine within the self is most likely attending to one thing totally. The attentional patterns are focused. From this vantage point, the "centeredness" of Zen meditation (Kapleau, 1965) and bio-energetics (Lowen, 1967), the emphasis toward body and mind integration in Gestalt therapy (Perls, Hefferline, and Goodman, 1951), and the recent emphasis on dance therapy (Pesso, 1969) could be viewed as examples of therapies seeking to help the individual become more totally integrated and synchronous. Indeed, the goal of many (perhaps all) helping theories is to develop a more integrated, genuine, authentic human being. Most therapies in some way focus on self-synchrony through paying in-depth *attention* to the self. *However, self-synchrony does not necessarily mean synchrony with others.*

Genuineness in relationship, Elizabeth Ivey suggests, requires attention to the self *and* to the other. Movement synchrony as described by Condon is possible at conscious or unconscious levels. The therapist and patient who move together verbally and nonverbally, freely and easily, have accomplished this feat by attending to one another. It is clearly the therapist's responsibility to initiate synchrony or genuineness, but at the same time the therapist's task is to help the client return to synchronous and genuine relationships with the world at large. The term "out of sync" describes the problem well. Laing's elegant book of poems *Knots* (1970) illustrates the great difficulties we all have in developing genuine synchronous relationships with others. *The Politics of Experience* (Laing, 1967), of course, carries deep implications for concepts of genuineness, for clearly sociocultural standards and incongruencies make the problem of achieving genuineness even more difficult. Laing raises the questions of who is ultimately the most dissynchronous, the insane individual or the insane world.

Genuineness was a special characteristic of Fritz Perls. He was, at least during therapy demonstrations, virtually always in tune with himself. Those who have observed him "work" with clients in front of a large group will recall that he would be either fully with a client or not with the client at all. In the latter cases, Perls would state that the client was unwilling to "work" and dismiss the individual summarily. However, if the client were willing to put him or herself fully into Perls' skilled hands, charismatic wonders would follow. Unfortunately, Rogers' definition of genuineness fails to consider the important matter of charisma. Basic to charismatic therapists and "guru" types is a basic belief in self and one's ability to effect change. It may be seen that the definition of genuineness quoted from Rogers fails to provide a warning that being *oneself* totally may not be sufficient to help another individual and, in fact, may be a danger. Lieberman, Yalom, and Miles' (1972) important study of casualties in encounter groups reveals that charismatic (and we suspect genuine in relation to self) group leaders produced more casualties than more conservative types who developed relationships *with* their groups.

The answer to the dilemma posed by the above is that charisma and self-certainty must be balanced by a *genuineness-in-relationship*. Attending skills, appropriate use of immediacy and concreteness, positive regard, respect, empathy, and warmth for the *other individual* are vital for positive personality growth and change. Due to the increased precision made possible by video, the microtraining research and training format, and some of the carefully constructed studies in nonverbal communication such as those of Condon, it is now possible to determine far more precisely just how genuine a helper is both in terms of self and relationship with others.

A scoring system for genuineness has been presented by Ivey and Gluckstern (1976b) and may serve as a basis for examining the degree of genuineness occurring in alternative approaches to behavioral change. Finally, it should be observed that the microtraining skill of direct-mutual communication is specifically oriented to training dyads in the development of a genuine relationship.

SUMMARY

Empathy has been presented as a broad construct in this chapter. It appears that attending skills provide a behavioral definition of empathy as defined by Rogers. At the most basic level, empathy consists of hearing the client's world as he or she sees it. Attending skills provide the vehicle for the communication of empathy.

Higher levels of additive empathy are possible through the use of various influencing skills. The advanced helper can give directions, self-disclose, or interpret, thus adding to the client's experience. However, the ineffective use of influencing skills can be damaging not only to advanced empathy but also to the total relationship. Thus, additional qualitative dimensions of helping were stressed as being important to developing and sustaining an empathic relationship.

The concept of positive regard was defined as selective attention to positive aspects of the helpee. Most (perhaps all) significant helping theories focus on the positive dimensions of client experience with the expectation that *clients can be helped*. This belief that therapy, counseling, and interviewing can "do something" seems basic to all theoretical orientations.

Warmth and respect were presented as supplementary to positive regard. Warmth is viewed as primarily a nonverbal communication of positive feelings through gesture, touch, and/or vocal tone. Respect is defined as more verbally oriented and was contrasted to the "put-down," the negative valuing of self or others' experience. In a more positive vein, respect was defined as (1) enhancing statements about the other, and (2) statements which appreciate and support differences of belief and opinion. One may show respect even though one may not agree with what another person says or does.

Concreteness was presented as a fairly simple and direct construct which may be viewed most clearly in relationship to its opposite—vagueness. The importance of a concrete and specific approach to helping was stressed.

Immediacy was defined at an elementary level in terms of the tense of the helper or helpee's sentence structure. Present tense discussion is viewed as the more important and powerful approach to helping, but past tense and future tense exploration can be valuable as well. Different theoretical orientations may use different tense structures in their communication between helper and helpee. Mehrabian and Wiener's work on the linguistic dimensions of immediacy was mentioned prominently and provides more extensive and refined definitions which are well substantiated by research.

Confrontation was defined as the clear delineation of discrepancies or incongruities in the helpee or helper. A confrontation may focus on discrepancies in the helpee (or the helper) *or* on discrepancies in the relationship between helper and helpee. Some helping theories believe that the resolution of discrepancies is the major function of the helping interview. Bandler and Grinder's work was emphasized as an important linguistic contribution to a more in-depth understanding of confrontation.

The final construct delineated in the chapter was genuineness, which was contrasted with phoniness and fakery. A helper who assumes a "professional stance" as a facade to keep away from clients is a classic example of the failure to be genuine in the interview. The goal of being genuine in the interview is seen as the key to an impactful style of helping. At the same time, genuineness and attention solely to the self unless guarded against can lead to a charismatic attitude potentially dangerous to the client. Thus, full genuineness in the helping relationship demands that the helper be in genuine, authentic contact with self but perhaps more importantly also within his or her relationship with the helpee.

An empathic relationship between client and counselor, interviewer and interviewee, and therapist and patient is vital to growth. The nature of that empathic relationship will vary from theoretical orientation to theoretical orientation. All helping theories in some way use attending skills; most use dimensions of interpersonal influence.   Virtually all will use the "1-2-3" pattern of attend, influence, and check out.   All effective helping theories focus on positive, forward-moving aspects of the helpee and stress the fact that the helpee *can* act to change his or her world.   Differing degrees of warmth and respect will be shown by different helpers.   Levels of immediacy and confrontation will vary, although the resolution of incongruities is basic to most theories of helping.   While some helpers may succeed for a time with a professional facade, ultimately the person must be congruent and genuine within the self and within the relationship with the helpee. The style of empathy varies with the orientation and the individual but must be present in some form for therapeutic gain.

SECTION III

APPLICATIONS OF MICROTRAINING SKILLS IN THE HELPING PROCESS

The chapters in the preceding section were designed to provide the reader with a firm understanding of the role of attention, attending skills, and influencing skills as viewed within the microcounseling framework. Further, Section II demonstrated that the microcounseling skills serve to impart qualitative dimensions such as empathy, positive regard, and genuineness. The goal of this section is to demonstrate how microtraining skills are inherently a part of most dyadic or group interactions regardless of theoretical, cultural, or individual orientation. The central purposes of this section are to present specific applications of the microcounseling format to (1) the analysis of alternative theoretical orientations to counseling and psychotherapy, (2) the analysis of the cultural environmental-contextual situation in which helping operates, and (3) the examination of the individual and cultural competencies which may be demonstrated by the effective helper in reaching a maximum number of clients successfully. A secondary thrust of this section is to examine applications of microtraining in the teaching of skills in many alternative settings and, further, to detail ways in which microtraining relates to several other systematic training programs such as human resource development and Interpersonal Process Recall.

Chapter 7 presents several theoretical orientations to the helping process. Different therapists are examined in their emphasis on microtraining leads. It will be found, for example, that different helpers have different patterns of use of microtraining skills. Carl Rogers and the client-centered helpers tend to use paraphrases, reflections of feelings, and summaries, whereas Fritz

157

Perls and Gestalt therapists use directions, questions, and interpretations more frequently. The sentences generated by these
two helpers are very different, as are the sentences generated by
their helpees.

Microtraining gives special attention to cultural variables in
the helping process. People from differing cultures have varying
patterns in their uses of helping skills. Early research on applications of microtraining to issues of cultural expertise will be presented in Chapter 8. The essence of this chapter is that people
from different cultural and socioeconomic backgrounds will
generate different sentences and use different microtraining skills
and qualitative conditions.

Chapter 9 considers the matching of helper and helpee.
Different helpers undoubtedly are more effective with some
helpees than others. Some beginning ideas for the bringing together of helpers and helpees will be presented. In addition, the
concept of "cultural expertise" in the helper will be presented
as a potential goal statement and outcome variable for helping.

Chapter 10 will demonstrate the applications of the microtraining framework in several alternative settings. Microtraining
has been used for teacher training, speech therapist training, parent training, psychiatric patient training, and a whole array of
teaching/training combinations. These several applications will
be summarized, with special attention being given to the psychoeducational role of the helper.

This section will conclude with a discussion of other well-
known systematic programs in helper training in Chapter 11.
Most of these systems have elements in common with microtraining, and similarities and differences of these programs will be
examined.

Chapter 7

MICROTRAINING SKILLS USED
BY COUNSELORS AND THERAPISTS OF
DIFFERING THEORETICAL ORIENTATIONS

PROFESSIONAL HELPERS *differ markedly from each other in their use of microtraining leads.* They attend to different aspects of the client communication. They vary in their use of reflection of feeling, self-disclosure, questioning techniques, and interpretation. The purpose of this chapter is to examine how the microtraining framework may be used to examine the overt behavior of several alternative approaches to the helping process.

Assuming that helpers do indeed differ markedly in their use of helping leads, what is the effectiveness of each approach to helping? Claims for the effectiveness of one method over another are many, but proof to that effect is generally lacking. In fact, the question is more often asked, "Does psychotherapy do any good?" The many careful reviews of this subject (e.g. Bergin, 1971; Eysenck, 1966; Meehl, 1955; Meltzkoff and Kornreich, 1970; Strupp and Bergin, 1972) are conflicting in their opinions. It seems that one can use the data to prove what one wants to believe. Sloane et al. (1975) suggest that the deeper the commitment of the researcher to the helping process, the more likely that findings will demonstrate that therapy is helpful.

Actual studies comparing the effectiveness of alternative approaches to helping are relatively rare. One of the most cited studies in this area is Paul (1966; 1967), who examined undergraduates enrolled in a public speaking course who suffered from anxiety during presentations. Insight-oriented helping (client-centered and analytic) was provided for five interviews and com-

159

pared for its effectiveness with a Wolpe (1958; 1961) systematic desensitization procedure and two control groups, one an attention-placebo and the other a no-treatment. The three groups which received attention improved; however, the systematic desensitization group improved most significantly. A two-year follow-up revealed continuation of this pattern. A variety of other studies have demonstrated that behavioral approaches are more effective than psychodynamic (e.g. DiLoreto, 1971; Gelder, Marks, and Wolff, 1967; Bandura, Blanchard, and Ritter, 1969).

A carefully constructed comparative study is that of Sloane, Staples, Cristol, Yorkston, and Whipple (1975). Three behaviorally oriented and three psychoanalytically oriented therapists were compared over a four-month period. They found that both groups were improved as compared to waitlisted patients. Perhaps most importantly, they found that the two treatments were differentially effective with different types of patients. The analytically oriented helpers were more successful with patients who had a higher socioeconomic status and less overall pathology. Behavior therapy was more effective with hysterical and manic types of patients and was more effective on an overall basis.

An increasingly popular question among professional helpers is *Which therapy with which individual and what conditions?* The Sloane et al. studies provide an important clue to the answer of this question and help explain the contradictory discussions on the effectiveness of therapy found in the literature. Given differing problems and differing personal histories, different clients need different types of therapy and counseling.

Microtraining and the psychoeducator model provide a framework wherein the issue of comparative effectiveness of helpers may be evaluated in more detail in the future. Specifically,

1. Microtraining skill categories provide a framework wherein we may observe what a helper is doing in the interview. The Ivey Taxonomy (Fig. 2) applies skills analysis as related to differing theoretical orientations and provides an overview of helping styles.

2. The model of the effective individual described in Chapter 9 provides a map of specific outcomes for short-term be-

Taxonomy of Helper Behavior

(Revised)

Examples of use of microcounseling leads by differing theoretical orientations.

		NON-DIRECTIVE	MODERN ROGERIAN ENCOUNTER	BEHAVIORAL	ANALYTIC	TAVISTOCK	FAMILY THERAPY	GESTALT	ECLECTIC, TRAIT AND FACTOR
MICROCOUNSELING LEAD*									
Attending Skills	Open question			X	X		X	X	X
	Closed question			X			X	X	X
	Minimal encourage	X	X	X			X	X	X
	Paraphrase	X	X		X		X		X
	Reflection of feeling	X	X		X		X		X
	Summarization	X	X	X	X		X		X
Influencing Skills	Directions			X			X	X	X
	Expression of content		X	X			X		X
	Expression of feeling		X				X		X
	Influencing summary		X	X			X		X
	Interpretation				X	X	X	X	X
FOCUS									
	Helpee	XX	XX	XX	XX		X	XX	XX
	Helper		X				X		X
	Dyad or group		X		X	XX	XX		X
	Other people			X	X				X
	Topic (facts, info.)			X					X
	Cultural-env. context.			X					X

PRIME ISSUE OF MEANING (Topics likely to be attended to or reinforced)	FEELINGS	RELATIONSHIP	BEHAVIOR PROBLEM-SOLVING	UNCONSCIOUS MOTIVATION	AUTHORITY LEADERSHIP RESPONSIBILITY	FAMILY INTERACTION SYSTEMS	HERE AND NOW BEHAVIOR	VARIES
AMOUNT OF HELPER TALK-TIME	Low	Med.	High	Low	Low	Med.	High	Varies

Behavior counts on eye contact, body language, and verbal following are possible and valuable as well.

---

*Direct-mutual communication is not listed as it is a skill which is a combination of several other skills in a systematic interpersonal interaction.

Figure 2.

havior on the part of the helpee. These same dimensions can be used to measure long-term outcome, especially when combined with carefully constructed "do-use-teach" contracts, "homework," or systematic practice of behavior learned in the interview in settings other than the interview.

A general model of outcome — the individual with cultural expertise — is missing from most studies of psychotherapeutic effectiveness. If the effective individual is a person who can generate an infinite number of responses to life situations and can commit self to a course of action, the major task of professional helping is to diagnose the specific deficits of the helpee (be they attitudinal or behavioral) and institute specific helping procedures to meet those specific needs.

This chapter will present a preliminary statement on the treatment procedures of several approaches to helping (client-centered, trait and factor, behavioral, Gestalt, family therapy, and medical interviewing). The verbal behavior of several helpers will be observed and classified. Helper behavioral effect on the helpee will also be considered. Out of such specific analysis it should be possible at some future date to specify which treatment is likely to be most effective for certain types of individuals. The following analysis examines only microtraining skills and does not consider qualitative dimensions or specific verbal content. Full consideration of these issues would require a book in itself.

CLIENT-CENTERED HELPING

The classic Rogerian model consists primarily of minimal encourages, paraphrases, reflections of feeling, and summarization. However, careful analysis reveals an almost interpretive flavor to some helper statements. The case of Mrs. Oak in *On Becoming a Person* (Rogers, 1961) illustrates the typical style of helping used in client-centered counseling.

Rogers first presents an excerpt from the eighth interview as an example of how behavior which at first appears negative may show itself later as positive:

It is in the eighth interview that Mrs. Oak rolls back the first layer of defense, and discovers a bitterness and desire for revenge underneath.

C 1: You know over in this area of, of sexual disturbance, I have a feeling that I'm beginning to discover that it's pretty bad, pretty bad. I'm finding out that, that I'm bitter, really. Damn bitter. I—and I'm not turning it back in, into myself . . . I think what I probably feel is a certain element of "I've been cheated." (*Her voice is very tight and her throat chokes up.*) And I've covered up very nicely, to the point of consciously not caring. But I'm, I'm sort of amazed to find that in this practice of, what shall I call it, a kind of sublimation that right under it—again words—there's a, a kind of passive force that's, it's pas—it's very passive, but at the same time it's just kind of *murderous.*

T 2: So there's the feeling, "I've really been cheated. I've covered that up and seem not to care and yet underneath that there's a kind of a, a latent but very much present *bitterness* that is very, very strong." (Reflection of feeling)

C 2: It's very strong. I—that I know. It's terribly powerful.

T 3: Almost a dominating kind of force. (Paraphrase)

C 3: Of which I am rarely conscious. Almost never . . . Well, the only way I can describe it, it's a kind of murderous thing, but without violence. . . . It's more like a feeling of wanting to get even. . . . And of course, I won't pay back, but I'd like to. I really would like to.*

The first statement of the helper is primarily a reflection of feeling. He repeats her words "I've been cheated" as if they were an emotion and feeling. He selectively attends to the emotional word "bitterness" and ignores the stronger "murderous" feelings. The second statement of the helper may be classified as a paraphrase which catches the essence of the emotion's impact on the client.

The client, on the other hand, starts with a fairly broad statement. The therapist by focusing on the emotions makes the issue and the *emotions* underlying the statement much clearer, and in her final statement, the client talks about a feeling of "getting even."

---

*From Carl Rogers, *On Becoming a Person.* Copyright © 1961. Reprinted by permission of Houghton Mifflin Co.

In this case, the helper has focused clearly on immediate here and now emotions; past experience has been ignored. The helpee is making "I" statements and expressing feelings in the present tense. The therapist's handling of even this short segment could be compared to that of an analytically oriented helper, who might have paid more attention to past causes of present distress. Other helpers would have asked for a specific and concrete example of the client's problems and then instituted treatment to solve identified issues. A feminist helper might focus on this case as an issue experienced by many women.

Rogers presents Mrs. Oak again on the same issue in interview thirty-one.

> Up to this point the usual explanation seems to fit perfectly. Mrs. Oak has been able to look beneath the socially controlled surface of her behavior, and finds underneath a murderous feeling of hatred and a desire to get even. This is as far as she goes in exploring this particular feeling until considerably later in therapy. She picks up the theme in the thirty-first interview. She has had a hard time getting under way, feels emotionally blocked, and cannot get at the feeling which is welling up in her.

> *C 1:* I have the feeling it isn't guilt. (*Pause. She weeps.*) Of course I mean, I can't verbalize it yet. (*Then with a rush of emotion*) It's just being *terribly hurt!*

> *T 1:* M-hm. It isn't guilt except in the sense of being very much wounded somehow. (Reflection of feeling)

> *C 2:* (*Weeping*) It's—you know, often I've been guilty of it myself but in later years when I've heard parents say to their children, "stop crying," I've had a feeling, a hurt as though, well, why should they tell them to stop crying? They feel sorry for themselves, and who can feel more adequately sorry for himself than the child. Well, that is sort of what—I mean, as though I mean, I thought that they should let him cry. And—feel sorry for him too, maybe. In a rather objective kind of way. Well, that's—that's something of the kind of thing I've been experiencing. I mean, now—just right now. And in—in—

> *T 2:* That catches a little more the flavor of the feeling that it's almost as if you're really weeping for yourself. (Reflection of feeling, overtone of interpretation)

> *C 3:* Yeah. And again you see there's conflict. Our culture is such that—I mean, one doesn't indulge in self-pity. But this isn't—I mean, I feel it doesn't quite have that connotation. It may have.

T 3: Sort of think that there is a cultural objection to feeling sorry about yourself. And yet you feel the feeling you're experiencing isn't quite what the culture objected to either. (Reflection of feeling, paraphrase)

C 4: And then of course, I've come to—to see and to feel that over this—see. I've covered it up. *(Weeps.)* But I've covered it up with so much *bitterness,* which in turn I had to cover up. *(Weeping) That's* what I want to get rid of! I almost don't *care* if I hurt.

T 4: *(Softly, and with an empathic tenderness toward the hurt she is experiencing)* You feel that here at the basis of it as you experience it is a feeling of real tears for yourself. But *that* you can't show, mustn't show, so that's been covered by bitterness that you don't like, that you'd like to be rid of. You almost feel you'd rather absorb the hurt than to—than to feel the bitterness. *(Pause)* And what you seem to be saying quite strongly is, I do *hurt,* and I've tried to cover it up. (Summary) *

The first therapist statement from this section of the interview is a reflection of feeling and opens the client to more in-depth exploration of her emotions. However, she focuses on the idea of children crying for themselves ("other person" focus) and then talks about her feelings which are parallel. The therapist's second comment takes the two ideas from the client's last comment and puts them together with a summary reflection of feeling (with overtones of an interpretation).

The client at 3 feels heard (a common indication of this is a "yeah," "yes," or "right" from the helpee) and is able to discuss some of her ambivalent feelings as they relate to the culture. The therapist reflects these ambivalent feelings. The therapist at 4 provides a summary including both content and feelings but has a primary emphasis on feelings. The summary brings together the attitudes and feelings of many interviews, and the client at 5 sees herself from a new perspective, but through her own words. Note that the focus of the helper's comment has ten references to the helpee ("you" and "I"). The more names and personal pronouns, the more personalized the helping interview.

This interaction is characteristic of client-centered helping.

---

*From Carl Rogers, *On Becoming a Person.* Copyright © 1961. Reprinted by permission of Houghton Mifflin Co.

The focus is completely on the client. The helper does not self-disclose (but may say that he or she fails to understand) and only rarely interprets or asks a question (and the question most likely to be asked is the check-out "Am I hearing you accurately?"). The emphasis is clearly here and now, present tense communication. Concreteness of emotions is sought but not concreteness of ideas or action.

This type of helping produces a helpee who is able to verbalize freely about emotions, can see the complexity and ambivalences of emotional experience, and is able to focus on self. This helpee is able at interview thirty-one to generate new sentences to describe her situation. Attitudinal and expressive styles of the client between interviews eight and thirty-one show significant changes. Important among these changes is the ability of the client to see positive strengths in the emotions and behavior which represent her life.

However, imagine that the helpee came into therapy already able to self-disclose in the here and now and to move freely into complex and ambivalent feelings but faced an immediate crisis decision in regard to a marriage or a job. Given these circumstances, the client-centered model may be less effective. Specifically, the client already possesses skills associated with this mode of helping and needs to solve a problem *now*. Or, if the client were from a low income area and unable to verbalize freely, and if the most immediate issue were a missing welfare check, the slow unfolding of emotions would be unlikely to produce significant results.

It is suggested that each therapeutic procedure does succeed (given enough time), but the crucial issue of *success for what purpose* should be raised. Some people would profit from this type of treatment, others would be more impatient and have less need for the fifty-plus interviews often associated with long-term client-centered counseling. Finally, it should be mentioned that Rogers in his more recent statements (e.g. Rogers, 1970) has moved more toward self-disclosure and sharing of thoughts and feelings. This influencing dimension of more immediate and sharing involvement provides more rapid change and learning but remains in much the same mold as client-centered counseling, as the focus of conversation will remain primarily on the client and the helper will engage in self-disclosure with primary emphasis on here and now feelings to facilitate client self-exploration.

TRAIT AND FACTOR HELPING

Trait and factor helping is most often associated with vocational counseling. The trait and factor helper is interested in assembling as much data as possible to help the client make a decision, learn more about self, or solve a particular problem. This type of helper will often be found asking questions and giving advice (expression of content). The counselor in the state employment office may be frequently characterized as having interviews which consist of asking a series of questions to bring out data and then suggesting a job. The "two-step dance" of many professional helpers in employment services is a most limited view of trait and factor helping. Such a case is presented in Patterson's (1973) popular text on theories of personality and does not adequately depict the possibilities of trait and factor helping.

Trait and factor approaches can be and are supplemented by all skills of the microtraining framework. True trait and factor helping demands that the individual, the job, the culture, the family, and all relevant factors be considered before making a decision. True trait and factor helping will include helping the client explore feelings, may include self-disclosure on the part of the helper, and may even at times include the techniques of the Gestalt therapist or psychoanalyst. Trait and factor helping at its best is an eclectic approach, taking aspects of all theories for the benefit of the client.

The following interview illustrates some of the skills a helper might use in an educational planning interview with a student:

Helper 1: So, you wanted to talk about how things are going at college? (Open question)
Helpee 1: They're not going.
Helper 2: Not going? (Minimal encourage)
Helpee 2: No. My classes this quarter are just—I don't know.

I had like history, English, liberal arts, what every freshman gets. Those were interesting, but now that I'm in business with stuff like econ, business math. They're just so dead—I don't know. (Expression of content and feeling)

Helper 3: You're a sophomore? (Closed question, note topic jump)

Helpee 3: Right.

Helper 4: And the subjects you have don't seem to have much life where last year they seemed to have more interest and vitality for you. You find things you're taking don't have much life for you. (Paraphrase and reflection of feeling)

Helpee 4: Right. And—I don't know—you hear a lot about the sophomore slump and I keep thinking maybe I am in that—I don't know.

Helper 5: I would like to know a bit more about how you have been feeling. You say the courses are kind of dead. (Expression of content, minimal encourage)

Helpee 5: I don't know—I used to enjoy school. I'm on a scholarship, and I've got to keep my grades up. I feel so much pressure, but I've lost interest in my work. It's hard to study. Last year I had a 3.4, but now I am down to 2.2. I'm not failing anything, but still. . .

Helper 6: So far I've heard that last year was a lot more exciting for you, that you are really concerned about how this term is going. Can't help but wonder if you are studying what you are most interested in. (Summary followed by an interpretation)

In the opening stages of this trait and factor interview, the helper alternates between questions so as to ensure covering basic diagnostic data about changes in college performance while also examining the helpee's feeling about his present situation. The reflections of feeling have brought out important information (pressure, lack of interest in present courses, a "dead" feeling, the scholarship, and other data) which needs to be explored later in the session. The interpretation ("Can't help but wonder if you are studying what you are most interested in") is a common diagnostic impression of counselors engaged in vocational counseling and will need extensive further checking.

The helper in later stages of the interview asks questions or supports discussion about which courses have been enjoyed most, feelings about present academic performance, the importance of teacher presentation style in course enjoyment. As a result of questioning and reflection techniques, the following exchange occurs:

Helper: You were saying that you avoided business and math in high school, yet here you are, but one teacher in high school did make you feel that business might be appropriate. (Summary)

Helpee: He wasn't a stereotyped business teacher. No glasses or conservative dress. He wasn't real flashy either. He was a little gangly and had freckles on his face. He was just my type of person. Everyone really liked him . . . he was a once in a lifetime teacher. You know, he kinda looked like me.

This interchange provides the helper with a clue which may help explain some of the helpee's motivation toward the business field. Through a broad range of techniques, the trait and factor helper attends to the helpee and brings out as much data as possible. One may note a tendency to focus on past history, with a strong emphasis on concreteness.

Toward the end of the interview, the helper introduces the possibility of vocational testing:

Helper 1: Sam, we have talked quite a while now, and I feel I have started to get to know you, some of your interests and some of your concerns. One thing that might be helpful for a broader understanding would be for you to take some occupational tests. (Summary and expression of content)

Helpee 1: Oh.

Helper 2: Sounds like the idea doesn't turn you on too much. Tell me more? (Reflection of feeling, open question)

Helpee 2: Well, I took those things in high school and they didn't tell me much. Seemed like a waste of time. But, if you think they'd be helpful. . .

Helper 3: It's going to be your choice. Tests *can* provide new data and information. But they are only worth what you put into them. . . and even then they have to be taken with a grain of salt. (Expression of content)

Helpee 3: I don't know. . . do you think they would really help?

Helper 4: They help many students, and they might be useful to you. Before you decide, would you like to have me tell you about some of the options for testing and what you could expect? Then you could react to the possibilities and decide what you want. (Expression of content, closed question)

This interchange is important and is missing from too many trait and factor interviews. Once again, we see that the reflection of the client's nonverbal feeling at "Oh" was basic. It does little good to take tests until the client is ready for them.

Looking back over these brief excerpts, it may be seen that the trait and factor vocational counselor uses a very different helping style from the client-centered counselor. A wide array of skills are used. The focus may be on the client one moment, an external topic (e.g. tests, high school, courses) the next, on other people (family, teachers), or on the cultural-environmental context. All must be considered for trait and factor helping to operate effectively.

The client in this case behaves very differently from Mrs. Oak in the client-centered interview. While emotions are expressed, they are not the central focus of the session. The client talks about concrete happenings in daily life and expresses both feeling and content freely. The client may ask the helper for information by asking a question. In the later stages of helping, the client may act to interpret his own life direction.

It may be seen that the helpee in this case might well benefit from the long-term client-centered approach. Several instances occur where one might be tempted to explore feelings and attitudes in more depth. The helper, however, chose to use feelings and attitudes as reference points related to eventual life decisions. Similarly, it could be stated that perhaps Mrs. Oak might have benefitted from a trait and factor vocational approach. Some feminist therapists have stressed the importance of meaningful work in helping women find personal identities and satisfactions.

Which is more effective—trait and factor counseling or client-centered counseling? They have different objectives and will accomplish different things. Either can be done poorly or well. The client interested in changing his or her major has a deficit and need in that area and will most likely profit from the approach of the trait and factor helper. At another point in his life, this client might well profit from the deep exploration of feelings. Which method of helping is more effective? It depends on the needs, values, and goals of the helper and helpee.

BEHAVIOR THERAPY

Perhaps the most directive form of helping is behavior therapy. In structure, behavior therapy is not unlike trait and factor helping. The helper tries to bring out as much data as possible first, then synthesizes these data into a coherent treatment plan, and finally administers the plan. The skills used are similar to those of the trait and factor helper just presented. However, emphasis on emotions will vary. In the case presented here, little attention is given to emotions. The ultimate focus of behavior therapy is more on treatment than it is on diagnosis.

Therapist 1: Dr. N. has written to me about you, but I want to approach your case as though I knew nothing about it at all. Of what are you complaining? (Open question)

Mrs. P. 1: I'm afraid of sharp objects, especially knives. It's been very bad in the past month.

Therapist 2: How long have you had this fear? (Closed question)

Mrs. P. 2: It began 6 years ago when I was in hospital after my first child was born. Two days later my husband brought me some peaches and a sharp knife to cut them with. I began to have a fear that I might harm the baby with it.

Therapist 3: How long had the knife been with you when it occurred to you that it might harm the baby? (Closed question)

Mrs. P. 3: I don't believe I let him leave it overnight, that night; or else we left it that night and then the next day—I think you could say—I told him to take it home. I can't remember exactly; I know I just didn't want it around. From that day to this I don't mind using knives as long as I'm with someone, but when I'm alone with the children I just don't want them around.

Therapist 4: Can you remember in what way the thought first came into your mind that you might hurt the baby? (Closed question)

Mrs. P. 4: I can't remember.

Therapist 5: Now since that time, generally speaking, has this fear been the same all along, or has it got better or worse? (Closed question)

Mrs. P. 5: Well, right after we moved about 5 months ago I felt a little bit better about it. At first, when I got home from the hospital, I made my husband take all the knives away from the house. I didn't want them around, so he took them to my mother's. I brought a couple back from her house when we moved. But I couldn't—after I brought them—I couldn't use them. I couldn't keep them out where I could see them and might pick one up and, you know—use it sometime.

Therapist 6: So what do you say in general—that the fear has been much the same? (Paraphrase) *

In the above section, the helper begins with an open question and then continues with closed questions to find out the information needed for treatment. This is a pattern characteristic of many diagnostic interviews, regardless of theory. In the above series, the helper obtains a general picture of Mrs. P.'s major concern. The interview continues in much the same fashion, with the therapist asking a variety of open and closed questions about family, personal background, parents, and present and past status. Most questions are closed and oriented toward assisting the therapist to obtain data from Mrs. P.

A midinterview interchange between helper and helpee is interesting and illustrates how sharply behavioral approaches differ from psychoanalytic and client-centered. Both would be inclined to have the client expand in depth on the fears expressed.

Therapist 1: Did you have any particular fears when you were a child? (Closed question)

Mrs. P. 1: Well, no. Not that I know of. But when I was 8 years old our house burned down. I was on my way home from school and the fire engines passed us. It was in January and it was snowing like anything and somebody told us that our house was on fire. And that was a fear . . . it was. My parents lost almost everything they had. And I know they . . . oh, 5 or 6 years after that every time I would hear a fire engine I would get so nervous if I was in school I would have to get up and leave. I wouldn't leave the school, but I would have to get out of the class—but things like that don't bother me now.

Therapist 2: Did you have any other such experiences, or any other fears at all when you were a child? (Closed question)

Mrs. P. 2: No.

Therapist 3: Well, now, you said that you didn't get on very well at school. Apart from the fact that your studies were difficult, how did you like school? (Paraphrase, open question)

Mrs. P. 3: I liked it fine. I mean I just played right along.

---

*From Joseph Wolpe and Arnold Lazarus, *Behavior Therapy Techniques,* 1966. Courtesy of Pergamon Press, Elmsford, New York.

Therapist 4: Well, did you always do badly at your classes? (Closed question)

Mrs. P. 1: Yes.

Therapist 5: What about sports? How were you at them? (Closed and open questions)

Mrs. P. 5: I might have taken after father in sports. I did well.

The therapist ends the session with the following comments:

Well, I've got enough of the important background information. I will give you one or two questionnaires to do as homework, and then next time you come here, we'll talk of the treatment procedures. We'll probably be doing a special kind of treatment called desensitization. It involves deep muscle relaxation and other special procedures. That is all of now. (Influencing summary).*

Throughout this interview, the dominant mode has been closed questions. An occasional paraphrase, open question, or reflection of feeling may appear, but these are minimally important. This interview is but a single example, and some behavior therapists will use emotionally oriented skills to a greater degree. Morganstern (1976), for example, makes a clear case that the client must feel he or she has been *heard* and suggests paraphrasing and reflection of feeling as useful in behavioral assessment. A recent and carefully constructed dissertation by Seidenstücker (1976) studies this issue utilizing the microcounseling model and presents a flexible but systematic format for behavioral assessment.

The behavior therapist feels free to give specific directions to the client. The building of a systematic desensitization hierarchy requires the asking of questions and the giving of specific directions to work through the hierarchy. Of course, the clearest example of the behavior therapist giving directions is in deep muscle relaxation. For example,

I am now going to show you the essential activity that is involved in obtaining deep relaxation. I shall again ask you to resist my pull at your wrist so as to tighten your biceps. I want you to notice very carefully the sensations in that muscle. Then I shall ask you to let go gradually as I diminish the amount of force I exert against you. Notice as your forearm descends that there is decreasing sensation in the

---

*From Joseph Wolpe and Arnold Lazarus, *Behavior Therapy Techniques,* 1966. Courtesy of Pergamon Press, Elmsford, New York.

biceps muscle. Notice also that the letting go is an activity, but of a negative kind—it is an "uncontracting" of the muscle. In due course, your forearm will come to rest on the arm of the chair, and it may then seem to you as though relaxation is complete. But although the biceps will indeed be partly and perhaps largely relaxed, a certain number of fibers will still be contracted. I shall therefore say to you, "Go on letting go." Try to continue the activity that went on in the biceps while your forearm was coming down. It is the act of relaxing these additional fibers that will bring about the emotional effects we want. Let's try it out and see what happens (Wolpe and Lazarus, 1966, p. 62).

Sexual therapy, a major "new" thrust in helping procedures as this book is being written, has long been a successful domain of behavioral therapists. Semans as long ago as 1956 wrote in clear terms about systematic methods to stop premature ejaculation. The techniques of progressive stimulation, but stopping before climax and then beginning again were delineated. Patients were taught via direct instructions what to do and how to behave sexually. Wolpe and Lazarus' (1966) *Behavior Therapy Techniques* details Semans' work and the efforts of many others in behavioral psychology. It is fascinating but tragic that techniques of directive helping available as much as twenty years ago are only now beginning to be used to their full potential.

Again the question may be asked Which therapy is most effective? Data suggest that client-centered and analytic therapies have been relatively ineffective with sexual and many behavioral problems. However, the data are beginning to accumulate (Sloane et al., 1975) that while behavioral approaches may be more effective for some problems, insight-oriented therapies may be more appropriate for others. Once again, we find that the outcome of behavior therapy is different as the techniques and purposes were different. Perhaps the question as to which technique is best is ultimately naive, as in the past we have failed to see the rich dynamics of the interpersonal process and that clients with differing concerns have different needs.

GESTALT THERAPY

The master charismatic therapist was undoubtedly Fritz Perls. The following is taken in entirety from *Gestalt Therapy Ver-*

batim (Perls, 1969) and represents a classic example of Perls' work with dreams.

BEVERLY*

Beverly 1: I guess I'm supposed to say something. I don't have any interesting dreams. Mine are sort of patent.

Fritz 1: Are you aware that you're defensive?. . . I didn't ask you in only to bring dreams. (Interpretation)

B. 2: You asked for them last night and I was afraid that would disqualify me. If I could manufacture a few. . .

F. 2: Now you have a very interesting posture. The left leg supports the right leg, the right leg supports the right hand, the right hand supports the left hand. (Expression of content)

B. 3: Yeah. It gives me something to hang onto. And with a lot of people out there you kind of get some stage fright. There are so many of them.

F. 3: You have stage fright and there are people outside. In other words you're on stage. (Reflection of feeling, paraphrase)

B. 4: Yeah, I suppose I feel that way.

F. 4: Well, what about getting in touch with your audience. . . (Open question)

B. 5: Well they look very good. They have wonderful faces.

F. 5: Tell this to them. (Direction)

B. 6: You have very warm faces, very interested, very interesting . . . with—with a lot of warmth.

F. 6: So then shuttle back to your stage fright. What do you experience now? (Direction, open question)

B. 7: I don't have any more stage fright. But my husband doesn't look at me.

F. 7: So go back to your husband. (Direction)

B. 8: You're the only one that looks self-conscious. Nobody else looks self-conscious at me. (laughter) You sort of feel like you're up here, don't you? Or sort of like your youngster's up here?. . . No?

X: (from audience, yells) Answer!

Husband: She's the one who's up there and she's trying to place me up there.

F. 8: (to husband) Yah. You've got to answer. (to Beverly) You have to know what I feel. (Direction)

B. 9: Well he doesn't usually answer. Did you want him out of character? (much laughter)

F. 9: So, you are a clobberer. (Interpretation)

---

*From Frederick Perls, *Gestalt Therapy Verbatim*, 1969. Courtesy of Real People Press, Moab, Utah.

B. 10: You need an ashtray.

F. 10: "I need an ashtray." (Fritz holds up his ashtray) She knows what *I* need. (laughter) (Expression of content)

B. 11: Oh, no—you have one. (laughter)

F. 11: Now *I* get stage fright. (laughter) I always have difficulties in dealing with "Jewish mothers." (laughter) (Expression of feeling)

B. 12: Don't you like "Jewish mothers"?

F. 13: Oh, I love them. Especially their matzo-ball soup. (laughter) (Expression of feeling)

B. 14: I'm not a gastronomical Jewish mother, just a Jewish mother. (chuckles) I don't like gefilte fish either. I guess I'm a pretty obvious Jewish mother. Well, that's not bad to be. That's all right. Matter of fact, that's good to be.

F. 14: What are your hands doing? (Open question)

B. 15: Well, my thumbnails are pulling at each other.

F. 15: What are they doing to each other? (Open question)

B. 16: Just playing. I do this often. See, I don't smoke, so what else are you gonna do with your hands. It doesn't look good to suck your thumbs.

F. 16: That's also the Jewish mother. She has reasons for everything. (laughter) (Interpretation)

B. 17: (jokingly) And if I don't have one I'll make one up. (chuckles) The ordered universe. What's wrong with being a Jewish mother?

F. 17: Did I say there's something wrong with a Jewish mother? I only say *I* have difficulties in dealing with them. (Closed question, expression of feeling) There is a famous story of a man who was such an excellent swordsman that he could hit even a raindrop, and when it was raining he used his sword instead of an umbrella. (laughter) Now there are also intellectual and behavioristic swordsmen, who in answer to every question, statement, or whatever, hit it back. So whatever you do, immediately you are castrated or knocked out with some kind of reply—playing stupid or poor-me or whatever the games are. She's perfect. (Interpretation)

B. 18: I never realized that.

F. 18: You see? Again the sword. Playing stupid. I want once more to restate what I said earlier. Maturation is the transcendance from environmental support to self-support. The neurotic, instead of mobilizing his own resources, puts all his energy into manipulating the environment for support. And what you do is again and again manipulate me, you manipulate your husband, you manipulate everybody to come to the rescue of the "damsel in distress." (Interpretation)

B. 19: How did I manipulate you?

F. 19: You see, again. This question, for instance. This is very important for maturation—change your questions to statements. Every question is a hook, and I would say that the majority of your questions are inventions to torture yourself and torture others. But if you change the question to a statement, you open up a lot of your background. This is one of the best means to develop a good intelligence. So change your question to a statement. (Expression of content, direction)

B. 20: Well, th—that implies that, ah, there's a fault to me. Didn't you intend it so?. . .

F. 20: Put Fritz in that chair and ask him that question. (Direction)

B. 21: Don't you like Jewish mothers? Did you have one that you didn't like?

Well, I like them. They're just a very difficult lot to deal with.

Well, what makes them so difficult?

Well, they're very dogmatic and very opinionated and inflexible and the box that they construct for themselves to grow in is a little narrower than many. They're less easy to therapize.

Does everybody have to be subject to your therapy?

No. (laughter)

(to Fritz) Did you ever switch chairs like this with yourself?

F. 21: (laughing) Oh yes—*Oh!* Even *I* get sucked in! (laughter)

B. 22: You said you had problems with Jewish mothers. (laughter)

Husband: Do you understand now why I didn't answer? (laughter and applause)

F. 22: That's right, because you see how a Jewish mother doesn't say, "You shouldn't smoke so much." She says, "You need an ashtray." (laughter) Okeh. Thank you. (Summary)

The microtraining framework reveals immediately that Perls used many directions and occasional interpretations.* He shared his observations and his experience of the client. While the attending skills are present, they appear mainly as questions (which

---

*It is recognized that some Gestalt-oriented helpers believe that Gestalt therapy does not use interpretation. Analysis of actual typescripts suggests that interpretation is not uncommon in this helping mode. We would suggest that the definition of interpretation as "renaming" of life experience is crucial here. Fritz Perls did not hesitate to rename the world as he saw it.

are, of course, closely related to directions). Perls' pattern of microtraining skills is vastly different from the helper orientations studied thus far.

Also important in analyzing Perls' work are the qualitative conditions. Particularly, it may be noticed that Perls' immediacy (present tense communication in particular) is extremely prominent. His questions and observations are particularly concrete and specific. Perls' emphasis on positive aspects of the client is perhaps less than that of Rogers. However, we simultaneously see a respect for the client's ability to work with difficult material. The main ingredients for Gestalt from a microtraining point of view appear to be here and now conversation, directions, and immediate here and now feedback focusing on the client's observable behavior. Confrontation of discrepancies in verbal and nonverbal behavior is common. Interpretations are used occasionally and appear to serve the purpose of helping the client look at herself from a new perspective.

The client's response to Perls is one of openness, manifested by frequent expressions of feeling and sharing of observations through expression of content. She is able to participate fully in the exercise and ask questions herself. She speaks in the present tense, and, in the exercise where she switches chairs, she is able to interpret her own behavior. In this way, her behavior becomes much like that of Perls himself. Some would comment that Perls' most successful clients were those most able to become similar to the confrontive and talented helper.

Again, which therapist is most effective? The issue may be raised this time in a new light. In each case, we see the helpee becoming a little bit more like the helper through the process of therapy or counseling. The client-centered helpee explores feelings and looks at self positively. The trait and factor helpee explores many facets of the self in a broad fashion. The client of the behaviorist thinks in terms of overt behaviors and acts in accordance with the overall plan of the professional helper. Those who worked with Perls often became similarly confrontive, lived more in the here and now, did not hesitate to express their feelings, and simultaneously attempted not to push their world view on others — "you do your thing, I'll do mine."

The question of which therapy is more effective, then, becomes Which therapy produces the most effective individual? Until a common definition of the effective individual is agreed upon, all therapies can make a strong case that their orientation is the most effective.

FAMILY THERAPY

Family therapy has been described as "the delicate flower" (Grinder and Bandler, 1976). Families grow and develop through the relationship of individuals. An individual may be effective alone but toxic in a family relationship. When one considers that a family, whether consisting of two people or ten, consists of a multiple network of relationships, the complexity of family therapy becomes apparent.

Focus dimensions of microtraining are particularly important in family therapy. In United States culture, many individuals see themselves primarily as *individuals* and secondarily as members of a family. This may be contrasted with some Asian cultures, where family takes precedence over the individual. In the past, *individual* therapy and counseling have been focused on helping the individual adapt and adjust to the existing family, believing that the family structure is a given. The West Coast family therapists, under such pioneers as Satir (1964; 1972), Haley (1963), and Erickson (Haley, 1973), work with a very different focus in their sessions. The major focus of family therapy is the *family* and its network of interrelationships. While individuals are often the focus of conversation and helping leads, ultimately the family structure is the most important dimension. Many family therapists claim allegiance to the anthropologist Gregory Bateson (cf. 1972), who delineated families themselves as a major issue for helping long before techniques for working with families were systematically developed. Further, Bateson worked closely with many prominent therapists in clarifying how his concepts could be translated from anthropology to therapy with individuals and families (e.g. Jackson, 1968a,b).

The clearest delineation of family therapy to date, in our

opinion, is that of Bandler and Grinder (1975) and Grinder and Bandler (1976). Using the underlying constructs of family therapy, they have added transformational grammar and the structure of language to training in family therapy. The result is a most powerful and clear package, explaining much of what happens in family therapy. They also point out that individual therapy, of necessity, must often rely on client statements of what transpired in the "real world." Family therapy offers a chance for the therapist to see and hear the real interaction in the context of the therapy period.

> In the context of family therapy . . . there is no need for the therapist to rely on a re-creation of some scene from the past as the communication process unfolding before him is the real thing — the process which forms the basis for the client's modeling (picture of the world). By carefully attending to the communication process—the presence or absence of incongruity in the communications among family members, or the systematic avoidance or deletion of certain types of messages— and by questioning the family members about what they are most aware of, the therapist can identify deletions, distortions, and generalizations which are preventing the family members from achieving together the experiences which they want.*

The above quote suggests in itself several tactics and skills which may be required from a microtraining point of view for successful family therapy. First, there is the need for "careful attending"; second, the focus must be on the family *and* the relationships of individuals within that family; finally, a variety of skills (questioning and interpretation, particularly) are used to help the family "reinterpret" their mutual experience of one another.

Grinder and Bandler (1976) and Bandler and Grinder (1975) give special attention to "semantic ill-formness" in the sentences produced by the family. Many families are "stuck" with repetitive stock phrases to describe their experience of one another. A major goal of family therapy is to help the family get "unstuck" and view itself and its members in new and creative ways. We have suggested that the effective individual is one who

---

*From Grinder, J. and Bandler, R., *The Structure of Magic,* Vol. 2. Palo Alto, California: Courtesy of Science and Behavior Books, 1976.

can generate a maximum number of nonverbal and verbal sentences (Ivey, 1977). Similarly, we would suggest that *the effective family is one which can generate a maximum number of effective nonverbal and verbal sentences and behaviors to act in the world with a maximum number of other individuals, families, and groups.*

Grinder and Bandler present a segment from an early session of family therapy. This segment presents only the son (George) and the father (Matt). As the full family is explored, the relationships become even more complex. This segment, however, provides an early introduction as to how microtraining can be used to analyze the behavior of the family therapist.

1. *Therapist:* Well, George (a ten-year-old boy), I've heard from all of the family members except you—tell me, what do you want? (Open question)
2. *George:* I want respect.
3. *Matt:* (The father in the family) (Smiling broadly) Yes, that I believe.
4. *George:* (Explosively) SEE!! That's just what I'm talking about—I don't get any respect from anyone in this family.
5. *Therapist:* Wait, George; you sound real angry to me. Can you tell me what just happened with you? (Reflection of feeling, open question)
6. *George:* I . . . I . . . oh, never mind; you wouldn't understand anyway.
7. *Therapist:* Perhaps not, but try me—did the way you just responded have something to do with something your father did? (Closed question)
8. *George:* Yeah, I ask for respect and HE (pointing at his father, Matt) just laughs right out loud, making fun of me.
9. *Matt:* That's not true, I didn't . . .
10. *Therapist:* Be quiet for a moment, Matt. (Turning to George) George, tell exactly what happened with you just then. (Direction)
11. *George:* I asked for respect and my father started making fun of me—just the opposite.
12. *Therapist:* George, tell me something—how, specifically, would you know that your father was respecting you? (Open question)
13. *George:* He wouldn't laugh at me—he would watch me

when I say things and be serious about it.

14. *Therapist:* George, I want to tell you something I noticed and something that I can see right now. Look at your father's face. (Expression of content direction)

15. *George:* Yeah, so what?

16. *Therapist:* Well, does he look serious to you—does he look like he's taking you seriously right now—like he, maybe, respects you for what you're saying and doing right now? (Closed question)

17. *George:* Yeah, you know, he does look like he is.

18. *Therapist:* Ask him, George. (Direction)

19. *George:* What? . . . ask him . . . Dad, do you respect me? Are you taking me seriously?

20. *Matt:* Yes, son . . . (softly) . . . I'm taking you seriously right now. I respect what you're doing.

21. *George:* (Crying softly) I really believe that you do, Dad.

22. *Therapist:* I have a hunch right now that Matt has more to say, George; will you take him (indicating Matt) seriously and listen to him? (Interpretation, closed question)

23. *George:* Sure . . .

24. *Matt:* Yeah . . . I guess I do have something to say. A minute or so ago when you first said that you wanted respect, George, I smiled and said, "Yes, that I believe" but I guess you only saw the smile and didn't hear what I said (crying quietly) , and then, when you became so angry, I suddenly remembered how I never believed my father respected me, and I'm grateful (turning to the therapist) that you helped me straighten this out with George.

25. *Therapist:* That's right—a message that's not received the way you intended it is no message at all. Matt, is there some other way that you can show George that you care for him besides telling him that you respect him? (Interpretation, closed question)

26. *Matt:* Huh . . . some other way besides telling him . . . I don't know. . .

27. *Therapist:* I have another hunch—that, maybe, there's a rule in this family, maybe a rule that you, Matt, learned in your father's family, that the men in the family don't touch one another to show their affection and love. Do you catch what I mean, Matt? (Interpretation, closed question)

28. *Matt:* . . . Wow . . . I guess . . . I really connected on that one . . .

29. *Therapist:* Well, maybe it's time for you to try to connect in a new way with your son. (Direction)

30. *Matt:* (Moving slowly and awkwardly at first, then more smoothly, quickly crosses over to George and holds him close.) *

The pattern of interactions in this example is typical of what can happen in family therapy. The therapist begins with the typical open question. George answers with what Grinder and Bandler term a *nominalization,* "I want respect." The sentence is also a surface structure with many underlying meanings. Respect is a term which cannot easily be defined in terms of concrete words or observable behavior. Immediately, the task of the therapist becomes to denominalize the important term respect and get at the deep structure and underlying meaning of the sentence. Respect is a qualitative condition underlying the microtraining process. The reader may find it helpful to reread the definition of respect in Chapter 6 and compare the statements presented there with the denominalization of respect in this family therapy segment.

The therapist at 5 reflects feeling (focus on George and the therapist) and then asks an open question in the first attempt to denominalize respect. The therapist at 12 completes the process with the open question (which is highly concrete — note the word "specifically" — and focuses on therapist, son, and father). At this point (George, 13), the term respect is rounded out with an operational definition on which the father can act if he chooses.

A crucial point in the interview turns on the therapist's action at 22 ["I have a hunch right now that Matt has more to say, George; will you take him (indicating Matt) seriously and listen to him?"]. The focus is on the therapist and the two clients, and while the comment is at first vague ("hunch"), the nominalization "take seriously" is more concrete — especially as respect has just been operationally defined. The microtraining skill is an interpretation followed by a closed question. The purpose of the therapeutic intervention is the denominalization of the surface structure of the relationship.

Matt (24) realized that his reaction to his son was a surface

___
*From Grinder, J. and Bandler, R., *The Structure of Magic,* Vol. 2. Palo Alto, California: Courtesy of Science and Behavior Books, 1976.

reaction on his part to the deep structure of his relationship with his own father years ago. Matt is able to interpret his own experience from a new and more creative point of view. The segment closes with another interpretation and an implicit direction leading to the dramatic climax.

Family therapy contains many of the dimensions of the broad-based communication skills of direct-mutual communication. The focus is most often on more than one individual or on an individual in relationship. The conversation remains primarily in the here and now present tense for the family interaction is there. There is no need to return to the past for data. The process of denominalization described by Bandler and Grinder is basically the result of the "1-2-3 pattern" of attending, influencing, and checking out through asking for further clarification in a cycle amplified and clarified by the family therapist.

The question may be asked If family therapy at its most successful dimensions so closely resembles the process of direct-mutual communication, would it be appropriate to train families directly in effective communication skills in a preventive program, thus lessening the need for therapy with disturbed families? The answer, of course, is patently obvious. If dimensions of effective helping can be clearly delineated, they should be moved immediately into educational-prevention programs for all. This will not eliminate the need for therapy, but it may result in more effective and productive individuals and families. Gordon's "parent effectiveness training" (1970) and Guerney's "relationship enhancement" (1977) are two fine programs.

This examination of family therapy and other helping theories has thus far been solely *within* a standard United States cultural base. There is need for a return to a further examination of cultural patterns in communication as cited in Chapters 8 and 9. The family is the prime transmitter of the culture to the individual. If personality change is to occur and to maintain itself, the family network of relationships must change. If the family is to change and maintain change, this change must be in relationship to the culture. Personality characteristics, family structure, and the culture are a circular causal system. Mead (1951) has stated, ". . . the method of child rearing, the presence of a particular literary tradition, the nature of domestic and public architecture, the religious beliefs, the political system, are all conditions within which a given kind of personality develops."   Anthropological concepts are too often missing from family therapy. Radical feminist therapists in particular have objected to family therapy as a transmitter of traditional cultural values.   Indeed, Grinder and Bandler (1976) state that one of the values of the family therapist is to keep the family intact.   This is a cultural value statement.   Regardless of the value structure of the individual, it seems clear that much family therapy as it now exists operates within traditional United States cultural patterns.

The family patterns endorsed by many family therapists could be compared to those of China.   Tien (1976), for example, comments on differences between United States and Chinese answers to the question "Why did you come to the University?"   Students in the United States give the answer "so that I can get ahead," "to better myself," "so that I can get myself a job."   All of these answers focus on the individual.   Tien points out that the United States national goal of self-fulfillment is "completely antithetical" to that of China.   Answers to the same question in China resulted in the following which sound strange to individual-focused United States citizens: "to serve the people." "to serve the revolution," "to build socialism."   All these answers are societal-focused.

The family in China, as does the United States family, transmits a culture.   However, the Chinese family serves an entirely different purpose in terms of cultural goals.   The values, ideas, and systems of communication all focus on the individual as a part of society.   The family in China produces a different type of person than the family produces in the United States.   Which is the "right" family structure and the "correct" national point of view will best remain as a value question for the reader.

The important point of anthropological considerations is that *the family is the repository of culture and transmits what the individual is to become.*   Family therapy as presently constituted works within cultural bounds and thus serves to maintain present cultural patterns.   Within the culture, this serves as an important maintenance function. However, when one considers issues of cross-cultural communication, family programs which fail to at least present individuals and families with the sociocultural implications of their interpersonal relationships are incomplete at a minimum and dangerous at worst. It is dangerous in that people who are unaware of cultural differences are ill-equipped to deal with others different from themselves. The culturally effective family and family member must have a maximum number of responses and sentences available to communicate with a maximum number of individuals, families, groups, and cultures.

Therapy which does not consider the family, the institutions of society, and sexual and cultural boundaries is incomplete. Thus, it may be suggested that the individually oriented helping theories discussed in this chapter (and presented in Appendix III) all fail to take full account of the cultural base of helping.

THE MEDICAL INTERVIEW

Thus far, this chapter has stressed the microtraining analysis of therapy and counseling sessions. Microtraining can be used for other types of interpersonal communication. One interesting example is the medical diagnostic-prescriptive interview. This type of session occurs most frequently when the patient goes to the physician on a routine office visit. The diagnostic-prescriptive interview could be considered as consisting of three key segments: (1) the oral history, (2) the physical examination, and (3) the concluding diagnosis and prescription for treatment.

The following case has been abstracted from an actual diagnostic-prescriptive interview and will illustrate how microtraining skills can be used to analyze interviews other than counseling and therapy. The oral history phase will be considered first:

> *Physician:* Hi, John, how are you? (Open question)
> (As the interview is with a twelve-year-old child, this open question is in some ways *closed,* as it is so open as to be vague. More structure, such as "how have things been going in school?," might get more opening data from the patient. This is, of course, true only if the physician wants to establish a relationship with the patient.)
> *Patient:* O.K., I guess.

Physician: Well, what's troubling you today? (Open question)
Patient: My eye is runny.
Physician: Tell me more about it? (Open question)
Patient: Well, it's itchy, it's been running, and it hurts. (Expression of content and feeling)
Physician: I see, have you had a cold too? (Closed question)
Patient: Yes.
Physician: Have you been taking any medicine for all this John? (Closed question)
Patient: Mom's been giving me Triaminic®.
Physician: Let's see now. Have you had an earache? (Closed question)
Patient: Yes.
Physician: When did all this start? (Closed question)
Patient: Two weeks ago.
Physician: Could you tell me how it started? (Open question)
Patient: First, I had a little cold. Then my cold got worse, then a little earache, and now my eye is all runny.
Physician: Let me ask you some questions now. Is anyone else in your family sick? (Closed question)

In the oral history phase, the physician asks open questions to obtain the broad picture of what has occurred. Then, closed questions are asked to determine the many factors which might be causative. Dudley and Blanchard (in press) found that experienced physicians asked open questions in the early phases of the interview, and during the later phases, as their diagnostic impression was formulated, they asked closed questions to verify their impressions. Inexperienced physicians, on the other hand, tended to ask many closed questions, failing to give the patients opportunity to explore and summarize *their* view of the problem.

The first phase of this type of interview requires attending skills on the part of the diagnostician. While questioning is usually the predominant mode, paraphrasing could be used profitably to help patients express themselves with less of a sense of inquiry and urgency. If the physician is interested in emotional factors, reflection of feeling would help assess the patient's emotional state. At the conclusion of the oral history phase, a summarization of the patient's complaints, e.g. "John, you have been saying that you have . . .," is useful in that the patient is told that she or he was *heard*. This followed by the open *and* closed question "Is there anything I missed?" permits the patient to add anything else considered important.

The second phase of the diagnostic-prescriptive interview is the physical examination. While attending skills are still used frequently, influencing skills of directions and expression of content (particularly information giving) appear prominently.

> *Physician:* I'd like to look at you now John. Take off your shirt. (Expression of content, direction)
> Now I'm going to listen to your heart. This may be a little cold. (Expression of content—information giving. This lets the patient know what is going to happen)
> *Physician:* That sounded fine. (Expression of content—reassurance) Now turn your head, I want to look in your ear. (Direction, expression of content—information giving) You've got a big red ear drum there. Has your ear been hurting long? (Expression of content—information giving, closed question)
> *Patient:* Yeah, about a week.
> *Physician:* What have you been doing for your ear? (Open question)
> *Patient:* Mom put a heating pad on it one night.

During this phase of the interview the physician gave directions, continued part of the oral history through open and closed questions, and told the patient what was being done to him through expressions of content of the information-giving type. Some physicians would conduct the examination without a word, or they might give only directions. This physician indicated to the patient what was going to happen and gave some of the results of observations as well as giving directions. Reflections of feeling or questions about feelings could have been used to open the child to more self-disclosure.

The final phase of the interview is the diagnosis and prescription phase. What does the patient have and what can be done about it?

> *Physician:* Well, John, it seems that you have pinkeye. The symptoms you told me about—the runny nose, the sore throat, the red ears, the red eye—and what I've seen in the physical all add up to pinkeye. (Summarization and interpretation)
> *Patient:* Is that serious?
> *Physician:* No, but it is contagious. I'll write out a prescription

here that will take care of it very quickly. (Expression of con-
tent—information giving and reassurance.)
Patient: That's good.
Physician: Are you allergic to anything? (Closed question)
Patient: No.
Physician: I'm going to start you out on some medicine. Do you
want liquid or pills? (Expression of content, closed question)
Patient: I have trouble taking pills.
Physician: O.K. You've got to take this for ten days, four times
a day. (Direction)

The final phase of the session continues with the physician
clarifying needs for cleanliness, giving further information about
the illness, and specifying directions for care and treatment. The
session ends with the instruction for the child to return in ten
days.

This is obviously a most routine office visit for the family practice or pediatric physician. The experienced physician goes
through these phases of the interview with little thought of what
is occurring. The beginning physician (or nurse or medical
technician) could benefit from training in diagnostic and treatment procedures important in routine office visits. The failure to
ask open questions may result in missing important data. The
poor giving of directions may result in a patient not taking medicine or ignoring the physician's advice. The ability of the physician to express him or herself clearly and succinctly may be as
important as the accurate diagnosis of patient illness.

The three phases of this brief interview are interesting in that
the first phase of oral history is concerned primarily with attending to the patient through questions. The second phase is often
a balance of attending and influencing skills in that questions continue to be asked, but the physician gives some information from
observations and gives many directions. The final phase is usually
devoted primarily to influencing skills. The diagnostic impression is parallel with the psychiatrist's interpretation in a therapy
session and in this case was presented as a summary/interpreta-
tion. After this information is given to the patient, directions for
treatment are suggested.

Medical interviews such as this can be criticized for the central focus on the illness, with only peripheral focus on the patient and the family network. However, if the physician takes time to focus on the patient, the family system, and the unique personal needs of that patient, valuable time may be lost. Thus, while skills such as reflection of feeling and paraphrasing plus self-disclosure on the part of the physician concerning his or her reactions to the patient or parallel life experience may humanize the interview, they cannot be part of every session or the medical interview will become indistinguishable from the psychiatric or counseling session. The task of the busy physician is to find a balance between complete focus on the illness and an overly extensive focus on the individual who has the illness. Most physicians err on the side of the illness, thus contributing to the patient's impression that he or she is not a person but rather a set of symptoms.

Again, the question may be asked Was this an effective interview? This depends once again on the value structure of the observer. Technically, this physician covered all medical bases carefully. The oral examination was extensive and well done, the physical examination covered all important points, the diagnosis was considered correct, and the prescription was appropriate. The physician appeared self-confident and believable and thus receives high marks for professional performance. *But,* why wasn't a parent present at this session? Who else may come into contact in the family and perhaps contract the illness? Are there overriding emotional complications which might explain this particular illness at this particular time? If such issues are of importance to the observer, then this interview may be judged as less effective — particularly on an emotional-relationship plane.

The extensive use of questions in medical interviews has been disputed by Gazda, Walters, and Childers (1975). They have demonstrated that it is possible to use more Rogerian-facilitative skills to bring out patient data. Early evidence indicates more patient satisfaction with this nontraditional approach to communication. They list several reasons why questioning techniques may be inappropriate in the medical interview in that they place the patient in a dependent relationship, force the patient into the physician's frame of reference, and may cause the physician to miss underlying emotional factors important to the case.

SUMMARY

Several varying types of interviewing, counseling, therapy, and diagnostic sessions have been presented in typescript form. The purpose of this chapter is to illustrate that different interviewers use different skills to achieve widely different objectives. Yet, each of the interviewers uses microtraining skills. They use different skills in varying combinations with varying verbal content, but all can be identified as using specific skills with specific foci with varying emphases on qualitative dimensions.

We have seen that the client-centered helper focused solely on the client. Through reflections of feeling, minimal encourages, paraphrases, and summarizations, the client-centered helper deals with helpee feelings toward self and the world. In more recent varieties, client-centered helping now includes self-disclosure as an important element of effective communication.

The trait and factor helper in the vocational counseling example used a broad variety of eclectic techniques, including extensive use of open and closed questions, reflection of feeling, directions, and expression of content (particularly information giving).

A case study of a behavior therapist was presented, and it was observed that open and closed questions, expression of content (advice and information), and directions were important in this orientation to helping. It was pointed out that behavior therapists will vary widely in their use of such skills as paraphrases and reflections of feeling.

The Gestalt therapist was the most active individual helper presented. Interpretation and directions plus extensive questioning were basic to the brief interview-demonstration.

A family therapy case excerpt was presented, and the microtraining skills of the therapist included all dimensions of the microtraining framework. Questions, directions, and self-disclosures were particularly important in helping the family members understand their experience in the here and now, present tense world. Interpretations at key points suggested the way toward new action.

The question was asked throughout these five segments as to

which therapeutic method is the more effective. The answer to this question, it is suggested, lies in the value structure of the observer. If one believes that expression of client feelings is central, then client-centered helping is the more effective framework. If vocational decision and consideration of a broad range of factors for making this decision are important, trait and factor helping is the more effective. If quick insight into depth problems from a here and now perspective is valued, the work of Gestalt therapy is most effective. If one takes a broader view of helping, the family therapy session which explored interpersonal support systems may be considered to be the most effective.

From a cultural point of view, however, all the above interviews could be criticized as operating within a single cultural perspective. Issues of sexual, racial, religious, ethnic, or cultural identity are unlikely to be considered in most individual or family therapy situations. The concept of the culturally effective individual suggests that the communication responses which permit the individual to reach the largest number of people are the most effective. Full effectiveness demands consideration of cultural perspectives.

A final segment presented an analysis of a diagnostic-prescriptive session of a typical office visit with a family physician. Microtraining skills were used to analyze the physician's behavior, and it was found that in the early phases of the session, the physician used attending skills to bring out data from the patient. In the middle phases of the session (the physical examination), influencing skills were coupled with attending skills to bring out further data and verify the diagnosis. The final phase of the session, wherein the diagnosis was presented and prescriptions for action were suggested, involved primarily influencing skills.

It is suggested that microtraining skills may be used to examine a wide variety of communication sessions. They can be and have been used to examine the process of communication in group interviews, medical sales within a drug company, the process of an employment interview, family communication, faculty meetings — an infinite number of possibilities. In each of these cases, it seemed that the individual or group which has the maximum number of communicative responses available to communicate with a maximum number of individuals will be maximally effective. Thus, it was suggested that a goal common to all helping theories would be to increase the behavioral response repertoire through removal of blocks or conflicts or "splits," thereby providing the helpee with new and alternative verbal and nonverbal sentences which would enable him or her to communicate with a maximum number of individuals.

Chapter 8

THE CULTURAL-ENVIRONMENTAL-CONTEXTUAL IMPLICATIONS OF MICROTRAINING*

M OST HELPEES SEE THEIR PROBLEMS as residing in their inability to manage their lives or personal inadequacy to solve the problems which they face. Primary focus of counseling and therapy traditionally has been to help clients and patients achieve objectives such as "self-actualization," "development of a better self-concept," "more individualization," or to "achieve personal goals." Indeed, until the last few decades, virtually all helping theories focused on the *individual,* and for many the "I-Thou" relationship between interviewer and interviewee has been considered ideal. Community psychology and family therapy have helped to change the emphasis from that of the individual to that of the system within which the individual resides. Whereas traditionally the goal would be to improve the self-concept of the housewife who has a lowered image of herself due to being "stuck" in the home, a community approach would see the primary issue as helping the housewife to organize a day-care center which would enable her to get out of the house. Family therapy, on the other hand, might insist on the family members coming in to discuss the woman's concepts in light of the family system, with the overall goal of this approach being to help the system accommodate some of the frus-

*The term "culture" in this book is used in its broadest sense. Individuals who come from different parts of the world will be viewed as exemplifying cultural differences, as will be men and women and people of different ethnic groups or subcultures in the United States. In essence, culture will be used in this book to denote different patterns of life history among groups or individuals.

trated needs of this family member rather than solely working on the improvement of her self-concept.

Although both of these approaches have served to shift the focus away from the individual in a helping relationship, the central belief of helping professions has been shaken more profoundly by the black power and black identity movements, which have demonstrated the importance of sociocultural issues in individual development.   Hispanic and Asian identity movements have closely paralleled black awareness.   This in turn has been followed by massive emphasis on women's liberation and the new feminism. Gay liberation, ethnic pride movements, the Gray Panthers (for older individuals), welfare rights groups, and other advocacy coalitions have evolved rapidly in recent years.   *Common to all these movements is an emphasis on the cultural-environmental-contextual factors impinging on individual development.*

From a cultural-environmental-contextual perspective, the focus of helping moves from an individual emphasis to the relationship of that individual to the society in which one lives.   The classic statement of this point of view may be found in Ryan's (1971) *Blaming the Victim.*   In the introductory pages of this book, Ryan points out that a black child enters the slum school and is blamed for failure.   The child often comes from a home without books, speaks a distinct and varied dialect (forbidden in the middle-class school), and suddenly is expected to perform in a middle-class fashion.   When the child fails to "measure up" to standards completely foreign, the child is blamed for the failure. If the school is relatively "enlightened," the child may be excused from failure because of "cultural deprivation" or "disadvantagement."   Each way, the child and the child's situation are the responsibility of the child.   He or she must act to remedy the situation.

Ryan speaks of this child as *victim.*   He asks "What is wrong with the victim?"

> . . . no one remembers to ask questions about the collapsing buildings and torn textbooks, the frightened, insensitive teachers, . . . the relentless segregation, . . . the irrelevant curriculum, . . . the insulting history book, . . . or the self-serving faculty of the local teachers' college. (P. 4)

If the professional helper were to *focus* on the cultural-environmental-context, the subject of the question, reflection of feeling, or interpretation would be the school, the teacher, or society. On the other hand, most helpers *focus* on the individual and unconsciously attempt to help the individual *adapt* to cruel and unusual treatment from society and institutions.

Women too are victims. The most desired patient for the psychoanalyst is the middle-aged housewife who is hysterical and/or depressed. Years of income can be produced helping this woman adapt to her comfortable split-level home and suburban life. The analyst (or other professional helper) typically will focus on the individual and her unique history leading to this problem. Chesler (1972), in a powerful statement in *Women and Madness,* states clearly that the helper who seeks to adapt this woman to her life situation fails to see the problem as a *woman's issue.* Chesler points out that women in particular have been "ripped off" by the psychiatric profession and led to believe that their "problems" are *their fault* and sole responsibility.

Women's consciousness-raising groups and feminist therapy have helped change the situation. Women are encouraged to see their concerns as cultural and societal in origin, thus freeing them for later individual and group action to find fuller selfhood *and* interrelationships with other women. Consider the following example:

> Counseling of women with a focus primarily on individual issues misses the fact that simply being a woman in a sexist environment may be the most important issue. The helper who focuses solely on the individual may fail to see the important environmental issues influencing behavior.

Woman: My husband objects to me taking a job.

Helper A: *You* seem worried and upset about this. What have *you* been doing to help him understand *your* needs? (Focus on the individual may be helpful, but promotes belief that the woman is responsible for any change.)

Helper B: This is a problem many women have experienced. *Society* has established rules that women are to serve their husbands. *The women's movement* views this not as your problem, but as a problem of our culture. How do *you* react to that? (Focus on the cultural-environmental-context-

ual issues gives the woman a chance to see how she inter-
acts with the world.)   (Ivey and Gluckstern, 1976b, p. 62).

The basic issue in the use of microtraining for consciousness
raising, interracial counseling, feminist therapy, gay therapy, or
other activist orientations to helping is a full awareness of the importance of focus on the cultural-environmental-contextual situation from which the individual comes.   Sole focus on "I-Thou"
helping may be naive and, in fact, dangerous for some clients.
There are those who would call "I-Thou" helping without supportive societal and contextual considerations pacification programs
and political indoctrination (Halleck, 1971; Szasz, 1961; Steiner,
1975).

Microtraining has only recently ventured into the area of
cultural-environmental-contextual issues.   Ivey and Gluckstern
(1974a,b), in discussing the concept of focus, fail to mention this
dimension, although it appears prominently in their later (1976a,b)
work.   Research and training giving consideration to these issues
is only beginning but does offer some promising early findings and
methods.   The purpose of this chapter is to summarize several
approaches to bringing broad sociocultural issues into the helping
process via microtraining techniques.

PRESENT EXPERIMENTAL WORK

Ivey and Gluckstern (1974c) have used their Basic Attending
Skills videotape package as a format to teach nonsexist counseling.
The model of teaching involves an approach similar to an introductory attending behavior workshop or training session (see
Appendix I).   Specifically, trainees in a role-playing session develop an example of a deliberately sexist counseling session.   The
stereotypical model provides the basis for individual or group discussion of what sexism is and how it may appear in the interview.
A positive and a negative modeling tape exhibiting sexist and nonsexist helping is then shown, and further practice sessions follow.
This simple and basic exercise has proven effective many times in
training and workshop sessions.   We believe it provides a basic
model for beginning work in cross-racial counseling, ethnic
counseling, gay therapy, or any of a variety of cultural-environ-

mental-contextual situations.

A typescript of the videotape of ineffective and effective attending behavior is included in Appendix II. While originally developed for training in attending behavior, this videotape and
typescript proves equally effective as a model illustrating how sexism operates in many helping interviews. Particularly important
is the concept of selective attention. In the negative modeling
tape, it may be observed that the male helper consistently topic
jumps and ignores the female helpee's assertive statements while
supporting traditional feminine roles through attention to family
and husband's opinions. For example,

> *Al 1:* Norma, I had heard that you were active in getting the
> Valley Women's Center started. I'd like to hear a little bit more
> about how that happened.
>
> *Norma 1:* Well, I guess it's almost been four years ago that it
> started because it's almost been; and I kind of wonder, I guess
> it was just a lot of women. . .
>
> *Al 2:* (Interrupting) Four years ago now, I remember, I came
> here about four years ago.
>
> *Norma 2:* Well, what happened. . . I think it was about five,
> almost six years ago that the women's liberation movement be-
> gan. But it was about four years ago that there was a really
> big push on the campus to get something going.
>
> > *Comment:* During Norma 1 and 2, Al sits with arms closed,
> > occasionally breaking eye contact. He opens up
> > and moves forward when talking about himself at
> > Al 2.
>
> *Al 3:* Did you feel there was a need to do something?
>
> *Norma 3:* Well, when I first started out I didn't. I almost got
> kind of. . .
>
> *Al 4:* (Interrupting) What did your husband think when you
> got into that? (The helper leans forward with interest.)
>
> *Norma 4:* I think he, I think he was humoring me. I think he
> was like most men, not really paying much attention.
>
> *Al 5:* Yeah, it is kind of funny sometimes.
>
> *Norma 5:* Yeah, well I think that men, and I don't think my
> husband is any different really. . .
>
> > *Comment:* The same pattern again appears. Whenever the
> > helpee expresses herself, the helper moves back,
> > breaks eye contact. If she talks in an unassertive
> > traditional female role, eye contact is maintained.

The positive attending skills model, on the other hand, shows the male helper responding positively to the helpee's assertiveness.

Al 1:   Norma, you've been saying you've had a long term relationship with the women's movement and it might be more helpful right now if you could share with me a little bit about what some of your feelings are right now at this moment.

Norma 1:   Oh, my feelings are really very positive in terms of the women's movement 'cause I'm not sure if there hadn't been some pioneers out there to have raised my consciousness I would have pretty much gone on the way I was. Maybe less externally conflicted, but maybe more internally conflicted. I think that the women's movement forced me to act on my own behalf. I think that would be the best way to describe it. And that process of acting has developed for me a whole area of growth that I'm enjoying. In some ways when I say I'm ambivalent, the result of the women's movement is I pushed ahead in areas that I never thought I was going to push ahead in before. And in that process of pushing ahead, of course, I probably alienated some people. And somehow that's O.K. because I'm feeling better about myself.

Al 2:   So you feel better about yourself, and I hear you saying that you really like the idea that you're acting. Can you give something a little bit specific of where you have acted and felt good about yourself?

Comment: The helper pays close attention through eye contact, head nods, and body language as the helpee states positive things about herself. This is reinforced by the selective attention to the positive things about her new role. It would have been possible, for example, to selectively attend to her alienating people, and thus the conversation would head in a very different direction. The helpee's longer verbal statements should also be noted.

Norma 2:   Oh well, I think that pretty much the whole job I've taken, the fact that I am willing to take a job that has responsibilities, that I have the need to assert myself, to explore new ways of acting. I think one of the really exciting things about that as a woman, well maybe not as a woman, that I began to find all sorts of skills that I would have said "No, no that's not for me." But as I began to assert myself, I realized that if you're going to go ahead in this area, you are going to have to have certain competencies that you kept denying you had. And as I got in touch with the, it's just very exciting.

Al 3:   In a sense, you really feel good about yourself and what's happened to you as a result of being part of the movement.

The pattern of nonverbal communication in this videotape is particularly interesting. The breaks in eye contact in the first session (about 40 in number) and distracting nonverbal gestures (20-plus) appear at times when the helpee is attempting to assume a nontraditional role. Eye contact is maintained when the helpee talks about (at the helper's instigation) maintaining a traditional feminine role. In the positive modeling tape, eye contact breaks are reduced to three (at seemingly appropriate times), and there are far fewer disruptive gestures. The male helper's nonverbal communication supports the female helpee as she moves toward a nontraditional definition of self.

A black-white team at the University of Massachusetts, composed of Bailey Jackson, Allen Ivey, Judy Katz, and Craig Washington, has developed an experimental set of training tapes for counseling on racial issues. The first set of tapes is constructed in a similar fashion to those of the Ivey-Gluckstern tapes previously discussed. A variety of pairings of counselors and counselees is made, however. Blacks are teamed with blacks, whites with whites, and blacks with whites both as counselor and client. There are six examples of positive and negative same-race and different-race counseling. The method of teaching is similar to basic microcounseling training in terms of role-playing ineffective helping followed by discussion and identification of issues. Modeling tapes are then viewed, followed by additional practice sessions.

Black-white training has been enriched by Jackson's "Black Identity Theory" (1975a) and his "White Identity Theory" (1975b). Jackson points out that it is naive to believe that counseling theory can be transferred directly to any black or white person. People come from different backgrounds and have different views of their world, particularly as they view the world from a racial perspective. Black identity theory poses four stages of aspects of black consciousness. The first level is termed "passive acceptance." The black individual copes with a white world by attempting to "get by" and act like white people. The term "Uncle Tom" has been used by some blacks to describe this orientation. The second level is "active resistance," where the black person rejects white patterns of life. "Personal energy is put into rejecting whites and building a power structure . . . that will realize the same rewards for blacks that they have for whites" (p. 22). The term "black militant" has been applied to some individuals of this orientation. A third level is termed "redirection" and is perhaps being represented by the "Black pride" movement, wherein whites become irrelevant but are not actively rejected. Emphasis is on personal and group pride in Blackness. Jackson poses a fourth level, "internalization," which combines aspects of the preceding three levels and an increased sense of personal and cultural identity*.

The importance of this theoretical orientation to counseling cannot be overstressed. At its most basic level, the theory states the obvious but often forgotten point that black people have widely varying views of the world and cannot be all treated the same. Jackson and Ivey were conducting a workshop in a southern black college, and the role-played helpee enacted a black with a level one orientation while the helper enacted a level two orientation. Her comment after two minutes of attempting to counsel a person with a completely different world view was "I simply can't talk to this man!" Out of such experiences, we have come to believe that different skills are required when people of differing world views come together. Simply coming from the same racial background is not enough. In the case above, the level two helper was encouraged to use attending skills and hear the point of view of the level one helpee. If appropriate, at a later

---

*There are interesting parallels between Jackson's four stages of black identity development and Satir's (1972) communication categories developed by people under stress. She identifies the *placater* who seeks to please and "go along," the *blamer* who places other people as responsible for problems, the *computer* who appears ultra-rational and reasonable, and the *distracter* who moves in many different directions. If more positive terms were identified for these categories of response and the distracter redefined as a person who uses aspects of the other three categories for effective communication, very direct and clear patterns between Jackson and Satir are apparent. There is some logic to this approach, as family communication structure is very much the basis for any individual's identity as a cultural being. Further, there are times when it is appropriate to placate, blame, or use rational approaches to solve problems.

point, the helper could engage in self-disclosure which might even take the form of consciousness-raising.

Basic to counseling on racial and cultural issues is an awareness of one's own world view and a sensitivity to the world view of the other. This clearly implies that attending skills are first and foremost in importance in any counseling or helping session of this type. However, where in traditional helping the focus is always on the individual, this approach to helping demands a clear focus on the cultural context and world view of the helpee as an essential dimension of effective helping.

Jackson's theory of black identity development has a parallel in white identity. Jackson points out that whites are not aware of themselves as whites and basic consciousness-raising to the fact of whiteness may be a major problem for the helper committed to this area. The stages of white identity theory are roughly parallel to those of black identity theory with the major exception that white theory has one additional stage below level 1, wherein active rejection of Third World people takes place.

The women's movement, gay liberation movement, or ethnic pride movements all may be viewed from the context of Jackson's theory. His system provides an enriching way of examining cross-cultural helping and suggests specific actions in specific settings. While no formal research has been conducted to date on the combination of microcounseling with Jackson's theoretical structure, clinical efforts and numerous workshops reveal this to be an effective addition.

In summary, experimental work with microcounseling and cultural-environmental-contextual issues is in the elementary beginning stages. The concept of focus appears to be of prime importance. One cannot work with these important issues unless they are actually discussed in the helping interview. The success of focusing on these issues is most dramatically illustrated by the black and women's movements and the many important personal changes that have been made with many people. Jackson's theoretical structure of black identity development provides a broad frame of reference for examining a vast arena of cultural awareness issues in the personal development of whites, women, and gays. Finally, it is important to realize that different skills and different qualitative conditions (cf. Chapter 6) are necessary when working with individuals with varying views of the world.

A DIRECT TRAINING APPROACH FOR CO-COUNSELING

McDermott (1976b) sought to attack some of the above issues via a direct training modality rather than through a theoretical approach. He explored three key issues in another cultural-environmental-contextual area, mental health in the inner city. He asked three main questions: (1) do low income peers have innate counseling skills in their common life experience, a common idiom, and consequent empathic understanding? (2) can they be trained via microcounseling? (3) can they co-counsel each other under professional supervision? Microcounseling training was combined with some of Carkhuff's (1969a,b) facilitative conditions.

McDermott trained thirty-six Hispanic and Chinese peer counselors from the Lower East Side of New York, of whom 80 percent either had been on welfare in the last four years or found it necessary to work a six- or seven-day week. They were an upwardly mobile group in that all had enrolled in a "miniversity" and were engaged in college-level work. The age of the trainees ranged from twenty-two to fifty-nine, with an average of thirty three. None of the trainees had studied psychology in any form. The training was over a four-month period, with fourteen sessions of four hours each. A single "micro-skill" was emphasized in each session. By the end of the second class, McDermott comments, the "danger flag was flying," as promised resources of co-trainers did not materialize and he found insufficient time to observe everybody. He selected four trainees who appeared particularly able and employed them in the course as "peer trainers," and this added dimension provided more interpersonal openness and more extensive feedback.

The microcounseling skills used for training were similar to those presented in this text but were reworded in an appropriate fashion for this group, and translations into the languages of the trainees were made available as well (McDermott, 1976a). Sample titles for skills included "communication of prizing" (e.g. posture), "paraphrasing of feelings," "letting your insides show" (i.e. self-disclosure), and "confrontation: defining a contradiction." McDermott comments that he had made attempts prior to this study to work with Carkhuff's facilitative conditions, but they had proved too abstract to teach low income people. Within the microtraining skills he selected, he incorporated some of these core conditions of helping.

After the instructor's explanation and role-play of the skill of the day, three groups of twelve trainees internal to the study itself were developed. Each group practiced the skill in dyads by three different methodologies: (1) peer trainers gave feedback until the trainees reached a minimally facilitative use of the skill; (2) no observer gave feedback, but the practicing dyads reported their reactions about skill acquisition back to an instructor-led T-group; (3) a combination of the previous two. McDermott found that the trainees were able to improve their performance on the "Skill Discrimination Index" (Carkhuff, 1969a), were able to increase their attention to the client affect, demonstrated more of the facilitative conditions emphasized in the training program, and demonstrated greater personal growth as measured by the Personal Orientation Instrument (POI) (Shostrom, 1966). The first group showed highest gain in skill acquisition. The second group showed highest gain in awareness of sexual and cultural issues surrounding counseling; they also showed high gain in skill acquisition. The third group showed mixed gains and rather inconclusive results.

Perhaps more important than the statistical design or the results reported above are the data collected from personal journals maintained by participants. Many reported specific instances of increases in self-confidence and assertiveness. However, the prime emphasis in the journals was on internal experiencing during the class sessions. For example, a Hispanic trainee reported

> The (co-) counselor helped me in my conflict by empathizing with me, and by encouraging full exploration of myself and by encouraging me to express my feelings . . . My negative feelings were surfaced. The feelings I had were imaginary. . . Now if I am confronted to speak in front of a class, I will be less apprehensive. I know I won't be laughed

at or ridiculed. . . . Since the (co-) counseling sessions I am moving more towards action (McDermott, 1976b, pp. 141-142).

A Chinese student reported

. . . I was helped to explore the problem which happened to me a couple of weeks ago. First I didn't want to express my oppression to the Counselor ———, because I know that as a Chinese and influenced by Chinese traditional culture, I find myself more conservative than most people. . . When I explored (this issue) and expressed the whole thing outwardly, I felt more comfortable than having them hidden inside of me (McDermott, 1976b, p. 141).

These students' reports, combined with the finding that the Hispanic group showed more interpersonal growth than the Chinese group on the POI on feeling and interpersonal sensitivity dimensions, seem to reflect cultural differences. Other cultural differences were demonstrated by the Chinese group which scored higher than the Hispanic group on "synergistic awareness," including the nature of man. As such, the importance of a focus on cultural-environmental-contextual dimensions formulated previously is readily apparent. Of course, it must be recognized that the POI is a culturally biased instrument, and these findings must be viewed most tentatively. However, they do support the existence of cultural-environmental differences among trainees and the importance of the trainer's focusing on these issues if training is to be maximally effective.

The major focus of McDermott's research was to investigate peer co-counseling as a strategy to root out cultural bias on the part of professional mental health workers. When low income people of the same sex, ethnic class, and other criteria of peer status counsel each other by reversing counselor and counselee roles, there is automatically excluded from the counseling relationship most of the imported cultural imperialism and socioeconomic elitism often attending counseling relationships. If oppression enters the counseling relationship, it is the low income peer who brings it in—frequently in the form of "internalized helplessness" (McDermott, 1976b, pp. 11-12). More common in this study, however, was the positive introduction of concepts of oppression, chauvinism, and prejudice in peer co-counseling sessions. The insights about the effects of cultural-environmental-contextual issues on personal lives gained by participants was an important benefit in this study. Freire's *Pedagogy of the Oppressed* (1972) talks in detail about the need to assist low income people to define their own problems and discuss their own solutions. There is evidence that the skills training and co-counseling in McDermott's study provide a more concrete and systematic method to reach Freire's ends. The study also illustrates the flexibility of the model's technology, which can be applied to virtually any helping theory orientation. That is, the skills taught during the McDermott study were drawn from Carkhuff (1969a,b) as well as those defined in this text, and the training was apparently effective. Additionally, the program demonstrates the effectiveness and benefit of systematic peer training with large groups. Finally, the crucial "bottom line" in this study for microtraining is that low socioeconomic groups of varying racial backgrounds can profit and change through microtraining style workshops and classes. As such, this study verifies clinical experience of the authors in training a wide array of client groups from varying racial, ethnic, sexual, and cultural backgrounds.

MICROTRAINING IN INTERRACIAL COMMUNICATION

The issue of how majority and minority individuals can communicate effectively is a major concern of the helping profession. Most studies and efforts in this area have been conducted in terms of black-white communication. Most typically, sensitivity training and encounter groups have been used (e.g. Katz, 1975; Rogers, 1970; Wilkinson, 1973). The sum and substance of the encounter approach has been increased communication during the session, but with little generalization after the training. An often-quoted study by Banks, Berenson, and Carkhuff (1967) examined the effects of race on helping and the attitudes of black helpees toward four helpers of varying experience levels. They found that the relatively inexperienced black helper was perceived as most effective, and none of the helpees would consider returning to the most experienced white helper. The white helper, however, was functioning at a relatively low level. Though experienced, he was not fully competent. Banks (1972) found that similarity of racial pairings results in greater self-exploration. Carkhuff (1971b) summarizes the issue ably when he states that given equality of competence, people seem to prefer counselors of similar racial backgrounds; however, competence is to be preferred over incompetence regardless of racial or cultural background.

Efforts to date suggest that successful interracial counseling and therapy occur despite limitations and problems. The work cited earlier in this chapter represents microtraining's future thrust in this area. However, the psychoeducator model of Authier et al. (1975) suggests the importance of directly teaching interracial or intercultural communication skills to clients of both majority and nonmajority backgrounds. While it may be important to train counselors, therapists, and helpers in communication skills, a more immediate and potentially more helpful approach is to teach individuals from different cultures effective communication directly through a psychoeducational approach.

Noel (1976) conducted such a psychoeducational training program in a high school in an upper-middle-class community which had a history of infrequent and relatively poor communication between black and white students. She trained sixteen black-white pairs of students (eight male, eight female) in sharing their experiences of being black or white in the high school environment. Experiencing was defined in Gendlin's (1962) terms as the sharing of moment to moment experiences and feelings. Experiencing was further operationalized by teaching five of the components from the direct-mutual communication manual (Ivey and Gluckstern, 1976b). The student pairs went through a basic microcounseling training paradigm with pre- and posttraining videotaping, although no video models were presented.

Results on a wide variety of measures revealed increased facility and depth of communication in the students. The students rated themselves more highly after training, as did external observers viewing randomized tapes. A particularly interesting finding of the study was that no significant differences between black and white students in self-disclosure was demonstrated in any of the videotapings. This finding directly contradicts the bulk of the research literature which indicates that blacks are less self-disclosing than whites (e.g. Jourard and Lasakow, 1958; Dimond and Hellkamp, 1969). Slight differences between males and females in the predicted direction (more self-disclosure for females) was found.

Evaluation of the study following the training and posttesting revealed that students felt the experience was of benefit, as is indicated in most microcounseling studies. However, the more important fact is that the videotape clearly demonstrated improved communication after training.

Noel's study, of course, is subject to important limitations. The scales used were subjective as opposed to the behavioral counts now preferred in microtraining research. There is no evidence of generalization of learned behavior; it has become an axiom of microtraining research and practice that generalization of learned behavior must be planned as part of a training program as skills learned in the massed practice of microtraining are gradually lost.

Nonetheless, Noel's study represents a pioneering effort in a difficult and complex area. This study and that of McDermott may be considered roughly comparable to the first microcounseling study of attending behavior which was subject to similar limitations (Ivey, Normington, Miller, Morrill, and Haase, 1968). We hope these studies represent the first of a series of increasingly precise and controlled studies on the role of microtraining in teaching skills and understanding in interracial communication and helper training.

An important and fascinating extension of microtraining for youth is represented by Bradley's work (1976) on "interpersonal skill development" for inner-city youth. Bradley was concerned about assisting young Afro-American youth from the inner city to communicate more effectively with their environment and with each other. Concentrating on the skills of attending behavior, he first taught some of the standard middle-class means of communication. He then extended this training to job interviewing and taught these young people how to apply for a job. For youth on the job in a restaurant, he developed mini-microtraining units such as "a complaining guest," "an accident to a guest's clothing," and "the late-arriving reservation." The experiential learning of the microtraining workshop provided a safe place for learning job skills.

THE CROSS-CULTURAL TRIAD

Still another effort to transcend language and cultural barriers is the work of Paul Pedersen of the University of Minnesota. Pedersen introduced at the Ninth International Congress of Ethnological and Anthropological Sciences in Chicago in 1973 an important paper which serves to move the microcounseling framework beyond its present cultural limitations to a new and broader perspective. Pedersen defines the problem of cross-cultural communication in professional helping as follows:

> Kagan (1964) and Schwebel (1964) suggest that counselor education programs may actually be contributing to the encapsulation process, implanting a cultural bias however implicit in their curricula. Counselors tend to become "addicted" to one system of cultural values in a dependency that is counterproductive to effective counseling (Morrow, 1972).
>
> Helpers who are most different from their helpees, in race and social class, have the greatest difficulty effecting constructive changes, while helpers who are most similar to their helpees in these respects have the greater facility for appropriate helping (Carkhuff and Pierce, 1967). Mitchell (1970) goes so far as to say that most White counselors cannot be part of the solution for a Black client since they are so frequently part of the problem. Williams (1970) likewise asserts that the White mental health worker cannot successfully counsel the "Black Psyche." Ayres (1970) and Russel (1970) describe an implicit or sometimes explicit bias in the counseling process itself that is frequently perceived as demeaning, debilitating, patronizing and dehumanizing.
>
> In cross-cultural counseling there is a greater danger of mutual misunderstanding (McFayden and Winokur, 1956), less understanding of the other culture's unique problems (Kincaid, 1969), a natural hostility that destroys rapport and greater negative transference toward the counselor (Vontress, 1971). Thomas (1962) points out the danger of confusing a client's appropriate cultural response with neurotic transference. Middleton (1963), Woods (1958) and Trent (1954) suggest numerous other sources of difficulty for the White professional counseling Blacks. Ignorance of one another's culture contributes to resistance in opposition to the goals of counseling. This resistance is usually accompanied by some feelings of hostility, threat or unwillingness to allow the stranger access to a client's real feelings (Pedersen, 1973, pp. 5-6).*

*Used by permission of Paul Pedersen.

To combat these many problems of counseling across races and cultures, Pedersen has developed a modification of the microcounseling paradigm in which the trainee counselor is matched with two persons, the first a counseling ,client, the second an "anti-counselor." The counselor is ordinarily from one culture, while the client and the anti-counselor come from a second culture. The client portrays the usual client role, while the anti-counselor explicates cultural aspects of the client's issues (Pedersen, undated).

The model presupposed by Pedersen in a cross-cultural setting is that there are three main forces occurring in a helping interview: (1) the experiential world of the helper, (2) the experiential world of the helpee, and (3) the for-the-most-part unconscious sociocultural experiences of the two.* The task of the anti-counselor is to clarify the cultural dimensions of the client's world. The anti-counselor and counselor generally do not speak to each other: An open struggle for power and control of the interview often occurs, and the counselor trainee becomes very aware of the unsaid thoughts and feelings of the helpee from another cultural setting.

The specific operation of the cross-cultural coalition model could be described in the following steps:

1. A *trainee* is selected who wishes to increase his or her understanding of cross-cultural issues.

2. Two individuals of another culture agree to assist the trainee's growth. They are ordinarily given advance in-

---

*Pedersen, in a personal communication (June, 1976), commented that the third force in the helping interview is broader than defined here. He states that the counselor and client bring years of socialization into the interview. "I see this third element as a third 'presence' almost in the sense of demonic possession coming from those troubling aspects of the client's life-space that made counseling necessary. To some extent the counselor contributes to that 'problem' by not understanding the client's culture. . . The task of the anti-counselor is not to *clarify* the cultural dimensions of the client's world (although that is hopefully the effect), but rather to fight for survival *against* the whole counseling alternative using the anti-counselor's cultural similarity with the client as the weapon." In this way, the client's *resistance* to the counseling process is made explicit. If the counselor is authentic, the client will move to the counselor; if the anti-counselor is more authentic, the client will move away from the counselor. The strong polarization of counselor and anti-counselor is basic to the Pedersen model.

struction in the model so as to serve more effectively as joint trainers. One individual serves as the *client* and discusses a real or role-played problem. The second individual, the anti-counselor, acts as an alter-ego to the client, giving constant emphasis to counselor errors and to the cultural background of the client. The anti-counselor constantly points out conscious or unconscious cultural biases on the part of the counselor and works actively against the counselor to sabotage the interview.

3. The counselor, client, and anti-counselor engage in a five- to ten-minute microcounseling-style session. However, all three individuals are on camera. The client may speak to either counselor or anti-counselor, but they may not speak to each other. In many cases, the counselor and anti-counselor end up vying for attention in a power struggle of two cultural viewpoints.

4. Pedersen has developed video vignettes depicting varying types of triad counseling situations. His vignettes include black/white, Asian/white, Hispanic/Anglo, and other cultural pairs. The model has also proved effective in male-female training. The appropriate model is shown to the group and discussed. The single skill emphasis of microcounseling is not stressed. The vignettes are designed to open broad areas of cultural discussion and reduce helper defensiveness.

5. The counselor, client, and anti-counselor view their own tape, and the client and anti-counselor give direct, immediate, and often powerful feedback to the counselor. In ideal conditions, the debriefing session following the interview is also taped. Thus, the helper is able to view self under two important and highly stressful situations. Pedersen also uses the two tapes for later critiquing in large groups.

Let us now consider an example of the program in action. In Episode Two of Pedersen's vignettes, we find a white male counselor working with a female graduate student from Ecuador. The anti-counselor is a woman graduate student from Brazil. The counselor appears open and honest when confronted by the client's problem that she is considered a flirt by campus males and she states that they are always trying to take sexual advantage of her. The anti-counselor moves freely about the room, sometimes standing directly between the counselor and the client (thus symbolizing the gap between two counselors). The anti-counselor constantly speaks of the fact that Spanish-speaking women cannot trust looser, more sexually aggressive United States males. Despite these handicaps, the counselor, through careful attending skills used in a concrete fashion, is able to clarify the problem. Just as the counselor appears to be truly reaching the client and starts to relax, the anti-counselor goes to work with a vengeance. The anti-counselor points out that the counselor is trying to get the client to "do what Americans do," which means eroding her identity as a Latin female. She points out to the client that the counselor is sitting with his legs open—a sexually provocative gesture in the culture of the client. She speaks to the client in Spanish. The counselor becomes tight in reaction to this cultural coalition, and the counselee verbalizes a strong desire to leave.

This brief summary shows some of the problems in cross-cultural communication and some of the specific aspects of the triad model which help illuminate crucial issues. Knowledge gained by trainees from this vignette includes many points, among them the continued importance of nonverbal communication in the interview and the crucial barrier of language. Viewing such a tape, trainees learn once again the importance of counselor genuineness in the interview, the importance of attending skills, and the need to be able to express oneself clearly via self-expression and influencing skills. The counselor's defensiveness manifested itself in posture, verbal denial, and some inability to attend to the central issues of the client. The counselor was easily taken off the track and attempted to justify his behavior rather than honestly state the situation as it was. Pedersen points out that all counselors make mistakes and the important issue is how counselors deal with their errors after they have been made. He suggests the skill of "recovery" as an important helping dimension. The reactions of the counselor, the client, and the anti-counselor to the vignette were as follows:

Doctor Robert Flint — Counselor

This experience gave me an insight into the fact that I tend to see foreign students as more vulnerable and fragile than Americans. This erroneous perception leads me to forget some basic principles of counseling and leaves myself open to manipulation and avoidance of their problem as I become entangled with *my* problem — a high N-Nurturance which can be very disruptive to counseling. My desire to "perform," to be a "good" counselor who can "help" the client and overcome "the problem" is usually under good control, but escapes my control easily when I encounter a person from another culture whose behavior I do not feel secure interpreting.

Client

My participation in the role-playing situation as well as viewing the edited videotape of the different role playings made me increasingly aware of the importance of the concept of the *anti-counselor*. The anti-counselor overwhelmed me at times, forcing me to express myself and feel in ways that I wanted to avoid, to the point that I felt frustrated when the role-playing session ended. This situation was not unrealistic; on the contrary, it reminded me of my past feelings and reactions when interacting with another individual such as a counselor or friend. After the role-playing, I had a clearer understanding that, under similar circumstances, the source for the interference had come from within me. The communication barriers I had felt in the past were not unlike those that I experienced when in the role playing the anti-counselor physically interfered between the counselor and me by getting up, or by talking to me in Spanish and mentioning my cultural values and beliefs. The latter in particular reminded me of situations in which intercultural values had blocked communications, especially when the other individual was not aware of my cultural background.

Elizabeth Gama — Anti-Counselor

Playing the role of a problem, which I myself have faced, was a real "trip." I was more than just the anti-counselor — I was the personalized hidden self, out in the open, exposing all contradictions, value conflicts, fears, expectations . . . that "are not supposed" to come out. We were completing each other. She, asking for help, wanting to grow; I, the fear of changing, of facing myself and society (Pedersen, 1973, p. 27).

The cross-cultural coalition model provides an opportunity to identify the client's issue from a broader perspective. Most helpers are satisfied to understand a client's background from their own theoretical perspective, completely unaware of how cultural blinders are limiting their ability to see the world as it is. As in microtraining, the cross-cultural model provides an opportunity for safe practice in learning the ways of another group or culture. Further, the triad model has implications beyond cross-cultural helping. It could be stated that no two individuals ever come from the same precise cultural background. Jails are cultures, different schools are cultures, ethnic neighborhoods are cultures, being handicapped is a cultural experience. The experiences of men and women are different. As such, the triad model can be employed effectively in numerous training situations where people come from different backgrounds. Pedersen believes that *all* counseling is cross-cultural to a greater or lesser extent. He points out that helpers can no longer assume that words and past experiences mean the same thing to their helpees that they do to them. At the same time, counseling between cultures is possible. Pedersen states that the two basic mistakes made by counselors are (1) underemphasizing the importance of the client's culture—"they are just like the rest of us"—and (2) overemphasizing cultural differences to the point that the other individual is considered deviant or is treated as a rare and fragile specimen.

The triad model is exciting and dynamic. The question may be asked, however, "Does it work?" Less systematic and precise (at least at present) than most approaches to microcounseling, can cross-cultural training via this model make a difference in helper behavior? Is it effective across subgroups and cultures?

The early evidence is encouraging and impressive. On a clinical basis, workshops in triad training have been successful in settings as varied as Japan, Latin America, and the United States and with groups ranging from prisoners to drug-dependent clients to male and female counselors. The model is always well received and is a highlight of any training workshop. Thus, it seems safe to conclude that the triad model can be used in virtually any setting with almost any type of group. Analysis of semantic differential scores reveals marked improvement in perceptions of helper effectiveness in cross-cultural settings. Pedersen, Holwill, and Shapiro (1976) have studied comparison groups of people trained via this method. Using the Carkhuff (1969a,b) scales of empathy, they found significant changes on all dimensions. Further research will delineate the process more completely and its effectiveness with a variety of individuals and groups.

SUMMARY

Research and training methods in the cross-cultural aspects of microtraining are clearly in their infancy. At this point, it seems clear that microtraining—with appropriate variations—is an effective technology for application to a wide variety of cultural-environmental-contextual situations.

This chapter began with statements about the failure of the helping professions to consider vital socioeconomic and cultural issues underlying the practice of helping. Discussing counseling psychology as "the innocent profession," Ivey (1973a) has commented on the excessive emphasis on the individual in the helping professions. While we must ultimately work with people as individuals, the failure to take into account family, large group, institutional, and cultural considerations is a failure to look at the full gestalt of the individual. Professional (and paraprofessional) helpers focus so much on the individual person that they may fail to see the context from which that individual comes. If a problem is lack of money, a reflection of feeling about how he or she feels about being hungry fails to meet the issue. If the problem is racial or sexual discrimination, the sexual or racial issue must be faced squarely and the degree to which it determines an individual's problem must be assessed. This definition may even mean that the professional helper moves out of his or her office and begins to act as an advocate for the fellow person whom we often term as helpee, client, interviewee, or patient.

The most powerful and direct method for cross-cultural training appears to be that of the cross-cultural triad model of Pedersen. Lively and exciting, it provides every individual with a meaningful introduction and then substantial practice in a variety of cultural issues in counseling. At this time, we consider the Pedersen model the most powerful technique for cross-cultural training.

However, it is our belief that moving all trainees directly into the Pedersen model may be inappropriate. Naive, inexperienced trainees can "wilt" under the pressure and barrage of words of the cross-cultural coalition model. Clinical experience suggests that training in basic microcounseling skills before induction into the rigorous methods of Pedersen is wise. If an individual knows what he or she is doing in terms of specific microtraining behaviors, the Pedersen model is learned more quickly and more profit seems to ensue. We believe this is because the trainee has labels for what is happening and skills to deal with crisis situations.

McDermott's work with low socioeconomic level individuals is particularly important, as it demonstrates that microtraining can work effectively with Chinese and Hispanic populations. Further, the fact that significant co-counseling benefits resulted is impressive and highly supportive of the psychoeducator model. At the same time, this study shows that the microtraining model can be integrated successfully with the well-known Carkhuff training system. The ultimate benefits of this combination of methods remain to be seen, particularly as this text presents a redefined set of concepts for teaching the qualitative dimensions of helping.

Microtraining's work in cultural-environmental-contextual issues must begin with careful systematic study of the highly specific dimensions of the training series in sexism and racism mentioned in conjunction with Ivey and Gluckstern and Jackson et al. When one considers that the basic study of attending behavior was conducted over ten years ago, one hopes that it does not take another ten years to clarify fully the microtraining implications of cross-cultural helping.

The preliminary study from the psychoeducator model by Noel clearly demonstrates that microcounseling techniques can be used to teach more effective communication skills to individuals from differing racial backgrounds. The direct training of clients in communication skills used in varying cultures may be ultimately a most important use of the microtraining paradigm.

Chapter 9

TOWARD IDENTIFYING CULTURALLY RELEVANT PROCESSES AND GOALS FOR HELPERS AND HELPEES*

T HIS CHAPTER will define the goal of helping as increasing people's competencies in the generation of verbal and nonverbal sentences. Microtraining seeks to develop a helper who has *"the ability to generate an infinite number of responses to any helpee statement"* (Ivey and Gluckstern, 1976a, p. 1). Chapter 7 on alternative theories in helping and Chapter 8 on cultural uses of microtraining illustrate the infinite array of possible responses available for any helper as content dimensions are added to basic skills.

However, it is clearly inappropriate to focus solely on creative new responses. Obviously, some responses are more effective in some situations than others. Certain theories are likely to be more effective with certain problems than others. Differing cultural and subcultural groups appear to require different approaches. *The central purpose of this chapter is to explore the possibility of determining the most appropriate method of helping for particular clients and client groups.*

Sue (1977) presents four conditions for counseling the culturally different. Interestingly, the model he provides for exam-

---

*Portions of this chapter are reprinted or adapted from Allen E. Ivey, The culturally competent individual, *Personnel and Guidance Journal, 55(7).* Copyright 1977, American Personnel and Guidance Association. Reprinted with permission. This chapter provides only a rudimentary introduction to issues of racism, sexism, and their like. See Katz and Ivey (1977) for a more complete statement on these issues.

ining cultural issues in counseling also is useful in comparing the appropriateness of alternative theoretical models of helping for different individuals within a single culture. This chapter will begin with a review of Sue's four conditions for counseling. This will be followed by a detailed examination of what makes for cultural expertise and the relationship of microtraining dimensions to personal effectiveness. Finally, this chapter will consider some issues, currently beyond the scope of microtraining, which must be considered as a more culturally relevant view of the helping process evolves over the next several years.

FOUR CONDITIONS FOR EXAMINING THE HELPING PROCESS

Approximately 50 percent of Asian-Americans, blacks, Chicanos, and Native Americans terminate counseling after the first interview. This may be compared with a 30 percent rate for Anglo or white clients (Sue, McKinney, Allen, and Hall, 1974; Sue and McKinney, 1975; Sue, Allen, Conaway, in press). Sue (1977) points out that "many Third World clients find the values of counseling to be inconsistent with their life experience." This same point could and should be extended to the counseling process as a totality. Many white-majority (at least "majority" in the United States) clients do not return for counseling either. It is clear that the helping profession is not reaching all those whom it could serve.

The client enters the helping process with a cultural, language, and social class heritage as well as having a unique personal history as an individual. The helping professions have too long assumed that individuals coming to them are of relatively similar background. Following Sue's (1977) thinking, it seems clear that (1) there must be a knowledge of a person's cultural background and experiences, (2) the characteristics of the helping process and values in particular theories of helping must be made more explicit, and (3) it should be possible to compare and contrast a helpee's needs with helping systems to determine if they are consistent, inconsistent, or — entirely possible — not even remotely connected.

Sue talks about four conditions for examining helping. The

conditions rest upon *processes* of helping (e.g. nature of theory, the skills a helper uses) and the *goals* of helping (e.g. insight, self-actualization, behavior change, here and now living). A client may be exposed to appropriate process and appropriate goals, appropriate process and inappropriate goals, inappropriate process and appropriate goals, or inappropriate process and inappropriate goals.

Condition I—Appropriate Process, Appropriate Goals

The helpee's life goals are considered, and the helper has available an array of processes, competencies, and skills to help the client achieve his or her ends. The effective helper will *know* the cultural background of the helpee and will have a grasp of several alternative methods which may be of assistance. These methods may range from direct advice and information giving to complex therapeutic techniques to direct instruction in skills via the psychoeducator model. In all these, necessary adaptations must be made to insure individual and cultural appropriateness.

Low socioeconomic level helpees, for example, may be concerned with survival on a day-to-day basis. Advice and suggestions are appropriate processes to achieve goals, and the microcounseling skill of expression of content with a focus on the helpee and the topic, e.g. food stamps, may be the most useful process skills to achieve the goal of survival. By way of contrast, a client coming in for a sexual difficulty may have the goal of successful sexual functioning, and the appropriate process may be a behavioral approach with skills of questioning, information giving, directions, and a prime focus on the helpee. On the other hand, if the middle-class helpee feels vaguely alienated from self and family, the goal may become oriented toward self-fulfillment and actualization of potential, and the processes may move more toward reflective attending skills, self-disclosure, interpretation, or direct-mutual communication on the part of the helper. Given a certain helping goal, it seems increasingly apparent that different means or processes may be used to achieve that goal. For example, the goal of self-actualization may be reached through Rogerian, Gestalt, or analytic processes. It may be noted in each case above that different processes oriented toward different goals could be utilized. A reflection of feeling might be of little use to the person seeking food stamps, while it might be helpful for the individual with a vague feeling of alienation. Conversely, advice and information might be useful in one case and not in the other. At a broader level, behavioral approaches may be the most effective processes for resolution of immediate sexual problems and analytic methods the most effective for discovering underlying long-term causes. The appropriateness of the process and the appropriateness of the goal are crucial considerations for the helper in meeting the needs of a particular helpee.

A pilot study conducted by Jude Berman of the University of Massachusetts in conjunction with Allen Ivey illustrates the potential of this approach. Groups of white males, white females, and Third World people were shown video stimulus vignettes of white and black helpees presenting job-related counseling problems. At the conclusion of the vignette, the observers were asked to write "what they would say if they were the counselor in the situation." The responses were then classified according to the Ivey Taxonomy. In terms of microcounseling skills, white males tended to ask more questions, white females used more reflection and paraphrasing, and Third World people more advice and interpretation. In addition, white groups focused primarily on the job problem as being individual or "I"-centered, whereas Third World people more often stressed the cultural and societal dimensions which often make individual job-search virtually impossible.

These are early findings, but they show real promise for future verification and study. It does appear that cultural, sexual, and group differences in terms of use of dimensions of the Ivey Taxonomy may lead to further delineation of the specific skills of helping suitable for differing cultural, socioeconomic, and personal backgrounds. Cross-cultural workshops in helping skills reveal clearly that peoples of differing cultural backgrounds respond differently to aspects of the microtraining paradigm. These experiences require research data to provide verification and amplification of clinical observations.

This preliminary research supports Sue's contention that

different groups and individuals need varying helping approaches. The most effective helper will be the one who can generate the most culturally and individually appropriate verbal and non-verbal helping sentences to communicate with a maximum number of individuals.

Condition II—Appropriate Process, Inappropriate Goals

The helping process selected may be in touch with the client's culture and/or personal needs but still may be oriented toward goals which are incompatible. Sue cites the example of using behavior modification to eliminate "fighting behavior" in a black ghetto student. The process is systematic and structured and takes much of the middle-class mystique out of helping, but the end goal puts the problem in the hands of the individual rather than the society which produced the problem. It is through procedures such as this that helping has been termed a pacification program by some experts (e.g. Steiner, 1975).

Generally speaking, professional helping has been much more effective in delineating processes than in delineating goals. A client may be brought into an interview seeking relief from anxiety. Behavior, existential, Gestalt, and psychoanalytic methods all have processes which encompass basic microtraining skills and may be useful in alleviating the problem. However, the different goals of "behavioral change," "being," "living in the here and now," and "insight" may be more or less appropriate depending on the needs and background of the individual helpee. The radical therapist or feminist helper might view all the processes above as relatively effective but would see them in terms of leading the helpee toward an inappropriate goal. The goal they might stress would focus more on society's effect on the individual, and the process might include consciousness-raising efforts.

Jackson's (1975a,b) black identity theory (discussed in the previous chapter) provides another illustration of the importance of relating process and goals in the helping session. If two black individuals were in a helping relationship, but the helper had a different consciousness level or world view from the helpee, it might be possible for the helper unconsciously to use effective processes to achieve goals counter to those of the helpee. This issue, of course, is complicated immensely when the helper and helpee are of different racial backgrounds. Similarly, the goals for low feminist consciousness male helpers with women may be inappropriate, even though processes of helping may be highly appropriate and effective. With the best of intentions, it is possible to achieve wrong ends. Jackson's theory is particularly helpful here, as it is one of the few helping theories which speaks directly to goal issues.

Which goal is appropriate for which client is an important value question which helping has yet to examine fully.

Condition III—Inappropriate Process, Appropriate Goals

"More often than not, counselors tend to use inappropriate strategies in working with the culturally different. Early termination is most likely to occur when the process is antagonistic to the values of the client and forces him/her to violate some basic personal values" (Sue, 1977). The helper "with the best of intentions" and appropriate goals may fail because the process is incompatible with personal values of the helpee.

Many Third World people, for example, find the value concepts of Carl Rogers and nondirective helping especially compatible in terms of respect for individuals and valuing empathy and warmth. However, the Rogerian process of paraphrasing, reflection of feeling, and summarization plus self-disclosure in more recent versions is incompatible with cultural patterns. Blacks, for example, may find the patient waiting and reflective tone of a Rogerian helper antagonistic even though values may be common. Many blacks find that self-disclosure is not comfortable for them (cf. Jourard and Lasakow, 1958; Dimond and Hellkamp, 1969) and thus are unwilling to share themselves when they don't know where the helper "is at."

In a similar fashion, many majority people find nondirective, client-centered helping uncomfortable. An action-oriented society such as the United States does not always have the patience to wait for the Rogerian mirror. On the other hand, many individuals find the quick, powerful approach of Gestalt unwelcome, or the technician-oriented behavior modification "dehumanizing," or the interpretive, insight-oriented analytic therapies "unrealistic" or oriented too much toward pathology.

Given any one individual, the helper's goal may be "noble" and in touch with the helpee's, but the process must also fit the individual and cultural background of the client. It seems unrealistic to expect any one helping theory to be able to reach *all* people. Yet it is apparent that many professionals are still arguing that their therapy or helping system is the "most effective."

Condition IV—Inappropriate Process, Inappropriate Goals

When process and outcome are not in synchrony with the helpee, it is most likely that early termination will occur. And in this type of helper-helpee matching, early termination may indeed be desired for the protection of the helpee. Sue talks about Asian-Americans who "may value restraint of strong feelings and believe that intimate revelations are to be shared only with close friends" and cites question asking, interpretation, and reflection of feeling as completely inappropriate. Goals and processes of helping are antithetical to cultural values.

Similarly, a majority of clients may come to the helping process with concerns which are also based on broad cultural or subcultural differences. An individual may come from a strong religiously-oriented home to a therapist who comes from an antireligious analytic orientation. The goal of "oneness with God" may conflict with such an orientation, and the client who might have been comfortable with some open sharing of thoughts and experiences coupled with some advice is frustrated by constant interpretation of every behavior and thought. The therapist is simultaneously frustrated, as he or she may have used very similar processes to good effect in the preceding interview with another client of a different background with different expectations.

Sue's work — designed as a study of cultural differences — has broad implications for the helping profession. It provides a general map and explanation of some very basic issues many helpers have missed. The ideas expressed here are mainly theoretical at this point, but it may be anticipated that research will verify some suggestions and sharpen others. It seems very safe at this point, however, to say that different people will respond differently to different helpers and helping theories. The larger the skill repertoire and cultural knowledge of the helper, the more individuals who may be reached.

CULTURAL EXPERTISE AND THE EFFECTIVE HELPER

Granted that different processes and goals are suitable for different client populations, a framework for more general objectives of helping is still needed. As stated in the introduction to this chapter, microtraining seeks to expand the response repertoire of the helper and enable him or her to generate an infinite number of responses to any helpee statement. Part of that response repertoire are the single skills, qualitative conditions, and alternative theoretical orientations delineated in earlier chapters.

The purpose of this section is to define the concept of cultural expertise and discuss its application to helper *and* helpee growth and change. In briefest form, *cultural expertise may be defined as the ability of an individual to generate verbal and nonverbal* sentences to communicate with a maximum number of individuals within a particular cultural setting* (Ivey, 1977).

Chomsky's work in linguistics (cf. 1957; 1965; 1968) provides the underlying framework for the idea of cultural expertise, although the concept is very different from ideas developed by Chomsky. Chomsky points out that individuals theoretically can use grammar to generate an infinite number and array of sentences. These sentences can be used to describe and communicate one's picture of the world. In truth, people have the capacity (or competence, in Chomsky's terminology†) to generate an infinite

---

*The concept of a nonverbal sentence is chosen over "behavior," as behavior is seen as a limiting concept which often exists without a sequential context. The concept of nonverbal sentence provides sequence and meaning for behavior.

†A potentially confusing issue is the term "competence." Chomsky distinguishes between competence and performance. A person is theoretically competent to generate an infinite array of sentences but may be unable to perform or demonstrate those sentences. Behavioral objectives terminology (cf. Mager, 1962; Burns and Klingstedt, 1973) tends to equate competence with performance. In our discussions, we will not deal with Chomsky's distinction but work with a more generalized definition of competence and expertise in the behavioral objectives' sense. Chomsky, of course, is talking only about verbal communication.

number of verbal and nonverbal sentences but are often limited in their ability to do so. Limitations in the ability to generate a full array of sentences — verbal and/or nonverbal — may come from limited education or social experience ("behavioral deficit"), emotional "blocks," Gestalt "splits" or "impasses," denial, projection, or any of an array of terms used by the helping profession to indicate the inability of a person to perform routinely.

Due to a lack of educational experience or to personal-emotional difficulties, many individuals are often *stuck* with routine and stereotyped patterns of words and behaviors. These words and behaviors represent the verbal and nonverbal sentences which people have generated to describe their world. The task of the counselor, interviewer, therapist, or psychological educator is to assist these individuals to generate new and more creative sentences to represent experience, thus unfreezing their approach to the world.

Thus, a major application of microtraining is in identifying new ways to help people increase their communication competence, to increase their behavioral repertoire, remove splits or impasses, resolve polarities . . . and in general to increase the number of verbal and nonverbal sentences people can generate. Microtraining, of course, is not a true generational grammar. Rather, it is a classification of many verbal and nonverbal sentences which has many characteristics of a true generational grammar. There are an infinite number of helping leads just as there are an infinite number of sentences; one can always think of a new microtraining lead to replace an old one. Each microtraining lead has a specific set of rules which define its use, and we know that using certain leads brings about certain predictable changes in client behavior. The taxonomy of microtraining leads makes possible the attachment of meanings to sounds and behaviors whereby one person's thoughts and behaviors can become another's. When helpers add theories of helping to their behavioral repertoire, e.g. Rogers, Freud, behavioral, their possibilities for responses multiply enormously.

This same basic objective, of course, may be applied to the counseling or psychotherapy client. A client may enter the helping relationship with a particular problem, polarity, confusion, or block with complete inability to generate any sentences to describe the situation or issue. After skillful work with the helper, the client is able to name or describe what is happening from new frames of reference. This in itself represents the first stage of helping, where clients are now able to generate at least several sentences to describe their life situations. Further work in the interview should lead to a client who can view the problem from a totally new and fresh perspective which is relevant to finding new solutions to old difficulties.

It is suggested that the basic competencies of the effective helper have direct analogies to competencies sought for effective helpees. Thus, both helper and helpees can aim to increase their ability to generate new sentences which hopefully will enable them actively to work through problem-related areas. Further, skills of verbal and nonverbal communication which make for effective helping also are relevant simply to being an effective person. Also, skills and qualities such as reflection of feeling, paraphrasing, giving of directions, and self-disclosure, concreteness, and respect are as useful to helpees as they are to helpers. While the central focus of the ensuing discussion will be on the helper, it is important to keep in mind that competencies identified and suggested for the helper have direct parallels for the helpee.

Let us now turn to a general definition of cultural expertise.

The culturally experienced and effective individual is able to generate an appropriate array of verbal and nonverbal sentences in his or her own culture. The individual becomes conversant with the fact that definitions of cultural expertise vary from culture to culture, subculture to subculture, and even from family to family or individual to individual. *Full* cultural expertise implies abilities in strength, knowledge, job skills. For purposes of this discussion, cultural expertise refers only to verbal and nonverbal communication competencies.

General notions about cultural expertise may be useful. However, the pragmatic question of the specifics of the culturally effective individual needs to be delineated as well. In effect, what does the culturally experienced and effective individual look like? How does one behave? What does one say and do to communicate cultural expertise?

First, let us consider the culturally ineffective individual who may be found in any large psychiatric institution. This person's nonverbal behavior is immediately determinable as markedly different from cultural norms. Eye contact may be bizarre, with constant staring or frequent eye contact breaks; the eyes may be on the floor. Unusual body language may be found in stereotyped or random movements. Vocal tone and speech rate may be noted as inappropriate. The verbal patterns may include "flight of ideas" and movement from topic to topic. Mixed verbal and nonverbal messages will be prominent. Racist or sexist slurs may be even more common than in the culture in general. This person is unable to generate verbal and nonverbal sentences which permit communication of the self.

Ivey (1973b), in work with psychiatric patients, demonstrated that teaching simple, culturally related skills, i.e. appropriate verbal and nonverbal behavior, to patients was sufficient to obtain release from the hospital. The thrust of the "media therapy" clinical effort was to illustrate that patients who can demonstrate culturally appropriate communication in terms of eye contact, body language, vocal tone, and verbal following behavior are minimally equipped to function within a culture.

As alluded to above, the transfer of cultural concepts from one culture to another must be done with care if cultural expertise is to be achieved. For instance, a workshop on counseling skills ran aground in Alaska when trainers stressed the importance of eye contact. It turned out that this particular group of Eskimos dealt with personally relevant material sitting side by side and specifically *not* maintaining eye contact. Similarly, eye contact may be a sign of hostility among certain Southwest Native Americans or among certain blacks. Hall (1976) studied film clips of Anglo and Native American walking styles and noted many differing patterns of body movement. What is appropriate verbal following behavior in one culture may be considered rude in another. The United States culture, for example, tends to be more direct in expression, while some Asian cultures leave the most important dimension of a conversation unsaid. Thus, attending may be considered a cultural universal, but it is not possible to state that attending manifests itself in the same fashion in the various subcultures of a society.

The first dimension of cultural expertise has been detailed in preceding paragraphs (patterns of nonverbal and verbal communication). It seems sufficient to add that minimal competence with one cultural subgroup, e.g. white majority males, does not ensure competence with another cultural subgroup, e.g. females. This point is important, as it suggests that we need not call men "sexist" but can rather describe them as ineffective and lacking cultural expertise. Similarly, individuals who appear effective within white middle-class culture are not necessarily equally skilled with those of another cultural grouping. Such individuals may not be "racist" but may be considered culturally inexperienced and ineffective. This, however, does not deny the reality of racism and sexism.

Figure 3 presents the Ivey Taxonomy of microtraining skills as it relates to the concept of cultural expertise. The taxonomy presents an orderly classification of skills which individuals use for communication and professionals use for counseling, psychotherapy, and psychological education. It will be noted that the IT focuses on the word "appropriate," and this is in accord with Sue's point that *appropriate* processes and goals are necessary for effective helping relationships. It may also be noted that the taxonomy is a process-oriented grouping of skills and does not deal with value issues and specifics of important cultural differences. Hall's *The Silent Language* (1959) is one map or framework for examining systematically communication differences among cultures. Chapter 8 represents microtraining's efforts toward a research-based cultural framework for helping. This issue is obviously in the early stages of development.

In the preceding section, we detailed how different skills and different theories may be appropriate for different individuals who seek help in the interview. The IT also stresses the qualitative dimensions of helping as well. Ways of showing respect or

THE CULTURALLY EXPERIENCED INDIVIDUAL

The individual with cultural expertise behaves appropriately to the culture and is able to generate an infinite array of verbal and nonverbal sentences to communicate with a maximum number of people. Few are competent in all skills with all members of their culture, and none is experienced with all cultural subgroups or with those of totally different cultural backgrounds. Each of the dimensions below is measurable.

1. The culturally experienced individual uses *culturally appropriate basic skills:* eye contact, body language, tone of voice, rate of speech and loudness, verbalization on acceptable topics. Style of usage of these skills varies with the cultural group.

2. The culturally experienced individual uses *culturally appropriate communication skills* to hear others and describe the self: attending skills of open and closed questions, minimal encourages, paraphrases, reflections of feeling, summarizations *and* influencing skills of directions, expressions of content, expressions of feeling (self-disclosure), influencing summarizations, and interpretations. These skills will be differentially appropriate in different cultures.

3. The culturally experienced individual uses *culturally appropriate qualitative skills* as an added dimension to communication: concreteness, respect and warmth, immediacy, confrontation, genuineness. Again, these skills vary as to use in different cultures.

4. The culturally experienced individual can *focus skillfully on a variety of culturally appropriate subjects:* self, other individuals, topics, group, cultural-environmental-contextual issues.

Figure 3.

immediacy, for example, will vary from culture to culture and from individual to individual within a single culture. It is inappropriate to take a helping technology and apply it to any group or any individual without careful consideration of the full range of available alternatives for communication. In effect, *communication of* empathy will vary from culture to culture.

To sum up, the effective helper will demonstrate skills of effective communication. Moreover, the helpee, as a result of working with an effective helper, will gain more and more skills, thus becoming more like a fully functioning, culturally experienced person. There are direct analogies between the skills of the helper and the skills which the helpee eventually attains and/or develops.

Appendix VII delineates the specific competencies of the helper and helpee in considerable detail. Discussed in this appendix are general competencies of helping associated with attending and influencing skills such as those outlined in the Ivey Taxonomy and in this chapter, competencies which may be used in determining the ability of the helper performing in alternative theoretical orientations, and competencies in producing specific client or patient outcomes. All these competencies are presented in some detail with specific outcome criteria and measurement suggestions.

"MATCHING" HELPER AND HELPEE

Thus far, we have indicated that the helper needs to have appropriate processes and goals available if he or she wishes to communicate effectively with the helpee. A standard of cultural expertise was presented as showing how the microtraining taxonomy might be related to issues of appropriateness in the helping process. The taxonomy appears to provide a map of some issues important in developing communication in the interview. The question to be considered only briefly in this section is *How can we determine which method of helping is most appropriate with which individual at what time?*

Currently, research on this basic issue in helping is incomplete. Microtraining has only recently entered the field as a systematic method to study this issue. However, presently available data suggest the following for consideration:

1. *Alternative theoretical orientations such as Gestalt, Rogerian, trait and factor, etc., use very differing patterns of helping skills.* The conversational conventions — both verbal and nonverbal — seem effective for different ends. Clients who wish to look at their feelings toward themselves will do well to consider nondirective helping. Those who wish to examine their past may prefer analytically oriented methods. Those who wish to solve specific problems may prefer trait and factor or Gestalt methods. The processes are different, and the goals are in many ways very different. Helping needs to consider matching the goals of the client with the goals of the helping intervention.

2. *All theoretical orientations seem to have much in common.* Particularly important among these are a constant focus on the individual (while simultaneously generally ignoring societal-cultural issues) and an emphasis on freeing the individual from polarities, blocks, mixed messages, etc., so that the client can get "unstuck" and generate new and more creative ways of interacting with his or her world. Regardless of theory or method, it seems that all helping methods seek to add to the client's repertoire of verbal and nonverbal behavior. The most direct approach to this issue, of course, is the psychoeducational framework, which teaches skills directly and immediately without the indirectness associated with counseling, interviewing, and therapy. If freeing the individual for more creative responses is a general goal, it may be possible to test the efficiency of different helping methods to achieve this end. While helping methods have broadly conceived goals which differ markedly from each other, commonalities such as this may point the way toward research which enables us to determine which method is more effective for specific ends.

3. *Data from anthropology, sociology, and now increasingly from interviewing suggest that individuals of differing cultural and subcultural backgrounds have differing needs and will respond differently to theories of helping including microcounseling.* Early research suggests this as an important and promising area for matching helper and helpee. However, the specification of appropriate variables has only begun, and *no* specification of variables will ever cover the wide range of individual variation which exists in a culture. Thus, while matching on these characteristics may generally be sought, we must remember that individual differences and individual treatment probably will always be necessary.

4. *Research presented in Chapter 8 on the cultural-environmental-contextual in microtraining suggests that this video approach may be used as a laboratory to sort out the many variables in cross-cultural helping.*

5. *Out of research and evaluation in the helping interview and the cultural dimensions of that process may emerge a unified explanation of the helping process.* Basic to that explanation appears to be Sue's (1977) concept of four conditions of helping with consideration of culturally appropriate processes and goals. The model of the culturally effective individual provides some aspects of the necessary matching between helper and helpee.

Thus, in no way is it possible for microtraining to answer the question of "which therapy for which individual under what conditions?" But, at this time we do appear to have some clear ideas of what should not be done and what represents some inappropriate matches of helpers and helpees. Perhaps in a future statement it will be possible to give more complete guidelines as to what represents appropriate behavior on the part of the helper in the interview.

Finally, it must be noted that the culturally experienced and effective helper appears in many ways similar to the culturally effective helpee. It seems logical that identifying specific high level skills of the helper and teaching them directly to the helpee may be a useful adjunct or supplement — and in some cases a complete replacement — to the helping interview.

SUMMARY

This chapter has presented preliminary data and thinking for determining the most appropriate method of helping a particular client or client group. Sue has developed a model for counseling the culturally different which appears to have implications for all helpees. His framework posits appropriate and inappropriate processes and goals in the helping interview. In an ideal helping relationship, the helper will use appropriate helping processes and appropriate goals for each helpee. However, a variety of less desirable matches are possible. For example, the helper may use appropriate processes with inappropriate goals, or inappropriate processes with appropriate goals, or both goals and processes may be inappropriate. A number of examples of each type of goal and process dimension were delineated.

The concept of cultural expertise was then presented. The culturally effective and experienced individual is able to generate a wide array of verbal and nonverbal sentences so as to communicate with a maximum number of individuals. The Ivey Taxonomy was presented as it relates to this concept, and specific microtraining skills were examined for their relevance under cultural scrutiny. It is suggested that the IT may serve as a vehicle to compare communication among peoples of different cultures or among therapists of differing orientations within standard United States helping theories.

Finally, the issue of matching helper and helpee was discussed. While it was indicated that effective matching is not possible at this time, the helping field does seem to be at a stage where ineffective matches of helpers and helpees may be identified and thus awkward helping sessions avoided. Later research and clinical observation may lead to more detailed and precise specification of desired helping relationships. However, it was stated that individual variation within a culture may never be fully planned for, and thus having a maximum array of responses available is even more necessary.

Chapter 10

MICROTRAINING AS USED IN OTHER SETTINGS

KAY GUSTAFSON

T HE TERM *microtraining* refers to the general training format characterized by single skill emphasis, presentation of models, feedback—often through observational media, and positive supervision. This general paradigm has been most extensively used in the microteaching program to train undergraduate teaching students in basic teaching skills and in the microcounseling program to train graduate counseling students in basic counseling skills. The possible range of microtraining, however, is in no way limited to these skills or these populations. Conceivably, one could design a program to teach nearly any skill to nearly any trainee using a microtraining paradigm. In addition, the format itself is open to modifications to suit particular situations or trainees. This flexibility of microtraining in terms of innovations with new populations, variations in skills, and adaptations of the format has been aptly demonstrated by many of the exciting new programs to be summarized here. A major trend in these innovations has been the extension of training beyond academia to work settings and directly to clients themselves.

Before exploring these applications to new populations, however, we will examine some changes in the microtraining of the original target populations — students of teaching and counseling. In general, this presentation will be organized in terms of trainee populations, with variations in skills and format noted within each group.

TEACHER TRAINING

The original microtraining package, microteaching, was developed at Stanford University by Allen (1967), Aubertine (1967), and their colleagues. The microteaching format is basically identical to that of microcounseling except that the skills are basic teaching skills, the teacher instructs a small group of students (four or five) for a longer period (five to twenty-five minutes), and the teacher's lesson is designed as a small, self-contained unit as opposed to the microcounseling practice interviews which are open-ended and terminated at a fixed time by the supervisor.

A formal "package" of film models of microteaching skills is now sold commercially. Allen, Ryan, Bush, and Cooper (1969) have developed eighteen microteaching skills and organized them into the following five "skill clusters":

1. Response repertoire
   a. Verbal responses
   b. Nonverbal responses
   c. Verbal and nonverbal responses
2. Questioning skills
   a. Fluency in asking questions
   b. Probing questions
   c. Higher order questions
   d. Divergent questions
3. Creating student involvement
   a. Set induction
   b. Stimulus variation
   c. Closure
4. Increasing student participation
   a. Reinforcement
   b. Recognizing attending behavior
   c. Silence and nonverbal cues
   d. Cueing
5. Presentation skills
   a. Completeness of communication
   b. Lecturing

c. Use of examples

d. Planned repetition

The literature on microteaching has become extensive, and research efforts suggest that microteaching techniques facilitate learning and make teacher education less ambiguous. Turney, Clift, Dunkin, and Traill (1973) report that over half of American teacher education institutions utilize some form of microteaching. Although long established in training primary and secondary teachers, Perlberg and Bryant (1968) have introduced microteaching into the college setting in group and individual models. More recently, Perlberg, Peri, and Weinreb (1970) have extended the microteaching model to the professional training level in the training of dental educators at Tel Aviv University in Israel.

Despite this popularity of the microteaching approach, some evidence suggests the need to supplement the teaching skills outlined previously with basic counseling or relationship skills similar to many of the microcounseling skills. Although the goals of microteaching are to teach skills which increase student participation and involvement, Chadbourne's (1975) recent analysis of the model films revealed a traditional teacher-centered approach, with a lack of attention to affect and interpersonal process (out of 2,000 teacher statements, only four reflection of feeling statements were counted). Microteaching skills tend to focus on control of students and imparting information. It would seem that the use of some microcounseling skills might assist teachers in listening more effectively to children, particularly if education is viewed as a two-way process.

In response to this need, a behavioral objectives curriculum in human relations training (Ivey and Rollin, 1972) was utilized as a regular portion of the teacher training program at the University of Massachusetts. In this program, a variety of learning techniques including microtraining are used in human relations hierarchies based on behavioral objectives. Each hierarchy focuses on a single human relations skill area in a "do-use-teach" model. Programs were developed in over thirty areas, ranging from self-control of physiological responses to listening skills and from empathy to organizational change.

Participants are first asked to demonstrate their ability to engage in, for example, attending behavior as taught in the microtraining framework. However, demonstration of the ability to engage in a behavioral skill is insufficient in itself and raises a major question, namely "How can the behavioral skill be transferred to daily life?" As a final step, the trainee must demonstrate the ability to teach some aspect of attending behavior to others. Trainees have taught attending behavior to children, family, and friends using many innovative methods and concepts which the project staff have in turn used to enrich and enliven their own teaching. Additional skills are currently being developed, and a human relations laboratory-library is anticipated, wherein students may be oriented to the skills content of the program and self-select those skills appropriate to their own needs. The involvement of individuals in selecting their own areas for behavioral change may prove an important and facilitating method for increasing individual personal growth.

In a much shorter (six-hour) workshop format, Hemmer (1974) also used a microtraining approach to train education students in the facilitative skills of openness, sharing of experiences, listening, and feedback. This proved to be a workable and one of the most popular aspects of the entire teacher training program. The success and popularity of this program points to the need the trainees felt for these type of skills and to the flexibility of the microtraining format in fitting the needs and limitations of various settings.

Finally, microcounseling has recently been joined with the well-known classroom tool, the Flanders Interaction Analysis System (FIAC) (Flanders, 1970). The FIAC has been widely used to analyze student-teacher interaction and to encourage more "indirect," i.e. more student-centered, teaching. However, the FIAC simply points out that teachers are oriented to content and not to pupils and provides no systematic instruction in how to change behavior. Bradley (1976) designed a study in which teacher classrooms were studied via the FIAC, microcounseling training was instituted, and a posttraining FIAC analysis was conducted.

All of these microcounseling skills training programs offer an exciting enhancement to the training of future elementary and secondary teachers. Even greater need for such training may exist, however, among teachers of higher education and supervisory teachers. A modification of the Enriching Intimacy Program (discussed in detail in the next chapter) has also been used to teach the behavioral components of genuine, warm, empathic relating to a variety of persons connected with medical education (Authier and Gustafson, 1975b). Trainees have ranged from M.D.s and nurses to librarians, veterinarians, and media personnel. In addition, Bradley (1975a) has used microtraining with supervisory teachers to help them learn to relate more effectively to the teachers they supervise.

The two major areas of change in the microtraining of teachers would thus seem to be the addition of training in basic human relations skills to the microteaching training and the extension of training in both these areas to teachers in higher education. Both of these changes emphasize the belief in the two-way (teacher/ student) nature of effective teaching and the importance of modeling, as a teacher, the kind of communication wanted from the students.

COUNSELOR TRAINING

As the microcounseling program has been refined and expanded in recent years, graduate students in counseling and clinical psychology have remained primary trainee populations. In addition to the training in the basic microcounseling skills, however, these groups have been the targets of microtraining in an exciting variety of more specialized types of skills. The skills of the programs to be reviewed here have ranged from training in different aspects of interventions such as timing, to training in skills related to a specific type or school of therapy, to training in the skills of other counselor roles such as consultation or supervision. Many of these have been quite limited programs, but they do suggest several possibilities for more widespread adoption and future developments. The format throughout has remained basically a microtraining paradigm, although some modifications in structure will be noted as we briefly explore each of these skills packages.

Rather than focus on the content of counselor verbalizations, Elsenrath, Coker, and Martinson (1972) chose to focus on timing aspects. Using an audiotaped programmed teaching program incorporating a microteaching component, they successfully trained undergraduate dormitory counselors to (1) increase the length of silence before responding to interviewee statements and (2) decrease the length of their own responses.

Also concerned with time, but in the broader sense of phases of a single interview, Greenall (1969) has developed a series of short videotape excerpts which represent positive and negative behavioral models of various phases of the interview. Section one of his videotape focuses on beginning the interview and presents models of positive and negative seating relationships, listening to client's viewpoints, and noting the client's feeling. Each specific point is identified by commentary. Section two of the tape focuses on observing the client's nonverbal communications, while section three focuses on responding to the client. In these sections, listening and questioning skills are stressed. The final section of the tape illustrates methods of summarizing the interview, giving advice, and terminating the session.

Rather than focusing on single skills and letting the trainee place them into a larger framework at a later point, Greenall provides a structure wherein the trainee may actually see the relevance and place of specific skills in the actual interview setting. The danger of the single tape, however, is that the trainee can be overwhelmed by too much data or information. To avoid this difficulty, a revised edition of Greenall's program treats each section of the tape as a complete program in itself, and more time is spent focusing on the specific skills he wants to convey to the trainee. Each section builds on the previous section.

Used in this way, Greenall's method could be a particularly promising one. It may be very desirable to combine the broad conceptual framework he suggests with the single skills approach. The Enriching Intimacy Program, which will be described in detail in the next chapter, also combines a broader conceptual framework (respect—empathy—genuineness) with a single component skills emphasis. In both programs, each phase builds on the prior phase.

A related program developed by Thielen (1970) also focuses on the development of a broader skill—accurate empathic responses. Rather than focus on component skills in a traditional microtraining format as the Enriching Intimacy Program does, he utilizes some interesting format modifications and remains concentrated on the global skill. Thielen's method is a three-hour session in which the counseling supervisor, the trainee, and counselee work together for mutual facilitation. The thirty-minute presession includes only the supervisor and trainee. The trainee reads a written manual on accurate empathy, views a tape with three levels of empathy demonstrated, and role-plays empathy. The supervisor and the trainee then plan for the upcoming session and discuss how they can use the tri-relationship for "maximum help for all concerned." Next, the trainee and supervisor hold a thirty-minute co-counseling session with the client. During this session, both operate as counselors and seek to develop an understanding of the client. The supervisor and the trainee hold a thirty-minute postsession in which the trainee rates the supervisor's and his or her own behavior against the description in the written manual. Role playing of specific behaviors and appropriate feedback are part of this session. If necessary, the models of empathy are again shown. A second thirty-minute co-counseling session is then held with the client. Near the end of this session, the client is encouraged to give feedback to the trainee. A final postsession of forty-five minutes reviews the entire procedure and stresses the skills taught within the session. This procedure was found to facilitate trainee ability to respond in standardized counseling situations and also increased the trainee's self-concept.

Thielen's use of microtraining techniques in conjunction with co-counseling, the complex counseling skill of empathy, and the actual counseling of a client illustrates an interesting modification of the basic microtraining framework. The juxtaposition of different media and approaches seems a particularly promising avenue for counselor training, especially when complex skills of therapy are under consideration.

The programs developed by Elsenrath, Greenall, and Thielen each focused on skills related to some aspect of generalized counseling technique. Several other programs, however, have been developed to train counselors in the specialized skills related to a particular mode or school of counseling. The first of these groups to be presented here is Wallace, Horan, Baker, and Hudson's (1975) training program for counseling graduate students in decision-making counseling. Their focus was on counseling aimed at facilitating client decision making. They selected eleven counselor behaviors that operationally defined the process of helping clients arrive at wise decisions. These behaviors were as follows: (a) define the problem as one of choice; (b) explain the decision-making paradigm; (c) identify possible alternatives; (d) gather relevant information from the client; (e) present relevant information to the client; (f) request that the client identify advantages and disadvantages for each alternative; (g) present any additional advantages and disadvantages for each alternative to the client; (h) request that the client select the most promising alternative; (i) verbally cue and reinforce the client for gathering additional information about the most promising alternative; (j) help the client implement the alternative; and (k) maintain neutrality concerning what the client ought to do. They found the microcounseling format significantly more effective than a traditional (lecture-reading-films) method of promoting student acquisition of decision-making counseling skills.

Similarly, Flowers and Goldman (1976) have successfully used a program similar to microtraining to train mental hospital paraprofessionals in the techniques of assertion training.

Turning from individual counseling skills to group counseling skills, Moreland (1973) has developed a set of nine basic group facilitation skills. These include expectation clarification, external to internal focus, refocusing from the individual to the group, group-oriented meaning attribution, encouraging thematic sequential mutual self-disclosure, facilitator nonverbal behavior, confrontation, the silent member, and introduction of action and exercises into the group's work. This approach has been used to train graduate students at Southern Illinois University as beginning group facilitators in personal growth groups. The manuals differ from the traditional microcounseling model in that they combine both descriptions of facilitator behaviors and a particular philosophy of group process. The basic behaviors would seem to be applicable across many types of group counseling, however, and trainers in other settings may want to edit and rewrite the philosophy to match their own approach.

These three programs only begin to touch the possible therapy approaches which could be defined in terms of specific component skills and taught to therapists within a microtraining format. The behavioral approaches would be the most easily adapted, but nearly any school of therapy could potentially be taught in this manner. Such programs would seem to be a possible major area of future development of microtraining for the counseling student populations. A second major area of possible development is the definition and training of other aspects of the counselor's role aside from direct client contact. Indeed, the skills needed in two such important counselor roles, those of consultation and supervision, have already been trained within microtraining formats.

Goodwin, Garvey, and Barclay (1971) developed a program called microconsultation to train school psychologists in the skills needed to serve as behavioral consultants to classroom teachers. The program concentrates basically on the skills needed to conduct with the classroom teacher a behavioral analysis of his/her classroom and identify those environmental changes which may help a student to learn new ways of behaving. The consulting behaviors trained were in two major categories: (1) structuring the interview—explaining behavior analysis, targeting problem behavior, and maintaining rapport—and (2) environmental assessment—identifying target behaviors, antecedents, consequents, and reinforcers, interpreting learning terms, summarizing, planning change, collecting data, and rehearsing behavior. The focus of Goodwin's program throughout is not on training the counselor to work as a behavioral analyst on a primary change agent level but rather on training in how to work with a classroom teacher to enable that teacher to learn to be a behavioral analyst for his/her own classroom. The microconsultation training is specifically for a consultation role.

The second major counselor role that has been trained under a microtraining format is a supervising role. Moore (1974) has systematically trained mental health professionals to supervise paraprofessionals. Using a combination of microcounseling technology and the Moore and Delworth (1972) behavior change training models, he trained five specific tasks in the process of supervising, each of which included specific behavioral strategies for task accomplishment. The tasks were as follows: assess the paraprofessional's beginning skill level, teach the paraprofessional how to make use of supervision, teach the paraprofessional the necessary skills for successful completion of the job, help the paraprofessional deal with ambivalence and anxiety about being evaluated, help the paraprofessional identify and eliminate over-extension.

For the graduate counseling student population, then, the basic microcounseling skills packages have been supplemented by training in the skills of specific aspects of basic counseling, in those related to particular therapy modes and in those related to consultant and supervisory roles. The flexibility of the micro-training format is impressive. Hopefully, these experimental programs are the forerunners of many more innovative applications of microtraining in the skills of therapy approaches and roles. Equally notable to this expansion of skills packages for counseling students has been the extension of basic microcounseling training to paraprofessionals and professionals in other fields. This extension is the focus of the next section.

PARAPROFESSIONAL COUNSELOR TRAINING

The training of paraprofessionals has been a particularly fruitful area for the concise and specific microcounseling approach, in that time limitations and limited trainee backgrounds characterize most such programs. Counseling aides (Haase and DiMattia, 1970; Cowles, 1970), drug counselors (Gluckstern, 1972, 1973; Authier and Gustafson, 1975a; LaFrance, 1970), campus peer counselors (Dorosin, D'Andrea, and Jacks, 1976; Scroggins and Ivey, 1976), dormitory counselors (Danish, 1970), day camp leaders (Zeevi, 1970a,b), hot line volunteers (Zeevi, 1970a,b; Hearn, Uhlemann, and Evans, 1975), manpower counselors (Greenall, 1969), employee assistance interview counselors (Munz, Villa, Slipow, Reynolds, Minski, Gustafson, and Authier, 1976), and teaching aides (Collins, 1970) have all received some form of microcounseling training as part of their preparation. Most of the paraprofessional programs have concentrated on training in basic counseling skills and have not been leaders in the development of new skills packages. They have been important, however, in demonstrating the applicability of the micro-counseling approach to a wide range of ages and educational levels as well as the flexibility of the format itself. Many of these programs have involved successful and ingenious modifications of the format to fit particular limitations of the training situation. Several of these programs will be discussed in later chapters, and these will not be presented here as we focus on the format innovations for this population.

One such format is the individualized approach adopted by Cowles (1970) in microtraining mental health paraprofessionals in a junior college. He did not preselect skills but instead had each trainee briefly interview a volunteer client. Trainees were asked to select the skills on which they would like to improve. Individual behavioral training programs were devised where necessary. Clinical observation revealed that this was an especially successful and popular feature of the training program.

Zeevi (1970a,b) made an effort to blend dyadic experience in microtraining with group process. Microtraining was a regular part of the paraprofessional training program at the Jewish Community Center of Springfield, Massachusetts. Attending behavior concepts were taught in three different areas: (a) leadership training programs for teenagers, (b) training leaders for the Center's day-camp program, and (c) training volunteers for the "hot line," a telephone counseling and referral service for teens operated by Springfield College. The dyadic instruction phase followed group training procedures similar to those employed by

Haase and DiMattia with paraprofessionals. Each trainee alternately acted as a listener and an expresser and obtained feedback from the group and the supervisor. The group process phase involved informal group exercises in self-expressive and attending behavior. This often included mutual feedback between an individual and the group on the verbal and nonverbal behavior trained in the dyadic phase.

In the area of lay drug counselor training, Gluckstern (1972; 1973) also combined some microtraining with other group approaches. She preceded her forty-hour drug information and counseling skills training phase by a twenty-hour structured encounter experience designed to "unfreeze" the volunteers and thereby facilitate openness during later parts of the training program. She found that the trainees did learn the skills and maintained them over a period of seven months. Two program features which seem to have influenced retention here and which may be useful additions to future programs were the continued self-supervision in counseling skills that the trainees provided as they listened to one another's tapes in their peer "support groups" and the self-rating forms that the trainees completed and returned after each field counseling session to evaluate their use of the skills learned during training.

LaFrance (1970) also applied the microcounseling model to train counselors in a faculty-student drug education and counseling center. He found that the specific skills of microtraining are taught most effectively as an adjunct to group process. When a specific issue in drug education or treatment comes up and the need for a specific skill is apparent, LaFrance employs on-the-spot microtraining with videotape equipment. He has found that the immediate use of the framework has been effective in imparting counseling skills. He states that more traditional forms of microtraining have proven less successful and that these students feel a greater sense of immediacy and involvement in training through this more spontaneous method.

Hearn, Uhlemann, and Evans (1975) modified the microcounseling manuals for hot line workers and compared microcounseling and sensitivity training. They concluded that microcounseling leads to better performance with respect to specific skills and that both microcounseling and sensitivity training lead to better performance than no training with respect to general skills.

The area of peer counseling is a growing area of paraprofessional activity, especially on college campuses, which has necessitated adaptations of the microcounseling programs to serve a large paraprofessional counselor population with rapid turnover. Student interns working in the Division of Student Services of LaGuardia Community College of the City University of New York are required to participate in training in twelve microcounseling skills as part of the peer counselor training program offered by the Human Development Center. This center is a centralized continuing resource for all of the campus peer counseling programs.

In a similar area, Danish (1970) trained one large group consisting of 250 dormitory counselors in direct-mutual communication. The counselors divided into dyads and talked for five minutes. A programmed text was passed out, and an experienced couple demonstrated various types of open communication on the stage. The dyads then discussed among themselves how their session compared with the model and the text. Second and third five-minute sessions were then conducted. During the session, a roving group of previously trained counselors met with groups around the room. This use of previous trainees as trainers is reinforcement of their previous learning through an implementation of the do-use-teach model. Elizabeth Collins used a similar large group do-use-teach approach in an experimental program in the Dade County school system in Miami, Florida, where she taught attending skills to a group of high school students who serve as teacher aides. These students, who assist English teachers, are, in turn, teaching attending behavior to fellow students as part of their duties.

The *Stanford Observer* (1975) has reported that well over 100 peer counselors, trained by professionals, are helping at the University in such varied fields as job hunting, homosexuality, contraceptives, study habits, and minority and foreign student concerns. They are taught with microtraining-type videotapes, role-playing, and workbooks in a seven-week course. Evaluation by Dorosin, D'Andrea, and Jacks (1976) reveals that trainees are skilled and that student use of professional helpers seems to be increased by successful peer counseling programs.

Work settings are also beginning to apply the peer counselor concept in employee assistance programs. A modified microtraining format was recently used (Munz et al., 1976) to train interviewer/counselors for the Public Health Administration's assistance program for its own employees. The role of these interviewers, who come from all levels within the various agencies and who perform these duties in addition to their regular jobs, is to provide a confidential referral service to community agencies for their troubled peers. This intensive program combined microtraining in basic relationship skills with a group support base and specific issue-oriented teaching.

In reviewing these applications of microtraining to a wide variety of paraprofessional trainees, the possibilities for modifications and additions to suit particular circumstances or populations are evident. Hopefully, this speaks for the flexibility and vitality of the microtraining format and is only the beginning of other creative modifications. Indeed, such modifications are by no means limited to paraprofessional training programs. Clear support for this contention is apparent in the programs developed for the other important new consumer groups for basic counseling skills—students of related helping professions.

TRAINING IN THE RELATED HELPING PROFESSIONS

The extension of microtraining beyond psychology to a variety of other helping professions is a particularly exciting development in that it may be a sign of some lessening of traditional professional provincialism and may point to the possibility of greater sharing and cross-fertilization between the fields in the future. As in paraprofessional training, the basic relationship or counseling skills have been applied across fields and adopted virtually unchanged, but format modifications to meet equipment and time limitations have been abundant.

In a training program for social workers at Indiana University, Bloom (1970) modified the microcounseling format to accommodate for the lack of videotape equipment. He rewrote several of the manuals and used role playing and discussion in groups of three with the third person serving as the feedback mechanism. A similar triad arrangement has been used by several trainers in large workshop formats where videotape equipment is sparse. In these cases, available video units are used to show model tapes and, on a rotating or voluntary basis, for practice interviews. Such a format has been used by Authier and Gustafson to train social work students in the Enriching Intimacy Program.

The health care professions constitute an important group in both the prevention and early identification of emotional problems. Fortunately, the value of a humanistic approach to the treatment of the whole person and the need for training in relationship skills are being increasingly recognized in the health fields. Among the health professions, psychiatric nursing personnel (Authier and Gustafson, 1976b; Hearn, 1976), medical students (Moreland, Ivey, and Phillips, 1973; Authier and Gustafson, 1974), physician assistants (Gustafson and Authier, 1976), speech therapists (Irwin, 1970), and family practice residents (Authier, 1976) have been trained in microcounseling skills. The Enriching Intimacy Program has been used with medical students (Gustafson, 1975) and is a regular course in the first-year physician assistant curriculum at the University of Nebraska Medical Center. The class has been conducted in both a regular quarter course and weekend marathon formats. The eight-session relationship skills course offered to the freshman medical students at the same institution alternates small group microcounseling skills training sessions with sessions centered on the review of videotaped interviews which two of the trainees have conducted with patients during the prior week. This opportunity to apply or see the skills in a more "real" setting and to give and receive feedback on their usage is designed, in part, to improve generalization.

The University of Nebraska Medical Center Family Practice Residency Program carries this a step further by providing a two-day marathon modified microtraining workshop in the Enriching

Intimacy skills and subsequently requiring regular supervisory reviews, including frequency counts of skills usage of videotaped interactions with actual patients for each resident. First-year residents are taped each month, second-year every two months, and third-year as needed or requested. To further enhance generalization, the model tapes used in training are segments taken from actual previous resident-patient interaction. This modification of the microtraining format was adapted in part to fit the rigorous time demands of a residency program. Although the format continues to focus on specific skills and makes heavy use of videotape feedback, it condenses the presentation of a number of skills into a shorter time span, uses limited role-play practice, and relies heavily on extended practice and feedback on the usage of all the skills in longer interactions.

The flexibility of the microtraining format demonstrated by these programs was previously noted. Perhaps more importantly, however, these programs point to an increased flexibility of thinking in labeling or categorizing the uses and value of the micro-counseling skills. The recognition of the usefulness of basic counseling skills to this variety of professionals who are not always, or even usually, defined as counselors suggests that these skills may be conceptualized as basic communication or relationship skills. This reconceptualization in turn suggests their potential usefulness in other relationships and opens the door for the extension of microcounseling training to many new groups. Until this point, all of the trainee populations we have considered have been helpers or providers of services of some type. In the next section, however, we are turning to programs aimed at the direct training of the usual recipients of help—students, psychiatric patients, counseling clients, and, most exciting of all, people in general who wish to learn how to relate to others more effectively. This psychoeducational shift in emphasis from helper to helpee training is the trend in microtraining today which offers the greatest potential for expanded application of the paradigm as well as continued creative modifications to fit the needs of these populations.

STUDENT TRAINING

As noted before, fortunately, the importance of offering teachers specific training in communicating more effectively with their students is being recognized today. The value of such systematic training for students has received much less attention. Yet if teachers can be taught specific skills to increase their effectiveness as teachers, a reasonable assumption is that students can also be taught specific skills to increase their effectiveness as students.

One important aspect of the student role is the basic microcounseling skill of attending behavior. Ivey and Hinkle (1970) convincingly demonstrated the power of simple attending by teaching a group of six college students attending behavior and then videotaping their seminar in a psychology course. By deliberately varying their level of attending behavior on preset signals, the students were able to dramatically change the teaching style of the teacher who remained unaware of their manipulation. Perhaps most significantly, however, their feigned attending became real attending as the professor became more involved with them. Students generally do not realize the power they have to influence their classroom experiences. Through the judicious use of attention and listening skills, students can have more involvement in the direction of their learning than most would consider possible. This experiment demonstrates the joint responsibility of teacher and student for what goes on inside the classroom.

Middle-class students often develop the skills of being successful students naturally. Other students, particularly those from disadvantaged backgrounds, have not learned the behavioral dimensions of "studenting." Microtraining procedures offer an avenue to teach students some aspects of successful academic work. Many of the microcounseling skills may be applicable to students, and further efforts are needed to identify specific studenting skills. Luckily, the same skills that are useful as students also apply in many other roles of the person's life. Training in basic communication skills can thus have the double effect of enhancing both the present learning experience and future living.

Bradley (1975b) addressed himself specifically to the problems of disadvantaged students. He has used microcounseling training as a direct, systematic interpersonal skills development program for inner city youth. The microtraining format has been adapted for nonreaders and is designed to be relevant to inner-city residents. The course is offered as part of a vocational education class, and usually the first skills are something like "listening skills for the salesperson." Soon, however, other areas of interpersonal communication—vocational or social—are covered. Reading is not required. The teacher may explain the skill or use a videotape of another person explaining the skill. Role-plays set up in a familiar, culturally relevant setting by volunteers doing as many things wrong as possible are very useful in capturing the interest of the members. Small groups discuss, develop good models, and practice. Central to this approach is that the specific skill being developed is defined and presented in concrete form by the group itself. The skills trained are those seen as needed and useful by the trainees. A favorite topic is "another dull meal with your mate."

Aldrige and Ivey (1975) taught junior high school students the skills of attending behavior via a microtraining format. Data reveal that this younger population can be taught skills of microtraining as easily as adults. Many junior high students are shy and cannot talk to members of the opposite sex easily. Training in skills of self-expression appears to be useful to these youngsters. Direct-mutual communication has also been found to be useful as a skill to facilitate marital communication (Andes, 1974), and it would seem that this, plus other skills such as parenting skills (Bizer, 1972), might be useful as an addendum to marriage and the family courses in college and high school.

Schwebel (1970) used a combination of informal small groups plus specific behavioral material in a way which was content relevant to his course while also enhancing his students' skills. He utilized four microcounseling skills in a thirty-member undergraduate introduction to clinical psychology course. The first assignment given to the class is to outline "what a clinical psychologist would have to know about you in order to begin to understand you." Schwebel states that this is then discussed among the students in small groups and used by them as a basis on which to develop interviewing topics useful in understanding others. Before their first interview with a fellow student, microcounseling manuals are introduced. Interviewing and the interviewer then become the focus of discussion for the following two weeks. Schwebel's students thus had the opportunity to look at counseling from an experiential point of view and learn some skills which improved their participation and learning in discussions.

Crabbs and Jarmin (1976) advocate using microcounseling skills as an integral part of continuing education workshops in any field. Microcounseling skills are introduced early (somewhere between the get-acquainted activities and the content phase of the workshop) to provide the optimum experience for the participants to be facilitative listeners through the remaining part of each program. Explanations and models of the skills are specifically adapted to fit that group. Such an approach has been used with parents, high school students, YMCA staff members, administrators, and local business personnel as part of their workshops or courses on other subjects and has been judged by the participants to enhance the learning experience as well as being useful in their lives outside the course at work and home. The basic microcounseling or communication skills taught in these programs seem to improve performances at all levels from junior high through adult education. It seems likely that they would be equally helpful early in grade school also. Modifying the microcounseling procedure for these young groups would be an interesting future project.

A second possible use of microtraining with students is as a direct instructional format in teaching the specific component skills of an occupation or related to employment in general. In fact, this has been done. DiMattia (1970) has used an individual approach to teach college students skills of presenting themselves successfully in an employment interview. Microtraining has been adapted with some success for executive training programs in industry. It has been used as a system of sales training in an insurance company and in pharmaceuticals. Early evidence in one evaluation of sales training indicated a 20 percent increase in sales in a single state. Basic business skills have been taught to distributive education students (sales trainees in high school who are released part of the day). The steps in pole vaulting, equipment assembly, letter composition, or many other skills could probably be adapted to a microtraining format as well. The efficiency of microtraining may be questionable for many simple skills, but for many complex tasks, the single component skills emphasis of microtraining may promote an efficient and effective teaching procedure.

PSYCHIATRIC INPATIENT TRAINING

Just as the focus of microtraining in education has broadened to include student training as well as teacher training, the focus of microtraining in psychology has expanded to include the direct training of patients or clients as well as therapist or counselor training. Probably resulting from a combination of their usually evident deficits in interpersonal skills and their captive accessibility, hospitalized mental patients have been the primary trainees in the application of microtraining within psychoeducation.

One view of hospitalized mental patients is that they are individuals with behavioral deficits rather than "sick" people. In such a view, patients are seen as lacking behavioral skills and alternatives. The treatment of choice then becomes supplying individuals with a variety of alternative behaviors which may be adapted to better their situation. Increasingly, training in specific skills is being accepted as the therapy of choice. The many therapy programs working from the philosophy of therapy as education reviewed by Authier, Gustafson, Guerney, and Kasdorf (1975) represent a range of different formats. The components of microtraining in some combination, however, are frequent parts of these programs. Indeed, a few have explicitly adopted a microtraining format.

As discussed previously, Donk (1972) adapted the microtraining framework to instruct hospitalized mental patients in the skills of attending behavior. He found that patients could readily learn listening skills. Further, he rated ward behavior and found that patients who had learned attending behavior demonstrated improved ward adjustment as compared to nontreatment controls.

Similarly, Orlando (1974) successfully trained three chronic, locked-ward patients (including one diagnosed as retarded and schizophrenic and one as organic brain syndrome) to take a therapist role through the sole use of three skills: attending, empathic nodding, and reflection of feeling. More explicit trainer coaching was used during the practice interviews with this severely distributed population, but learning and use of the skills on the ward did occur.

Freiband and Rudman, at the Northampton, Massachusetts, Veterans Administration Hospital, have explored the uses of media therapy (Higgins, Ivey, and Uhlemann, 1970; Ivey, 1973b) with hospitalized patients and again have clinically demonstrated that it is possible to teach patients a variety of behavioral skills. Media therapy is an individualized form of microcounseling in which the involvement of patients in selecting behaviors that they would like to change is very important. Most often, patients identify behaviors similar to those of the microtraining paradigm such as maintaining eye contact, verbal following, and postural or other nonverbal changes. However, this method may involve repeated videotaping, counting, and practice of such unorthodox skills as "sitting on my hands" to avoid disturbing gestures, or the development of more socially acceptable behaviors than hitting to be "one up" on others. Later, the more orthodox microcounseling relationship skills may be the goal. Model tapes may or may not be used as appropriate. Other patients may be involved in role-plays. Training usually involves a series of mutually defined skills and may be supplemented by other procedures such as relaxation training and "homework" such as daily audiotaping via cassette recorder of fifteen-minute conversations on the ward and counting the specific behaviors under training. The length of training on any given skill is competence rather than time based. In an effort to support generalization to the home setting of newly learned ward behaviors, a "me-kit" consisting of a handbook of materials and skills developed by the patient and his/her trainer during the stay at the hospital is often presented upon leaving. Family media therapy sessions have been found to increase maintenance of new behaviors.

A practical means of systematically applying training in relationship skills to nearly the entire population of a psychiatric inpatient unit is illustrated by the Step Group Program (Authier and Gustafson, 1976a). This modified microcounseling format blends training in basic relationship skills with group therapy. The program consists of three levels of steps of groups. Three specific skills are emphasized in each step group. The skills are as follows: Step I—relaxed posture and appropriate gesturing, eye contact, and verbal following; Step II—open questions, making questions into statements, and reflection of feeling; Step III—confrontation, feedback, and self-disclosure. All new patients begin in Step I, and promotion to the next higher step is based entirely on skills usage in the meeting. Each meeting begins with a definition and discussion of the skills of that step. Videotape models are provided in one current setting, and typed cards are used in another. The group leader specifically gives feedback and reinforces and models skills usage during the meeting and in a weekly progress note. The homogeneity of skills level within a group, the visible reinforcement, and the individual pacing have made the program a popular activity among both staff and patients. Preliminary research data show a strong correlation between step level membership and ward personnel ratings of communication in other settings (Petrick, 1976).

Further, the Step Group Program points to a possible use of microcounseling as an adjunct to many types of group therapy for either inpatients or outpatients. In many types of group therapy, a "pre-group" training session in basic interaction skills is a useful possibility in terms of norm clarification and facilitating interaction. Supplementing this suggestion is the possibility of referring individuals who have difficulties relating to the group process to microtraining and then returning them to the regular group. For example, a group often demonstrates, at a profound level, that an individual cannot listen to others' feelings. However, they usually do not tell him or her what behaviors should be engaged in for change. Referral for microtraining in specific skills may be useful because it can provide skills or alternatives which the individual can use to facilitate self-change. Simultaneously, group pressure may motivate an individual to learn a new behavior where there would have otherwise been no interest.

Keil (1968) developed a detailed plan for training groups of mental patients in job interviewing skills in two four-hour periods. The first period focused on application forms, dress and appearance, appropriate mannerisms, and an "asset search." Patients learned how to explain hospitalization and their past history. In each area, patients role-played possible ways of handling situations with employers. Videotaped models of appropriate behavior were presented, against which patients could compare themselves. The second two-hour session focused specifically on the job interview. Patients role-played a minimum of two job interviews. Positive and negative behaviors were identified, and positive reinforcement for appropriate behavior was given by the trainer. While formal research data on this program are not available, some patients previously judged "hard-core and unemployable" by the placement office of the hospital found jobs after training.

OUTPATIENT TRAINING

Turning to outpatient counseling clients, Haase, Forsyth, Julius, and Lee (1971) adapted the microtraining paradigm to teach clients accurate expression of feelings prior to initiation of counseling and found that clients then expressed more emotion in the first session of actual counseling. They suggested that where clients have a deficit in their ability to express themselves, microcounseling training can be especially suitable as a preparation for the therapy phase. Here again, however, the major trend is to view the training as the therapy itself rather than as a preparation for the "real thing."

Edward Aldrige of the Northampton State Hospital, Massachusetts, has employed the teaching of specific communication skills as a basic part of a family therapy program with the disadvantaged. He taught mothers of "problem children" basic attending skills or, put more simply, how they can listen to their children.

Gormally, Hill, Otis, and Rainey (1975) used a microtraining approach for training situationally nonassertive clients. The specific behaviors trained included proper breathing while speaking, focus on goals of situation, eye contact, congruent body movements, voice loudness, voice modulation, sending one piece of information at a time, and avoiding undue hesitations. In assertive expression, they found that microtraining increased self-rated and objectively rated assertiveness as compared to insight-oriented counseling control. Galassi, Galassi, and Litz (1974) utilized a similar approach to assertive training and found significant improvements on several self-ratings—eye contact, length of interaction, and assertive content.

Assertive training is only one potential microtraining-based therapy, however. Although the behavior therapies are the most easily viewed as "teachable" and immediately adaptable to a microtraining format, theoretically, any set of changes or skills that can be defined in behavioral terms could be taught to clients using a microtraining format. Again, other therapeutic modalities such as the Step Group Program may enhance the effectiveness of both.

PEOPLE TRAINING

Teachers, students, helpers, and helpees all have the common characteristic of being people. They all can learn through a microtraining format a variety of better ways to relate to other people in their working and living. Logically, what is helpful to these people may also be very useful to people in many other roles. Perhaps the most exciting direction of growth in relationship skills training is the offering of such training to people in general who desire it. The aim, then, is enhancement, growth, or prevention rather than remediation.

Several of the student programs covered previously fall into this category. Many families, couples, and working units can benefit from microtraining, skill-building, and relationship enhancement. One rewarding application of the Enriching Intimacy Program has been with a church group who felt they were a close unit but who wanted to relate to one another even more intimately and effectively.

Microtraining workshops or dyadic sessions can be conducted as personal growth sessions or skill development sessions. The prime thrust of this book is toward skill development. However, when partners or small groups work on microtraining skills, they almost inevitably start discussing real issues of immediate concern to them. The trainer then has the choice of moving these individuals back to prime emphasis on skills or encouraging them to use practice time as personal growth and interpersonal communication periods. McDermott's (1976a) work with inner-city people illustrates this point and is discussed in considerable detail in the chapter on cross-cultural counseling. He developed microcounseling training programs and used an innovative blend of standard and new ideas for skills. The skill was introduced, and then small groups worked on the skill, discussing real problems. In the process of acquiring skills, the individuals worked through real problems and made new life decisions.

Thus, it is possible to extend all present microtraining work to personal growth for an infinite variety of populations. The method is simple. The training workshop is announced as being focused on personal growth with a secondary emphasis on skill development. Regular microtraining procedures are used in the workshop, but skills emphasis is secondary. Video modeling tapes are used to discuss how the individual is growing and changing while using the skills. The attending workshop from Ivey and Gluckstern (1974a,b) presented in Appendix I is a model which can be used for this type of training. In effect, a microtraining personal growth workshop appears much the same as a skill development session, with the major difference being what is emphasized during the small group sessions. It is even possible to divide a training group into those who want prime emphasis on skills and those who wish to focus on personal issues and then conduct training simultaneously with people who have very different experiences in their practice sessions.

Another program is Malamud's (1971) Self-Understanding Workshops, where members create "second chance" families from among themselves. These "families" attempt to provide members with a second chance at growth opportunities which may not have been present in their actual childhood families. Utilizing the behavioral concepts of microcounseling, he developed interesting affective exercises to facilitate communication, two of which are quoted below:

> Sharing Feelings. I tell the group, "I have to present a paper at a professional meeting this Saturday, and I feel scared to death." I ask each member to respond to me with a single sentence. I reply to each sentence with either an "Ugh" or a "thank you." For example, if somebody says to me, "You shouldn't be nervous. After all, you're a psychologist!" I answer, "Ugh, I don't want to talk to you anymore." But if, on the other hand, a student in the group says to me, "Gee, I have felt that way too," I say, "thank you, I'd like to tell you more." So I go around in this way. It is a simple thing, but they get the point: Some ways of responding may turn people off, and other ways may encourage further self-disclosure. After I have modeled this exercise, I ask for a volunteer to take my place with self-disclosure of his own.
>
> In a variation of this exercise, I divide the group into two subgroups, A and B. I place myself in group A. I express a feeling, for example, "I don't know why, but I just don't like to be touched." I tell members in group A, "Each of you pretend that this is your feeling, and that you have just expressed it. Now each member in group B will respond in turn to this feeling of yours with a single sentence. See whether this sentence makes you feel closer to or more distant from the responding person. If closer, raise your hand. The number of raised hands constitutes the "score" for each responder." For example, following are two B members' quite different responses to the above feeling with their scores in parentheses: "OK, I won't touch you." (5) "You have a right not to like being touched, but perhaps talking about it might help." (12) After each member in group A has presented a feeling for response from group B, the two groups exchange roles, and people in the B group offer feelings to be responded to by the A group.*

Malamud's imaginative work is especially relevant, as it underlines the fact that the microtraining framework is only one route toward accomplishing a specific goal. This recognition of the

---

*Reprinted from Malamud, D.: The second chance family: A medium for self-directed growth. In Blank, L., Gottesegen, G., and Gottesegen, M. (Eds.): *Encounter: Confrontations in Self and Interpersonal Awareness*, 1971. Courtesy of Macmillan Company.

differing learning styles of individuals is particularly needed as the range of possible microtraining trainees is expanded to include people in general. If we wish to teach another person attending behavior or self-expressive behaviors, the microcounseling framework is just one viable training alternative. Single behavioral skills can be taught in many ways. If a person has the desire, he can learn attending behavior or psychological interpretation skills simply by reading about them or hearing someone else talk about them. However, most individuals learn quickly and efficiently in a stimulating situation. Microtraining provides such a situation for many people, but there are other routes to learning these skills.

The variety of programs reviewed here suggest a multitude of possible uses and adaptations of all or part of the microtraining paradigm. Population, skills, and format have, in turn, each been the prime target of modification. Within counseling, the development of new varieties of therapeutic skills for use in training both the therapists at all levels and the clients directly is the current major area of growth. Beyond traditional counseling, the extension of training efforts to nonclients in growth-oriented programs is a major development offering very exciting potential.

Fortunately, a structured educational workshop approach is becoming a very accepted form of self-enrichment, and much of the stigma of seeking such help is diminishing. Although the published examples of these types of programs are scarce, the possibilities are tantalizing, and hopefully your imaginations will suggest many other untried opportunities.

Future changes, however, must be based on their relevance and appropriateness for the group involved. It would be easy to suggest that virtually any area of human endeavor can be broken down into identifiable skills and that the skills can be taught with measurable results. However, while microtraining and microcounseling are useful methods of instruction, they are not the only methods, nor are they necessarily an effective way of instruction for all people in all settings. Rather, it is more reasonable to see the microtraining framework as another vehicle to impart information and realize that like all other teaching vehicles, the quality of the teacher or supervisor is ultimately a most important dimension. The supervisor must *model* the skills being taught.

SUMMARY

Originally developed for the training of teachers and counselors, microtraining has since shown its versatility in a myriad of settings with an almost infinite number of training populations. The present chapter first summarized uses of the framework in counseling and teaching and attempted to show that these areas still offer rich opportunities for new exploration and development.

Extensive attention has been given to microtraining as a paraprofessional training vehicle, and an array of uses of the framework were presented. Similarly, related helping professions such as social work, nursing, medicine, and speech therapy have found the framework useful.

Client populations appear to profit also from systematic training. The chapter summarizes work with training of students, psychiatric inpatients, outpatient counseling and therapy clients, and also "people training." The psychoeducational model implies that teaching developmental skills of living to helpee populations will be an increasingly important role for the professional helper of the future.

Chapter 11

PACKAGED SKILL TRAINING PROGRAMS

MICROCOUNSELING is not the "only" means of training the effective helper or helpee. That is, there are several ways to help people become more competent. Prior chapters focused on the concept of effective outcomes of training from a more theoretical point of view. The purpose of this chapter then is to demonstrate that from a structural point of view much of what is currently being offered in the way of skill training programs includes microtraining components which add to their effectiveness. The five basic dimensions of the microtraining format are single skills, feedback, modeling, practice, and supervision. The programs discussed therefore will have two or more of these basic components as part of their structural format. Additionally, unlike those discussed in Chapter 10, the programs considered will be those which can for the most part stand on their own; hence, the title "packaged" shall apply.

Many of these skills training programs have been developed to meet the needs stressed in Chapter 2. Perhaps most important in this regard was Hobbs' (1964) "Third Revolution," the paraprofessional movement. The fact that more appropriate delivery of mental health services was dependent upon involving nonprofessional manpower made short-term effective training programs with wide applicability necessary. A major asset of most of the training programs which were developed to meet this need is their structured nature. That is, in contrast to traditional didactic methods, these more structured programs emphasize systematic experiential exercises and are based on the acquisition of specific competencies. Additionally, most of these programs focus on skills important for dealing with others in a helping way.

Although there are major differences among the programs, most are concerned with providing a basic set of skills which would have applicability across the broad range of paraprofessional roles.

Guerney (1964; 1977) developed one of the first programs to meet the rising need for more paraprofessionals in the mental health field. Although *Filial Therapy* is not appropriate to include as one of the "packaged programs" to be presented here, it is essential to note that it served as the springboard for the psychoeducational model, a second important development responsible for the expansion of skill training programs. Indeed, Guerney and his associates (Guerney, 1969; Guerney and Flumen, 1970; Guerney, Guerney, and Stollak, 1971; Guerney, Guerney, and Stollak, 1973; Guerney and Stover, 1967) have been primarily responsible for the promulgation of the viability of using skill training as a therapeutic modality. This movement arose to help meet the needs of people to cope with the increasingly technological and complex environment. Since there were not enough mental health professionals to meet these demands, the movement in essence was designed to help people become their own therapeutic agents, especially within the "interpersonal realm." The role of the practitioner using such a model, according to Guerney, Guerney and Stollak (1973), is that of "teaching personal and interpersonal attitudes and skills which the student can apply to solve present and future psychological problems and to enhance his and others' satisfaction with life." Their line of deduction was that interpersonal skills are often symptoms of good mental health; interpersonal skills are effectively taught to professional and nonprofessional helpers; if these skills can be taught to a training population, then they should be able to be taught to a patient population.

Although the foregoing has logical appeal, many barriers needed to be broken before the movement actually took force. As discussed in a previous chapter, such things as allowing therapeutic interaction to be open to public scrutiny, giving up the medical model and status which accompanies it, i.e. being a doctor, considering oneself a teacher rather than a therapist, and requiring the helper to view the patient as someone who is lacking in interpersonal skills rather than someone who is sick, thus violating the theoretical and value structure of many professional helpers, were just a few of the obstacles which needed to be overcome.

To move to a psychoeducator model, a systematic reconceptualization of the helper role from one-to-one healing with primarily supportive and sometimes indirect teaching tasks to that of a teacher with direct teaching tasks is essential. This is particularly true with regard to "therapists" implementing the "packaged programs" as part of their therapeutic programs. Those who were able to make that shift have done just this, and indeed one program (Structured Learning Therapy, Goldstein, 1973) was developed specifically to meet this need.

This chapter will not pretend to be an exhaustive list of all those packaged programs in existence but instead will present some of those which can logically be viewed as structurally related to a microtraining format, from a program which is a direct modification of the microcounseling format, namely the Enriching Intimacy program (Authier and Gustafson, 1973), to one which does not have any direct relationship to microcounseling yet does employ basic microtraining components which add to its effectiveness, the Human Resources Development Model (Carkhuff, 1969a,b; 1972). Also, the discussion will include programs which have been in existence for a sufficient period of time to have compiled some data as to their effectiveness. The presentations of the programs themselves will include a brief discussion of factors leading to the development of the program, a brief description of the program, including a discussion of the various microtraining structural components of the program, and a summary of the evidence demonstrating the effectiveness of the program.

ENRICHING INTIMACY: A BEHAVIORAL APPROACH

Enriching Intimacy: A Behavioral Approach (Authier and Gustafson, 1973), a relationship skills training program, was developed in part as one means of demonstrating the predictive validity of many of the microcounseling skills. That is, although microcounseling as a training technique had ample evidence demonstrating its effectiveness, there was little solid evidence in 1971 demonstrating that microcounseling skills were related to client outcome criteria. The therapist's attitude of empathy, genuineness, and warmth/respect, on the other hand, were indicated to be related to outcome (e.g. Truax, 1961; Truax and Wargo, 1966, 1967a,b; Dickenson and Truax, 1966; Rogers, Gendlin, Kiesler, and Truax, 1967; Carkhuff and Truax, 1965). It seemed logical, therefore, to attempt to teach such therapist characteristics via a microtraining paradigm.

The Experiential-Didactic program (Truax and Carkhuff, 1967) was demonstrated to be an effective means of imparting these central therapeutic ingredients; however, for the most part the program is time consuming, and the efficiency of its training format is questionable in many settings. Furthermore, even the effectiveness of the training format was somewhat questionable in that of seventeen studies cited by Carkhuff (1969a,b), only two resulted in increased manifestations of the attitudes above a rating of three, the minimally facilitative level as defined by the scales to measure these conditions. Further, the two studies which did result in increases above this minimally facilitative condition were 100-hour training programs with Ph.D. candidates, thus placing into question the practical applicability of the E-D program. However, perhaps the single most limiting aspect of the E-D program stems from the lack of specificity; that is, the format of this training program fails to specify behavioral components of empathy, genuineness, and warmth/respect. Thus, even though they talk about shaping these three qualities, just what behaviors the E-D program is shaping are obscure.

The Enriching Intimacy (E.I.) program attempted to overcome this deficit, as well as other seeming shortcomings of the E-D program, by teaching via a microtraining format specific behaviors which, on the basis of face validity, their correspondence with theoretical descriptions of the dimensions, and in a few cases, their research-derived relationships, were demonstrated to be aspects of empathy, genuineness, and warmth/respect. The program is divided into four stages: (1) teaching the behavioral components of respect, (2) teaching the behavioral components of empathy, (3) teaching the behavioral components of genuineness, and (4) an integrative group phase. The structural format of the program, as alluded to, follows the microtraining format quite closely. Thus, within each skill learning phase, model tapes, five-minute practice sessions with role playing which are simultaneously videotaped, and immediate feedback during the review sessions are all part of the training program. Additionally, operational definitions of each behavioral component are discussed, and for the most part the skills are focused on singly. Perhaps a brief description of each phase of the training program will better clarify the relationship of the E.I. program with the microtraining format as well as make more lucid how such complex therapist characteristics as respect/warmth, empathy, and genuineness can be taught behaviorally.

Respect, or warmth, is taught during the first phase of the Enriching Intimacy program, as it is felt that the behaviors which comprise respect/warmth are basic to being empathic and genuine as well. The behavioral components of respect demonstrate for the most part that being respectful or warm toward someone is merely demonstrating that you are willing and interested in listening to what the client is telling you. Additionally, it is demonstrating respect for the individual's worth, integrity, and abilities. As such, it is apparent that many of the skills of microcounseling, such as attending behavior, minimal encourage to talk, open question, and paraphrasing, are all basic to being respectful. Indeed, modified microcounseling manuals (Ivey and Gluckstern 1976b) are used in the teaching of respect.

The major difference between E.I. and microcounseling then is the way these skills are integrated into a "global model tape" demonstrating poor and good respect. A poor global example demonstrates one person interviewing another using poor examples of the skills of respect mentioned above, while the good example demonstrates a role-play in which all the skills are used accurately. The contrast between the poor and the good examples is marked, and generally trainees are surprised to find that merely using the handful of behaviors discussed above either accurately or inaccurately can make such a difference in the amount of respect one conveys.

Just as the skills are drawn largely from the microcounseling program, so is the training format itself. Again, perhaps the main difference is the emphasis during the first part of training on the larger concept of respect and all which this entails, especially regarding the behavioral components. The trainees review the poor and the good models of the "poor respect" tape, with ample time allowed for discussion. During the discussion the point is clearly made that it was the manifestation or lack thereof of the attending skills, the minimal encourages to talk, the open invitation to talk, and paraphrasing which made the poor and the good samples of the global respect tapes so drastically different. With this emphasis in mind, the students then begin to focus on learning the specific skills which comprise respect, focusing on them one at a time. The format is identical to the microtraining format in that the trainees read an operational definition, view a good and a poor example model tape of the skill, conduct role-plays which are videotaped, and then review the videotapes for immediate feedback. Each trainee usually takes as many turns as necessary until competency with the skill has been demonstrated.

Phase two of training comprises the empathy portion of Enriching Intimacy. The behavioral components, as alluded to, consist of many of the behavioral components of respect, but for the most part, the use of the skills, especially the nonverbal skills, is intensified. Thus, eye contact may be more intense; facial expression may be showing more than interest, perhaps even concern; and seating distance may be closer, perhaps even with touching occurring. The main difference with regard to verbal skills is their focus on feelings. Here the reflection of feeling skill is identical to the reflection of feeling skill of the microcounseling paradigm, but in addition, the skills of confrontation, self-disclosure, and changing questions into statements are skills unique to the program. Nevertheless, even these have some resemblance to the skills taught during the influencing portion of microcounseling.

The format for the empathy training portion is similar to that of the respect portion of training with two major exceptions. The first exception is that there is a large emphasis given to identification of feelings, and a feeling word list is used for this purpose. Once the trainees have expanded their feeling word vocabulary, they listen to audiotapes of clients' statements of personal concern in an attempt to identify as accurately as possible the feelings the client is expressing. The second exception, related to the above, involves the trainees' viewing silent videotapes as a way of helping them become more aware of the nonverbal components of feelings. Other than these two exceptions, though, the training involves the trainees' focusing on one skill at a time, following the traditional microtraining format.

Genuineness comprises the third phase of training and once again follows a structured microtraining format. The focus here from the Enriching Intimacy point of view is that whereas empathy allows one to be more accurate in the identification of others' feelings, genuineness is the means of training people to be more aware of their own feelings when they are interacting with others. Again, the basic respect skills are stressed as the basic components of being genuine, but in addition to that, a verbal skill of feedback is taught as a means of conveying the helper's feelings to the helpee. Congruency between verbal and nonverbal behavior is stressed as being the key to being genuine, and the feedback skill is used as one means of accomplishing this. As defined by the E.I. program, feedback is "telling the other person the effect that his/ her behavior is having on you." During the training of the feedback skill, emphasis is given to being as specific and accurate as one can be when practicing the skill. This portion of training helps the helper become more aware of personal feelings and teaches the ability to express these feelings to another. Self-disclosure is another skill emphasized during genuineness training which serves to underscore the interrelationship between being empathic and being genuine. The final task during genuineness training is for the participants to conduct a role-play situation which they foresee as being one in which they would have the most difficulty being genuine. This approach allows the trainee to become even more aware of personal feelings involving a particularly threatening situation, helps him/her to become aware of reactions during stressful situations, and teaches a way of dealing with the stress in a constructive fashion with the helpee.

The final phase of the Enriching Intimacy program is the group session phase. The purpose of the group sessions is twofold: (1) to allow the trainees a forum in which to integrate the three global skills of empathy, warmth/respect, and genuineness and (2) to allow an opportunity for them to explore their motivations for wanting to be helpers. The role of the supervisor during this format is really that of a group facilitator helping the trainees to focus as honestly as possible on the various motivations for choosing a helping profession. Additionally, reinforcement is given when trainees use certain of the skills emphasized in the previous three phases of training or are seen as manifesting high levels of one of the more global skills. Sometimes more didactic intervention is called for, and often a trainee will be asked to re-phrase a comment in order to make it more empathic, more genuine, or more respectful.

Does the Enriching Intimacy program work? To date, two studies have been completed which have examined the effectiveness of the Enriching Intimacy program. The first study (Gustafson, 1975) was conducted with eighteen medical students who were randomly assigned to the E.I. program, the E-D condition (Truax and Carkhuff, 1967), and a no-training control condition. Each training group met for twenty-two hours with their respective trainers, who were evaluated as to their levels of empathy, respect/warmth, and genuineness. Moreover, the trainers were rated on the student/supervisor relationship questionnaire and the interview instructor evaluation questionnaire.

No significant differences were found between trainers. The evaluations of the trainees resulted in two significant findings. The E.I. group showed a significant increase in respect/warmth rating in contrast to the control group, and the E-D group showed a significant increase in empathy rating in contrast to the control group. These findings were not confirmed by any other measure of interaction with either patients or peers, however. The greater enthusiasm of the E.I. trainees was shown in their higher program evaluations and the loss of two members of the E-D group.

The findings, then, were not very impressive with regard to the E.I. training program. However, the initial skill levels of the subjects was a large confounding variable which may have undermined the effectiveness of the program. That is, the program was taught to medical students who the term before had received an interviewing course in which several of the microcounseling skills were stressed. As such, all subjects, regardless of whether they were in the Enriching Intimacy group, the Experiential-Didactic program, or the no-treatment control group, had many of the skills which were to be emphasized by the E.I. program. Indeed, perusal of the preskill levels of the subjects demonstrates that they were all above the minimally facilitative conditions before even beginning the training! If nothing else, then, the study demonstrated the effectiveness of the microtraining format emphasizing basic microcounseling skills for helping people to relate empathically, warmly, and genuinely. Supporting this notion further is the Toukmanian and Rennie (1975) study which found that microcounseling significantly increased ratings of empathy. Impressive is the fact that microcounseling trainees were not only more empathic than no-training control subjects but gained significantly more on empathy than did trainees receiving Carkhuff's more structured modification of the E-D program, i.e. Human Relations Training.

The second study designed to study the effectiveness of the E.I. program was conducted with physician assistants (Gustafson and Authier, 1976). Fifteen subjects were randomly assigned to a marathon training group in E.I., a ten-week E.I. group which met for two hours each week, and a no-training control group. The study was designed to test whether offering the E.I. program in a workshop format was equally as effective as offering it as a course over a period of weeks. Additionally, the study allowed for study of the effectiveness of the program itself. Results of the study indicated that, as hypothesized, the marathon and weekly session groups did not differ significantly in the use of the skills taught. More important in terms of effectiveness of the program itself, the results demonstrated that both the marathon and weekly session groups differed significantly from the no-training control group in the use of the skills trained. Finally, it should be noted that although the trained groups did not significantly differ from the control group in their manifestation of empathy, respect/warmth, and genuineness posttraining, the trend was in that direction. Thus, as with the Gustafson study, it seems that perhaps more time would be needed if significant changes in the manifestation of the central therapeutic ingredients of empathy, respect/warmth, and genuineness were to be obtained via the E.I. program.

Subjective evidence indicates the E.I. program is effective with such populations as nurse aides, social work students, church group members, medical students, medical educators (Authier and Gustafson, 1975b), and family practice residents. The evidence from all these training programs demonstrates the training to be well received in that the participants found the course enjoyable, reported the training to be worthwhile, and would recommend it to others. Although all this evidence is encouraging, more studies need to be conducted before one can state unequivocally that the program is efficacious.

STRUCTURED LEARNING THERAPY

As the title implies, this approach to training has grown out of the psychoeducator model. Goldstein (1973) developed Structured Learning Therapy (SLT) because he felt that more traditional treatment approaches were more the function of middle-class life-styles and professional preferences and were not at all responsive to the needs, life-styles, and environmental realities of the lower-class patient. He concludes,

> . . . . we have presented above an immense amount of evidence indicating that our traditional psychotherapy techniques are simply and grossly both inadequate and inappropriate for the lower-class patient. Perhaps our most adequate professional contribution to the lives of lower-class patients, or at least a very major one to which we have given grossly insufficient attention, may be in adding to their repertoire of specific social, interpersonal, and personal skills (p. 68).

With regard to a treatment approach designed to meet the needs of the lower-class patient, he stresses,

One such approach appears to be what we have termed structured learning therapy, in which explicit focus can be placed upon skill training—via the use of modeling, role playing, and social reinforcement—to enhance patient autonomy, assertiveness, internal controls, role taking abilities, sense of mastery, social interaction skills, accuracy of affective perception and communication, tolerance for frustration and ambiguity, and a host of other useful behaviors in which he may be deficient (p. 69).

It is immediately apparent, then, that SLT employs many of the teaching modalities of the microtraining paradigm. Indeed, even the single skill emphasis is used during most of the early training. Later training emphasizes more complex skills and includes three to eight basic skills per model.

SLT in its most recent form consists of four training phases: (1) modeling, (2) role playing, (3) social reinforcement, and (4) transfer of training. The headings of these phases imply obvious similarities to the microtraining structure. A brief description of each phase follows in an attempt to make clear the relationship between the microtraining format and Structured Learning Therapy.

The first phase emphasizes modeling, a central microtraining component as well. The SLT modeling phase is different from the modeling phase of microcounseling, however, in that audiotapes rather than videotapes are employed. This phase of SLT involves the training population listening to a didactic presentation of the rationale of the training format and its effectiveness. The patient population then listens to a model tape emphasizing a certain learning point. As alluded to, this learning point approach is similar to the single skill approach in microtraining. The model tapes themselves are somewhat different, though, in that a narrator usually sets the scene, actors then portray the learning point, and the narrator then recapitulates the vignette, restating the learning points and urging their continued use. In this respect, the narrator serves one of the functions of the supervisor in the microtraining format, as generally it is the narrator who sets the stage for the importance of learning a particular skill to be modeled as well as summarizing the skill and entertaining any questions which might be raised regarding the appropriateness of its use.

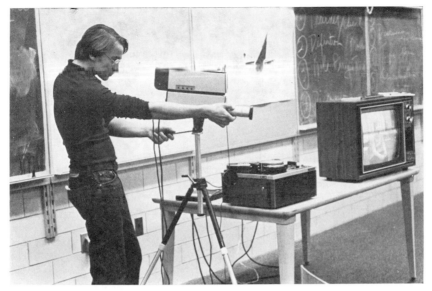

Illustration 1. Equipment for a microtraining session need not be complex. Here we see a small camera, a half-inch video unit, and a monitor. Skills for running this equipment can be learned easily in from five to ten minutes.

Illustration 2. Discussion of single skill units in small groups with the assistance of printed manuals is a feature of all microtraining workshops. Groups of four tend to be most effective and provide ample opportunity for role-playing.

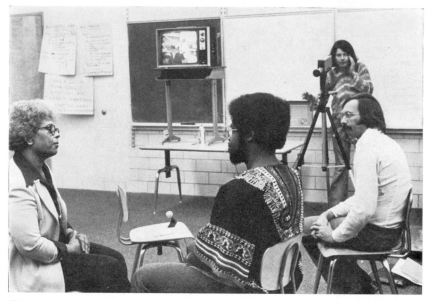

Illustration 3. A typical video filming session. Here we find a helper with a role-played helpee. A camera person is giving prime attention to the helper-trainee. The fourth individual is concerned with process observation and behavior counts.

Illustration 4. Observation of the helper's performance is a high point of microtraining. Here the instructor is reviewing a practice session with a trainee.

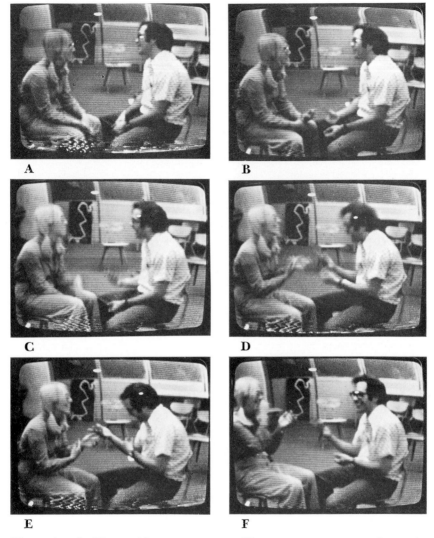

Illustration 5. These videotape segments illustrate movement synchrony in a microtraining role-play session. The helper and helpee are discussing a mutually meaningful issue. Note first in Illustration 5A that their postures are in a rough "mirror image" of each other. This was not planned, but happened spontaneously in the interview. Illustration 5B shows the hands beginning to rise together, which is followed through in 5C, 5D, and 5E. Illustration 5E represents the completion of the transaction. The time elapsed for this series of movements is less than a second, and it is not possible to distinguish helper from helpee. As helpers become able to "tune in" with their clients, movement synchrony often appears spontaneously. Such complex movements cannot be planned, but we have found that the helper, by deliberately assuming the posture of the helpee, can facilitate deeper levels of communication and the development of movement synchrony.

The second phase of SLT involves the patient population role playing the skill which was emphasized during the modeling phase. This phase is practically identical to the role-playing practice phase of microtraining in that one person plays the helpee and another the helper attempting to use the skills emphasized during the training session, with the other trainees in the group observing how well the helper follows the learning points, saving his/her comments for later discussions. One very basic difference between SLT and microcounseling is in the means of giving feedback. That is, SLT does not videotape these role-plays as a means of stimulating discussion following the role-play. Both programs emphasize the microtraining component of feedback, but microcounseling employs both videotape and verbal feedback while SLT emphasizes only verbal feedback as a shaping process.

Social reinforcement serves as the third phase of SLT. This phase is seen as a means of "shaping" a trainee's behaviors to ensure that the learning point is acquired by him or her. The trainers are encouraged to provide social reinforcement according to several rules:

1. Provide reinforcement immediately after role plays which follow the learning points.
2. Provide reinforcement only after role plays which follow the learning points.
3. Vary the specific content of the reinforcements offered.
4. Provide enough role-playing activity for each group member to have sufficient opportunity to be reinforced.
5. Provide reinforcement in an amount consistent with the quality of a given role play.
6. Provide no reinforcement when a role play departs significantly from the learning points (except for "trying" in the first session or two).
7. In later sessions, space out the reinforcement so that not every good role play is reinforced (Goldstein, 1973, p. 10).

The specific instruction regarding administration of social reinforcement is a strength of SLT, since it very obviously incorporates learning theory as a means of enhancing skill acquisition. Microcounseling differs some from this approach in that social reinforcement is not stressed quite so specifically. The final step of the social reinforcement phase of SLT involves the replaying of the model tape once all trainees have had an opportunity to practice the role playing. The purpose, of course, is to summarize the learning point(s) for the trainees, thus leaving them with the learning points firmly in mind.

The fourth phase of Structured Learning Therapy is the transfer of training phase. Since the overall goal of Structured Learning Therapy is to help the patient in real-life environments, this is a crucial phase. Indeed, Goldstein has only recently added this portion to the SLT training format, as he feels that it is where most training programs fall short. As a means of guarding against this, his recent work has included "on-the-ward transfer trainers" to help transfer and stabilize the learning points in the ward situation. Additionally, homework is urged, and contracting with the patient is used as a way of insuring that the patient will attempt the learning points at home. Specificity is stressed, and the patients are reinforced when they report their various attempts to engage in skills while in their home environments. Sometimes, written contracts involving note taking while at home are employed as a way of helping to analyze how the practice of the learning skill went in the home setting. The parallels between this phase and the "do-use-teach" contracts of microcounseling are obvious.

The research evidence for Structured Learning Therapy is impressive in that it has been found to be an effective technique for patients who heretofore were seen as recalcitrant. One such study (Gutride, Goldstein, and Hunter, 1972b) studied 106 psychiatric patients. These subjects were randomly assigned to seven weeks of SLT—five weeks of SLT plus two more weeks of on-the-ward training (transfer of training phase) —seven weeks of social companionship therapy, and a no-treatment control group. Therapy goals were to increase mealtime social behavior. Results show that SLT patients improved more than social companionship therapy or no-training, and that when differences occurred between the SLT groups, the improvement in the SLT group receiving ward training was greater than that of the SLT group receiving seven weeks of training without the transfer of training portion of the therapy. Gutride, Goldstein, and Hunter (1972a) also demonstrated Structured Learning Therapy to be a reliable treatment for asocial psychiatric patients. An interesting finding of this study was what the authors term a "mutual inhibition" of treatment effectiveness between Structured Learning Therapy and psychotherapy. That is, they found that both Structured Learning Therapy and psychotherapy influenced a number of dependent measures, but that in combination, although there were a small number of criteria, Structured Learning Therapy inhibited psychotherapy.

Further research will need to be conducted to explore this finding, as it is the opposite of the subjective impressions of other psychoeducators. Both Media Therapy and Step Group Therapy, two microcounseling-related therapeutic approaches, generally seem to have an enhancing effect on other therapeutic procedures. Perhaps Structured Learning Therapy, with emphasis on specific life-coping skills rather than "counseling-related or relationship skills," could be the contributing factor. Still, the results are impressive for Structured Learning Therapy, again attesting to the effectiveness of a psychoeducator approach as a treatment modality.

Structured Learning Therapy has also been used to train paraprofessional counselors (Goldstein, 1973). One such study involved using SLT to train paraprofessionals to be empathic (Goldstein and Goedhart, 1973). This study, which was conducted as part of two experiments, is the most impressive to date and thus will be presented in some detail. The first experiment involved seventy-four student nurses. The pre- and posttraining involved these student nurses responding to a set of thirty common problematic situations involving nurse-patient interactions. The training program itself consisted of

1. A presentation and discussion of the meaning and nature of empathy
2. Distribution and discussion of the Carkhuff Empathy Scale, highlighting concrete examples of the five levels presented
3. Discussion of such supporting topics as
   a. Means for identifying patients' feelings

   b. Means for communicating to patients that their feelings
      are understood
   c. Empathy versus sympathy
   d. Empathy versus diagnosis of their evaluation
   e. Empathy versus directiveness or questioning
4. Initial modeling in which all thirty situations alluded to
   above were enacted by the two group leaders
5. Role playing which involved reading one of the thirty
   situations and having one of the group members respond,
   first on a volunteer basis and later taking turns
6. Further modeling, role playing, and social reinforcement.

These several procedures consumed a ten-hour period, offered
during two consecutive days. Immediately following the final
stage of training, the trainees were asked to respond to a different
form of the thirty problematic situations than they responded to
in pretraining. A follow-up measure was taken one month following training. The nursing staff involved in this study demonstrated significant gains in empathy, both immediately following
training and one month later.

A second part of this investigation consisted of using the same
format with ninety subjects in a different psychiatric hospital.
These subjects consisted of twenty staff nurses, forty attendants,
and thirty other high patient contact staff (O.T., R.T., etc.). Although essentially a replication study, this second study explored
the effect of structured learning plus transfer of training as compared to structured training only and a no-training control. The
major findings of Experiment 1 were replicated in that both training groups showed significantly greater empathy than the no-
training control group, but in addition to this, the structured
learning training plus transfer of training group showed the highest level of empathy.

The results of the above study thus demonstrate that Structured Learning Therapy can be used as a counseling training
program. Although it is not warranted to discuss the therapeutic
effectiveness of Structured Learning Therapy in more detail here,
it should be noted that the transfer of training portion of this
explicitly psychoeducator approach to training is possibly the key

factor of its purported effectiveness. Indeed, this is the most important step of any psychoeducator therapeutic endeavor. It is this phase of educational training as a therapeutic modality which tends to make these models more effective than more traditional models of therapy. In essence, the direct learning approach teaches the trainees skills which will be useful in helping them cope with stresses when they are back in their home environments. This is contrasted to psychoanalytic and other more esoteric approaches where the patient gains insight perhaps but is not taught skills to cope with those problems which continue to arise in spite of the insight. Sometimes the increased insight worsens the presenting problems, as the person is more aware of the problem areas. As such, it would seem that the teaching of coping skills would be an important adjunct to more traditional therapeutic approaches, and, of course, this is our thrust.

INTERPERSONAL PROCESS RECALL

The most recent update of Interpersonal Process Recall (Kagan, 1975a), which first became available in manual form in 1971, stated that it was developed in order to address the fundamental questions:

> Can we improve the ways in which people relate to each other?
> Can reliable methods be developed to teach people to live with each other without inflicting pain?
> Can we improve the mental health of our own society? (p. 74)

After four years of controlled studies, Kagan concluded that therapeutic behavior was too complex to be learned by most students through any type of supervised experience. As such, Kagan and his coworkers formulated the teaching strategy based on the principle of counselor or therapist developmental tasks. Kagan writes,

> Tasks were designed so that they were specific enough that the majority of students can be expected to grasp the concrete or learn the skills, yet not be so finite as to be of dubious relevance to the complex dynamic behavior of counselor or therapist as a positive influence on human interaction (p. 76).

The teaching strategy designed to impart these developmental tasks consists of didactic presentation of concepts, stimulation exercises, interpersonal affective stress, video and physiological feedback, study of oneself in action, feedback from clients, and finally, understanding of skill at dealing with the complex bilateral impacts which occur when two people are in a relationship with each other.

Once again, then, it is clear that at least some aspects of the microtraining paradigm are utilized in the Interpersonal Process Recall method. The didactic portion with the written descriptions of materials which are to be learned and the role playing with the video feedback are two obvious similarities. Two obvious differences, on the other hand, are the individual and mutual recall portions. However, it should be noted that micro-counseling supervisors often use some aspect of the former recall method when exploring how the trainee felt during the role-play and the videotape feedback portions of microtraining. Even the mutual recall method has been integrated as an alternative use of microcounseling and has been found to be an effective variant (Welch, 1976). Welch has presented evidence that I.P.R. paired with microcounseling is a useful combination. Thus, again the difference between microcounseling and other training skill programs becomes lessened as useful components of each are combined and modified for a particular need.

The I.P.R. program itself is offered in seven units: (1) response mode training, (2) stimulus affect training, (3) role playing, (4) inquirer role training, (5) colleague-client recall, (6) mutual recall, and (7) summary. These will be discussed in some detail below in an attempt to demonstrate the structural similarities and differences of I.P.R. and microtraining. Unit one consists of helping the student learn four characteristics of therapeutic response — exploratory, effectiveness, listening, and honest labeling. This part of the training consists of students being shown vignettes with an actor-client making a statement followed by an interviewer response to that statement in one of the four modalities. Several client types and interviewer types are presented for each of the four sets of concepts, and then a student practices the new response roles with a series of simulated clients on film who look directly at them and make statements of varying complexity. Again, obvious aspects of the microtraining paradigm are apparent, such as specific skills and student practice. The differences, of course, are the simulated clients on film and the nature of the skills themselves.

Unit two is the stimulus affect portion of the training, which is designed to help the student become more aware of personal feelings which might interfere with effectiveness in human interactions. The stimulus affect tapes are used in four ways: (1) in small groups, (2) in pairs, (3) simultaneous video recording the student's reaction to the vignette, and (4) videotaping the student's reaction to the tape while simultaneously recording physiological changes. The latter is especially exciting, as it has great research potential.

In unit three, the student conducts a role-play or interaction with a real client, which is videotaped and then reviewed. During the review, the student is encouraged to relive the session in as much detail as possible, with the primary focus being on subjective feelings rather than on specific skills used. Thus, although the videotaped role-play is similar to microtraining, the feedback emphasis is quite different. That is, here the emphasis is on the trainee's reactions rather than the particular skill he or she may or may not have been using during the session. Discussion then revolves around how the trainee might deal with these feelings during future sessions. Further, the discussion allows for a sort of desensitization process to occur.

Unit four involves training the students in the inquirer role. The basic assumption for this phase of training is that the recall process is a useful skill for the students to have when they conduct their own sessions. The hope then is that the trainee will examine his or her feelings in future sessions with clients, eventually using this ability for self-supervision and training.

Unit five is utilized mainly to help the student expand the client's wants, perceptions, and aspirations, and to learn something of how clients avoid, deny or suppress, or learn to grow unchanged. The major modality during this unit is having a student conduct an inquiry and videotape review similar to that described in unit three with a client who has been interviewed by a fellow student. The focus again is on facilitating the client's re-living the session and exploring the subjective feelings that arise as the tape is reviewed. In this way, a counselor can learn to be a more effective inquirer and at the same time learn more or less experientially how the client was feeling during various portions of the interview and the kinds of interventions the client found to be either stimulating or meaningless.

Unit six is perhaps the most complex portion of the I.P.R. method, as it entails mutual recall. Whereas before the student was not receiving direct feedback from the interviewed clients, this unit focuses on direct feedback from the clients on perceptions of the helper and the interaction. In this session, both client and student share their moment-to-moment impact on each other. These mutual recall sessions are led by an inquirer who seeks to help both client and student talk and listen openly to each other.

Unit seven, the final section, summarizes observations which Kagan and his colleagues have made about human interaction. As such, it is designed to provide a theoretical framework to enable trainees to understand the meaning of some of the experiential learning in which they have engaged. Finally, the recapitulation allows the trainees to assimilate all that they have learned, using their own conceptual frameworks.

As might be expected, due to its longevity, the program has ample evidence attesting to its efficacy. Goldberg (1967), using an earlier version of the model, was the first to provide clear-cut evidence supporting the I.P.R. as an effective counseling training model. This study compared the I.P.R. with traditional supervision, which included a student supervisor observing each interview through a one-way mirror and then immediately spending an hour viewing a session with the student (audiotapes of the interview were used whenever the supervisor or the student so designated). Although the I.P.R. model did not include affect stimulation films, the I.P.R. model was still found to be significantly different from the supervisor training model as rated on the Affective Response Scale (Goldberg, 1967; Kagan, 1971) and the

Wisconsin Orientation Scale, which is designed to measure the client's willingness to talk about personal or factual matters.

Later studies (Grzegorek, 1970; Dendy, 1971; Archer and Kagan, 1973) found the I.P.R. to be an effective training program for counselors of the state prisoners in Michigan, teaching staff and undergraduate students respectively. Indeed, Archer and Kagan (1973) found that the same undergraduates could in turn train other undergraduates, so that the peer-instructed students scored significantly higher than other students who experienced an encounter group of similar duration. Further, the study demonstrated that the I.P.R.-trained students were the ones who were chosen by dormitory residents as students who "would be able to talk about a personal problem."

A recent cost/benefit analysis of the I.P.R. revealed conflicting results (Kingdom, 1975). This study failed to demonstrate the I.P.R. to be any more effective than traditional supervision when the dependent variables were empathy level, client satisfaction, and supervisor ratings of client's self-reported inhibition. On the positive side, however, I.P.R. was found to significantly affect the client's level of self-exploration over time, a crucial outcome variable.

Consistent with the psychoeducator movement, a study by Resnikoff, Kagan, and Schauble (1970) used eight hours of I.P.R. as an adjunct therapy with clients at a college counseling center and found the I.P.R. clients to be statistically different from clients receiving equivalent treatment time. Unfortunately, a replication study was unable to confirm the earlier finding. Perhaps the main reason for these conflicting results is the fact that eight hours may not allow enough exposure to consistently affect measurable outcome.

Indeed, the time factor may be the largest deterrent to the I.P.R. being used on a more practical level, either within a therapeutic setting or as a training modality for helpers. Although significant differences between traditional supervisory and I.P.R. models have been found in as few as eight to ten hours, most people who have conducted the program find that thirty to fifty hours of total time is desirable. The amount of time needed to present the total package is understandable, since the I.P.R. is one of the most complete programs in existence as far as attempting to train all aspects of the very complex dynamic behavior of a therapy or interview session. The alternative use of the I.P.R. mutual recall session in conjunction with microcounseling training, which was discussed earlier, might be a way of shortening the total training time. Used in this way, the trainee could be integrating several of the microcounseling skills during an interview with a real client and then have the client give reactions and feelings toward the trainee's interviewing style. This approach has been found useful as a means of helping the trainee grow, as many trainees express themselves more openly during the second session. Additionally, the client's reaction and feelings toward the trainee's interviewing style are invaluable.

HELPING SKILLS: A BASIC TRAINING PROGRAM

In response to the burgeoning need for structured training for paraprofessionals, Danish and Hauer (1973a,b) developed their program. They felt that more than anything, paraprofessionals needed to learn basic skills which would enable them to build a strong relationship with helpees. Danish states, "The graduate of the program should have skills to facilitate the development of trust and rapport between himself/herself and the helpee" (1974, p. 1). Danish and Hauer felt that by teaching basic relationship skills, a broad enough foundation would be laid to enable people to provide assistance to the helpee, whether the helper be a policeman, a mental health counselor, or any of a wide array of professional and nonprofessional helpers. Additionally, they felt the training process for teaching the skills should follow a "skill-learning" format which involved identification of explicit behavioral objectives, practice or application of the skills to be learned, self-learning by group discussions, a rationale for learning, sequential presentation, active training participation, the use of modeling, and the use of immediate feedback concerning the appropriateness of trainee responses.

In an attempt to teach the basic skills required to form an effective relationship, the Helping Skills program is taught in six stages: (1) understanding needs to be a helper, (2) using effective nonverbal behavior, (3) using effective verbal behavior, (4) using effective self-involving behavior, (5) understanding others' communication, and (6) establishing effective relationships. Further, each of these stages is taught via the process alluded to above. More specifically then, the process of training for each stage involves (1) defining the skill in behavioral terms, (2) presenting a rationale for the skill, (3) identifying a skill attainment level, (4) modeling of effective and ineffective examples of the skill, (5) allowing opportunity for extensive supervised practice of the skill, and (6) assigning homework to assist the generalization process. Although it is obvious that some components of the microtraining approach are employed, perhaps a brief description of each stage of the program will serve to make more lucid the similarities and differences between Helping Skills: A Basic Training Program and microcounseling.

Stage one of the program emphasizes the importance of understanding one's need to be a helper. The authors contend that this has been a much-neglected area of paraprofessional training in the past and have incorporated more of an emphasis on these needs into their program for that very reason. Moreover, they maintain that helpers are people first, and that training only in response modes overlooks the effect that the person who is the helper has on the helping process. The procedure followed during this stage involves alternating between the group and the dyadic discussions. Sometimes models, either live or on film, are observed as a means of stimulating discussion. Homework is also assigned during this stage. The 122-page training manual which accompanies the program also consists of behavioral checklists and room for written evaluations by dyadic partners, which also enhance one's understanding of the need to be a helper.

The second, third, and fourth stages of the program are very similar to microcounseling in both the content and the training process used. Several of the skills, such as eye contact, posture, open questions, and self-disclosure, are very similar to the skills taught in the microcounseling format. Additionally, the process of operationally defining skills, using models, and role playing followed by feedback and discussion is very similar to microtraining. A major difference again is the behavioral checklists and the homework assignments, although certainly the new microcounseling skill manuals incorporate reevaluations and homework assignments as well.

The fifth stage of the program is designed to make the trainee more sensitive to the behavior of others. The understanding guide, which is broken into general movements, general appearance, general verbal response pattern, and general verbal tone, is used. Danish and Hauer have done an excellent job of breaking down into manageable learning components the way in which a person presents, and as such, this is really a strong point of the program. Additionally, the format allows the trainee to understand more fully another person's behavior. The procedure here involves practice in using the understanding guide by viewing either a live or a filmed model of a person engaging in helpee-like behaviors.

Stage six of the program involves integrating the specific skills which were emphasized throughout the first five stages. Here, didactic instruction is given as to the various means to form or establish an effective relationship with a helpee. A group discussion then follows, in which implications and processes in establishing effective relationships occur. Next, the groups break into dyads, with one individual being the helper and the other the helpee. Following this, the trainees observe models of a person using ineffective communication skills and then return to their dyads to role play, using ineffective communication skills. The trainees next observe the models using effective communication skills. Afterwards, the trainees assemble as a group and discuss the differences in behavior when good and poor communication skills are used. Finally, homework involving the individual having the opportunity to be a helper for about twenty minutes is requested. It is recommended that these sessions be audiotaped and the tape be evaluated using a checklist. One interesting difference with regard to a procedure of this format as compared to microcounseling is the viewing of the model tape after an initial role play. Again, the use of the homework assignment and systematic checklist at the end of the training session is another aspect of the program which is unique.

The question of the effectiveness of written homework and written evaluation as opposed to videotape feedback is open to scrutiny, but when one does not have the advantage of video equipment, certainly having some written evaluation form would be of benefit. Also, with regard to transfer of training, it would seem that the use of both might help the generalization process. Of course, as with the other programs discussed, the brief description given here does not do complete justice to the program. There are probably several other differences and similarities which could be described between the program and microcounseling, but rather than belabor this point, let us turn to the effectiveness of the Helping Skills program.

Like the E.I. program, the research evidence reflecting the effectiveness of the Helping Skills program is limited due to its being a relative newcomer to the counselor training field. One of the more recently published articles to date is that reported by Danish, D'Augelli, and Brock (1976). This study compares pre- and postaudiotapes of 126 trainees, all but nine of whom were undergraduates. The authors hypothesized that the trainees' post-training would have more content and affective responses, employ fewer direct questions and advisory responses, and employ more open questions. All but the fourth hypothesis were confirmed; that is, for some reason, the trainees failed to employ more open questions. The authors admit to limitations of not using real clients and only using a six-minute sample of helping behavior as well as not using a control group, but they still seem encouraged that the program did achieve most of its goals. Further, they claim that the study suggests that the helping skills program can accomplish its training goals with paraprofessional personnel acting as trainers, since the trainers were four graduate-level students who had received the training previous to the study.

Two other research projects designed to test the effectiveness of the Helping Skills program are noteworthy. The first is of particular value since it focuses on an often-neglected portion of skills training, namely retention of skills after training is completed. McCarthy, Danish, and D'Augelli (in press) conducted a study with twenty-six trainees engaged in three helping interviews—before training, immediately following training, and seven months later. Although high skill levels immediately following training were not generally maintained, at follow-up they remained higher than pretraining levels. Additionally, two specific verbal responses, affective responses and closed questions, were at posttraining levels. Two other specific verbal responses, advice giving and self-disclosure, while not significantly different pretraining and posttraining, were significantly different at follow-up, suggesting that the skills were somehow incorporated into the response repertoire without more specific training. This is a particularly interesting finding since an ancillary variable of the study explored the relationship between those trainees who were engaged in formal helping activities in the interim and those who were not, and found a remote relationship to exist. Needless to say, the conflicting results of this follow-up study demonstrate the need for more follow-up projects, not only with the Helping Skills program but with all skill training programs. Hopefully, such exploration would clarify some of the inconsistencies demonstrated here.

The other noteworthy evaluation of the Helping Skills program was conducted by D'Augelli and Levy (in press), in which human service paraprofessionals in a youth service agency were studied. These workers had previously completed the ten-week Helping Skills training program. Using simulated helping interviews, they were compared to an untrained volunteer staff. It was found that training made a significant impact on trainees' verbal helping responses. Indeed, trainees were found to be using significantly more content responses, affective responses, open questions, and less closed questions than the volunteers. Importantly, this study also included follow-up as part of its design. Data from the two-month follow-up evaluation demonstrated that the skill level was maintained for certain responses, whereas others either returned to pretraining levels or for some reason increased, although not significantly. Specifically, content responses were found to decrease significantly at follow-up to levels similar to pretest levels. Further, although affective and open responses demonstrated no change over training, these responses were used significantly more at follow-up than at pretesting. Thus, it seems that passage of time affects response maintenance in a complex way, thereby again indicating the need for more follow-up studies which should allow for some clarification of the variables affecting response maintenance. Finally, it should be noted that some of the more complex response modes of the Helping Skills program were not affected by training, suggesting that either the program is not effective in imparting these more complex skills, e.g. advice-giving, self-involving, self-disclosing, or that more time is needed before these more complex skills become a part of a trainee's repertoire. The latter explanation seems to be more the case, as in the McCarthy et al. study at least self-disclosing responses, while not significantly different from pretest, at the posttest level were significantly different at follow-up. However, the fact that the D'Augelli and Levy study used only a six-minute analogue interview suggests either the artificial nature of the interview or the short duration of the interview may have been responsible for the more complex skills not being demonstrated.

HUMAN RELATIONS TRAINING

As discussed at the beginning of this chapter, the Carkhuff Human Relations Training program (Carkhuff, 1969a,b) is not directly related to the microtraining format. Indeed, many would consider aspects of it the forerunner of microcounseling. Such is the case, because the Carkhuff training program was developed from the Truax and Carkhuff (1967) Experiential-Didactic program, which was discussed in Chapter 2 as one of the first systematic counselor training programs. Furthermore, as discussed earlier, the Human Relations Training program was one of the first which attempted to focus on specific therapist qualities, differentiating good therapists from poor therapists as part of its training format. Additionally, the Carkhuff training program attempts to integrate all sources of learning, i.e. experiential, didactic, and modeling, in a more systematic way than was accomplished in the more traditional counselor training programs. Indeed, Carkhuff

developed the Human Relations Training as he felt even the Experiential-Didactic program he developed with Truax was less
systematic than it might be. His thinking appears to have been
that the E-D program was quite effective with persons in training
to become professional counselors but that lay counselors and
paraprofessionals needed a still more systematic approach. Additionally, the Human Relations Training program emphasizes
skill training in concreteness, self-disclosure as part of being
genuine, confrontation, and immediacy, which were not systematically trained in the earlier work.

Although the above would seem to indicate that the content of
Human Relations Training is very similar to that of microcounseling, this is not the case. For the most part, Human Relations
Training consists of training in several core counselor conditions,
such as empathy, genuineness, respect, and concreteness, which
are essentially the affective and paralinguistic aspects of interpersonal communication. Further, these core conditions by their
very nature are for the most part global characteristics rather than
specific behaviors. Nevertheless, some specific behaviors, such as
reflections, open-ended inquiries, and confrontation, are trained
as part of helping trainees to become more proficient in the core
conditions. Microcounseling, on the other hand, as has been
stressed throughout this book, focuses on the hierarchy of well-
defined specific counselor behaviors. It seems to us that the microcounseling content tends to emphasize the linguistic determinants
of some of the Human Relations Training core conditions (see
especially Chapter 6, where the qualitative facilitative conditions
are reviewed from a microcounseling point of view).

Perhaps, then, the main difference between the two systems is
in the training process. Even here, though, there are many commonalities, such as the use of modeling, role playing, immediate
feedback, and the like. Three major differences between the two
instructional techniques do exist, however, First, Human Relations Training uses two training phases, the first of which consists
of a discrimination training phase during which trainees learn to
differentiate levels of counselor communications by listening to
audiotaped recordings of counselor models but get no practice at

counseling. The second training phase is communication training, wherein trainees role play and learn through actual practice. The microtraining format, of course, does not have a discrimination training phase and instead uses role playing as its focal point of training, hence providing trainees with experiences in counseling from the outset of the training program. The development of the Microcounseling Skills Discrimination Index, however, is a beginning effort of microcounseling in this area (see Appendix IV). Second, videotape rather than audiotape is used as the means for presenting models as well as for training feedback purposes. Third, the feedback of the Human Relations Training consists of using objective ratings of trainee level of communication which provide direct confrontation and feedback to the trainee regarding his or her level of performance instead of the videotaped feedback as described above.

Since the Human Relations Training program is a further extension of the Truax and Carkhuff Experiential-Didactic program discussed in detail in Chapter 2, it seems warranted here to discuss only those aspects of the program which differentiate it from the earlier one. Some of these have been mentioned above, e.g. the Human Relations Training program's emphasis on concreteness, confrontation, and immediacy. Moreover, the Human Relations Training program does not include the group psychotherapy phase of training as part of its experiential format as did the E-D program. Finally, there seems to be an even greater emphasis on the modeling of the various skills by the trainer. Carkhuff (1969a) states, "The trainer is the key ingredient insofar as he offers a model of a person who is living effectively" (p. 201). As such, the effects of modeling seem to be given a higher emphasis than they were in earlier training. Moreover, the very nature of some of the additions to the Human Relations Training program make the didactic portion of that program much more detailed, almost to the point where it has a specific skills rather than a core condition focus. As such, the Human Relations Training program has components which make the program more similar to the microtraining format than the E-D program. The content similarity is also apparent when one considers that confrontation is taught by both the Human Relations Training and microcounseling programs.

Not surprisingly, the Human Relations Training program is found to be effective with a variety of populations, ranging from teachers (Carkhuff and Griffin, 1971) to resident assistants (Mitchell, Rubin, Bozarth, and Wyrick, 1971) to psychiatric patients (Pierce and Drasgow, 1969; Vitalo, 1971). The last population, i.e. psychiatric patients, is of most interest here since it demonstrates once again the effectiveness of a psychoeducator model of treatment. Thus, these two studies will be presented in some detail below.

Similar to some of the other counseling programs discussed, Human Relations Training has served as an impetus for training in communication skills to patient populations without particular focus on specific roles or problem areas, largely as an extension of the counseling training system. Pierce and Drasgow (1969) drew from the Human Relations Training program in an attempt to assess the effects of training in interpersonal functioning upon psychiatric inpatients. Training essentially consisted of teaching a reflection of feeling skill via explicit instruction and feedback-ingraded practice. The trainer's role was conceptualized as a behavior-shaper, with major emphasis on verbal reinforcement of increasingly longer feeling-oriented interactions between a specific and rotating dyad. After providing a verbal listing of common feelings, the trainer instructed and reinforced a patient to identify in one word the feeling expressed in a sentence from another patient, then to build that word into a sentence, and gradually to increase the length of the interaction between the two patients assigned roles as listener and understander from two sentences to fifteen to twenty minutes. Pre-post assessments of the learning were rated by use of the Truax (1967) rating scales for empathy, positive regard, genuineness, and concreteness. The results indicated that the training group demonstrated significant improvement in interpersonal functioning and improved significantly more than any of the four control groups. A similar study by Vitalo (1971) was also conducted to assess the effects of training in interpersonal functioning upon psychiatric inpatients. Two groups of five patients each from the wards of two psychiatric hospitals were trained via the Human Relations Training program. The training leader's role was reported to consist of using direct instruction methods, directing patients' practice, responding, reinforcing and correcting patients' responses, suggesting alternative more facilitative responses, i.e. modeling, and progressively shaping the patients' behaviors. The dependent measure consisted of the Truax and Carkhuff (1967) rating scales. The results indicated that the trainees/patients demonstrated significant improvement from the pre- to the postmeasures of the facilitative interpersonal functioning skills.

Still another study, designed to assess the effects of Human Relations Training in the treatment and counseling of parents of emotionally disturbed children (Carkhuff and Bierman, 1970), suggests training as a preferred mode of treatment with outpatient populations. Ten parents of emotionally disturbed children were taken off the psychiatric clinic waiting list and offered systematic training in interpersonal skills. The results indicated significant improvement in the level of communication discrimination between parents and to some degree between the parents and their children. Traditional indexes of child behavior demonstrated general improvement, but the changes were not significant.

Needless to say, the results of the above studies were very encouraging for the psychoeducator model of treatment. It is important to note that the role of the therapist in all of these studies was one of a trainer in specific skills. Further, the training tasks involved teaching modalities common to all teaching endeavors, that of providing verbal or written didactic instruction, that of providing models, either live or audio, that of providing or arranging feedback on performance, and that of administrating or coordinating an integrated program. It is heartening to see "therapists" use extensions of the Human Relations Training programs as a means of treatment, and it is our hope that, as evidence continues to demonstrate the effectiveness of the psychoeducator model, to use Carkhuff's terminology, training will indeed be the "preferred mode of treatment."

Before summarizing the commonalities of the various programs described to this point, mention needs to be made of several programs which, although not packaged in the sense that they include videotapes, films, a leader's manual, or what have you, still focus on the helping relationship. In this vein, Brammer's manual, *"The Helping Relationship"* (1973), discusses quite specifically many of the skills the helper needs in order to help another person and conceptualizes the interview as a totality. *Intervention in Human Services* by Schulman (1974) is another text which provides ideas on how to be most helpful. Her book is particularly useful in that it talks specifically about intervention from various theoretical frameworks. Other texts designed to enhance mental health via the psychoeducator model are Egan, *The Skilled Helper* (1975), Gazda, *Human Relations Development— A Manual for Educators* (1973), and Goodman, *Companionship Therapy* (1972). Certainly there are others which could be mentioned at this point, but as indicated earlier, this chapter is not meant to be an exhaustive survey of the various helping programs but instead merely a discussion of some of those which are offered in such a way as to stand on their own and which have components of the psychoeducator model adding to their effectiveness.

SUMMARY

Throughout this edition, we have made clear that microcounseling is not the only way to help people become more effective helpers or helpees. This chapter in particular was designed to demonstrate that several programs are available which are effective means of meeting this end. However, it was suggested that some of the dimensions of the microtraining format often add to these other training programs' effectiveness. Additionally, like microcounseling, they were designated as programs which for the most part could stand on their own and hence were considered "packaged" programs.

Emphasis was given to two primary factors responsible for the growth of such "packaged" programs. First, Hobbs' "Third Revolution," the paraprofessional movement, was designated as a major force. Second, the psychoeducator movement with emphasis on helping people to become their own therapeutic agents, especially in the interpersonal realm, was cited as the other major force. Bernard Guerney and his associates were cited as being particularly influential with regard to the psychoeducator movement taking hold.

The programs actually discussed ranged from the Enriching Intimacy program, one which is a direct modification of the microcounseling paradigm, to Human Relations Training, which, although developed before microcounseling, was demonstrated to have similar microtraining components. The intermediate programs discussed were Goldstein's Structured Learning Therapy, Kagan's Interpersonal Recall, and Danish and Hauer's Helping Skills program.

Caution was given regarding these programs not being considered the only ones in existence but rather ones which were for the most part forerunners of some of the more current skill training programs. Additionally, these programs were given emphasis due to their having some research data backing their effectiveness. Indeed, readers were advised of several which were not included but which would be worthwhile to explore based on the particular needs of their agencies.

Microcounseling and the programs described in this chapter serve two purposes: (1) training helpers in the skills of counseling and therapy and (2) as psychoeducational vehicles. The reader is referred to some useful sources which the authors have found helpful in the psychoeducation approach.* Some of these works represent packaged approaches to achieve psychoeducational objectives, others are theoretical pieces helpful in orienting the trainee to underlying issues in training, and still others represent interesting approaches to sharing the mysteries and complexities of the helping process with the public.

---

*Alberti and Emmons, 1970; Anderson and Love, 1973; Arbuckle, 1976a,b.; Berne, 1964; Bessell, 1970; Bessell and Palomares, 1971; Bry, 1976; Carkhuff and Berenson, 1967; Connolly and Bruner, 1974; Delworth, 1973; Dinkmeyer and Dreikurs, 1963; Dreikurs, 1948; Fast, 1970; Harris, 1967; Hurst, 1976; Krumboltz and Krumboltz, 1972; Lambert, 1972; Maslow, 1971; Patterson and Guillion, 1968; Pfeiffer and Jones, 1969, 1970, 1971, 1973; Raths, Harmin, and Simon, 1966; Schutz, 1967; Simon, Howe, and Kirschenbaum 1972.

SECTION IV

ALTERNATIVE APPLICATIONS OF MICROTRAINING IN TEACHING AND RESEARCH

Alternatives, options, different routes . . . if one were to characterize microtraining at this juncture, the main theme appears to be a multitude of different ways to use basic skills with different populations under varying conditions. The purpose of this final section is to expand further the multipotential framework.

Special attention is given in Chapter 12 to "Using Microtraining as a Teaching Tool." Alternatives for using the single skills approach in one-to-one training and small group training are discussed. Extensive discussion is given to maintenance of learned behavior via competency standards and follow-up training. Ideas for developing training materials, both written and videobased, are presented.

Chapter 13 is entitled "Research Related to Microtraining," and over 100 research studies directly relating to the paradigm are presented in summary form. An array of needed alternatives for future research is presented.

The concluding chapter, "Microtraining: An Open System," reiterates the main theme of the book. The technology and metatheory which is microtraining offers considerable latitude for development and new innovations. The reader is urged to take ideas from the framework, shape them, and adapt them to fit the special needs and background of specific groups who may need training. Further, a large number of unresolved issues exist within the paradigm which will require further clinical and research effort to clarify.

Chapter 12

USING MICROTRAINING
AS A TEACHING TOOL

MICROTRAINING AND MICROCOUNSELING represent an open system, an approach to interviewing training which allows for alternatives and variations. While the basic framework has been demonstrated to be effective in a multitude of research and training situations, it is still possible to alter the skills being taught, the order of materials presented, and to adapt the model to fit virtually any situation. Trainers who take the microtraining model and mold it to their own unique setting and trainee population will find that this results in the most powerful and enjoyable learning experience. This chapter is concerned with providing an array of data which illustrates that microtraining can be used in many different situations under highly varying conditions to meet the special needs and interests of the individual trainer and trainee.

We believe that one of microtraining's major contributions is in the area of competency-based helper training. The specificity of the model and the clear effects on both helpers and helpees make a most effective and useful training system. This chapter provides the background for a competency-based helper training program, and those oriented to this model are encouraged to turn to Appendix VII, where a series of examples of specific competencies are presented. Suggestions for adapting competencies to fit many different orientations to helping are presented.

The chapter also presents specific suggestions for effecting and launching a microcounseling training program and summarizes major alternatives for adapting the framework to varying settings. Specifically, we will present data on methods of teaching microcounseling skills to individuals, using microtraining in group settings, the do-use-teach contract which promotes generalization of learned skills to new settings, how to develop microtraining materials and video modeling tapes, a consideration of the role of the client in microtraining, the alternative uses of video equipment, still other alternative microtraining models, and ethical considerations in microtraining.

The material discussed here will be of most interest to individuals wishing to train others in microtraining skills. It is this training dimension which relates microtraining to the psychoeducator model. The effective helper of the future will be actively involved in teaching others the important skills of helping and interpersonal communication.

TEACHING MICROCOUNSELING SKILLS TO INDIVIDUALS

There is a very real danger that the teaching of microcounseling skills can become mechanical and fixed, particularly if one becomes too ruled by specific methods. After one has learned the procedures and enjoyed the first flush of success, it is possible to develop a routine in which the supervisor loses personal involvement with the trainees. When this happens, we have often observed that the trainees learn the skills being taught but are not enthused by the procedures and have trouble generalizing newly learned behaviors to the actual counseling setting.

We have learned that teaching the specific skills of counseling involves important supervisory-counseling skills. As noted earlier, the supervisor must model the skills being taught. For example, it is possible to teach attending behavior to a trainee and fail to attend to the trainee's questions and possible resistance toward the entire procedure. The supervisor in such situations must listen to the trainee and observe individual needs of the moment. A trainee may be concerned over the cosmetic effect of seeing him or herself on television for the first time. The supervisor can facilitate learning by helping the trainee talk out feelings. A trainee may feel incapable of engaging in the behavior being taught. At such points, superior counseling and supervisory skills are essential if trainee growth through microtraining is to occur. The confidence and competence of the trainer is as important as the material being taught.

With some trainees, supplementing the regular program with role playing is most helpful. Occasionally, a modern Rogerian approach is useful. The supervisor might say to the trainee, "I have the feeling right now that you are anxious about going on videotape." Such leads can help the trainee explore him or herself and accompanying attitudes. However, it is essential that the supervisor not simply role play reflection of feeling; such behavior is most effective when the supervisor really cares about the trainee and seeks to develop a more mutual relationship. This live-modeling approach adds to the genuineness of the encounter.

When teaching attending behavior, the entire session is begun in a casual and friendly (but organized) fashion. Trainees are welcomed and invited to inspect the television recording facility. Questions regarding the experience are often raised, and much can be done at this stage to alleviate anxiety.

After the initial five-minute videotaping session, the first task of the supervisor is to establish a more genuine relationship with the trainee. This may be done by a variety of means, but basically the supervisor must attend to the client and respond to immediate needs, even if this means delaying the training procedures. Generally speaking, the question "How did it go?" or "How do you feel?" provides sufficient material for the sensitive trainer to determine how best to establish a relationship with that particular individual. With nervous trainees, we have occasionally instituted informal instruction in systematic relaxation. Most trainees, however, are relatively relaxed and eager to move forward with the instructional procedures.

Throughout the supervisory session, we provide opportunities for the trainee to interact with us in any way he or she chooses. If the trainee is resistant, we may use this resistance as a leverage to obtain a deeper relationship. Trainees are encouraged to examine the meaningfulness of the skill which we are teaching. However, when confronted with a good deal of talk or resistance on the part of the trainee, we sometimes suggest a short-term contract in which the trainee agrees to "try on" the skill during this session and we will talk on the issue at greater length later. During this phase we often make the point that "This is simply one view of counseling. All we are asking you to do is 'try on' some new and specific behavior. If you like it, you may continue it. If not, feel free to forget it. Unless the behavior fits and feels natural, it will be of no use to you." This "if you listen to me, I'll listen to you" contract has proven most fruitful and has resulted in subsequent changes or additions to our basic training procedures.

When viewing the modeling tape or reviewing the five-minute tape made by the trainee, it is usually helpful to stop the tape and give the trainee an opportunity to react—or you may wish to give specific reactions of your own. However, it is vital that the trainee not be overwhelmed by data. Sometimes too many behaviors are taught at once, or a specific skill is described in too minute detail. Microtraining procedures are not concerned with producing effective counselors in one session. The primary concern is helping trainees to grow with time. As such, it is preferable that most trainees be given one to three specific suggestions as to how they might improve. Otherwise, the suggestions are forgotten, and a trainee is made more tense.

Basically, all we ask of our trainees is some improvement from their starting point. While most reach criterion levels rather quickly, others require several sessions. Some trainees are better in their first five-minute session than others are after several training units. Our approach has always been to reward improvement and not to judge the level of effectiveness. We find that this approach usually brings even the most "unpromising" trainee to satisfactory performance. As such, microtraining is a highly individualized process.

In summary, the above points center on the counseling and supervisory skills of the trainer. If a unique and meaningful relationship with the trainee can be established, improvement in both immediate and future performance seems almost inevitable. If the supervisor finds him or herself becoming bored or losing effectiveness with the process despite these suggestions, it may be wise to ask another individual with similar supervisory skills to serve as a replacement. A procedure such as microcounseling requires personal involvement if it is to succeed, and like all things, one eventually finds a need for change.

Microcounseling is well defined procedurally, so that relatively untrained individuals such as paraprofessionals or students can be utilized as trainers. In such settings, the counseling or personnel supervisor becomes a roving consultant, assisting the staff to actually run the training program. A basic model to train paraprofessionals has been explored by Haase and DiMattia (1970) and since has been elaborated upon by Gluckstern (1973). A major suggestion for the utilization of paraprofessionals in training of others is that adequate training in supervisory skills be added to basic training in the microcounseling model.

GROUP INSTRUCTION IN MICROTRAINING

Microcounseling in its first presentation was considered a one-to-one training modality. However, it is not always possible to have time to spend with individuals. Counseling must often be taught in group or classroom settings. Ivey and Gluckstern (1974a,b; 1976a,b) have given special attention to developing group methods for teaching microtraining skills. Research indicates (cf. Gluckstern, 1973; Hearn, 1976; Scroggins and Ivey, 1976) that group instruction can be as effective as individual instruction if careful attention is given to classroom plans or workshop designs and sufficient practice in the skill being taught is provided. A competency-based approach to group instructions is most effective if participants in the group demonstrate each specific skill or quality before being considered "trained."

Group instruction in microcounseling skills involves the same basic dimensions as the one-to-one approach but supplements the basic framework with the following dimensions of group process.

Step 1: Creating a learning environment. When teaching microcounseling skills to groups, one must first start with the group and its unique needs. Get-acquainted exercises, "name games," and information concerning the timing of the workshop or class are important in starting any session. The specific goals and competencies emphasized in the session are clarified for the trainees.

Step 2: Training. The specific skill is introduced with lecture, study of the microtraining manuals, and observation of videotape models. Live modeling of the specific skills and demonstrations by the trainer are encouraged. Large and small group exercises may be employed to role play the skill being taught. Clarity of presentation is vital, for it is not possible to know how well every individual understands one's presentation.

Step 3: Practice. Whereas Step 2 is devoted to providing a basic cognitive understanding of the concepts of the workshops, real learning occurs during the practice session, for it is here that trainees must demonstrate that they can *do* what is being taught in the training session. Small groups, usually consisting of four people, are organized, with specific roles given to each trainee. One of the trainees serves as leader of the group, a second as co-leader, and the two other members serve as helper and helpee. The co-trainers guide their pair through the skill practice session until the helper gains competence. At this point, roles shift, and a new helper trainee is designated. This pattern continues until all in the group have demonstrated the ability to engage in the skill. The trainer moves from group to group to answer questions and assist with problems that may arise.

The ideal practice session provides each small group of four to six participants with video units. However, audio cassette recorders and skilled observation and behavior counts from the small group members themselves can provide a suitable alternative.

Step 4: Extensions. Training and practice provide only beginnings. Microcounseling skills will soon be lost unless specific contracts are made for taking the learned behavior out of the laboratory workshop setting and into actual interview situations. Behavioral contracting for *using* the skills learned within the training framework helps "set" the learning and makes generalization to real-life situations possible. Advanced trainees complete their demonstration of full competence by teaching learned skills to other people in one-to-one or workshop form.

Step 5: Evaluation and feedback. Small groups and the leader(s) meet in the final stages of a workshop and determine whether or not each individual has met the objectives of the single skill. If full competency has not been demonstrated in practice sessions, individuals can work further to enhance their skills before moving on to other aspects of training. The behavioral contracts discussed in the preceding paragraph may also be examined to determine student ability with each workshop.

Workshop designs of this nature take trainees in groups of 4 to 100 through the entire microcounseling conceptual framework. With careful use of small group interaction and follow-through on levels of competency, trainees can achieve counseling skills equal to those trained via one-to-one microtraining.

The systematic workshop format is also most useful in introducing microtraining and communication constructs to paraprofessionals and groups of lay people. A wide variety of lay groups, ranging from normal children through extremely troubled psychiatric patients, have participated successfully in such workshops. The content and definition of the skills, of course, changes to fit the needs of the unique population served.

Personal growth workshops also may be conducted using microtraining materials. The same workshop designs are used, but participants are encouraged to use practice sessions for in-depth exploration of personal concerns. Groups of four (or more) may be formed in which each member practices the specific skills, e.g. self-disclosure, attending, open questions, etc., but prime attention is given to personal issues. The skills provide a structure which gradually moves a small group of people to greater exploration. At the same time, the skills help ensure that the growth groups are truly "helpful." A special advantage of this approach as compared to traditional T-groups is that people become aware of what is going on in a group in terms of specific behaviors and are better able to transfer newly learned behavior beyond the training group. Of course, transfer of behavior is greatly facilitated by the use of the do-use-teach contracts which will be outlined in the ensuing section.

THE DO-USE-TEACH CONTRACT

Instructional procedures in counseling, interviewing, or therapy most often have stressed *understanding* as basic to successful performance as a helper. Cognitive understanding, however, does not mean the ability to engage in helping and to impact on another person's life. The do-use-teach contract has been developed in microtraining workshops to ensure that learned behavior maintains itself (cf. Ivey, 1971; Ivey and Rollin, 1972; Ivey and Gluckstern, 1974b, 1976b).

The do-use-teach contract is based on the simple but obvious fact that behavior which is not clearly developed and performed or used in one's daily life is likely to be rapidly lost. Haase, DiMattia, and Guttman (1972) found that microtrained paraprofessionals who did not practice or use their skills during the ensuing year after training lost the skills (although retraining could rapidly bring them up to criterion levels once again). Maintenance and generalization of microcounseling skills should be programmed rather than expected or lamented.

The first aspect of a do-use-teach contract is doing or performing the indicated skill. The competencies of microtraining cited in this chapter are doing-oriented. Unless a trainee can demonstrate specific competencies, we have no guarantee that real learning has occurred. When microtraining research or training programs have been less effective, it is because criterion levels of performance have not been stressed. A verbalization from a helpee that he or she has the ability to demonstrate the skills is not adequate. Specific examples of effective helping need to be demonstrated on video- or audiotape. Small groups can monitor each others' behavior, but some specific method of checking out the ability of the individual to perform the skills is necessary. Some individuals master the competencies easily and quickly; others need several recycles of training before minimum competencies can be demonstrated.

Weinrach (1976) has given special attention to the do-use-teach framework and has extended the original model. He stresses highly specific behavioral contracting in which individuals test out their ability with the skill with real interviews, friends, or family. He uses a simple contract "I agree to use (name of skill or concept) with (name of individual) under these specific conditions: _____. I will note the reactions I get and report back to my training group" (p. 312). Weinrach reports the following from his trainees:

> Betty, a 23-year-old teacher, reported that she selected her boyfriend because he never seemed to tell her what was bothering him when he was upset. Betty decided to use eye contact as her first skill the next time her boyfriend appeared upset. Betty reported back to her group that after attending to her boyfriend with improved eye contact, he slowly began to talk about himself. In another situation, Mark, a 45-year-old counselor, indicated that his wife always complained that he cross-examined her. He decided to use open-ended questions the next time they discussed household finances. Mark reported ecstatically to the group that for the first time he understood how his wife felt (p. 312).

Using microcounseling skills outside of the workshop in such exercises helps cement the skill and convince trainees of their value in the interview.

Ivey (1973b), in work with psychiatric patients, used a more behavioral approach in which specific counts were made of agreed-on behaviors defined in the media therapy sessions. One manic patient had a problem with consistent topic jumping and was given an audio-cassette recorder to carry on the ward. He had a contract to have three conversations per day with other patients. The conversations were recorded and then analyzed for the specific number of topic jumps. A wide variety of behavioral contracts to use microtraining skills are possible, and some are identified in Appendix I, where a model workshop in attending behavior is presented.

"You don't know what you are doing until you can teach it to someone else" has long been a model of those involved in microtraining. Real mastery of a skill occurs when one can teach it to others and have them demonstrate the skill. "Teach" contracts similar to the "use" contracts cited above by Weinrach are developed to encourage trainees to share what they have learned with others. Participants may employ newly learned skills to teach effective communication to families, friends, church groups, children, or any of a wide variety of populations. The nature of the teaching may range from the replication of systematic microtraining one-to-one or workshop methods to extremely informal teaching of skills. As in all microtraining sessions, the beginning trainer should make sure that trainees can demonstrate specific competencies. Verbalizations that an individual understands the concepts are insufficient.

Ivey stressed this point in his work with media therapy and psychiatric patients. A patient who could demonstrate good attending skills in the training session and use them on the ward had made a good beginning. Real mastery and progress, however, showed when some patients began teaching their own families listening skills. Similarly, trainees begin to show real professional competence when they are able to share their skills with others through teaching what they have learned, thus entering the psychoeducator model. The systematic and specific methods of microtraining make entry into the psychoeducational model clear and direct.

The effective helper should not only understand what he or she is doing but should be able to demonstrate this behavior in a workshop setting and achieve measurable competence. Further, the effective helper is able to generalize learned behavior beyond the training situation to work in interviewing practice *and* daily life settings. Finally, the truly effective helper is able to enter into the psychoeducational model and teach what has been learned to others with demonstrable effects on their behavior. "You don't know what you are doing until you teach it to someone else."

Whether one decides to use microtraining for group or individual training, the careful development of material for training is central. The following section discusses central issues surrounding the filming of videotapes to present models of effective helping.

DEVELOPING MICROTRAINING MATERIALS AND VIDEO MODELING TAPES

When developing materials for microcounseling, for groups or individuals, one learns more about the skills than do those who will eventually be taught. Much thought and care must go into developing written or programmed materials which communicate the underlying concepts of a basic skill. Similarly, developing a video or film sequence to illustrate the behavior in question is a demanding task. However, with some basic guidelines, the task is pleasant and an important learning experience for the person who develops the materials.

As such, a possibility which one may wish to consider in materials development is simply giving students the problem of defining the skills of interviewing in behavioral terms. With some guidance from the trainer, this can be a successful method of teaching basic skills. This approach, however, takes a good deal of time and equipment and perhaps should be reserved for advanced trainees who may go into counseling or personnel supervision.

The first step in developing materials for microtraining is the selection of the skill or specific behavior. If the skill is defined as attending behavior, a good way to begin is to place models of poor attention on videotape, for it is relatively easy to model ineffective interviewing. Once one views the ineffective model, it becomes possible to identify the specific behaviors which comprise effective demonstration of the behavior in question. Individuals who model ineffective listening on videotape typically avoid eye contact, show physical discomfort, and engage in topic jumping and interruption. Viewing these negative behaviors, then, makes it possible to develop positive models representing an antithesis. (A typescript of an attending behavior model tape is presented in Appendix II.)

If the behavior to be developed was focused on positive responses to a negative employee, the first model might have the interviewer alternately ignoring and interrupting the employee, thus demonstrating a generally ineffective confronting approach (the word "generally" is inserted, as we have found that virtually any behavior is appropriate in some situations). The positive model then might consist of attending behavior plus certain expressive skills such as direct-mutual communication and giving factual information to the employee. Through this method, new skill tapes using the basic concepts of microtraining can be adapted to many situations.

Having identified general positive and negative models of the behavior in question, it is then feasible to establish more complete working models of the behavior. As an example, one attending behavior model consists of a one-minute segment without sound, illustrating positive attention on the part of the interviewer. (During this segment the trainer talks with the trainee about the importance of nonverbal communication and points out eye contact and physical posture patterns.) This is followed by a minute of a soundless negative model with poor eye contact patterns and a closed or tight physical posture. Next, the sound comes on and a minute of poor verbal following behavior is shown in which the interviewer topic jumps, talks about himself, and interrupts. A final two-to-three-minute segment consists of the counselor engaging in positive attending behavior both verbally and nonverbally.

Written manuals are most helpful to supplement the model tapes. We have found that brief manuals are preferred to detailed instructions. The manuals presented in Appendices I and V are focused on a few key aspects of the skill and are designed to cue the trainee to a quick overview. Experience has revealed that these generalized models are effective, but in some cases, manuals should be rewritten to meet the special needs of unique trainees. For example, when working with younger children, the language of the manual needs simplification. With psychiatric patients, even less material may be desirable. Translation of the manuals into the language of the training group is clearly important. Further, it should be stressed that training in microcounseling skills with a manual *alone* can produce significant behavior change in the interview. Video models enrich and enliven the experience, self-observation brings learnings to personal levels, and the rapport between trainee and trainer facilitates speed and depth of learning. Yet, the fact remains that well-developed written materials in many cases are sufficient for improvement in helping performance.

The reflection of feeling modeling tapes, typically five to seven minutes in length, consist of three examples, one negative and two positive. The negative model focuses on objective content and ignores obvious feelings on the part of the client. The positive models demonstrate emotional responses to the client's utterances. A similar format is used for paraphrasing.

The summarization modeling tape has varied in length from five to ten minutes. In this model, a client discusses a problem with the counselor, who uses attending behavior and reflection of feeling. At crucial points, the counselor summarizes the client's thoughts and emotions over the session to that point. Two summarizations are positive, two negative.

After trainees have demonstrated their ability to engage in the specific attending skills, an integration of these skills is presented on a fifteen-minute model tape. The helper goes through each of the attending skills, and the trainee is expected to classify and rate the different skills being used. Solely attending skills are used, thus demonstrating that an effective interview can be conducted without the influencing skills. In the integration of skills model tape, Ivey and Gluckstern (1974c) include interviewing errors so that both positive and negative aspects of helping may be considered. Trainees at the completion of the attending skills sessions are expected to produce an interview in which all attending skills are demonstrated during the model interview.

The modeling tape for self-expression takes the form of an individual unable to express self clearly followed by one who demonstrates culturally sanctioned methods of self-expression. The directions model tapes are similar. A teacher gives ineffective and then effective directions to a class; a "physician" gives directions to a patient on how to take a prescription; finally, a helper demonstrates effective and ineffective directions through relaxation training. It may be noted that the influencing skills model tapes broaden the concepts of microtraining to include areas other than interviewing, counseling, and therapy.

The modeling tapes for self-disclosure present a father talking first ineffectively with his son about coming home at late hours; this is followed by an excerpt in which self-disclosure is used as a method for better family communication. Then, a counselor

demonstrates self-disclosure in a helping interview. This model
tape presents a large number of self-disclosures with variations in
focus and immediacy. Trainees are encouraged to score and rate
the many self-disclosures for their varied effectiveness.

The interpretation model tape begins with an example of psychological imperialism (the forcing of a helper's beliefs on the
helpee), with the helper making a strong interpretation and then
forcing that interpretation on the helpee. A model tape then
follows with the helper presenting an array of interpretations
which once again may be scored and rated by the trainees.

The final integration of skills model tape of the Ivey and
Gluckstern (1976c) series is presented in typescript form and discussed in detail in Appendix III. The major objective of this tape
is to demonstrate all the microtraining skills and to provide a
setting wherein the qualitative dimensions of helping may also be
evaluated. At the conclusion of microtraining workshops,
trainees are expected to present videotapes in which they demonstrate all the skills of helping and rate their tapes for the qualitative dimensions as well.

While model tapes for all the qualitative dimensions of helping have not been developed, Authier and Gustafson (1973)
have demonstrated that such is certainly possible. In each case, the
following steps are helpful: (1) develop a negative model of
the qualitative dimension. For example, if concreteness is the
quality being taught, vagueness of expression should be the mode
of the helper on the tape; (2) develop a positive tape in which
concreteness is demonstrated; (3) check to make sure that extremely clear differences between the two tapes may be seen by
even the most novice helper. Exaggeration of the negative model
tape may be necessary to make the concept clear. We have found
that the qualitative dimensions can be taught along with the specific skills of microtraining. Ivey and Gluckstern (1976b), for
example, teach one qualitative skill with each influencing skills
workshop.

The direct-mutual communication modeling tape follows the
common microtraining format of a negative example with two
people completely failing to listen followed by two positive models
illustrating different dimensions of the skill. In this case, written

programmed material was integrated with video models illustrating specific aspects of open communication among pairs of individuals. We have found that those who have worked in T-groups or sensitivity training are best at providing models of direct-mutual communication.

It can be seen that modeling tapes for each skill have tended to take a slight different form. Those who have utilized micro-counseling in their training programs have consistently adapted the modeling tapes and skills to suit their own particular needs and theoretical persuasions. We do not particularly commend the above approaches to video modeling tapes but have found them effective in our setting.

Once a video modeling tape has been developed, it is possible to develop a written manual. Samples of manuals are available in the appendix. Each manual has gone through several revisions in an attempt to make the concept more specific to the population being taught. When teaching attending behavior to children, for example, a simple statement of about a paragraph in length seems appropriate. When working with advanced clinical graduate students, more sophisticated and theoretically oriented statements may be useful.

A most useful training device to supplement model skills tapes is the stimulus vignette of a client expressing a variety of emotions and/or problems. For attending skill training, Ivey and Gluckstern have developed a series of short (10 to 30 seconds) presentations in which role-played helpees portray varying emotions (single emotions, mixed emotions, mixed verbal and nonverbal emotions). The task of the classroom or workshop participant is to label the emotions presented and then to suggest a specific microtraining lead which might be used to facilitate client growth. Some trainees are naturally quite expert in labeling emotions, while others are rather primitive in their vocabulary and ability to recognize emotional expression in the helpee. This training is most helpful in aiding many people in expanding their emotional vocabulary. Haase and DiMattia (1970), for example, found that some beginning paraprofessionals could not reflect feelings until this more elementary training in recognizing and labeling emotions was provided.

More detailed stimulus vignettes are provided in the influencing skills model tapes. The vignettes are from one to two minutes in length, and a helper using attending skills draws out a role-played helpee. The tape is then stopped and trainees are asked to (1) make an attending summarization of the helpee's problem, (2) note their own emotional reactions to the helpee, (3) note their own parallel life experiences, and (4) present a self-disclosure or interpretation, depending on the skill being taught. A typescript of one of these vignettes is presented in Appendix V. The stimulus vignettes have proven popular with trainees and have resulted in important learnings. Among these has been increased awareness of the fact that different people attend to different issues, again underscoring the importance of cultural and subcultural dimensions of helping. A useful group exercise is to have summarizations of the key problem of the helpee presented by the trainees; invariably, the issues selected as central vary extensively from individual to individual. This is followed by comparison of emotions raised in respect to the helpee, and once again, wide individual differences are noted. Finally, self-disclosures and interpretations, which vary equally widely, are used. Out of this exercise trainees learn about how they respond and sometimes project their own experience on the helpee in a group context in which they see others doing the same thing. Further, the wide array of potentially helpful responses to facilitate helpee growth is made extremely clear.

CLIENTS IN THE MICROTRAINING PROCESS

It is the client who provides the life and rationale for microcounseling and microtraining processes. Designed as a bridge between classroom theories of counseling and interviewing and actual practice in the field, microtraining provides maximum realism with a minimum of danger to clients and/or prospective counselors.

A major question in the early stages of research in microcounseling centered on how real the five-minute sessions would be. Would paid and volunteer clients be representative of those whom counselors might interview at later points, or would these be artificial and contrived sessions? Clinical observation by numerous individuals has revealed that the sessions are indeed real; clients talk about real issues and concerns, and except for the length of the sessions, very real parallels to actual counseling exist.

Clients appear to enjoy and appreciate the opportunity to participate in microcounseling training sessions, willingly cooperate with filling out evaluation forms, and usually volunteer to return for more sessions. On many occasions when we have paid clients to serve as research subjects, we have found them saying they benefitted from the sessions and therefore did not wish to accept payment. To date, observation and follow-up of clients have not found any individuals who feel negatively toward the process. Nonetheless, it seems desirable to have fully trained professional counselors or supervisors on hand to supervise the work of a microcounseling clinic.

When volunteer clients are not readily available, role playing between pairs of counseling or interviewing trainees has proven effective. In role-played sessions, we have found that the situation becomes surprisingly real, and preliminary evidence suggests that this approach to microtraining may be as effective as more usual methods. As experimentation with role playing has continued, we have found that many pairs of trainees prefer to talk about real concerns rather than taking someone else's role. Needless to say, sessions of this nature become concerned with problems of real depth, and this method of training requires careful supervision by experienced staff. The potential for personal and professional growth, however, is important in such sessions and can be followed up by counseling, referral, or group sessions.

With advanced trainees, Kagan and Krathwohl's Interpersonal Process Recall (1967) methods have proven most effective. Clients remain in the microtraining session and discuss their reactions with the trainee and his supervisor. This immediate and direct feedback from the client's world has proven most helpful in promoting trainee growth. Trainees are often more able to listen to their clients than their supervisors. Welch (1976) has demonstrated the effectiveness of combining Interpersonal Process Recall with microcounseling.

Finally, it should be observed that microtraining procedures in the "skill of being a client" may be useful. The vicarious therapy of Truax et al. (1966) has demonstrated the validity of pretraining a client prior to counseling sessions. Clients who have been taught skills to use in counseling sessions tend to view counseling more positively and benefit more from sessions. Haase, Forsyth, Julius, and Lee (1971) have applied the microtraining framework to college counseling center clients and found that client pretraining facilitated subsequent interviews. Although microcounseling procedures were not used, a closely parallel study by Whalen (1969) demonstrated that video modeling films could facilitate group-encounter processes.

While the preceding examples have focused on counseling and therapy, useful analogies can be drawn to personnel or employment interviewing. It appears that volunteer clients from work settings will perform successfully as microtraining clients. However, evaluation may concern employees as much or more than students in a course. Some may fear that promotions or raises depend on their performance. Under such conditions, role-played sessions may be preferable. Skillful, honest supervision seems essential, because such fears can only damage the effectiveness of the microtraining sessions.

Realness is important to microtraining. If sessions seem artificial, awkward, or stereotypic, the supervisor will want to look at his or her relationship with trainees and clients. Any procedure which is as clearly defined as microtraining has the danger of becoming stereotyped and losing touch with original goals. Our experience suggests that failures in microcounseling are often failures of the supervisor to relate with trainees and volunteer clients on a personal basis.

VIDEO EQUIPMENT

The basic dimensions of focusing on a single skill of interviewing, feedback, supervision, and practice can be accomplished without video equipment. However, videotape and the resulting pictorial and sound feedback is an impressively powerful tool.

Foremost in value is feedback from interviewing sessions. The trainees have the opportunity to view themselves in action, and there can be no dispute about what happened in a session when it appears on videotape. Trainees can see what is liked about themselves and what they might wish to change. Simultaneously, they have the opportunity to view video models of other interviewers demonstrating the specific skill. Bandura and Walters (1963) have conclusively demonstrated the importance of modeling in human learning processes. Trainees learn new interviewing skills more quickly and easily when they see skills demonstrated by experts.

Many trainees are nervous about their first sessions in front of a video camera, and some special attention may have to be paid to a cosmetic effect of concern over physical appearance during the first microtraining session. However, if a positive and supportive supervisor is present, video anxieties appear to dissipate. It is particularly helpful if primarily positive aspects of the first five-minute session are stressed. Trainees are anxious to learn the skills and are quite capable of pointing out where they failed to engage in the skill being taught.

Stoller (1965) has pointed out the importance of "focused feedback" in therapeutic work with videotape. Focused feedback means that the supervisor focuses training only on a single dimension of the trainee's behavior and does not try to remake the trainee all at once. When one sees a trainee committing six or seven errors in the course of a five-minute session, it is tempting to try to rearrange the trainee's total performance for the next session. We have found it preferable to say to the trainee, "We do not expect you to produce a perfect interview, we only want to see improvement in this one area." Not only does this reassure the trainee, but he or she is also gratified to see improvement in the specific area, whereas if all skills were stressed at once, improvement might be painfully slow. Interestingly, we have also found that stressing a single skill and omitting reference to other problems often result in improvement in other areas which have been ignored. Even though microtraining divides counseling into specific dimensions, these dimensions are related, and improvement in one area brings improvement in others as well.

Videotape equipment has been blessed with improved reliability and simplicity in recent years. Systems only slightly more complex than audiotape recorders now exist. In one recent study, we used junior high school students as videotape operators. Videotape cassettes, streamlined portable recorders and cameras, and compatible systems between competing companies all facilitate videotape use. Equipment costs have been reduced dramatically in recent years and can be expected to be further lowered.

Two models of equipment use can be identified. One is represented by studio-type operations in which videotape equipment is centrally located, with quality light and sound systems, technicians, and supporting services all available. While the reliability of equipment is improved under such systems, it has been found that use of equipment diminishes. We favor a less complicated and less expensive model of equipment usage. Videotape systems are sufficiently reliable and durable that they can be used on a take-out basis much as audiotape recorders or film systems in any school. Experience has proven that microtraining can be successful in a studio-type environment with a concealed camera (which, of course, has been shown to the trainee and client prior to the session) or with the supervisor running portable equipment in the same room as the trainee and the client.

Individuals must find their own way to use video equipment. There are many models of video laboratories that can be developed with split screens, special effect generators, and other useful techniques. Such special equipment may be most helpful in research settings which require detailed examination of specific dimensions. For general use, however, inexpensive, portable equipment will prove satisfactory. In effect, all that is needed for microtraining with video equipment is the equipment, a trainee, a client, a supervisor, and a room. The less complicated the operation, the more likely that the equipment will be used extensively.

ALTERNATIVE MICROTRAINING MODELS

The original microcounseling model has been outlined in Chapter 1. There are, however, a multitude of other models, which can include the basic dimensions of focusing on a specific skill, provision of a written or programmed manual, demonstration via modeling of the skill to be taught, and reward of appropriate trainee behavior.

Group models of training have proven most effective. For example, six to eight trainees may be taught attending behavior together. They are paired for the first five-minute sessions and are each videorecorded. All trainees then receive instruction via a manual, view a modeling tape, and finally criticize their tapes as a group. The final five-minute sessions are again videorecorded and observed. The total time elapsed is approximately two hours.

Original microtraining sessions had trainees attempt positive behaviors in the first five-minute sessions. While this has been effective, recent experimentation has suggested that having trainees deliberately demonstrate negative behavior in the first five-minute session results in better learning of skills. In demonstrating what reflection of feeling or attending behavior is not, trainees more readily grasp the skill. Teaching by contrast has become a standard part of microtraining procedures. This approach has been helpful to those trainees who are concerned and anxious over their television appearance. When a person demonstrates negative behavior in the first session, improvement in the second session is certain. This, in turn, seems to free the individual for later growth.

Audiotape may be substituted for videotape but has a danger of focusing on words alone and missing the vital nonverbal dimensions of the encounter. However, if used in a group situation or with skilled supervision, feedback on trainee performance is still available. Models of the skill may be demonstrated or role played by the supervisor.

Most individuals will learn attending behavior skills within a one-hour cycle of counsel-recounsel. Complex skills such as reflection of feeling, summarization, and interpretation require two cycles of from ninety minutes to two hours each. For those who do not learn the behaviors within a two-hour period, recycling for another session is recommended. Most trainees learn the specific skills when sufficient recycling is permitted.

The five-minute session for microtraining is an arbitrary figure. Some have criticized this length as insufficient for any real counseling to occur. Observation, however, reveals that five minutes is a substantial period for most skills. Time variations of from three to ten minutes have been explored, with satisfactory results. More complex skills such as interpretation and summarization seem to require a longer period of time. Basically, the length of the session depends on the skill, the individual, and the supervisor.

Special modifications in the microcounseling skill may be necessary for some trainees. For example, when teaching attending behavior to younger children or especially anxious individuals, the three dimensions of eye contact, verbal attention, and physical attention may be more than is possible to learn at one sitting. In such a case, it is recommended that the single skill of eye contact be taught, then nonverbal attention, and finally verbal following patterns. These skills may be integrated into attending behavior at a later point. Justifying the approach is the work of Polanyi (1966) on tacit knowing cited earlier. As one learns a specific skill, it eventually becomes habituated and integrated into a larger whole, allowing the individual to move to higher levels of growth and expression. Koestler (1964) also describes the same phenomenon.

An effective group program in counseling skills has been used in some classrooms. Students who have been introduced at a prior time to the basic microtraining framework are advised that they are to identify a specific skill of counseling. They select their own skill and develop their own modeling tapes and written materials.

Even sharper breaks with the basic microcounseling model are possible. Telling individuals about the skill and demonstrating it in a brief role-playing situation sometimes proves sufficient for the skill to be learned and generalized. Microcounseling skills can be and have been taught with the first five-minute session eliminated, with modeling tapes omitted, with or without a supervisor, and with changes in order of presentation of materials. Further, informal observation suggests that skills are taught most effectively when the supervisor changes the model to suit peer preferences and needs. People seem to need to own what they are doing, and adaptation of the basic model tends to produce more involvement. Microtraining is sufficiently flexible that an almost infinite number of changes are possible. What does seem important, however, is that the four basic dimensions of single skills, feedback, models, and supervision are included in some form.

ETHICAL CONSIDERATIONS

We have found that microcounseling and its videotape methods are useful tools for training. While teaching the direct-mutual communication skill, we have found trainees expressing themselves openly and freely. Further, a volunteer or paid client may sometimes open an important problem area. In short, we are dealing with *people* and with a powerful method of effecting human change.

The confidence of microtraining clients must be kept. It is not permissible to show videotapes of training sessions without the client's (and trainee's) signed permission. Even if permission is granted, professional ethics demand careful consideration of what types of materials are presented to what types of groups outside of the training sessions.

For the occasional volunteer client who discusses a problem which requires further counseling or follow-up, a professional staff supervisor should be available throughout microtraining sessions. If microtraining sessions are run by advanced graduate students or paraprofessionals, regular supervision and examination of their work are essential.

The trainee's rights must also be protected. He or she is entitled to the same professional and personal respect that is accorded to microtraining clients. Trainees, when role playing clients or developing skills focusing on sharing their own feelings, may show themselves in need of further counseling. Follow-up counseling and referral services should be available.

Both trainees and clients should be fully aware of videotape equipment. All our trainees and clients are shown video equipment before they begin their sessions. While it happens most rarely, if a client or trainee decides against videotaping, the session should proceed with the camera turned off. At a later date, when the trainee or client is more secure, videotaping can proceed.

Finally, microtraining is not a panacea. It is a new and promising method of interviewing and client training. Further research to determine parameters of effectiveness and generalization is needed. The training procedures of microcounseling should not be seen as equipping an individual to be fully effective as a counselor but as a bridge between theoretical methodology and actual practice. Much more goes into producing an effective counselor or interviewer than microtraining techniques alone. At the same time, research and clinical data have now accumulated to the extent that we can speak with considerable confidence of the power and effectiveness of the microtraining model. These techniques are powerful means for producing personal growth and professional development. As with any powerful tool, this method can be used for good or ill. Constant reference to and awareness of confidentiality and ethical practice are essential.

Chapter 13

RESEARCH
RELATED TO MICROTRAINING

JERRY KASDORF AND KAY GUSTAFSON

T HIS CHAPTER sets forth a large number of research studies developed under the microtraining rubric or which are cited because of closely related methodological issues. The material is designed as a broad survey of critical issues in microtraining and goes into considerable detail in areas where research is extensive; it also attempts to indicate places where further research is most clearly needed. The chapter summary brings together the central findings of the many studies. It should be emphasized that this chapter will discuss primarily studies not mentioned in detail in earlier chapters.

The First Edition of *Microcounseling* (1971) cited the extreme complexity of interviewing, counseling, and psychotherapy as the chief barrier to meaningful research. One of microcounseling's objectives is to delineate the process of helping in more explicit terms so that process and outcome variables in the interview may be related from a new point of view. This focus on small, distinct units of behavior is perhaps the most significant conceptual contribution of the microtraining paradigm. Fortunately, this emphasis simplifies not only the training but the evaluation of that training as well. Over the past several years, a veritable plethora of studies utilizing the microtraining format have appeared. This research has clarified several issues and has led to progressively more refined techniques in terms of experimental designs and dependent measures. Still, the most salient outcome of research in microtraining has been to reiterate the complexity of the interviewing process and to suggest many areas needing further investigation.

The microtraining paradigm provides an opportunity for controlled, systematic laboratory research in which the interview may be studied under naturalistic conditions. The specificity of the format allows careful delineation of what happens in an interview. Behaviors manifested by the interviewer may be identified and quantified and then related to the interviewee's responses. The feasibility of teaching these interviewer behaviors to different populations of trainees and the generalization of these behaviors beyond training sessions can be studied. In addition, personality correlates of learning and the contributions of the separate components of the microtraining paradigm to trainee learning can be systematically investigated with ease.

Microtraining has value in more than a laboratory research setting, however. It is also organized as a format ideally suited to evaluative research—the examination of whether or not a program achieves its objectives. Oetting (1976) has made the following statement:

> Scientific inquiry is aimed at the advancement of scientific knowledge. There is little need for such research to be immediately useful or practical, but there must be great concern for making sure that any contribution that is made is stated as accurately as possible and that the exact relationship between independent and dependent variables is known. *Evaluative research has a different purpose.* (Italics ours.) It is aimed at collecting data that will help in making decisions about programs. . . If the best estimate by the evaluator is that the program works, then further effort might be devoted to it, including further evaluation; if not, then staff time and effort are needed elsewhere (p. 11).

Clearly, the most extensive use of microtraining is in day-to-day practical operation of clinical training programs. Considerable effort has been expended in an array of evaluative or action research studies on the effectiveness of microtraining with numerous groups. These studies complement and support the experimental-laboratory research approach and, despite the absence of rigorous design, suggest additional areas for further study and examination.

This chapter summarizes key aspects of experimental and evaluative research in microtraining and suggests some future uses and improved methods for utilizing the paradigm. Six main areas discussed are (1) identification and measurement of behavioral skills, (2) studies assessing the efficacy of microtraining programs, (3) studies assessing the contributions of components of the microtraining format, (4) investigations of therapy dimensions, (5) studies of personality aspects of microtraining, and (6) studies of further extensions of microtraining.

RESEARCH ON BEHAVIORAL SKILLS
Identification of Behavioral Skills

The most obvious research use of the microtraining format is in identifying and labeling discrete behavioral skills of interviewing. A large number of specific interviewing skills have been experimented with to date. In addition, other areas, such as sales, interpersonal communication, teaching, and problem solving, provide ample opportunity for development of an infinite array of skills.

During development, two criteria are applied in evaluating a microcounseling skill. Each skill must be (1) objectively identifiable and (2) readily transferable. Either ideas stemming from direct observation of interview behavior or, more often, theoretical concepts of previous researchers served as the initial impetus for the definition of most of the current microcounseling skills.

Once this general skill area is selected, developing and refining a new interviewing or communication skill is a straightforward matter. A satisfactory video-modeling tape of the skill to be learned and studied is produced. Concomitantly, written manuals describing the skill and its conceptual framework are produced. The entire procedure generally follows these steps:

1. A general idea of the skill is developed and agreed to by the research staff. Extensive discussions or criticisms of the skill are not conducted until the skill is seen on videotape.
2. A negative model is videotaped, and a deliberate effort is made to demonstrate the absence of the skill in question.

In developing reflection of feeling, for example, an effort was made to ignore all feelings expressed by the client.

3. The model is reviewed, the specific negative behaviors are labeled, and behaviors for a positive model of the skill are identified.

4. A positive modeling tape is produced. This, combined with the negative tape, provides a framework for final production of the skill, the written manual, and eventual specifications.

Once identified, the next step involves training others to see if the skill is readily transferable. If not, it has probably not been described adequately or divided into behavioral units discrete enough to be comprehensible by trainees.

Identification of new skills has primarily evolved from the attempts of Ivey and his colleagues (1971, 1974) to operationalize and teach skills considered facilitative to counseling. New skills have evolved from observational methods in which positive or negative interview behavior is defined and codified under a systematic framework. The first publication describing microcounseling (Ivey, Normington, Miller, Morrill, and Haase, 1968) dealt with three specific types of skills: attending behavior, reflection of feeling, and summarization of feeling. Since that time, a plethora of studies have been conducted with new populations, examining attending and other basic skills and their components. Further expansions of the model to new populations included work with children (Goshko, 1973), inner-city high school students (White, 1974), parents (Bizer, 1972; Durrett and Kelly, 1974; Rizzo, 1976; Sadler and Seyden, 1976), teachers (Ivey and Rollin, 1972), librarians (Jennerich, 1974), medical students (Moreland, Ivey, and Phillips, 1973), medical residents (Cassata, 1974), and a wide array of paraprofessional populations (e.g. Authier and Gustafson, 1975a; Dorosin, D'Andrea, and Jacks, 1976; Gluckstern, 1973; Haase and DiMattia, 1970; Terrell, 1976).

Expression of content and expression of feeling were first studied in client behavior by Gluckstern (1972, 1973) and then extended to helpers by Sherrard (1973), Chadbourne (1975), and Hearn (1976). The general conceptual frame of self-disclosure came from the earlier research by Jourard (1971a,b) and was influenced by the work of Doster (1972), Carkhuff (1969a,b), and Wiener and Mehrabian (1968). Interpretation is the least studied microcounseling skill, but early work by Rollin (1970) and Sherrard (1973) suggest the viability of the microtraining definition.

Higgins, Ivey, and Uhlemann (1970) utilized the microtraining model to study the concept of direct-mutual communication which parallels in some ways Kagan's (1975a,b) more recent work on Interpersonal Process Recall and "mutual recall." Ivey and Gluckstern (1976b) have recently pointed out the similarity between effective mutual recall and direct-mutual communication and behaviors included in Carkhuff's levels 4 and 5.

Recently, factor analysis has been employed to isolate new skills and to identify old ones more precisely. The use of factor analysis in microtraining studies began with Crowley and Ivey's (1976) analysis of the skill of direct-mutual communication. Randomly selected statements from interview sessions before and following training were scored by raters on a five-point "Interpersonal Process Scale," an adaptation of the Carkhuff facilitative scales. The ratings were then factor analyzed to determine what types of comments were most facilitative to interpersonal interaction. This analysis revealed nearly twenty factors in both pretraining and posttraining sessions, which accounted for about 80 percent of the variance in both cases. The major difference in verbal statements after training, which were rated significantly higher in facilitative conditions by judges, was the focus on increased reference to the individuals engaged in the process of communication as opposed to references to things or abstract topics. There was also a marked increase in the "degree of emotional expressiveness" as represented by affective word count.

The study just described was an adaptation of the work of Zimmer and Park (1967) who applied factor analytic procedures to two sessions of experienced counselor-client interactions. Each counselor communication was rated on Strupp's (1960) warm-cold, five-point scale and the results factor analyzed. The facilitative factors identified were restating and understanding, minimal activity—present cognitive, minimal activity—future affective, unstructured invitation, reflection of school conflict, supportive communications, clarification, probing, cognitive interpretation, and affective interpretation. Zimmer and Anderson (1968), using positive regard and empathy scales, again identified similar components. Later work by Zimmer and his associates (Zimmer and Cowles, 1972; Zimmer and Pepyne, 1971) found that the global dimensions often utilized as dependent measures, such as empathy, warmth, and genuineness, can be specified more precisely in terms of specific types of responses that are the components of these dimensions, such as reflection of feeling, open-ended questions, and attending behavior. It might be expected that specifically identified facilitative behaviors would lead to better learning and retention of desired skills than vague global concepts that are not easily delineated or transferable.

The discussion thus far has centered on the identification of the helping skills. The same approach for identification of skills can be used on other areas as well. An outstanding example of this may be found in the application of microcounseling to the training of physicians' representatives by a large pharmaceutical concern (Nuttall and Ivey, in press). These representatives are responsible for introducing new products to the practicing physician and keeping the busy practitioner aware of new trends in drug treatment. Interestingly, the time allotment for the representative-physician contact is often only five minutes—the recommended microtraining time frame for skill learning and practice.

The interview was examined, and specific skills were identified. While open questions, paraphrases, and summaries were selected as being important from the microcounseling paradigm, other skills particular to the sales situation were also selected for individual training. A systematic program was then developed on the basis of the identified skills, and representatives from one state were trained. While the first criterion for success of training is ability to engage in the trained skills, a second criterion for success of this particular program was increased dollar volume of drug sales. Baseline data on sales in this state were compared with later data following training, and indications were that the program was effective. This represents an evaluative research model in an action setting with yoked (ability to engage in skills) and unyoked (dollar sales) evaluation criteria.

Representatives throughout the country are now being trained, and a complex control group design has been established to test the effectiveness of the program. These more controlled findings will, of course, lead to acceptance or rejection of the program and further modification in the training designs.

This pharmaceutical firm example is important, as it illustrates rather concretely the ideal framework for microtraining research. First, the interview was studied carefully and replicable skills were identified. Second, these skills were taught in laboratory sessions so that the clarity of the skills was increased. Third, a systematic program for training was written and tested. Fourth, an evaluation research design was employed in a single state to test the program, and fifth, a carefully constructed national program was instituted to test the value to the entire sales program, with specific outcome criteria which transcended learning of the skills.

Needless to say, it is not always possible for the diffuse enterprise of professional and paraprofessional helpers to engage so systematically in such evaluation projects. However, the same steps applied in this project might be considered a model framework for the development and evaluation of microtraining-based programs in many other skill areas.

Measurement of Skills

The issue of transferability of skills refers to the simple question "Was the skill learned?" Developing functionally meaningful indices to test interviewee acquisition of identified behavioral skills has been more difficult than first assumed, however. The first study on attending behavior (Ivey et al., 1968) utilized a Likert-type five-point rating scale (reliability .84) of five specific behavioral dimensions. Since that time, numerous studies have employed this type of scale, usually with high interrater reliability

(Guttman and Haase, 1972; Haase and DiMattia, 1970; Haase, DiMattia, and Guttman, 1972; Jennerich, 1974; Wallace, Horan, Baker, and Hudson, 1975).

Recently, several authors have questioned the value of such rating scales. The bulk of this discussion has centered on the concept and measurement of "empathy," often considered the cornerstone of facilitative skills (Blaas and Heck, 1975; Caracena and Vicory, 1969; Chinsky and Rappaport, 1970; Heck and Davis, 1973; Kiesler, Mathieu, and Klein, 1967; Kurtz and Grummon, 1972; Zimmer and Anderson, 1968). Although the focus has been on empathy ratings, the criticisms are relevant to the use of this method of measurement for other skills as well.

Perhaps the most cogent argument against the Likert-type rating scales of empathy ratings is the report by Rappaport and Chinsky (1972) of an earlier study conducted by Truax (1972) that demonstrated no significant differences on empathy ratings by judges whether or not they were made (a) with both counselor and client responses present or (b) with only the counselor's responses. This has led several researchers (Caracena and Vicory, 1969; Chinsky and Rappaport, 1970; Heck and Davis, 1973) to question the clarity of empathy. Blaas and Heck (1975) point out that judges may be responding to a "counseling style" rather than specific behaviors which may or may not be facilitative. Further, considerable disagreement has occurred when counselors, clients, and objective judges rate counselor empathy (c.f. Kiesler, 1966; Bozarth and Grace, 1970; Feitel, 1968; Fish, 1970; Burstein and Carkhuff, 1968; Caracena and Vicory, 1969; Hansen, Moore, and Carkhuff, 1968; Kurtz and Grummon, 1972; McWhirter, 1973). Hill and King (1976) point out that differences in measuring instruments may account for these conflicting results. Often empathy is measured by a pencil-and-paper test on the part of the client and/or counselor such as the Barrett-Lennard Relationship Inventory (Barrett-Lennard, 1962) or the Truax Relationship Scale (Truax and Carkhuff, 1967), while judges make their discrimination of empathy on the basis of listening to counselor responses. Therefore, two different types of measuring instruments are used.

Perhaps more importantly, Hill and King point out that counselors are trained in counseling skills, while judges are given special discrimination training and clients are not given any training at all. The result is a differential level of awareness on the part of these groups. Hill and King found that when all three groups were taught the same skills, these differences disappeared. For similar reasons, Toukmanian and Rennie (1975) have suggested that efforts be directed toward both (a) identifying the discriminanda different types of raters use in applying scales to the therapy transaction and (b) more clearly operationalizing the scale to increase the probability that different types of raters are responding to similar discriminanda.

In view of the difficulties with rating scales, and in line with the behavioral emphasis of microtraining, direct behavioral counts have been employed by Aldrige (1971) and Aldrige and Ivey (1975) with reported reliabilities of .90 or better on such dimensions as number of breaks in eye contact and number of hand movements. Important in the high reliabilities attained in this work was a carefully planned eight-hour training series for raters. Many others have used frequency counts with varying degrees of reliability. For a teaching paradigm like microtraining where the aim is to teach discrete, identifiable behavioral skills, the most direct measure of the trainee's ability to use the skills is frequency counts of that skill. Frequency counts, however, must still be viewed with some caution, for they do not indicate the appropriateness of response.

This fact is underscored in a study by Frankel (1970). He trained counselors in reflection of feelings and collected several pre- and posttraining measures, including the Counselor Verbal Response Scale (CVRS) (Kagan, see Appendix IV) and the Response to Feeling Scale (RF-J). The CVRS was designed to measure the frequency of counselor statements directed to the emotional content, while the RF-J scale was designed to measure the accuracy of a counselor's responses to a client's feelings. He found that his training format (a quasi-microtraining format) had significantly increased the frequency of feeling response but not the accuracy of those responses. Similarly, Lea (1975) found that explicit instructions themselves increased the frequency of reflection of feelings but not the rated level of empathy. This is important since many studies concentrate on the frequency of certain types of responses and ignore accuracy and/or appropriateness.

In studies focusing on improving eye contact, the dependent measure is often number of breaks in eye contact. A perfect score using this criterion would be produced by a constant stare, certainly not appropriate in most cases. Current microtraining manuals, incidentally (Authier and Gustafson, 1973; Ivey and Gluckstern, 1976b), emphasize *variable* eye contact and cultural variability in what constitutes "appropriate eye contact." This is a beginning, for one skill, in defining norms for desirable frequencies. With more complex skills, however, the issue of timing and desirable frequencies also becomes much more complex. Timing issues represent a challenging area of future research.

One alternative to a strict frequency count was utilized by Dudley and Blanchard (in press), who took time sampling measures with encouraging results. Taped interviews were divided into consecutive ten-second segments. Each differential behavior was assessed as occurring or not occurring during every third segment. Each of the behaviors was scored as occurring if that behavior was displayed at any time during the ten-second segment being rated. The time sampling measures were later converted to percentages. The interrater reliabilities reported using this method were as follows: Relaxed Posture—100%; Eye Contact—100%; and Minimal Encourages—89%. This appears to be a promising method for collecting measurements on certain interview behaviors.

A second alternative to strict frequency counts is to include ratings on qualitative dimensions with the quantitative measures. Most recently, the Ivey Taxonomy, discussed more completely in another chapter, has been used to count each behavior on three dimensions: (1) the skill, (2) the focus or subject of the sentence, and (3) concreteness, respect, etc. This procedure alleviates much of the criticism of frequency counts alone but again depends on the clarity and reliability of the scales used to rate the more qualitative dimensions.

A relatively new measure of microskills learning which may be used alone or in conjunction with ratings or frequency counts is the Microcounseling Skills Discrimination Scale (MSDS) (Lee, Zingle, Patterson, Ivey, and Haase, 1976). The MSDS was developed to measure ability to discriminate between effective and ineffective verbal and nonverbal helping messages. Both trained and naive groups have been found to successfully discriminate between effective and ineffective helping messages, although the trained groups yielded a greater range of discrimination. Discrimination scores on the MSDS have also shown substantial correlation with other scales measuring discrimination. Scroggins and Ivey (1976), for example, found that student residence hall counselors could learn to discriminate effective from ineffective leads at close to professional levels as a result of brief microtraining. In using this scale in future studies, however, caution is required in assessing the meaning of improved discrimination, as Carkhuff (1969a,b) and Carkhuff and Banks (1970) have shown that the ability to discriminate a skill does not necessarily imply the ability to communicate that same skill.

The primary emphasis in this discussion of skills measurement has been on evaluating the efficacy of the training procedure, that is, on answering the question "Were the skills learned?" The frequency counts used in most microtraining research provide direct and clear answers to this question. Remaining, however, is the additional question of "How useful are these skills in terms of improved counseling ability and ultimately in terms of client outcome?"

Capelle (1975a,b) emphasized the use of independent criteria when assessing the efficacy of training in counselor skills. He points out that it is not enough to demonstrate that subjects change in the desired way and direction that they are being taught; one must also demonstrate that the newly learned skills have effectively improved one's counseling skills on independent criteria. In this vein, other measures used in microtraining studies include adaptations of Kagan's Counselor Verbal Response Scale, Carkhuff's empathy scale, counselor self-concept ratings, variations of semantic differential scales, talk-time ratios, mean duration of utterance of counselors, Matarazzo's Therapist Error Checklist, microcounseling's Counselor Effectiveness Scale, or any of several other possible outcome/process measures. Several of these instruments may be viewed in Appendix IV. Unfortunately, the value of many of these measures is too often limited by their own lack of validation. This represents a needed trend in microtraining research. A second needed trend, to be discussed more fully later in this chapter, is the emphasis on direct assessment of clients' responses to specific microcounseling skills.

Not enough information is presently known to determine the best dependent measures for all the skills. Methods are needed to better assess the appropriate degree, frequency, and timing of skill usage. As more meaningful dependent measures are developed, more skills can be identified and tested. Theoretically, microtraining could be utilized to teach techniques as varying as systematic desensitization (this point has been discussed more fully in this and previous chapters), encounter groups, and rational-emotive therapy. The microtraining paradigm forces one to examine therapeutic techniques and identify the components of these techniques, thus removing the vagueness and magic so often attributed to therapy and also facilitating research investigation of their effects.

STUDIES OF THE EFFECTIVENESS
OF THE MICROTRAINING PROGRAM

The procedures and measures utilized to assess the efficacy of microtraining have become progressively more sophisticated. Earlier evaluation research studies often were unable to employ control groups, and few studies compared the relative merits of microtraining with other training formats. Capelle (1975a) noted that many microcounseling studies have not employed experimental designs that allow accurate or valid assessment of microtraining efficacy. Another problem making assessment difficult has been the highly variable training formats and assessment procedures employed in microtraining studies. Often, results of studies employing different measurements, different subject instructions, different interview goals, and different training variables are compared to one another.

Basic Studies of Trainee Outcome

The early studies of Ivey et al. (1968) demonstrated that microtraining could be a powerful and efficient paradigm for teaching interview skills. Attending behavior in students was significantly improved in these studies. However, only one of the three studies in this monograph employed a control group, and the clients were coached. A short time later, Moreland, Phillips, Ivey, and Lockhart (1970) demonstrated that these interview skills could be effectively utilized in interviews with uncoached clients. Ten beginning clinical psychology graduate students received intensive microtraining in six skills (attending behavior, minimal encourages, open invitation, reflection of feeling, summarization, and paraphrasing). At the end of training, the trainees interviewed the same client for another thirty minutes. Specific interviewing skills and general interview effectiveness were evaluated.

Counselor responses were codified by two independent raters into separate categories representing the six skills. Attending behavior, open invitation, reflection of feeling, and summarization improved on both quantitative and qualitative measures. The attending behavior scale revealed significant improvement. The number of closed-ended questions was reduced, while the number of minimal encourages and paraphrases remained the same. It was also found that the trainees decreased in the number of errors on the Therapist Error Checklist (Matarazzo, Phillips, Wiens, and Saslow, 1965). These data suggest that the trainees were more effective interviewers after microtraining and that the specific behaviors they had learned became integrated into their skill repertoire. The lack of a control group limits the generalization of results, however.

In a controlled study, Kerrebrock (1971) trained high school academic advisors in attending behavior, reflection of feeling, and expression of feeling. The microcounseling-trained group used the two latter skills significantly more frequently than the control group.

As these and other studies have demonstrated, the effectiveness of the microcounseling program is in teaching basic counseling skills. However, these studies have underscored the importance of both the retention and the generalization of these skills to the actual counseling setting, if indeed microcounseling is to be seen as a truly effective training format.

Haase and DiMattia (1970) looked at the retention issue in their study which effectively taught paraprofessionals attending behavior, expression of feeling, and reflection of feeling. A one-year follow-up (Haase, DiMattia, and Guttman, 1972) with the same subjects revealed nonverbal aspects of attending behavior and the verbal construct of expression of feeling still high. However, verbal following and reflection of feeling ratings, while still higher than pretraining, had regressed. Further, discussion with these paraprofessionals revealed that relatively few of them had had the opportunity to practice learned skills during the one-year delay between testing. Although identified as paraprofessional counselors, they were used on the job in primarily clerical tasks. Skills which are not practiced are likely to be lost.

More recently, Scroggins and Ivey (1976) microtrained residence hall counselors in a two-and-one-half day (20-hour) workshop format followed by one hour per week for six weeks of follow-up training. The skills of attending, open questions, minimal encourages, paraphrasing, reflection of feeling, and summarization were stressed. Analysis of pre- and posttraining tapes revealed that the microcounseling trainees improved significantly in minimal encourages, paraphrasing, reflection of feeling, and summarization, as well as on an overall rating of empathy, as compared to a no-training control group. A one-year follow-up interview indicated that the skills were generally maintained. Reflection of feeling and open-ended questions increased in frequency, but not significantly. Closed-ended questions and summarization evidenced a significant decline. The overall ratings were nearly identical. Despite this similarity, it is interesting that the pattern of skills used seemed to have changed somewhat over the year.

These results are encouraging but nevertheless must be viewed with some caution, as only twenty-one of the original ninety-eight counselors were involved in the follow-up data. The extension of the original training over six weeks, the use of competency-based workbooks, and the opportunities for the trainees' use of the skills in their daily lives as residence hall counselors are possible factors contributing to the retention of skills in this study.

Gluckstern (1972, 1973) also found that her paraprofessional trainees maintained their performance in a six-month follow-up study. These paraprofessionals met monthly for follow-up training and were working actively with clients. However, individual patterns of skill usage clearly changed over time. In contrast, Hearn (1976) trained psychiatric nurses and found in a one-month follow-up that the learned behaviors had decreased. Hearn attributed this to (1) possible failure to bring all trainees to full competence and (2) lack of opportunity to practice the skills on the ward.

The importance of opportunity and support for use of the skills in the work setting was echoed by Savicki (1975) in his work with juvenile court workers. The needs for building incentive for use of the skills into the work setting plus refresher courses and consistent monitoring were suggested. Guttman and Haase (1972) further suggest implementing a behavioral training model in which counselor skill acquisition is contingent upon client responses rather than rewards from the supervisor. This reward based on client response would more closely approximate the stimulus conditions in a counseling session and could thus help maintain the learned behaviors in the actual work setting.

The Guttman and Haase (1972) study is particularly significant in that it is nearly the only study which has focused specifically on generalization of the microcounseling skills from training to actual counseling interviews. They found that the microtraining group, in comparison to a control group, evidenced greater learning and retention of the skills of reflection of feeling and summarization of feeling. Generally, they showed a large increment in ability after training, which extinguished to some degree at the first counseling session one week later, and then improved by the third counseling session, but not back to the posttraining level.　The investigation of this learning curve and factors influencing skills retention over a longer period of time is needed.

The investigation of the use of trained skills in the real work setting, instead of with coached or experimental clients, is a much-neglected microcounseling research area.　Naturalistic investigations similar to that of Spooner and Stone (1977), who studied the maintenance of specifically trained counseling responses in actual client interviews across time from (1) the end of prepracticum training, (2) during practicum, and (3) on the job three to nine months after students had left the training setting, would be an important addition to the microtraining literature.

In summary, preliminary evidence on generalization and retention of microcounseling skills is mixed but encouraging. Training to criteria, follow-up and refresher training, and reinforcement in the work setting seem to influence skills retention. The do-use-teach contracting, as advocated by Ivey and Rollin (1972) and Weinrach (1976), may be useful in ensuring that microcounseling trainees retain their newly acquired skills in their "back-home" counseling setting.

The above factors may be particularly important as microtraining is extended to new trainee populations engaged in various work settings.　Two sets of studies reveal contrasting results that might be partially explained by subject types and that may have important implications for future training formats.　Moreland, Ivey, and Phillips (1973) trained first-year medical students using a microtraining format in attending behavior, minimal activity, open-ended questions, paraphrases, reflections of feeling, and summarization.　During posttraining interviews, the subjects demonstrated significant improvement in attending behavior and reflection of feeling.　They also demonstrated a significant increase in "good" responses and a significant decrease in "poor" responses on the Therapist Error Checklist.　No significant changes occurred in the use of open-ended questions, paraphrases, and summarization.　In a later study conducted by Authier and Gustafson (1975a) using paraprofessional drug counselors as subjects and using essentially the same dependent measures, no significant training effects occurred.　However, in a second very similar study training psychiatric nurses, Authier and Gustafson (1976b) did find significant improvement in the supervised group's use of opposite and microcounseling skills. A possible explanation for these contrasting results may be in the initial skill levels of the trainees.

Supporting this possibility are the findings of Dalton, Sundblad, and Hylbert (1973) and Dalton and Sundblad (1976). The first study compared a modeling-learning condition (consisting of a brief, didactic presentation, viewing of a modeled counseling interview, and a covert practice session) with a treatment control group involving reading relevant material only and a no-treatment control in the acquisition of empathic understanding as measured by the subjects' written responses to the Carkhuff Helpee Stimulus Expressions. The second study replicated the first study, collected data, and then trained the modeling-learning- and the information only- control groups using Carkhuff's systematic training format. Both studies found that subjects who completed the modeling-learning procedure showed significantly higher levels of functioning as compared to either of the control groups in their respective studies. Comparing across the two studies, however, the subjects in the earlier study functioned at a significantly higher mean level of communicated empathy as compared to those in the second study, both before and following exposure to the modeled learning experience. In fact, the lower functioning subjects in the second study required the additional ten-hour systematic training to approach the levels of functioning (2.38 vs. 2.47) of the first study's subjects after only the briefer model-learning experience.

These results are consistent with Carkhuff's (1969a) previous finding that individuals functioning at initially low levels of communicated empathy learned the behaviors more slowly than individuals functioning at initially higher levels. Taken a step further, these studies indicate that complex behaviors, particularly when used with novice counselors, need to be learned to a specified criterion level, as Ivey and Gluckstern (1976a) have suggested. Specifically, trainees who "go through" a microtraining program are not necessarily competent in the skill taught. Detailed attention must be given during training to make sure that the trainee actually can demonstrate the skill in question. New training materials in microcounseling stress competency-based performance objectives to ensure that trainees have actually learned and can demonstrate the skill. This point may be very relevant in explaining the contrasting Moreland et al. and Authier and Gustafson findings cited earlier. If it is true that the medical students and psychiatric nurses were functioning initially at a higher level than the paraprofessional drug counselors, they may have been able to show significant improvement in the short training times, whereas the paraprofessionals may not have been able to reach that criterion in the same time.

An appropriate conclusion, then, would seem to be that when complex behaviors are taught, future training formats should require criterion performance on each skill before moving on to the next skill. Moreover, high structure situations combined with preestablished criterion performances might be especially important when training novice or paraprofessional counselors. Studies indicating the necessity for highly structured formats when teaching complex skills will be reviewed in our later consideration of the structural components of the microtraining format.

In addition, the type of trainee and the goal of the work setting may be important influences on program design. Several studies have demonstrated significant improvement in attending behavior after minimal microtraining. Lynch and Magoon (1975), however, did not. They compared pre- and posttraining attending behavior scores after a brief microtraining program using college faculty advisors as subjects. One group was exposed to a two-hour microtraining session, a second group to a two-hour microtraining session without videotaped feedback, and a third group received written instructions only. Immediately after the training, each advisor conducted a ten-minute videotaped advising session with a coached student advisee. Judges rated eye contact (time in contact and number of breaks), physical attentiveness (number of shifts in posture), verbal following behavior (i.e. advisor's statement referring to a topic previously mentioned by the advisee), and time talked by the advisor. Additionally, the

Counselor Effectiveness Scale (CES) was completed by the advisor (self-rating) and the advisee (advisor rating). No significant differences emerged. No pretest measures were taken, but the time-advisor-talked measure was revealing. Advisors in the study made a small number of statements but consumed between 71 percent and 82 percent of the total talk-time. Had the advisors spent more time listening, the results might have been different. One is much more apt to score high on attending behavior when one is talking compared to when one is listening. Further, previous studies have shown that on less complex tasks, such as attending behavior, instructions alone may suffice to alter behavior significantly. Since no pretraining interviews were conducted, it is not possible to tell if this occurred in this study. Nevertheless, as alluded to, the goal of the interview seems to be an important determinant of interview behavior. For example, interviews that have as their goal advising or formulating diagnoses would dictate different types of interviewing behaviors. That is, one might expect more interviewer talk-time and more closed-ended questions in a diagnostic interview than in a therapy interview. The goal of the interview is thus a variable which deserves further attention, both in evaluating research outcome across studies and as an important factor in designing training programs and selecting the skills to be taught.

Comparisons of Microtraining to Other Training Formats

Recently, a few studies have been reported that have included a control group and that have directly compared microtraining with other training formats. This type of experiment probably represents the most cogent evidence for microtraining.

The Moreland, Ivey, and Phillips (1973) study previously alluded to also provides some comparative data. Twelve microtraining subjects were compared to twelve subjects who received more traditional interview training. Data analysis of the pre- and posttraining interviews indicated that both groups significantly decreased their use of closed-ended questions and significantly increased their use of open-ended questions and summarizations. On the attending behavior and reflection of feelings measures, the microtraining subjects demonstrated significantly greater improvement than the comparison subjects. Finally, there were no categories in which the comparison group demonstrated significantly more improvement than the microtraining group.

Although they did not employ a control group, DiMattia and Arndt (1974) compared microcounseling techniques to reflective listening techniques in the teaching of attending behavior to introductory counseling students. Reflective listening techniques (Randolph, Howe, and Achtermann, 1968) involve the use of structured and unstructured responses in teaching trainees to make clients feel understood. With the exception of posture, the two methods were found to be equally effective in teaching attending behavior.

Toukmanian and Rennie (1975) compared the differential effectiveness of Human Relations Training (HRT) and Microtraining (MT) with twenty-four undergraduate students randomly assigned to one of the two training conditions. The HRT subjects received training in Carkhuff's seven core counselor conditions, while the MT subjects were trained in the use of attending behavior, minimal activity responses, verbal following behavior, open inquiry, and reflection of feeling. Pretraining and posttraining interviews with coached clients were audiotaped for each subject. Dependent measures included typical measures for both of the two types of training programs. Assessment of empathy responses, a primary component of HRT training, and three MT measures (open invitation, closed inquiry, interpretation and advice) were taken and compared with a control group. Compared to the no-training control group, both groups of experimental subjects significantly improved on both sets of training criteria. However, on the empathy measures, the MT group improved significantly more than the HRT group. This lends support to the notion that training in specific component skills in a systematic fashion is more effective than training in less well-defined global skills.

In a related study, Gustafson (1975) compared a modified microcounseling format called Enriching Intimacy (EI) with a modified HRT training format termed Experiential-Didactic

(ED), along with a control group, on the dimensions of empathy, warmth-respect, and genuineness. In contrast to Toukmanian and Rennie (1975), the study utilized dependent measures common only to HRT. The results showed that on the five-point empathy ratings, the ED group had significantly improved compared to the control group but was not significantly different from the EI group. On the five-point warmth-respect rating, the EI group improved significantly more than the control group but was not significantly different from the ED group. Neither group was significantly different from the control group on genuineness ratings. The results from the other dependent variables, however, might have been more meaningful had the author employed measures commonly used in microtraining as well as those employed in HRT training.

Another comparative study completed by Dunn (1975) compared microcounseling with empathy group training, self-instruction training, an attention placebo training group, and a no-treatment control group. Each trainee underwent three hours of training or placebo training and conducted four ten-minute taped interviews. Tapes of the interviews were rated by three trained judges on Accurate Empathy and frequency of reflective statements. Coached clients rated the trainees on Accurate Empathy and The Confederate Client Relationship Questionnaire.

Microtraining and empathy group trainees evidenced the most rapid rate of skill acquisition and the highest level of skill acquisition. The self-instruction group, although somewhat lower in level of skill acquisition, was not found to be statistically significantly different in any of the measures. All three of these groups improved significantly more on the measures than the attention-placebo and no-treatment control groups. However, this study may reflect the importance of instructions more than the efficacy of training. The instructions included the following:

> . . . You are expected to listen carefully to what he is saying to you. From time to time, the client will give you cues or draw you into the conversation with a pause or a question. At these points, communicate to the client that you are indeed paying attention to him and really listening to him. In a statement or two, attempt to feed back to the client the essence of what he has just communicated to you, the con-

tent of his statements, and more importantly the feelings you sense are behind his statement. Be brief and concise, but try to let the client know you are sensitive to his current feeling.

The study illustrates the potential limitation of generalizing results when using coached clients, especially with overly specific instructions. Obviously, clients are not going to intentionally pause from time to time to cue the counselor that it is now time to reflect feelings. Additional generalization limitations were created by the subject selections, who were all female volunteers from sororities at a midwestern university. Further, no interjudge reliabilities were reported for the dependent measures. This may have been especially important because other studies have shown that one can significantly increase the frequency of reflection of feelings with specific instructions but not necessarily the accuracy of those reflections.

Three studies have compared a microcounseling program with a program combining microtraining and some techniques of Interpersonal Process Recall (Kagan, 1975a). Fletcher (1972) found a significant difference in the improvement in reflection of feelings of the combined training group over the microtraining group and the client feedback group. The lack of a control group and low interrater reliabilities in this study make the conclusions tenuous, however.

In a more complete study, Boyd (1973) compared a microcounseling model including three forms of recall interrogation (client, counselor, and mutual recall) with a microcounseling model including supervisor review of taped interviews and a no-treatment control group. Microtraining, regardless of the additions, was found to be effective in teaching the verbal response set. Behavioral supervision was associated with greater gains than the recall interrogation.

This finding contrasts with that of Welch (1976), who compared a combined microcounseling-Interpersonal Process Recall group involving viewing a client recall session with a trained inquirer with a *nonsupervised* microcounseling group and a quasi-control group which had only read a description of the target skills. Beginning counselors were trained in attending behavior and evaluated on eye contact, talk-time, verbal following, open questions, counselor focus, and client focus. Analysis of highly reliable frequency counts revealed that the combined treatment group achieved a significantly higher level of functioning on five of the six skills, open questions being the exception. This exception is consistent with Gluckstern's (1972) finding that trainees did not improve in related skills which were not specifically trained. The finding of no difference between the individual, nonsupervised microcounseling group and the instruction-only group on this simple level of skills is also consistent with the results of previous studies. The difference in the Boyd and Welch results may relate to the supervision variable. It is interesting that the addition of IPR feedback in the same short forty-five-minute period did enhance even this simple skill beyond the effect of instruction alone. The replicability of these findings and further consideration of the role of supervision with more complex skills needs to be studied. These are exciting studies in that they are beginning to explore the interplay between these two successful video feedback training programs. Hopefully, this will prove a fruitful arena for future investigation.

In a postmeasures-only design, Evans, Uhlemann, and Hearn (1975) compared microcounseling training with sensitivity training and a no-treatment control group for prospective hot line workers. Microcounseling participants received training in attending behavior, open-ended questions, minimal encouragements, paraphrasing, and reflection of feeling during a weekend workshop. Posttraining audiotaped pseudocalls were rated on empathy and assessed on frequency of specific skills and the Therapist Error Checklist (TECL). For analysis, frequencies of the microcounseling skills taught were combined to one general measure called open invitation to talk. This was compared to closed inquiry and advice giving. Compared to the sensitivity and control groups, microcounseling trainees emitted more good responses and were rated as more empathic. Both training groups used more open invitations to talk than the control group. Microcounseling trainees gave less advice than controls. The lack of pre-post comparisons in this study limits the conclusions regarding training efficacy. The confirmation of positive post-microtraining changes on the interaction quality measures unrelated to the microcounseling format is important.

In a well-conducted study, Hearn (1976) compared the efficacy of three methods of teaching counseling skills: microcounseling training, sensitivity training, and programmed learning. An attention-placebo group was included for comparative purposes. All subjects participated in pretraining, posttraining, and one-month follow-up interviews with pseudoclients. Twenty-minute interviews conducted on each of these occasions provided the following data for analysis: (1) behavioral counts of counselor responses, (2) focus of counselor responses, and (3) focus of client responses. Additionally, all interviews were evaluated by means of the TECL. Following the final interview, each subject was evaluated by the immediate supervisor on the Nursing Staff Performance Inventory.

The microcounseling training condition proved more effective on several measures. On postinterviews, it resulted in more reflections of feeling, less advice giving, more client-focused and less other-focused responses, a greater ability for clients to focus on their own concerns, more good responses and fewer fair responses, and less total errors in response during posttraining and follow-up interviews. The next most effective method of training was programmed learning. It resulted in the emission of less advice-laden responses, more good and less fair responses on the TECL, and more good responses and less total errors on the TECL during follow-up interviews. The effects of sensitivity training did not differ significantly from the attention-placebo control procedures.

The study is notable for several reasons. For one, it is a well-designed study, including an attention-placebo group. Second, it included a follow-up measure. Third, it employed several independent criteria in the assessment procedure, including changes in the client.

In summary, microcounseling appears to be an effective method of producing rapid behavior change in trainees. However, it is evident that to maintain these skills one must thoroughly learn them during training or be in a setting where they are reinforced after initial learning. Ivey has suggested devising stringent learning criteria during training to insure later retention. Program evaluation studies will continue to be valuable on a practical level in decisions to implement or retain programs and in establishing criterion levels and program lengths or designs for specific trainee populations. On a more scientific level, however, future studies need to pay closer attention to experimental design, statistical analysis, and dependent measures employed, and they need to carefully consider the importance of instructions and interview goals.

Studies of Client Outcome

Through the implementation of client measures, indirect support has accumulated on the positive effects of trainees' use of the microcounseling skills on their clients' behavior.

At the most basic level of talk-time, Kelley (1971) found that clients who talked with trained interviewers participated more actively and talked more in the interview. Their mean duration of utterance increased, while number and length of counselor utterances decreased. The original attending behavior study (Ivey et al., 1968) found that microcounseling trainees talked 47 percent of the time in the first interview and 33 percent in the second, whereas figures for the control group were 42 percent and 37 percent. Although not explicitly measured, this decrease in interview time also implies more active client participation.

The first study that focused in detail on the relationship of microtraining and its effect on client behavior was conducted by Gluckstern (1972, 1973). She found that clients of microtraining workshop participants moved from talking about external topics and other people to talking about themselves after their helpers had been trained. Concomitantly, she found increases in expression of feeling as opposed to expression of content in these clients. Unfortunately, this early study by Gluckstern did not contain a control group. However, more recently, Hearn (1976) attained results similar to those of Gluckstern and included three comparison groups in her study. She used the Ivey Taxonomy to study increased focus on self as opposed to external topics. Additionally, microtraining subjects in her study demonstrated superior performance when compared with subjects trained with a sensitivity approach, a programmed text, and a film. Welch (1976) also found significantly greater references to self as opposed to topic or counselor references from the clients interviewed by the integrated IPR-microcounseling trained group. This group had shown a significant increase in eye contact, talked less, made fewer topic changes, and focused on the client more than a microcounseling-only and a quasi-control instruction-only group. In an analogue study, Meyers (1973) found that potential clients change a trainee's performance after microtraining more frequently than before microtraining.

These studies attest to changes in client behavior as microcounseling skills are used. In addition, the Ivey Taxonomy, as Hearn (1976) demonstrated, is a viable measuring device. The controlled situation of microtraining offers a promising laboratory for these important variables in counseling process and outcome. This is a relatively new area of microtraining research, and there is a need for many more client outcome studies, both on the level of immediate interpersonal responses and on the more general level of improved functioning outside the counseling session. The immediate effect on responses and the interaction of the two participants is of great interest from the more scientific-experimental point of view, while "back-home" client behavior change on the more general scale remains the central outcome variable of clinical program evaluation. Ultimately, the value of any counseling skill must be evaluated on its value in helping clients. Of course, all of the problems of defining and measuring client outcome which trouble all outcome research are again operative here and represent a real challenge for future researchers.

Our focus on client outcome to this point has been on clients who have been interviewed by microcounseling trainees. A second way to look at client outcome is to focus on clients who themselves have been microcounseling trainees. Of course, this trend to direct training of clients is a part of the broader psycho-education movement which defines therapy as teaching and has been discussed at length throughout this book.

Donk (1972), on a small group basis, and Ivey (1973b), on an individual media therapy basis, used the microtraining format with psychiatric inpatients. Their research, however, is more at a clinical case level and needs careful and systematic extension.

Haase, Forsyth, Julius, and Lee (1971) utilized the microtraining paradigm for training clients in the accurate expression of feeling prior to initiation of counseling. They compared the microtraining clients with a regular initial interview group and an untreated control group. Judges' ratings of the accurate expression of feelings of these clients revealed significant differences between all groups. Clients who received the microtraining treatment were significantly more able to accurately express their feelings than either the regular interview or control group clients. This study demonstrates the potential use of microtraining as a pretraining system for clients entering therapy or counseling. In an analogue study, Stone and Stebbins (1975) also demonstrated that a video model of self-disclosure is an effective means of pretraining "clients."

The generality of the effectiveness is teaching facilitative skills was further expanded by Atkinson (in press) in a quasi-microtraining format. Working with inmates in a federal correctional facility drug abuse programs, he successfully significantly increased inmates' use of reflection of feeling and minimal verbal response compared to a control group of inmates.

Further examples of direct client training in inpatient and outpatient settings will not be considered here, as they are covered in more detail in Chapter 10. This is an exciting use of microtraining research in that training outcome and therapy or counseling outcome are the same thing. Of course, all of the issues related to research with other trainee populations still apply, and the need to relate client learning to longer-term client improvement is still vital. Evidence on generalization, at least from training sessions to ward behavior, has been encouraging in the Donk (1972), Orlando (1974), and Petrick (1976) studies (see Chapter 10 for details). In addition, Durrett and Kelly (1974) trained parents as therapeutic agents to their disturbed children, using a combination of microcounseling and behavioral rehearsal procedures, and investigated the degree to which the eight skills learned in the fifteen hours of training transferred to parent-child interactions. Results indicated a significantly greater increase in total child talk-time in a structured family interview, as compared to control. Subjective reports also indicated improved communication between spouses.

STUDIES OF COMPONENTS OF THE MICROTRAINING MODEL

The relative importance of several dimensions of the microtraining model and other training models have been systematically studied by numerous authors. Many of these studies have been concerned with the structure of the microtraining format and its influence on teaching desired communication skills. These studies have focused on the major components of microtraining such as supervision, modeling, feedback and self-observation, and instructions.

The importance of *supervision* in teaching communication skills has been studied by several investigators, and conflicting results have been reported. Goldberg (1970) and Frankel (1970) found supervision unnecessary to teach accurate reflection of feeling, while Hutchcraft (1970) and McDonald and Allen (1967) found supervision to be one of the most potent factors of the microtraining paradigm. Kelley (1971), in contrast, found differences on some dependent measures but not on others. Forge (1973) found an individualized microcounseling format which involved neither peer nor supervisor feedback to be more effective than a quasi-control group which only involved reading the manuals. A supervisor-led group and an independent peer feedback group showed nonsignificant improvements when compared to the quasi-control group.

Authier and Gustafson (1975a, 1976b) found no significant improvement in skills for either a nonsupervised microtraining group or a supervised microtraining group in their earlier study. In their later study, opposite results occurred; that is, they found significant skill improvement for both microtraining in general and for the supervision variable. In another study, two types of supervision, with and without modeling, were compared in brief empathy training (Payne, Weiss, and Kapp, 1972). Experiential supervision consisted of the supervisor attempting to form an empathic relationship with the trainee in the discussion of the experimental task. In the more structured didactic supervision task, supervisors again attempted to establish a positive interpersonal relationship but additionally offered specific information on empathy and discussed their techniques with the trainee. Following training, subjects responded to training tapes and were rated for empathy responses on Carkhuff's five-point scale. Results showed significantly higher means for those trained under the didactic method.

In a similar analogue study, Payne, Winter, and Bell (1972) compared techniques-oriented supervision, where the supervisor focused on the trainee's techniques in terms of specific feedback on empathy and specific modeling of more empathic responses, to counseling-oriented supervision, where the supervisor avoided direct suggestions and focused on establishing an empathic supervisory relationship, to placebo supervision, which focused on client psychodynamics, and to a no-treatment control group. The effects of presupervision modeling or no modeling were also examined. Ratings of audiotaped responses to client stimuli were made. Of the supervised groups, only the techniques-oriented supervision trainees showed significant improvement in rated level of empathy. The meaning of this result for supervision is clouded, however, by the fact that the control group, which received only the presupervision modeling, also improved significantly.

The somewhat conflicting results seen in the studies on supervision accentuates the need to specify clearly both dependent and independent variables, and to ensure that results are not overgeneralized when they are reported. The above studies involved different skills, instructions, subject types, and data analyses, yet the results are often considered under the rubric of effects of supervision on microtraining outcomes. Additional research is needed to clarify the relative importance of supervision in microtraining. Furthermore, studies should talk about the effects of supervision on microtraining with a specific skill under specific conditions. For example, Authier and Gustafson (1976a) taught six different skills but analyzed their data and reported the results in terms of total skill scores. This may be a dubious procedure, as a more recent study (Scroggins and Ivey, 1976) has shown. In that study, it was found that subjects had changed on six-month posttraining scores on overall evaluation measures, but on specific skill measures they had actually increased scores on some skill measures and decreased scores on others. This suggests that global scores may hide actual performance changes by subjects.

The importance of *instructions* in imparting communication skills was illuminated by Doster (1972) in his work on eliciting self-exploration. In his study, subjects underwent one of six instruction programs prior to interviews: (1) minimal instructions on appropriate interview behavior (MI), (2) detailed instructions (DI), (3) observational model (OM), which consisted of observing a videotaped model demonstrate behavior consistent with the detailed instructions, (4) role rehearsal of appropriate interview behavior (RR), (5) DI + OM, and (6) DI + RR. Results revealed the importance of the instructional component in modifying self-exploration. Detailed instructions were the single most effective component for self-exploration in follow-up. Similarly, Carr (1974) found lecture plus practice to be equal to microtraining with peer staffing or with supervisor staffing in teaching basic attending behavior to counseling students.

Modeling is another component of microtraining that has been shown to be effective in teaching new skills and strengthening previously learned ones (Bandura, 1969; Eisenberg, and Delaney, 1970; Dalton, Sundblad, and Hylbert, 1973; Lauver and Brody, 1975; Perry, 1975; Thomas, 1974). Several studies have attempted to assess its relative potency in the overall microtraining schema. Of these, many have also combined the modeling component with different types of instructions.

Kuna (1975) studied the effect of lecture, reading, and modeling in training beginning counselors in the skill of restatement. Restatement was defined as repeating what the counselee has said more or less in his exact words, making no attempt to clarify or interpret what has been said. This skill is roughly equivalent to microcounseling's minimal encourage and general verbal following of attending behavior. Trainees were evaluated on their verbal responses to ten audiorecorded client statements. As compared to a control group, instruction through lecture produced a significant increase in skills competency. Instruction was thus sufficient for learning of this relatively simple skill.

Turning to the somewhat more complex skill of reflection of feeling, Goldberg (1970) trained undergraduates under four training conditions and rated the trainees' pre- and posttraining audiotaped responses to taped client stimuli on a five-point scale. She found that instructions were not significantly more effective than the control treatment, models were significantly more effective than instructions, and models plus instructions were significantly more powerful than models alone.

Studying an even more complex skill, interpersonal openness, Whalen (1969) assessed the relative efficacy of modeling and instruction in a group setting. She compared a model plus detailed instructions to a model plus minimal instructions only. For this quite complex skill, both a model and detailed instructions were found to be necessary for improved performance.

Training nursing students in the similar skills of direct-mutual dyadic communication, Forti (1975) found that an approach utilizing video models plus trainer feedback was effective in teaching trainee dyads to express feelings about themselves to each other, but that a programmed text in addition to the models and feedback was needed to teach the more complex skill of expression of feelings for each other in a here and now context.

In a study which included two levels of skill competency, Uhlemann, Lea, and Stone (1976) attempted to determine the relative importance of instructions, modeling, and their combined effect in teaching reflection of feeling and empathy. They used low-functioning elementary school students as determined by scores on the Carkhuff Communication Index (Carkhuff, 1969a, b) and trained them in reflection of feeling. The fifty subjects were randomly assigned to five training conditions: instruction only, modeling only, instruction plus modeling, modeling plus instruction, and a control group. A subsequent interview with the coached client was scored for frequency of reflection of feelings and level of empathic communication by scores on the Communication Index. The results revealed that the instruction and instruction-plus-modeling groups reflected feelings significantly more often than the modeling, modeling-plus-instruction, and control groups. However, on the more complex behavior of empathy, the instruction-plus-modeling and modeling-plus-instruction groups scored significantly higher than the instruction, modeling, and control groups. The results demonstrate that frequency of responses may be influenced by instructions alone on relatively simple behaviors, but this does not necessarily hold true for more complex behaviors.

In assessing the effects of these training components across studies, it is especially important to note the specific measurement techniques employed. For example, the differences in the findings of Goldberg (1970) and Uhlemann et al. (1976) for the training of reflection of feeling are difficult to evaluate in that different measures were employed, that is, a rating scale and frequency counts. The differences in results possible from two different rating procedures is further highlighted in a study by Perry (1975), who assessed the relative efficacy of instructions and no-instructions and three modeling conditions (high empathy model, low empathy model, and no model) in training counselor empathy. In written responses to a client's taped verbalizations, instructions had no effect on empathy ratings, but subjects hearing a high empathy model exhibited significantly higher empathy scores. However, in actual interviews, there were no significant differences between groups. A possible explanation is that knowing what to do and feeling comfortable doing it in a real interpersonal situation may be very separate issues, greatly related to practice. Again, the importance of an experiential approach to training interviewing skills, such as that used in the microcounseling paradigm, is readily apparent, especially if the skills are complex or potentially threatening to the trainee. A second possible explanation for these surprising results may be that empathy ratings are often affected by nonverbal cues (Lee, Zingle, Patterson, Ivey, and Haase, 1976) which were not available to judges for ratings of the written responses but which were present on the videotapes for the interview ratings.

This latter speculation is corroborated in a study by Stone and Vance (1976), who studied the effects of instructions, modeling, and rehearsal and their combinations in training college students in empathic communications. They used two measures of empathy skill, one based on a written response to sixteen standardized stimulus statements and the second based on a verbal response to a client disclosure. The level of empathic communication increased over time for all training groups but not for the no-treatment control groups on the written responses. However, in the pseudointerview measure, the combination of training methods facilitated performance, while no improvement was shown by groups experiencing a single training method. Again, written responses to statements as a measure of empathy were quite different from verbal responses. In addition, this study lends further support to the conclusion that for the efficient imparting of complex skills, both instructions and modeling components are essential.

Further evidence for the efficacy of instructions for teaching simple skills and for the importance of the modeling component for more complex skills is provided by Perkins and Atkinson (1973). They studied the relative merits of a lecture plus discussion, lecture plus modeling, and lecture plus role playing in teaching attending behavior, reflection of feeling, and summarization of feeling. All three groups maintained eye contact significantly longer than a control group in a posttraining interview. Reflection of feeling responses were recorded a significantly greater proportion of time for the lecture-discussion and lecture-modeling treatment, while the most complex behavior, summarization, which occurred in less than 5 percent of the responses, occurred significantly more frequently only for males in the lecture-modeling group. The study once again demonstrates that the frequency of relatively simple communication behaviors, such as eye contact, can be significantly increased by instructions only, while more complex behaviors, such as summarization of feeling, are significantly increased in frequency when a modeling component is included in the training format.

Further evidence for the hypothesis that the complexity of the behavior to be learned should determine the degree of structural components to be included in training is supplied by McDonald and Allen (1967). They varied the methods of microtraining treatment in training teachers in a series of controlled studies. They were searching for important variables in microtraining and systematically included or omitted key aspects of the microtraining treatment. Video modeling tapes proved to be the most effecive variables for describing the behavior to be learned, but the presence of a supervisor facilitated learning from the model. The authors concluded that the full complement of microtraining methods (feedback, modeling, supervision with cueing and discrimination) was the most effective way to impart skills. If the behavior is relatively simple, they suggest that simple instructions may be sufficient; however, as behavior becomes more complex, the importance of including all the microtraining components of training is increased.

Their conclusion was echoed by Wallace, Horan, Baker, and Hudson (1975), who studied graduate counseling students' acquisition of a complex complement of skills called decision-making counseling under three instructional methods. The process of helping clients arrive at wise decisions was operationally defined in terms of eleven specific sequential counselor behaviors. Audiotaped interviews with coached clients were rated on a Likert-type scale for each of the eleven behaviors. In both the original study and a replication, the full microtraining model involving lecture, written handout, model tape, videotaped practice, and supervisor feedback was found to be significantly more effective than either the lecture and handout or the lecture, handout, and videotaped model methods. Thus, for this complex skill package, both explicit instructions and models as well as practice and feedback are needed.

The question of the need for skills practice and *feedback* for each trainee on a given skill has become particularly relevant as shorter group workshop formats have increasingly been used. Due to time demands, these workshops may only require each trainee to participate as either the helper or the helpee in the practice interview of a given skill. In view of the current emphasis on criterion levels and the "do-use-teach" model, the adequacy of the short workshop format has been questioned. Rizzo (1976), however, found that full participation (lecture, model tapes, manual, self-observation, practice, and feedback as the helper, as well as observation of two other helper-helpee interactions), partial participation (same as full except trainee acts only as the helpee), and passive training (lecture, model, manual, and observation of three helper-helpee interactions) were equally effective in training parents of retarded children in open invitation to talk or in reflection of feeling. Rizzo concluded that the potency of group training components minimized the effects of participation in individualized training components, suggesting that large numbers of trainees can benefit from microcounseling workshops without receiving individualized training and practice on each skill. These results need to be replicated with more complex skills, longer skills packages, and/or marathon formats, however. In addition, the trainees in the study were upper-middle-class, well-educated parents, so the generalizability of this finding to other populations must be investigated. This focus on trainee type leads to the final section in our discussion of the effects of the structural components of microtraining.

As has been mentioned earlier in this chapter, the interaction of the initial skills level of the trainees and the degree of structure must be considered both in evaluating research and in designing training programs. In a suggestive study, Kriesel (1975) compared complete sixteen-and-one-half hour microcounseling training in five basic microcounseling skills and an additional skill called focus on values with a skills practice group which focused on verbatim supervision feedback, group process, and some role playing. The skills practice group emphasized many of the same kinds of skills, but instruction was less specific and no video models or feedback were employed. On five-point scale ratings of sampled posttraining interview behavior with a client from a local pastoral counseling center "recruited" for the study, the microcounseling group performed significantly better than the skills practice group only on open invitation to talk. Then, the students were split into low, medium, and high groups based on the clients' pretraining ratings of empathy. It was found that the low empathy students increased significantly in empathy as perceived by clients during the posttraining interviews as a result of microcounseling training, while they showed no change as a result of skills practice training. The higher functioning students showed a different pattern, and their ratings of empathy were less affected by the training. This finding would lend tentative support to the need for more structured training for lower functioning trainees. Unfortunately, this study did not include a no-training control group, used posttest-only behavioral measures, and mixed undergraduate and graduate theology students. Nevertheless, the findings do suggest the need for more attention to the interaction of trainee skills levels and the structural components of microtraining.

In summary, the studies concerned with the relative importance of supervision, instructions, and modeling suggest that maximum treatment results in maximum behavior change. However, the complexity of the behavior to be learned and the level of experience of the subjects may lessen the importance of some of the training components. In short, the standard microtraining paradigm appears to be the most effective method of imparting skills. When behaviors are relatively simple, however, shortening the basic microtraining framework may prove equally effective, thereby enhancing the efficiency of the training model.

Several studies have demonstrated the effectiveness of micro-training in abbreviated training formats. In one such study (Dalton and Sundblad, 1976), the effects of a single modeling presentation were compared with the same modeling presentation followed by ten hours of systematic training (patterned after Carkhuff, 1969a,b), with subjects receiving systematic training only, and with subjects receiving neither modeling nor systematic training. The difference in mean level of functioning following the modeled learning experience alone and following systematic training alone was not significant. Systematic training by itself did not demonstrate itself to be a superior method of developing empathic response behavior compared to the much briefer modeled experience. Both groups were significantly superior to the control group, as was the combination of the modeling experience followed by the systematic training experience. The results supported an earlier study (Dalton et al., 1973) demonstrating that communication of accurate empathic understanding can be rapidly and significantly influenced by observation of a model.

Frankel (1971) altered the training sequences for three different groups of undergraduate females in training reflection of feelings. A model-feedback (MF) group was provided with information about reflection of feeling, followed by a counseling session with another undergraduate, a videotape model presentation, another practice counseling session, a videotape playback session, and finally a third practice counseling session. In the second group, feedback-model (FM), the positions of presentation of the videotape playback and videotape model presentation were reversed, with model presentation occurring just prior to the final counseling session. The third group received only the information component but conducted three practice counseling sessions as did the other two groups. The results indicated that the training did not improve the accuracy of counselor focus on client feeling. However, as predicted, greater frequency of reflection of feeling occurred after a single presentation of a videotape model, videotape feedback, or the combination of the two than in the reading-only condition. The results further accentuate the fact that frequency counts are relatively easy to influence compared to accuracy measures of empathy.

Savicki (1975) tested the efficacy of a modified group design to see if an abbreviated format can produce improvement in skill performance. No baseline taping was done prior to each microcounseling skill session. Rather, groups immediately saw videotaped presentations of didactic input and of examples of the specific skills. After watching skill model tapes, the groups practiced that skill. Working in triads, one interviewed, the second role played, and the third collected behavioral observation data on the interviewer's skill performance. Immediately following the practice session, clients filled out a subjective impressions report, rating how they reacted to the interviewer. The triad then rotated positions until all subjects participated in all three positions. Then, their videotape was replayed and feedback given.

One week after the final training session, subjects reviewed their baseline tapes and rated their own baseline performance. Subsequently, they conducted a ten-minute session with a "new" role-played client from another group. This interview served as the posttraining measure of interviewing skills and as the basis for posttraining self-ratings.

Comparisons of pre-post performance ratings showed significant change on all skills and supported the contention that experienced personnel can improve their performance on the basic microcounseling skills using an abbreviated format. Self-ratings of perceived counselor effectiveness also increased, indicating increased self-confidence with training. Although the results have limited generalizability due to the absence of a control group, Savicki suggested that by including a wide range of skills in a microcounseling program with experienced individuals, one can use the microtraining format as an interviewing assessment device. Recently, Ivey has created a classification system (Ivey Taxonomy) to aid in this assessment procedure. An example of this type of assessment is shown in Appendix III.

These encouraging results regarding abbreviated microtraining formats should be viewed with some caution, however. Retention of skills over time must be considered. For example, Hutchcraft (1970) examined varying modeling procedures and retention of the learned skills. Change occurred on four variables: frequency of counselor interruptions, frequency of counselor zero response latency, total number of counselor responses, and total duration of counselor talk-time. He found that individuals trained with the most complete modeling procedure learned the skills most effectively but that the skills were not maintained over a twenty-four-hour delay period. Hutchcraft concluded that applied practice in learned skills is needed following training for retention. Future studies with abbreviated microtraining format will allow for delineation, inspection, and evaluation of individual training components; however, the effects of these components on retention as well as immediate learning needs to be considered in such evaluation. Considering the complexity of the data we are dealing with, future research possibilities are unlimited.

INVESTIGATIONS OF THERAPY PROCESS

As demonstrated in a previous chapter, an interesting use of microcounseling technology is to analyze various therapeutic approaches. A relatively unexplored use of microtraining technology is the video- or audiotaping of therapeutic interviews and then identifying and codifying the behaviors involved. At the most basic level, this could focus only on the interviewer's or therapist's behavior. The behaviors of effective and ineffective therapists within one setting or orientation could be examined. In addition, differences in the helping styles of therapists of differing theoretical schools of therapy or in different settings could be delineated, much as they were in Chapter 7. If the clients' behaviors were similarly identified and coded and multiple samples taken, this method could eventually be used to investigate the interview process itself, that is, client-therapist changes over time. In this way, it may be possible to identify in a more empirical way the similarities and differences of existential, psychoanalytic, behavioral, and other therapies and to study the effects and relative effectiveness of various helping styles with specific clients or problem areas.

To date, a limited number of studies examining therapist styles applying a microtraining technology or variations thereof have been completed. The earliest study focused on relating style to effectiveness. Normington (1969) took videotapes of four experienced counselors who had helped develop modeling tapes of reflection of feeling and presented them to two expert counselors and sixty-eight high school students. The experts and students agreed in their ratings and ranked all four counselors in the same order. Normington noted that the semantic differential items defining the more skilled counselor included high ratings on such words as close, meaningful, helpful, secure, strong, active, industrious, and efficient. The counselor who received lowest ranking received low ratings on such words as deep, close, skillful, competent, meaningful, and helpful. While the data are interesting, the specific behaviors contributing to the ranking were not identified.

In a somewhat more behaviorally oriented study, Hayden (1975) studied several relationships between the verbal behavior of twenty experienced therapists and their peer-rated effectiveness. The more effective the therapist was perceived, the higher the levels of empathy, positive regard, and genuineness, and the more likely the therapist was to use "inner focus" (Rice, 1965) and "experiential confrontation." Although this research was correlational, similar future research needs to be conducted and an even more explicitly behavioral emphasis taken. The Ivey Taxonomy could be used to more specifically delineate the behaviors of the effective therapists from the ineffective therapists, thereby allowing for a more explicit use of microtraining technology than cited above.

The basic methodology for such a study could follow the model of Authier (1973), who audiotaped the actual initial interviews of psychiatric residents and then from each interview coded fifty time-sampled therapists utterances as being one of five basic microcounseling skills, one of the opposite skills, or in a miscellaneous category. The total frequency of microcounseling skills was significantly greater than the total frequency of opposite skills. The microcounseling skills comprised 81 percent, the opposite skills 10 percent, and the miscellaneous category 9 percent of all therapist utterances. This model of audiotaping actual counseling sessions and counting the therapist utterances could be combined with ratings on many other dimensions and the relationships between the measured abilities studied.

In considering therapist behavior and especially in assessing the effectiveness of that behavior, the setting and goal of the interview must not be ignored. Indeed, the different goals and concomitant different mix of skills necessary to achieve these goals by therapists of different persuasions have been depicted in Chapter 7. Nevertheless, a more systematic research approach such as that suggested above would allow for the study of the mix of therapist behaviors used in different settings and would be valuable additions to the literature.

In this vein, Dudley and Blanchard (in press) assessed differences in the interviewing behavior of experienced (Board Certified Psychiatrists) and inexperienced (second-year medical students) therapists assigned the task of interviewing and diagnosing a patient on the basis of the interview. They found that experienced interviewers used more prompts to keep the patient talking, asked more open-ended questions, changed topics less frequently, and showed a different pattern and rate of asking questions. Experienced therapists used more open questions in the early part of the interview and closed questions later as they tended to near a diagnosis. In considering the influence of the goal of an interview, it would be interesting to contrast the behaviors used in these initial diagnostic interviews with those used in later therapy sessions.

In a very different setting, styles of telephone counseling with college undergraduates were compared in two studies reported by Libow and Doty (1976). Results indicated significant participant preference for active advice giving compared with an empathic approach on an overall call evaluation and on helpfulness-of-call and helper likeability ratings. Interestingly, the advice-giving role was rated most favorably by callers when it was preceded by an empathic interview. The results reiterate how different therapeutic situations demand different therapist behaviors. The hot-line dialogue could be further delineated by the use of the Ivey Taxonomy, and the microtraining paradigm could be applied to determine what specific components of the two styles of telephone counseling led to the surprising results. Apparently, someone calling in on a hot line wants fast action advice and has little time for supportive techniques. Another possible explanation for these findings is that a large part of empathy ratings are related to non-verbal behaviors which are not available to hot-line clients.

In perhaps the first study to use an explicit microcounseling technology to explore therapist style, Sherrard (1973) used the Ivey Taxonomy to codify behavior of different group leadership styles. Typescripts of four different group leaders, each representing a different style, were compared. The leadership styles selected were "didactic-experiential" (Carkhuff), "Bion-type process group" (Goldberg), a vocational development group (leader unspecified), and "group-centered" (Lifton). Two trained graduate students were able to classify the behaviors of the group leaders along three primary dimensions (attending/nonattending; focus; verbal responses), with interrater reliabilities ranging from a low of .80 on verbal responses to a high of .94 on attending behavior responses. Significant differences in group leader behaviors consistent with expectations were shown. Specifically, Carkhuff used more directions and more information statements, Goldberg used interpretation as the primary skill, Lifton reflected feeling and shared information, while the vocational leader focused primarily on information giving and paraphrasing of content. The study demonstrates how the Ivey Taxonomy might be used to differentiate important dimensions of successful therapists of differing persuasions. Identifying the specific behaviors of differing therapies would prove useful in understanding the process more thoroughly and enhance transmitting it to others.

Thus far, we have concentrated on therapist behavior. For a complete picture of the process, however, client behaviors must also be coded. As discussed in Chapter 7, one might expect Perls', Ellis', and Rogers' clients to differ significantly. Yet, to date, microcounseling technology has not been utilized to explore this very important area. Indeed, research in this area would allow for an understanding of these dimensions, which may lead to a more efficient and valid rationale for selecting a therapist or an approach for a given client. Ultimately, the changing relationship of the counselor's and client's behaviors across time could be examined. These are lofty goals, and work is yet to be done on applying microcounseling technology to these areas as well. The work that has been done with "clients" as reviewed earlier has usually focused on a training context and has not looked at client behavior in actual counseling sessions. However, the approaches beginning to be applied in that context could be used with real sessions in the future.

For example, Durand (1971) did demonstrate a novel use of the Counselor Effectiveness Scale (CES) in investigating the interpersonal process occurring in a dyad during the course of a modified microtraining program emphasizing attending behavior and affective discrimination. CES ratings were completed at four points in the training by both members of a dyad of trainees such that they rated themselves and the other person. Although the experimental group's "self" ratings were not statistically different from the control group's, they showed a different and interesting pattern. The trained group's "self" ratings dropped dramatically at point two (after supervisor feedback on their initial listening skills), approximated the level of point one at point three, and leveled out over the remainder of the treatment. At the same time, the trained group's "other" rating decreased rapidly over time periods two and three and then increased abruptly between periods three and four, but not to the high point found at point one. These changing views of self and other were related to learning stages and the threat of seeing oneself as deficient in certain areas.

Although the Durand study occurred in a training context, it is notable in that the focus was partially on process. The approach of repeated taping and rating not only of the CES but other measures (including behavior counts) could be applied to ongoing therapy interactions as well. Many studies in therapy-related areas suggest possible applications of such microtraining methodology to explore therapy process.

For example, the concept of client-therapist "complimentarity" and its relation to outcome was studied by Dietzel and Abeles (1975). They found that therapists with successful client outcomes as compared to therapists with unsuccessful client outcomes as measured by pre-and post-MMPI inventory data were complimentary initially, somewhat less complimentary during the middle stages of therapy, and approximated the initial level of complimentarity at the termination of treatment. In other words, they were more warm and empathic initially, more confronting once a relationship was established, and then reverted back to a supportive role once clients began achieving their stated goals. In microcounseling terminology, the progression of therapy for the successful therapists changed from attending skills to influencing skills and back to attending skills with the progression of therapy. The confirmation of these shifts through documented behavioral changes on a system like the Ivey Taxonomy would be an exciting delineation of therapy process.

The application of microtraining technology to investigating therapy process is in its infancy. The potential for examining therapist behavior, client behavior, and their interrelationship and for relating these behaviors to a number of theoretical constructs of the therapy literature exists for future research.

STUDIES OF DEMOGRAPHIC AND PERSONALITY VARIABLES

The importance of demographic personality characteristics of trainees subjected to microtraining has been relatively neglected to this point. Are different personality types affected differently by microtraining? Does microtraining effect personality change? These are largely unanswered questions that must be decided with future research. Presently, however, a modicum of investigators have begun addressing the question of the influence of personality characteristics on microtraining.

Rennie and Toukmanian (1974) compared the acquisition of counseling skills in introverted and extroverted counselor trainees as defined by scores on the Eysenck Personality Inventory (EPI) under low (experiential) and high (didactic) structure training conditions. The results were surprising. The subjects failed to demonstrate differential learning under conditions of either high or low trainer intervention, regardless of whether they were introverts or extroverts. However, there was a tendency toward a significant interaction effect for personality factors and testing occasions, suggesting that different learning patterns may have been operating for the introverts and extroverts. In a related paper, Rennie and Toukmanian (1976) concluded that low neuroticism or low trait anxious students tended to gain more in empathy during training than high neuroticism peers.

Kloba and Zimpfer (1976) divided 104 high school sophomores into two groups, based on a dependency-independency rating, and compared them in acquisition of the helping skill of open-ended comments when using high status or no prescribed status models. Results from the posttest-only design indicated that both groups of adolescent trainees exposed to a high status model used open-ended comments significantly more than trainees whose model's status was not indicated. However, independent trainees employed open-ended comments significantly more than dependent trainees, regardless of the status of the model. No interaction was found.

Noel (1976) microtrained high school students in direct-mutual communication and found improved communication effectiveness but no sex or race differences. Sodetz's (1972) micro-training study with beginning counselors also found no sex differences.

Chasnoff (1976) studied the relationship between ambiguity tolerance and the learning of video modeled interview behavior. Although the high ambiguity tolerance trainees performed somewhat better, she found no significant differences in the learning of high and low ambiguity tolerant trainees. These results suggest that training models like microtraining which employ video models may be useful in diminishing the detrimental effects to learning previously attributed to low ambiguity tolerance. Further research may be helpful in identifying the effects of different learning strategies in overriding the negative effects of specific personality characteristics.

Meyers (1973) found microtraining useful in effecting a positive change in the counselor trainee's feelings toward the interview situation. Scroggins and Ivey (1976), however, found no significant personality changes on the Personal Orientation Inventory following microtraining. This finding is not unexpected in that microcounseling is not oriented to personality change. The relationship of skills training and usage to personality change will become an increasingly important area, however, as the psychoeducator movement gains prominence and direct client skills training is more frequently employed as therapy. Perhaps the most important study in this area to date is that of McDermott

(1976b), discussed in Chapter 8 in detail, who found that personal growth can occur through microtraining sessions if impetus for such growth is designed into the training.

These studies represent a beginning of research into the personality factors involved in microcounseling studies. In future research, sex and personality characteristics of raters, clients, trainees, trainers, or models could be varied and studied. Additionally, interactions of personality characteristics with specific training methodologies and personality changes following training can be examined. Many possibilities exist, and hopefully this largely unexplored region will entice researchers in the near future. However, for these changes to occur, specific training keyed *behaviorally* to the outcome measures may be necessary.

STUDIES OF FURTHER EXTENSIONS OF MICROTRAINING

Primarily, we have been talking about the use of microtraining to identify and teach facilitative skills of communication. However, the applicability of microtraining is manifold, and numerous studies have been conducted to demonstrate this fact. Most of the studies cited here represent extensions of the microtraining paradigm into new areas, often with new trainee populations. These extensions raise the question of the generalizability of past findings and thus call for reinvestigations of many aspects of the microtraining model in these new areas. In addition, adaptations of the format and combinations with existing models of that field are often required and are open to investigation.

An attempt to modify paraprofessionals' attitudes toward crisis intervention utilizing a quasi-microcounseling format was conducted by Larke and English (1975). The authors first gathered raw data on successful and unsuccessful attempts at crisis intervention. Next, the interview data were analyzed, actors trained, and then a videotape made. Following completion of the videotape, seventy-five students were randomly assigned to one of five groups: videotape modeling with guided participation, videotape modeling, didactic case presentation with guided participation, reactive control, and a nonreactive control group. The results indicated that the videotape modeling with guided participation was by far the most powerful condition influencing attitudes toward a specific individual. However, the video approaches were not superior in influencing attitudes in general. This study accentuates the importance of the feedback components inherent in the microcounseling format and suggests that model presentation alone without further practice and continuous feedback may severely weaken a training program.

In a novel but important study utilizing modeling and videotape feedback, Arnkoff and Stewart (1975) attempted to modify problem-solving behavior by teaching individuals the components of effective problem-solving behavior. Fifty-six male student volunteers were randomly assigned to one of four training conditions: modeling, videotape feedback, modeling plus videotape feedback, and a control group. After training, they were given problems to solve and were rated on the questions they asked, number of questions asked, percentage of essential questions asked, organization of information, and number and rating of solutions. For the measures involving summarization and organization of the information, there were no significant treatment effects. In those measures dealing with asking questions, training and modeling in particular led subjects to seek more information in dealing with the problem. In terms of the quality of information requested, the videotape feedback condition changed the subjects' behavior the most. Modeling was more effective in gathering more information, but the videotape feedback was better in helping subjects discriminate important information. The results support the importance of feedback in improving the quality of responses and also support the notion of collecting both quantitative and qualitative data.

Chadbourne (1976) utilized the Flanders Interaction Analysis Categories (FIAC) and the Ivey Taxonomy to determine if commercial films for teacher training programs dealt with the affective as well as the cognitive components of students' learning. After analysis, it was determined that the training films represented a model of relatively traditional teaching. Teachers in the film did not express their own feelings or support student expression of feelings, they did not reinforce students' focus on themselves, and they completely ignored group process. Therefore, the analytic process found that the behavioral outcomes of the film were inconsistent with the goals of the program, which were to deal with both the cognitive and affective components of learning. The important point of the study is, however, that proper delineation of skills with adequate assessment devices allowed for clear analysis of the program. This is inherent in the microtraining format. In a recent study, Bradley (1976) has found that the combination of interaction analysis and microcounseling was effective in training teachers to be supervisors of other teachers. Interaction analysis was used to examine a videotaped conference between the supervisor-trainee and a classroom teacher, with the aim of identifying specific supervisor behaviors that contributed to making the conference less successful. The microcounseling format was then used to develop the behaviors needed to improve the supervisory process.

Reeder and Kunce (1976) found that a technique similar to microcounseling was effective in the treatment of heroin addicts. Working with a strategy called "vicarious behavior induction," subjects viewed a series of videotapes developed to depict a model demonstrating coping behavior in solving problems related to maintaining drug abstinence. These subjects were compared with a group of subjects who had viewed a lecture about coping behavior (video lecture). Subjects who participated in the video modeling group had substantially better vocational outcomes 30, 90, and 180 days after treatment than those who participated in the video lecture group. Not only is this procedure somewhat novel, but it presents impressive outcome data. The content of the video model procedure, interestingly, dealt with job interviewing among other coping skills. With the addition of role playing following the video model procedure, the effectiveness of this model might be increased even more. The vicarious behavior induction technique has also been used largely by rehabilitation programs with delinquent boys, disadvantaged persons, psychiatric patients (Cook, 1975), and psychiatric aides (Cook, Kunce, and Sleater, 1974).

A format employing many of the basic components of micro-training called learning training has been used successfully to teach parents of adolescents to respond empathically to their children (Guzzetta, 1976). Surprisingly, however, whether or not the children participated with their parents made little difference.

Two recent studies have demonstrated how assertion training can readily be adapted to a microtraining format. Flowers and Goldman (1976) report a technique that utilizes microcounseling as one component of their training program. Trainees first complete a thirty-item (Rathus, 1973) self-report of their own assertive behavior and then participate in two five-minute microcounseling sessions, once as a counselee and once as a counselor. In the five-minute interaction, one trainee discloses a problem in which he or she is having difficulty in self-assertion. Then, the other trainee attempts to help the discloser with the problem during the five-minute interaction. It is noteworthy that good communication skills are important regardless of theoretical bent. In the second study, Gormally, Hill, Otis, and Rainey (1975) integrated all of the components of microtraining in teaching assertive behavior to volunteer subjects. Instructions of the skill, modeling, role-played practice that is videotaped, videotape replay with trainer comments and reinforcement, and additional practice of the skill were all included in this program. Results indicated that microtraining subjects compared to an insight-oriented counseling control group increased significantly more on self-rated and objectively rated assertiveness ratings.

Finally, in an action research project aimed at developing a couple's relationship-building program, Andes (1974) utilized video and small group feedback to train couples in conflict resolution. Conflict resolution was defined as a complex behavioral chain of sixteen different skills, including many of the microcounseling communication skills. The couples' mutual communications improved over the course of the workshop and remained improved four months later. This and similar efforts point to the flexibility of the microtraining format to combine with a variety of approaches and the great potential of communication skills training within a psychoeducational model as a preventative as well as remedial measure for improving interpersonal relationships.

The possible extensions of microtraining to new skill areas with new trainees seem almost limitless. The studies cited throughout this chapter have already included the microtraining of many new skills. In addition, Saltmarsh and Hubele (1974) successfully taught giving, taking, and seeking behaviors, and Miller, Morrill, Ivey, Normington, and Uhlemann (1973) taught techniques of assessing clients' attitude toward tests. Further extensions of microtraining, many of which include new skills and new training populations which have not yet been fully researched, are presented in Chapter 10.

SUMMARY AND IMPLICATIONS

Each question answered within the microtraining research framework seems to bring forth new issues worthy of still further examination. Microtraining increasingly appears to be a paradigm which is sufficiently precise for experimental rigor but is simultaneously practical for action research in applied clinical settings. The bridge between experimental laboratory and applied practice seems particularly evident as the literature is summarized. The purpose of this section is first to summarize what we know about varying areas of research and second to suggest areas where inquiry may most likely be directed with maximum probability of success and value.

The most clearly defined area of microcounseling research at present is in the development of new skills. A relatively specific and workable method for identifying and testing behavioral skills makes it possible for other investigators to examine each skill and cross-validate results. This specificity of process and outcome variables results in a clarity of communication which has not often been possible. A large number of identified skills were summarized in the first section of this chapter. For future work, two main directions are apparent: (1) development and testing of an infinite array of new skills suitable for business, communication, government, or any other human endeavor; (2) systematic action and experimental testing of these skills to determine their value and transferability with yoked and unyoked outcome criteria.

The first section of this chapter closed with an examination of alternative means to measure skills. While a large number of instrumentation thrusts are obviously possible, we are currently recommending instrumentation which relates directly to the training process, e.g. specific behavioral counts via the Ivey Taxonomy, *plus* one or more external, unyoked measures. Not enough information is known about the appropriate degree, timing, and frequency of skill usage. Further work in instrumentation and examination of the process of skill usage throughout an entire interview or series of interviews is needed.

The effectiveness of the microtraining method has been demonstrated in several studies which illustrate that newly learned skills can be retained and integrated into interviewing practice. However, patterns of skill acquisition (and skill decay) seem to vary from skill to skill and from group to group and individual to individual. Clearly, people learn and can demonstrate microtraining skills after one-to-one or group training, but how long and under what conditions are the skills maintained? What type of practice is necessary to maintain high level performance? Does an individual gradually leave the formal skills learned as he or she develops a unique personal style of helping? We are still unclear as to how effectively skill training is integrated into naturalistic interview settings, and more work in this area seems imperative. We also know with certainty that skills learned which are not practiced subsequently will soon extinguish.

There is evidence that low functioning people need more structure and training in simple skills than high functioning individuals. A simple skill such as attending behavior may be a "natural" behavioral style for many, but for those who have difficulty in attending, careful structured learning seems necessary. Criterion standards need to be established for trainees before moving on to a new skill. There has been a tendency in some microtraining research to "train" people but not to make sure that trainees are able to reach a specified level of functioning. "Going through" training does not produce competency; rather, clear performance standards are needed. Complex skills appear to require more structured training than simple skills. A myriad of research questions arise in this area: What are basic competencies required for minimal level helping? What sequencing of training is most effective? What basic competencies should be required? What are the competencies and skills of differing theoretical approaches to helping?

A few studies have begun to compare microtraining with other training formats, and the results are generally favorable. At the same time, there is evidence that microtraining when combined with other training formats such as Interpersonal Process Recall is even more effective. The question may not be which training system is most effective but which training system or systems are most effective, with what type of individuals, under what conditions? The emphasis in this book and in Ivey and Gluckstern (1976a,b) is to suggest wherever possible the systematic combination of microcounseling with other avenues to training. The question of searching for a "best" method of training seems to us an obsolete and misleading question.

The publication of this volume brings forth the first array of client outcome studies, and they seem to suggest that changes in helper behavior directly result in client verbal and nonverbal changes. These studies are consistent in their results, but much more research in this area is needed. Particularly valuable would be information on client verbal and nonverbal behavior throughout an entire naturalistic interview or, better yet, a series of interviews. Data thus far suggest that client verbalizations are heavily determined by helper behavior and that a certain pattern of client behavior may be expected when working with a helper of a particular theoretical orientation. The media therapy and step group therapy approaches have not been fully explored, and the therapeutic value of microtraining as an alternative and supplement to traditional approaches to helping needs in-depth examination.

The most extensive literature on microtraining consists of studies examining the several components of the model. An oversimplification of the data is that "more is better." Specifically, if all components of the microtraining model are used (instructions, model tapes, supervision, feedback, and self-observation), maximal effectiveness is likely. However, it seems equally clear that differ ent people respond differently to separate parts of the training model. Some profit most from instructions, others from models, etc. With less complex skills, instructions seem adequate, but with more complex skills such as reflection of feeling, more components of the training format are necessary. *Practice,* a central issue in development and maintenance of skills, has not been studied adequately as a training component in itself. Our clinical experience has revealed that practice with a skill and demonstration of specific skill acquisition is perhaps even more important than the components of the training model. A careful examination of the literature cited here might lead to this conclusion, but a clearer indication of the importance of practice and performance ability with a skill seems needed.

Implied from the above summaries is the vital importance of more complete investigations into the therapy process itself. The section "Investigations of Therapy Process" summarizes several studies, all of which seem rich in implications for further work. Perhaps the central question of these which can eventually be examined systematically is the age-old issue of "Which therapeutic method for which individual at what time under what conditions?" The systematic approach of microtraining seems to be at the verge of helping answer many questions in this crucial area.

Personality as related to microtraining has not yet been a fruitful area, and few studies have been completed to date. What does exist is the general suggestion that certain types of personality, e.g. low neurotic independent, and high functioning, learn more rapidly and effectively than others. The above statement must be made most tentatively due to extremely limited data. To date examination of microtraining as a personal growth vehicle has produced mixed results. In some cases, personal functioning seems to improve after microtraining, while in other cases, no effect was demonstrated. It is suggested for the future that if personal growth and improved adjustment are goals, then such training will have to be systematically introduced into microtraining sessions. One route toward this avenue is giving trainees specific personal growth topics around which they may practice the separate helping skills in real, rather than role-played, situations.

However, perhaps the most crucial and promising area for research in the next several years will be the examination of cultural patterns of skill use as discussed in Chapters 8 and 9. Helping has been operating consistently within a predominantly white middle-class socioeconomic perspective. The temptation will be to continue in the same mold. Too long we have assumed that our research findings and our helping methodologies are sufficient for use with all people. We believe that this assumption is now appropriate for empirical testing. What processes and goals are most appropriate for an inner-city youth, an upper-socioeconomic-level white divorced woman with no job experience, a thirty-five-year-old Chicano migrant worker, a black college graduate, an Appalachian coal miner, a second-generation Polish high school student, or an eighteen-year-old woman who dropped out of the eighth grade due to pregnancy? The idea that a single theory or single set of helping skills is appropriate for all these different individuals seems totally inadequate. It is our hope that the small beginning presented in this volume will be a stimulus to extensive research over the next several years. The concept of "cultural expertise" shows promise but needs validation and extensive experimental support. Racism, sexism, and oppression are factors inherent in many, perhaps most, helping sessions whether one works with majority or minority individuals. Unless the helping profession starts dealing with these issues systematically, our efforts are ultimately self-defeating.

Thus, we can see that the microtraining format has been demonstrated to be a viable research paradigm for many issues varying from personality variables through therapeutic process to client outcome. Indeed, as stated earlier, the flexibility of the microtraining format as it combines with other training techniques and the great potential of skills training within a psychoeducational model point to microcounseling as a remedial/preventive tool as well as an educational/developmental means to improve the human condition.

Chapter 14

MICROTRAINING: AN OPEN SYSTEM

Microtraining is a structural and methodological approach to interviewing training. As such, it provides an infinite array of possibilities for conceptualizing the helping process. As a *technology*, it may be shaped and adapted for individual and group training, certain portions may be deleted or emphasized according to the needs of the trainee(s), and the system may be applied to populations as varying as psychiatric patients and medical students, counselors and clinicians, social workers and speech therapists, teen-age peer counselors and teachers, and parents and children. As an evolving *metatheory* concerning the helping process, the skill framework presented here may be used to describe many aspects of alternative theoretical orientations to helping, provides a beginning framework for examining all-important cultural issues in helping, and potentially describes the interview in terms wherein the outcome variable of helping—cultural expertise—may be examined in measurable terms directly related to counselor or therapist actions.

This extreme flexibility of microtraining is simultaneously a major strength and a major weakness. Strength shows in the value of the framework for research and examination into ever-changing research and training situations, for there seems to be no end to the alternative uses of the framework. The potential weakness lies in a possible diffuseness to these efforts which may lack inherent conceptual sense and may lead to trainers claiming more for the system than is justified, a possible rigidity in some who claim they have found *the* correct way of operating, and even a loss of some of the key concepts which hold the program together. When these issues are considered, it becomes readily apparent that it is necessary to examine some basic assumptions and values of the framework and to reiterate them for emphasis.

The purpose of this concluding chapter is twofold: (1) to reiterate and reemphasize some basic foundation beliefs of the microtraining system and (2) to indicate some likely important future directions for training and research. The options for microtraining are many—they are most meaningful when the trainers take these techniques and concepts and shape and adapt them to meet their own framework and the needs of the people whom they would teach and train.

THE NECESSARY AND SUFFICIENT CONDITIONS OF MICROTRAINING

Each individual is unique and responds differently to the several parts of the microtraining paradigm. While many find self-observation of their videotape performance to be the most important aspect of the experience, others find videotape models illustrating how the skill is demonstrated most valuable. Still others consider the written manual defining one specific skill or the assistance of an effective, warm supervisor the most important dimension of their learning interviewing techniques.

Clinical experience has revealed that there is no one way in which microtraining is most effective. Rather, evidence suggests that individuals respond to different aspects of the training paradigm. Some appear to need the support of the written word, others the relationship with an understanding supervisor, while still others apparently could change simply by watching themselves perform without benefit of external influence. As people do indeed differ, the multimedia approach of microtraining appears to be one way in which unique differences can be recognized and utilized for each individual's growth. In the same vein, it may be anticipated that microtraining itself may be an inappropriate vehicle for teaching some individuals interviewing skills. In such cases, alternatives may be considered, ranging from traditional training techniques to in-depth supervisor-trainee relationships such as those proposed by Kell and Mueller (1966) or Wideman (1970). An additional possibility is the combination of microtraining with other systematic approaches to helper training which are detailed in Chapter 11.

As noted earlier, McDonald and Allen (1967) in their research noted that different trainees responded most favorably to different parts of microtraining. The same observations were made by Higgins, Ivey, and Uhlemann (1970) examining media therapy. It is suggested that there are no necessary and sufficient conditions for successful microtraining. The question seems to be not which method is best, but *which method, with what individual, under what conditions is best?*

THE IMPORTANCE OF EMPHASIS
ON SINGLE SKILLS

Where microtraining has proven ineffective, the inevitable explanation has almost always been that the supervisor or trainee has been unable to focus on a single dimension of the counseling relationship. The supervisor may comment that the trainee had so many errors in the interview that it was necessary to work on more than one problem. A frequent result of such emphasis is that nothing is learned, the trainee is discouraged, and the supervisor is frustrated. We cannot urge too strongly—*in microtraining, teach only one skill at a time.*

It is important to repeat, with additional emphasis, earlier comments on training. It does not seem helpful to try to remake the trainee all at once. When one sees a trainee committing several errors in one five-minute session, it is tempting to try to rearrange the total performance. When this is tried, failure almost always follows. If a more casual approach is taken, improvement seems to be rapid. ("Don't worry about that error. We are concerned with gradual improvement. Focus on this single dimension.") This is sometimes facilitated by noting instances where the trainee did successfully engage in the skill in the first session and emphasizing this strongly in the supervisory session.

Stoller (1965), in his pioneering work with focused feedback, stresses a similar point. In his therapeutic group work, he emphasizes only one dimension of client behavior at a time, using this as a lever to produce larger changes at a later point. We do not expect therapists to remake a client in one interview, but somehow counselor trainers expect that same miracle from themselves.

Gendlin and Rychlak (1970) explore the issue of teaching single skills and cite the intrinsic reinforcement that comes with learning a new skill. Studies by Bank (1968), Bear (1968), and Lovaas (1968) are examples wherein an individual obtains a sense of confidence and mastery while learning a new skill. Similarly, we have observed trainees participating in microtraining sessions, who at first lacked self-confidence in their ability to interview, gradually develop increasing confidence as they learn new skills. It might be suggested that one important result of learning a single skill is a generalized feeling of mastery. This sense of mastery in turn results in increased ability to learn and in meaningful individual integration of the skills.

Stressing a single skill and omitting reference to errors in the interview not only results in improvement in the skill in question but often brings improvement in other areas as well. However, it may be particularly difficult for sophisticated trainees to focus on only one aspect of the interview. It can be helpful to have them specify what they see themselves doing in the interview and then ask them to teach the supervisor their specific skills. The values of such an approach are twofold. First, the supervisor may learn new skills of interviewing, and second, the sophisticated trainee is given an opportunity to look at him or herself from a new perspective and may learn the importance of the motto, "You don't know what you are doing unless you can teach it to someone else." Another alternative is to present the broad array of available skills and have the trainee select the skill he or she wants to learn rather than requiring learning the skills in a certain order.

The importance of single skills in microtraining cannot be emphasized too strongly. It is believed that this dimension may be the most important aspect of the entire microtraining framework. Nothing is more discouraging to a beginning interviewer than the feeling that he or she must be expert in all things simultaneously.

Along with the emphasis on single skills is the necessity of seeing that trainees can *demonstrate competency* in the skills. Going through a single skills training session does not ensure ability to engage in the skill. Further, trainees must have the opportunity to test out their new behaviors in their daily life environments and use the interviewing skills in their work. Microtraining skills are lost unless practiced and utilized. The do-use-teach contracts are an important part of ensuring that single skill training lasts and generalizes from the laboratory session or training workshop. Where possible, group and individual follow-up and further supervision facilitates learning and growth. Trainees who develop informal self-supervision groups and rate and classify their skills find these modalities are powerful allies in helping retain and improve their learning. In sum, learning which is not practiced and generalized will eventually disappear.

TOWARD OPENING THE HELPING PROCESS TO INSPECTION AND ANALYSIS

Writing connected with microtraining over the years has emphasized the importance of "demystifying" and clarifying the helping process (c.f. Ivey et al., 1968; Ivey, 1973a, 1974c; Ivey and Leppaluoto, 1975; Ivey and Weinrach, 1976; Katz and Ivey, 1977; Weinrach and Ivey, 1975). Underlying all these papers has been the general theme that helping is an important process which must be made public and shared openly and clearly within and without professional circles. We believe this is in the tradition of Carl Rogers, who opened the helping process to scrutiny with typescripts, audiotapes, and films of his work. Rogers has served as a personal and as a professional model to encourage helpers to examine their work before others. His willingness to be open and be criticized for his efforts has helped many of us look at ourselves in new ways.

The presentation of this book has been designed as a small effort to encourage professionals and those whom they train to open their sessions for examination. The training tapes for modeling which a person develops provide an opportunity to demonstrate to trainees that he or she is also a real person. Ivey and

Gluckstern, in their modeling tapes (1974c, 1976c), have attempted to discuss real concerns and personal issues touching their lives. Our experience has been that the modeling of openness on the part of trainers results in trainees who in turn are more personally open and willing to examine themselves and share their reactions with others.

Further, the specific skills emphasis of microtraining appears to be a non-threatening way to analyze and share one's opinions in the supervisory session. Rather than saying, "that lead was ineffective" (or worse), we find supervisors—be they peer-group supervisors or professional trainers—commenting, "You asked a closed question and got a very short answer from the helpee." This factual type of labeling results in very free interchanges between supervisor and trainee and within small peer training groups that results in rapid growth both personally and professionally.

The sharing of helping skills with the lay public can develop out of the specificity and deliberate openness of the microtraining workshop. Clearly, the important helping skills must be shared with the world at large whenever possible. People can help one another as well as professionals. The question which is yet to be fully answered is "Which skills, under what circumstances, should be shared with lay population?" With minor modifications, the attending skills can be shared with most people, and clinical and research experience has been that such training is popular and effective. The influencing skills, we believe, should be shared with more care and deliberation. Microtraining and the psycho-education movement will be explored in more depth in the following section.

TEACHING BEHAVIORAL SKILLS TO CLIENTS

The real frontier in microtraining may well be transferring this method to the classroom, the community mental health center, and the home. If microtraining has proven useful in teaching behavioral skills to counselors, teachers, and a variety of other individuals, the next logical step would be a more extensive exploration of systematic methods of imparting communication skills to people in general.

One could view the skills of interviewing presented here as simply one catalog of skills needed for effective daily interaction. The wife needs not only to attend to her husband but also needs to recognize and listen to his emotions. She should be able to express herself directly and clearly. The child in the classroom can profit from attending and self-expression skills. Early work with psychiatric patients suggests that this complex group also can profit from a behavioral skills approach.

An important question in teaching behavioral skills lies in the genuineness of the encounter. As such, direct-mutual communication, a skill which is not considered learned unless it is forgotten and truly spontaneous, seems essential. Microtraining is only one avenue to teach this skill. Although not generally labeled as such, it has been strongly emphasized in encounter and sensitivity groups. One suggestion for helping individuals communicate more openly and honestly with one another may be an approach which combines some of the advantages of specificity of microtraining with the less easily definable aspects of group work. For example, it may be useful for some individuals to begin the process of behavior change in an encounter group. In the group, skills they lack may be defined, and they then may be referred to microtraining to learn these skills. Similarly, some may wish training in communication skills before entering the rigors of an encounter group.

Microtraining in specific communication skills may be a useful addition to school curricula in human relations education. A particular value of microtraining is goal specificity. It tends not to examine individual problems but rather to teach more effective methods through which human beings may communicate with one another. As such, microtraining may prove a useful method of introducing concepts of affective education into the schools.

The workshop in Appendix I is presented as if for beginning counselor trainees. However, this same design, with appropriate modifications, has been used with parents, couples, children, Sunday School classes, business people, community groups, and many others. The concept of cultural expertise has permitted adaptations of microtraining to be used successfully with a large number of people from differing social and cultural backgrounds. The key to microtraining as a psychoeducational tool for personal development appears to be careful diagnosis of the individual or population to be trained and then making appropriate changes in the model. The media therapy or self-directed self-expression framework presented in Appendix VI illustrates one individually oriented approach using microtraining skills in an individually prescribed program of psychoeducation.

ALTERNATIVE THEORETICAL PERSPECTIVES AND MICROTRAINING

Whereas in the first edition of this work microtraining was presented as a theoretical model, the emphasis here is on microtraining as an evolving metatheory about different theories of the helping process. This final section will bring together some commonalities and distinctions of the helping process as seen from a microtraining perspective. It is stressed that the metatheoretical aspects of microtraining are only in their infancy, but this approach seems to raise some questions for future areas of theoretical exploration and research.

Attention and attending behavior have been presented as underlying concepts of all helping theories. We believe that helpees talk about what helpers listen to or selectively reinforce through attending. It appears that all helpers use basic attending skills and that most use them in a white middle-class perspective. Closely related to these constructs are cultural considerations which reveal that patterns of attention and attending behavior may differ markedly from group to group. Thus, while attending appears to be a cultural universal, it is clearly unwise to assume that the observable behaviors of attending are similar across cultures and groups.

Similarly, different theories attend to different issues. As pointed out in Chapter 3, key points or pauses may occur in the helping interview. At these points, therapists or counselors tend to move in very different directions. At several points in the Appendix III typescript, hiatus points appear where helpers of different persuasions would behave very differently. However, once a helper has embarked on a conversational island, the distinctions between alternative theories become less clear.

It was also suggested that a central purpose of all helping theories is to assist the client in generating an increased array of verbal and nonverbal sentences. While the goals and sentences associated with different theories vary greatly, they all seem to be concerned with helping the client get "unstuck" from stereotyped responding through resolving mixed thoughts and feelings, coping with polarities, resolving "splits" or impasses, untangling transactions, or adding to a behavior repertoire.

A common route toward this general goal appears to be clarifying the meaning of the helpee's present verbal and nonverbal sentences. Bandler and Grinder (1975) term this process denominalization, and the concept of concreteness in helper and helpee verbalizations appears to be an important common thread in most helping. We have suggested that the client comes to the helping interview with a surface structure sentence, e.g. "I can't cope with my children," and the task of the helper is to find the meanings, behaviors, and words which represent the underlying structure of that sentence and accompanying behavior. Needless to say, study of psycholinguistics and sociolinguistics (c.f. Conville and Ivey, 1975) and general semantics will be an important future thrust of the helping professions. The process of denominalizing and clarifying sentences occurs in vastly different ways in different theories. The meanings that clients finally have to define the deeper structure of their sentences will depend heavily on the words and meanings of the helper with whom they are working.

The above point may be basic in explaining why some helpers are effective and others ineffective. If, indeed, a central purpose of helping is to clarify personal meanings, the helpers who have a fairly clear set of definitions of what is happening will be more effective than the helper who has no idea of where he or she is heading. This seems to be a case where "some direction is better than no direction." At some point in the future, it may be possible to define which directions are most helpful, but accomplishment of this task seems to be somewhat in the distance for helpers of today.

Common to most helping theories also are the "core conditions" such as empathy, concreteness, immediacy, warmth and respect, etc. However, we have pointed out that these constructs are heavily culturally based and middle-class as defined in most helping theories. Appropriate immediacy for one group may be inappropriate for another. Further, emphasis on these dimensions appears to vary from theoretical orientation to theoretical orientation. For example, whereas Gestalt tends to emphasize here and now behavior, analysts may spend the bulk of their time on the past, and behaviorists may plan for the future. It seems inappropriate to apply these core conditions indiscriminately as is often done in today's professional helping. They are important dimensions, but their use must be monitored to fit the needs of each unique client or group.

Common to most helping theories is a focus on the helpee. Most conversation in helping sessions will center on the client, and this seems most appropriate. However, the degree of emphasis on the helper, the mutual relationship of the dyad or immediate group, the amount of talk about external topics or significant others will vary extensively from theory to theory. Finally, very few helping theories focus on the cultural-environmental-contextual framework of the helpee. Feminist or ethnic-racial consciousness groups appear to be emphasizing this dimension more than any theory. We have suggested that the failure of psychological theories to consider context and society is a major limitation. As this book is being written a new trend is developing of a serious strand of thought which criticizes helping as too individual or "self" oriented. Some would argue that hoary terms of the helping profession such as "self-actualization" may be in error.

Finally, all helpers use microtraining skills. However, different helpers of different theoretical orientations use skills very differently, as was outlined in Chapter 7. One theory uses questions extensively, another considers them inappropriate. Another favors self-disclosure, while another considers it unprofessional and potentially destructive. Some work actively to discourage interpretation, while others consider it the prime skill in the interview. This simple point that *different helpers use different skills* has been found important in psychotherapy and counseling theory classes taught by the authors. Rather than teach the theory, we have found that direct analysis of typescripts, films, or videotapes of prominent helpers is an effective way to begin study of a theory. The students or trainees classify the microtraining leads of the helper and note the use of the qualitative conditions. The verbal content and sentence structure of the helper (and the helpee) are then examined in detail, with special emphasis on key words and phrases of the helper which tend to reappear over the interview (for example, the words "responsible" and "choice" appear frequently in rational-emotive therapy). Out of this analysis, we have found that students can begin to anticipate the key dimensions of a helping theory. Rather than looking at the "why" of a theory first, we have found that students can build their own explanations and understand a theory in more depth using this approach.

These clinical observations, of course, need to be carried further through formal research. Coupled with the material presented in this brief summary of some key aspects of microtraining metatheory, it should be possible to identify the specialized skills and techniques of even the most highly skilled and/or esoteric therapist or helping method. For the employment interviewer or vocational counselor, the major emphasis may be self-expression skills, such as how to impart information, and paraphrasing skills emphasizing how to help an individual make a decision. Relationship and phenomenological counselors may find reflection and summarization of feeling skills most essential in early stages of therapy, but direct-mutual communication with its emphasis on here and now interactions may prove more important in later communication. Behavioral psychologists may wish to consider relationship skills as preparatory to involvement in the direction of the interview. Within the microtraining paradigm, it should be possible to develop specialized skills for use in behavior modification. Especially suitable for this purpose is the possibility of conditioning certain verbal response classes in the counseling session.

The specialized techniques of dynamically oriented theories

may be clarified through use of microtraining. Techniques used by Gestalt therapy with the "hot seat" or in dream interpretation could be taught within a microtraining framework. The use of body cues, important in Gestalt therapy, is another feasible area for microtraining. The value of a trainee exploring these powerful techniques under more controlled practice should be apparent. Jungian or Freudian trainees may find interpretation a useful beginning point for developing more sophisticated interpretation skills. An especially difficult interpretation may be role played and a variety of alternative interpretations explored and compared with role models of expert therapists.

Microtraining is not wedded to any one theoretical orientation. Rather, it is a system which can be used in any of a wide variety of different concepts of interviewing training. It may be seen that microtraining is now at a stage whereby the basic skills approach to helper training may be applied systematically to virtually any theoretical orientation to helping, thus clarifying its process and enabling adherents to produce competent helpers more quickly. We realize this statement has the danger of moving beyond presently available data and research. Our clinical experience clearly suggests that this is possible, and the strong statement is made in the hope that some researcher will take the challenge of applying microtraining systematically to training in specific theoretical orientations and delineate where the above statement is true and where it is false. Out of such research, microtraining is changed, shaped in new directions, and develops as a broader conceptual framework.

CULTURAL CONSTRUCTS AND MICROTRAINING

The first edition of this book barely mentioned the concept of culture. Challenging (and often painful) experiences over the past few years have revealed clearly the cultural bias of microcounseling in its early forms and the similar white middle-class Western bias of other helping theories as well. We now believe that helper training which does not consider issues of culture at least in a broad sense is incomplete at best and most likely dangerous to the helpee.

The specificity of the microcounseling model made consideration of cultural issues imperative. It is fairly easy to say that
everyone should be "empathic" in a helping relationship. This
relatively abstract term makes it possible to gloss over important
cultural differences. However, when one says "maintain eye contact to be empathic," one soon learns that eye contact is inappropriate in many cultures. It was an array of such experiences
coupled with increasing awareness of anthropological, sociological,
and linguistic considerations that led to some of the early research
in microtraining on cross-cultural dimensions cited in Chapter 8.
We believe the "how" of empathy varies with cultural background.

Sue's (1977) model of four conditions for cross-cultural
helping delineated in Chapter 9 provides an important and highly
useful framework for future delineation of what skills and techniques are appropriate in cross-cultural communication and in
helping interviews. His model should lead to a clearer conception
of what skills are appropriate with what individual from what
cultural group under what conditions. Within that frame,
Roberts (1975) provides a statement that could be considered an
elaboration of the microtraining concept of cultural-environmental focus. He talks about a seven-stage set of "boundaries"
which need to be considered for full personhood. The first is the
"personal boundary," and it may be noted that the helpee focus
concept relates closely to this concept. The next boundary is
sexual. An individual needs to have a sense of self as a sexual
being as well as a person. The family boundary is also important,
and the family therapy movement illustrates the value of consideration of family as related to sexuality, sex roles, and the personal
boundaries. Ethnic, provincial (area of the country, or city),
social class, and cultural boundaries are the remaining four dimensions of Roberts' system. Study of cultural factors must take into
account all seven boundary systems and *also* consider how they
relate with one another.

It seems clear that microtraining has a major task for future
clinical and research focus as it seeks to unravel some of the
complexities of these important cultural-environmental-contextual

dimensions of helping. At some point, it may be anticipated that cultural universals of helping and systematic differences among cultures for helping may be defined. Further, it seems important that "maps" (or carefully documented frameworks) of some specifics of appropriate and inappropriate counseling techniques be defined for cultural groupings.

TOWARD A DEFINITION OF THE EFFECTIVE INDIVIDUAL

The concept of cultural expertise has been introduced as leading toward systematic study of outcome variables in the helping process. It is suggested that the culturally effective and experienced individual has behaviors which are closely analogous to those of the competent helper. A specific definition of the culturally effective individual is that he or she is able to

1. Generate a maximum number of verbal and nonverbal sentences to communicate with self and others within the culture.
2. Generate a maximum number of sentences to communicate with a variety of *diverse groups* within the culture and, where possible, with diverse groups in other cultures.
3. Formulate plans and act on the many possibilities which exist in a culture and reflect on these actions.

It has been suggested that the Ivey Taxonomy of microtraining skills may also be applied to study the communication expertise of the helpee. In fact, when helping interviews are scored or rated on the IT, helpees are rated on the same dimensions as helpers.

As evidenced by the content of Chapter 13, the bulk of microtraining research thus far has been on helper behavior. It now seems that we can turn more extensive attention to the outcome variable of helping—the helpee. There is preliminary evidence that the conversational patterns of helpers show fairly quickly in the conversational patterns of their clients. The IT and the concepts of cultural expertise would seem to offer a framework whereby baseline measures of client verbal and nonverbal behavior may be taken at the beginning of helping and process changes noted during and following the institution of a counseling, therapy, or psychoeducational program.

If the skills of cultural expertise as identified thus far prove valid, then it may be possible to test the comparative effectiveness of alternative approaches to helping. For a very simple example, should diagnosis reveal that a helpee is able to generate sentences only in the past tense, thus dwelling constantly on the past, the goal might become to enable this person to talk about what is happening now or in the future. Three treatment options might be Gestalt therapy, psychoanalysis, and psychoeducation. The Gestalt approach with its here and now emphasis could be expected to produce present tense verbalizations, the analytic might be expected to keep the client in the past tense at least for the first several months or years, and a psychoeducational program might direct attention immediately to training the individual to monitor the tense of statements. All three procedures would be expected to produce results, but they would go about their efforts in differing ways. Through research, it may be possible to determine eventually which approach is the treatment of choice.

The above oversimplified statement shows the magnitude of the problem of determining comparative effectiveness of alternative approaches to helping. Further, it illustrates once again that microtraining has a way of opening up more questions for specific research efforts. The precision of microcounseling serves as a helpful framework to consider the rich complexities of the world.

Along with the psychoeducational model, we anticipate that examination of dimensions of the culturally effective and experienced individual will take more and more of microtraining's time and effort. As cultural expertise is defined more fully and precisely, we anticipate that the psychoeducational model will come to the fore more frequently as the treatment of choice. However, this itself is a clinical opinion and needs to be substantiated by further research and investigation. Microtraining provides many answers, but it always seems to point the way to an ever-increasing array of alternatives.

ALTERNATIVES

Microtraining has been presented as a highly specific and clearly identified method of teaching interviewing skills. The potential value of this specificity has been continually stressed. Simultaneously, an effort has been made to show that this framework can be adapted in many ways, that it can be used for a multitude of purposes, and that it appears to be most effective when it meets the individual needs and desires of the supervisor and trainee.

Experience and research has led to the conclusion that specific commitments to single skills and general adherence to the microtraining framework leads to the greatest benefit for the largest number of trainees and clients. This same experience and research, however, has also resulted in an increased awareness of individual differences and the need to adapt any training program to the needs of the teacher and the learner.

Several varying models for counseling and interviewing training have been presented. They have been complicated by the suggestion that a major emphasis in training should be with clients rather than interviewers. The question then becomes "What commitment to action is most appropriate?" The confusion of the beginning interviewer or the troubled client requires a commitment to action and action itself. Microtraining represents one such commitment. Other commitments for interviewing training such as the Rogerian and analytic models have been presented. It is not believed that any one model is the *right model;* rather, it seems important that the counselor-trainer commit himself or herself to action in a consistent, integrated manner.

Thus, there are many alternatives for teaching individuals interviewing skills. These range from long-term psychoanalysis to encounter procedures to direct cognitive instruction. The goal of all is to facilitate human development. It is believed that microtraining is simply one more method through which human growth may occur.

REFERENCES

Alberti, R., and Emmons, M.: *Your Perfect Right.* San Luis Obispo, Impact, 1970.

Aldrige, E.: The microtraining paradigm in the instruction of junior high school students in attending behavior. Unpublished dissertation, Amherst, University of Massachusetts, 1971.

Aldrige, E., and Ivey, A.: The microcounseling paradigm in the instruction of junior high school students in attending behavior. *Canadian Counsellor, 9*:138-144, 1975.

Allen, D. (Ed.): *Micro-teaching: A Description.* Stanford, Stanford Teacher Education Program, 1967.

Allen, D., and Ryan, K.: *Microteaching.* Reading, A-W, 1969.

Allen, D., Ryan, K., Bush, R., and Cooper, J.: *Teaching Skills for Elementary and Secondary School Teachers.* New York, General Learning, 1969.

Allen, K., Hart, B., Buell, J., Harris, F., and Wolf, M.: Effects of social reinforcement on isolate behavior of a nursery school child. *Child Development, 35*:511, 1964.

Anderson, N., and Love, B.: Psychological education for racial awareness. *Personnel and Guidance Journal, 51*:666-670, 1973.

Andes, D.: An evaluation of a couples' relationship-building workshop: The use of video and small group feedback in teaching communication skills. Unpublished dissertation, Amherst, University of Massachusetts, 1974.

Arbuckle, D.: Comment. *Personnel and Guidance Journal, 54*:434, 1976a.

Arbuckle, D.: The school counselor: Voice of society? *Personnel and Guidance Journal, 54*:427-430, 1976b.

Archer, J., Jr., and Kagan, N.: Teaching interpersonal relationship skills on campus; a pyramid approach. *Journal of Counseling Psychology, 20*:535-541, 1973.

Arnkoff, D., and Stewart, J.: The effectiveness of modeling and videotape feedback on personal problem solving. *Behavior Research and Therapy, 13*:127-133, 1975.

Atkinson, D.: Effects of media training on inmate interpersonal relationship skills. *Criminal Justice and Behavior* (in press), 1977.

Aubertine, H.: The use of microteaching in training supervising teachers. *High School Journal, 51*:99-106, 1967.

Authier, J.: Analysis of therapists' objective verbal behaviors during the initial psychiatric interview. Unpublished dissertation, Portland, University of Portland, 1973.

Authier, J.: Personal Communication. Omaha, University of Nebraska Medical Center, 1976.

Authier, J., and Gustafson, K.: Enriching intimacy: a behavioral approach. Unpublished training manual, Omaha, University of Nebraska Medical Center, 1973.

Authier, J., and Gustafson, K.: Using video to develop communication skills. *Biomedical Communications, 2:*10, 38-42, 1974.

Authier, J., and Gustafson, K.: Application of supervised and nonsupervised microcounseling paradigms in the training of paraprofessionals. *Journal of Counseling Psychology, 22:*74-78, 1975a.

Authier, J., and Gustafson, K.: Developing relationship skills in medical educators. *Biomedical Communications, 3:*18, 29, 35, 38, 1975b.

Authier, J., and Gustafson, K.: Step group therapy-training: A theoretical ideal. Unpublished paper, Omaha, University of Nebraska Medical Center, 1976a.

Authier, J., and Gustafson, K.: The application of supervised and nonsupervised microcounseling paradigms in the training of registered and licensed practical nurses. *Journal of Consulting and Clinical Psychology, 44:*704-709, 1976b.

Authier, J., Gustafson, K., Guerney, B., Jr., and Kasdorf, J.: The psychological practitioner as a teacher: A theoretical-historical and practical review. *The Counseling Psychologist, 5:*31-50, 1975.

Ayllon, T., and Azrin, N.: *The Token Economy: A Motivational System for Therapy and Rehabilitation.* New York, Appleton, 1968.

Ayres, G.: The disadvantaged: An analysis of factors affecting the counselor relationship. Paper presented to the Minnesota Personnel and Guidance Association Mid-Winter Conference, Minneapolis, Minnesota, February, 1970.

Bandler, J., and Grinder, R.: *The Structure of Magic I.* Palo Alto, Sci & Behavior, 1975.

Bandura, A.: Psychotherapy as a learning process. *Psychological Bulletin, 58:*143-159, 1961.

Bandura, A.: *Principles of Behavior Modification.* New York, HR&W, 1969.

Bandura, A., Blanchard, E., and Ritter, B.: The relative efficacy of desensitization and modeling approaches for inducing behavioral, affective, and attitudinal changes. *Journal of Personality and Social Psychology, 13:*173-199, 1969.

Bandura, A., Lipher, D., and Miller, P.: Psychotherapists' approach-avoidance reactions to patients expressions of hostility. *Journal of Consulting Psychology, 24:*1-8, 1960.

Bandura, A., and Walters, R.: *Social Learning and Personality Develop-*

ment. New York, HR&W, 1963.

Bank, P.: Behavior therapy with a boy who had never learned to walk. *Psychotherapy,* 5·150-153, 1968.

Banks, G.: The differential effects of race and social class in helping *Journal of Clinical Psychology, 28*:90-92, 1972.

Banks, G., Berenson, B., and Carkhuff, R.: The effects of counselor race and training upon counseling process with Negro clients in initial interviews. *Journal of Clinical Psychology, 23*:70-72, 1967.

Barrett-Lennard, G.T.: Dimensions of therapist response as causal factors in therapeutic change. *Psychological Monographs, 76*:(43, Whole No. 562), 1962.

Bateson, G.: *Steps Toward an Ecology of Mind.* San Francisco, Chandler, 1972.

Bayes, M.: Behavioral cues of interpersonal warmth. *Journal of Counseling Psychology, 39*:333-339, 1972.

Bear, D.: Some remedial uses of the reinforcement contingency. In Shlein, J. (Ed.): *Research in Psychotherapy.* Washington, D.C., American Psychological Association, 1968, Vol. III, pp. 3-20.

Berenson, B., and Mitchell, K.: *Confrontation.* Amherst, Human Resource Development, 1974.

Bergin, A.: The evaluation of therapeutic outcomes. In Bergin, A., and Garfield, S. (Eds.): *Handbook of Psychotherapy and Behavior Change.* New York, Wiley, 1971, pp. 217-270.

Bergin, A., and Suinn, R.: Individual psychotherapy and behavior therapy. In Rosenzweig, M., and Porter, L. (Eds.): *Annual Review of Psychology.* Palo Alto, Annual Reviews, 1975, pp. 509-556.

Berne, E.: *Games People Play.* New York, Grove, 1964.

Bessell, H.: *Methods in Human Development: Theory Manual.* El Cajon, Human Development Training Institute, 1970.

Bessell, H., and Palomares, U.: *Human Development Program for Institutionalized Teenagers.* El Cajon, Human Development Training Institute, 1971.

Betz, B.: Bases of therapeutic leadership in psychotherapy with the schizophrenic patient. *American Journal of Psychotherapy, 11*:1090-1091, 1963.

Beutler, L., Johnson, D., Neville, C., and Workman, S.: Some sources of variance in "accurate empathy" ratings. *Journal of Consulting and Clinical Psychology, 40*:167-169, 1973.

Birdwhistell, R.: The kinesic level of investigation of the emotions. In Knapp, P. (Ed.): *Expression of the Emotions in Man.* New York, International Universities Press, 1963.

Birdwhistell, R.: Some body motion elements accompanying spoken American English. In Thayer, L. (Ed.): *Communication: Concepts and Perspectives.* Washington, D.C., Spartan, 1967.

Bizer, L.: Parent program in behavioral skills. Unpublished manual, Amherst, Massachusetts, Regional Public Schools, 1972.

Blaas, C., and Heck, E.: Accuracy of empathy ratings. *Journal of Counseling Psychology, 22:*243-246, 1975.

Blanchard, E., and Young, L.: Clinical applications of biofeedback training. *Archives of General Psychiatry, 30:*573-589, 1974.

Blocksma, D., and Porter, E.: A short-term training program in client-centered counseling. *Journal of Consulting Psychology, 11:*55-60, 1947.

Bloom, M.: Personal communication. Indianapolis, Indiana University, School of Social Work, 1970.

Boyd, J.: Microcounseling for a counseling-like verbal response set: Differential effects of two micromodels and two methods of counseling supervision. *Journal of Counseling Psychology, 20:*97-98, 1973.

Bozarth, J., and Grace, D.: Objective ratings and client perceptions of therapeutic conditions and counseling center clients. *Journal of Clinical Psychology, 26:*117-118, 1970.

Bradley, C.: Microcounseling: a tool for the preparation of supervisors. *Journal of Industrial Teacher Education, 13:*24-31, 1975a.

Bradley, C.: Systematic interpersonal skill development for inner city youth. Unpublished paper, Philadelphia, Temple University, 1975b.

Bradley, C.: Interpersonal communication skills: The marriage of interaction analysis and microcounseling. Unpublished manuscript, 1976.

Bradley, C.: Systematic interpersonal skill development for inner-city youth: A microcounseling approach. *Educational Technology* (in press), 1977.

Brammer, L.: *The Helping Relationship.* Englewood Cliffs, P-H, 1973.

Bry, A.: *TA for Families.* New York, Har-Row, 1976.

Buber, M.: *I and Thou.* New York, Scribner, 1970.

Burns, R., and Klingstedt, J.: *Competency-Based Education.* Englewood Cliffs, Educational Technology, 1973.

Burstein, J., and Carkhuff, R.: Objective, therapist and client ratings of therapist-offered facilitative conditions of moderate to low functioning therapists. *Journal of Clinical Psychology, 24:*240-241, 1968.

Capelle, R.: Microcounseling vs. human relations training: A critical review of the literature. Unpublished manuscript, Downsview, Ontario, York University, 1975a.

Capelle, R.: The effects of systematic counselor training vs. counseling instructions on counselor-focused and client-focused criteria. Unpublished paper, Downsview, Ontario, York University, 1975b.

Caracena, P., and Vicory, J.: Correlates of phenomenological and judged empathy. *Journal of Counseling Psychology, 16:*510-515, 1969.

Carkhuff, R.: *Helping and Human Relations.* New York, HR&W, 1969a, Vol. I.

Carkhuff, R.: The counselor's contribution to facilitative processes. Mimeographed manuscript, Buffalo, State University of New York, 1968. Cited in Carkhuff, R.: *Helping and Human Relations.* New York, HR&W, 1969b.

Carkhuff, R.: *Helping and Human Relations.* New York, HR&W, 1969b, Vol. II.

Carkhuff, R.: Principles of social action in training for new careers in human services. *Journal of Counseling Psychology, 18:*147-151, 1971a.

Carkhuff, R.: *The Development of Human Resources.* New York, HR&W, 1971b.

Carkhuff, R.: Training as a mode of treatment. *Journal of Counseling Psychology, 18:*123-131, 1971c.

Carkhuff, R.: The art of helping: A guide for developing skills for parents, teachers and counselors. Amherst, Human Resource Development, 1972.

Carkhuff, R., and Banks, G.: Training as a preferred mode of facilitating between races and generations. *Journal of Counseling Psychology, 17:* 413-418, 1970.

Carkhuff, R., and Berenson, B.: *Beyond Counseling and Therapy.* New York, HR&W, 1967.

Carkhuff, R., and Berenson, B.: *Teaching as Treatment: An Introduction to Counseling and Psychotherapy.* Amherst, Human Resource Development, 1976.

Carkhuff, R., and Bierman, R.: The effects of human relations training upon child psychiatric patients in treatment. *Journal of Counseling Psychology, 17:*157-161, 1970.

Carkhuff, R., and Griffin, A.: The selection and training of functional professionals for inner-city pre-school. *Journal of Clinical Psychology, 27:* 163-175, 1971.

Carkhuff, R., and Pierce, R.: Differential effects of therapist race and social class upon patient depth of self-exploration in the initial clinical interview. *Journal of Consulting Psychology, 31:*632-634, 1967.

Carkhuff, R., and Truax, C.: Training in counseling and psychotherapy: An evaluation of an integrated didactic and experiential approach. *Journal of Consulting Psychology, 29:*333-336, 1965.

Carr, S.: An evaluation of peer-staffing as a microtraining paradigm in pre-practicum counselor education. Unpublished dissertation, University of Southern Mississippi, 1974.

Cartwright, R.: Psychotherapeutic process. *Annual Review of Psychology, 19:*387-416, 1968.

Cassata, D.: Techniques for enhancing communication skills in therapeutic situations. Paper presented to the International Communication Association, New Orleans, 1974.

Chadbourne, J.: The efficacy of the Ivey Taxonomy of group leader behavior for use with classroom teachers. Unpublished dissertation, Amherst, University of Massachusetts, 1975.

Chadbourne, J.: Creative uses of microtraining skills. In Ivey, A., and Gluckstern, N.: *Basic Influencing Skills: Participant Manual.* North Amherst, Massachusetts Microtraining, 1976, pp. 190-193.

Chasnoff, S.: The effects of modeling and ambiguity tolerance on interview behavior. *Counselor Education and Supervision, 16*:46-51, 1976.

Chesler, P.: *Women and Madness.* New York, Avon, 1972.

Chinsky, J., and Rappaport, J.: A brief critique of the meaning and reliability of "accurate empathy" ratings. *Psychological Bulletin, 73*:379-382, 1970.

Chomsky, N.: *Syntactic Structures.* The Hague, Mouton, 1957.

Chomsky, N.: *Aspects of the Theory of Syntax.* Cambridge, MIT Pr, 1965.

Chomsky, N.: *Language and Mind.* New York, HarBrace J, 1968.

Coleman, J.: *Abnormal Psychology and Modern Life.* Chicago, Scott F, 1965.

Collins, E.: Personal communication. Miami, Dade County Public Schools, 1970.

Condon, W.: Method of micro-analysis of sound films of behavior. *Behavior Research Methods and Instrumentation, 2*:51-54, 1970.

Condon, W.: Multiple response to sound in dysfunctional children. *Journal of Autism and Childhood Schizophrenia, 5*:37-56, 1975.

Condon, W., and Ogston, W.: Sound film analysis of normal and pathological behavior patterns. *Journal of Nervous and Mental Disease, 143*:338-346, 1966.

Condon, W., and Sander, L.: Synchrony demonstrated between movements of the neonate and adult speech. *Child Development, 45*:456-462, 1974.

Connolly, K., and Bruner, J.: Competence: Its nature and nurture. In Connolly, K., and Bruner, J. (Eds.): *The Growth of Competence.* New York, Acad Press, 1974.

Conville, R., and Ivey, A.: Sociolinguistics and the counselling process. *Canadian Counsellor, 10*:6-12, 1975.

Cook, D.: Vicarious behavior induction: A modeling strategy for rehabilitation change. Monograph 1, Arkansas Studies in Rehabilitation. Arkansas Rehabilitation Research Training Center, 1975.

Cook, D., Kunce, J., and Sleater, S.: Vicarious behavior induction and training psychiatric aides. *Journal of Community Psychology, 21*:293-297, 1974.

Cowles, D.: Personal communication. Greenfield, Massachusetts, Mental Health Center, 1970.

Crabbs, M., and Jarmin, H.: Microcounseling: Making it work for you. *Personnel and Guidance Journal, 54*:329-331, 1976.

Crowley, T.: The conditionability of positive and negative self-reference emotional affect statements in a counseling type interview. Unpublished dissertation, Amherst, University of Massachusetts, 1970.

Crowley, T., and Ivey, A.: A factor analytic study of communication patterns in media therapy. Unpublished paper, Amherst, University of Massachusetts, 1970.

Crowley, T., and Ivey, A.: Dimensions of effective interpersonal communications: Specifying behavioral components. *Journal of Counseling Psychology, 23:*267-271, 1976.

Dalton, R., Jr., and Sundblad, L.: Using principles of social learning in training for communication of empathy. *Journal of Counseling Psychology, 23:*454-457, 1976.

Dalton, R., Jr., Sundblad, L., and Hylbert, K.: An application of principles of social learning to training in communication of empathy. *Journal of Counseling Psychology, 20:*378-383, 1973.

Danish, S.: Personal communication. Carbondale, Southern Illinois University, 1970.

Danish, S.: A training program in helping skills. Paper presented to the American Psychological Association Convention, New Orleans, 1974.

Danish, S., and Brodsky, S.: Training of policemen in emotional control and awareness. *Psychology in Action, 25:*368-369, 1970.

Danish, S., D'Augelli, A., and Brock, G.: An evaluation of helping skills training: Effects on helpers' verbal responses. *Journal of Counseling Psychology, 23:*259-266, 1976.

Danish, S., and Hauer, A.: *Helping Skills: A Basic Training Program.* New York, Behavioral Publications, 1973a.

Danish, S., and Hauer, A.: *Helping Skills: A Basic Training Program— Leaders Manual.* New York, Behavioral Publications, 1973b.

D'Augelli, A., and Levy, M.: The verbal helping skills of trained and untrained human service paraprofessionals. *American Journal of Community Psychology* (in press).

Davitz, D.: *The Communication of Emotional Meaning.* New York, McGraw, 1964.

Deikman, E.: Individual differences in response to a Zen meditation exercise. *Journal of Consulting Psychology, 29:*135-145, 1963.

Delworth, U.: Raising consciousness about sexism. *Personnel and Guidance Journal, 51:*672-674, 1973.

Dendy, R.: A model for the training of undergraduate hall assistants as paraprofessional counselors using videotape techniques and Interpersonal Process Recall (IPR). Unpublished dissertation, East Lansing, Michigan State University, 1971.

Dickenson, W., and Truax, C.: Group counseling with college underachievers: Comparisons with a control group and relationship to empathy, warmth and genuineness. *Personnel and Guidance Journal, 45:*243-247, 1966.

Dietzel, C. and Abeles, N.: Client-therapist complementarity and therapeutic outcome. *Journal of Counseling Psychology, 22:*264-272, 1975.

DiLoreto, A.: *Comparative Psychotherapy.* New York, Aldine-Atherton, 1971.

DiMattia, D.: Personal communication. Amherst, University of Massachusetts, 1970.

DiMattia, D., and Arndt, G.: A comparison of microcounseling and reflective listening techniques. *Counselor Education and Supervision, 14:* 61-64, 1974.

Dimond, R., and Hellkamp, D.: Race, sex, ordinal position of birth and self-disclosure in high school students. *Psychological Reports, 25:*235-238, 1969.

Dinkmeyer, D., and Dreikurs, R.: *Encouraging Children and Parents to Learn.* Englewood Cliffs, P-H, 1963.

Donk, L.: Personal communication. Grand Rapids, Pine Rest Christian Hospital, 1969.

Donk, L.: Attending behavior in mental patients. *Dissertation Abstracts International, 33:* Order No. 72-22,569, 1972.

Dorosin, D., D'Andrea, V., and Jacks, R.: A peer counselor training program: Rationale, curriculum, and evaluation. Unpublished paper, Cowell Student Health Center, Palo Alto, Stanford University, 1976.

Doster, J.: Effects of instructions, modeling and role rehearsal on interview verbal behavior. *Journal of Consulting and Clinical Psychology, 39:*202-209, 1972.

Dreikurs, R.: *The Challenge of Parenthood.* New York, Duell, 1948.

Dudley, W., and Blanchard, E.: Comparison of experienced and inexperienced interviews on objectively scored interview behavior. *Journal of Clinical Psychology* (in press).

Duncan, S.: Nonverbal communication. *Psychological Bulletin, 72:*118-137, 1969.

Dunn, R.: Comparative effects of three counselor training techniques on reflection of feeling. Paper presented to the Canadian Psychological Association Annual Meeting, Quebec City, June, 1975.

Durand, H.: Teaching listening behavior: A videotape technique for the improvement of effective discrimination. Unpublished dissertation, Pittsburgh, University of Pittsburgh, 1971.

Durrett, D., and Kelly, P.: Can you really talk with your child? A parental training program in communication skills toward the improvement of parent-child interaction. *Group Psychotherapy and Psychodrama, 27:*98-109, 1974.

Eble, R.: Estimation of the reliability of ratings. *Psychometrica, 16:*407-424, 1951.

Egan, G.: *The Skilled Helper.* Monterey, Brooks-Cole, 1975.

Eisenberg, S., and Delaney, D.: Using video simulation of counseling for training counselors. *Journal of Counseling Psychology, 17:*15-19, 1970.

Ekman, P., and Friesen, W.: Nonverbal behavior in psychotherapy research. In Shlien, J. (Ed.): *Research in Psychotherapy.* Washington, D.C., American Psychological Association, 1968, Vol. 3, pp. 179-216.

Ekman, P., and Friesen, W.: Nonverbal behavior and psychopathology. In Friedman, R., and Katz, M. (Eds.): *The Psychology of Depression.*

Washington, Winston, 1974.

Ekman, P., and Friesen, W.: *Unmasking the Face.* Englewood Cliffs, P-H, 1975.

Ekman, P., Friesen, W., and Ellsworth, P.: *Emotion in the Human Face.* New York, Pergamon, 1972.

Ekstein, R., and Wallerstein, R.: *The Teaching and Learning of Psychotherapy.* New York, Basic, 1958.

Elsenrath, D., Coker, D., and Martinson, W.: Microteaching interviewing skills. *Journal of Counseling Psychology, 19:*150-155, 1972.

Evans, D., Uhlemann, M., and Hearn, M.: Microcounseling and sensitivity training with hotline workers. Unpublished paper, London, Ontario, University of Western Ontario, 1975.

Exline, R., Gray, D., and Schuette, D.: Visual behavior in a dyad as affected by interview content and sex of respondent. *Journal of Personality and Social Psychology, 1:*201-209, 1965.

Exline, R., and Winters, L.: Affective relations and mutual glances in dyads. In Tompkins, S., and Izard, C. (Eds.): *Affect, Cognition, and Personality.* New York, Springer, 1965.

Eysenck, H.: *The Effects of Psychotherapy.* New York, International Science, 1966.

Eysenck, H., and Eysenck, S.: *Eysenck Personality Inventory Manual.* San Diego, Educational and Industrial Testing Service, 1968.

Fast, J.: *Body Language.* New York, Evans, 1970.

Feitel, B.: Feeling understood as a function of a variety of therapist activities. Unpublished dissertation, New York, Teacher's College, Columbia University, 1968.

Fiedler, F.: A comparison of therapeutic relationships in psychoanalytic, non-directive, and Adlerian therapy. *Journal of Consulting Psychology, 14:*436-445, 1950a.

Fiedler, F.: The concept of an ideal relationship. *Journal of Consulting Psychology, 14:*239-245, 1950b.

Fiedler, F.: Factor analyses of psychoanalytic, non-directive and Adlerian therapeutic relationships. *Journal of Consulting Psychology, 15:*32-38, 1951.

Fiedler, F.: Quantitative studies on the role of therapists' feelings toward their patients. In Mowrer, O. (Ed.): *Psychotherapy: Theory and Research.* New York, Ronald, 1953.

Fish, J.: Empathy and the reported emotional experiences of beginning psychotherapists. *Journal of Consulting and Clinical Psychology, 35:*64-69, 1970.

Fisher, T., Reardon, R., and Burck, H.: Increasing information seeking behavior with a model-reinforced videotape. *Journal of Counseling Psychology, 23:*234-238, 1976.

Flanders, N.: Analyzing Teacher Behavior. Reading, A-M, 1970.

Fletcher, J.: Increasing skills of offering acceptance. Unpublished dissertation, Seattle, University of Washington, 1972.

Flowers, J., and Goldman, R.: Assertion training for mental health paraprofessionals. *Journal of Counseling Psychology, 23*:147-150, 1976.

Foote, N., and Cottrell, L., Jr.: *Identity and Interpersonal Competence.* Chicago, U of Chicago Press, 1955.

Forge, H.: Comparison of three variations of microtraining in teaching basic interviewing skills to counselor trainees. Unpublished dissertation, Kansas City, University of Missouri-Kansas City, 1973.

Forti, L.: Media therapy: An evaluation of the effects of programmed instruction and video taped models on microcounseling behaviors. Unpublished dissertation, Washington, D.C., American University, 1975.

Frankel, M.: Videotape modeling and self-confrontation techniques: An evaluation of their effects on counseling behavior. Unpublished dissertation, Rochester, University of Rochester, 1970.

Frankel, M.: Effects of videotape modeling and self-confrontation techniques on microcounseling behavior. *Journal of Counseling Psychology, 18*:465-471, 1971.

Frederick, C.: *EST: Playing the Game the New Way.* New York, Delta, 1974.

Freiband, W., and Rudman, S. Personal communication. Northampton, Veterans Administration Hospital, 1970.

Freire, P.: *Pedagogy of the Oppressed.* New York, Herder & Herder, 1972.

Galassi, J., Galassi, M., and Litz, M.: Assertive training in groups using video feedback. *Journal of Counseling Psychology, 5*:390-394, 1974.

Gazda, G.: *Human Relations Development: A Manual for Editors.* Boston, Allyn, 1973.

Gazda, G., Walters, R., and Childers, W.: *Human Relations Development: A Manual for Health Sciences.* Boston, Allyn, 1975.

Gelder, M., Marks, I., and Wolff, H.: Desensitization and psychotherapy in the treatment of phobic states: A controlled inquiry. *British Journal of Psychiatry, 113*:53-73, 1967.

Gendlin, E.: *Experiencing and the Creation of Meaning.* New York, Free PRESS of Glencoe, 1962.

Gendlin, E., and Hendricks, M.: Rap manual. *Changes.* Chicago. Mimeographed, undated, cited in Rogers, C.: Empathic: An unappreciated way of being. *The Counseling Psychologist, 5*:2-10, 1975.

Gendlin, E., and Rychlak, J.: Psychotherapeutic processes. In Mussen, P., and Rosenzweig, M. (Eds.): *Annual Review of Psychology.* Palo Alto, Annual Reviews, 1970.

Gluckstern, N.: Parents as lay counselors: The development of a systematic parent program for drug counseling. Unpublished dissertation, Amherst, University of Massachusetts, 1972.

Gluckstern, N.: Training parents as drug counselors in the community.

Personnel and Guidance Journal, 51:676-680, 1973.

Goldberg, A.: A sequential program for supervision of counselors using the Interpersonal Process Recall technique. Unpublished dissertation, East Lansing, Michigan State University, 1967.

Goldberg, E.: Effects of models and instructions on verbal behavior: An analysis of two factors of the microcounseling paradigm. Unpublished dissertation, Philadelphia, Temple University, 1970.

Goldstein, A.: *Structured Learning Therapy: Toward a Psychotherapy for the Poor.* New York, Acad PR, 1973.

Goldstein, A., and Goedhart, A.: The use of structured learning for empathy enhancement in paraprofessional psychotherapist training. *Journal of Community Psychology, 2*:168-173, 1973.

Goodman, G.: *Companionship Therapy.* San Francisco, Jossey-Bass, 1972.

Goodwin, D., Garvey, W., and Barclay, J.: Microconsultation and behavioral analysis: A method of training psychologists as behavioral consultants. *Journal of Consulting and Clinical Psychology, 37*:355-363, 1971.

Gordon, T.: *Parent Effectiveness Training.* New York, Wyden, 1970.

Gormally, J., Hill, C., Otis, M., and Rainey, L.: A microtraining approach to assertion training. *Journal of Counseling Psychology, 22*:299-303, 1975.

Goshko, R.: Self-determined behavior change. *Personnel and Guidance Journal, 51*:629-632, 1973.

Greenall, D.: Manpower Counselor Development Program. Unpublished manual, Vancouver, British Columbia, Department of Manpower and Immigration, 1969.

Greenspoon, J.: The reinforcing effect of two spoken sounds on the frequency of two responses. *American Journal of Psychology, 68*:409-416, 1955.

Grinder, R., and Bandler, J.: *The Structure of Magic II.* Palo Alto, Sci & Behavior, 1976.

Grzegorek, A.: A study of the effect of two emphases in counselor education, each used in connection with simulation and videotape. Unpublished dissertation, East Lansing, Michigan State University, 1970.

Guerney, B., Jr.: Filial therapy: description and rationale. *Journal of Consulting Psychology, 28*:303-310, 1964.

Guerney, B., Jr. (Ed.): *Psychotherapeutic Agents: New Roles for Non-Professionals, Parents, and Teachers.* New York, HR&W, 1969.

Guerney, B., Jr.: *Relationship Enhancement: Skill Training Program for Therapeutic Problem Prevention and Enrichment.* San Francisco, Jossey-Bass, 1977.

Guerney, B., Jr., and Flumen, A.: Teachers as psychotherapeutic agents for withdrawn children. *Journal of School Psychology, 8*:107-113, 1970.

Guerney, B., Jr., Guerney, L., and Stollak, G.: The practicing psychologist as an educator: An alternative to the medical practitioner model. *Pro-*

*fessional Psychology, 2:*276-282, 1971.

Guerney, B., Jr., Guerney, L., and Stollak, G.: The potential advantages of changing from a medical to an educational model in practicing psychology. *Interpersonal Development, 2:*238-245, 1973.

Guerney, B., Jr., and Stover, L.: The efficacy of training procedures for mothers in filial therapy. *Psychotherapy: Theory Research and Practice, 4:*110-115, 1967.

Guerney, B., Jr., Stover, L., and DeMeritt, S.: A measurement of empathy in parent-child interaction. *Journal of Genetic Psychology, 112:*49-55, 1968.

Gustafson, K.: An evaluation of enriching intimacy—a behavioral approach to the training of empathy, respect-warmth, and genuineness. Unpublished dissertation, Amherst, University of Massachusetts, 1975.

Gustafson, K., and Authier, J.: Marathon versus weekly enriching intimacy relationship skills training for physician assistants. Unpublished paper, Omaha, University of Nebraska Medical Center, 1976.

Gutride, M., Goldstein, A., and Hunter, G.: Structured learning therapy for increasing social interaction skills. Unpublished manuscript, Syracuse University, 1972a.

Gutride, M., Goldstein, A., and Hunter, G.: The use of modeling and role playing to increase social interaction among schizophrenic patients. Unpublished manuscript, Syracuse University, 1972b.

Guttman, M., and Haase, R.: The generalization of microcounseling skills from training period to actual counseling setting. *Counselor Education and Supervision, 12:*98-107, 1972.

Guzzetta, R.: Acquisition and transfer of empathy by the parents of early adolescents through structured learning training. *Journal of Counseling Psychology, 23:*449-453, 1976.

Haase, R., and DiMattia, D.: The application of the microcounseling paradigm to the training of support personnel in counseling. *Counselor Education and Supervision, 10:*16-22, 1970.

Haase, R., DiMattia, D., and Guttman, M.: Training of support personnel in three human relations skills: A systematic one-year follow-up. *Counselor Education and Supervision, 11:*194-199, 1972.

Haase, R., Forsyth, D., Julius, M., and Lee, R.: Client training prior to counseling: An extension of the microcounseling paradigm. *Canadian Counsellor, 5:*9-15, 1971.

Haase, R., and Tepper, D.: Nonverbal components of empathic communication. *Journal of Counseling Psychology, 19:*417-424, 1972.

Hackney, H.: Construct reduction of counselor empathy and positive regard: A replication and extension. Unpublished dissertation, Amherst, University of Massachusetts, 1969.

Hackney, H., Ivey, A., and Oetting, E.: Attending, island and hiatus behavior: A process conception of counselor and client interaction.

Journal of Counseling Psychology, 17:342-346, 1970.

Haley, J.: *Strategies of Psychotherapy.* New York, Grune, 1963.

Haley, J.: *Uncommon Therapy.* New York, Norton, 1973.

Hall, F.: *The Silent Language.* New York, Doubleday, 1959.

Hall, E.: *Beyond Culture.* Garden City, Doubleday, 1976.

Halleck, S.: *The Politics of Therapy.* New York, Science, 1971.

Hansen, J., Moore, C., and Carkhuff, R.: The differential relationship of objective and client perceptions of counseling. *Journal of Clinical Psychology, 24*:244-246, 1968.

Harris, T.: *I'm OK, You're OK.* New York, Avon, 1967.

Hayden, B.: Verbal and therapeutic styles of experienced therapists who differ in peer-rated therapist effectiveness. *Journal of Counseling Psychology, 22*:384-389, 1975.

Hearn, M.: Three modes of training counsellors: A comparative study. Unpublished dissertation, London, Ontario, University of Western Ontario, 1976.

Hearn, M., Uhlemann, M., and Evans, D.: Microcounseling and sensitivity training with hotline workers. Paper presented to the Annual General Meeting of the Canadian Psychological Association, Quebec City, June, 1975.

Heck, E., and Davis, C.: Differential expression of empathy in a counseling analogue. *Journal of Counseling Psychology, 20*:101-104, 1973.

Hemmer, J.: Altering elementary school teachers' facilitative communication skills with microcounseling. Unpublished paper, Amherst, University of Massachusetts, 1974.

Higgins, W., Ivey, A., and Uhlemann, M.: Media therapy: A programmed approach to teaching behavioral skills. *Journal of Counseling Psychology, 17*:20-26, 1970.

Hill, C., and King, J.: Perceptions of empathy as a function of the measuring instrument. *Journal of Counseling Psychology, 23*:155-157, 1976.

Hobbs, N.: Mental health's third revolution. *American Journal of Orthopsychiatry, 34*:822-833, 1964.

Hurst, J.: Skills dissemination: Guidelines for counseling psychologists. Report of the sub-committee on skills dissemination. Report to Division 17, Counseling Psychology, American Psychological Association. Fort Collins, Counseling Center, Colorado State University, 1976.

Hutchcraft, G.: The effects of perceptual modeling techniques in the manipulation of counselor trainee interview behavior. Unpublished dissertation, Bloomington, Indiana University, 1970.

Irwin, R.: Personal communication. Columbus, Ohio State University, 1970.

Ivey, A.: The intentional individual: A process-outcome view of behavioral psychology . *The Counseling Psychologist, 1*:56-60, 1970.

Ivey, A.: *Microcounseling: Innovations in Interviewing Training.* Springfield, Thomas, 1971.

Ivey, A.: Counseling psychology: The innocent profession. *The Counseling Psychologist, 4*:111-115, 1973a.

Ivey, A.: Media therapy: Educational change planning for psychiatric patients. *Journal of Counseling Psychology, 20*:338-343, 1973b.

Ivey, A.: Adapting systems to people. *Personnel and Guidance Journal, 53*:137-139, 1974a.

Ivey, A.: Microcounseling and media therapy: The state of the art. *Counselor Education and Supervision, 13*:172-183, 1974b.

Ivey, A.: The clinician as a teacher of interpersonal skills: Let's give away what we've got. *The Clinical Psychologist, 27*:6-9, 1974c.

Ivey, A.: Invited response: The counselor as teacher. *Personnel and Guidance Journal, 54*:431-434, 1976.

Ivey, A.: Cultural expertise: Towards systematic outcome criteria in counseling and psychological education. *Personnel and Guidance Journal, 55*:296-302, 1977.

Ivey, A., and Alschuler, A. (Eds.): Psychological education: A prime function of the counselor. Special issue of the *Personnel and Guidance Journal, 51*:581-692, 1973.

Ivey, A., and Gluckstern, N.: *Basic Attending Skills: Leader and Participant Manuals.* North Amherst, Microtraining, 1974a, 1974b.

Ivey, A., and Gluckstern, N.: *Basic Attending Skills: Videotapes.* North Amherst, Microtraining, 1974c.

Ivey, A., and Gluckstern, N.: *Basic Influencing Skills: Leader and Participant Manuals.* North Amherst, Microtraining, 1976a, 1976b.

Ivey, A., and Gluckstern, N.: *Basic Influencing Skills: Videotapes.* North Amherst, Microtraining, 1976c.

Ivey, A., and Hinkle, J.: The transactional classroom. Unpublished paper, Amherst, University of Massachusetts, 1970.

Ivey, A., and Hurst, J.: Communication as adaptation. *Journal of Communication, 21*:199-207, 1971.

Ivey, A., and Leppaluoto, J.: Changes ahead: Implications of the Vail Conference. *Personnel and Guidance Journal, 53*:747-752, 1975.

Ivey, A., Moreland, J., Phillips, J., and Lockhart, J.: Paraphrasing. Unpublished manual, Amherst, University of Massachusetts, 1969.

Ivey, A., Normington, C., Miller, C., Morrill, W., and Haase, R.: Microcounseling and attending behavior: An approach to pre-practicum counselor training. *Journal of Counseling Psychology, 15:* Part II (Monograph Separate) 1-12, 1968.

Ivey, A., and Oetting, E.: Microcounseling innovations and analysis of interview process. Paper presented to the Convention of the American Personnel and Guidance Association, Dallas, 1966.

Ivey, A., and Rollin, S.: A behavioral objectives curriculum in human relations: A commitment to intentionality. *Journal of Teacher Educa-*

*tion, 23:*161-165, 1972.

Ivey, A., and Rollin, S.: The human relations curriculum: A commitment to intentionality. *British Journal of Educational Technology, 5:*21-29, 1974.

Ivey, A., and Weinrach, S.: The six deadly myths of counseling. *Pennsylvania Personnel and Guidance Journal, 4:*76-80, 1976.

Jackins, H.: *The Human Side of Human Beings: The Theory of Reevaluation Counseling.* Seattle, Rational Isl, 1965.

Jackson, B.: Black identity development. *Meforum: Journal of Educational Diversity and Innovation, 2:*19-25, 1975a.

Jackson, B.: White identity development. Unpublished paper, Amherst, School of Education, University of Massachusetts, 1975b.

Jackson, D.: *Communication, Family and Marriage.* Palo Alto, Sci & Behavior, 1968a.

Jackson, D.: *Therapy, Communication and Change.* Palo Alto, Sci & Behavior, 1968b.

Jahoda, M.: Current concepts of positive mental health. Monograph Series #1, Joint Commission on Mental Health, New York, Basic, 1958.

James, M., and Jongeward, D.: *Born to Win: Transactional Analysis with Gestalt Experiments.* Reading, A-W, 1971.

James, W.: *The Principles of Psychology.* New York, HR&W, 1890.

Jennerich, E.: Microcounseling in library education. Unpublished dissertation, Pittsburgh, University of Pittsburgh, 1974.

Jourard, S.: *Self-Disclosure.* New York, Wiley, 1971a.

Jourard, S.: *The Transparent Self.* New York, Van N-Rein, 1971b.

Jourard, S., and Lasakow, P.: Some factors in self-disclosure. *Journal of Abnormal and Social Psychology, 56:*91-98, 1958.

Kagan, N.: Three dimensions of counseling encapsulation. *Journal of Counseling Psychology, 2:*361-365, 1964.

Kagan, N.: Influencing human interaction (a filmed six-hour mental health training series and accompanying 186-page instructor's manual). East Lansing, Michigan State University, 1971.

Kagan, N.: *Influencing Human Interaction.* East Lansing, Michigan State University, 1972.

Kagan, N.: Can technology help us toward reliability in influencing human interaction? *Educational Technology, 13:*44-51, 1973.

Kagan, N.: *Influencing Human Interaction.* Washington, D.C., American Personnel and Guidance Association, 1975a.

Kagan, N.: Influencing human interaction — Eleven years with IPR. *Canadian Counsellor, 9:*74-97, 1975b.

Kagan, N., and Krathwohl, D.: Studies in human interaction. Research Report No. 20, East Lansing, Michigan State University, Educational Publication Services, 1967.

Kagan, N., Krathwohl, D., and Farquhar, W.: IPR-interpersonal process recall: Stimulated recall by videotape. Research Report No. 24, East Lansing, Michigan State University, Bureau of Educational Research Services, 1965.

Kagan, N., and Schauble, P.: Affect simulation in interpersonal process recall. *Journal of Counseling Psychology, 16*:309-313, 1969.

Kapleau, P.: *The Three Pillars of Zen.* Boston, Beacon Pr, 1965.

Kasamatsu, A., and Hirai, R.: An electroencephalographic study on the Zen meditation (Zazen). *Folio of Psychiatry and Neurology, Japanica, 20*:315-336, 1966.

Katz, J.: A systematic handbook of exercises for the re-education of white people with respect to racist attitudes and behaviors. Unpublished dissertation, Amherst, University of Massachusetts, 1975.

Katz, J.: One feminist's view of a counseling session. In Ivey, A., and Gluckstern, N.: *Basic Influencing Skills: Participant Manual.* North Amherst, Microtraining, 1976, pp. 188-190.

Katz, J., and Ivey, A.: White awareness: The frontier of racism awareness training. *Personnel and Guidance Journal, 55*:485-489, 1977.

Kaufmann, P.: Selected communication variables and their effect upon advisee satisfaction with advisor-advisee conferences. Dissertation, Ames, Iowa State University, undated.

Keil, E.: The utilization of videotape in job pre-training for mental patients. Unpublished paper, Fort Collins, Colorado State University, 1968.

Kell, B., and Mueller, W.: *Impact and Change: A Study of Counseling Relationships.* New York, Appleton, 1966.

Kelley, J.: The use of reinforcement in microcounseling. *Journal of Counseling Psychology, 18*:268-272, 1971.

Kennedy, D., and Thompson, I.: Use of reinforcement technique with a first grade boy. *Personnel and Guidance Journal, 46*:366-370, 1967.

Kennedy, J., and Zimmer, J.: A comparison of the reinforcing value of five stimuli conditions and the production of self-reference statements in a quasi-counseling situation. *Journal of Counseling Psychology, 15*:357-362, 1968.

Kerrebrock, R.: Application of the microcounseling method using videotape recordings to the training of teachers in basic counseling techniques. Unpublished dissertation, Los Angeles, University of Southern California, 1971. *Dissertation Abstracts International, 32*:740A, University Microfilms No. 71-21, 470, 1971.

Kiesler, D.: Some myths of psychotherapy research and the search for a paradigm. *Psychological Bulletin, 65*:110-136, 1966.

Kiesler, D., Mathieu, P., and Klein, M.: Summary of the issues and conclusions. In Rogers, C., Gendlin, E., Kiesler, D., and Truax, C. (Eds.): *The therapeutic relationship and its impact: A study of psychotherapy with schizophrenics.* Madison, U of Wis Press, 1967.

Kincaid, M.: Identity and therapy in the Black community. *Personnel and*

Guidance Journal, 47:884-890, 1969.

Kingdom, M.: A cost benefit analysis of the Interpersonal Process Recall technique. *Journal of Counseling Psychology, 22*:353-357, 1975.

Kloba, J., Jr., and Zimpfer, D.: Status and independence as variables in microcounseling training of adolescents. *Journal of Counseling Psychology, 23*:458-463, 1976.

Koestler, A.: *The Act of Creation*. New York, Dell, 1964.

Kriesel, H.: The teaching of basic counseling skills to theology students: A comparison, within a values context, of the microcounseling paradigm with the skills practice approach. Unpublished dissertation, Claremont, School of Theology, 1975.

Krumboltz, J.: Changing the behavior of behavior changers. *Counselor Education and Supervision, 6*:222-229, 1967.

Krumboltz, J., and Krumboltz, H.: *Changing Children's Behavior*. Englewood Cliffs, P-H, 1972.

Kuna, D.: Lecturing, reading, and modeling in counselor restatement training. *Journal of Counseling Psychology, 22*:542-546, 1975.

Kurtz, R., and Grummon, D.: Different approaches to the measurement of therapist empathy and their relationship to therapy outcomes. *Journal of Consulting and Clinical Psychology, 39*:106-116, 1972.

LaFrance, R.: Personal communication. Amherst, University of Massachusetts, 1970.

Laing, R.: *The Politics of Experience*. New York, Ballantine, 1967.

Laing, R.: *Knots*. New York, Vin Random, 1970.

Lambert, W.: *Language, Psychology, and Culture*. Stanford, Stanford, U Pr, 1972.

Larke, J., and English, R.: Effects of videotape case presentation with guided participation in training paraprofessional helpers. Working paper No. 90. Rehabilitation Research and Training Center in Mental Retardation. Eugene, University of Oregon, 1975.

Lauver, P., and Brody, G.: The relative effectiveness of self-modeling as a procedure for teaching basic interviewing skills. Paper presented to the American Educational Research Association Annual Meeting, Washington, D.C., 1975.

Lea, G.: Effects of instructions and modeling on the training of a low functioning population in the reflection of feeling. Unpublished master's thesis, Ontario, University of Western Ontario, 1975.

Lee, D., Zingle, H., Patterson, J., Ivey, A., and Haase, R.: Development and validation of a microcounseling skills discrimination index. *Journal of Counseling Psychology, 23*:468-472, 1976.

Levy, L.: *Psychological Interpretation*. New York, HR&W, 1963.

Libow, J., and Doty, D.: An evaluation of empathic listening in telephone counseling. *Journal of Counseling Psychology, 23*:532-537, 1976.

Lieberman, M., Yalom, I., and Miles, M.: *Encounter Groups: First Facts*.

New York, Basic, 1972.

Lindsley, O.: An experiment with parents handling behavior at home. *Johnstone Bulletin, 9:*27-36, 1966.

Lovaas, O.: Some studies in childhood schizophrenia. In Shlein, J. (Ed.): *Research in Psychotherapy.* Washington, D.C., American Psychological Association, 1968, Vol. III, pp. 103-121.

Lowen, A.: *The Betrayal of the Body.* New York, Macmillan, 1967.

Luria, A.: The origin and cerebral organization of man's conscious action. Paper presented to the XIX International Congress of Psychology, London, 1969.

Luthe, W.: Autogenic training: Method, research, and application in medicine. In Tart, C. (Ed.): *Altered States of Consciousness.* New York, Wiley, 1969, pp. 309-319.

Lynch, R., and Magoon, T.: Microtraining for college faculty advisors: Some constraints and suggestions. Unpublished paper, University of Maryland, 1975.

McCarthy, P., Danish, S., and D'Augelli, A.: A follow-up evaluation of helping skills training. *Counselor Education and Supervision* (in press).

McDermott, D.: *A Manual for Peer Counselors.* New York, Full Circle Associates, 1976a.

McDermott, D.: A study of peer counselors' acquisition of skills and personal growth. Unpublished dissertation, Yellow Springs, Union Graduate School, 1976b.

McDonald, F., and Allen, D.: Training effects of feedback and modeling procedures on teaching performance. Unpublished report, Stanford, Stanford University, 1967.

McFayden, M., and Winokur, G.: Cross-cultural psychotherapy. *Journal of Nervous and Mental Disorders, 123:*369-375, 1956.

McWhirter, J.: Two measures of the facilitative conditions. A correlation study. *Journal of Counseling Psychology, 20:*317-320, 1973.

Mager, R.: *Preparing Instructional Objectives.* Palo Alto, Fearon, 1962.

Mahl, G.: Gestures and body movements in interviews. In Shlien, J. (Ed.): *Research in Psychotherapy.* Washington, D.C., American Psychological Association, 1968, Vol. III, pp. 295-346.

Malamud, D.: The second chance family: A medium for self-directed growth. In Blank, L., Gottsegen, G., and Gottsegen, M. (Eds.): *Encounter: Confrontations in Self and Interpersonal Awareness.* New York, Macmillan, 1971.

Maslow, A.: Deficiency motivation and growth motivation. In Jones, M. (Ed.): *Nebraska Symposium on Motivation.* Lincoln, University of Nebraska Press, 1955, pp. 8, 20, 24, 25, 27.

Maslow, A.: *The Farther Reaches of Human Nature.* New York, Viking Pr, 1971.

Matarazzo, J., and Wiens, A.: Speech behavior as an objective correlate of empathy and outcome in interview and psychotherapy research: A review with implications for behavior modification. *Behavior Modification,* 1977, in press.

Matarazzo, J., Wiens, A., Matarazzo, R., and Saslow, G.: Speech and silent behavior in clinical psychotherapy and its laboratory correlates. In Shlien, J. (Ed.): *Research in Psychotherapy.* Washington, D.C., American Psychological Association, 1968, Vol. III, pp. 347-394.

Matarazzo, R.: Research on the teaching and learning of psychotherapeutic skills. In Bergin, A., and Garfield, S. (Eds.): *Psychotherapy and Behavior Change.* New York, Wiley, 1971, pp. 895-924.

Matarazzo, R., Phillips, J., Wiens, A., and Saslow, G.: Learning the art of interviewing: A study of what beginning students do and their patterns of change. *Psychotherapy: Theory, Research and Practice, 2:*49-60, 1965.

Matarazzo, R., Wiens, A., and Saslow, G.: Experimentation in the teaching and learning of psychotherapy skills. In Gottschalk, L., and Auerbach, A. (Eds.): *Methods of Research in Psychotherapy.* New York, Appleton, 1966, pp. 597-635.

Maupin, E.: Individual differences in response to a Zen meditation exercise. *Journal of Consulting Psychology, 29:*135-145, 1965.

May, R.: *Love and Will.* New York, Norton, 1969.

Mead, M.: The study of national character. In Learner, D., and Lasswell, H. (Eds.): *The Policy Sciences.* Stanford, Stanford U Pr, 1951, pp. 70-85. Cited in Kaplan, B.: *Studying Personality Cross-Culturally.* New York, Har-Row, 1961, p. 48.

Meehl, P.: Psychotherapy. *Annual Review of Psychology, 6:*357-378, 1955.

Mehrabian, A.: *Nonverbal Communication.* New York, Aldine-Atherton, 1972.

Meltzkoff, J., and Kornreich, M.: *Research in Psychotherapy.* New York, Atherton, 1970.

Meyers, M.: Effects of micro-interviewing skills training on counselor trainees' feelings toward interview situation and on potential client preference. Unpublished dissertation, Kansas City, University of Missouri, 1973.

Middleton, R.: Alienation, race, and education. *American Sociological Review, 28:*973-977, 1963.

Miller, C., Morrill, W., Ivey, A., Normington, C., and Uhlemann, M.: Microcounseling: Training in assessment of clients' attitudes towards tests. *Counselor Education and Supervision, 13:*14-23, 1973.

Miller, C., Morrill, W., and Uhlemann, M.: Microcounseling: An experimental study of pre-practicum training in communicating test results. *Counselor Education and Supervision, 9:*171-177, 1970.

Mitchell, H.: The Black experience in higher education. *The Counseling Psychologist, 2:*30-36, 1970.

Mitchell, K., Rubin, S., Bozarth, J., and Wyrick, T.: Effects of short-term training on residence hall assistants. *Counselor Education and Supervision, 10:*310-318, 1971.

Moore, M.: Training professionals to work with paraprofessionals. *Personnel and Guidance Journal, 53:*308-312, 1974.

Moore, M., and Delworth, U.: Initiation and implementation of outreach programs (technical report number II). National Institute of Mental Health, Grant #1 ROIMH 18007, 1972.

Moreland, J.: A descriptive taxonomy of group facilitation skills. Unpublished paper, Carbondale, Southern Illinois University, 1973.

Moreland, J., and Ivey, A.: Interpretation. Unpublished manual, Amherst, University of Massachusetts, 1969.

Moreland, J., Ivey, A., and Phillips, J.: An evaluation of microcounseling as an interviewer training tool. *Journal of Clinical and Consulting Psychology, 41:*294-300, 1973.

Moreland, J., Phillips, J., Ivey, A., and Lockhart, J.: A study of the microtraining paradigm with beginning clinical psychologists. Unpublished paper, Amherst, University of Massachusetts, 1970.

Morganstern, K.: Behavioral interviewing: The initial stages of assessment. In Hersen, M., and Bellack, A.: *Behavioral Assessment.* New York, Pergamon, 1976, pp. 51-76.

Morrow, D.: Cultural addiction. *Journal of Rehabilitation, 38:* 30-32, 1972.

Mosher, R., and Sprinthall, N.: Psychological education: A means to promote personal development during adolescence. *The Counseling Psychologist, 2*(4):3-82, 1971.

Mueller, W., and Kell, B.: *Coping with Conflict: Supervising Counselors and Psychotherapists.* New York, Meredith, 1972.

Munz, V., Villa, V., Slipow, J., Reynolds, D., Minski, H., Gustafson, K., and Authier, J.: Public Health Employee Assistance Program: Interviewer/Counselor Training Workshop. Unpublished manual, Washington, D.C., Roy Little John Associates, 1976.

Murray, E.: The content analysis method of studying psychotherapy. *Psychological Monographs, 70:*(Whole No. 420), 1956.

Noel, W.: Experiencing as systematic training: Its effect on communication between black and white high school students. Unpublished dissertation, Amherst, University of Massachusetts, 1976.

Norman, D.: *Memory and Attention: An Introduction to Human Information Processing.* New York, Wiley, 1969.

Normington, C.: A comparison of counselor ratings by high school students and experts. Paper presented to the American Personnel and Guidance Association Convention, Las Vegas, 1969.

Nuttall, E., and Ivey, A.: Research for action: The tradition and its implementation. In Goldman, L. (Ed.): *Research and the Counselor.*

New York, Wiley (in press).

Oetting, E.: Evaluative research: An orthodox science. *Personnel and Guidance Journal*, 55:11-15, 1976.

Orlando, N.: The mental patient as therapeutic agent: Self-change, power and caring. *Psychotherapy: Theory, Research and Practice*, 11:58-62, 1974.

Patterson, C.: The counseling practicum: An ethical issue. *Counselor Education and Supervision*, 7:322-324, 1968.

Patterson, C.: Foreword. In Carkhuff, R.: *Helping and Human Relations*, Vol. II. New York, HR & W, 1969b.

Patterson, C.: *Theories of Counseling and Psychotherapy*. New York, Harper & Row, 1973.

Patterson, G., and Brodsky, G.: A behavior modification program for a child with multiple problem behaviors. *Journal of Child Psychology and Psychiatry*, 7:277-295, 1966.

Patterson, G., and Guillion, E.: Child Training: A Manual for Parents. Rantaul, Rantaul Press, 1968.

Paul, G.: *Insight vs. Desensitization in Psychotherapy*. Stanford, Stanford U. Pr, 1966.

Paul, G.: Insight versus desensitization in psychotherapy two years after termination. *Journal of Consulting Psychology*, 31:333-348, 1967.

Payne, P., Weiss, S., and Kapp, R.: Didactic, experiential, and modeling factors in the learning of empathy. *Journal of Counseling Psychology*, 19:425-429, 1972.

Payne, P., Winter, D., and Bell, G.: Effects of supervisor style on the learning of empathy in a supervision analogue. *Counselor Education and Supervision*, 11:262-269, 1972.

Pedersen, P.: A cross-cultural coalition training model for educating mental health professionals to function in multicultural populations. Paper presented to the IXth International Congress of Ethnological and Anthropological Sciences, Chicago, September, 1973.

Pedersen, P.: Manual: A cross-cultural training model for counselors. Unpublished paper, International Student Adviser's Office, Minneapolis, University of Minnesota, undated.

Pedersen, P., Holwill, C., and Shapiro, J.: A cross-cultural training procedure for classes in counselor education. Unpublished paper, International Student Adviser's Office, Minneapolis, University of Minnesota, 1976.

Pepyne, E.: The control of interview content through minimal social stimuli. Unpublished dissertation, Amherst, University of Massachusetts, 1968.

Pepyne, E., and Zimmer, J.: Verbal conditioning and the counseling interview. Unpublished paper, Amherst, University of Massachusetts, 1969.

Perkins, S., and Atkinson, D.: Effect of selected techniques for training resident assistants in human relations skills. *Journal of Counseling*

*Psychology, 20:*89-94, 1973.

Perlberg, A., and Bryant, D.: Video recording and microteaching techniques to improve engineering instruction. Unpublished paper, Champaign, University of Illinois, 1968.

Perlberg, A., Peri, J., and Weinreb, M.: Using microteaching techniques and immediate feedback with closed-circuit television to improve teaching in dental education. Unpublished paper, Tel Aviv, Tel Aviv University, 1970.

Perls, F.: *Gestalt Therapy Verbatim.* Moab, Real People, 1969.

Perls, F., Hefferline, R., and Goodman, P.: *Gestalt Therapy.* New York, Delta, 1951.

Perry, M.: Modeling and instructions in training for counselor empathy. *Journal of Counseling Psychology, 22:*173-179, 1975.

Pesso, A.: *Movement in Psychotherapy: Psychomotor Techniques and Training.* New York, NYU Pr, 1969.

Petrick, S.: An evaluation of a combined group therapy and communication skills training program for psychiatric inpatients. Unpublished dissertation, Lincoln, University of Nebraska, 1976.

Pfeiffer, J., and Jones, J.: *A handbook of structured experiences for human relations training,* Vols. I, II, III, IV. Iowa City, University Associates, 1969, 1970, 1971, 1973.

Phillips, E.: Achievement place: Token reinforcement procedures in a homestyle rehabilitation setting for "predelinquent" boys. *Journal of Applied Behavioral Analysis, 1:*213-223, 1968.

Phillips, J., and Kanfer, F.: The viability and vicissitudes of behavior therapy. *International Psychiatry Clinics, 6:*75-133, 1969.

Phillips, J., Lockhart, J., and Moreland, J.: Minimal encourages to talk. Unpublished manual, Amherst, University of Massachusetts, 1969a.

Phillips, J., Lockhart, J., and Moreland, J.: Open invitation to talk. Unpublished manual, Amherst, University of Massachusetts, 1969b.

Phillips, J., and Matarazzo, R.: Content measures of novices' interview techniques. *International Mental Health Research Newsletter, 4:*11-12, 1962.

Pierce, R., and Drasgow, J.: Teaching facilitative interpersonal functioning to psychiatric patients. *Journal of Counseling Psychology, 16:*295-298, 1969.

Polanyi, M.: *The Tacit Dimension.* Garden City, Doubleday, 1966.

Quay, H., Werry, J., McQueen, M., and Sprague, R.: Remediation of the conduct problem child in the special class setting. *Exceptional Child, 31:*509-515, 1966.

Randolph, N., Howe, W., and Achtermann, E.: Self-enhancing education: Guidance and counseling. Unpublished manuscript, Cupertino, Cupertino Union School District, 1968.

Rappaport, J., and Chinsky, J.: Accurate empathy: Confusion of a construct. *Psychological Bulletin, 77:*400-404, 1972.

Raths, L., Harmin, M., and Simon, S.: *Values and Teaching.* Columbus, Merrill, 1966.

Rathus, S.: A thirty-item schedule for assessing assertive behavior. *Behavior Therapy, 4:*398-406, 1973.

Reeder, C., and Kunce, J.: Modeling techniques, drug abstinence behavior, and heroin addicts: A pilot study. *Journal of Counseling Psychology, 23:*560-562, 1976.

Reivich, R., and Geertsma, R.: Observational media and psychotherapy training. *Journal of Nervous and Mental Disorders, 148:*310-327, 1969.

Rennie, D., and Toukmanian, S.: Acquisition of counseling skill by introverted and extroverted counselor trainees under conditions of experiential and didactic training. Paper presented to the Symposium on Personality and Applied Psychology, Canadian Psychological Association Annual Meeting, Windsor, June, 1974.

Rennie, D., and Toukmanian, S.: Effects of counselor trainee extroversion and neuroticism on empathy gain duration training. Unpublished manuscript, Ontario, York University, 1976.

Resnikoff, A., Kagan, N., and Schauble, P.: Acceleration of psychotherapy through simulated videotape recall. *American Journal of Psychotherapy, 12:*10-16, 1970.

Rice, L.: Therapist's style of participation and case outcome. *Journal of Consulting Psychology, 29:*155-160, 1965.

Rizzo, S.: A comparison of effects of variations in microcounseling training with groups of parents of the developmentally disabled. Unpublished dissertation, Philadelphia, Temple University, 1976.

Roberts, D.: Treatment of cultural scripts. *Transactional Analysis Journal, 5:*29-35, 1975.

Rogers, C.: *Client-Centered Therapy.* Boston, HM, 1951.

Rogers, C.: The necessary and sufficient conditions of therapeutic personality change. *Journal of Consulting Psychology, 21:*95-103, 1957a.

Rogers, C.: Training individuals in the therapeutic process. In Strother, C. (Ed.): *Psychology and Mental Health.* Washington, D.C., American Psychological Association, 1957b.

Rogers, C.: A theory of therapy, personality and interpersonal relationships as developed in the client-centered framework. In Koch, S. (Ed.): *Psychology: A Study of a Science, Vol. III, Formulations of the Person and the Social Context.* New York, McGraw, 1959, pp. 184-256.

Rogers, C.: *On Becoming a Person.* Boston, HM, 1961.

Rogers, C.: *Carl Rogers on Encounter Groups.* New York, Har-Row, 1970.

Rogers, C.: Empathic: An unappreciated way of being. *The Counseling Psychologist, 5:*2-10, 1975.

Rogers, C., and Dymond, R. (Eds.): *Psychotherapy and Personality Change.* Chicago, U of Chicago Pr, 1954.

Rogers, C., Gendlin, E., Kiesler, D., and Truax, C.: *The Therapeutic Relationship and Its Impact.* Madison, U of Wis Press, 1967.

Rogers, J.: Operant conditioning in a quasi-therapy setting. *Journal of Abnormal and Social Psychology, 60*:247-252, 1960.

Rollin, S.: The development and testing of a performance curriculum in human relations. Unpublished dissertation, Amherst, University of Massachusetts, 1970.

Russel, R.: Black perceptions of guidance. *Personnel and Guidance Journal, 48*:721-729, 1970.

Ryan, W.: *Blaming the Victim.* New York, Vin Random, 1971.

Sadler, O., and Seyden, T.: Groups for parents: A guide for teaching child management to parents. *Journal of Community Psychology, 4*:3-63, 1976.

Saltmarsh, R., and Hubele, G.: Basic interaction behaviors: A microcounseling approach for introductory courses. *Counselor Education and Supervision, 13*:246-249, 1974.

Sartre, J.: *Nausea.* New York, New Directions, 1964.

Sartre, J.: *No Exit.* New York, Vin Random, 1946.

Satir, V.: *Conjoint Family Therapy.* Palo Alto, Sci & Behavior, 1964.

Satir, V.: *Peoplemaking.* Palo Alto, Sci & Behavior, 1972.

Savicki, V.: Abbreviated group microcounseling training with experienced juvenile court workers. Unpublished paper, Monmouth, Oregon College of Education, 1974.

Savicki, V.: Some data and speculations concerning maintenance of basic interviewing skills for experienced interviewers. Unpublished paper, Monmouth, Oregon College of Education, 1975.

Scheflen, A.: *Stream and Structure of Communicational Behavior.* Bloomington, Ind U Pr, 1969.

Scheflen, A.: *Communicational Structure: Analysis of a Psychotherapy Transaction.* Bloomington, Ind U Pr, 1973.

Schulman, E.: *Intervention in Human Services.* St. Louis, Mosby, 1974.

Schutz, W.: *Joy.* New York, Grove, 1967.

Schwebel, A.: Personal communication. Columbus, Ohio State University, 1970.

Schwebel, M.: Ideology and counselor encapsulation. *Journal of Counseling Psychology, 2*:366-369, 1964.

Scroggins, W., and Ivey, A.: An evaluation of microcounseling as a model to train resident staff. Unpublished manuscript, University, University of Alabama, 1976.

Seeman, J.: A study of nondirective therapy. *Journal of Consulting Psychology, 13*:157-168, 1948.

Seidenstücker, E.: Konstruktion und evaluation eines trainingsprogramms fur klinische interviews. Inaugural-Dissertation, der Universitat Regensburg, 1976.

Semans, J.: Premature ejaculation: A new approach. *Southern Medical Journal, 49:*353-358, 1956.

Sherrard, P.: Predicting group leader/member interaction: The efficacy of the Ivey Taxonomy. Unpublished dissertation, Amherst, University of Massachusetts, 1973.

Shor, R.: Three dimensions of hypnotic depth. *International Journal of Clinical and Experimental Hypnosis, 10:*23-38, 1962.

Shostrom, E.: The Personal Orientation Inventory. San Diego, Educational and Industrial Testing Service, 1966.

Simon, S., Howe, L., and Kirschenbaum, H.: *Values Clarification.* New York, HR&W, 1972.

Skinner, B.: *Science and Human Behavior.* New York, Macmillan, 1953.

Sloane, R., Staples, F., Cristol, A., Yorkston, N., and Whipple, K.: *Psychotherapy Versus Behavior Therapy.* Cambridge, Harvard U Pr, 1975.

Snyder, W.: An investigation of the nature of nondirective therapy. *Journal of General Psychology, 33:*193-223, 1945.

Sodetz, A.: The effect of videotape microcounseling on counselor behavior. Unpublished dissertation, Columbia, University of Missouri, 1972.

Spooner, S., and Stone, S.: Maintenance of specific counseling skills over time. *Journal of Counseling Psychology, 24:*66-71, 1977.

Stanford Observer: Students learn the deep value of peer counseling. Stanford University Alumni Newspaper, April, 1975.

Steiner, C. (Ed.): *Readings in Radical Psychiatry.* New York, Grove, 1975.

Stokes, J., and Romer, D.: Microcounseling Skills Discrimination Index: A methodological note. *Journal of Counseling Psychology* (in press).

Stoller, F.: TV and the patient's self-image. *Frontiers of Hospital Psychiatry, 2:*1-2, 1965.

Stone, G., and Stebbins, L.: Effect of differential pretraining on client self-disclosure. *Journal of Counseling Psychology, 22:*17-20, 1975.

Stone, G., and Vance, A.: Instruction, modeling and rehearsal: Implications for training. *Journal of Counseling Psychology, 23:*272-279, 1976.

Stover, L., Guerney, B., and O'Connell, M.: Measurements of acceptance, allowing self-direction, involvement, and empathy in adult-child interaction. *The Journal of Psychology, 77:*261-269, 1971.

Strupp, H.: An objective comparison of Rogerian and psychoanalytic techniques. *Journal of Consulting Psychology, 19:*1-7, 1955a.

Strupp, H.: Psychotherapeutic technique, professional affiliation, and experience level. *Journal of Consulting Psychology, 19:*97-102, 1955b.

Strupp, H.: The effect of the psychotherapist's personal analysis upon his techniques. *Journal of Consulting Psychology, 19:*197-204, 1955c.

Strupp, H.: *Psychotherapists in Action.* New York, Grune, 1960.

Strupp, H.: *Patients View Their Psychotherapy.* Baltimore, Johns Hopkins, 1970.

Strupp, H., and Bergin, A.: *Research in Individual Psychotherapy: A*

Bibliography. Chevy Chase, National Institute of Mental Health, 1972.

Sue, D.: Counseling the culturally different. *Personnel and Guidance Journal. 55:*422-425, 1977.

Sue, S., Allen, D., and Conaway, L.: The responsiveness and equality of mental health care to Chicanos and Native Americans. *American Journal of Community Psychology* (in press), 1977.

Sue, S., and McKinney, H.: Asian-Americans in the community mental health care system. *American Journal of Orthopsychiatry, 45:*111-118, 1975.

Sue, S., McKinney, H., Allen, D., and Hall, J.: Delivery of community mental health services to black and white clients. *Journal of Consulting and Clinical Psychology, 42:*794-801, 1974.

Sullivan, H.: *The Interpersonal Theory of Psychiatry.* New York, Norton, 1953.

Swets, J., and Kristofferson, A.: Attention. In Mussen, P., and Rosenzweig, M. (Eds.): *Annual Review of Psychology.* Palo Alto, Annual Reviews, 1970, pp. 339-366.

Szasz, T.: *The Myth of Mental Illness.* New York, Dell, 1961.

Terrell, T.: The effects of microtraining in attending behavior on response behavior and attending behavior of paraprofessional orientation leaders. Unpublished dissertation, Mississippi State, Mississippi State University, 1976.

Thielen, T.: The immediate effects of an abbreviated co-counseling supervision approach in teaching empathic skills to counselors-in-training. Unpublished dissertation, Bloomington, Indiana University, 1970.

Thomas, A.: Pseudotransference reactions due to cultural stereotyping. *American Journal of Orthopsychiatry, 32:*894-900, 1962.

Thomas, G.: Using videotaped modeling to increase attending behavior. *Elementary School Guidance and Counseling,* 35-40, 1974.

Tien, J.: Everyone getting ahead—Nobody left behind: Education in the People's Republic of China. *Harvard Graduate School of Education Bulletin, 20:*16-22, 1976.

Toukmanian, S., and Rennie, D.: Microcounseling vs. human relations training: Relative effectiveness with undergraduate trainees. *Journal of Counseling Psychology, 22:*345-352, 1975.

Trabasso, T., and Bower, G.: *Attention in Learning: Theory and Research.* New York, Wiley, 1968.

Trent, R.: The color of the investigator as a variable in experimental research with Negro subjects. *Journal of Social Psychology, 40:*281-287, 1954.

Truax, C.: The process of group psychotherapy: Relationships between hypothesized therapeutic conditions and intrapersonal exploration. *Psychological Monographs, 7:*(Whole No. 511), 1961.

Truax, C.: Effective ingredients in psychotherapy: An approach to unraveling the patient-therapist interaction. In Stollak, G., Guerney, B., Jr., and Rothberg, M. (Eds.): *Psychotherapy Research: Selected Readings.* Chicago, Rand, 1966, pp. 586-594.

Truax, C.: A scale for the rating of accurate empathy. In Rogers, C., Gendlin, E., Kiesler, D., and Truax, C. (Eds.): *The Therapeutic Relationship and Its Impact. A Study of Psychotherapy with Schizophrenics.* Madison, U of Wis Pr, 1967, pp. 555-568.

Truax, C.: The meaning and reliability of accurate empathy ratings: A rejoinder. *Psychological Bulletin, 77*:397-399, 1972.

Truax, C., and Carkhuff, R.: Experimental manipulation of therapeutic conditions. *Journal of Consulting Psychology, 29*:119-124, 1965.

Truax, C., and Carkhuff, R.: *Toward Effective Counseling and Psychotherapy: Training and Practice.* Chicago, Aldine, 1967.

Truax, C., Carkhuff, R., and Kodman, F.: The relationships between therapist offered conditions and patient change in group psychotherapy. *Journal of Clinical Psychology, 21*:327-329, 1965.

Truax, C., Carkhuff, R., Wargo, D., Kodman, F., and Moles, E.: Changes in self-concept during group psychotherapy as a function of alternate sessions and vicarious therapy pretraining in institutionalized mental patients and juvenile delinquents. *Journal of Consulting Psychology, 30*:309-314, 1966.

Truax, C., and Mitchell, K.: Research on certain therapist interpersonal skills in relation to process and outcome. In Bergin, A., and Garfield, S. (Eds.): *Handbook of Psychotherapy and Behavior Change.* New York, Wiley, 1971.

Truax, C., and Wargo, D.: Antecedents to outcome in group psychotherapy with hospitalized mental patients: Effects of therapeutic conditions, alternate sessions, vicarious therapy pre-training and patient self-exploration. Unpublished manuscript, Fayetteville, University of Arkansas, 1967a.

Truax, C., and Wargo, D.: Antecedents to outcome in group psychotherapy with juvenile delinquents: Effects of therapeutic conditions, alternate sessions, vicarious therapy pre-training and client self-exploration. Unpublished manuscript, Fayetteville, University of Arkansas, 1967b.

Truax, C., and Wargo, D.: Psychotherapeutic encounters that change behavior: For better or worse. *American Journal of Psychotherapy, 22*: 499-520, 1966.

Turney, C., Clift, J., Dunkin, J., and Traill, R.: *Microteaching: Research, Theory, and Practice.* Sydney, Sydney University Press, 1973.

Tyler, L.: *The Work of the Counselor.* New York, Appleton, 1953.

Uhlemann, M., Lea, G., and Stone, G.: Effects of modeling and instructions on low-functioning trainees. *Journal of Counseling Psychology, 23*:509-513, 1976.

Ullmann, L., and Krasner, L.: *Case Studies in Behavior Modification.* New

York, HR&W, 1965.

Vitalo, R.: Teaching improved interpersonal functioning as a preferred mode of treatment. *Journal of Consulting and Clinical Psychology, 35:* 166-171, 1971.

Vontress, C.: Racial differences: Impediments to rapport. *Journal of Counseling Psychology, 18:*7-13, 1971.

Wahler, R.: Setting generality: Some specific and general effects of child behavior therapy. *Journal of Applied Behavioral Analysis, 2:*239-246, 1969.

Wallace, W., Horan, J., Baker, S., and Hudson, G.: Incremental effects of modeling and performance feedback in teaching decision-making counseling. *Journal of Counseling Psychology, 22:*570-572, 1975.

Watzlawick, P., Beavin, J., and Jackson, D.: *Pragmatics of Human Communication.* New York, Norton, 1967.

Wawrykow, G.: Video vs. audio feedback in training therapists varying in openness to experience. Unpublished thesis, Waterloo, University of Waterloo, 1970.

Weinrach, S.: A model for the systematic generalization of counseling skills. *Counselor Education and Supervision, 15:*311-314, 1976.

Weinrach, S., and Ivey, A.: Science, deception, and psychology. *Bulletin of the British Psychological Society, 28:*263-267, 1975.

Welch, C.: Counsellor training in interviewing skills: Interpersonal Process Recall in a microcounseling model. Unpublished dissertation, Montreal, McGill University, 1976.

Werner, A., and Schneider, J.: Teaching medical students interactional skills. *New England Journal of Medicine, 290:*1232-1237, 1974.

Whalen, C.: Effects of a model and instructions on group verbal behaviors. *Journal of Consulting and Clinical Psychology, 33:*509-521, 1969.

White, M.: Guidance through counseling in the inner-city high school: The development of a structured counseling program. Unpublished dissertation, Amherst, University of Massachusetts, 1974.

Whiteley, J.: Counselor education. *Review of Educational Research, 30:* 173-187, 1969.

Whitley, D., and Sulzer, B.: Reducing disruptive behavior through consultation. *Personnel and Guidance Journal, 48:*836-841, 1970.

Wideman, J.: Growth and development in counselor education. Unpublished dissertation, Cambridge, Harvard University, 1970.

Wiener, M., and Mehrabian, A.: *Language Within Language: Immediacy, A Channel in Verbal Communication.* New York, Appleton, 1968.

Wilkinson, C.: Problems in black-white encounter groups. *International Journal of Group Psychotherapy, 23:*155-165, 1973.

Williams, R.: Black pride, academic relevance, and individual achievement. *The Counseling Psychologist, 2:*18-22, 1970.

Wolpe, J.: *Psychotherapy by Reciprocal Inhibition.* Stanford, Stanford U

Pr, 1958.

Wolpe, J.: The systematic desensitization of neuroses. *Journal of Nervous and Mental Disease, 112*:189-203, 1961.

Wolpe, J., and Lazarus, A.: *Behavior Therapy Techniques.* New York, Pergamon, 1966.

Woods, F.: Cultural conditioning and mental health. *Social Casework, 39:* 327-333, 1958.

Woodworth, R., and Schlosberg, H.: *Experimental Psychology.* New York, HR&W, 1954.

Wrenn, C.: *The Counselor in the Changing World.* Washington, D.C., American Personnel and Guidance Association, 1962.

Yalom, I., Houts, P., Newell, G., and Rand, K.: Preparation of patients for group psychotherapy. *Archives of General Psychiatry, 17:*416-427, 1967.

Zeevi, S.: Development and evaluation of a training program in human relations. Unpublished dissertation, Amherst, University of Massachusetts, 1970a.

Zeevi, S.: Microtraining in a community center. Unpublished paper, Amherst, University of Massachusetts, 1970b.

Zimmer, J., and Anderson, S.: Dimensions of positive regard and empathy. *Journal of Counseling Psychology, 15:*417-426, 1968.

Zimmer, J., and Cowles, K.: Content analysis using fortran: Applied to interviews conducted by C. Rogers, F. Perls, and A. Ellis. *Journal of Counseling Psychology, 19*:161-166, 1972.

Zimmer, J., and Park, P.: Factor analysis of counselor communications. *Journal of Counseling Psychology, 14:*198-203, 1967.

Zimmer, J., and Pepyne, E.: A descriptive and comparative study of dimensions of counselor response. *Journal of Counseling Psychology, 18:*441-447, 1971.

Zimmerman, E., and Zimmerman, J.: The alteration of behavior in a special classroom situation. *Journal of the Experimental Analysis of Behavior, 5:*59-60, 1962.

Zubec, J.: Behavioral and EEG changes after prolonged perceptual deprivation. *Psychonomic Science, 1:*57-58, 1964a.

Zubec, J.: Behavioral changes after prolonged sensory and perceptual deprivation. *Perceptual and Motor Skills, 18:*413-420, 1964b.

Zubec, J.: Effects of prolonged sensory and perceptual deprivation. *British Medical Bulletin, 20:*38-42, 1964c

Appendix I

A SAMPLE ATTENDING BEHAVIOR
WORKSHOP*

T HE FOLLOWING PAGES present how a workshop in attending behavior is conducted with a large group. The session is one of
fourteen similar systematic sessions presented in the *Basic Attending Skills* and *Basic Influencing Skills* series (Ivey and Gluckstern,
1974a,b; 1976a,b).

It will be useful to turn to Appendix II from time to time,
as a typescript of a sample modeling tape with baseline and posttest microcounseling sessions illustrates the concepts of this workshop. In an ideal setting, all participants will engage in a baseline interview before engaging in training. Important in all microcounseling workshops is the establishment of clear competencies
of performance. It is possible to engage in microtraining as a
teaching exercise and still not have participants who can demonstrate or *do* the skills. Appendix VII outlines some general competencies for people who have gone through skills training. In
cases where research has not found marked behavior change
among trainees, one of the primary causes is failure of the trainer
to ensure that people have achieved improvement and/or minimal
competence in the basic skill.

The *Leader Manual* of *Basic Attending Skills* is presented first,
followed by the *Participant Manual*. Readers will want to refer
to the *Participant Manual* as they read so as to clarify the connections between the suggested exercises and trainee material.

*The material from the videobased series *Basic Attending Skills* is reproduced
verbatim by permission of Microtraining Associates, Inc., Box 641, North Amherst,
Massachusetts, 01059. Information on similar workshops may be obtained from
that address.

BASIC ATTENDING SKILLS LEADER MANUAL
ALLEN E. IVEY AND NORMA B. GLUCKSTERN

ATTENDING BEHAVIOR: EYE CONTACT, POSTURE, AND VERBAL FOLLOWING

Workshop #1

Introductory Comments on Attending Behavior Workshop

As this is the first workshop in the series, we have provided a substantial number of exercises and alternatives. Approximately six to eight hours would be required to complete all the exercises in the suggested order.

Further, we have not given suggested time frames for each exercise, as they can be completed rather quickly or may be extended for considerable periods of time depending on the needs and interests of the group involved with the training. Thus, the leader will have to plan approximate time frames for the workshop sessions. Hopefully, these times will be flexible so that the inevitable changes in workshop design are possible as you obtain feedback from the group.

We cannot stress too strongly the importance of the single skills concept. Nothing destroys a microcounseling workshop faster than a leader who permits the group to move beyond the skill to efforts to "solve the problem" immediately. This is one of the basic difficulties of the beginning counselor, and many groups also find themselves in the same bind. A firm hand by the leader may be required to keep the group on task. Where necessary, take time out to "process" individual and group reactions to "what is happening," but suggest that problem solutions can be worked on outside the group.

Some major alternatives to the highly structured workshop presented here are suggested. We have used all of them with success.

1. A "bare-bones" three-hour workshop would entail activity 1 (warmup and introductions), activity 2 (the video lecture on microcounseling), activity 4 (reading the manual), activity 5 (viewing the modeling tape), activity 6 (second

viewing of tape with behavioral counts), and activity 7 (practice with attending skills), plus activity 13 (windup session and feedback).

2. A more "existential" approach is one in which the group is given the problem. . . ."define what listening is not" (activity 3). The group(s) then develops its own conceptions of what effective helping would be and develops its own video modeling tapes of effective and ineffective helping without the benefit of lectures, manuals, or videotape models. The resultant product of the group can then be compared with the microcounseling constructs. In some cases, we have suggested that the group(s) select the three most important things they would teach beginners. We have used this approach from behavioral and existential theoretical frameworks with equal success. The results sometimes resemble the microcounseling skills; other times, quite different and interesting conceptions are developed.

3. These materials, of course, can be used with the regular individual training methods of microcounseling as outlined in the original microcounseling book. The book also outlines numerous other alternatives for teaching individuals or groups the skills of interviewing via these methods.

STEP 1: CREATING A LEARNING ENVIRONMENT

Microcounseling is a skills-oriented approach designed to help people relate to people more effectively. But before you teach skills, it is best to recognize that you are working with real people who have anxieties, concerns, and expectations related to the workshop. The first thing that you must do as a trainer is to help them and yourself deal with this reality and reduce as quickly as possible personal anxieties in this situation. There are a number of ways in which you can help provide a warm and receptive learning climate.

A standard format we use in many workshops follows:

Activity 1: Individualized recognition

Microcounseling is about people. We'd like you to get to know one person now. Find one person in the room you don't know at all or don't know well. Your task is to introduce them with one fact about them that interests you.

Call the group together and go around with the introductions.

Return to your pairs and determine what the two of you would like to gain from this workshop. Negotiate your differences into one statement where possible.

Call the group together and go around the room collecting the data on newsprint, writing down the needs and objectives of each pair for all to see.

Summarize main trends of the group and post on newsprint as a constant reminder of the needs of this particular group. Refer to it from time to time or when necessary.

..... alternative to activity 1

If the group is larger than twenty, we suggest the following:

Find one individual you don't know and get to know them so you can introduce them and one fact to someone else.

Next, find another pair of individuals and introduce the person you have just met with the one fact you selected.

Now, find a group of four individuals and once again introduce yourselves to one another.

Having introduced each other, on a sheet of newsprint list the objectives the members of your group have for the workshop.

Ask the groups to post their newsprint on the wall with masking tape and to note what the different groups have had to say.

Leader then summarizes, processes the procedures, and answers questions from the group.

Activity 2:   The purpose and methods of this workshop

Present videotaped mini-lecture "What is Microcounseling?" Discuss the lecture and its implications for this workshop. It will ordinarily be wise to underline the importance of the *single skills* approach and how it will seem difficult for some people in the early stages.

. . . . . alternative to activity 2

The leader can give a mini-lecture to the group outlining the single skills approach and the strengths and limitations of microcounseling from personal perspectives.

Important points to stress at this stage of the workshop seem to be:

a. Learning how to help is a difficult task. Microcounseling simplifies the process by selecting single skills to work on one at a time.

b. It may feel awkward and unnatural to use single skills at first. But if one is willing to practice them and learn them well, they soon become natural habits.

c. There is no one "right way" to counsel or to help. Each of us will have to find our own natural style of being with other people.

d. This workshop stresses listening skills, a place where beginning counselors often falter. . . .*they talk too much!* There is more to counseling than presented in this workshop. Don't expect to be a "super-counselor" at the end, but if you involve yourself, you'll be on the road to helping people more effectively.

STEP 2: TRAINING

Activity 3: What helping is not

Ask for two volunteers, one to serve as a helper, one to serve as a helpee. This pair will be videotaped. Their task, "to show what listening is not."

The helpee is asked to share a real present or past concern and simply to be him or herself. (Some, however, prefer that the helpee role play a specific problem.)

The helper is asked to do the worst possible job of helping, in effect "Do everything you can think of which represents ineffective helping; do things which you have seen or imagined the ineffective helper doing."

This task usually puts the group at ease, and the volunteers usually do a fine job of demonstrating what helping is not.

Videotape the pair for a two- to five-minute period. Then show the videotape. If the tape does not demonstrate enough negative factors, ask the pair to do it again, but to exaggerate a little more.

Have the group brainstorm or list everything they saw which represented what helping is not. The leader keeps a list of these behaviors on a sheet of newsprint, writing everything down, but in cases where the comments are non-behavioral, asks questions as to what observable behaviors led to that observation.

For example, many people say the helper appeared tense or nervous. Write that down, and then ask what it was that the helper did which indicated nervousness. Nervousness becomes behaviorally specified when the group is able to say "hand wringing," "sitting in tight position (i.e. arms crossed)," "frowning," etc.

This may be followed by a mini-lecture or discussion in which the many things that helpers and counselors do that are wrong are emphasized. It is most helpful at this point, however, to suggest strongly that all of us can't expect to do everything right at once. Reaffirm the importance of single skills. The purpose of microcounseling training is not to be perfect but rather gradually to learn to do a better job.

. . . . .alternative to activity 3

Use the small groups of eight developed earlier. Have each group select a pair to demonstrate what counseling is not. Each group then puts on newsprint all the dimensions that occur to them as important in depicting the ineffective helper.

Activity 4:   Read manual on attending behavior

Refer participants to the workshop handbook and have them read the information on attending behavior. This may be followed by discussion and questions (see page 436).

Activity 5: *View video modeling tape on attending behavior*

Show the videotape straight through with no comments or reactions until the end. Allow discussion and reactions. Important in discussion may be the observation that attending skills certainly do not solve all the problems of effective counseling but that they serve as helpful beginnings. Once again, the *single skill* concept of learning should be stressed. (See Appendix II.)

Activity 6: *Behavioral counts of attending behavior*

Have the students turn to the behavioral rating sheets (see page 439) and divide the large group into four equal subgroups. Group 1 is to count the number of eye contact breaks in the effective and ineffective modeling tapes; group 2, the number of distracting gestures; group 3, the number of verbal topic jumps; group 4 is to make more subjective qualitative ratings on the five-point scale.

Show the video modeling tapes of attending behavior once again. Stop the tape after the ineffective model and record the behavioral counts and subjective ratings on a sheet of newsprint. Then show the effective attending model and once again record the behavioral counts and subjective ratings. You will find fairly good correspondence of ratings among the members of each group, but some variance. Depending on your orientation, you can discuss the issue of interrater reliability or, we prefer, the fact that different people interpret the same data differently. For example, most people feel that the effective attending tape has at most one distracting gesture; some, however, note four or five. This difference in rating provides an opportunity to point out that nonverbal gestures have different meanings to individuals with varying backgrounds and that there probably is no "correct" gesture or attending style for any one individual (see also Attending Manual 1a, page 440).

STEP 3:   PRACTICE

Activity 7:   Practice with attending skills

Break the group into triads. Each member of the triad in turn is to serve as helper, helpee, and observer. Each person should engage in an attending practice session with a helpee for five minutes while the observer takes notes. The helpee and the observer then should take about five minutes to provide specific feedback to the helper.

Thus, a minimum of one-half hour should be spent in which each individual has an opportunity to practice the basic skill of attending. Stress the importance of each individual finding his or her own unique style of attending.

. . . . .alternatives and supplements to activity 7

At this time, we often like to introduce Attending Manual la (page 440). For those who clearly understand and can perform the basic skills, observation of personal styles of attending adds involvement.

It is often important to restate the single skills emphasis of microcounseling. Some participants find themselves so involved in the role-played or real problems of the helpee that they work more on problem solving than on learning the skill of attending. We have found that strong emphasis on the importance of skill practice is vital here. We suggest that those who wish to continue working on the problem make individual contracts to meet following the workshop session.

The effectiveness of this activity can be enhanced if each participant records his/her sessions on audiotape and the triad together makes specific behavioral counts and subjective ratings.

Still another alternative is to have one triad videotape their interaction and play this videotape for the entire group, focusing both on behavioral counts and qualitative ratings of performance.

Never forget to stress that we do not expect "Super-

Counselors." Participants are merely requested to learn the difference between attending and nonattending. In our busy American culture we want perfection at once and may be impatient to solve problems quickly without doing the important basic listening first.

Activity 8: Windup on attending behavior

This time is used for feedback and process comments by the entire group.

A good way to begin is to give the participants the sentence stem "I learned...," going around the room quickly getting "I learned" statements from as many participants as possible.

Sum up, provide opportunity for questions. Where appropriate, relate learning to original demand and interest sheets posted around the room on newsprint.

STEP 4: EXTENSIONS

Activity 9: Do-use-teach mini-lecture

Show the videotaped mini-lecture which describes the importance of the do-use-teach framework. As an alternative, the leader may wish to give the lecture in person. This lecture makes the following points:

a. Most learning is focused toward understanding. We sit in classes and are tested to determine if we know what has been talked about. We have no evidence that we can do or use what we have learned-thus the do-use-teach framework.

b. Do is experiential in nature. We have just experienced attending behavior with our bodies. You probably found that actually doing the exercise was a vastly more important exercise than learning about it cognitively. We consider understanding only a prelude; doing is learning!

c. We learn things in parts and by practicing can put them together into larger wholes.

d. But being able to *do* something does not mean we can

use it. Vital to this workshop is making a contract to get outside this immediate setting and test out the concepts in a new situation. You will shortly be asked to develop some ideas for using attending behavior in other settings and perhaps even developing some tests for these new uses here. Attending behavior has been used in groups, parent training, interpersonal interaction, training of psychiatric patients, etc. But most specifically, we would like *you* to use attending in some specific situation.

e. "You don't know what you are doing until you can teach what you have learned to someone else." In microcounseling, we are interested in demystifying the counseling/helping process and hope that many in this group will be interested in teaching what they have learned to someone else. It is not necessary to use the format of this workshop to teach the skill. Use other ways to teach the same skills—that's OK!

f. Don't just understand—do-use-teach.

Activity 10:   Identifying extensions

After viewing the tape or listening to your lecture, ask the group to brainstorm as many uses of attending behavior as they can think of.

Record them on newsprint.

Activity 11:   Developing the do-use-teach contract

Break group into groups of four. Each group is to complete the do-use-teach contract form in the student workbook (see page 441) .

Activity 12:   Let's teach each other

The leader repeats basic points for the need to teach and in addition explains that the workshop has been designed to make things so explicit that participants should be able to begin the process of teaching now.

The leader then allows ten minutes for groups of four persons to develop a presentation, role-play, or teaching activity stemming from the concept of attending behavior.

Each group will then make a presentation to the larger group.

. . . . .alternative to activity 12

The leader follows the above format but assigns specific tasks to groups. The idea of assigning specific tasks is that a beginning group may find teaching and designing the methodology too difficult.

The following are suggestions for groups of four:

1. Role-play a family in which the father and mother talk to each other while the children misbehave. It may be noted that parents tend to respond to and attend to their children most often when they engage in "deviant" patterns of behavior. Another view is simply that the children are seeking attention. Why not attend in the family?

2. Ask for a volunteer. The volunteer is to give an extemporaneous presentation on a specific topic of interest to him or her and the group. He or she is to go outside the room and prepare the talk. While the volunteer is gone, the members of the group determine that they are going to attend to him for a time, but upon a specific signal will cease attending, and then once again upon a signal start attending again.

   As an alternative, five members of the group sitting in one area of the room could be especially attentive on signal, and then cease attending. The remainder of the group is to engage in minimal attending skills, showing some interest but not much. An observer is to note the effect of attending on the speaker.

3. Role-play the effect of attending on a husband-wife argument.

4. Role-play a teacher displaying attending and non-attending behaviors toward children in several classroom situations, e.g. discipline, a reading group, talking with an individual child who has a problem, etc.

Special attention may be paid to nonverbal behaviors of the teacher.

5. Demonstrate how to develop a microcounseling video training tape in attending behavior. This could be for any of a variety of populations.

STEP 5: EVALUATION AND FEEDBACK

Activity 13:   Windup session

Mini-lecture by leader summarizing the basic concepts of attending behavior and the need to follow through on action contract.

. . . . .alternatives to activity 13

Simply call the session to a halt with "That's enough. . .let's break . . . I think you've got the point."

Feedback to the trainer may be obtained through asking the group to finish the sentence stem "I appreciate . . . " "I liked especially . . . " "I need more of . . . " "I want from the training more . . . . "

Use evaluation form attached (see page 444). We recommend against using standard written evaluations in each session, but this form has been provided for those who prefer this method of feedback.

SELECTION FROM BASIC ATTENDING SKILLS PARTICIPANT MANUAL

ALLEN E. IVEY AND NORMA B. GLUCKSTERN

SESSION 1: ATTENDING BEHAVIOR
A Central Skill of Helping

The first thing that the helper must learn is to *listen* to the helpee. But what is listening? We all know what it is, but defining the term precisely is another matter. The central goal of this first session in microtraining is to help you identify what listening is and to consider the many implications of this definition.

The exercises in this workshop are organized around the following objectives and/or concepts:

1. You will first be asked to think through your feelings as you enter new situations. Many of your feelings and thoughts will be similar to those of the person whom you might wish to help. A helper should never forget what it feels like to seek assistance.
2. You will identify what listening is not. Through this exercise, you will be able to identify some very specific behaviors which relate to effective listening.
3. Three key aspects of listening will be defined in Micro-counseling Manual 1. Compare them with your definitions.
4. You will view a videotape of ineffective and effective listening and demonstrate your ability to count specific listening and nonlistening behaviors.
5. The concept of selective attention will be presented in Microcounseling Manual 1A. You will want to start examining the topics to which you give most attention.
6. Knowing about the concepts of this workshop is inadequate for performance; you will have the opportunity to practice and demonstrate that you can engage in the skills of attending behavior.
7. Through a "do-use-teach" contract you will demonstrate your ability to take the concepts of listening to situations beyond this training session.

At the completion of training in attending, you should have mastered the following competencies: (1) ability to define attending behavior, (2) ability to count attending behaviors in videotapes or films, (3) ability to demonstrate the skills of attending yourself in a demonstration interview, and (4) ability to *use* attending behavior in settings beyond this training session.

Beginning the workshop

What were some of your reactions as you came here today? What did you expect? Were/are you concerned about the impression you will make on others? What are your feelings toward the trainer?

When you begin a counseling or helping interview with another person, that individual will also be facing a new beginning.

Helpees have many of the same feelings and thoughts as you.

Record some of your thoughts and feelings about beginnings and new situations here.

_____

_____

_____

_____

_____

We hope that you will remember that people you may meet in a helping relationship are people just like you. They have many of the same feelings you did. At the same time, many of their feelings and thoughts will be different. We hope you will listen to them.

What listening is not!

List below your observations of what helping/counseling is not. As you make your list, check to see if what you list represents observable behavior, something that can see (The helper may appear anxious, true, but what do you *see* that makes you think he/she is anxious? Is he/she wringing his/her hands, sitting in an uptight position, stammering?).

_____

_____

_____

_____

_____

Attending Behavior: A Description
Microcounseling Manual 1

The most basic skill of helping is listening to those whom you would help. But what is listening? We use the term "attending behavior" to make listening specific and observable. Attending behavior is a basic, rather simple skill, but with many, many profound implications.

Three key dimensions comprise attending behavior:

1. Eye contact. If you are going to talk to someone, look at them. No need to stare, just be aware that you are talking to another person. You will also want to notice "eye contact breaks"—when you look away, you are sometimes telling the person you are working with that you aren't really with them. Later on, you will start noticing that eye contact breaks on the part of the helpee give you clues as to where that other person "is at." More on that later.

2. Attentive body language. We usually think that counseling is a verbal relationship. In truth, some estimates say that 85 percent of our communication is nonverbal. Think for a minute . . . how should your body communicate that it is listening? Find your own natural listening style, and check with others to see how it "comes across." The basic attentive listening posture in our culture is a slight forward trunk lean with a relaxed easy posture. *But, find your own style*—being yourself is most important.

   Later on, you will want to start looking for small signs of tension (frowns, tense mouth or chin, clenched fists, marked shifts in body posture at key times in the interview) in both yourself and the client. But for now, simply assume a relaxed body position and communicate that you are involved.

3. Verbal following. A frequent basic question of beginning helpers is "What do I say?" We say, don't get uptight, take whatever the helpee has said and respond to it in a natural way. Direct whatever you may say to what the helpee has just said or said earlier in your session. The helper never needs to introduce a new topic—simply stay with what has already been said. In summary, don't topic jump.

While we do not stress vocal tone as one of the three basic dimensions of listening, do notice your tone of voice. For some people, this is a key in communicating that you care about and are involved with others. Certain vocal tones communicate caring and involvement regardless of the words. Your voice is indeed an instrument; don't hesitate to use it.

In briefer form, your goal in interviewing is to be a good listener through the use of specific, observable behaviors:

1. Using varied eye contact to communicate with the helpee.
2. Using a natural, *relaxed* posture and gestures. No need to sit rigid and "professional." Use your body to communicate your involvement.
3. Staying on the topic. Don't topic jump or interrupt. Simply note what the helpee has said and take your cues from him/her. There is no need to go into your own head to think of what to say. The helpee has already told you. If you get lost and can't think of anything to say, simply hesitate a moment and think of something said earlier that interested you. Go back and make a comment or ask a question about that topic. You are still attending! This simple point has been a lifesaver to many helpers.

There is no need to talk about yourself or give answers when you attend to someone else. Your main responsibility as a helper is to assist helpees in finding their own answers. You'll be surprised how able they are to do this if you are willing to attend.

A final point is to respect yourself and the other person. Ask questions or make comments about things that interest and seem relevant to you. If you are truly interested in what is being said, attending behavior often follows automatically. But remember, the more interested you are, the harder it sometimes becomes to keep yourself quiet and *listen* to the other person.

The definition of attending behavior presented here is in terms of the most common form of listening in American and Western culture. However, *patterns of eye contact, body language, and verbal following vary markedly from culture to culture.* Eye contact among some Southwest Native Americans may represent a hostile act. Researchers have found significant differences between some blacks and whites. While everyone uses some form of attending behavior, the specific pattern of these three key dimensions varies among individuals and groups.

Rating and Behavioral Count Sheet for Attending Behavior

Check or rate the following specific dimensions of attending.

	INEFFECTIVE MODELING TAPE	EFFECTIVE MODELING TAPE	(USE EXTRA SPACE FOR OTHER RATINGS YOU MAY USE IN THIS WORKSHOP)	
NO. OF EYE CONTACT BREAKS				
NO. OF EXTRANEOUS, UNNATURAL MOVEMENTS				
NO. OF TOPIC JUMPS				
TOTAL NONATTENDING				

It is not easy to count the specific behaviors above all at once. You may prefer to rate the dimensions on the five-point scale provided below:

5 maximally facilitative	Use of behavior significantly adds to and enriches the communication.
4 facilitative	Use of behavior adds to and enriches communication.
3 minimally facilitative	Use of behavior slightly adds to communication.
2 lacks facilitative skill	Use of behavior detracts from communication. (Normal conversation is usually at this level.)
1 destructive	Use of behavior significantly hinders communication.

Rate each dimension from 1 - 5	INEFFECTIVE MODELING TAPE	EFFECTIVE MODELING TAPE	(USE EXTRA SPACE FOR OTHER RATINGS YOU MAY USE IN THIS WORKSHOP)	
EYE CONTACT				
BODY LANGUAGE				
VERBAL FOLLOWING				
VOCAL INTONATION				
OVERALL SUBJECTIVE RATING				

Extensions of Attending Behavior
Microcounseling Manual 1a

The purpose of this manual is to summarize some further implications of attending behavior with special reference as to individual helper "style." The essential point of this manual is summarized below:

> *Helpees talk about what helpers listen to.* At first glance attending and attending skills impress the beginner as "non-directive" in nature. While nondirectivists may use these skills, attending skills lead as much as they follow.

> For example, a client may say "I'm really uptight right now. The exam I've got ahead is awful. What will my parents do if I fail?" All of the following responses are attending:
> "You're tense right now."
> "What is your exam about?"
> "Again, you feel your parents are on you."
> "You fear failure in other situations too?"

The response selected by the helper often says more about the helper than it does about the helpee. Notice what topics you selectively attend to. What topics turn you on, turn you off? What do you zero in on? What do you avoid?

The three aspects of attending behavior provide you with important cues as to what your "style" is. For example, where do you break eye contact? Do you unconsciously avert your eyes when someone talks about religion, thereby indicating that this is a topic you don't care to hear about? Do your eyes brighten when the helpee talks about sex and you find that all your helpees are talking about this area? Careful examination of videotapes will reveal clear points where you reinforce certain helpee comments and extinguish others.

Similarly, note your pattern of body language in relation to specific topics. Where do you sit forward, move back, tighten a fist, relax, tense yourself? Also, note that your body language communicates to your helpee and vice versa. This is termed "movement contagion" and is a variable which can only really be studied by videotape.

The examples above illustrate the importance of selective attention in verbal following. *Once again, helpees talk about topics which you are willing and able to listen to.*

Summarize in your notes key points and note your patterns of selective attention both verbally and nonverbally. It will give you a clue as to your natural "style." Finally, note your "percent of talk-time." Some helpers talk too much. Attending is about listening. Do you give your helpee enough "air-time" on topics of interest to him or her? Use a stopwatch and check it out.

Do-Use-Teach Contract

You first had an opportunity to understand what the concept of attending behavior was about. You then experienced the ideas of attending behavior first hand. The time is now to decide what they mean to you and how they can or cannot be used in your own life space.

We know from past workshops that the concepts taught are often useful. We find ourselves concerned that they are not used as widely in as many different settings as possible. What we would like you to do now is think about how you might like to *use* the concepts of attending behavior outside this room.*

Some ways that people have used attending in their own lives include the following:

1. A beginning helper tried it with a helpee when she didn't know what to do.
2. A shy person who coudn't talk to anyone tried attending and found it provided an opening wedge in conversation.
3. A man in trouble with his boss tried deliberate attending and discovered he was missing some crucial messages.
4. At the family dinner table, a husband and wife found they weren't listening to their children. They were too busy talking with themselves.
5. A depressed individual found that going out and deliberately attending to someone else helped him get out of himself.

---

*This statement may sound like a demand to some who do not find attending their cup of tea. Our suggestion to those of you, then, at this time is to recall our first comment in the mini-lecture. Attending is not for everyone, take what you can from the concept, but, more important, develop your own ways to use and teach listening skills. Check them out with others and see how they go. Be yourself!

6. A woman uptight about the lesbian movement deliberately used attending skills and learned another point of view.
7. A teacher tried it in a staff meeting and noted that very few people listen.
8. A student deliberately attended to her teacher and to her surprise found the teacher talking to her and no one else!

Teachers, parents, children, patients, counselors, helpers—we can all profit by more deliberate listening. And the time to use attending skills is when we begin to lose control of ourselves, we feel lost, we don't know what to do. Using attending all the time in a deliberate fashion would be tedious and tiresome. Only use it when you feel lost or want to hear someone more carefully than usual.

Personal experience with using attending is crucial. Our helping skills should not be just used in the interview; they have meaning in our daily lives as well.

What do you want to do to test out the value of attending in your own life? _____

_____

_____

Talk with someone about your plan to use attending. Is it specific enough? Will it work? Can you arrange a time to get together with this individual to report how your contract worked out?

Teach

Next, we would like you to think about someone or some group with whom you might like to test your understanding of and facility with attending behavior by teaching them what you have learned today.

Teaching someone else about attending behavior has taken many forms:

1. Using this same workshop format to teach teachers, parents, peer counselors, hot-line operators, etc. these same listening skills which you have learned.
2. Simply telling people about the concepts often proves helpful.
3. Redefining listening skills in your own way. After all, you

don't have to use eye contact, body language, and verbal following as the terms. Some might prefer very differing use of words.

4. Going home and developing a mini-workshop within this framework to teach your own family the importance of attending.

5. If you are helping someone in a counseling session, try teaching them these basic skills. Especially helpful to depressed individuals or those with weak social and interpersonal skills.

6. Direct instruction of psychiatric patients in listening skills.

7. Teaching children in elementary school the importance of these dimensions.

8. Teaching college or high-school students to attend to their professors and teachers. The effect of attending and nonattending on those making presentations is dramatic.

To whom and when would you like to teach attending behavior? And how would you do it? Write it below and make a contract with someone in the group to actually do it.

_____

_____

_____

DO ⎞ YOU DON'T KNOW WHAT YOU ARE DOING
USE ⎬ UNTIL YOU CAN TEACH IT TO SOMEONE
TEACH ⎠ ELSE!

Evaluation and Feedback Form on Attending Behavior

Name (Optional)

1. What is *your* definition of attending behavior?_____

_____

2. What is *your* natural style of listening or attending?_____

_____

3. Rate yourself on the following dimensions as you see yourself.

	EXCELLENT 5	4	MEDIUM 3	2	POOR 1
EYE CONTACT					
BODY LANGUAGE					
VERBAL ATTENTION					
INTONATION					
OTHER DIMENSIONS					

4. Rate the workshop on the following dimensions on the same five-point scale.

INTRODUCTORY MINI-LECTURE					
VIDEO MODELING TAPE					
2ND ATTENDING LECTURE					
PRACTICE SESSIONS					
THE WRITTEN MANUAL					
ENVIRONMENT OF WORKSHOP					
CLARITY OF WORKSHOP					
THE TRAINER'S ABILITY					
OTHER					

5. What would you like to see improved? What did you like best?

Appendix II

ATTENDING BEHAVIOR MODELING TAPE TYPESCRIPT AND ANALYSIS*

THIS IS A TYPESCRIPT of the model tape used in the *Basic Attending Skills* series. In the first tape, the counselor demonstrates ineffective helping. The role-played helpee is discussing some of her attitudes toward feminism.

The camera in this model tape is focused solely on the helper, and the helpee is not seen except as the camera comes in over her shoulder. This is to provide a clear focus on the *helper* as the object of study. As training moves to more advanced levels, it is also important to present the helpee or client on videotape.

Ineffective Attending Example

After a brief introduction, the camera focuses on the helper who is sitting with arms closely folded across the chest. As he asks the first question, his arms open and his hands move to his lap. As he completes his opening statement, his arms return to the closed position. He maintains eye contact and his posture (with the exception of his arms) represents an attending stance.

Al 1: Norma, I had heard that you were active in getting the Valley Women's Center started. I'd like to hear a little bit more about how that happened.

Norma 1: Well, I guess it's almost been four years ago that it started because it's almost been; and I kind of wonder, I guess it was just a lot of women. . .

Al 2: (Interrupting) Four years ago now, I remember, I came here about four years ago.

---

*Taken from *Basic Attending Skills Leader Manual* (Ivey and Gluckstern, 1974a).

445

Norma 2: Well, what happened . . . I think it was about five, almost six years ago that the women's liberation movement began. But it was about four years ago that there was a really big push on the campus to get something going.

> *Comment:* During Norma 1 and 2, Al sits with arms closed, occasionally breaking eye contact. He opens up and moves forward when talking about himself at Al 2.

Al 3: Did you feel there was a need to do something?

Norma 3: Well, when I first started out I didn't. I almost got kind of . . .

Al 4: (Interrupting) What did your husband think when you got into that? (The helper leans forward with interest.)

Norma 4: I think he, I think he was humoring me. I think he was like most men, not really paying much attention.

Al 5: Yeah, it is kind of funny sometimes.

Norma 5: Yeah, well I think that men, and I don't think my husband is any different really . . .

> *Comment:* The same pattern again appears. Whenever the helpee expresses herself, the helper moves back, breaks eye contact. If she talks in an unassertive traditional female role, eye contact is maintained.

Al 6: Well, what motivated you? You had some desire to prove yourself or something?

Norma 6: Yeah, well, I suppose in some ways. At that time it wasn't to, it really wasn't to prove myself. I think that I was conscious of the fact that there were a lot of, my consciousness had been raised in some sense. I'd always tried to achieve more, I had never been really content.

Al 7: Now back in college. By the way, where did you go to college?

Norma 7: Southern Connecticut.

Al 8: Your consciousness was raised there?

Norma 8: No, I think I kind of went to school like most people. Most women did . . .

Al 9: (Interrupting) Then your husband was a little bit more comfortable at that time.

Norma 9: With the role I played. Yes, I think much more so. He saw this as sort of a hobby. Women go to school to amuse themselves. I don't think he took me very seriously at that point, while I was going to school.

> *Comment:* The pattern continues. Almost at the same point that the helpee talks about her husband not taking her very seriously, the "helper" breaks eye contact and cracks his knuckles, giving an extremely bored appearance.

Al 10: Well, along that line then, you're still pretty active I guess.

Norma 10: Yeah, I think that I see myself as a role model for other women, because I'm clearly, heavily into a career, the kind of things that the women's movement talks about.

Al 11: Well, what about your kids? How do they like this?

Norma 11: I guess they're ambivalent about it, I think they're very proud...

Al 12: (Interrupting) Say, where is Bill now? (The helper again interrupts as she talks about positive accomplishments.)

Norma 12: Oh, he's living in New York now. He has a job in a school and is really very happy with what he's doing.

Al 13: What school does he work at?

Norma 13: I don't really know the name. It's a Junior High. Oh, I guess somewhere in the Bronx, he's been working . . .

Al 14: (Interrupting) Yeah, I know the Bronx well.

Norma 14: It's difficult, but I think he's excited at having a chance to teach in an . . .

Al 15: (Interrupting) Well anyway, Norma, I'm really glad that you got into the women's movement. I think it's really important that we get good people like you doing things. I think it's great. I think you're doing a good thing. I think it will give you a lot of satisfaction too.

> *Comment:* The tone of voice does not indicate support. The helper picks lint off his clothes as he makes the above statement as if "brushing off" or discounting the client.

Norma 15:　Well, I guess I'm pleased with having done it, you know...

Al 16:　(Interrupting) Some women get terribly aggressive about these things, but you don't seem to.　Am I right?

Norma 16:　That depends on what your view is, or what you mean about aggressive.　I'd have to ask you what you mean about a woman being aggressive, about being in a women's movement.　What sort of things are you referring to?

Al 17:　Well I think that some women are in to do an authority thing and you seem willing to accept your place.　I think it's important for women to be actualized and to realize themselves.　How do you react to that?

Norma 17:　Well I guess I'm having trouble dealing with that because there's some ... (End of tape).

Summary of ineffective interview.　Using the "Rating and Behavioral Count Sheet for Attending Behavior," behavior counts were made by the authors.　Thirty-nine eye contact breaks were observed, twenty-three nonverbal body language "distractors," and twelve topic jumps.　The definition of an eye contact break at first sounds easy and relatively precise.　However, different people define eye contact breaks differently because of their past experience.　One person may count an eye contact break as only occurring when the person turns the head, while another may count every time the person glances away.　Similarly with distracting body language movements, what is *distracting* to one person may not be to another.　Thus, in workshops on attending behavior, individuals are urged to first make their own definitions of what constitutes these behaviors and then to compare their definitions with others.　For research purposes, it is possible to define these categories relatively precisely, but for training, it is more valuable to focus on the fact that *different people see the same situation differently.*　Counts on eye contact breaks in this session have ranged from eight to sixty, nonverbal distractors from five to forty-five, and topic jumps from four to seventeen in workshops conducted by the authors.

The timing of attending and non-attending behaviors is also

important in this five-minute interview. Careful observation of the videotape shows that the male helper exhibits attending behavior when the woman helpee talks about a traditional feminine role, and he fails to attend when she talks about a more assertive self. This is a classic example of *selective attention*. By selecting certain things to attend to, the helper is determining what the helpee is able and willing to talk about. The specific behaviors of eye contact breaks, nonverbal distractors, and topic jumps provide clear examples for the beginning helper to identify in the interview.

Other factors could also be rated and/or counted in this session. The percent of talk-time is about equal. Helping is for the client, not for the helper. Talk-time in seconds or number of words can be measured. The helper has a quick "response-latency" in that he interrupts and hesitates very little between the end of the client's comments and his next statement. This can be measured in seconds. The helper's eye blinks and patterns of head nods can be examined. Subjective qualitative analysis using five-point scales can be conducted. This particular interview would rank at the lowest level of facilitative conditions.

Effective Attending Example

We can now turn to the more effective interview on the video modeling tape. In the following example, the helper attempts to engage in the specific behaviors of attending. As the segment begins, the camera again focuses on the helper. The helper in this tape is turned partially away from the helpee, but he does maintain eye contact and an attentive posture throughout. The posture would have been more appropriate if the helper had sat and faced the helpee more directly. While this is an important point to observe, it would not be stressed with the beginning helper. All that is sought in the early phases of training is *improvement* from low baseline behavior.

Al 1: Norma, you've been saying you've had a long-term relationship with the women's movement, and it might be more helpful right now if you could share with me a little bit about what some of your feelings are right now at this moment.

Norma 1: Oh, my feelings are really very positive in terms of the women's movement, 'cause I'm not sure if there hadn't been some pioneers out there to have raised my consciousness I would have pretty much gone on the way I was. Maybe less externally conflicted, but maybe more internally conflicted. I think that the women's movement forced me to act on my own behalf. I think that would be the best way to describe it. And that process of acting has developed for me a whole area of growth that I'm enjoying. In some ways when I say I'm ambivalent, the result of the women's movement is I pushed ahead in areas that I never thought I was going to push ahead in before. And in that process of pushing ahead, of course, I probably alienated some people. And somehow that's OK because I'm feeling better about myself.

Al 2: So you feel better about yourself, and I hear you saying that you really like the idea that you're acting. Can you give something a little bit specific of where you have acted and felt good about yourself?

> *Comment:* The helper pays close attention through eye contact, head nods, and body language as the helpee states positive things about herself. This is reinforced by the selective attention to the positive things about her new role. It would have been possible, for example, to selectively attend to her alienating people, and thus the conversation would head in a very different direction. The helpee's longer verbal statements should also be noted.

Norma 2: Oh well, I think that pretty much the whole job I've taken, the fact that I am willing to take a job that has responsibilities, that I have the need to assert myself, to explore new ways of acting. I think one of the really exciting things about that as a woman, well maybe not as a woman, that I began to find all sorts of skills that I would have said "No, no that's not for me." But as I began to assert myself, I realized that if you're going to go ahead in this area, you are going to have to have certain competencies that you kept denying you had. And as I got in touch with the, it's just very exciting.

Al 3: In a sense, you really feel good about yourself and what's happened to you as a result of being part of the movement.

Norma 3. Oh, very much so, I have absolutely no regrets, I think I've always had conflicts, but they're different conflicts now, but the conflicts I'm dealing with now, I'm willing to deal with.

Al 4: So you say you feel good about yourself. At the same time, there are some conflicts that you feel able to deal with. Would you like to share one of your conflicts, for example? (Helper adds facilitative gestures.)

Norma 4: Oh, clearly that any woman who functions both in a family role and a career role has personal problems in terms of their own lifestyle. It's clear that that's one. I think another one is working with men and being willing to say, "Look, I can in fact define or take the leadership, that in fact you are working for me and are going to take orders from me, or not orders. But recognizing that I am in a position to have final decisions making power." That's more like it. The worry is to make decisions. I think one of the most exciting aspects is the person I am now working for I have a great deal of respect for, and I still have conflicts with, but one of the things he has been teaching me is to say "No." And he says to me, every once in a while, "O.K. Norma, say no." And that's a new thing for me to say to somebody, "No." And that I don't feel guilty about it, and that I don't feel that somehow I have no right to say no. So it's moving from a passive role to an active role, an assertive role, a decision making role.

Al 5: So to kind of sum up this brief segment, I just asked if you had any feelings of problems or concerns and you kind of went through a couple with perhaps your family, dealing with men as being a changed woman in a changing world is not always easy. And yet you kind of end up saying that you feel kind of good about yourself and what's happening. (Helper adds facilitative gestures.)

Norma 5: Alright, very much so.

Summary of effective interview. In this example, the authors count seven eye contact breaks (none major), two body language distractors, and no topic jumps. In workshops, most participants count zero to two eye contact breaks, but up to twenty-five have been counted. Distracting body language movements range from zero to ten. At most two topic jumps are noted. The important thing, once again, is not the "correct" number of items counted but the search for an improvement in the second session.

Important in microtraining sessions is *improvement,* giving the trainee a feeling of accomplishment. In a few rare cases, the goal for a trainee may be more eye contact breaks (to remove a constant stare), or to have more gestures (even though they might be awkward at first) for a wooden helper.

Other possibilities for comparison with the first session include number of interruptions or response-latency time of the helper (in this case the helper moves from seven to zero interruptions), percent of talk-time (it may be observed that the helpee gets considerably more "air-time" in the second session), and other behavioral counts. The number of positive facilitative gestures could be counted, and subjective scales of interviewing competence could be used. On a five-point scale, this interview would rank at about a middle "three," as the responses are interchangeable with the helpee.

Finally, it is important to note the *selective attention* aspects of the second interview. The helper had strongest head nods and supportive gestures when the helpee was affirming herself and her capabilities. He tended to sit still and ignore negative aspects of the self, although he provides in Al 4 an opportunity for her to explore conflicts. The verbal attention was given primarily to positive things about her statements and reinforces her desire to maintain a nontraditional woman's role.

These same data could be used to teach basic attending skills, or they could be used as sample material to teach concepts of sexism. In the first case, the emphasis is on specific behavior; in the second, the emphasis is on what the helper selectively attends to and reinforces in client verbal and nonverbal behavior.

Appendix III

TYPESCRIPT AND SCORING OF A DEMONSTRATION INTEGRATION OF SKILLS INTERVIEW*

MICROCOUNSELING SKILLS do not exist in a vacuum. They are used with real people in real interviews, counseling sessions, and therapeutic hours. The demonstration interview presented here was designed to illustrate the microtraining skills as they might be used in an actual interview.

This session has the following important parameters:

1. It was designed as a role-play. However, the issues discussed were real.
2. The session was completed in a video studio with technicians present. In addition, a small video unit was run by the helper so that he could demonstrate how video replay can be integrated into the regular helping interview.
3. The helper wished to demonstrate the attending skills in order. It may be noted that he planned to start with a closed question to be followed by an open question. These are followed in turn by a minimal encourage, a paraphrase, a reflection of feeling, and a summarization. Needless to say, we do not recommend following any prescribed "menu" of skills. This interview was designed in this way to show how skills can be integrated into an interview in a deliberate fashion.

---

*The typescript is taken from *Basic Influencing Skills Participant Manual* (Ivey and Gluckstern, 1976b) and is used by permission of Microtraining Associates, Inc., Box 641, North Amherst, Massachusttes, 01059. A videotape of this interview is available from Microtraining.

4. Following the one-by-one presentation of skills, the helper attempted to demonstrate all microtraining skills and dimensions. A few deliberately less effective responses were used to illustrate how these moments affect the interview.

This typescript is discussed in detail in Chapters 4, 5, and 6, where material from this session is used to illustrate the several microtraining skills. The typescript is representative of one of the final competencies required of individuals who go through *Basic Attending Skills* and *Basic Influencing Skills* training workshops. Trainees are expected to produce typescripts of their helping sessions in which their and the helpee's responses have been scored and rated. While this book has not given prime attention to helpee behavior, we do stress that helpees can be rated on the same dimensions of communication effectiveness as helpers.

TYPESCRIPT FOR ANALYSIS — AL IVEY AND JOAN CHADBOURNE

Following is a typescript of an interview between Al Ivey and a role-played helpee. The interview was unplanned, with the exception that Al's original goal was to move through the microtraining skills one by one. This was possible for the attending skills but more difficult for the influencing skills. Scoring of the helper and helpee statements follows the typescript, plus process comments by the participants.

Al 1: Do you mind if we videotape this session?

Joan 1: No, that's okay.

Al 2: Could you tell me how things have been going?

Joan 2: Well, things have been going generally pretty well. I'm clerking now. The children are all in school. Seem to be okay. And my life generally seems pretty good, except now that I'm in a man's world, uhm, my life is really different. I— before I was doing paraprofessional work with women and was in women's groups, and really my whole life evolved around women. And now I'm working with men, and I've started seeing men, ah . . . and I'm not quite sure how to handle some of these men-women relationships.

Al 3: You're not quite sure how to handle these new relationships?

Joan 3: No, ah. . . there's one man who thinks he's in love with me. And the whole idea of someone really loving me and wanting me to be *his*. And it's like he wants to own me for the rest of his life. . . . That makes me feel terrible. And maybe something's wrong with me, but I don't want to be owned. I don't want to be someone's woman.

Al 4: The thought of someone just owning and controlling you——

Joan 4: Yeah.

Al 5: It just gives you—I get right now a feeling, a very tight feeling. Is that right?

Joan 5: Yeah, and it's tight, and it's a question and I guess because you're a man, and I know that you have a good marriage. It's—I'm sort of wondering—that's not the way it's supposed to be, is it? I mean, good marriages don't mean that you own each other? Do they?

Al 6: So, if I can put it together, what you've been saying is that this business of ownership has really got you going emotionally. And at the same time, you're not really quite convinced that that's the way it has to be.

Joan 6: I hope not.

 Comment: This ends the opening phase of the interview. Al has gone through in order six microcounseling skills. The minimal encourage at Al 3 is interesting in that he selectively attended to "new relationships." If he had reinforced "children," "woman in a man's world," "paraprofessional work with women," or some other key construct from Joan 2, the interview would have headed possibly in very different directions. Some feminist helpers object strongly to this at first seemingly unimportant lead. The summary at Al 6 puts together what is to be the topic for the remainder of the session. This clarifying of what helper and helpee will talk about early in the interview seems to be characteristic of most helping sessions, regardless of theoretical orientation. The negotiation for what is to be the topic of a session occurs early in most interviews, and the topic selected often says as much about the helper as the helpee.

Al 7: Maybe it would help if you could give me a more specific example of what's been going on?

Joan 7: Well, a clear example. Ah . . . this man whose name is George was very, very busy for awhile and I didn't see him. And that was fine. I had briefs to prepare, and I just, I was very, very busy with the girls and my work. That was fine with me not to see him. And, all of a sudden he's not so busy, and he called me up and said, "You know, I'm coming right over" after three weeks of not seeing him. "I, you know, I want to be with you. And I have three weeks free, and I want to be with you as much of the time as possible." And I said Heyyyyy. Now *I* have a case to prepare. Now I'm busy. He said, "Oh, I won't interfere, but, you know, I'd like to be here all the time." That doesn't seem fair.

Al 8: So what you're saying is that it was okay for him not to see you when he was busy, but now when you're busy he doesn't come across that it's okay with him.

Joan 8: It's like my work isn't important but his is.

Al 9: Your work isn't as important, but his is.

Joan 9: Yeah.

Al 10: I can't help but wonder—would you share a little bit about how it makes you feel inside? Even right now as you talk, I see something.

Joan 10: There's tension right here, and I feel like going. . . Leave me alone. Get away from me. You're intruding into my life. And, it's it's, I feel tight and defensive. It's like I don't want anybody to get in if that's the way. I'm going to be taken advantage of that way. Nobody's going to get in. But, (pause).

Al 11: I get the feeling right now that you feel you just want to close him off. Yet at the same time, I hear something else. . . But it's almost an unheard thing.

Joan 11: Unheard thing is, ah, . . . but I don't want to spend the rest of my life alone. Ah, I do want a relationship with a man. Ah, is it just this man, or is it, is it that I need to be so separate?

Al 12: Hmm (pause). Let's stop just for a moment and let me just feed back to you what I've been hearing so far. You've been saying that you're in your new law apprenticeship? Okay. And yet the real issue is the man. And how can you be yourself and be a professional. And how can you put yourself in a warm, human way with him as well. And, undergirding it is that feeling that he really wants to control you rather than allow you to be. Am I hearing you accurately?

Joan 12: I guess I don't feel that it's so much control as really own.

Al 13: Own, even more than control, then?

> *Comment:* This series of exchanges serves to clarify further the opening definition of the problem to be explored. Al 7 is a particularly clear example of concreteness and Joan 7 reveals a helpee who is able to be concrete and specific. Note that the tense changes to present (from past) at Al 10 and Joan later commented that this exchange was a place where she felt particularly heard. At Al 12 we see a clear example of movement synchrony where helper and helpee mirror one another's body movements. The word "control" represents a mild interpretation or renaming on the part of the helper and is clarified by the helpee. This series of verbal exchanges could be called clarification of the problem which leads to exploration in the next few leads.

Joan 13: Yeah. It's like parading me down the street. You know—here, here's my property. That's part of it. Now, you know, now, Joan I want you to do this. But, you know, even when he gives me something it's like come over right now. I have something for you. And I might be in the middle of doing something.

Al 14: I see. Okay. Could I share one of my own experiences like this? This is from the past. I know that I had a need, and maybe still do, to control, to own, my wife. And I can remember in the past where I've set up conditions and so forth where she was to do things. And . . . looking back on it I know that for me this was coming from my own point at that point from the feeling of not being sure of myself in my relationship to women. Ah, how does that come across to you?

Joan 14: It's funny. I can really believe that about you, but somehow for him—I'm just so frightened of him—that that may be it, but I don't want to deal with his insecurity. I guess it's . . .

Al 15: Right now you're saying that you are really frightened of him.

Joan 15: Frightened that he could ooze into my life and take over. And also disgusted that why should I have to deal with that in order to have a warm relationship with a man.

Al 16: Yeah. How can you deal with that?

Joan 16: I know the difference—you gave your example—the difference is that I know you're doing something about it. You've changed.

Al 17: You said you'd like to deal with it. Ah, am I hearing that accurately? That you'd like to deal with him more effectively, or be with him more?

Joan 17: Yeah. Or just tell him to get out of my life. I don't know which I want to do.

> *Comment:* The self-disclosure at Al 14 is past tense and relatively cognitive in nature. The nonparallel self-disclosure moves the helpee more to a past tense discussion of her relationships. Al 15 illustrates the helper returning to basic attending skills when the influencing leads are ineffective. Note the present tense dimension of the lead.
>
> Note that Al 16 represents a clear example of the hiatus period in the interview (see Chapter 3). This is a point at which the session could head in several very different directions. Although present tense sentence structure is used, the selective

attention to the word "deal with" implies a future orientation as well. This segment of the interview could be termed exploration, but leading to action. It may be observed from the scoring form following the typescript that virtually all helper leads except the self-disclosure have been attending (parallel) in nature.

The following lead represents a clear example of an alternative behavior at the hiatus point. A Gestaltist might have opted for the "hot seat"; an analyst might have interpreted; a behavior therapist might have started some form of systematic instruction; a feminist therapist might have pointed out how this is a typical woman's problem and started an assertion training or consciousness-raising program.

Al 18: Okay. Let's not try to resolve that right now. Let's do an exercise that we've done in the past. Stop for a moment. And would you just sort of close your eyes and just sort of imagine what you might like your relationship to be like. Regardless of how it is now—what would you like it to be? How would you like to respond to him? Just think for a moment.

Joan 18: (pause) I can see us both having very important professions. Coming in at the end of the day. Having a warm hug. Exchanging some of the things that happened during the day. Ah, each having some time with the children, the girls. (pause) Taking turns cooking. Taking turns doing things around the house. Ah, and me having some time that was for Joan, alone. And, that I didn't have to beg for that. Or I didn't have to make excuses. Or I didn't have to take it just when he was busy doing something else. But it was legitimate. And I could say that I really need to go to the woods, or I need to go to my office. All right, would you take the girls out for the afternoon, because I really want to be in the house by myself right now. And I wouldn't have to apologize for that.

Al 19: That's a nice fantasy, I think.

Joan 19: Yeah, (laugh) I like it!

Al 20: You like it. I can share—I guess I would say that I share even at this moment the same fantasy, and also tell you from my experience that it hasn't been and isn't necessarily all that easy. It really isn't. And yet, it's something that I want. And apparently you want for you very much too. Is that right?

Joan 20: Oh, yeah. It's just my own space. To own myself. And to come out and to love and be giving and to exchange intellectually. And go back.

Al 21: So maybe at this moment it might be helpful if you would visualize: how do you respond to him, for example when he comes in? . . .That's when he makes you feel like this?

(Note: Following the question, Joan physically tightens her shoulders.)

Joan 21: A lot of times . . . . Or sort of stiffen up. It's the stiff upper lip.

Al 22: The stiff upper lip.

Joan 22: And, you know, what's coming next? Be prepared. Be on guard.

    Comment: Al 18 represents a direction where Joan tells how she would like the world to be. One may note immediately the discrepancy between "what is" and "what is desired." Again, different helpers of different theoretical orientations would use that discrepancy in many different ways. Yet most would seek to resolve it. The self-disclosure at Al 20 is more present tense in nature. However, it would have been more powerful if he had self-disclosed in the present tense about his reactions to Joan at that moment. Note the "check-out" ("Is that right?"), allowing Joan room to agree or disagree with his statement. This represents the beginning of the action phase of the interview.

Al 23: Let's stop and take a look at the videotape and let's take a look at yourself in that "what's-coming-next?" posture, and so forth.

(The videotape is rewound briefly.)

You might want to move out front so you can see a little bit, Joan. I'd like you to tell me if this is the way you come across to him quite often.

(The videotape is viewed briefly.)

That's back a little farther. We'll come up to it in a minute. (pause) Let's move ahead just a little bit.

(The videotape is viewed and then "stop-framed" on Joan who is holding her shoulders tightly.)

Is that the type of experience that you have in relationship to him quite often?

Joan 23: Um-hm.

Al 24: I know I'd feel awfully uptight if I looked like that. Sometimes I do look like that.

Joan 24: Yeah. My whole back is straight and tight. (pause)

Al 25: Okay? . . . Let's turn the videotape on again. Ah . . . you say that you find yourself responding to him a lot like that? Is that right?

Joan 25: I'm feeling very strongly right now that what I need to do is say good-bye to him. But it really—that this isn't a situation that I can continue to work on. And that it's not time for me to be that involved anyway.

> *Comment:* This is the main action of this session. Joan is confronted with the discrepancy between what happens to her in relationship to this man and the fantasy of what she would like life to be like. She resolves the discrepancy herself with a renaming or reinterpretation of the events. Note that the helper has been involved primarily in influencing skills at this phase of the interview, yet Joan clearly makes her own decisions. A behavioral helper might seek more clearly delineated actions she could take in the future, again an analyst might interpret, while the existential-humanist might be searching for the meaning of her behavior.

Al 26: How would you like to respond to him? I mean first I've got to say that I've heard you say that you really want to be done with it.

Joan 26: Hmm.

Al 27: How would you like to respond to him? What might he say to you to make you come across like this?

Joan 27: Would you repeat the question?

Al 28: What might he say that makes you come across like this?

Joan 28: It's a kind of coming in and sometimes taking hold of me before I've had a chance to slowly move together. Uhm . . . It's the demanding tone of voice.

Al 29: Um-hm. So what you're really saying, loud and clear then is that you've really seen yourself on videotape makes you say that you don't want to deal with this person anymore.

Joan 29: No, I don't. I'm not getting anything from it anymore. . . . And I guess one of the big questions was, was there something wrong with me, so that I would never have a relationship with a man, or was it, was there something in this relationship that was difficult.

Al 30: I see.

Joan 30: And it seems like maybe it isn't just something wrong with me. That this is a special kind of interaction between him and me that really isn't very good.

Al 31: So what I hear you saying is that you basically are putting your own new views on this situation. Before I heard you struggling this way and that way. Now I hear you saying I'm going to look at this a little differently. You will reinterpret the situation. Ah, is this the way I want to be? Ah, you know, you could perhaps be with him, you know, more strongly, relaxed, but you're telling me, I hear you pretty clearly that that isn't something that you want to do.

Joan 31: I'm not ready to do that now. The relationship isn't important enough. My career is more important, and my children are more important. And that's where my energy should be going rather than my energy to hold myself—defend myself—from some person.

Al 32: So what I hear you say, it sounds like before you were coming from "What should I do?" "What's right?" I hear you struggling. I hear you very instantaneously saying "What do I want?" And then you're saying: "This is what I want."

Joan 32: And I know from that feeling I had when I was telling you both from looking at myself and from the feeling I had inside when I told you how I feel with him that that just really —I know the answer now.

Al 33: Okay. Ah, let me just check out a little bit more, and then I think you better respond to me honestly. You perhaps sense a little puzzlement in my face right now? I hear you loud and strong saying—

Joan 33: You've said that three times!

Al 34: I've said that three times. I'm not used to people . . . . and you've done it in the past sometimes, becoming quite that definitive that quickly. And my experience is, "is that where you're really at?" How do you react to me doubting you a little bit and so forth?

Joan 34: Lots of people seem to doubt, but when I make a decision that comes from my gut, it's made. And I don't make it from my head. It's a whole decision, and most people don't understand how I do that but that's a process that works for me, and I really need somebody to help me start feeling, and experiencing, and seeing myself. Sometimes it happens, and sometimes it doesn't. But, yeah, you really helped me make a decision then.

Al 35: So another way to look at it: as we began by saying you were afraid of this guy owning you. And we end by saying you want to own yourself.

Joan 35: I do own myself.

Al 36: . . . That you *own* yourself, and you know where you want to go.

Joan 36: Yeah. That was really good.

Al 37: You sound really sure.

Comment: This clarification of the decision process phase of the interview represents a particularly interesting set of exchanges. The helper at Al 26 has a great deal of difficulty hearing the quick decision of the helpee. Note also the sentence structure "How would you like to respond to him?" This puts the female in the passive role and could be considered an example of unconscious sexism in the interview. It is also a cultural way of viewing women's roles, for we have observed feminist helpers using the same sentence structure.

The bulk of exchanges in this segment of the section focus on the helper assimilating and hearing accurately what Joan has decided. We believe that deliberate returning to attending skills when the helper makes an error is one of the best routes toward "recovery." All helpers will occasionally make errors in a session. The issue is not whether one makes errors or not, but how one recovers from less effective helping leads.

Al 33 illustrates one route toward recovery from error which moves beyond simple attending. Here, he self-discloses in the here and now present tense and admits his puzzlement. He asks Joan for a reaction to his behavior via the check-out implicit in the questioning tone of his voice. She comments later that the honest admission of confusion was helpful to her.

In the following segment, a new area for exploration is opened. At Joan 37, she says she feels "very, very sure" of her decisions. However, videotape replay reveals a questioning puzzled look on her face which leads to the helper suggesting that perhaps there is something else she might want to share.

Joan 37: I feel very, very sure.

Al 38: That comes across to me. Okay. Anything else you would like to share?

Joan 38: Yeah. I really know that that's the right decision. On the other hand, it's . . . the other half is how do I go about having a relationship with a man? That fantasy is very nice, and I'd really like to find a person and fulfill some of that fantasy at least. Or at least start working toward it.

Al 39: That fantasy, the warmth——

Joan 39: The sharing——

Al 40: The nonownership, the sharing, as you mentioned. This is something that you'd like very, very much.

Joan 40: And the individual space.

Al 41: So, there's a real question there. You know what you want. Now the question is apparently you decided to close off the relationship. But what you also know what kind of relationship you want. And yet, closing this off leaves you . . . where?

Joan 41: Ah, it leaves me by myself, which is okay for a while. I think the really big question is, is there someone—somewhere, or do I just sort of sit and wait, which is my usual process. I don't go out and look for men. Ah . . . will he come to my door? Uhm, or will I be sitting at my table and waiting for a long, long time?

Al 42: I'd like to suggest another frame of reference for looking at this. Ah, first of all, I've heard, and I've got to say I really like the way you make a decision that you feel good with. On the other hand, I also hear you turning on and turning off this guy. You came in saying how can you work it out? You looked at yourself on video and said no. Ah, I hear, you know, in this almost "either-or" in relationships . . . assuming a different frame of reference in that you want it all one way or all another way. That may be a little bit of a challenge right now. Now how does that sound? Come back at me.

Joan 42: Um, I didn't quite understand the—maybe. . . the either-or thing: it gets to a point. And then it's like in *Fiddler on the Roof* he said "On this hand—and on this hand—and on this hand—and on— No, I won't do it on this hand." And that's sort of the way it is. Like it gets over here far enough, and you're off the edge. Um, I'm not sure that it is either-or. But there is a breaking point.

Al 43: That really isn't very helpful. But there is a breaking point.

Joan 43: Um-hm. But I never know when it's really going to come. Or when it's going to come. It creeps up.

Al 44: It creeps up?

Joan 44: Yeah, it surprises me. My process of decision making.

Al 45: . . . So, let me give you a little feedback in terms——

Joan 45: That would be helpful.

Al 46: You mentioned that I am a man. I guess that's obvious. You're a woman. Ah, I like it. I like the way you're responding now. You're coming across soft and easy to hear. At the same time, I like you when you come across strong and sure of yourself. I find myself being a little wary of you becoming superstrong. And I also find myself a little puzzled when you come across superunsure. You haven't been much of that today. Ah, so you come across to me in many, very different ways. And I guess, underlying that, my reaction to you is a very positive feeling. And yet, as a man, I kind of, as a person, I sometimes wonder just where you're going to jump next? And this puzzles me. In a sense this makes me close up. How do you respond to that?

Joan 46: I think that's one of the reasons why I say that I'm going to sit here and wait. Because somebody has to, uhm, . . . it's hard to follow me. I never know what to expect next. So how could you know what to expect next? And you have to be very facile and easy on your feet, or, or else not attend to me a lot. And that's okay not to attend to me a whole lot.

Comment: Al 46 represents a specific example of direct-mutual communication. The statement begins with an attending phase, in which he indicates what he has heard from her. This is followed by an influencing phase, where he draws on his own personal experience and perceptions of her and follows this by a check-out, allowing her to respond. Joan does not respond directly but does comment on this later in the processing session (see Al 50 to Joan 54).

This phase of the interview represents another opening and clarifying phase. The question at hand is what are the helper and helpee going to talk about next. The issue appears at Joan 41, where she confronts herself and discrepancies in her behavior. A more appropriate lead at Al 42 might have been a reflection or summary of that discrepancy rather than the interpretation. Again, this represents the hiatus point where different helpers would use different leads.

Following are comments by Al and Joan as they processed the videotape they are viewing. It may be noted that some of their discussion parallels the Interpersonal Process Recall methods of Norman Kagan.

Al 47: We've just completed our simulated interview which in one sense was not necessarily all that simulated because the issues that we discussed are at least very analogous to the real issues that Joan and I have perhaps sometimes discussed in the past. Ah, maybe we might come on. Put, put both of us on camera now and discuss the last interview to some extent. I might say, Joan, that as you know I was going to do a menu of different microtraining skills and I found that this was in one sense first a limiting factor, but I think I did get through basically all the specific skills that I wanted to. But more important than going through the skills is what were your reactions to this interview? What were high points, low points? Where was I on, where was I off? This might be useful.

Joan 47: The things that were really useful were . . . You gave me a direction (see Al 18). You told me to fantasize and that was very helpful. The videotape (see Al 23) . . . a lot of your self-disclosure of content and self-disclosure of feelings and the summary (see Al 14, 20). Uhm, the one time that you didn't understand my decision-making process—that was very helpful for me (see Al 26-34). It gave me a lot of insights into how other people respond to me. And then when you summarized your feelings at the very end of not quite knowing where I was after the interpretation (see Al 46). That was very helpful, too.

Al 48: So, just to select out one of those. One thing that was useful to you was like you came on very clear on the videotape. This was a decision for you. And, in fact, rather than me going along with it, and so forth, me reacting where I was, being puzzled and so forth, was more helpful than if I just bought it.

Joan 48: Yes.

Al 49: I see.

Joan 49: That really made me feel like: Hey, you're listening. You're willing to give who you are back to me. And I need that because other people in the world respond similarly. So that was really helpful for me.

Al 50: I see. And the videotape type of reaction. I was a little surprised that you responded that strongly to it. But then on the other hand, I worked with videotape enough that nothing really should surprise me. I've seen this type of thing before. Ah, you mentioned the summary self-disclosure, summary expression of feeling and reactions, I gave a lot of my reactions to you in different places. Now, how did you respond to that when I said I responded in different ways to you (see Al 46) ?

Joan 50: Again, that was really helpful. I think that was very real . . . . And it sort of illustrates some of the things that have happened between us.

Al 51: Yeah. And we've just gone back to look at the tape. What did you see yourself doing after I said I was in relationship to you?

Joan 51: I topic jumped (see Joan 46) .

Al 52: You topic jumped. Then started talking "about" rather than yourself or me——

Joan 52: And also rather than here and now, what we were talking about, I went to there and then, and just left you out of it completely.

Al 53: And this is something that can happen to anybody that does self-disclosure because the helpee or the person that you're talking with may just plain choose to leave. And you left at that point.

Joan 53: I sure did.

Al 54: And even though you left, how did you feel about it?

Joan 54: Ah, it was really a very right on—I think it, I left almost because you were so right on. And I know that that's the way you respond, and that that's the way you feel. And it was so honest. And I guess I was just not right ready to come back and be honest with you.

Al 55: Another place where we really seemed to go a little off track was on the either-or which I saw as an interpretation presenting you with another frame of reference. And you seemed to not really be too crazy about that (see Al 42).

Joan 55: Yeah. It was the (groping) Yeah, you said switch off and on. And I think that was part of it. The either-or was okay. Because that's true, but it's on a continuum, and you said switch. And it was just that one word, I realized, that made me say no. It's not like "yes-no." It's "yes-no" and "maybe's" in between.

Al 56: You feel I was laying a trip on you at that moment?

Joan 56: No.

Al 57: You didn't feel I was?

Joan 57: I just thought that you really hadn't . . . .

Al 58: One concern that I do have with interpretation is that interpretation has to be used with real judgment and real care. And I could have gone with an analytic interpretation, a Freudian, or I could have looked at your behavior. A whole variety of things could have been done. And yet, I think it is a different frame of reference. And what we really wanted to illustrate at this point was an interpretation. And they don't always work. That's why the check-out is important. (See check-out in Al 42).

Joan 58: And also you and I have a relationship that it was okay for me to say no.

Al 59: Okay. I think we might sign off at this point (their camera crew giving the signals). Thanks so much, Joan.

Ivey Taxonomy Scoring Form

| | MICROTRAINING SKILLS | | | | | | | | | | | | ATTENDING AND/ OR PARALLEL | FOCUS | | | | | | QUALITY | | | | |
| | ATTENDING | | | | | | INFLUENCING | | | | | | | | | | | | | | | | | |
HELPER STATEMENT NUMBER	CLOSED QUESTION	OPEN QUESTION	MIN.ENCOURAGE	PARAPHRASE	REFLECT. FEELING	SUMMARIZATION	DIRECTIONS	EXPRESSION CONT.	EXPRESSION FEEL.	SUMMARIZATION	INTERPRETATION	DIRECT-MUTUAL C.		HELPEE	HELPER	DYAD	OTHERS	TOPIC	CULT-ENV.-CONTXT.	CONCRETENESS	IMMEDIACY	RESPECT	GENUINENESS	CONFRONTATION
1	X												+	X				X		C	H	+	1	
2		X											−		X			X		−	P		1	
3			X										+	X			X			C	H		2	
4				X									+	X			X			−	H		2	
5					X								+	X						C	H	+	2	
6						X							+	X			X			C	H		1	X
7		X											+	X						C	P		1	
8				X									+	X			X			C	P		2	X
9			X										+	X			X	X		−	H		2	X
10		X											+	X						C	H		2	X
11				X	X								+	X	X					C	H		2	X
12									X		X		+	X						C	H	+	1	X
13			X										+	X						C	H		2	
14								X	X				(+)		X		X			C	P	+	1	X
15				X									+	X						C	H		2	
16		X											+	X						−	H		2	
17			X										+	X			X			C	H	+	2	
18							X						−	X						C	H		2	
19			X										+		X			X		−	H	+	2	
20								X	X				+	X	X					C	p/h	+	2	X
21		X		X	X								(+)	X			X			C	p/h		2	X
22		X											+	X						C	H		2	
23	X					X							+	X						C	H	+	2	X
HELPEE STATEMENT																								
1								X					+					X		−	H		1	
2								X	X				+	X		X	X	X		C	p/h	+	1	X
3								X	X				+	X						C	p/h		2	X
4			X										+	X						−	H		2	
5	X							X	X				+		X		X			C	H	+	1	
6			X										+	X						−	H		1	
7								X					+	X			X			C	p/h		2	X
8												X	+	X			X	X		C	H		2	X
9			X										+	X						−	H		2	
10									X				+	X			X			C	H		2	
11								X	X				+	X			X			C	h/f		2	X
12								X	X				+	X						C	H		2	X
13								X					+	X			X			C	p/h		2	
14								X	X				+	X	X		X			C	p/h	+	2	
15									X				+	X			X			C	H		2	X
16								X			X		(+)		X					C	p/h	+	2	X
17								X					+	X			X			C	H		2	X
18								X	X				+	X			X	X		C	F	+	2	
19									X				+	X						−	H	+	2	
20									X				+	X						C	f/h		2	
21									X				+	X						C	H		2	
22								X					+	X						−	P		2	
23			X										+	X						−	H		2	

Ivey Taxonomy Scoring Form (cont'd)

HELPER STATEMENT NUMBER	CLOSED QUESTION	OPEN QUESTION	MIN.ENCOURAGE	PARAPHRASE	REFLECT. FEELING	SUMMARIZATION	DIRECTIONS	EXPRESSION CONT.	EXPRESSION FEEL.	SUMMARIZATION	INTERPRETATION	DIRECT-MUTUAL C.	ATTENDING AND/OR PARALLEL	HELPEE	HELPER	DYAD	OTHERS	TOPIC	CULT.-ENV.-CONTXT.	CONCRETENESS	IMMEDIACY	RESPECT	GENUINENESS	CONFRONTATION
24									X				+		X					C	p/h		2	
25			X				X						+	X			X			C	p/h	+	2	
26	X		X										(+)	X			X			V	f/h	(−)	1	
27	X												−	X			X			V	F	(−)	0	
28	X												+	X			X			C	P		0	
29			X										+	X			X			C	H	+	1	
30		X											+	X						−	H		1	
31					X								+	X						C	p/h		1	X
32					X								+	X						C	p/h		2	X
33					X				X				+	X	X					C	H		2	X
34								X	X				+	X	X					C	p/h	+	2	X
35				X									+	X						C	H		2	X
36		X											+	X						C	H		2	
37						X							+	X						C	H		2	
38	X								X				+	X	X					C	H	+	2	
39		X											+	X						−	H		2	
40			X	X									+	X						C	H		2	
41	X				X								+	X						C	H	+	2	X
42										X	X		+	X			X			C	p/h	+	1	X
43			X										+	X			X			−	H	+	2	X
44			X										+	X			X			−	P		2	
45			X										+	X	X					−	H		2	
46								X	X			X	+	X	X	X				C	H	+	2	X
HELPEE STATEMENT																								
24									X				+	X						C	H		2	
25								X	X		X		(+)	X			X			C	H	+	2	X
26		X											+	X						−	H		1	
27				X									+		X					C	H	+	1	
28								X	X				+	X			X			C	P		1	
29										X			+	X			X			C	p/h		2	X
30											X		+	X			X			C	p/h	+	2	X
31											X		+	X			X			C	H	+	2	X
32											X		+	X						C	p/h	+	2	X
33								X					+		X					C	H		1	
34								X	X				+	X	X		X	X		C	p/h	+	2	X
35								X					+	X						C	H	+	2	
36									X				+	X						−	p/h	+	2	
37									X				+	X						C	H	+	2	
38								X					+	X			X			C	h/f		2	X
39		X											+				X			−	H		2	
40								X					+	X						C	H	+	2	
41								X					+	X						C	h/f	+	2	X
42								X	X				+	X			X			C	p/h		1	X
43								X					+	X			X			−	P		2	X
44								X	X				+	X			X			C	H		2	X
45		X											+				X			−	H	+	2	X
46								X	X		X		−	X						V	p/h		1	

COMMENTARY ON THE AL AND JOAN VIDEOTAPE

The *Basic Influencing Skills Participant Manual* presents an array of discussions on the demonstration videotape from several theoretical and personal perspectives. Basically, different people view the tape differently. Depending on the theoretical orientation of the reader or microtraining participant, the session is good, bad, or indifferent. In microtraining workshops, we seek to stress this point—different people have widely varying values as to what should occur in helping sessions.

Following is information concerning the scoring of the videotape, taken from the *Basic Influencing Skills Participant Manual*. Also included is a statement and review of the interview from Joan Chadbourne nineteen months after the interview was taped. Perhaps the "bottom line" for evaluating the success of an interview is what a client determines its value to be over time.

The Scoring of the Videotape

Attending and/or parallel responses. During the session Al had forty-three attending responses and three nonattending. Joan had forty-five attending responses and one nonattending. The general conclusion may be reached that a reasonable level of attending was achieved by both helper and helpee.

Inexperienced helpers may have many topic jumps. Helpees who wish to avoid issues may also show frequent shifts of verbal attention.

The times at which Al had clear topic jumps were at Al 2 (he moved from permission to videotape to start the interview), Al 18 (he gave the direction to fantasize), Al 27 (where he was clearly lost and not hearing Joan correctly). Some marginal attending responses were at Al 14 (where he self-disclosed, but the self-disclosure was not truly parallel to where Joan was "at" at that moment. Contributing to the problem here was his shift from Joan's present tense discussion to his past experience), Al 21 (where he gives a direction not fully related to the situation; primarily saving this lead from a lower rating was the reflection of Joan's present feeling state), and Al 26 (he is not really hearing Joan but goes through the motions only to break down at Al 27).

Joan, an effective helpee, stayed on the topic at every point except Joan 46, after which she asked that the session be terminated. In the process discussion afterwards, Joan (see Al 50 through Joan 54) indicates that this statement was "right on" and she did not wish to talk about that issue at that time on videotape.

Microtraining skills. Allowing for double scoring of some responses, Al and Joan presented the following pattern of skills:

Attending Skills			Influencing Skills		
Al	Joan		Al	Joan	
2	1	closed questions	4	1	directions
10	0	open questions	4	25	expression of content
11	6	minimal encourages	7	21	expression of feeling
9	0	paraphrases	0	3	summarizations
6	0	reflections of feeling	2	5	interpretations
5	0	summarizations	2	0	examples of DMC

The preceding chart reveals the following about Al: (1) he demonstrates the ability to present each of several microtraining skills in a single helping session. This could be considered a recommended competency for anyone participating in this program; (2) he shows forty-three attending and nineteen influencing responses; (3) on his less successful influencing leads, he routinely returns immediately to attending skills to reenter participation in the interview (see Al 12, 13, for example). This follows the theory that attending skills should form the most important basis of *all* helping sessions and be the choice of the helper when other alternative leads are not successful.

Joan, again, appears as an effective helpee. She was able to discuss content issues of substance and remained constantly in touch with her emotions throughout. Some helpees are unable or unwilling to deal with emotions. She was able to reinterpret her life experience on five different occasions. She did not move into a mutual relationship with the helper but on occasion was able to share some of her reactions toward him.

Focus. The following pattern of focus may be observed, allowing for double or multiple scoring of some responses.

Al	Joan	
42	39	Helpee
11	6	Helper
1	0	Dyad (more if the definition were liberalized)
13	17	Others
7	11	Topic
0	1	Cultural-environmental-context

The prime focus of this interview was on the helpee. Research indicates that many beginning helpers become so interested in the details of the client's lifestyle or extraneous topics that "others" or "topic" becomes the central focus of the session. If Al's objective was to assist Joan in focusing on Joan, the interview was successful. Clients tend to place their focus where the helper places his or her focus.

In many cases, the focus was multiple as Joan explored her relationship to George, the man she eventually decided was not for her. The focus pattern of seeing oneself in relationship to others is a potential source of growth. If the session were moving toward DMC and here-and-now encounter, the mutual focus ("I," "you," "we") of Al 46 might appear prominently.

Important statements of Joan (Joan 8, 25, 34) combine several foci dimensions where she appears to be bringing together herself in relation to her surroundings.

Quality dimensions. The newer and less-researched and developed aspects of microtraining workshops reveal additional information of value.

Concreteness was demonstrated by Al in thirty-four of his responses and by Joan in thirty-three. Al was scored for vagueness twice (Al 26, 27) where he failed to understand what Joan was doing at the moment. Joan was scored for vagueness at Joan 46 where she did not wish to talk about or react to Al's direct-mutual communication comment of the moment. However, it may be stated that both helper and helpee were able to remain relatively concrete and specific throughout the helping session.

Thirty-nine of Al's statements were in the "here and now," while Joan was in this tense in forty-two statements. Past tense ratings showed fourteen for Al and sixteen for Joan. Two of Al's statements were rated for future tense dimensions, while five of Joan's were in this category. The large predominance of here and now, present tense statements indicates most likely a theoretical bias of Al and a willingness of Joan to work "in the moment." The interplay of past experiences with present experience shows at Joan 29, 30, and 31. The ability to relate present tense experience with past experience is an important one in the skillful helpee and is basic for sensing patterns in one's life.

The scoring of respect via the criteria suggested in the training program was more difficult since respect can be shown in a variety of ways. Basically, statements of the helper or helpee were scored "+" if (1) they contained a clear, positive statement about the self (e.g. Joan 37), (2) they contained a clear, positive statement about the other (e.g. Al 19), or (3) they contained a relatively clear statement allowing for differences. The latter is frequently shown in the check-out of the helper after an interpretation or self-disclosure. The check-out shows respect by allowing people to differ with the opinion of the helper (see Al 42). Sixteen "+" and two "−" were scored for Al, eighteen "+" for Joan.

Genuineness ratings, more subjective in nature, reveal the following pattern: level 2: Al 33, Joan 36; level 1: Al 11, Joan 10; level 0: Al 2, Joan 0. These are typescript ratings and do *not* take into account additional nonverbal dimensions which might possibly lower the scores of both individuals. Level 2 appears to represent a level where both helpee and helper are working together, level 1 where they are communicating; level 0 appears to be scored when lack of understanding appears. Al 27, 28 represents clear level 0 genuineness, where he is so startled by Joan's reaction that he is unable to cope effectively. It is not until Al 33 where he honestly states his confusion that level 2 genuineness returns. Joan's drop at Joan 46 may also be noted. Finally, it should be observed that unless *both* helper and helpee are functioning at relatively high levels *together,* scores on this subjective scale will be low.

Confrontation (the noting of discrepancies within the self or in relationship to others) was noted in nineteen of Al's and twenty of Joan's statements. Both helper and helpee appeared able and willing to openly discuss and confront discrepancies in themselves and in relationship to each other.

In summary, both helper and helpee appeared to demonstrate the qualitative dimensions of helping. Further, and perhaps most important, when these dimensions deteriorated, they were able to take steps to repair the damage and to continue to work on the issues.

Summary of scoring and rating. You will want to examine the leads for the techniques of scoring. It is possible that you will want to develop additional criteria to make the scoring of the several dimensions yet more specific. The Ivey Taxonomy continues to undergo constant revision, and your suggestions for clarifying and changing scoring dimensions are welcome. Genuineness, for example, still rests on a subjective scale. Eventually it will be necessary to identify more clearly and in specific terms exactly what is meant by this concept.

One of Al's most effective helping leads is shown at Al 12, where he interprets (albeit incorrectly), focusing on the helpee. He is simultaneously concrete, in the present tense showing respect, and confrontive. His misuse of the word "control" lowers his score on genuineness, but even this error brings Joan in the following statements to increased clarity about the issue of "ownership." The directions at Al 18 and Al 23 are crucial to clarifying Joan's present state. The direct-mutual communication statement at Al 46 shows potential but was not received by Joan at this time.

The ineffective responses at Al 27, 28 are marked by failure to attend, vagueness, a future orientation (whereas Joan was in the present), lack of respect, lack of genuineness, and absence of confrontation. Need we say more! Al's ability to note his failure and recover via attending skills (primarily the paraphrase and summarization) is typical of experienced counselors who rely on attending after putting their "foot in mouth." The old motto of "when one is lost, off the track, etc., return to attending skills" was essential to Al's regaining participation in the session. If he had stuck with his view of Joan's behavior, he might eventually have changed Joan's mind for her or lost a helpee.

Joan demonstrates the effective helpee at several points. Joan 25 is especially clear. Here she expresses content and feeling, reinterprets her life experience, focuses on herself and George, and is simultaneously concrete, in the present tense, showing respect, being genuine, and confronting discrepancies within herself and in relation to others. *The fully functioning helpee is very similar to the fully functioning helper.*

Basic Influencing Skills also provides several critiques of this interview including a rather sharp examination by a feminist critic (Katz, 1976). Important in all evaluations of the interview is that different people view the same event quite differently. Chadbourne (1976) provides her impressions of the interview at a six-month follow-up point and her more recent observations at nineteen months postinterview follow-up are presented below.

NEW DIMENSIONS OF THE MICROCOUNSELING INTERVIEW

Joan Warrington Chadbourne*

I appreciate this opportunity to reexamine the interview we had nineteen months ago. This time, I want to focus on it from the vantage point of the newly defined dimensions of quality. I also see a new sexist issue for myself on which I want to comment.

Six months after the experience, I commented on our interview and your creative use of microcounseling skills (Chadbourne, 1976). At that time, I stated that the first segment of the interview, through Joan 25, had a high quality of interaction. The second segment, which followed my intuitive decision after confronting myself via videotape, was spent dealing with your response to my decision-making process. The latter segment was of a much lesser overall quality.

I saw your confusion about my intuitive (feminine) process as a product of your sexist conditioning. The rational, linear thought process, generally defined as masculine, is the only decision-making model which is accepted in our society. You were

*Joan Warrington Chadbourne is Assistant Professor, Counseling, University of Connecticut, Storrs.

unaccepting of my more intuitive mode.

A year after my original commentary, other factors emerge as relevant. The most outstanding new insight is embarrassing to me. My own sexist and nonassertive behavior pattern is clear in the typescript. During the second segment of the interview, after you have become confused, I try to make excuses for your doubts (Joan 34 and 46), rationalize my process (Joan 31, 34, and 38), and focus on your helpfulness in segment one (Joan 34 and 36). My behaviors are meant to save your male ego, a typical non-feminist behavior. You were confused by my process. We had a very concrete and immediate issue. If I had confronted you and/or told you what I was experiencing (genuineness), we would probably have achieved much more direct-mutual communication and the second segment of the interview would have been of a higher quality.

Attending to dimensions of quality has a strong impact on the direction and the outcome of an interview. Some examples taken from the typescript and alternatives which were possible illustrate the importance of the quality dimensions.

Most statements are scored concrete on the concrete-vagueness scale; I would like to point out several examples of you asking me to be more concrete and the results. In Al 7, you asked for a specific example connected to my conversation about marriage and ownership. This question had a major influence on the direction of the interview. At that point, we could have talked about ownership feelings I had in relation to you or in general. However, you helped me to describe and later to experience myself in one particular relationship in which I felt owned. That specific example led to a very real decision which I acted upon.

Al 18 is a very interesting request for concreteness through fantasy. I responded with specific examples; however, if I had not, you could have requested more specific details. In fantasy, people have the opportunity to see details they do not normally notice.

You provided a similar opportunity for me "to realize the full deep structure of [my] key verbalizations," through the videotape experience. The use of fantasy and videotape are my favorite interventions in the interview. Both were very facilitative; these experiences made my words *feel* concrete, real, and specific.

The second segment of the interview, from Al 26, might have been very different if either of us had changed the quality of our statements to *more* immediate, genuine, and confrontative ones. In addition, the underlying issue was our relationship, and the focus needed to be on our dyad rather than on topic or either one of us.

Bringing the interaction to the now with a focus on our dyad would have changed the outcome of the second segment of the interview. Joan 31 "defend myself against some person" and Joan 41 "it leaves me by myself" could have been brought to the now by asking how I was experiencing those feelings now, with us. Joan 34 "lots of people" was a *deliberate* vague and general response. Forcing me to deal directly with you would have dramatically changed the interaction. We were dealing with you and me and how we relate, but neither of us directly focused on our own interactions. You did some confrontation at Al 46 which could have brought a focus on us, but I deliberately chose not to respond with a here and now focus on us.

The comments on the second segment come from my own Gestalt and existential orientation. A more analytical helper might have gotten into my conflict with authority when it became obvious that I would not relate to you about your confusion.

It is important for the readers to know that we were advisor and graduate student and that we had a pact not to discuss our interpersonal process. As advisor and graduate student we were, in that relationship, and now as colleagues we are, very productive; the pact was useful. However, in the interview, I certainly maintained the pact and kept the second segment from being too immediate and from focusing on us.

During the interview the pact was a handicap because the issue we were dealing with was my quick and intuitive decision-making process and your doubtful response to it. This segment of the interview is a powerful example of the influence of the helper-helpee relationship and the need for that relationship to be discussed.

The interview is a very real experience for me. While rereading it and preparing these comments, I easily recall the tension I had talking about ownership and George, the excitement during the fantasy, the awareness which emerged while viewing the video-tape, the sureness and satisfaction from making the decision, my frustration, and my decision not to deal directly with you when you were confused and doubting my process. The first segment of the interview was really exceptionally helpful and exciting; you were creatively using your skills. You really facilitated important insight and behavior.

I must add a personal note, especially to other professional women who are searching. I have been able to integrate my professional and personal lives. A confident, nonsexist man helps, and so does joy and confidence in oneself as a professional woman.

Appendix IV

INSTRUMENTATION USEFUL IN
MICROTRAINING RESEARCH

RESEARCH IN MICROCOUNSELING and microtraining has gone through an evolutionary process. We began with subjective five-point scales and a semantic differential instrument for rating counselor effectiveness; the next movement was into direct behavior counts; the most recent research has been in several diverse areas such as counting and classifying interviewing leads via the Ivey Taxonomy, the development of a Microcounseling Skills Discrimination Index, and the achievement of contracted behavioral objectives with the "do-use-teach" framework.

This appendix presents several instrumentation thrusts of microtraining plus instruments developed by R. G. Matarazzo, Robert R. Carkhuff, and Norman Kagan which are useful supplements to evaluation of microtraining's effectiveness. In addition, scales by Bernard Guerney and his associates are presented in brief form as an alternative for use when working with special groups.

Most, perhaps all, of the scales presented in this section should be recognized as culturally related instruments. It is our belief that research on the helping process has come all too often from an unconscious cultural bias. This does not deny the value of the instruments presented here or elsewhere. However, each research instrument needs to be evaluated as to its appropriateness for a particular cultural or subcultural group.

SUBJECTIVE FIVE-POINT SCALES

The first microcounseling research project (Ivey, Normington, Miller, Morrill, and Haase, 1968) was heavily based on subjective rating scales with polar opposites. The scale below, with modifications, has been used in several studies. The original scale used seven raters who rated three-minute segments of videotapes which had been prepared for use in the project. Interrater reliability using Fisher's Z transformation was .843. Three of the seven raters were tested over a twenty-four-hour period with randomized tapes of the same material, and *intra*rater reliability of .842 was established. These reliability ratings are characteristic of other studies of which Rollin's (1970) r. of .898 with two independent raters is an example. Thus it seems safe to say that this scale has reasonable reliability, despite the fact that it relies on relatively subjective ratings.

ATTENDING BEHAVIOR RATING SCALE

ADAPTED BY STEPHEN A. ROLLIN* AND ALLEN E. IVEY

EYE CONTACT
____1. Inattentive, loses eye contact frequently, avoids eye contact, may stare inappropriately.
____2. Avoids prolonged eye contact, uncertain as to attentiveness, may break eye contact consistently on certain topics or stare on occasion.
____3. Somewhat attentive, does not vary eye contact consistently.
____4. Consistent eye contact, generally appropriate.
____5. Observes closely, varies use of eye contact, always attentive.

POSTURE, MOVEMENTS, AND GESTURES
____1. Tense, unnatural, uncomfortable, may fidget excessively.
____2. Too relaxed—sloppy; somewhat tense or rigid, slightly nervous, some inappropriate gestures.
____3. Comfortable generally but may appear too tense or too relaxed in relation to client. May show lack of variation and few facilitative gestures.
____4. Comfortable, attentive, appropriate gestures.
____5. Natural, comfortable, attentive, variation, body movements and gestures in synchrony with client.

---

*Stephen A. Rollin is Associate Professor, Counselor Education, Florida State University, Tallahassee, Florida.

VOCAL TONE AND SPEECH RATE (Optional)

___1. Irritating, shrill, distracting, inappropriate affect as reflected in voice modulation, extremely slow or rapid speech rate, may also be represented by complete monotone.

___2. Some hesitancy, uncertainness, monotonic or unexpected tonal variety. May be too fast or slow. Inappropriate affect may be shown.

___3. Relatively little change in tonal quality, stereotyped, surface affect primarily.

___4. Pleasant and clear, some variation provides good source of stimuli. Speech rate appropriate to situation.

___5. Articulate, considerable variation in tone and feeling, appropriate affect as reflected in voice modulation. Appropriate speech rate.

VERBAL ATTENDING BEHAVIOR

___1. Changes topic abruptly and frequently, interrupts, may talk about self and own ideas to exclusion of other.

___2. Frequent topic changes or focus on irrelevant material, may make noncontributory statements or questions, allows sidetracking.

___3. Generally stays on topic but may miss important data and allows some sidetracking, neglects to label or explore important content or feelings.

___4. Stays on the topic consistently, does not introduce data from own experience unless clearly relevant to the helpee, accurate reflections and paraphrasing.

___5. Not only stays on topic but assists helpee in delving deeper into the topic. Labels and explores important content and feelings, may again use personal material, but clearly the prime attention is given to the helpee.

Another subjective scale is the "Accurate Reflection of Feeling Scale," which has yielded interrater reliabilities of .64 to .92 in the original microcounseling studies. This scale was adapted from the Truax and Carkhuff (1967) format and suggests that subjective empathy ratings such as those stressed by Truax and Carkhuff may be appropriate measures of microtraining outcome. The following scale was developed primarily by Cheryl Normington and was used in the first microcounseling research report (Ivey, Normington, Miller, Morrill, and Haase, 1968).

MEASUREMENT OF ACCURATE RESPONSE TO FEELING

CHERYL J. NORMINGTON

INTERVIEW SEGMENT #					
1	2	3	4	5	
0	0	0	0	0	Inaccurate responses to content.
1	1	1	1	1	Slightly accurate responses to content.
2	2	2	2	2	Often accurate responses to content.
3	3	3	3	3	Always accurate responses to content.
0	0	0	0	0	Ignores obvious feelings.
1	1	1	1	1	Inaccurate responses to obvious feelings.
2	2	2	2	2	Slight accuracy toward obvious feelings.
3	3	3	3	3	Often accurate toward obvious feelings.
4	4	4	4	4	Always accurate toward obvious feelings.
0	0	0	0	0	Can't rate concerning deeper feelings.
1	1	1	1	1	Concern with deeper feelings & occasionally accurate with regard to them.
2	2	2	2	2	Frequently accurate toward deeper feelings.
3	3	3	3	3	Almost always accurate toward deeper feelings. May occasionally hesitate or err but corrects quickly & accurately.
4	4	4	4	4	Unerringly accurate and unhesitant toward deeper feelings.

Still another subjective rating scale used in microcounseling research has been the Ideal Therapeutic Relationship scale developed by Jerry Authier. This scale consists of fourteen items derived from the criteria isolated by Fiedler (1950a,b; 1951) as characteristic of the ideal therapeutic relationship. The scale requires trained raters to rate the trainees on a five-point Likert-type scale for their videotaped pre- and postinterviews. A rating of 1 indicates either that the characteristic was not manifested or manifested to a very low degree, while a rating of 5 indicates that the characteristic was manifested at an extremely high degree. The sum of the ratings across all fourteen items serves as an overall indicator of each trainee's manifestation of an ideal therapeutic relationship. Thus, the larger the total score, the more ideal the therapeutic relationship, with a maximum score of 70 reflecting an "ideal therapeutic relationship."

The Ideal Therapeutic Relationship scale has been used in five studies to date. The interrater reliabilities have ranged from .41 to .91. In all cases, these reliability coefficients were significant at at least the .05 level of probability.

THE "IDEAL THERAPEUTIC RELATIONSHIP" SCALE

JERRY AUTHIER

Fourteen statements are listed below which have been identified as being most characteristic of the "ideal therapeutic relationship." Please rate the preceding interview on a scale ranging from 1 to 5 along each of these dimensions. Circle a rating of 5 if the interview is highly characterized by the statement, an intermediate rating if the interview is somewhat characterized by the statement, and a 1 if the statement is not a characteristic of the interview.

1. An empathic relationship exists between the therapist and the patient.

    1_____2_____3_____4_____5

2. The therapist and the patient relate well.

    1_____2_____3_____4_____5

3. The therapist sticks closely to the patient's problems.

    1_____2_____3_____4_____5

4. The patient feels free to say what he likes.

    1_____2_____3_____4_____5

5. An atmosphere of mutual trust and confidence exists between the therapist and the patient.

    1_____2_____3_____4_____5

6. Rapport between the therapist and the patient is excellent.

1_____2_____3_____4_____5

7. The patient assumes an active role.

1_____2_____3_____4_____5

8. The therapist leaves the patient free to make his own choices.

1_____2_____3_____4_____5

9. The therapist accepts all feelings which the patient expresses as completely normal and understandable.

1_____2_____3_____4_____5

10. The therapist manifests a tolerant attitude toward the patient.

1_____2_____3_____4_____5

11. The therapist is understanding.

1_____2_____3_____4_____5

12. The patient feels that he is really understood.

1_____2_____3_____4_____5

13. The therapist is really able to understand the patient.

1_____2_____3_____4_____5

14. The therapist really tries to understand the patient's feelings.

1_____2_____3_____4_____5

BEHAVIORAL COUNTS

Microcounseling's emphasis on observable behavior makes possible rather specific counts to determine the existence or non-existence of specific behaviors. A wide variety of behaviors have been noted and duly counted. The first behavioral count method of microtraining was counting the number of topic jumps from a typescript of the Ivey, Normington, Miller, Morrill, and Haase (1968) series of studies.

A typescript of all interviews was completed and rated for verbal attending behavior by two trained raters. If a counselor comment followed the verbal comments of the client, it was scored "plus." If it did not follow, it was scored "minus." If disagreement between the two ratings occurred, the statement was not used. Of 1,904 ratings, the two raters disagreed on only 114, thus illustrating consistent agreement as to verbal attending behavior. Each counselor was scored for the percentage of verbal attending behavior in each session held with a client (p. 3).

In the original study, the above behavioral count system proved effective, as it did again with Aldrige (1971) and Aldrige and Ivey (1975). However, Moreland, Ivey, and Phillips (1973) did not find this measure as effective in differentiating trained and untrained groups. The explanation for this incongruency now appears to be in the original level of communication competence of trainees. The Ivey et al. and Aldrige and Ivey studies used relatively naive subjects, i.e. beginning counselors and junior high school students, whereas the Moreland, Ivey, and Phillips study was conducted using medical students. Examination of results in other studies (c.f. Hearn, 1976; Chadbourne, 1975; Sherrard, 1973) now leads us to conclude that topic jumps appear as important variables for improvement in less sophisticated groups. However, talented individuals may already have this skill at their disposal and should not be expected to change this particular behavior as a result of microtraining.

Aldrige (1971) also counted broken eye contact, arm and hand movements, leg and foot movements, whole body movement, and expressive gestures. Although not all findings were significant between control and experimental groups, microtraining subjects markedly lowered their whole body movements (marked shifts in posture) and number of eye contact breaks. The experimental group had a slight increase, although nonsignificant, in expressive gestures which are considered positive and facilitative.

Virtually any type of behavior is amenable to counting for pre- and postevaluation of trainees in microcounseling research. The "Rating and Behavioral Count Sheet for Attending Behavior" of the *Basic Attending Skills* program (see Appendix I) is a typical example of behavioral counts used in microcounseling research. Ivey and Gluckstern (1976b) talk specifically about the use of operant charts in self-directed self-expression workshops and in the media therapy framework:

> . . . it is useful with some trainees to count specific behaviors in each training session and place them on operant charts so that improvement in behavioral skills may be observed over time . . . very precise

definitions of behaviors are necessary. The client may say, "I look tough." The task of the helper is to make the abstract concept "tough" operational. In the case of the demonstration videotape, tough was defined as harsh verbal tone, chewing gum, high per cent of talk time, and several specific nonverbal gestures . . . [It is possible to] develop behavioral counts on each of these measures and chart the progress of the helpee through several training sessions (p. 36).

It was this approach that Ivey (1973b) used in modifying behaviors of psychiatric patients. Sample behaviors included interruptions, eyes downcast on the floor, short steps when walking, extensive topic jumps, etc. Always important in work with patients was the clarification of behavior in operational and countable terms. Both the therapist and the patient in this case counted the behaviors. Goshko (1973) used the same approach with success with children who set about modifying their own behaviors.

Behavior change in the laboratory, of course, is not behavioral change on the ward, in the classroom, or in the family. Ivey found that the "do-use-teach" contract with specific counts and feedback was important in assisting patients to generalize newly learned behavior to the ward. One patient, for example, was given an audiotape cassette recorder "with the assignment that he was to tape-record a 15-minute conversation every day and then listen to the tape counting the number of times. . .he caused an unnecessary topic jump" (Ivey, 1973b, p. 340). Goshko worked toward generalization of learned behavior of children to the classroom setting through similar procedures and obtained the support of the teacher in maintaining learned behavior. Weinrach (1976) has elaborated on this system.

Authier and Gustafson have used a categorization scheme which relies both on behavioral counts for verbal utterances and a subjective Likert scale for nonverbal behaviors. Their scheme is somewhat unique in that it includes a microcounseling skill and its respective opposite. The general research design that the categorization scheme is used for is a pre-post design which has videotaped segments as data being analyzed.

Generally, the videotaped pre- and postinterviews are rated independently by two judges who have been trained on practice tapes until a .80 interrater reliability level is reached. The tapes

CODING SHEET

Rater_____ Interviewing Time   Tape No._____

	0 - 4 minutes	5 - 8 minutes	9 - 16 minutes	16 - 20 minutes
minimal encourage to talk				
open question				
closed question				
feeling oriented question				
fact oriented question				
paraphase				
question— statement				
multiple choice question				
reflection of feeling				
ignores feeling				
confrontation				
attacking or not confronting				
self-disclosure				
inappropriate or incomplete S. D.				
feedback				
non-discussion of obvious own reaction				
misc.				
Verbal Following	1 2 3 4 5 6 7	1 2 3 4 5 6 7	1 2 3 4 5 6 7	1 2 3 4 5 6 7
Posture	1 2 3 4 5 6 7	1 2 3 4 5 6 7	1 2 3 4 5 6 7	1 2 3 4 5 6 7
Eye Contact	1 2 3 4 5 6 7	1 2 3 4 5 6 7	1 2 3 4 5 6 7	1 2 3 4 5 6 7

are then rated by the raters, who are "blind" in that they are unaware of the pre or post status of the interview and the experimental or control conditions. Generally, the coders are asked to
categorize each therapist's utterance as either one of the microcounseling skills, one of the respective opposite skills, or a miscellaneous skill. An utterance is operationally defined as any therapist verbalization which is either responded to by the patient, or
which has a latency period of over two to three seconds. Finally,
this format is generally used to rate thirty-minute tapes, with the
coders rating the first eight utterances of each fifth of the tape
until a total of forty utterances has been categorized.

Modified versions of the categorization scheme which follow have been used in a number of studies. Interclass correla-
tions using Eble (1951) formula estimated interrater reliability
for all studies at the .90 level or above. Needless to say, such high
coefficients have always been highly significant.

Generally speaking, the behavior count format will be most
effective with less sophisticated or more disturbed populations.
As the communication competence of the individual develops, the
quality and category of verbal interaction through such dimensions as stressed in the Ivey Taxonomy will prove more fruitful for
research. However, at beginning levels, behavior counts such as
those described here will undoubtedly continue to be important
and effective.

COUNSELOR EFFECTIVENESS SCALE

The Counselor Effectiveness Scale (CES) has been used frequently in microtraining research and therefore, the scales and
data on its development are included in this manual.

The CES has been primarily used to measure client attitudes
toward the counselor. When used in evaluating the counselor
before and after microtraining sessions, it has proven to be a sensitive and useful instrument. However, we have also found the
instrument to be highly reactive to changes in the client's environment and thus do not recommend its use in other than immediate
pretraining and posttraining microcounseling sessions. However,

when using large samples, this reactivity may be of less importance.

The report on the development of the CES written by Richard Haase, Dean Miller, Allen Ivey, Weston Morrill, and Cheryl Normington follows.

Item Selection

Ninety-three items of the semantic-differential type (adjective continua) were randomly ordered in a semantic-differential format and comprised the initial pool. Estimates of item reliability and validity were obtained in the following manner: two graduate psychology classes (N=30) were asked to rate two videotaped models of counselors, with one model portraying desirable counselor behavior and the second portraying undesirable or ineffective techniques. Means, standard deviations, standard errors, and confidence limits (.05 and .01) were computed for every item on each of the two models. The standard error of each item served as a measure of its reliability, while the difference between confidence limits of the positive and the negative models served as a measure of validity of that item. The standard errors and confidence limits of every item were graphically plotted, and item selection for the final scales was completed by analyzing and selecting items which represented the most optimal combination of the two. Items were judged on the degree that they had low standard error (reflecting high agreement among raters) and a wide separation between confidence limits for the positive versus the negative model (a representation of that item's ability to discriminate). Two parallel forms of twenty-five items each were constructed on this basis.

Reliability

Parallel form reliability (coefficient of equivalence) was computed between form 1 and form 2 of the scale and yielded a value of +.975, which is significant beyond the .001 level of confidence. Raters consisted of students enrolled in a psychological testing course (N=18) who had no previous experience with either a semantic differential format or the scale under consideration. For all practical intents and purposes, they could be considered "naive" raters.

Interrater reliability was computed using Kendall's Coefficient of Concordance. Kendall's W allows one to obtain a measure of agreement between k judges who have made N observations. This obviated the need to compute $\frac{N(N-1)}{2}$ combinations of coefficients between individual judges and then proceeding to average these.

Undergraduate student raters (N=7) were utilized as judges and were asked to rate a videotape model of counseling on fifty observations made by these judges on the semantic differential format (25 on form 1 and 25 on form 2). Kendall's W was applied to these fifty observations and yielded a value of +.37, which is significant far beyond the .001 level of confidence. In essence, we now have information which indicates that all seven judges are utilizing essentially the same criteria of judgment. Hence, we are assured of significant interrater reliability of this scale.

Validity

The use of two radically different models of counselors allowed for a test of validity of the two scales by means of their ability to discriminate between rationally defined good model and rationally defined bad model of counselor behavior. The degree to which the scales can discriminate between these two models allows one to estimate the validity of the scales, i.e. whether the scale is actually able to measure or discriminate between effective and ineffective counselors. Undergraduate student ratings of both models (N=18) were obtained for both form 1 and form 2 of the scale. Means, standard deviations, and t values were computed. The results of the test of significance of the difference between mean ratings of model 1 and model 2 are presented below.

SIGNIFICANCE OF THE DIFFERENCE BETWEEN MODEL 1 AND
MODEL 2 AS RATED ON EACH OF TWO PARALLEL FORMS
OF A SCALE TO MEASURE COUNSELOR EFFECTIVENESS

Form	d.f.	Mean of Model		t	p
		1	2		
1	17	66.25	131.22	8.28	.001
2	17	65.00	134.44	10.60	.001

The results of the significance of the difference between the two models as measured by the forms of the scale under consideration are indeed encouraging. The fact that the items were originally drawn by a technique that utilized the same two models may indicate that further validity studies should be designed which utilize different counselors in different situations. Further work in this area shall be implemented.

Conclusions

It appears, at least tentatively, that the scale under consideration to measure counselor effectiveness is a promisingly reliable and valid instrument in short-term situations. It therefore seems tenable to apply this scale to experimental work. Further reliability and validity data on the scale, per se, are recommended.

COUNSELOR EFFECTIVENESS SCALE

R. Haase, D. Miller, A. Ivey, W. Morrill, and C. Normington

Scale #1

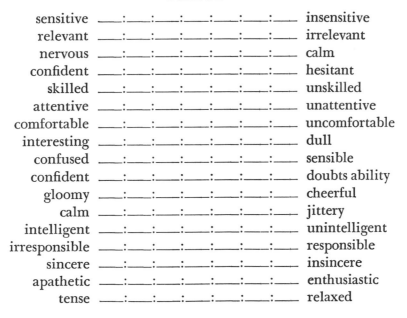

sensitive	insensitive
relevant	irrelevant
nervous	calm
confident	hesitant
skilled	unskilled
attentive	unattentive
comfortable	uncomfortable
interesting	dull
confused	sensible
confident	doubts ability
gloomy	cheerful
calm	jittery
intelligent	unintelligent
irresponsible	responsible
sincere	insincere
apathetic	enthusiastic
tense	relaxed

colorful ___:___:___:___:___:___ colorless
boring ___:___:___:___:___:___ interesting
formed ___:___:___:___:___:___ formless
unreal ___:___:___:___:___:___ real
sociable ___:___:___:___:___:___ unsociable
shallow ___:___:___:___:___:___ deep
careless ___:___:___:___:___:___ careful
polite ___:___:___:___:___:___ rude

Scale #2

skillful ___:___:___:___:___:___ clumsy
competent ___:___:___:___:___:___ incompetent
confusing ___:___:___:___:___:___ clear
meaningful ___:___:___:___:___:___ not meaningful
deep ___:___:___:___:___:___ shallow
sympathetic ___:___:___:___:___:___ unsympathetic
close ___:___:___:___:___:___ distant
socially inept ___:___:___:___:___:___ socially adept
decisive ___:___:___:___:___:___ indecisive
friendly ___:___:___:___:___:___ hostile
realistic ___:___:___:___:___:___ unrealistic
irritable ___:___:___:___:___:___ pleasant
passive ___:___:___:___:___:___ active
insecure ___:___:___:___:___:___ secure
strong ___:___:___:___:___:___ weak
nice ___:___:___:___:___:___ awful
erratic ___:___:___:___:___:___ stable
consistent ___:___:___:___:___:___ inconsistent
indifferent ___:___:___:___:___:___ conscientious
lazy ___:___:___:___:___:___ industrious
mature ___:___:___:___:___:___ immature
inattentive ___:___:___:___:___:___ attentive
social ___:___:___:___:___:___ antisocial
efficient ___:___:___:___:___:___ inefficient
helpful ___:___:___:___:___:___ unhelpful

MICROCOUNSELING SKILL DISCRIMINATION SCALE

Dong Yul Lee*

The Microcounseling Skill Discrimination Scale (MSDS) was developed by Dong Yul Lee, Allen E. Ivey, and Richard F. Haase. A description of the development and validation of this scale may be found in Lee, Zingle, Patterson, Ivey, and Haase (1976). In essence, research by these authors and by Scroggins and Ivey (1976) reveals that "expert" helpers rate videotaped segments differently than untrained helpers. After training in microcounseling, the responses of beginning helpers more closely resemble expert judgments of helping skills.

The instrument described here is still very much in the developmental stage. It also only describes two skills (reflection of feeling and paraphrasing). Stokes and Romer (in press) have suggested that the absolute ratings on the MSDS may confound individual use of the rating scale. They suggest "expressing each rater's judgments as a standard z score in terms of *his own* mean and standard deviation." In this way, it would be possible to identify individual gain more precisely. Stokes and Romer's argument should be reviewed in its entirety. Future work on the MSDS will need to consider these ideas plus the development of more extensive skill repertoire stimuli.

The Microcounseling Skill Discrimination Scale (MSDS) consists of forty-four interaction segments, with each segment made up of brief verbal exchanges initiated by the helpee and subsequently responded to by the helper. Half of the helper responses represent reflection of feeling, and the other half represent paraphrasing responses. Further, within the reflection of feeling and paraphrasing categories, half of the responses represent effective helper responses and the other half represent ineffective helper responses.

These forty-four interaction segments were derived from twenty-two helper statements representing a wide variety of

*University of Alberta, Edmonton. Now at University of Western Ontario, London, Ont. Doctor Lee is willing to share video segments with those who are interested in research on this instrument.

Microcounseling

helper problems, varying in emotional depth and content. The authors developed two alternative helping leads for each statement, one an effective response and the other an ineffective response. In this way, twenty-two helper statements were paired with twenty-two paraphrasing (11 effective, 11 ineffective) and twenty-two reflection of feeling (11 effective, 11 ineffective) responses, thus making up a total of forty-four interactions.

The above forty-four verbal interactions were then developed into two sets of videotaped segments, each of the sets differing only in the helper's *nonverbal* behaviors. In Set 1, the helper role-played the therapeutically effective nonverbal behaviors (i.e. eye contact, forward body-trunk lean, concerned facial expressions, .92 m distance from helpee), whereas in Set 2, the helper role-played the ineffective nonverbal behaviors (i.e. no eye contact, backward body-trunk lean, neutral facial expressions, 1.83 m distance from helpee).

The perceived quality or effectiveness of the helper responses in each segment may usually be rated on a five- or seven-point rating continuum. There may be two ways the MSDS can be scored. First, a discrimination score may be obtained by taking the sum of the absolute value of the deviations for each segment between a particular rater's rating and the mean value of a reference group of trained people in therapeutic communication. This type of discrimination score may be obtained from the two types of media by which these messages are presented; that is, from the typescript and from the videotaped segments of both Set 1 and Set 2.

The second type of discrimination a researcher might be interested in is the intraindividual differences in rating between Set 1 and Set 2. Recall that the two videotaped sets differ only in the helper's nonverbal behaviors, with Set 1 containing effective and Set 2 containing ineffective behaviors. Any reliable difference in rating between the two sets may then reflect the rater's sensitivity to nonverbal cues, while a zero difference would indicate insensitivity to the changes in nonverbal cues. So far, the research effort concerning the MSDS has been focused on the comparison between the untrained (high-school students and college undergraduates) and trained (graduate students in counseling and counselor educators) people in the helping relationship. The results can be summarized as follows: (1) regardless of the media by which the interaction segments were presented, both trained and untrained groups successfully discriminated between effective and ineffective verbal as well as nonverbal therapeutic messages. However, the trained raters, in contrast to the untrained raters, showed a greater *range* of discrimination by more negative ratings of the ineffective helper responses and more positive ratings of the effective responses; (2) nonverbal cues played a more critical role in reflection of feeling than in paraphrasing responses; (3) the discrimination score on the MSDS showed substantial correlation with other scales measuring discrimination in therapeutic message.

The MSDS can be used for various purposes in the training of therapeutic communications. For example, it may be used in assessing the counselor-trainee's ability to discriminate between effective and ineffective verbal and nonverbal messages. Also, the MSDS may be used in assessing the trainee's predeliction for rating of the therapeutic messages, that is, the trainee's relative weight given to verbal and nonverbal cues in the rating of therapeutic communication. The discrepancy score between two segments with identical verbal but different nonverbal cues would indicate the rater's reliance on the particular set of nonverbal cues in interpreting therapeutic messages.

The MSDS may also be a useful instrument in investigating the possible interaction of a set of nonverbal cues with a particular verbal message. Given the typescript MSDS interaction, for example, a researcher can easily vary any nonverbal cues of interest to him while keeping the verbal content constant. In the present form, only four nonverbal cues (eye contact, body-trunk lean, facial expression, distance) were varied between Sets 1 and 2. There is no reason why a researcher cannot develop further variations by including additional nonverbal cues such as vocal tone and gestures. Such variants of the MSDS might be a useful instrument in investigating not only the kinds of nonverbal cues that account for most of the therapeutic messages but also the setting under which maximum nonverbal by verbal message interaction occur. For example, given two identical verbal responses, which combination of a set of nonverbal cues would yield the greatest perception variances among raters?

Finally, it should be mentioned that by following the same procedures used by the present investigators, the MSDS may be expanded to other skills such as open-ended questions and summarizations.

MICROCOUNSELING SKILL DISCRIMINATION SCALE
D. Y. Lee, Allen E. Ivey, and Richard F. Haase

REFLECTION OF FEELING SEGMENTS   C = Client
Type-   H = Helper

script	Set 1		Set 2		Seg. #		
$\overline{X}$	SD	$\overline{X}$	SD	$\overline{X}$	SD		
5.3	1.7	3.6	1.3	2.5	1.1	1. C:	I know that the chances for the poor are very slim, and I want to get into something that will be a benefit to me and a credit to my own people. I'm not much of a classroom boy, and I want to know what. . . .what steps to take to prepare myself. My father is a minister, and I've been in the ministry for quite a few years. . . . If I can't be a good minister I don't want to be one at all. And yet I don't want to spend my life under the foot of somebody.
						H:	You feel that you should plan for a future that really gives you a lot of satisfaction and sense of contribution.
1.3	0.6	1.6	1.0	1.1	0.3	2. C:	I think I'm going to have to drop out of school. I can't go on any more. It's been bad since my

*Type-
script   Set 1   Set 2   Seg. #
$\overline{X}$ SD $\overline{X}$ SD $\overline{X}$ SD*

mother died last spring. There's just no need to continue having to put out the money any more.

H: You feel school is a pretty dull place. This may be true for many people.

4.4 2.0 4.1 1.8 1.9 0.6   3. C: I tried to be nice to my stepfather even if he does hate me. I try to be nice to him. It doesn't sink through his head. Like last night, I had a buddy over to the house. He didn't like my buddy. He was just hanging around watching TV, so he told me to go outside. He didn't want me to go back in.

H: You're terribly upset, confused, and disappointed. You wonder whether you're an important person to him.

6.3 0.5 2.9 1.8 1.5 0.7   4. C: So, like I said, he did go a little too far. I don't think he's basically a bad person. My mother always used to say that men would go as far as you'd let them, and I realize it was partly my fault too. If I had been surer of myself and told him to stop, he would have stopped. I don't understand why I didn't stop him.

Type-script		*Set 1*		*Set 2*		*Seg. #*
$\overline{X}$	SD	$\overline{X}$	SD	$\overline{X}$	SD	

H: Carol, you feel right now you're responsible, and you regret what happened. You're bewildered, curious, and somewhat confused too.

| 1.8 | 0.8 | 3.4 | 1.3 | 1.9 | 1.1 | 5. C: I really don't know what's wrong with me recently. I can't seem to concentrate on my courses or anything. . .and it's getting worse and worse. I'm falling further and further behind, and I just can't get caught up. And then I seem to fly off the handle. Why, just last weekend while I was home, my sister and I had a real battle. I don't know what my trouble is. |

H: You feel you can do the work if only you'd try harder. . . .Perhaps you know you shouldn't be a "loser" in this world of competition, but the fact that your grades are going down makes you more nervous.

| 5.4 | 1.8 | 2.5 | 0.9 | 1.9 | 1.1 | 6. C: I really like this guy an awful lot, and I've dated him five times. But. . .well. . .the trouble is he is Black. If my parents ever found out, it would be like a bomb explosion. They would pull me immediately out of school too. |

Type-						
script	Set 1		Set 2		Seg. #	
X SD	X	SD	X	SD		
						H: Carol, you're wondering which way you should go. It seems to be a choice between your boyfriend and your parents.
6.3 0.6	2.5	1.3	2.0	1.1	7.	C: (Shouting and pointing finger toward the helper) You *use* me just like all of the rest. You're just like the rest—you want something from me. That's all . . . I know what I'll do. I'll fail you. I'll lead you astray. You'll think I'm improving, but I'll fail. I'll be your failure case. *You* will be responsible.
						H: I sense you question the whole experience and all of my motives. Right now you're angry at me.
6.1 1.1	3.0	1.0	2.0	1.0	8.	C: I try to be nice to her. As I say, we have been roommates for six months, and we will be roommates for another two months, but . . .but as I say, she's awfully inconsiderate. . . .I just think a lot of what she does is on purpose, too. . .just to see what I'll do about it. I'm getting too upset.
						H: I hear you saying, Carol, you try awfully hard to get along, but nothing happens. You're really upset and troubled about it.

Type-script		*Set 1*		*Set 2*		*Seg. #*
$\overline{X}$	*SD*	$\overline{X}$	*SD*	$\overline{X}$	*SD*	

6.0 1.1 4.3 1.1 2.0 0.7 9. C: Well, I guess I *need* to be here. I don't know who else I could talk to about this. I feel awful, and I don't care if I die. My parents *can't* know, and I hope I never see Don again. . .*ever!* He was my boyfriend for two years, but I just don't care about it.

H: Carol, I sense you're terribly upset, depressed, and angry at Don. Many things are boiling up inside you right now.

2.3 1.7 3.8 2.3 2.4 1.0 10. C: It bothers me a lot. I don't think Cathy really loves me. I just don't think I'm *important* to her. She never tries to really understand how I feel about anything.

H: Cathy really bugs you, and you'd like to get back at her. . . .Perhaps you feel miserable because you have resentment against her but are unable to get back at her.

2.1 1.3 3.9 1.2 2.3 0.8 11. C: Well, you see, my parents met at King's College, and they've always had it in mind that I should go there. But. . .but I would rather. . . .

H: You know that King's College is a good school, but you don't want to be pushed away by your parents.

Type-script		*Set 1*		*Set 2*		*Seg. #*
$\overline{X}$	*SD*	$\overline{X}$	*SD*	$\overline{X}$	*SD*	

2.5 0.9 5.6 1.2 3.0 1.3   12. C: I just get so mad at my supervisor . . . .He's just a bunch of old sour grapes. Every time I come up with a creative idea, he knocks me down.

                                 H: Your supervisor is sometimes hard to work with. . .and, perhaps. . .it could also be true that you get angry at a lot of people, especially people in authority.

2.9 1.4 4.6 1.8 2.9 1.5   13. C: Well, Mrs. Smith sent me over here from the School of Music, and she said that I don't have the musical ability to keep on in the Music School. And she wants to know exactly what I'm suited for, but I know I'm. . .(pause). . .I know I still love music. But anyway she wants to be satisfied.

                                 H: You'd like to satisfy Mrs. Smith that music is a good field for you. Perhaps she thinks music is not for everybody.

6.7 0.4 5.6 1.6 3.4 1.3   14. C: So I did finally go to the doctor. And he said yes, I do need to have an operation. A major one, and right away. But I just *can't!* Since Jim and I are both in school now, there just isn't any money. And the baby is just five months. I'm awfully afraid, too.

Type-script		*Set 1*		*Set 2*		*Seg. #*
$\overline{X}$	SD	$\overline{X}$	SD	$\overline{X}$	SD	

H: You feel helpless, and scared . . . . and you're at a loss what to do. At this moment, you feel there isn't any way out.

6.2	0.8	4.0	2.1	1.9	1.1	15.

15. C: Well, (clears throat) I don't know how exactly to get started, but . . . .and my particular problem would be with my mother, and I . . . .well. . . .I'd like to be able to do something about it before I go home. I don't know how I can explain it, so maybe if you can . . . .I could start. . . (pause). . . I don't know where to start. I mean. . . .

H: A lot of things are going on right now. It's very difficult to get it out.

6.4	0.5	4.9	1.5	1.9	0.8	16.

16. C: Well, (sigh) I don't know. I'm sort of mixed up right now. I have been pre-med. And, well, I'm a senior now, but I have next year also, I've 19 hours to take, still, and I'm not sure now whether I want to become a doctor or not. I haven't been refused yet and I haven't been accepted either. And, well, I'm not sure in my own mind whether medicine would be the best thing for me.

Type-script		Set 1		Set 2		Seg. #	
X	SD	X	SD	$\overline{X}$	SD		
							H: I hear you saying, Dick, you're pretty confused about medicine as a future. A lot is going on right now.
2.9	1.9	6.1	1.1	3.4	1.2	17.	C: There's something about this town. It's an awfully *cold* town. Northerners are so blasted. . .uh! . . .indifferent. Oh I don't know, they're certainly not very warm or easy to know. I've been here since last summer, and I swear I don't know anybody at all.
							H: Northerners are really hostile to you, and they make you plenty angry. You seem to be raising a lot of questions about their customs and general ways of living.
1.5	1.1	5.5	1.1	3.8	1.5	18.	C: I just can't wait to get out of school . . . I'm so excited, I just want to get out and get started on my career. I know I'm going places!
							H: School is a real drag. You're bored and inefficient here. For many people, it may be painful to accept this, but I guess this is true.
1.4	0.6	4.9	1.4	2.8	1.0	19.	C: Henry loves me very much I think. You see the problem between us is really quite simple.

I don't love him. I only married him because I was supposed to marry. All my friends were getting married. I never felt any attraction. . . that is, I never found him attractive to me. Thank God we never had kids.

H: In some ways, you feel fond of and care for Henry. I suppose marital love is much more complicated than it appears to be. . . What I mean is. . .what I mean is that it could *change*. . .it's a kind of dynamic thing.

1.4 0.6 4.9 2.1 2.1 1.3 20. C: (In angry tone) We can't watch TV. She took a tube out so we couldn't watch it. When she wants to watch, she puts the tube back and makes sure we are all in bed before she watches it.

H: You like TV, especially the programs you miss.

1.3 0.9 4.0 1.6 3.5 1.7 21. C: Most of my problems started when I was at home because of my stepfather. He doesn't like us kids because he thinks we are higher class than he is. All he does is drink and drive around. He likes to kick us and beat us, and when we ask him for help, he turns his nose up. He doesn't

Type-script *Set 1* *Set 2* Seg. #
$\overline{X}$ *SD* $\overline{X}$ *SD* $\overline{X}$ *SD*

want to talk to us. . . .We don't have anybody to talk to. . . like a real father around the house.

H: You really care deeply for your stepfather, even though you wouldn't say this. Perhaps you might have a deep sympathy for him.

5.8 1.4 5.4 1.2 3.3 1.2 22. C: I thought maybe I could iron some of the wrinkles out. I'm always worrying about something —not big things, just little things. I can't get over the feeling that people are watching me. The way I worry about personal things and other things. . .When I see an ad in the paper, I worry about the things discussed in it although I know they aren't true.

H: I get several feelings from you, Dick. One is that you worry a good deal about unnecessary things, at the same time, the other is that you're concerned more about what you see as unnecessary worries.

PARAPHRASING SEGMENTS   C = Client
                                 H = Helper

| *Type-script* | | *Set 1* | | *Set 2* | | *Seg. #* |
| $\overline{X}$ | *SD* | $\overline{X}$ | *SD* | $\overline{X}$ | *SD* | |

5.0	1.8	4.0	1.8	3.0	1.0	1. C: Most of my problems started when I was at home because of my stepfather. He doesn't like us kids because he thinks we are higher class than he is. All he does is drink and drive around. He likes to kick us and beat us, and when we ask him for help, he turns his nose up. He doesn't want to talk to us. . . .We don't have anybody to talk to. . . .like a real father around the house.

H: Your stepfather wasn't there to talk to. I sense you want someone to listen to your problem, Dick.

1.4	0.9	1.8	1.0	1.3	0.4	2. C: I just get so mad at my supervisor . . .He's just a bunch of old sour grapes. Every time I come up with a creative idea, he knocks me down.

H: Oh, creative idea! It's very important for job performance.

6.3	0.9	2.3	1.2	2.3	1.0	3. C: Well, Mrs. Smith sent me over here from the School of Music, and she said that I don't have the musical ability to keep on in the

Music School. And she wants to know exactly what I'm suited for, but I know I'm. . .(pause). . .I know I still love music. But anyway she wants to be satisfied.

H: I hear you saying, Carol, your choice is to stay in music. A teacher has questioned your ability, and you're here because of her.

6.0 1.6 2.0 1.4 1.9 0.8 4. C: So, like I said, he did go a little too far. I don't think he's basically a bad person. My mother always used to say that men would go as far as you'd let them, and I realize it was partly my fault too. If I had been surer of myself and told him to stop, he would have stopped. I don't understand why I didn't stop him.

H: I hear you saying, Carol, you helped to create the situation for the excessive lovemaking but still can't understand why you didn't do more to change it.

1.1 0.3 2.1 1.1 1.9 0.9 5. C: (In angry tone) We can't watch TV. She took the tube out so we couldn't watch it. When she wants to watch, she puts the tube back and makes sure we are all in bed before she watches it.

Type-
script   Set 1   Set 2   Seg. #
$\overline{X}$ *SD* $\overline{X}$ *SD* $\overline{X}$ *SD*

		H: Watching TV with the tube gone does present a problem. Perhaps she had a bit of trouble with the tube in the past.

5.1 1.9 2.4 1.2 1.5 0.5   6. C: Well, I guess I *need* to be here. I don't know who else I could talk to about this. I feel awful, and I don't care if I die. My parents *can't* know, and I hope I never see Don again—*ever!* He was my boyfriend for two years, but I just don't care about it.

H: I hear you saying, Carol, that you have been going out with him for two years, but recently some things happened between you two which got you into a nightmare mess. . . .And yet, your relationship is not making any improvement.

6.3 0.9 1.1 0.3 1.3 0.6   7. C: I just can't wait to get out of school. . .I'm so excited, I just want to get out and get started on my career. I know I'm going places!

H: As I experience you, Dick, you see yourself as ready to get out and get started. You know you're heading for the top!

*Type-
script*   *Set 1*   *Set 2*   *Seg. #*
$\overline{X}$ SD $\overline{X}$ SD $\overline{X}$ SD

5.3 1.8   1.3 0.4   1.3 0.4   8. C: I tried to be nice to my stepfather even if he does hate me. I
try to be nice to him. It doesn't
sink through his head. Like last
night, I had a buddy over to the
house. He didn't like my buddy.
He was just hanging around
watching TV, so he told me to go
outside. He didn't want me to
go back in.

    H: Nothing you do works. He seems
to be the same, no matter what
you do.

5.3 1.5   3.3 1.4   2.3 1.0   9. C: Henry loves me very much I
think. You see the problem be-
tween us is really quite simple. I
don't love him. I only married
him because I was supposed to
marry. All my friends were getting married. I never felt any attraction. . .that is, I never found
him attractive to me. Thank
God we never had kids.

    H: Marriage for you was a duty,
something to be done because
most people do. I sense you're
about to make a decision.

1.8 1.0   1.6 1.0   1.4 1.0   10. C: I try to be nice to her. As I say,
we have been roommates for six
months, and we will be room-

mates for another two months,
but. . .but as I say, she's awfully
inconsiderate. . .I just think a lot
of what she does is on purpose,
too. . .just to see what I'll do
about it. I'm getting too upset.

H: Living with a roommate is often
a source of conflict. You know
. . .when two persons with different personalities become roommates. . . .six months may not be
long enough to get to know and
understand each other.

1.2 0.5 1.4 1.0 1.9 0.8 11. C: I thought maybe I could iron
some of the wrinkles out. I'm
always worrying about something
—not big things, just little things.
I can't get over the feeling that
people are watching me. The
way I worry about personal
things and other things. When I
see an ad in the paper, I worry
about the things discussed in it
although I know they aren't true.

H: Advertisements are often in error.
That's nothing unusual. As a
matter of fact, a lot of people
worry about the fact that there
are too many advertisements in
the paper. . . .We are bombarded
by these advertisements.

*Type-
script* *Set 1* *Set 2* *Seg. #*
X̄ SD X̄ SD X̄ SD

1.9 1.3 4.8 1.7 3.8 1.6 12. C: Well, you see, my parents met at King's College, and they've always had it in mind that I should go there. But. . .but. . .I would rather. . . .

H: Choosing a college is a decision for all students. . .You know all parents have some nostalgic feelings toward the schools that they attended a long time ago. It's nothing unusual.

2.1 1.1 4.9 1.0 4.4 0.9 13. C: It bothers me a lot. I don't think Cathy really loves me. I just don't think I'm *important* to her. She never tries to really understand how I feel about anything.

H: Understanding another person takes time, and perhaps that's the issue.

6.0 1.2 4.9 1.5 3.9 1.2 14. C: (Shouting and pointing a finger toward the helper) You *use* me just like all of the rest. You're just like the rest—you want something from me. That's all. I know what I'll do. I'll fail you. I'll lead you astray. You'll think I'm improving, but I'll fail. I'll be your failure case. *You'll* be responsible.

Type-
script   *Set 1*   *Set 2*   *Seg. #*
$\overline{X}$ SD $\overline{X}$ SD $\overline{X}$ SD

H: You expected me to be something different, but you learned that I'm one of the rest too. Failure on my part could be a reward for you.

5.5 1.9 6.3 0.7 5.0 1.2   15. C: I know that the chances for the poor are very slim, and I want to get into something that will be a benefit to me and a credit to my own people. I'm not much of a classroom boy, and I want to know what. . .what steps to take to prepare myself. My father is a minister, and I've been in the ministry for quite a few years. If I can't be a good minister I don't want to be one at all. And yet I don't want to spend my life under the foot of somebody.

H: I hear you saying you would like to get into something that will give you a lot of personal satisfaction as well as sense of contribution to the society. No single area strikes you at the moment.

6.1 1.0 5.0 0.9 4.3 0.8   16. C: I really don't know what's wrong with me recently. I can't seem to concentrate on my courses or anything. And it's getting worse and worse. I'm falling further and further behind, and I just

Type-script		*Set 1*		*Set 2*		*Seg. #*
$\overline{X}$	SD	$\overline{X}$	SD	$\overline{X}$	SD	

                                 can't get caught up. And then I seem to fly off the handle. Why, just last weekend while I was home, my sister and I had a real battle. I don't know what my trouble is.

H: You'd want to figure out what's been going on with you lately, Carol. You seem different to yourself.

1.5 0.6 3.8 1.7 3.0 1.5 17. C: Well, (sigh) I don't know. I'm sort of mixed up right now. I've been pre-med. And, well, I'm a senior now, but I have next year also. I've 19 hours to take, still, and I'm not sure now whether I want to become a doctor or not. I haven't been refused yet and I haven't been accepted either. And, well, I'm not sure in my own mind whether medicine would be the best thing for me.

H: Medicine is an important field to enter. Here you can help people. However, though, pre-med curriculum may be too dry and tedious even for serious students who want to be doctors.

2.8 1.8 4.9 1.4 4.9 1.4 18. C: So I did finally go to the doctor. And he said yes, I do need to have an operation. A major one,

| *Type-script* | | *Set 1* | | *Set 2* | | *Seg. #* |
| $\overline{X}$ | SD | $\overline{X}$ | SD | $\overline{X}$ | SD | |

and right away. But I just *can't!* Since Jim and I are both in school now, there just isn't any money. And the baby is just five months. I'm awfully afraid, too.

H: Who will take care of the baby is an important issue here. Especially when your baby is only five months old, it could be very difficult to leave her home and go to hospital.

| | | | | | | |
| 1.5 | 0.9 | 5.6 | 1.7 | 4.6 | 1.8 | 19. C: |

19. C: I really like this guy an awful lot, and I've dated him five times. But. . .well. . . the trouble is he is Black. If my parents ever found out, it would be like a bomb explosion. They would pull me immediately out of school too.

H: Parents have much to say in choosing a boyfriend. Perhaps this must be a shocking story even to your friends.

| | | | | | | |
| 1.7 | 0.9 | 6.0 | 0.5 | 5.4 | 1.6 | 20. C: |

20. C: There's something about this town. It's an awfully *cold* town. Northerners are so blasted. . .uh! . . .indifferent. Oh I don't know, they're certainly not very warm or easy to know. I've been here since last summer, and I swear I don't know anybody at all.

| *Type-script* | | *Set 1* | | *Set 2* | | *Seg. #* |
| X | SD | X | SD | X̄ | SD | |

H: This Northern town has been here for a long time. It's quite true that some people like this town and others don't. I would say it all depends upon individual tastes and preferences.

2.4	1.5	5.4	1.0	4.3	1.6	21.

C: Well, (clears throat) I don't know how exactly to get started, but. . . and my particular problem would be with my mother, and I . . .well. . .I'd like to be able to do something about it before I go home. I don't know how I can explain it, so maybe if you can . . . .I could start. . . (pause). . .I don't know where to start. I mean. . . .

H: So you have "interpersonal difficulties" with your mother . . . .or "generation conflict". . .maybe. . .

5.7	1.4	5.6	1.2	3.8	1.5	22.

C: I think I'm going to have to drop out of school. I can't go on any more. It's been bad since my mother died last spring. There's just no need to continue having to put out the money any more.

H: Since your mother's death, Dick, school doesn't make sense to you.

VIDEOTAPED SEGMENTS*

REFLECTION OF FEELING						PARAPHRASING					
Order	*V*	*NV*	$\overline{X}$		$\overline{X}$	*Order*	*V*	*NV*	$\overline{X}$		$\overline{X}$
1.	H	O	3.6	23.	X	2.5	1.	H	O	4.0	23.	X	3.0
2.	L	O	1.6	24.	X	1.1	2.	L	O	1.8	24.	X	1.3
3.	H	X	1.9	25.	O	4.1	3.	H	X	2.3	25.	O	2.3
4.	H	X	1.5	26.	O	2.9	4.	H	X	1.9	26.	O	2.0
5.	L	O	3.4	27.	X	1.9	5.	L	O	2.1	27.	X	1.9
6.	H	X	1.9	28.	O	2.5	6.	H	X	1.5	28.	O	2.4
7.	H	X	2.0	29.	O	2.5	7.	H	X	1.3	29.	O	1.1
8.	H	O	3.0	30.	X	2.0	8.	H	O	1.3	30.	X	1.3
9.	H	O	4.3	31.	X	2.0	9.	H	O	3.3	31.	X	2.3
10.	L	X	2.4	32.	O	3.8	10.	L	X	1.4	32.	O	1.6
11.	L	O	3.9	33.	X	2.3	11.	L	O	1.4	33.	X	1.9
12.	L	O	5.6	34.	X	3.0	12.	L	O	4.8	34.	X	3.8
13.	L	X	2.9	35.	O	4.6	13.	L	X	4.4	35.	O	4.9
14.	H	X	3.4	36.	O	5.6	14.	H	X	3.9	36.	O	4.9
15.	H	X	1.9	37.	O	4.0	15.	H	X	5.0	37.	O	6.3
16.	H	O	4.9	38.	X	1.9	16.	H	O	5.0	38.	X	4.3
17.	L	X	3.4	39.	O	6.1	17.	L	X	3.0	39.	O	3.8
18.	L	O	5.5	40.	X	3.8	18.	L	O	4.9	40.	X	4.9
19.	L	O	4.9	41.	X	2.8	19.	L	O	5.6	41.	X	4.6
20.	L	X	2.1	42.	O	4.9	20.	L	X	5.4	42.	O	6.0
21.	L	X	3.5	43.	O	4.0	21.	L	X	4.3	43.	O	5.4
22.	H	O	5.4	44.	X	3.3	22.	H	O	5.6	44.	X	3.8

    ↖——pair——↗   ↖——pair——↗

*Abbreviations

    V = Verbal content; H = High verbal content; L = Low verbal content

    NV = Nonverbal component; O = Effective nonverbal component:

    X = Ineffective nonverbal component.

    The above means are based on 7-point rating continuum, with 7 indicating positive (effective) and 1 indicating negative (ineffective) directions.

Notes

1. H indicates high level, and L indicates low level of the helper's *verbal* content.
2. O indicates effective (Set 1) and X indicates ineffective (Set 2) *nonverbal* behaviors of the helper.
3. Each paired segment, e.g. Segment #1 and #23, Segment #2 and #24, Segment #22 and #44, contains *identical* helpee and helper verbal statements but different *nonverbal* components. Thus, any difference in rating between paired segments for a rater may indicate the degree of rater's sensitivity to changes in nonverbal components. For example, zero difference might indicate that the rater made judgment exclusively on the basis of verbal component while oblivious to nonverbal components.
4. Mean is based on the rating of eight faculty members in Counselor Education. For further data see Lee, Zingle, Patterson, Ivey, and Haase (1976).

THE IVEY TAXONOMY

The Ivey Taxonomy (IT)—or variations of the same theme—is coming to be the most heavily used format for microtraining research. It seems logical to test for the presence or absence of specific behavior if that is what is being taught. If one wants to teach people how to tune in with another person's feelings, then it seems appropriate to count the number of reflections of feelings (or questions associated with feelings) pre-and posttraining.

The scoring and typescript of the interview in Appendix III provide clear examples of how the interview may be scored and rated for both verbal and nonverbal dimensions. Portions of the IT have been used in numerous studies with consistent success (cf. Moreland, Ivey, and Phillips, 1973; Sherrard, 1973; Chadbourne, 1975; Crowley and Ivey, 1970, 1976; Gluckstern, 1972, 1973; Hearn, 1976; Lee, Zingle, Patterson, Ivey, and Haase, 1976). Interrater reliabilities have ranged fairly widely depending on the degree of systematic training employed in teaching raters specific dimensions of the skills. Chadbourne (1975), for example, rated over 5000 statements from typescripts, and two independent raters reached 90.3 percent agreement overall. In this case, teachers were rated, and categories which occurred infrequently tended to have low interrater reliabilities, e.g. reflection of feeling occurred less than 0.10 percent of the leads. Moreland, Ivey, and Phillips (1973), on the other hand, working with a more sophisticated medical student population, had 100 percent interrater agreement in the same category. Sherrard (1973) added extra categories and used raters who had difficulty adapting to the behavioral approach of the IT. The reliabilities of his categories ranged from 53.8 percent for reflection of feeling (which in other studies usually presents the highest interrater reliability) to 93.8 percent for directions. Overall interrater agreement, however, was a satisfactory .877. Implications to be drawn from these data are the following:

1. Raters should receive clear instructions as to the skills being rated. Ideally, they should be able to engage in the skills themselves and demonstrate the competencies of microtraining.
2. If a single category is absent or appears infrequently, collapse categories or set up a general category of "other."
3. If rating tapes directly, stop the tape after each statement until all raters have made their determinations. Ideally, tapes should be presented at different times to independent raters who have met criterion levels of reliability before the study actually begins.

At this point, the qualitative conditions as defined within microtraining need extensive research. Clinical work in training and workshops suggests that high reliability should be possible with the relatively behavioral definitions of qualitative conditions suggested. Fortunately, the extensive work on these dimensions by Carkhuff (1969a,b) and many others provides a good foundation justifying the inclusion of these dimensions in the IT.

The discussion of the IT has thus far focused on behavior of the helper. *The most important advantage of the IT is that the same dimensions used to score helper behavior can also be used to score helpee behavior.* The IT thus provides a process measure for the effectiveness of alternative approaches to helping. The beginning client in therapy may topic jump frequently, have poor eye contact patterns, have difficulty making self-referent statements, and talk completely in the past tense or worry constantly about the future.   If helping is effective, this same client may be expected to engage in culturally appropriate verbal and nonverbal behavior, increase the number of statements about the self, talk in the present tense about personal feelings, and start reinterpreting or renaming his or her life experience.   In short, the effective or culturally experienced helpee may be expected to appear more and more like the effective helper.

While research on this point needs to be conducted, it is anticipated that the verbal and nonverbal sentence structure of the helper and helpee will become more similar through the course of a lengthy series of helping sessions.   Further, the IT makes possible the comparison of alternative approaches to helping.   It is expected that differential approaches will be differentially effective in achieving different ends.   One single outcome criterion for effective therapy or helping is perhaps naive—different approaches to helping and personal growth have differing views of what they would have people become.   At the same time, there is a common core to the helping process and that core can be identified more precisely through the IT and future extensions and modifications of the taxonomy.   The IT is not a closed system; it has changed and expanded several times in the past few years.   As the full dimensions of what constitutes cultural expertise become more evident, the IT will change and develop in new directions.

Examination of Chapters 4 through 7 will give preliminary indications of systematic methods for scoring interviews via the IT.   More detailed suggestions are found in Appendix III and in the *Basic Attending* and *Basic Influencing Skills* series (Ivey and Gluckstern, 1974a,b; 1976a,b) .

R. G. MATARAZZO THERAPIST ERROR CHECKLIST

A frequent research tool in microtraining has been R.G. Matarazzo's* "Check List of Therapist Behavior."   A special advantage

*R.G. Matarazzo is Professor of Medical Psychology, University of Oregon Health Sciences Center, Portland, Oregon.

of this instrument is that it was designed to measure therapy in general and was not conceived to measure any special orientation to helping. The categories are broad, yet reasonable interrater agreement seems to occur time and time again. Studies by Moreland, Ivey, and Phillips (1973), Hearn (1976), Matarazzo, Wiens, and Saslow (1966), and Matarazzo, Phillips, Wiens, and Saslow (1965) have all demonstrated the utility of this instrument. Percentage of interrater agreement on the instrument has ranged from 71 percent to 94 percent. Matarazzo (1971) comments that effective training in psychotherapeutic skills reduces errors, especially in faulty communication, but it is more difficult to reduce students' errors in terms of faulty role definition, that is, students who tend to be overly authoritarian or overly "social" in their helping roles. The latter point suggests some fruitful areas for microtraining research. See Matarazzo (1971) for a discussion of the process of counselor/therapist training and a listing of some studies using the Therapist Error Checklist.

R. G. MATARAZZO CHECK LIST OF THERAPIST BEHAVIOR
(Rev. 1976)

Therapist_____

Patient_____

General Quality of Statement

Good statement of question.

Fair statement—says generally right thing but partly ineffectual, embodying at least one error listed below, and no more than two.

Poor statement—embodies serious error, or multiple errors.

===

(Check as many as are applicable)

I. *Errors in Focus*

   Relevance

   Narrow focus or focus on irrelevant material

   Focus on symptoms in nonproductive manner

   Irrelevant or unprofessional statement, question, or humor

   Insufficient Direction

   Neglects to label or explore important content

   Allows sidetrack

   Fails to structure sufficiently—patient rambles

   Noncontributory statement, question, or behavior

   Allows problem behaviors to continue too long

   Fails to Respond Sensitively

   Stops exploration (changes topic, lack of response, etc.)

   Inaccurate reflection or question indicating lack of understanding of what patient has said

Asks patient own interpretation prematurely or other question to which he could not be expected to know the answer

II. *Faulty role definition—authoritarian or social*

Authoritarian

Argues—is authoritarian or dogmatic

Criticizes, belittles patient—condescending

Cross-examines patient (challenging)

Participates in criticism of another professional person

Gives information prematurely or advice inappropriately

Social

Makes personal reference or gives opinion inappropriately, prematurely, or seemingly for personal enhancement

Gives reassurance or agreement where inappropriate (when negative consequence to patient might result, when patient presses for substantiation of view *prior* to exploration)

Flatters patient

Laughter when inappropriate

III. *Faulty Facilitation of Communication*

Guesses facts (asking yes or no)

Asks yes, no, or brief answer question

Interrupts

Asks multiple questions in one comment

Awkwardness—abrupt

Interrupts silence while patient still appears to be trying to say something

Allows silence too long (patient appears embarrassed; therapist appears not to know what to say, patient appears to be through with communication)

Structures too much, makes long speech

THE CARKHUFF SCALE FOR EMPATHIC UNDERSTANDING

One of the most widely used scales in helping research is that provided by Carkhuff (1969b).* The five-point scale of empathic understanding is used as a baseline for many types of research. Due to the scale's wide use, we will not go into its validation and reliability but refer the reader to Carkhuff's text. There are, of course, some arguments about the scale. For example, Chinsky and Rappaport (1970) suggest that voice quality or other non-obtrusive variables may be critical in findings with the scale and suggest that accurate empathy ratings often lack independence. On the other hand, Beutler, Johnson, Neville, and Workman (1973) provide data suggesting that the present method of establishing subjective empathy is effective. It is our opinion that this widely used scale is a most valuable instrument for research.

Zimmer and Park (1967) and Zimmer and Anderson (1968) conducted factor analytic studies of empathy, and the resultant factors were closely allied to the microtraining skills discussed in this book. There does appear to be a close relationship between effective use of microtraining skills and accurate empathy. It may be noted that level 1 responses are defined in a manner similar to those lacking attending skills. Level 3 responses seem to be close to effective attending skills in that helper and helpee seem to have interchangeable responses. To reach levels 4 and 5, however, the helper must *add* to the communication. While this may be done with very effective attending skills, it is our belief that the influencing dimensions such as self-disclosure and interpretation are surer routes toward the highest levels of communication. (However, poor use of influencing skills will destroy even the best of attending skills.)

A special value of using non-microcounseling developed instrumentation is that skill outcome measures are not *yoked* to training procedures. The empathic understanding scale provides a good unyoked measure of helping outcome. However, there are those who argue that testing for outcome should relate to the treatment instituted. Those from a behavioral stance suggest that testing of

---

*Robert R. Carkhuff is Chairman of the Board, Carkhuff Institute of Human Technology, Pelham, Massachusetts.

behavior change should be tied directly to the helping intervention. In our opinion, both yoked and unyoked measures have value in helping research.

Readers are also urged to obtain Carkhuff's (1969a,b) statement for similar five-point scales for respect, concreteness, and other qualitative dimensions. Carkhuff Associates, Box 228, Amherst, Massachusetts, 01002, can provide additional and more recent information.

SCALE 1

EMPATHIC UNDERSTANDING IN INTERPERSONAL PROCESSES: A SCALE FOR MEASUREMENT*†

Level 1

The verbal and behavioral expressions of the first person either *do not attend to* or *detract significantly* from the verbal and behavioral expressions of the second person(s) in that they communicate significantly less of the second person's feelings than the second person has communicated himself.

EXAMPLES: The first person communicates no awareness of even the most obvious, expressed surface feelings of the

---

*This scale is derived in part from "A Scale for the Measurement of Accurate Empathy," which has been validated in extensive process and outcome research on counseling and psychotherapy (summarized in Truax & Carkhuff, 1967), and in part from an earlier version that had been validated in extensive process and outcome research on counseling and psychotherapy (summarized in Carkhuff, 1968; Carkhuff & Berenson, 1967). In addition, similar measures of similar constructs have received extensive support in the literature of counseling and therapy and education. The present scale was written to apply to all interpersonal processes and represents a systematic attempt to reduce ambiguity and increase reliability. In the process many important delineations and additions have been made, including, in particular, the change to a systematic focus upon the additive, subtractive, or interchangeable aspects of the levels of communication of understanding. For comparative purposes, level 1 of the present scale is approximately equal to stage 1 of the Truax scale. The remaining levels are approximately correspondent: level 2 and stages 2 and 3 of the earlier version; level 3 and stages 4 and 5; level 4 and stages 6 and 7; level 5 and stages 8 and 9. The levels of the present scale are approximately equal to the levels of the earlier version of this scale.

†From *Helping and Human Relations: A Primer for Lay and Professional Helpers*, Vol. II by Robert R. Carkhuff. Copyright © 1969 by Holt, Rinehart, and Winston, Inc. Reprinted by permission of Holt, Rinehart, and Winston.

second person. The first person may be bored or un-
interested or simply operating from a preconceived
frame of reference which totally excludes that of the
other person(s) .

In summary, the first person does everything but express that
he is listening, understanding, or being sensitive to even the feelings of the other person in such a way as to detract significantly
from the communications of the second person.

Level 2

While the first person responds to the expressed feelings of the
second person(s) , he does so in such a way that he *subtracts notice-
able affect from the communications* of the second person.

EXAMPLES: The first person may communicate some awareness of
obvious surface feelings of the second person, but his
communications drain off a level of the affect and
distort the level of meaning. The first person may
communicate his own ideas of what may be going on,
but these are not congruent with the expressions of
the second person.

In summary, the first person tends to respond to other than
what the second person is expressing or indicating.

Level 3

The expressions of the first person in response to the expressed
feelings of the second person(s) are essentially *interchangeable*
with those of the second person in that they express essentially the
same affect and meaning.

EXAMPLE: The first person responds with accurate understanding
of the surface feelings of the second person but may
not respond to or may misinterpret the deeper feelings.

In summary, the first person is responding so as to neither sub-
tract from nor add to the expressions of the second person; but he
does not respond accurately to how that person really feels be-
neath the surface feelings. Level 3 constitutes the minimal level
of facilitative interpersonal functioning.

Level 4

The responses of the first person add noticeably to the expressions of the second person(s) in such a way as to express feelings a level deeper than the second person was able to express himself.

EXAMPLE: The facilitator communicates his understanding of the expressions of the second person at a level deeper than they were expressed, and thus enables the second person to experience and/or express feelings he was unable to express previously.

In summary, the facilitator's responses add deeper feeling and meaning to the expressions of the second person.

Level 5

The first person's responses add significantly to the feeling and meaning of the expressions of the second person(s) in such a way as to (1) accurately express feelings levels below what the person himself was able to express or (2) in the event of ongoing deep self-exploration on the second person's part, to be fully with him in his deepest moments.

EXAMPLES: The facilitator responds with accuracy to all of the person's deeper as well as surface feelings. He is "together" with the second person or "tuned in" on his wavelength. The facilitator and the other person might proceed together to explore previously unexplored areas of human existence.

In summary, the facilitator is responding with a full awareness of who the other person is and a comprehensive and accurate empathic understanding of his deepest feelings.

THE AFFECTIVE SENSITIVITY SCALE
and
COUNSELOR VERBAL RESPONSE SCALE

NORMAN KAGAN*

Two other scales suitable for measuring unyoked outcomes of microtraining research are discussed below. Developed by Norman Kagan, they have demonstrated usefulness for both teaching and research purposes. The remainder of this section, written by Norman Kagan, describes the nature and function of these scales.

The Affective Sensitivity Scale consists of two forms (D and E) and is contained on two 16mm motion picture films. The scale consists of a series of personal encounters between two or more persons taken from actual interpersonal interactions. These encounters range from discussion between friends, couples, teachers, and students to physician-patient, counseling, and psychotherapeutic interactions. Each form consists of approximately thirty scenes, ranging in time from eight seconds to two minutes. After witnessing each scene, the examinee answers one or more multiple choice items. These items ask the examinee to select the responses which are most likely to be what one of the participants in the encounter is really saying to him or herself at the end of the scene. As was done in the development of the earlier version of the scale (which has been used extensively over the last dozen years), items were generated based on actual IPR recall responses of the participants as well as from ratings by people recognized as highly empathic. The new scale, unlike the old one, has excellent visual quality and, with the exception of one brief scene, excellent audio quality, despite being recordings of actual encounters.

In addition to total scale score, the wide range of interactions now permits the following profile to be constructed for each examinee: client sensitivity, interviewer sensitivity, child sensitivity, male sensitivity, female sensitivity, sensitivity in educational settings, health care settings, informal settings, group settings,

*Norman Kagan is Professor, Department of Counseling, Personnel, Services and Educational Psychology and Department of Psychiatry, Office of Medical Education Research, Michigan State University.

counseling settings, and psychotherapy settings.

The scale is machine scorable. It is available for purchase only from Mason Media, Box C, Mason, Michigan, 48854.

The Counselor Verbal Response Scale grew out of our need to develop a scheme for evaluating pre-to-post changes in interpersonal behavior. It was essential that there be high interjudge reliability, that the behaviors rated not be tied to any one counseling theory, and that the scale differentiate among known groups of effective and ineffective counselors and therapists. The method requires that a judge listen to an audio- or videotape interaction. Each client statement is listened to, and then the counselor's response is rated on each of the four dimensions of the scale. After twenty counselor responses have been dichotomized on each dimension, totals are then obtained. There is a maximum score of 20, and a minimum score of 0 is possible for each of the four dimensions.

In our first application of the CVRS, coefficients have averaged tape interjudge reliability of .84, 80, 79, .68, and 79. Our subsequent refining of the scale definitions and methods of training judges has resulted in a procedure which typically results in interjudge reliability of .85 and higher. The scale was found to significantly differentiate between trained and untrained counselors, between Master's level and Ph.D. level therapists, and also among trained and untrained physicians, nurses, corrections workers, teachers, and paraprofessional mental health workers. Research discussing this instrument may be found in Kagan (1975b), Werner and Schneider (1974), Kagan and Schauble (1969), and Danish and Brodsky (1970).

Incidentally, the dimensions are not used by effective counselors and therapists as a way of responding to every client statement. The specific elements are always included in the sessions of competent people but are rarely or never included in the interview behavior of counselors and therapists who are not considered competent by their peers or their clients. The elements then appear to be specific behavior which are within the *repertoire* of competent people but not within the repertoire of the less competent. In one sense they might be thought of as "symptoms" of effectiveness rather than core conditions. The scale items themselves are now taught to students as one of our training experiences and, in fact, the film used for such training is also an effective way of training judges. A fifty-four-minute film, "Elements of Facilitating Communication," defines the behaviors and provides simulated practice for students or prospective raters in using the dimensions. Whether one uses the film or not, it is important that each judge fully understands the dimensions and that high interjudge reliability is obtained prior to judge's rating experimental data. Users are urged to develop local norms.

Judges' training can be achieved through procedures described in the instructor's manual which accompanies the IPR film series. The manual is entitled "Interpersonal Process Recall—A Method of Influencing Human Interaction" and can be obtained through N. Kagan, 434 Erickson Hall, Michigan State University, East Lansing, Michigan, 48824, for $12.50. The film "Elements of Facilitating Communication" is available through the Multimedia Department of the American Personnel and Guidance Association, 1607 New Hampshire Ave., NW, Washington, D.C., 20009.

Exploratory responses to a person are those which encourage that person to stay deeply involved in the communication and yet at the same time give the person maximum freedom and latitude in what his or her next response will be. The response is such that the person is encouraged to become an active participant in the communication rather than a passive receiver of advice and knowledge. An exploratory response encourages the other person to explore further, to go more deeply, to expand, to elaborate, and also to assume a great deal of responsibility for the direction and content of the next statement. Exploratory responses indicate a willingness to have our comments modified or even rejected. Exploratory responses tend to establish an egalitarian partnership. Nonexploratory responses, even though they may be very gentle and well meaning, give the other person little opportunity to explore, to expand, or to express self freely. Nonexploratory responses usually take the form of true-false questions or multiple choice items. Nonexploratory responses frequently are characterized also by the counselor placing him or herself above the other person, establishing however gently an authoritarian leadership quality.

Listening responses are those which serve to "check out" the interviewer's understanding of what the other person has said. This is often a simple paraphrasing, but where the counselor did not understand or was confused, listening responses are those which also seek clarification from the other. Listening responses, then, are those which serve either to have the other clarify statements which were not understood or to have the other confirm the counselor's perceptions. What is communicated is an attempt to fully understand the other person's message. Nonlistening responses are those which do not check out the counselor's understanding, which may jump to erroneous conclusions, and which rely on unstated assumptions. Affective responses are those which focus and draw attention to the feelings of the other person. Affective responses usually focus on attitudes, fears, doubts, values—the music that goes along with the words. Affective responses are ones designed to help the other label, acknowledge, and talk about feelings. Cognitive responses focus on the facts, the data, the actual words. Cognitive responses are usually those which could have been made by reading a typescript of the other person's statements.

Honest labeling is being extremely frank but not punitive. Honest labeling responses are those which one might, for instance, say to a colleague about the client. Honest labeling responses typically are not those offered in social communications. They often seem "risky." Honest labeling responses are designed to communicate to the other person a willingness to deal directly and squarely with what was heard and to encourage the other person to be as honest as possible in labeling his or her own perceptions, attitudes, and reactions. Honest labeling may involve very intense, embarassing, or socially taboo themes. Honest labeling responses are often focused on the here and now relationship between the counselor and the client. Distorting responses, although they technically may deal with feelings, are often "formal and proper" and tend to tone down and cool off the other person's response. Avoiding and distorting responses often tend to communi-

Counselor Verbal Response Scale Rating Sheet

NORMAN KAGAN

	EXPLORATORY	NONEXPLORATORY	LISTENING	NONLISTENING	AFFECTIVE	COGNITIVE	HONEST LABELING	DISTORTING
1.								
2.								
3.								
4.								
5.								
6.								
7.								
8.								
9.								
10.								
11.								
12.								
13.								
14.								
15.								
16.								
17.								
18.								
19.								
20.								

cate to the other that the message was heard but avoided, that the
counselor is unwilling to deal with the things which both participants know are being said.

Each counselor statement is rated on each dimension until
twenty counselor responses have been dichotomized on each dimension (exploratory/nonexploratory, listening/nonlistening, af-
fective/cognitive, honest labeling/overweighting).

A SCALE FOR MEASUREMENT OF ADULT-CHILD INTERACTION

Thus far, all scales in this series have been primarily concerned
with the measurement of adult-adult interactional measures. It
seems only appropriate that an interesting scale by Stover, Guerney, and O'Connell (1971) be briefly summarized and suggested as
an important alternative type of measurement for empathy and related constructs. The three authors have developed a series of
scales: "Communication of Acceptance," "Allowing the Child
Self-Direction," and "Involvement." All scales are established
with five points and have well-established reliability (depending
on coder pair ranging from .48 to .98, but with most reliabilities
in the .90s).

Only one scale will be reviewed here, and the readers are urged
to examine the article cited above for further details. The scale
"Communication of Acceptance" may be described as follows for
evaluating parent-child communication:

1. *Verbal recognition and acceptance of feelings:* You're proud of how
   you fixed that; That makes you feel good. . .
2. *Verbal recognition and acceptance of behavior only:* You got it that
   time . . . You're hitting the mother doll.
3. *Social conversation or no conversation:* I'm not so good at building
   toys . . . These are nice toys.
4. *Slight or moderate verbal criticism stated or strongly implied:* That's
   cheating . . . No, not that way.
5. *Verbal criticism; argumentative, preaching:* It's not nice to feel that
   way; You're nasty . . .

(Stover, Guerney, and O'Connell, 1971, p. 262.)

The parallels between this scale and some of those described
earlier should be apparent. However, the import of making scales

relevant to the population studied should also be evident. Other scales described in this article focus on the parent's ability to allow a child to take the lead as opposed to forcing the child to follow the parent's directions and on the parent's degree of involvement with the child (ranging from being fully observant and giving high attention to completely withdrawing from or ignoring the child).

This conceptual frame for evaluating interaction is also elaborated in Guerney, Stover, and DeMeritt (1968), where an important measure of empathy in parent-child interaction is provided. This seven-point scale ranges from "highest level of empathic communication" through "open rejection." Interrater reliability ratings of .80 are reported, and validity data discussed in the article recommend its practicality and usability.

Finally, we would cite the array of interesting instruments prominent in Guerney's new book (1977) which focuses on husband-and-wife communication as well as family interaction. The appendix of this book provides data on the "Primary Communication Inventory," "Marital Communication Inventory," "Marital Adjustment Test," "Family Life Questionnaire," "Interpersonal Relationship Scale," "Handling Problems Change Scale," "Satisfaction Change Scale," "Relationship Change Scale," "Verbal Interaction Task," "Acceptance of Others Scale," "Self Feeling Awareness Scale," and "Relationship Questionnaire." Each of these scales shows promise for delineating specific aspects of effective communication and is closely allied to the straightforward family education techniques advocated by Guerney and his colleagues.

Appendix V

SAMPLES OF BRIEF MICROTRAINING
SKILL MANUALS*

BASIC TO ANY WORKSHOP or individual training in microcounseling is the brief one- to three-page manual which attempts to distill the essence of a skill into a short description. Sample manuals from the over twenty included in *Basic Attending Skills* and *Basic Influencing Skills* are presented here. These manuals were developed for beginning helpers and paraprofessionals. Those with reading difficulties will need simpler language, and Bradley (1975b) went so far as to put the basic concepts on videotape for inner-city youth who had reading problems. When working with teenagers or parents or medical students, special language appropriate to each group helps clarify the concepts.

The manuals for attending behavior are presented in Appendix I and are, of course, the most widely used and studied. The following manual, "Open Invitation to Talk," illustrates the importance of open and closed questions.

OPEN INVITATION TO TALK

The client comes into an interview with something that he/she feels is a problem. The initial task of the interviewer is to stay out of the interviewee's way so as to find out how the client sees his/her situation. Most useful in determining this is the technique of providing limited structure through the use of an open invitation to talk.

---

*The manual "Open Invitation to Talk" is taken from the First Edition of *Microcounseling*. The remainder of the manuals presented here are taken from *Basic Attending Skills* and *Basic Influencing Skills*.

Open: Could you tell me a little bit about your marriage?
or
How did you feel about that?
Closed: Are you married? Do you get along with your wife/husband?

It may be observed that the open comments provide room for the client to express his/her real self without the imposed categories of the interviewer. An open comment allows the client an opportunity to explore himself/herself with the support of the interviewer. A closed invitation to talk, on the other hand, often emphasizes factual content as opposed to feelings, demonstrates a lack of interest in what the client has to say, and frequently attacks or puts the client in his/her place. Closed questions can usually be answered in a few words or with a yes or no.

Crucial to open-ended questions is the concept of who is to lead the interview. While the interviewer does ask questions while using this skill, the questions are centered around concerns of the client rather than around concerns of the interviewer for the client. Questions should be designed to help the client clarify his/her own problems rather than provide information for the interviewer. A typical problem with closed questions is that the interviewer leads the client to topics of interest to the interviewer only. Too often an interviewer projects his/her own theoretical orientation onto the information he/she is trying to gather or imposes artificial structure too early. If the interviewer relies on closed questions to structure the interview, he/she is often forced to concentrate so hard on thinking up the next question that he/she fails to listen to and attend to the client.

Open invitations to talk are extremely useful in a number of different situations. The following are some examples:

1. They help begin an interview. (What would you like to talk about today? How have things been since the last time we talked together?)
2. They help get the interviewee to elaborate on a point. (Could you tell me more about that? How did you feel when that happened?)
3. They help elicit examples of specific behavior so that the

interviewer is better able to understand what the interviewee is describing.   (Will you give me a specific example?
What do you do when you get "depressed"?   What do you
mean when you say your father is hard to get along with?)
4. They help focus the client's attention on his/her feelings.
(What are you feeling as you're telling me this?   How did
you feel then?)

Go through the examples above again and give your supervisor
some possible closed-ended questions in each case above.   Then
change your closed questions to open questions.

A different type of manual is represented by Reflection of
Feelings.   Here, a quick definition is presented and then followed
by specific exercises which participants may use in individual or
small-group practice sessions.

REFLECTION OF FEELINGS

Let us begin with a very simple but important definition of responding to feeling as given in the *Microcounseling* text:

> Attending behavior could be described as being with the client
> physically and verbally. The construct of reflection of feeling . . . is
> often viewed as related to empathy or being with the client. It could also
> be described as *selective attention to the feeling* or emotional aspects of
> the client's expressions. By selectively attending and reflecting ob-
> served feeling states to the client, the interviewer is consciously rein-
> forcing emotional states while simultaneously extinguishing cognitive
> aspects by ignoring them.

Responding to feeling, then, may be specifically defined as tuning
out the cognitive aspects of a helpee's communication and re-
sponding only to the underlying emotional or feeling aspects.

How can you help others to express the central concerns they
are experiencing?   One excellent way is to listen for and respond
to the feelings of the client.   Try communicating "I can accurately sense the world as you are feeling and perceiving it," and
you can facilitate the client's movement toward more complete
self-awareness and self-understanding.

More specifically, being alert and responding to the *feeling* being expressed rather than attending solely to the *content* and decision issues is what is important in this skill. *What* the client is saying is the *content* portion of the message. One must also listen to *how* the client gives a message. For example, the client may speak more quickly when communicating enthusiasm, more slowly when communicating discouragement, etc. It is this *feeling* portion of the communication to which you are to pay attention.

In the example below, you will have an opportunity to select alternatives which indicate that you understand the client's feelings and internal emotions, the alternative which if spoken to the client would most likely evoke a response of "That's right!" Label each response as a question, paraphrase, minimal encourage, or response to feeling.

Example 1

Helpee: So I'm wondering if you can help me find a new major ... (pause) I suppose if I did find one, I'd just bungle things again ...

Helper: a. You really want to find another major, but you're not sure it would work out.

b. You feel that it's pretty futile to try again.

c. You'd just bungle things again ...

d. What majors are you considering?

e. Why do you feel that way?

Example 2

Helpee: What do you think I ought to do—run away, get a divorce, or just give in and take it?

Helper: a. There just doesn't seem to be any way out!

b. (Noting tears) You feel really low about your chances to resolve this right now.

c. Are you thinking seriously of running away?

d. Silence

e. You're really uptight about the marriage. It's really getting to you.

Example 3

Helpee: You know, it's funny, but when I talk to you, I just feel shaky. It's the silliest thing! Why should I do that?

Helper: a. Are you anxious in many situations?
            b. You wonder why you do this.
            c. Right now you feel very shaky talking to me; it
               confuses you to feel that way.
            d. Could you share with me a little more about how
               you feel toward me?
            e. You're laughing as you tell me you feel shaky and
               scared.

In the first example, *b* is the only reflection of feeling. Helper
lead *a* is a reasonably good paraphrase but ignores the underlying
emotional aspects of the helpee's communication. *C* may be
identified as a minimal encourage which has some feeling components in it, as the word *bungle* is affectively loaded. Helper
lead *d* is a question, of course, and tends to be a topic jump leading the helpee away from self-exploration into a new area.
Finally, *e* is another question which does partially respond to feeling, but the "why" dimensions tend to put the helpee on the spot
with a very difficult question to answer at this point.

Example 2 has two possible reflections of feeling—*b* and *e*.
Either could be appropriate. *B* tends to move the helpee to more
depth but may tend to cause muddling around in a very discouraging area. Despite this, we would prefer response *b* because the
counselor can later bring in more supportive and helpful data
after the full dimensions of feeling have been explored. The
temptation in moments like this is to comfort, give sympathy, and
provide answers. We believe it best to allow full emotional expression before moving on. Response *a,* a paraphrase, might very
well be as successful as the reflection of feeling, as it seems to catch
the essence of the client's state of being. *C* by outward appear-
ances would be a most ineffective question, unless the context
warrants it. The minimal encourager of silence might be very
effective but of course is not a reflection of feeling.

The final example has two reflections of feeling, *c* and *e*. *C* has
the advantage of here and now immediacy, *e* the advantage of
pointing out the mixed messages of feelings. Question *a* may be
a good approach *if* the feelings have already been explored and
are known and acknowledged; it does respond to emotion and give

the client room to explore. It would be unwise, however, if this is new information. Question *d* has immediacy and gives the client room to explore emotion, thus underlining the fact that one need not stick exclusively to reflections to help others express their emotions. Questions, however, still do not fully acknowledge the experience of the helpee. *B* impresses us as a rather minimal, minimal encourage.

In the space below, develop some of your own examples, try out some of your own responses, identify the reasons for your responses.

_____

_____

_____

_____

_____

Summary

In reflecting feelings, the following steps are most essential:

1. The feeling must be labeled. This may be through the actual words used by the helpee or through observation of nonverbal communication.

2. The helper uses a sentence stem such as "You seem to feel . . . ," "Sounds like you feel . . . ," "I sense you're . . ." and adds the labeled emotion.

3. A context may be added for additional clarification: "You seem to feel _____ when _____."

4. Reflections of feelings are most often useful if immediate here and now feelings in the interview are labeled and worked through.

Other manuals in the *Basic Attending Skills* series include advanced questions, paraphrasing, paraphrasing for decision making, reflection of complex ambivalent emotions, summarization, and integration of skills.

Following is the directions manual from *Basic Influencing Skills*. It may be noted that this manual includes aspects of the general skill of self-expression, a definition of what directions are, and a mention of the qualitative dimension of concreteness, particularly important in direction giving.

DIRECTIONS: PUTTING YOUR IDEAS ACROSS

Three dimensions of effective direction giving are stressed in this manual: (1) appropriate verbal and nonverbal behavior to support the direction; (2) concrete, clear directions; and (3) checking out with your helpee whether or not the directions were heard.

As a first step, however, *directions* should be defined. Some examples of verbal directions which might appear in a helping session include the following:

"Sit back in your chair, close your eyes, relax."

"Repeat what you just said, then repeat it again."

"After you leave here, count the number of times you find yourself putting yourself down to your friends."

"Have your right hand talk to your left hand."

"I want you to take a test."

The first dimension of effective direction giving is appropriate verbal and nonverbal self-expressive behavior to support the direction. Physicians often talk about the "white coat" effect—if the physician appears to know what is being talked about, the patient will be more inclined to follow instructions. Similarly, the most able direction givers of the helping profession have effective self-expressive behaviors of eye contact, vocal tone, and body language. Compare the effective helper with the weak or indecisive behavior of the parent or teacher who isn't quite sure what to do next to get the child or class to perform a certain activity.

It may be useful at this point to identify a model effective direction giver from your past experience and an individual who was less than effective. Give thought to their characteristic styles of self-expression.

Effective _____

_____

Ineffective _____

_____

A second dimension of effective direction giving is *concreteness* or clear verbal specificity. The more clear and direct the statement, the more likely that direction is to be heard. Compare:

"You try that again." versus "The first time you were looking at your hands. Say it again and look at me this time."

"Don't do that!" versus "One of our agreed-on rules in this group is to talk one at a time. O.K., let's start with Sue."

"Tell me more." versus "You just said you had a scary dream, then you wandered off to a discussion of dreams in general. Give me some specific things that happened in the dream that frightened you."

Further, when a series of directions must be given, it is more effective to give them *one at a time,* breaking them down step by step. For example, in teaching a microtraining session, don't give all the instructions for a group activity at once. First have the group break into small groups, *then* give the instructions. Later give additional instructions.

This leads to the third dimension of effective direction giving, the *"check-out."* Check out with your group or individual whether or not your directions were understood. Ask your helpee(s) to restate the direction. Or, ask if your directions were understood. Allow sufficient time to make sure your ideas were followed. The beginning direction giver often rushes at this point.

Specific examples of the check-out include the following:

"Could you tell me what I just said?"

"Are the directions clear? Do I need to say them again?"

"How does that suggestion come across to you?"

The first represents an open question seeking restatement, the second is a closed question allowing less participation, the third perhaps maximizes opportunity for the other to react to what you just said.

To sum up basic concepts of direction giving:

1. Use effective self-expression skills so you will be believable.

2. Be concrete and specific. One direction at a time is usually enough.
3. Check out to see if your directions were heard.

Leading toward the generalized skill of self-disclosure, *Basic Influencing Skills* presents three brief manuals on expression of feeling, expression of content, and the influencing summarization. With experienced helpers, these are simply read and discussed only briefly. With beginning helpers, each of the three manuals may be used for extensive practice before moving on to the more complex skill of self-disclosure.

Expression of Feeling, Expression of Content, and Summarization

The focus in this workshop will be on self-disclosure and its use in helping relationships. Self-disclosure will be presented in Microtraining Manual No. 6 as a broad construct consisting of several dimensions. The purpose of this manual is to examine *three* microtraining skills which are part of self-disclosure, but also are important skills in their own right.

The skills of expression of feeling, expression of content, and summarization will be presented here with illustrations of how these three skills could be used in situations other than self-disclosure. *Do not attempt self-disclosure until you can engage in these skills successfully.*

Expression of feeling

An expression of feeling is defined by any statement in which the helper expresses emotionally laden words. In a self-disclosure with expression of feeling we would find the following:

Helpee: Right now, I am really *fouled up*. My wife won't speak to me, I think I want to leave, but I am *afraid* to be alone. I'm just *confused*. (Expression of feeling, focus on self)

Helper: I sense in myself similar feelings of *hurt* and *frustration*. I want you to know that I am with you and *care.* (Expression of feeling, focus on self or helper plus focus on dyad)

However, expression of feeling could take other forms as well:

Helper: *Confusion* is something a lot of people face. They find the world a complex place which is *hard to cope with.* (Expression of feeling, focus on others)

Helper: The decision to leave or to stay is one which brings out many feelings — *change, loneliness, fear, challenge, stimulation.* (Expression of feeling, focus on the topic "leaving")

The effectiveness of these responses may vary. At any point, any one of them might be appropriate. But all are expressions of feeling. Crucial to the definition of an expression of feeling are the *emotionally laden or affective words* used.

An expression of feeling should be compared to a reflection of feeling (an attending skill). Both emphasize affective or emotionally laden words, but in the reflection of feeling, the focus is almost invariably on the helpee and the helpee's emotional experience. For example, "As I hear you, you're *terribly upset, worried,* and *confused* about what's happening right now."

The crucial dimension of an expression of feeling is the affective or emotional word. Expressions of feeling form an important part of the helpee's verbalizations as problems and concerns are explored. Some helpees (and some helpers) can profit from training in how to express their own emotions in counseling sessions.

Expression of content

Any statement which focuses on facts, ideas, information with minimal emphasis on emotional experience is classified as expression of content. The giving of advice, opinions, suggestions, and reassurance all represent expressions of content.

The following are expressions of content:

Helpee: Right now, I am really fouled up. My wife won't speak to me, I think I want to leave, but I am afraid to be alone. I'm just confused.

Helper: I can understand that. Sounds like you need to take some time and think it over. One need not rush into decisions. (Expression of content, focus on individual and topic) *Advice.*

That's tough, but you will be able to overcome the problem. (Expression of content, focus on individual) *Reassurance.*

Here are some alternatives for you to consider. See which fit your needs best. First, you could leave right now. Second, you could . . . etc. (Expression of content, focus on topic) *Suggestion.*

Sounds to me like the home situation is difficult. Many people in your situation have experienced the same issue . . . etc. (Expression of content, focus on topic) *Sharing information.*

It may be clearly seen that a wide array of possibilities for helping exist within this category of microtraining skills. The last item, "sharing information," is perhaps the most common expression of content type and represents the main style of daily conversation we all encounter. Any of these expressions of content may be useful in the helping interview. If used excessively, they may tend to deny the helpee's world and allow little chance for exploration of emotion.

Many more examples could be presented. Most conversations represent expressions of content. We get information from lectures, we learn about political opinions, parents tell us appropriate ways to behave.

If you were to listen to a single day's conversations, you would tend to find most of human interaction tends to focus on expression of content. While this may be necessary, it also results in people who are relatively unaware of emotional experience and who find it difficult to share their inner emotional world with others.

Influencing Summarization

The central purpose of summarization is to put your expressions of content and feelings together in a comprehensive form. Perhaps you have been working with a helpee on several issues during one interview and you have expressed several emotional reactions to the helpee, have given some advice and directions, and now would like to summarize what you have said in a more complete and comprehensive form. A periodic summarization will assist the helpee to sense the overall picture and direction of your thoughts.

In effect, summarizations are similar to expressions of feeling and expressions of content, except that the time period covered is longer and involves a broader range of issues. The time period of a summarization could be as short as five minutes or could be as long as a full interview; it could even include your impressions of several interviews. Such summaries have potential value to you to help organize your thoughts. . .and they have potential value to helpees as they can see "where you are coming from" more clearly.

Of course, it would be possible to have a summarization of your feelings or a summarization of content. As most summarizations involve both affect and content, this distinction is not ordinarily made.

Summarization as a self-expressive skill should be differentiated from summarization as an attending skill. The difference is on focus and on whom initiates the information. A summarization (attending) focuses on what the helpee has said. A summarization (influencing) focuses on what the helper has said.

Summarizations are also useful to the employer giving instructions and information to subordinates, the teacher giving data to students, the salesperson summarizing the merits of his or her product. Summarizations provide the opportunity to highlight key aspects of a conversation and to mark the things which others might desirably remember.

Examples of summarizations include the following:

To a helpee suffering from examination anxiety:

What I've been saying is that relaxation training is one route toward coping with your tension around exams more easily. I think I said that many people suffer similar problems but have overcome them through deliberate relaxation. I also said that the instructions I gave you would require practice and deliberate efforts on your part to *use* them. What are some of your reactions to our program right now?

To a helpee who has just lost a job:

We have been talking about a variety of things in this session and have been talking a lot about how you could go about obtaining a new position. The things I suggested were (1) develop a new resume (and we talked about some key steps in how that could be done), (2) go through a series of vocational tests (and we selected a group which seemed to interest you), (3) meet again next week at the same time. In the meantime, you'll be planning to interview for two new jobs using techniques we discussed.

To a training group in microcounseling:

During this session I used several different approaches to skills training. First we used video models of self-expression skills. Then we read a manual outlining some key points of these skills. This was followed by your practicing the skills and developing your own videotapes. At this point, we can develop a "do-use-teach" contract.

The above three summarizations represent information focused on what the helper said and did. Summarization as an attending skill focuses on what the helpee said and did. It would, of course, be most reasonable to summarize *both* what the helper *and* helpee said and did. This would be scored as a summarization in both the attending and influencing skills *and* with a focus on the helper and the helpee. For example:

During this past hour, you have commented on your problems with your six-year-old. You mentioned your fears of possible homosexual trends. I presented an interpretation that perhaps you were projecting some of your own fears about yourself on your child. Your reactions to that were diffuse and confused. I shared some of my feelings about your confusion and your fears as you expressed them—you came across to me as a person trying very hard to be perfect and fearful you wouldn't succeed. As we close out this hour, you look more relaxed—almost as if you want to try something new. Somehow you seem more confident to me. How does all this come across to you?

Before you can move to training in self-disclosure in the interview, it is necessary that you be able to express content, express feelings, and summarize your ideas clearly. Practice with these components will eventually lead to expertise and freedom in sharing yourself more openly with your helpees as intended in the global construct of self-disclosure.

Other influencing skill manuals to be found in *Basic Influencing Skills* include self-expression, self-directed self-expression, focus analysis, self-disclosure, three manuals on aspects of interpretation, direct-mutual communication, and integration of skills.

There are several qualitative manuals in the same series. Two are presented below. The first, concreteness, is brief and telegraphic, as trainees learn the concepts so readily.

Concreteness

Concreteness is a vital part of any helping relationship, and the ability to be specific is important in the use of other helping skills as well. A vague reflection of feeling is potentially less helpful than concrete and specific labeling of emotions. Concreteness on the part of the helper often facilitates the helpee in being more specific.

The exchange below could be rated as specific and concrete or vague and general. Rate each helper statement with a "C" or "V." Note also that helpees can be rated for the specificity of their statements. One task of the effective helper may be to assist a helpee in becoming more concrete.

——— *Helpee:* I feel lousy today.
——— *Helper:* I don't feel so good either. (Self-disclosure)
———   Give me a specific example of what you mean.
           (Direction)
———   You feel lousy. (Minimal encourage)
———   Could you share what's been happening that
           makes you feel that way? (Open question)
———   Right now, I find myself feeling a little lousy
           too. I just realized that I misinterpreted your
           comments about your family. (Self-disclosure)
——— *Helpee:* Yeah, I really felt you thought I was treating my
           kids wrong when I hit them. I think they de-
           served it, but the look on your face really got to
           me.
——— *Helper:* It really hurt you when I came across blaming
           you for what happened. (Reflection of feeling)
———   It really upset you. (Reflection of feeling)
———   I'm sorry. (Self-disclosure)
———   That isn't what I meant. (Self-disclosure)
———   And now, we seem to be at the same place we've
           often been. You try to express yourself and I
           seem to misinterpret what you mean. This is a
           pattern which occurs in many places—home, on
           the job, earlier with your parents. (Interpreta-
           tion)
———   You seem to have authority problems. (Inter-
           pretation)

Generally speaking, concrete expressions will facilitate the helping process. However, in early phases of helping, vague and more general expressions may *sometimes* be more helpful, as they allow more room for client self-exploration.

The second qualitative manual presented here, confrontation, is more complex. The description is longer, and an array of exercises follow the manual to help clarify and explicate the concepts.

Confrontation

The effective helper meets and copes with situations directly and forthrightly. The ability to express oneself clearly—to "say what you mean and mean what you say"—is central to any helping relationship. Confrontation—the accurate pointing out of discrepancies in an individual—is basic to self-directed self-expression and many other helping skills.

Confrontation is usually defined as a challenge and is often discussed as a conflict. A dictionary definition of confrontation is "to stand in the face of," "to face in hostility. . .to oppose." Given this definition, it may be seen that many self-disclosure statements could be classified as confrontations. For example, "I am going to stop you" is an expression of content; or "I am outraged by that" is an expression of feeling. Clearly, confrontations of this nature can either help or hurt. The effectiveness of these statements will depend on the context, the individual, and the specific timing of the intervention.

For purposes of this training manual, however, confrontation will be defined more narrowly as *the pointing out of discrepancies between or among attitudes, thoughts, or behaviors.* In a confrontation, individuals are faced directly with the fact that they may be saying other than that which they mean or doing other than that which they say.

The advantage of this definition is that it is clear and has been demonstrated to have considerable value in helping oneself or another person look at a situation more realistically and accurately. The definition of confrontation focuses heavily on the fact that people are not always *congruent* and consistent.

Helpee confrontations ("you") might include the following:

> "You say constantly that you are going to get up on time and get to work, but you never do."
>
> "You find yourself having mixed reactions to what I say. One side wants to agree, the other to fight and disagree."
>
> "You keep saying you love your wife, but you constantly bicker and argue."
>
> "Your words say you are comfortable talking about sex, but

your lack of eye contact always comes when we talk about the topic."

Self-focused confrontations ("I") used by the helper or helpee might include:

"I say I want to help myself stop smoking, but I just keep on."
"I think I intend to study, but I never start."

Dual-focused confrontations ("you" and "I") might include:

"Right now, *you* seem to be saying that *our* relationship has been good, but *my* experience—in this moment—is that *we* simply aren't communicating."
"*You* say that *I* understand *you,* but *I* feel puzzled and am not so sure that *I* do. *Let's* explore that some more."

The definition of confrontation presented above stresses the following factors:

1. A confrontation focuses on discrepancies between or among attitudes, thoughts, or behaviors.
2. A confrontation focuses on objective data. The more factual and observable a confrontation of discrepancies, the more helpful it may be. Confrontations are most effective when nonevaluative.
3. Confrontations may be focused on self, the helpee, or any other of the several dimensions of "focus."
4. Any verbal statement may be scored as containing or not containing a confrontation.
5. Finally, a confrontation is *not* a blunt statement of opinion or emotion which disagrees with someone else. These are expression of content or expression of feeling statements.

The objective nature of a confrontation—used appropriately with suitable timing—can be most helpful in aiding a client in self-examination or in helping people of varying opinions examine their differences.

Determining whether or not a confrontation is helpful is very much an individual matter. Confrontations used inappropriately may be destructive, at other times neutral. A positive confrontation leads to further self-examination of the discrepancies and possible resolution of varying trends. The issue of deciding whether or not a confrontation is helpful is complicated by the fact that the helper, the helpee, and an external "expert" may all view the same confrontation differently.

A possible goal is to work with helpees so that they notice and describe their own discrepancies, thus confronting themselves.

As a first step toward measuring the quality of a confrontation, we would suggest scoring a confrontation as "positive," "neutral," or "negative" ("+," "0," or "−"). Individual differences in ratings provide helpful data for discussion and more thorough understanding of confrontation and its effects. Further references and an alternative view of confrontation may be found in Berenson and Mitchell (1974) or Carkhuff (1969a,b).

Confrontation Exercises

The following excerpt from a video vignette provides an interchange which provides the opportunity for a confrontation.

Helper: Al, how are things going with Betty?

Helpee: Well, things are going very well. I, you know, I don't mind the fact, the fact that she's gone all the time anymore. I think it's okay that she goes out and works evenings at the office. That, that, yeah, that's okay. I mean, it's really, it's really fine. The kids and I went out and saw a movie last night. Ah ... and it was a good movie. So, it was okay. Yeah, I think things are going well. (All said in a flat monotone.)

Nonconfrontations from the helper might include the following:

Sounds like things are going better for you. (Paraphrase)

What you say sounds phoney to me. (Self-disclosure)

I've had similar situations where things were hard at the beginning and later got better. For example ... (Self-disclosure)

Confrontations might include the following:

> Al, you say that things are better, but your voice and expression suggest that perhaps it isn't there yet. (Paraphrase plus reflection of feeling)

> At this moment, I hear you saying that things are better, yet my experience with you is different. It reminds me of the time when I told my spouse that I didn't care for those late hours, but I was awfully angry inside and wouldn't admit it.   (Paraphrase plus self-disclosure)

Central to any confrontation is the pointing out of discrepancies. Confrontation is not disagreeing with the helpee. Many people think of a challenge such as "What you say sounds phoney to me" as a confrontation. While the statement may be based on discrepancies in the helpee's behavior, it does *not* point out clearly to the helpee what the discrepancies in behavior are. A confrontation must point out discrepancies clearly and precisely.

Following are some helpee statements. Make confrontive and nonconfrontive responses to each.

1. *Helpee:* I'm making plenty of money. $2.10 an hour. Only problem is that I seem to spend it faster than I make it. For my age, that's good money. I think I know what I'm doing and can take care of it.
   Nonconfrontive statement _____

   _____

   Confrontive statement _____

   _____

2. *Helpee:* My parents are getting along well. Oh, they argue now and then, but basically about minor things. They are really neat people; they never pressure me. I feel terribly guilty about not being able to get a job which they approve of.
   Nonconfrontive statement _____

   _____

   Confrontive statement _____

   _____

3. *Helpee:* (in angry voice with fists clenched) My wife and I never argue, we get along very well. The problem is my job; my boss doesn't understand me.

Nonconfrontive statement _____

_____

Confrontive statement _____

_____

4. *Helpee:* Drinking is no problem for me. I never drink before lunch.

Nonconfrontive statement _____

_____

Confrontive statement _____

_____

Other qualitative manuals in the *Basic Influencing Skills* series include respect, genuineness, and immediacy, plus manuals on the qualitative aspects of the cultural-environmental-contextual response and the check-out.

Finally, it is appropriate to consider the importance of video vignettes, short statements of problems or concerns by helpees. These are used to (1) teach participants how to label emotions, (2) help trainees learn to identify their own emotional reactions to clients, (3) develop alternative reflection of feeling, interpretation, or self-disclosure statements. The method of presenting a video vignette is simple. A helpee presents a short problem and usually is assisted in developing the problem by a counselor or therapist. At a crucial point, the exchange is stopped and trainees in small groups work through basic exercises. The following vignette is presented as it is used in self-disclosure, but it is also used as a prompt for other skills as well.

Video Vignettes*

In the following short video vignette, an actor will present a brief statement about himself as drawn out by a helper. Generate a series of self-disclosure responses to each vignette.

---

*From *Basic Influencing Skills.*

Long Hair

Helper: Billy, the last time you were here we were talking about getting your hair cut. What happened?

Helpee: Well, three weeks ago was my last haircut. Just before I went to my grandparents. And when you go to your grandparents, you really get your hair cut. Especially with my grandparents. They can't stand long-haired hippies. This is long-haired hippy. Before—oh boy . . . So anyway, when I got back, my father—it was the first time my father had seen the hair cut, and he said: yeah, well, it still looks pretty good. And my mother—I don't know if it was the day or the day after I came back—said: well, when are you going to get your hair cut the next time? Three weeks after the biggest haircut I've had since the last time I went to see my grandparents.

Helper: How'd that make you feel?

Helpee: Lousy. They ought to give me a chance to grow it out, at least. I mean, I can understand they don't like it as long as I like it. But still, there's got to be some compromise in there.

Key ideas of the helpee ―――――――――――――――――

Key emotions of the helpee ―――――――――――――――

Related ideas or experiences from your own life ――――――

The emotions that the helpee raises in you at this moment ――――

Self-disclosure statement ――――――――――――――――

(Examine each of the above statements for "I" focus, expression of feeling or content, tense, and parallelism.)

Appendix VI

MEDIA THERAPY: SELF-DIRECTED
SELF-EXPRESSION

Mㅌᴅɪᴀ ᴛʜᴇʀᴀᴘʏ (Ivey, 1973b) is a video system for training clients, helpees, and patients in single skills of living. Closely allied with assertion training and behavioral approaches to problem solving, media therapy is a step-by-step microtraining approach to aid helpees in making their own decisions about behaviors they wish to learn, develop, or change. The materials below are once again taken from *Basic Influencing Skills,* and additional material may be found there to amplify and clarify this process. Behavior count charts for use with this training are available in that manual.

Step 1: Videotape the Situation to be Analyzed

Self-directed self-expression is most easily presented to helpees as an opportunity to view oneself on television. Further, such self-viewing helps one identify strengths and weaknesses of communication. The helpee should be familiarized with the video equipment and encouraged to relax in any way possible. We have found that the attitude of the helper is most important here. If you are worried about the situation, the helpee will be concerned and potentially reluctant to go through the process. If you are relaxed and confident, e.g. have effective self-expression behaviors yourself, the helpee will tend to react the same way. An informal, casual, yet confident and professional attitude is appropriate.

The helpee must select a situation where he or she would like to improve his or her communication effectiveness. The situation may be real or role-played. Brainstorm with the helpee possible

situations for taping.   These may range from conversations with
an employer to family issues such as a son coming home late from
a date to dealing effectively with a welfare office.   *The more spe-*
cific the situation, the more effective the taping.   With some
helpees, a direct videotaping of a conversation between the helper
and helpee on an issue of mutual concern is helpful.

Videotape for three to five minutes a role-played or real situation.   Use the space below to take notes on the first step of the
self-directed self-expression process.

Step 2: View the Videotape, Define Behaviors

Before viewing the videotape and discussing the short segment, take time to check-out your helpee's internal reactions to the experience. Was it real? Was the experience anxiety provoking? Positive and/or negative thoughts? However, do not spend extensive time on this processing. Viewing of the videotape will prove more valuable than internal speculation. If videotape is not available, make the important distinction between general discussion and observation of specific behaviors.

View the videotape. Stop and start the tape at critical points. If the helpee notes anything either verbally or nonverbally, stop the tape. The helpee when asked may state, "I didn't like myself at that point. I looked stupid." "Stupid" is *not* observable behavior. Ask the helpee to define more precisely what he or she *saw* or *heard* that appeared stupid. Surprisingly, you will often find helpees able to define rather precise verbal and nonverbal behaviors closely related to the attending and self-expressive skills. Lack of attending may be defined as "I don't look at people" or "I interrupt too often." The objective of viewing the tape is to identify specific behaviors that the helpee might like to change or strengthen. The more specifically you define the behavior, the more successful your training session will be.

Many helpees focus only on the negative. Make a conscious attempt to find positive aspects of the helpee's behavior and don't hesitate to suggest that the helpee use these positive behaviors more often.

Define below aspects of the videotape viewing and specific behaviors that occur to you.

Step 3: Set Goals for Behavior Change

After developing a careful inventory of strengths that you and the helpee observe, list things that might be strengthened and/or changed in a repeat videotaping. Keep this list brief and introductory.

The helpee should then select *one* of the above behaviors as that which he or she would like to change or strengthen. Emphasize that people didn't learn all their present behaviors in a one to two hour session and one shouldn't expect to change them all in a short period of time. Self-directed self-expression works best with precise behaviors. For example, a person who comes across as "weak and insignificant" in a job interview may observe lack of eye contact or a hand gesture that is self-deprecating. Contract only for more frequent eye contact or for stronger hand movements—*not both.*

With some people—particularly in the advanced stages of work with videotaping in self-directed self-expression— brief training in microtraining skills such as open questions, paraphrasing, or directions may be useful. However, such training should be given only when asked for by the helpee. In self-directed self-expression, the helpee sets the goals, not the helper.

Use this space for the listing of goals and development of a possible hierarchy of items for behavior change. However, you will find that helpees who change one behavior successfully often change other behaviors as well.

Step 4: Second Videotaping: Viewing, and Observing Change

After a clear behavioral objective for change has been identified, videotape a second role-played or real situation closely allied to the first taping. In the viewing, give special attention to changes in the specific behavior. Note also possible changes in other behaviors as well.

With some helpees it is useful to count the number of instances of the specific behavior in the first session and compare this count with similar figures from the second session. Those clients who respond to a highly behavioral approach may want to set goals for the number of behaviors they wish in a specific setting.

With many helpees, it is wise to continue short practice videotape sessions to ensure learning of the behavior(s) selected. In some cases, it is appropriate to comment directly and immediately to the helpees *during* videotaping that they have forgotten to use the specific behavior agreed on.

Use this space for behavioral counts, observations of trainer behavior as they relate to helpee behavior, and for development of additional behaviors slated for change.

Step 5: Generalization of Learned Behavior

Assuming that the helpee has demonstrated ability to modify behavior in specific ways, it is important that plans be made to generalize the new concepts of self-expression beyond the laboratory. A role-played situation or a brief exchange on videotape is *not* real-life despite the power of this training format. Specific attempts to take behavior out of the training session to the world at large are essential.

The framework of the do-use-teach contract is one approach. The helpee could complete the following contract and report back to the helper the degree of success:

I agree to use _____
                          (Name of specific identified behavior)

with _____ under the
              (Name of individual or group)

following specific conditions: _____

_____.

I will report back my observations and experiences.

Supplementing this type of contract can be analysis of the effect of the behavior on the individual or group. For example, if the helpee desired to improve questioning skills, the helpee should be encouraged to note the effectiveness of these skills on those to whom he or she talks.

Appendix VII

COMPETENCY-BASED MICROTRAINING

The outcome variable of effective training is an effective trainee—a helper who can demonstrate specific competencies of helping with equally demonstrable effects on the helpee. The specificity of the microtraining model is ideal for those seeking accountability and measurement of counseling abilities. This section outlines specific competencies which microtraining participants may be expected to develop. These competencies are discussed under five main subheadings: (1) general competencies of helping, (2) competencies associated with attending skills, (3) competencies associated with influencing skills, (4) competencies in alternative theoretical orientations, and (5) competencies in producing specific client or patient outcomes. We believe that the general competencies of helping will be of interest even to those who question the wisdom of competency-based educational approaches.

GENERAL COMPETENCIES OF HELPING

The basic set of competencies desired in microtraining are broad in nature and allow considerable room for individual differences in style and theoretical orientation. Basically, these competencies focus on the helper being able to define what he or she is doing in the interview. No specific helping style is recommended or prescribed. The important issue is whether or not the trainee can recognize what happens in the interview and can communicate these observations to the trainer. Since general competencies of helping have wide application, they will be presented in considerable detail.

Ivey and Gluckstern (1976a, p. 1) describe the general competencies of the microtraining framework. The trainee is expected to demonstrate the following specific competencies:

1. *The ability to generate an infinite number of helping responses to any helpee statement.*
   Measurement: A videotaped client is presented who discusses a problem or concern briefly. Trainees write a wide array of helping responses. These responses may be from one specific theoretical orientation, or they may be from an eclectic framework.
   Comment: This competency focuses on the fact that there is no one single "right" statement to give to the helpee. Microtraining participants seem to be greatly relieved when they see that more than one response may be "correct." They also experience feelings of confidence and power as they demonstrate their ability to generate a wide array of helping responses, all of which may be potentially useful, irrelevant, or even harmful.

2. *The ability to classify helper and helpee statements and to rate the quality of the interaction.*
   Measurement: A videotaped or filmed helping session is shown, and participants rate and classify the behavior of the helper and helpee.
   Comment: The Ivey Taxonomy (see Appendix III) is used as the tool for helper and helpee response classification. This system of rating microcounseling skills and quality aspects of helping has proven effective in assisting trainees to understand *and later demonstrate* varying approaches to helping. This approach has been successful with methods ranging from Gestalt to nondirective to reevaluation co-counseling (Jackins, 1965).

3. *The ability to demonstrate specific microtraining skills, e.g. questions, directions, interpretation, in an ongoing helping interview, the style and theoretical orientation to be determined by the trainee.*
   Measurement: Trainees present their own individual style in a video- or audiotape interview. They demonstrate

their ability to engage in the skills that they consider most important.*

Comment: This, of course, is the central outcome competency. It is a competency which allows the trainee to counsel, interview, or do therapy in his or her unique style. At the same time, the trainee is asked to specify the skills used. If the trainee states a personal orientation as nondirective, the skills of nondirectivism (reflection, paraphrase, summarization) should be demonstrated. If the trainee states an orientation as Gestalt, the skills and qualities of that orientation, e.g. directions, present tense orientation, interpretation, should be presented. If eclectic, all skills should be demonstrated. No specific theoretical stance is demanded; what is required is that the person be congruent with the stated personal orientation to helping.

4. *The ability to demonstrate the qualitative dimensions of helping—concreteness, immediacy, respect, and genuineness —as operationally defined by microtraining.*

   Measurement: The helping interview in *3* above is to be rated on the qualitative dimensions of helping. See Appendix III for example scoring.

   Comment: Different helping theories demonstrate the qualitative dimensions of helping differently, but all show them in some fashion. The objective scales of microtraining may be used, or the more subjective dimensions of Truax (1967) or Carkhuff (1969a,b) serve as useful alternatives.

5. *The ability to use these skills beyond the interview in daily life interaction and teach them to others.*

   Measurement: Successful completion of "do-use-teach" contracts in which trainees agree to use behaviors and skills learned in microtraining sessions in their daily life and also teach them to others.

   Comment: We have found that helping skills are too often restricted to the interview. Reflection of feeling and self-

---

*An important issue in this competency, of course, is the cultural relevance of the desired style of the helper. Once the helper has defined personal style, it then becomes clear that this style's cultural appropriateness must be analyzed.

disclosure are concepts useful in daily life. The concepts of immediacy and concreteness can be useful in family interaction, work, and in most life interactions. Trainees who can use these skills outside of the training session and the interview have greater mastery of the concepts. Beyond this, the ability to teach helping skills to others is another way to cement learning and to expand the universe of helping people.

Through these five basic competencies, trainees can demonstrate their mastery of helping and their ability to act within and influence their culture. The competencies suggested here are specific and measurable, but they do not impose a strict, single world view on the helpee. The requirements are that the individual (1) know what he or she is doing; and (2) be aware of its probable effect on others.

The remainder of microtraining competencies will not be defined in as much detail as the above. For those who wish specific measurement techniques, rating scales, or more detailed outlines of competencies, *Basic Attending Skills* (Ivey and Gluckstern, 1974a,b) and *Basic Influencing Skills* (Ivey and Gluckstern, 1976a,b) may be referred to for additional information.

COMPETENCIES ASSOCIATED WITH ATTENDING SKILLS

Regardless of one's theoretical orientation or style of helping, one must listen to and attend to the helpee. If one is nondirective, attending skills alone are sufficient. If one is a behaviorist, an analyst, or a Gestalt therapist, attending skills remain the first and most basic competency. For unless one can hear the client accurately, the action or influencing dimensions of helping (directions, self-disclosure, interpretation) will likely be for naught. Thus, the trainee needs to be able to demonstrate basic competencies in attending as a first step in microcounseling or in any other approach to helper training.

The specific competencies stressed in attending skill training sessions include the following:

1. Ability to attend to the helpee.

Measurement: Examination of videotapes with special attention to eye contact patterns, nonverbal communication, and verbal following behavior.
2. Ability to ask open and closed questions.
3. Ability to demonstrate the use of the minimal encourage.
4. Ability to paraphrase accurately.
5. Ability to reflect feelings.
6. Ability to summarize the main strands of helpees' statements.
Measurement of 2 through 6: Presentation of video– or audiotapes of interviews in which these skills are presented and classified (Ivey and Gluckstern, 1976a, p. 3) .

It is again stressed that the attending behaviors as described in this book are culturally related. While microcounseling is rapidly gaining acceptance in other nations with varying cultures, adaptations of these skills are necessary. Further, within United States culture, subgroups will have varying patterns of use of these skills.

The helper who has culturally appropriate attending skills is able and ready to hear the helpee, diagnose problems, and provide necessary and sometimes sufficient conditions for personal growth in helpees.

COMPETENCIES ASSOCIATED WITH INFLUENCING SKILLS

The influencing skills are the "power" skills of helping. With power comes the ability to damage as well as help. Attending behavior which involves distortion can be a destructive experience, but that is not pure attending. Attending skills are almost universally helpful, as they assist the interviewee to clarify ideas and life experience. Influencing skills demand even more ability on the part of the helper and require a higher level of competence. A trainee should demonstrate clear abilities in attending dimensions before undertaking training in influencing skills. As such, the qualitative dimensions of helping are stressed along with the specific microtraining skills in training helpers in influencing helpees.

The specific competencies of influencing include the following:

1. Ability to engage in self-expressive behavior.
   Measurement: Examination of videotapes and audiotapes for patterns of eye contact, body language, vocal tone and rate, and ability to engage in a conversation on a culturally relevant topic.
2. Ability to demonstrate direction giving.
3. Ability to demonstrate expression of content, expression of feeling, and the influencing summarization.
4. Ability to self-disclose.
5. Ability to interpret a helpee's behavior.
6. Ability to engage in direct-mutual communication.
   Measurement: Presentation of videotapes or audiotapes in which the several skills are presented. With interpretation and self-disclosure, the ability to generate a wide variety of helping leads from differing theoretical orientations is stressed.
7. Ability to demonstrate the qualitative culturally relevant dimensions of helping—concreteness, immediacy, respect and warmth, confrontation, and genuineness.
   Measurement: Presentation of a videotape or audiotape in which these qualities of helping are demonstrated and scored.

The helper who is able to engage in and demonstrate all of these competencies is freed to make independent choices of the type of helper he or she wants to be. One need not slavishly commit oneself to a single therapeutic or counseling school but rather has the demonstrated competency to choose among alternatives and determine one's own direction of helping others.

COMPETENCIES IN ALTERNATIVE THEORETICAL ORIENTATIONS

Microtraining has been presented as a metatheory—a theory about helping theories. Many, perhaps most, professional helpers ultimately commit themselves to one or more theoretical schools of helping. Microtraining has now reached the point where it is possible to define rather precisely the behaviors of model helpers in varying orientations to helping (see Chapter 7). Out of this examination it becomes possible to outline microtraining programs in many specific types of helping theories.

Let us assume, for example, that the trainer is most interested in developing competent behavior therapists. The competencies which might be listed in a program of microtraining could be as follows:

1. Ability to ask questions, open and closed.
2. Ability to paraphrase and summarize (and, on occasion, reflect feeling) to check out the accuracy of data obtained from the helpee.
3. Ability to give directions clearly and precisely.
4. Ability to express content, i.e. give suggestions, information, or advice.
   Measurement: Presentation of videotapes or audiotapes demonstrating these skills.
5. Ability to conduct a deep muscle relaxation program.
6. Ability to conduct assertion training programs.
7. Ability to develop systematic desensitization hierarchies with a helpee.
   Measurement: These are more broadly based skills, but they can be defined precisely and presented as video models; the trainee, in turn, can demonstrate their use with a client.

This listing is quite similar to a behavioral assessment list developed by Seidenstücker (1976) for teaching behavioral helpers. These competencies are but a few examples of the use of competency-based helper training now possible using microtraining as a base. Similar programs could be developed for Gestalt therapists, sexual therapists, nondirectivists, encounter group leaders, analytic trainees, etc. In each case, underlying microtraining skills and qualitative dimensions can be selected and specific modeling tapes developed, and a systematic, highly concrete program for training in any of a wide variety of therapeutic orientations will be possible.

COMPETENCIES IN PRODUCING SPECIFIC CLIENT OR PATIENT OUTCOMES

The competence shown by the helper will in turn be demonstrated by competence in the helpee. The competent helper will produce verbal and nonverbal changes in the helpee. Some examples of helpee outcome competencies which the effective helper might be expected to produce include:

1. Ability to demonstrate verbal and nonverbal attending and self-expressive behaviors in accordance with the culture.
2. Ability to generate sentences with focus on self, others, group behavior, and the cultural-environmental-context.
3. Ability to engage in specific skills of attending (asking questions, encouraging others to talk, paraphrasing, reflecting feeling, summarization). Most people can ask questions and give minimal encourages; however, not everyone is capable of an accurate paraphrase or able to reflect feelings.
4. Ability to engage in the influencing skills (directions, expression of content and feeling, self-disclosure, interpretation). Most people are able to give directions and express content through advice and sharing information. Many self-disclose but do so inappropriately. The skills of renaming and reinterpreting life experience are available to relatively few.
5. Ability to be concrete in expression, to show respect and warmth to others, to be immediate rather than distant and apart in conversations, to be genuine, to confront discrepancies in self and others, and (as a broad construct) to assist others through empathy.

The measurement of these skills involves, of course, the same measurement techniques as are used for effective and skilled helpers. Appendix III illustrates how helpee behavior is rated. It is readily apparent that these competencies are the same as the competencies which the effective helper may be expected to demonstrate.

Although the complexity of all which is encompassed in the "effective helpee" makes it difficult to present an example for further clarification, it may be useful to examine the pattern of communication of the helpee in the Appendix III typescript. Throughout the interview, the helpee attends, utilizes a variety of communication skills, and demonstrates all the qualitative dimensions of communication. A particularly effective demonstration of the competent helpee or individual is shown at Joan 18, where she shares her fantasy of what she would like life to be like. Here she is simultaneously concrete, speaking appropriately on future dimensions, shows respect and genuineness, expresses feelings, and content, and also focuses on herself in relation to others and the topic of what life could be like. Her verbal and nonverbal behaviors are congruent. This example can be compared to the potentially ineffective helpee who might have avoided the task, i.e. topic jumped, broken eye contact, and expressed content in relation to a random external topic. The fantasy in response to the helper's direction follows:

Al 18: Okay. Let's not try to resolve that right now. Let's do an exercise that we've done in the past. Stop for a moment. And would you just sort of close your eyes and just sort of imagine what you might like your relationship to be like. Regardless of how it is now—what would you like to be? How would you like to respond to him? Just think for a moment.

Joan 18: (pause) I can see us both as having very important professions. Coming in at the end of the day. Having a warm hug. Exchanging some of the things that happened during the day. Ah, each having some time with the children, the girls. (pause) Taking turns cooking. Taking turns doing things around the house. Ah, and me having some time that was for Joan, alone. And, that I didn't have to beg for that. Or I didn't have to make excuses. Or I didn't have to take it just when he was busy doing something else. But it was legitimate. And I could say that I really need to go to the woods, or I need to go to my office. All right, would you take the girls out for an afternoon, because I really want to be in the house by myself right now. And I wouldn't have to apologize for that.

At Al 18, different helpers would have done very different

things at the hiatus period. The purpose of this discussion is not to evaluate the appropriateness of the helper response but to examine its effect on the helpee. In this case, the helpee responds competently.

The microtraining helper should be able to demonstrate that his or her interviewing behavior changes the behavior (verbal and nonverbal) of the helpee. The Ivey Taxonomy and the suggested competencies provide measurable means whereby helpers can demonstrate that they make a difference in the lives of their helpees. Beyond that, it seems logical that the stated goal of helping ("the effective individual is one who can generate a maximum number of verbal and nonverbal sentences to communicate with a maximum number of individuals, groups, and cultures") may be a beginning step toward a value statement of the most useful outcome variable for the helpee. If so, it may eventually be possible to compare the relative effectiveness of alternative modes of helping.

AUTHOR INDEX

SUBJECT INDEX